Merriam-Webster's
Pocket
Biographical
Dictionary

Merriam-Webster, Incorporated

Springfield, Massachusetts

A GENUINE MERRIAM-WEBSTER

The name *Webster* alone is no guarantee of excellence. It is used by a number of publishers and may serve mainly to mislead an unwary buyer.

Merriam-Webster™ is the name you should look for when you consider the purchase of dictionaries or other fine reference books. It carries the reputation of a company that has been publishing since 1831 and is your assurance of quality and authority.

Made in the United States of America
123456789NFWP99989796

Preface

Merriam-Webster's Pocket Biographical Dictionary gives basic information about notable persons both living and dead. Persons are generally entered under the name or title by which they are most commonly known. Entries typically consist of last name, personal names, birth and death dates, nationality, occupation, and a few brief pieces of information about their lives and accomplishments. Also included, when appropriate, are pseudonyms, original names, epithets, alternate names, reign names, and titles.

This dictionary shares many details of presentation with other members of the Merriam-Webster family, such as *Merriam-Webster's Collegiate Dictionary, Tenth Edition*. However, the nature of the material presented here requires special treatment of entries, and users of this dictionary need to be familiar with the following features.

Main entries follow one another in alphabetical order. Centered periods within the entries show points at which a hyphen may be put when the word is broken at the end of a line.

Transliterations of names from alphabets other than roman have been made as exact and consistent as possible. For most Chinese names, the traditional Wade-Giles system has been used. The Pinyin system has been used only for Chinese still living or recently deceased.

A number of names contain connectives like *d', de, di, van,* and *von.* With some exceptions, chiefly American or British names are not alphabetized under these connectives but rather under the principle element of their surname. If the surname of the person is usually construed as containing the connective, the entry appears at the principle element and the connective appears immediately after, separated by a comma:

Gogh, van ... Vincent

If the full name contains a connective which is not usually construed as an inseparable part of the surname, then the connective follows the person name:

Bee·tho·ven …Ludwig van

Variant spellings that are in common use appear at the main entry usually following the word *or*. If the variant spelling listed occurs significantly less frequently than the first, the variant follows the word *also*. If use of the variant spelling is limited in some way, an additional italic label is included to indicate the fact, as *Ar* or *L* for spellings or names that are most common in contexts where, respectively, Arabic or Latin spellings are commonly used. Variant spellings can also be shown after derivatives.

Birth and death dates about which there is little or no doubt are entered without qualification. Doubtful dates are followed by a question mark, and approximate dates are entered preceded by *ca* (circa). In some instances only the years of principal activity are given, preceded by the abbreviation *fl* (flourished). The dates of a reign or other term of office are enclosed in parentheses.

Derivatives are shown following a dash at the end of many entries. Such derivatives usually end in *-ian* or *-ic* and may function as adjectives or nouns or both. Derived adjectives mean "of or relating to (the person named in the entry)." Derived nouns mean "a follower of (the person named in the entry)."

Cross-reference entries are entries that direct the user from variant spellings or alternative forms of names to the main entry where they appear. Cross-reference entries appear only for forms that fall more than a page away from the main entry at which they appear.

Pronunciation information is either given explicitly or implied for nearly every name shown in boldface and for many alternative names and titles shown in roman or italic type. Pronunciation respellings are placed within reversed slant lines following the words to which they apply. Where the pronunciation is not indicated for a particular boldface entry, the pronunciation is to be inferred from an earlier indicated pronunciation.

A list of the pronunciation symbols follows this Preface.

Hyphens that are a fixed part of hyphenated compounds as *Jean-Jacques* or *Saint-Gaudens* are converted to a special double hyphen when the compound appears in lightface type and that hyphen comes at the end of a line. This indicates that the hyphen is to be retained when the word is not shown at the end of a line. Fixed hyphens in boldface words are always shown as short boldface dashes, which are a bit larger than ordinary hyphens, in this dictionary.

Guide words are shown in boldface type at the top left- and right-hand corners of each two-page spread. The guidewords are the first and last main entry on each spread.

Abbreviations used in this dictionary are listed in the section Abbreviations in This Work that follows this Preface.

Abbreviations in This Work

ABC American Broadcasting System
AD anno Domini
adj adjective
Ala Alabama
Am, Amer American
anthropol anthropologist
ANZUS Australia, New Zealand, United States Treaty Organization
Ar Arabic
archeol archeologist
Ariz Arizona
Ark Arkansas
Assn Association
astron astronomer
atty gen attorney general
Austral Australian
bacteriol bacteriologist
BC before Christ
Belg Belgian
biochem biochemist
Braz Brazilian
Brit British
bro brother
bros brothers
Bulg Bulgarian
ca circa
Calif California
Canad Canadian
cent century
chem chemist
Chin Chinese
Co company
Coll College
Colo Colorado
Confed Confederate
Conn Connecticut
criminol criminologist
d died
D Dutch

Dan Danish
dau daughter
DC District of Columbia
Dec December
Del Delaware
dir director
dram dramatist
Du Dutch
econ economist
ed edition
educ educator
Egypt Egyptian
emp emperor
Eng English
etc et cetera
ethnol ethnologist
esp especially
F French
ff following
Finn Finnish
fl flourished
Fla Florida
Flem Flemish
Fr French
Ft Fort
G German
Ga Georgia
gen general
Ger German
Gk Greek
gov governor
govt government
hist historian
Hung Hungarian
Ill Illinois
It, Ital Italian
Ind Indiana
Inst Institute
Jan January
Jp Japanese
Jr Junior
Kans Kansas
Ky Kentucky
L Latin
La Louisiana
lit literary
Lith Lithuanian
manuf manufacturer
Mass Massachusetts

math mathematician
Md Maryland
Mex Mexican
Mich Michigan
mil military
min minister
Minn Minnesota
Mo Missouri
Mont Montana
MP member of Parliament
Mt Mount
MVP most valuable player
n noun
N North
NASA National Aeronautic and Space Administration
NATO North Atlantic Treaty Organization
NBA National Basketball Association
NBC National Broadcasting Company
NC North Carolina
ND North Dakota
Nebr Nebraska
neurol neurologist
Nev Nevada
NFL National Football League
NH New Hampshire
NHL National Hockey League
NJ New Jersey
N Mex New Mexico
No North
Norw Norwegian
nov novelist
Nov November
NY New York
NZ New Zealand
Okla Oklahoma

Oreg Oregon
orig original,
   originally
Pa Pennsylvania
pat patented
Pers Persian
Penna Pennsylvania
Pg Portuguese
Phila Philadelphia
philos philosopher
physiol physiologist
Pol Polish
polit politician
Port Portuguese
prec preceding
pres president
prob probably
Pruss Prussian
pseud pseudonym
psychol psychologist
pub published
qv which see

RAF Royal Air
   Force
RC Roman
   Catholic
rev revised
RI Rhode Island
Rom Roman
Russ Russ
S South
SC South Carolina
Scot Scottish
SD South Dakota
SEATO South
   East Asia Treaty
   Organization
secy secretary
sen senator
Sept September
Serb Serbian
So South
sociol sociologist
Sp, Span Spanish

St Saint
Sw, Swed Swedish
Tenn Tennessee
theol theologian
Turk Turkish
U University
UN United Nations
US United States
USSR Union of
   Soviet Socialist
   Republics
usu usually
Va Virginia
vol volume
Vt Vermont
W west
Wash Washington
Wis Wisconsin
W Va West Virginia
WWI World War I
WWII World War II
zool zoologist

Pronunciation Symbols

ə   banana, collide, abut; raised \ə\ in \ə\, \ə\n\ as in battle, cotton, in \lə\, \mə\, \rə\ as in French table, prisme, titre

ˈə, ˌə   humbug, abut

ər   operation, further

a   map, patch

ā   day, fate

ä   bother, cot, father

ȧ   father as pronounced by those who do not rhyme it with *bother*

au̇   now, out

b   baby, rib

ch   chin, catch

d   did, adder

e   set, red

ē   beat, nosebleed, easy

f   fifty, cuff

g   go, big

h   hat, ahead

hw   whale

i   tip, banish

ī   site, buy

j   job, edge

k   kin, cook

ḵ   German ich, Buch

l   lily, cool

m   murmur, dim

n   nine, own; raised \n\ indicates that a preceding vowel or diphthong is pronounced through both nose and mouth, as in French bon \bōn\

ŋ   sing, singer, finger, ink

ō   bone, hollow

ȯ   saw, cork

œ   French bœuf, German Hölle

ō̄   French feu, German Höhle

ȯi   toy, sawing

p   pepper, lip

r   rarity

s   source, less

sh   shy, mission

t   tie, attack

th   thin, ether

th   then, either

ü   boot, few \ˈfyü\

u̇   put, pure \ˈpyu̇r\

ue   German füllen

ūe   French rue, German fühlen

v   vivid, give

w   we, away

y   yard, cue \ˈkyü\; raised \y\ indicates that a preceding \l\, \n\, or \w\ is modified by the placing of the tongue tip against the lower front teeth, as in French digne \dēnʸ\

z   zone, raise

zh   vision, pleasure

\   slant line used in pairs to mark the beginning and end of a transcription

ˈ   mark at the beginning of a syllable that has primary (strongest) stress: \ˈpenmənˌship\

ˌ   mark at the beginning of a syllable that has secondary (next-strongest) stress: \ˈpenmənˌship\

-   mark of syllable division

( )   indicate that what is shown between is present in some utterances but not in others: factory \ˈfak-t(ə-)rē\

÷   indicates that many regard as unacceptable the pronunciation immediately following: cupola \ˈkyü-pə-la ÷ -lō\

sic   indicates that the preceding pronunciation is correct despite the spelling: Kiribati \ˈkir-ə-bas—sic\

A

Aar·on \\'ar-ən, 'er\\ 14th cent. B.C. traditional founder of Hebrew priesthood; elder brother of Moses

Aaron Henry Louis 1934– — *Hank Aaron* Am. baseball player; played for Milwaukee/Atlanta Braves, Milwaukee Brewers 1954–76; set career home run record with 715

Ab·bey \\'a-bē\\ Edwin Austin 1852–1911 Am. painter & illustrator; *Harper's Weekly* staff illustrator; illustrated selections from the poetry of Robert Herrick, comedies of Shakespeare, etc.

Ab·bott \\'a-bət\\ Berenice 1898–1991 Am. photographer; known for portraits and for series on Manhattan in 1930s

Abbott George 1887–1995 Am. director, producer, playwright; wrote or cowrote close to 50 plays and musicals, including *On Your Toes* (with Richard Rogers and Lorenz Hart), *Damn Yankees*

Abbott Sir John Joseph Caldwell 1821–1893 Canad. polit.; prime min. (1891–92); dean of law faculty, McGill U. (1855–80)

Abbott Lyman 1835–1922 Am. clergyman & author; wrote *Christianity and Social Problems, Henry Ward Bucher, The Spirit of Democracy*, etc.

Ab·del·ka·der \\,ab-,del-'kä-dər\\ *or* **Abd al–Qā·dir** \\,ab-dəl-\\ 1808–1883 Arab leader in Algeria; led war of harassment against French and expanded territory; organized modern Algerian state

'Ab·dor·rah·man Khān \\,ab-,dȯr-rə-'män-'kän\\ *ca* 1844–1901 emir of Afghanistan (1880–1901); negotiated removal of British troops while leaving control of foreign affairs in British hands

Ab·dül·a·ziz \\,ab-,dü-lə-'zēz\\ 1830–1876 Ottoman sultan (1861–76); promulgated first Ottoman civil law code

Ab·dül·ha·mīd II \\,ab-,dül-hä-'mēd\\ 1842–1918 Ottoman sultan (1876–1909); promulgated first Ottoman constitution; opposed from within by Young Turks (1896–1908)

Ab·dul-Jab·bar \\ab-'dül-jə-'bär\\ Kareem 1947– — orig. *Lewis Alcindor* Am. basketball player; played for Milwaukee Bucks, L.A.-Lakers (1969–89); became NBA all-time leading scorer 1984

Abd·ul·lah \\,ab-də-'lä\\ 1882–1951 *'Abd Allāh ibn al-Husayn* emir of Transjordan (1921–46); king of Jordan (1946–51); led negotiations with British resulting in Arab revolt against Ottomans (1916)

Ab·dül·me·cid I \\,ab-,dül-mə-'jēd\\ 1823–1861 Ottoman sultan (1839–61); granted rights to citizens, including Christians; reorganized army, courts; fostered education

Abel \\'ā-bəl\\ Sir Frederick Augustus 1827–1902 Eng. chem.; invented cordite (1889, with Sir James Dewar) and the Abel tester for determining flashpoint of petroleum; wrote works on explosives

Ab·e·lard \'a-bə-ˌlärd\ Peter *F* Pierre **Alé·lard** *or* **Abai·lard** \ˌa-bā-'lär\ 1079–?1144 *husband of Héloïse* Fr. philos. & theol.; secretly married Héloïse and was as a consequence emasculated by hirelings of her uncle; became abbot of foundation of nuns headed by Héloïse; with Héloïse composed hymns, compiled their correspondence; wrote *Sic et non, Scito te ipsum*, etc.

Ab·er·crom·bie *or* **Ab·er·crom·by** \'a-bər-ˌkräm-bē, -ˌkrəm-\ James 1706–1781 Brit. gen. in America; commander of British forces in America in early stages of French and Indian War

Abercromby Sir Ralph 1734–1801 Brit. gen.; defeated French at Alexandria (1801); restored discipline, efficiency to British army

Ab·er·nathy \'a-bər-ˌna-thē\ Ralph David 1926–1990 Am. clergyman & civil rights leader; head of Southern Christian Leadership Conference (1968–77)

Ab·ing·ton \'a-biŋ-tən\ Fanny 1737–1815 née *Frances Barton* Eng. actress; created more than 30 characters, included Lady Teazle; a leader of English fashion

Abruz·zi Duke of the — see LUIGI AMEDEO

Abū al–Qā·sim *or* **Abul Ka·sim** \ə-ˌbül-'kä-səm\ *L* **Al·bu·ca·sis** \ˌal-byü-'kä-səs\ *ca* 936–*ca* 1013 Span. Arab physician & medical writer; author of medical compendium that greatly influenced European surgical practices for 500 years

Abū Bakr \ə-ˌbü-'ba-kər\ *ca* 573–634 1st caliph of Mecca; reputedly Muhammad's first male convert; his closest companion, adviser; chosen Muhammad's successor (632); began expansion of Islam into Arabia, Iraq, Syria

Abzug \'ab-zəg\ Bella 1920– née *Savitsky* Am. polit.; member U.S. House of Representatives (1970–76); a prominent activist in the feminist movement

Ach·e·son \'a-chə-sən\ Dean Gooderham 1893–1971 Am. statesman; secy. of state (1949–53); formulated Truman Doctrine (1947); helped formulate Marshall Plan (1947–48); wrote *Present at the Creation* (1969, Pulitzer prize), etc.

Ac·ton \'ak-tən\ 1st Baron 1834–1902 *John Emerich Edward Dalberg-Acton* \ˌdal-ˌbərg-\ Eng. hist.; a leader of English liberal Roman Catholic opponents of doctrine of papal infallibility; editor of *Cambridge Modern History*

Ad·am \'a-dəm\ Robert 1728–1792 & his bro. James 1730–1794 Scot. architects & furniture designers; used light airy style in architecture; created furniture in style made popular by Hepplewhite

Ad·ams \'a-dəmz\ Ansel Easton 1902–1984 Am. photographer; known for landscapes of Western U.S., esp. Yosemite; helped establish photography department at Museum of Modern Art

Adams Charles Francis 1807–1886 *son of J.Q.* Am. author & diplomat; minister to Great Britain (1861–68); edited letters of Abagail Adams (1840)

Adams Franklin Pierce 1881–1960 *known as F.P.A.* Am. journalist and humorist; wrote column "The Conning Tower"; wrote *Tobogganing on Parnassus*, *The Diary of Our Own Samuel Pepys*, etc.

Adams Henry Brooks 1838–1918 *son of C.F.* Am. hist.; teacher of history at Harvard; editor of *North America Review* (1870–76); wrote *The Education of Henry Adams* (1907), etc.

Adams James Truslow 1878–1949 Am. hist.; wrote *Founding of New England, The Epic of America, America's Tragedy*, etc.; edited *Dictionary of American History*, etc.

Adams John 1735–1826 Am. diplomat; 2d pres. of the U.S. (1797–1801); defense counsel for British soldiers accused of Boston Massacre (1770); helped John Jay and Benjamin Franklin negotiate peace treaty with Great Britain (1782)

Adams John Quin·cy \'kwin-zē, 'kwin(t)-sē\ 1767–1848 *son of John* 6th pres. of the U.S. (1825–29); U.S. Senator (1803–08); min. to Great Britain (1815–17); secy. of state (1817–25); helped formulate Monroe Doctrine (1823); member of Congress (1831–48)

Adams Maude 1872–1953 orig. *Maude Kiskadden* Am. actress; starred in *Little Minister* (1897–98), *Peter Pan* (1905–07), *Chantecler* (1910–11), etc.

Adams Samuel 1722–1803 Am. Revolutionary patriot; organized opposition to Stamp Act (1765); helped found Boston Committee of Correspondence (1772); signed Declaration of Independence; in U.S. Congress until 1781; gov. of Massachusetts (1794–97)

Adams Samuel Hopkins 1871–1958 Am. author and journalist; on staff of New York *Sun* (1891–1900), *McClure's Magazine* (1900–05); wrote *Average Jones, Success, The Harvey Girls*, etc.

Ad·dams \'a-dəmz\ Charles Samuel 1912–88 Am. cartoonist; created humorously macabre, ghoulish characters; work appeared frequently in the *New Yorker* (1940 ff.)

Addams Jane 1860–1935 Am. social worker; opened settlement house Hull-House, Chicago (1889); pres., Women's International League for Peace and Freedom (1919–35); helped found American Civil Liberties Union (1920); awarded (with Nicholas Murray Butler) 1931 Nobel peace prize

Ad·di·son \'a-də-sən\ Joseph 1672–1719 Eng. essayist, dramatist & poet; wrote essays for Steele's *Tatler* (1709–11); helped produce *Spectator* (1711–12); considered a master of English prose, esp. of periodical essay — **Ad·di·so·nian** \ˌa-də-'sō-nē-ən, -nyən\ *adj*

Ade \'ād\ George 1866–1944 Am. humorist & playwright; wrote *Fables in Slang, Breaking into Society*, etc., and plays *The Sultan of Sulu, Father and the Boys*, etc.

Ade·nau·er \'a-d°n-ˌaů(-ə)r, 'ä-\ Konrad 1876–1967 chancellor of West Germany (1949–63); helped form Christian Democratic Party (1945); first chancellor of postwar West Germany

Ad·ler \'äd-lər, 'ad-\ Alfred 1870–1937 Austrian psychiatrist; advanced theory of inferiority complex as explanation for psychopathy (1907); developed school of individual psychology — **Ad·le·ri·an** \äd-'lir-ē-ən, ad-\ *adj*

Ad·ler \'ad-lər\ Cyrus 1863–1940 Am. educ. & scholar; pres. Dropsie College (1908–24), Jewish Theological Seminary, NY (1924–40); edited *American Jewish Yearbook* (from 1899)

Ad·ler \'ad-lər\ Felix 1851–1933 Am. educ. & reformer; founder (1876) and lecturer, N.Y. Society for Ethical Culture; founded Workingmen's School (1880, later called Ethical Culture School); political and social ethics, Columbia U. (from 1902)

Ad·ler \'ad-lər\ Mortimer Jerome 1902–   Am. philos.; edited, with R.M. Hutchins, series *Great Books of the Western World* (1952); founded Institute for Philosophical Research (1952); wrote *The Idea of Freedom* (1958, 1961), etc.

Adri·an \'ā-drē-ən\ name of 6 popes: esp. **IV** (*Nicholas Break·spear* \'brāk-,spir\) 1100?–1159 the only Eng. pope (1154–59); crowned Frederick Barbarossa Holy Roman Emperor (1155); supposed to have issued bull giving Ireland to Henry II of England (1154)

Adrian Rom. emp. — see HADRIAN

Adrian Edgar Douglas 1889–1977 1st Baron of *Cambridge* Eng. physiol.; studied electrical activity of nerves and brain; awarded (with Sir Charles Sherrington) Nobel prize for physiology or medicine (1932)

Æ — see George William RUSSELL

Æl·fric \'al-frik\ *ca* 955–*ca* 1010 Eng. abbot & writer; called Grammaticus; wrote Latin and English grammar and glossary and two books of *Catholic Homilies* (990–92) and *Lives of the Saints;* considered greatest Anglo-Saxon prose writer of his time

Aeneas Silvius *or* **Sylvius** — see PIUS II

Aes·chi·nes \'es-kə-,nēz, 'ēs-\ 389–314 B.C. Athenian orator; opposed Demosthenes in Athenian assembly by advocating a policy of appeasement toward Philip II of Macedon

Aes·chy·lus \'es-kə-ləs, 'ēs-\ 525–456 B.C. Greek dram.; credited with creating true drama of action; wrote *Seven Against Thebes* (467), *Oresteia* trilogy (*Agamemnon, Libation Bearers, Eumenides*), *Prometheus Bound,* etc. — **Aes·chy·le·an** \,es-kə-'lē-ən, ,ēs-\ *adj*

Ae·sop \'ē-,säp, -səp\ Greek author of *Aesop's Fables;* prob. legendary; may have been a slave or adviser to King Croesus of Lydia — **Ae·so·pi·an** \ē-'sō-pē-ən, -'sä-\ *also* **Ae·sop·ic** \-'sä-pik\ *adj*

Aeth·el·berht \'a-thəl-,berkt\ *or* **Eth·el·bert** \'e-thəl-,bert, -thəl-, -,bərt\ *or* **Aed·il·berct** \'a-d'l-,berkt\ *d* 616 king of Kent (560–616); received Augustine and other missionaries sent by Pope Gregory I (597); issued first surviving Anglo-Saxon code of laws (604)

Aeth·el·red \'a-thəl-,red\ *or* **Eth·el·red II** \'e-thəl-\ 968?–1016 *the Unready* king of England (978–1016); purchased peace whenever unable to defend country against Danish and Norse invaders or put up ineffectual resistance

Afon·so I \ə-'fōn(n)-sü\ name of 6 kings of Portugal: esp. **I Hen·ri·ques** \ān-'rē-kish\ 1109?–1185 (1st king of Portugal; 1139–85); extended domain into Muslim territory; **V** 1432–1481 (reigned 1438–81); claimed throne of Léon and Castile through marriage to daughter of Henry IV; defeated by Ferdinand and Isabella (1476)

Aga Khan III \,ä-gə-'kän, ,a-\ 1877–1957 *Aga Sultan Sir Mohammed Shah* imam of a branch of Shiism (1885–1957); Indian representative at League of Nations (1932, 1934–37)

Aga Khan IV 1936–   *grandson of prec., Shah Karim* imam of a branch of Shiism (1957–)

Ag·as·siz \'a-gə-(,)sē\ Alexander 1835–1910 *son of J.L.R.* Am. zool.; curator, Harvard Museum (1874–85); made trips of zoological exploration to west coast of S. America (1875)

Agassiz (Jean) Louis (Rodolphe) 1807–1873 Am. (Swiss-born) naturalist; professor of natural history, Harvard (1847–73); began collections that became Harvard Museum of Comparative Zoology (1859); conducted expeditions to Brazil (1865), Cuba (1869), etc.

Agath·o·cles \ə-'ga-thə-,klēz\ 361–289 B.C. tyrant of Syracuse; eventually controlled most of Sicily; took title of king (ca. 304)

Agee \'ā-(,)jē\ James 1909–1955 Am. author; wrote film scripts for

African Queen (1951), *Night of the Hunter* (1955); wrote nonfiction *Let Us Now Praise Famous Men* (1941, pictures by Walker Evans) and novel *A Death in the Family* (1957, Pulitzer prize)

Ages·i·la·us II \ə-ˌje-sə-ˈlā-əs\ *ca* 444–360 B.C. king of Sparta (399–360); saved Sparta from Theban sieges (370–69, 362)

Ag·nes \ˈag-nəs\ Saint *d* A.D. 304 virgin martyr; martyred at Rome; patron saint of young girls

Ag·new \ˈag-ˌnü, -ˌnyü\ Spi·ro \ˈspir-(ˌ)ō\ Theodore 1918– Am. polit.; vice pres. of the U.S. (1969–73); resigned after pleading no contest to charge of taking bribes

Ag·non \ˈag-ˌnän\ Shmuel Yosef 1888–1970 Israeli (Austrian-born) author; often considered greatest writer in modern Hebrew; awarded (with Nelly Sachs) 1966 Nobel prize in literature

Agric·o·la \ə-ˈgri-kə-lə\ Gnaeus Julius A.D. 40–93 Rom. gen.; consul (77) and governor of Britain (77–84); conquered, pacified Britain to northern boundary of Perth and Argyll

Agrip·pa \ə-ˈgri-pə\ Marcus Vipsanius 63?–12 B.C. Rom. statesman; son-in-law, deputy of emperor Augustus whom he helped to power; as naval commander, largely responsible for defeat of Antony at Actium (31)

Ag·rip·pi·na \ˌa-grə-ˈpī-nə, -ˈpē-\ the elder *ca* 14 B.C.–A.D. 33 *dau. of Agrippa, wife of Germanicus Caesar, mother of Caligula*; banished to Pandataria where died of starvation, perhaps voluntarily

Agrippina the younger A.D. 15?–59 *dau. of prec. & mother of Emp. Nero;* may have poisoned husband Claudius after he adopted Nero as his heir

Agui·nal·do \ˌä-gē-ˈnäl-(ˌ)dō\ Emilio 1869–1964 Filipino leader; led Filipino forces in rebellion against Spain (1896–98); led uprising against U.S. control (1899–1901)

Ah·med III \ä-ˈmet, -ˈmed\ 1673–1736 Ottoman sultan (1703–30); forced into war with Russia (1711–13); defeated in invasion of Hungary (1716); lost territory in treaty (1718)

Ai·ken \ˈā-kən\ Conrad Potter 1889–1973 Am. writer; wrote verse, including "Preludes to Definition" and "Morning Song of Senlin"; novels and short stories, including "Strange Moonlight," "Silent Snow, Secret Snow," and "Mr. Arcularis"

Ai·ley \ˈā-lē\ Alvin 1931–1989 Am. dancer & choreographer; founded Alvin Ailey American Dance Theatre (1958); worked in multiracial, topical modern dance idioms

Ains·worth \ˈānz-(ˌ)wərth\ (William) Harrison 1805–1882 Eng. nov.; wrote historical romances, including *Rookwood, Guy Fawkes, Lancashire Witches,* etc., several illustrated by Cruikshank

Ai·shah \ˈä-ē-shə\ 611–678 *favorite wife of Muhammad;* helped foment opposition to caliph ʿUthmān; captured in Battle of the Camel against caliph ʿAli (656)

Ak·bar \ˈak-bər, -ˌbär\ 1542–1605 Mughal emp. of India (1556–1605); famed as administrator, reformer; abolished extortion, developed trade, tolerated many religions; brilliant patron of arts; built capital Fatehpur Sīkri (1570–86)

à Kempis — see THOMAS À KEMPIS

Aken·side \ˈā-kən-ˌsīd\ Mark 1721–1770 Eng. poet & physician; physician to the queen (1761); wrote *Pleasures of the Imagination, Odes on Several Subjects, Hymn to the Naiads,* etc.

Akhe·na·ton \ˌäk-ˈnä-t²n, ˌä-kə-\ *also* **Ikh·na·ton** \ik-ˈnä-t²n\ kin of Egypt (1379–1362 B.C.); 18th dynasty; reigned at first as Amenhotep IV but changed name with new religion of Aton, the sun disk; sometimes considered the first monotheist

Aki·ba ben Jo·seph \ä-'ki-vä-ben-'jō-zəf\ A.D. 40–135 Jewish sage & martyr in Palestine; founded rabbinical school at Jaffa; developed Midrash, new interpretation of oral law (Halakha)

Aki·hi·to \ä-kē-'hē-(ˌ)tō\ 1933–   emp. of Japan (1989–); his reign marked new era of Heisei, the "achievement of universal peace"

'Alam·gīr \'ä-ləm-ˌgir\ Muhī-ud-Dīn Muhammad 1618–1707 *Aurang·zeb* \ˌau-rəŋ-'zeb, ó-, -'zēb\ Mughal emp. of India; during his reign Mughal Empire reached greatest extent; his imposition of Muslim orthodoxy alienated others, provoked rebellions

Alanbrooke Viscount — see Sir Alan Francis BROOKE

Alar·cón, de \ˌä-ˌlär-'kōn, -'kón\ Pedro Antonio 1833–1891 Span. writer & statesman; minister to Norway and Sweden; wrote novels *El sombrero de tres picos* (1874), *El niño de la bola* (1878), chronicle *Diario de un testigo de la guerra de Africa* (1859)

Al·a·ric \'a-lə-rik\ ca 370–410 Visigoth king; conqueror of Rome; besieged Rome (408, 409); appointed Attalus emperor (409), deposed him (410); besieged, occupied, sacked Rome (410)

Alaric II d 507 Visigoth king; issued legal code; known as *Lex Romana Visigothorum* or *Breviarum Alaricanum*; defeated, killed by Clovis and Franks at Battle of Vouillé

Al·bee \'ól-(ˌ)bē, 'al-\ Edward Franklin 1928–   Am. dram.; wrote *Who's Afraid of Virginia Woolf?* (1962, filmed 1966), *A Delicate Balance* (1966, Pulitzer prize), *Seascape* (1975, Pulitzer prize), *Three Tall Women* (1994, Pulitzer prize), etc.

Albemarle Duke of — see George MONCK

Al·bé·niz \äl-'bā-(ˌ)nēs, -(ˌ)nēth\ Isaac 1860–1909 Span. pianist & composer; a leader of Spanish nationalist school; composed operas, zarzuelas, piano pieces, including *Iberia* (1906–09), etc.

Al·bers \'al-bərz, 'äl-bərs\ Josef 1888–1976 Am. (Ger.-born) painter; worked on experiments in color and geometry in series of paintings *Homage to the Square*, and drawings *Structural Constellations;* influenced Color Field and Op Art movements

Al·bert I \'al-bərt\ 1875–1934 king of Belgium (1909–34); reaffirmed Belgian neutrality, refused German demand for passage of troops (1914); led Belgian army in retreat to Flanders (1914) and led Belgian and French troops in final Allied offensive (1918)

Albert Carl Bert 1908–   Am. polit.; first elected to House of Representatives in 1946; speaker of the House (1971–76)

Albert of Saxe–Co·burg–Go·tha \'saks-'kō-ˌbərg-'go-tə, -thə\ 1819–1861 *prince consort of* Queen Victoria of Great Britain (1840–61); tutor and adviser to Victoria; set high moral standards for household and aristocracy

Al·ber·tus Mag·nus \al-'bər-təs-'mag-nəs\ Saint ca 1200–1280 *Albert* Count *von Boll·städt* \'ból-ˌshtet\ Ger. philos. & theol.; prepared commentaries on Aristotle; established place for natural science in system of Christian studies; recognized as greatest scholar of the day; wrote *Summa theologica* (incomplete), etc.

Al·boin \'al-ˌbóin, -bə-wən\ d 572 Lombard king (ca 565–572); led Lombards, Saxons, and others into northern Italy; established kingdom of Lombardy with capital at Pavia (569–72)

Albucasis — see ABŪ AL-QĀSIM

Al·bu·quer·que, de \ˈal-bə-ˌkər-kē, ˌal-bə-'\ Afonso 1453–1515 Port. viceroy & conqueror in India; named governor in India (1508); captured Goa (1510); took control (1510–1515) of Malabar coast, Ceylon, Sunda Isles, Malacca

Al·cae·us \al-ˈsē-əs\ *ca* 620–*ca* 580 B.C. Greek poet; wrote hymns, drinking and love songs, political odes

Al·ci·bi·a·des \ˌal-sə-ˈbī-ə-ˌdēz\ *ca* 450–404 B.C. Athenian gen. & polit.; persuaded Athens to join alliance against Spartans (431); later plotted against Athens; commanded Athenian fleet and won several victories over Sparta (411, 410)

Al·cott \ˈȯl-kət, ˈal-, -ˌkät\ Amos Bronson 1799–1888 Am. teacher, writer & transcendental philos.; established cooperative utopian community, Fruitlands, near Harvard, Mass. (1844–45)

Alcott Louisa May 1832–1888 *dau. of A.B.* Am. author; wrote *Little Women* (1868), *Little Men* (1871), *Jo's Boys* (1886), etc.

Al·cuin \ˈal-kwən\ *ca* 732–804 Anglo-Saxon theol. & scholar; introduced Anglo-Saxon scholarship into Frankish schools, sparking Carolingian Renaissance

Al·da \ˈäl-də, ˈȯl-, ˈal-\ Frances 1883–1952 *orig. Frances Davis* N.Z.-born soprano; at Metropolitan Opera, N.Y. (1908–29)

Al·den \ˈȯl-dən\ John 1599?–1687 *Mayflower* pilgrim; signer of Mayflower Compact; remembered for his part in legend involving Priscilla Mullins and Miles Standish

Al·der \ˈäl-dər\ Kurt 1902–1958 Ger. chem.; awarded (with Otto Diels) 1950 Nobel prize for chemistry for work in organic chemistry and discovery of Diels-Alder reaction

Al·drich \ˈȯl-drich\ Thomas Bailey 1836–1907 Am. author & editor; edited *Every Saturday* (1865–74), *Atlantic Monthly* (1881–90); wrote stories, including *The Story of a Bad Boy* (1870)

Al·drin \ˈȯl-drən\ Edwin Eugene Jr. 1930– Am. astronaut; member of Apollo XI mission; 2d man on moon

Alei·chem Sha·lom \ˌshȯ-ləm-ə-ˈlā-kəm, shō-\ 1859–1916 pseud. of *Sholem Ra·bin·o·witz* \rə-ˈbi-nə-ˌwits\ Am. (Russ.-born) humorist; wrote over 40 volumes of novels, stories, and plays in Yiddish; works include *Jewish Children, Tevye's Daughters,* etc.

Aleix·an·dre \ˌä-lek-ˈsän-dre\ Vicente 1898–1984 Span. poet; regarded as a Surrealist; wrote *La destrucción o el amor, En un vasto dominio*; awarded 1977 Nobel prize for literature

Ale·mán \ˌä-lā-ˈmän\ Mateo 1547–*ca* 1614 Span. nov.; wrote picaresque novel *Guzmán de Alfarache* (1599; part II, 1604)

Alemán Val·dés \väl-ˈdes\ Miguel 1902–1983 Mex. lawyer; pres. of Mexico (1946–52)

Alem·bert, d' \ˌda-ləm-ˈbar, -ˈber\ Jean Le Rond 1717–1783 Fr. math. & philos.; discovered partial differential equations; explained precession of equinoxes, rotation of Earth's axis; with Diderot edited the *Encyclopédie* (1746–54)

Al·ex·an·der \ˌa-lig-ˈzan-dər, ˌe-\ name of 8 popes: esp. **VI** (*Rodrigo Borgia*) 1431–1503 (pope 1492–1503); issued bull dividing New World between Spain and Portugal (1493); ordered execution of Savanarola (1498); instituted censorship of books (1501); greatly increased temporal power of papacy; patronized arts

Alexander III of Macedon 356–323 B.C. *the Great* king (336–323); son of Philip II; gained control over all Greece (335)

moved East into Persia; occupied Egypt, founded Alexandria (332); occupied Babylon; invaded northern India (326), withdrew (325–24) — **Al·ex·an·dri·an** \ˌa-lig-ˈzan-drē-ən, ˌe-\ *adj*

Alexander *Russ* **Alek·sandr** \ä-lik-ˈsän-dər\ name of 3 emps. of Russia: **I** 1777–1825 (reigned 1801–25); invaded by Napoleon (1812); helped defeat French army; entered Paris with allies (1814); formed Holy Alliance (1815); **II** 1818–1881 (reigned 1855–81); emancipated serfs (1861); expanded Russian territories in Caucasus, Central Asia (1868–81); killed by bomb in St. Petersburg; **III** 1845–1894 (reigned 1881–94); canceled liberal reforms of father; expanded Russian territory to border of Afghanistan (1884–85)

Alexander *Serb* **Alek·san·dar Obre·no·vić** \ä-lik-ˈsän-dər-ō-ˈbre-nə-ˌvich\ 1876–1903 king of Serbia (1889–1903); abolished Constitution of 1889; murdered by military; last of Obrenović family

Alexander Jane 1939– Am. actress; appeared in plays *The Great White Hope, Antony and Cleopatra*, in films *Kramer vs. Kramer*, etc.; chair, National Endowment for the Arts (1993–)

Alexander (Andrew) Lamar 1940– Am. polit.; gov. of Tennessee (1979–87); U.S. secy. of education (1991–93)

Alexander Harold Rupert Leofric George 1891–1969 1st Earl *Alexander of Tu·nis* \ˈtü-nəs, ˈtyü-\ Brit. field marshal; commanded invasions of Sicily (July 1943) and Italy (Sept. 1943); allied commander-in-chief in Italy (1944–45); gov.-gen. of Canada (1946–52)

Alexander I 1888–1934 king of Yugoslavia (1929–34); commanded Serbian forces in WWI; proclaimed kingdom of Serbs, Croats, and Slovenes (1918); established royal dictatorship (1929), took name Yugoslavia; assassinated by Croatian separatists

Alexander Nev·sky \ˈnev-skē, ˈnef-\ *ca* 1220–1263 Russ. saint & mil. hero; defeated Swedes (1240) and Germans (1242) in great battles; halted eastward drive of Swedes and Germans into Russia; canonized by Russian Orthodox Church (1547)

Alexander Se·ve·rus \sə-ˈvir-əs\ A.D. 208–235 Rom. emp. (222–235); defeated by Persians in Mesopotamia (232); bought peace from Alemanni (234); murdered by angry soldiers

Alex·is I Mi·khay·lo·vich \ə-ˌlek-səs-mi-ˈki̇-lə-ˌvich\ 1629–1676 *father of Peter the Great* czar of Russia (1645–76); gained control over eastern Ukraine (1654); suppressed great peasant revolt (1667–71); promulgated law code legitimizing serfdom (1649)

Alexis Pe·tro·vich \pe-ˈtrō-vich\ 1690–1718 *son of Peter the Great* czarevitch of Russia; opposed father's reforms; suspected of conspiring to usurp Peter; condemned to death, died before execution

Alex·i·us I Com·ne·nus \ə-ˈlek-sē-əs-ˌkäm-ˈnē-nəs\ 1048–1118 Byzantine emp. (1081–1118); defended empire against Sythians, Turks, Italian Normans; domain invaded by First Crusade (1096–99); founded Comnenian dynasty

Al·fie·ri \ˌal-fē-ˈer-ē\ Conte Vittorio 1749–1803 Ital. tragic poet; wrote tragedies using classical form, mostly about struggles against tyranny, including *Filippo, Antigone, Mirra, Saul*, etc.

Al·fon·so XIII \al-ˈfän(t)-(ˌ)sō, -ˈfän-(ˌ)zō\ 1886–1941 king of Spain (1886–1931); held Spain neutral during WWI; left Spain (1931) after elections returned large Republican majority

Al·fred *or* **Æl·fred** \ˈal-frəd, -fərd\ 849–899 *the Great* king of Wessex (871–899); recognized as ruler of all England not controlled by Danes (886); compiled laws; promoted learning; translated works of St. Gregory I, St. Augustine, Boethius

Alf·vén \(ˌ)al(f)-ˈvän, -ˈven\ Hannes Olof Gösta 1908–1995 Swed. astrophysicist; awarded 1970 Nobel prize in physics for his study of electrical and magnetic effects in fluids that conduct electricity

Al·ger \ˈal-jər\ Horatio 1832–1899 Am. author; wrote popular books for boys, including the *Ragged Dick* (1867), *Luck and Pluck* (1869), and *Tattered Tom* (1871) series

Al·gren \ˈol-grən\ Nelson 1909–1981 Am. author of naturalistic novels, including *Somebody in Boots* (1935), *Man with the Golden Arm* (1949), *Walk on the Wild Side* (1956), etc.

ʿAlī \ä-ˈlē, ˈä-lē\ *Ar* ʿAlī ibn Abī Tā·lib \-ˌi-bən-ˌä-bē-ˈtä-lib\ *ca* 600–661 *cousin & son-in-law of Muhammad* 4th orthodox caliph (656–661); invited to become caliph after murder of ʿUthmān; revered by Shiʿite branch as true successor to Muhammad

Ali Pa·şa \ˈpä-shə, ˈpa-; pə-ˈshä\ 1741–1822 *the Lion of Janina* Turk. pasha; held power over much of Albania, Macedonia, Thessaly, Epirus, the Morea

Ali \ä-ˈlē\ Muhammad 1942–   orig. *Cassius Marcellus Clay* Am. boxer; 1st and only boxer to win heavyweight championship 3 times; famous for flamboyant rhetorical style out of the ring

Al·lais \á-lā\ Maurice 1911–   Fr. econ.; awarded 1988 Nobel prize in economics for his theories on economic markets and the efficient use of resources

Al·len \ˈa-lən\ Ethan 1738–1789 Am. Revolutionary soldier; commanded Green Mountain Boys of Vermont (1770–75); seized Fort Ticonderoga with Benedict Arnold (May 10, 1775)

Allen William 1532–1594 Eng. cardinal; founded English Roman Catholic Seminary at Douai/Reims (1568); began Reims-Douai translation of Bible; served on commission to revise Vulgate

Allen Woody 1935–   orig. *Allen Stewart Konigsberg* Am. writer, actor, director; wrote and directed films *Annie Hall* (1977), *Hannah and Her Sisters* (1986), *Crimes and Misdemeanors* (1989), etc.

Al·len·by \ˈa-lən-bē\ Edmund Henry Hynman 1861–1936 1st Viscount *Allenby of Megiddo and Felixstone* Brit. field marshal; commanded cavalry in WWI (1914–15); in charge of Egyptian Expeditionary Force; took Beersheba and Gaza from Turks (1917), entered Jerusalem (1917), won victory at Megiddo (1918)

Allen·de Gos·sens \ˌyen-dā-ˈgô-ˌsen(t)s\ Salvador 1908–1973 Chilean Marxist; pres. of Chile (1970–73); overthrown in coup during which he died

Al·leyne \ˈa-lən, -ˌlēn, -ˌlän\ Edward 1566–1626 Eng. actor; built Fortune Theatre at Cripplegate with Philip Henslowe (1600), directed Lord Admiral's company (1600–03)

All·ston \ˈol-stən\ Washington 1779–1843 Am. painter; noted for dramatic subjects, use of light, atmospheric color; American Romantic; paintings include *Moonlit Landscape*, etc.

Al·ma–Tad·e·ma \ˌal-mə-ˈta-də-mə\ Sir Lawrence 1836–1912 Eng. (Du.-born) painter; known for historic idylls, genre scenes; excelled at textures, architectural detail; works include *Tarquinius Superbus* (1867), *Danse pyrrhique* (1869), *Wine Shop* (1869), etc.

Alt·man \ˈolt-mən\ Sidney 1939–   Am. (Canad.-born) biophysicist; awarded (with Thomas R. Cech) 1989 Nobel prize in chemistry for their discovery that ribonucleic acid (RNA) is able to assist chemical reactions in cells

Alva Duke of — see ÁLVAREZ DE TOLEDO

Al·va·ra·do, de \ˌäl-vä-ˈrä-thō\ Pedro *ca* 1485–1541 Span. conquistador; with Grijalva (1518) and Cortés in conquest of Mexico (1519–21); led expedition to Guatemala (1523–27); led expedition against Quito (1534); engaged in quest for Seven Cities of Cíbola

Ál·va·rez \ˈal-və-ˌrez\ Luis Walter 1911–1988 Am. physicist; awarded 1968 Nobel prize in physics for contributions to the knowledge of subatomic particles

Ál·va·rez de To·le·do \ˈäl-vä-ˌräth-thä-tō-ˈlä-thō\ Fernando 1507–1582 3d Duke of *Alba* \ˈal-ba\ *or Alva* \ˈal-va\ Span. gen.; master of military strategy; sent by Philip II to pacify Netherlands (1567); commanded brilliantly successful invasion of Portugal (1581)

Alvarez Quin·te·ro \kēn-ˈtā-rō\ Serafín 1871–1938 & his bro. Joaquín 1873–1944 Span. dram.; together wrote almost 200 plays about Andalusian life, including *La reja* (1897), *El amor que pasa* (1904), *Malvaloca* (1912), etc.

Ama·ti \ä-ˈmä-tē, ə-\ family of Ital. violin makers of Cremona: esp. Nicolò 1596–1684; teacher of Antonio Stradivari and of Andrea Guarneri; improved violin and developed grand Amati

Am·brose \ˈam-ˌbrōz\ Saint 339–397 bishop of Milan; considered architect of medieval church-state relations; works included *Hexaemeron*, *De bono mortis*, hymns, etc.; a doctor of the church — **Am·bro·sian** \am-ˈbrō-zhən, -zē-ən\ *adj*

Amen·ho·tep \ˌä-mən-ˈhō-ˌtep, ˌa-\ *or* **Am·e·no·phis** \ˌa-mə-ˈnō-fəs\ name of 4 kings of Egypt: esp. **III** (1417–1379 B.C.); **IV**— see AKHENATON

Amerigo Vespucci — see VESPUCCI

Am·herst \ˈa-(ˌ)mərst\ Jeffrey 1717–1797 Baron *Amherst* Brit. gen.; commanded expedition against French America; gov.-gen. of Brit. No. America (1760–63); commander in chief of British army (1772–75); Amherst Coll. and several U.S. towns named after him

Amis \ˈä-məs\ Kingsley 1922–1995 Eng. author; wrote *Lucky Jim, I Want It Now, The Old Devils,* etc.; also wrote James Bond novels under pseudonym Robert Markham

Amos \ˈä-məs\ 8th cent. B.C. Hebrew prophet; earliest prophet to have a book of the Bible named for him

Am·père \äⁿ-ˈper\ André-Marie 1775–1836 Fr. physicist; formulated mathematical basis of electrodynamics, including Ampère's law on force between two electrical currents

Amund·sen \ˈä-mən-sən\ Roald 1872–1928 Norw. polar explorer; navigated Northwest Passage, fixed position of North Magnetic Pole (1903–06); first to reach South Pole (Dec. 1911)

Anac·re·on \ə-ˈna-krē-ən\ *ca* 582–*ca* 485 B.C. Greek poet; famed for satires and for lyrics celebrating love and wine — **Anac·re·on·tic** \ə-ˌna-krē-ˈän-tik\ *adj*

An·ax·ag·o·ras \ˌa-ˌnak-ˈsa-gə-rəs\ *ca* 500–*ca* 428 B.C. Greek philos.; taught at Athens ca. 480–450; pupils included Pericles, Euripides, possibly Socrates; introduced dualistic explanation of universe — **An·ax·ag·o·re·an** \-ˌsa-gə-ˈrē-ən\ *adj*

Anax·i·man·der \ə-ˌnak-sə-ˌman-dər\ 610–*ca* 547 B.C. Greek philos. & astron.; credited with introduction of sundial, invention of geographical maps; often considered first thinker to develop a cosmology of the world — **Anax·i·man·dri·an** \ə-,nak-sə-'man-drē-ən\ *adj*

An·ders \'än-dərs, -dərz\ Władysław 1892–1970 Pol. gen.; fought Germany and Soviet Union at beginning of WWII; post-war leader of anti-communist Polish exiles

An·der·sen \'an-dər-sən\ Hans Christian 1805–1875 Dan. writer; best known for *Tales, Told for Children,* including "Princess and the Pea," "Ugly Duckling," "Emperor's New Clothes," etc.

An·der·son \'an-dər-sən\ Carl David 1905–1991 Am. physicist; awarded (with Victor Hess) 1936 Nobel prize for physics for discovering the positron; confirmed existence of mesons

Anderson Sir John 1882–1958 1st Viscount *Wa·ver·ley* \'wä-vər-lē\ Brit. polit.; home secy., min. of home security (1939–40); chancellor of the exchequer (1943–45); created viscount (1952)

Anderson Dame Judith 1898–1992 orig. *Frances Margaret Anderson* Austral. actress; played classical roles on stage, cruel, repressed matriarchs in films

Anderson Laurie 1947–   Am. performance artist; composer and performer of multimedia exhibitions, including *Duets on Ice, The Kitchen,* etc.; also produced films, recordings, art works

Anderson Marian 1897–1993 Am. contralto; first black singer at New York's Metropolitan Opera Company (1955); appointed delegate to U.N.(1958)

Anderson Maxwell 1888–1959 Am. dram.; wrote *What Price Glory* (1924, with Ernest Stallings), *Both Your Houses* (Pulitzer prize, 1933), *Key Largo* (1939), etc.

Anderson Philip Warren 1923–   Am. physicist; awarded (with John H. Van Vleck and Sir Neville F. Mott) 1977 Nobel prize for physics for helping develop semiconductor devices

Anderson Sherwood 1876–1941 Am. writer; wrote story collections *Winesburg Ohio* (1919), *Horses and Men,* etc.; autobiographies *Story Teller's Story, Tar: A Midwest Childhood;* pioneered psychological naturalism, use of vernacular prose

An·drás·sy \'ón-,drä-shē\ Count Gyula 1823–1890 Hung. statesman; first constitutional prime min. of Hungary (1867); foreign min. of Austro-Hungary (1871–79); maneuvered to check growth of Russian and Slavic power in Balkans

An·dre \'an-drē, än-(,)drā\ Carl 1935–   Am. sculptor; a leading exponent of minimalist art

André John 1750–1780 Brit. spy; appointed to negotiate with Benedict Arnold for betrayal of West Point to British (1779–80); captured and hanged

An·drea del Sar·to \än-'drā-ə-,del-'sär-(,)tō\ 1486–1530 *Andrea d'Agnolo* Florentine painter; works include frescoes on life of John the Baptist (1511–26), *Marriage of St. Catherine* (1512–13), *Pietà* (ca.1520), etc.; concerned with color, expression of emotion

An·dre·ot·ti \,än-drā-'ä-(,)tē\ Giulio 1919–   prime min. of Italy (1972–73; 1976–79; 1989–92); member of Christian Democratic Party

An·dret·ti \än-'dre-tē, an-\ Mario Gabriele 1940–   Am. (Ital.-born) automobile racer; winner of Indianapolis 500 (1969); Formula One world champion (1978); many other titles

An·drews \'an-,drüz\ Roy Chapman 1884–1960 Am. naturalist, explorer, author; headed expeditions (1916–30) throughout Asia; discovered dinosaur eggs, remains of Baluchitherium, evidence of ancient human life; wrote *Across Mongolian Plains* (1921), etc.

Andrews Julie 1935–   Am. (Brit.-born) actress; appeared on Broadway in *My Fair Lady* (1956), *Camelot* (1960), etc.; in films *Mary Poppins* (1964, Academy Award), *Sound of Music* (1965), etc.

An·dre·yev \än-ˈdrā-yəf\ Leonid Nikolayevich 1871–1919 Russ. author; wrote short stories notable for realism, pessimism, novels including *Gubernator* (1905), etc., plays

An·drić \ˈän-drich\ Ivo 1892–1975 Serbo-Croatian author; wrote lyrical meditations *Ex Ponto* (1918), novels, short stories; awarded 1961 Nobel Prize in literature

An·dro·pov \an-ˈdrō-ˌpóv\ Yuri Vladimirovich 1914–1984 Russ. polit.; pres. U.S.S.R. (1982–84); 1st secy. of communist party (1982–84)

An·dros \ˈan-ˌdräs, -drəs\ Sir Edmund 1637–1714 Brit. colonial gov. in America; gov. of province of New York and New Jersey (1674–81), then of "Dominion of New England" (1686); gov. of Virginia (1692–98), of Maryland (1693–94)

An·fin·sen \ˈan-fən-sən\ Christian Boehmer 1916–1995 Am. chem.; awarded (with Stanford Moore and William H. Stein) 1972 Nobel prize in chemistry for study of the chemistry of enzymes

An·ge·la Me·ri·ci \ˈan-jə-lə-mə-ˈrē-chē\ Saint 1474?–1540 Ital. religious & founder of Ursuline order after vision (1535); order was first teaching order for young girls; canonized (1807)

An·ge·li·co \an-ˈje-li-ˌkō\ Fra *ca* 1400–1455 *orig. Guido di Pietro* Florentine painter; outstanding painter of early Renaissance; chief works include altarpieces *Madonna della Stella*, *Deposition* in Florence, *Annalena Altarpiece*, etc.

An·gell \ˈän-jəl\ Sir Norman 1872–1967 *orig. Ralph Norman Angell Lane* Eng. author & lecturer; wrote *The Great Illusion* (1910), *The Great Illusion, 1933* (1933), other works on international affairs, finance, peace; awarded 1933 Nobel peace prize

An·ge·lou \ˈan-jə-ˌlō, -ˌlü\ Maya 1928–   *Marguerite Annie Angelou* Am. writer; wrote novels *I Know Why the Caged Bird Sings, The Heart of a Woman*, poems *And Still I Rise*, etc.

Ång·ström \ˈaŋ-strəm, ˈöŋ-\ Anders Jonas 1814–1874 Swed. physicist; a founder of spectroscopy; angstrom unit of length named for him; identified hydrogen in solar atmosphere (1862); published maps of solar spectrum (1868)

An·na Iva·nov·na \ˈa-nə-ē-ˈvä-nəv-nə\ 1693–1740 empress of Russia (1730–40); influenced War of Polish Succession (1733–35); allied with Austria in war against Turks (1736–39)

Anne \ˈan\ 1665–1714 *dau. of James II* queen of Great Britain (1702–14); reign marked by bitter party disputes, War of Spanish Succession; accomplished Act of Union with Scotland (1707)

Anne of Austria 1601–1666 *consort of Louis XIII of France* regent (1643–51) for her son Louis XIV; chose Cardinal Mazarin as prime min.; maintained absolute rule against nobles, defeated Fronde rebellion

Anne of Cleves \ˈklēvz\ 1515–1557 *4th wife of Henry VIII of England*; selected as wife for Henry to ally him with German Protestants against emperor; marriage soon annulled by Parliament at Henry's request

Annunzio, D' Gabriele — see D'ANNUNZIO

Anouilh \a-'nü-ē\ Jean 1910–1987 Fr. dram.; a major figure in the 20th century French theater; works include *Antigone* (1944); *L'Alouette* (1953), *Becket ou l'honneur de Dieu* (1959)

An·selm \'an-₁selm\ Saint 1033/34–1109 archbishop of Canterbury (1093–1109); wrote *Monologion, Proslogion, Cur Deus Homo*? canonized (1063?) and declared doctor of the church (1720)

An·tall \'òn-₁tòl\ József 1932–1993 prim. min. of Hungary (1990–93)

An·tho·ny \'an(t)-thə-nē, *chiefly Brit* 'an-tə-\ Saint *ca* 250–355 Egypt. monk; first Christian monk; organized communities of hermits (c. 305); subject of legends about temptations, struggles against forces of evil; viewed as founder of Christian monasticism

Anthony Mark — see MARCUS ANTONIUS

Anthony Susan Brownell 1820–1906 Am. suffragist; active from ca. 1850 in temperance, abolitionist, woman suffragist movements; with Elizabeth Cady Stanton organized National Woman Suffrage Association (1869)

Anthony *or* **An·to·ny** \'an-tə-nē\ **of Padua** Saint 1195–1231 Franciscan monk; named first Franciscan professor of theology by St. Francis (1223); canonized (1232) by Pope Gregory IX

An·tig·o·nus I \an-'ti-gə-nəs\ 382–301 B.C. *Antigonus Cyclops* gen. of Alexander the Great & king of Macedonia (306–301); invaded Egypt 305; revived pan-Hellenic League (302)

An·ti·o·chus \an-'tī-ə-kəs\ name of 13 Seleucid kings of Syria: esp. **III** *the Great* 242–187 B.C. (reigned 223–187); aggravated tension with Rome by harboring Hannibal (195); defeated by Romans at Thermopylae (191); completely defeated (190) by P. Scipio Africanus; **IV** *Epiph·a·nes* \i-'pi-fə-₁nēz\ *ca* 215–164 B.C. (reigned 175–164); fostered Hellenic culture; opposition to Jewish religion caused Wars of the Macabees (166–160); lost Jerusalem

An·tip·a·ter \an-'ti-pə-tər\ *ca* 397–*ca* 319 B.C. Macedonian gen.; left in command of Macedonia and Greece after death of Alexander the Great

An·tis·the·nes \an-'tis-thə-₁nēz\ *ca* 445–*ca* 365 B.C. Athenian philos.; studied under Socrates; founded Cynic school, teaching that happiness depends on moral virtue

An·to·ne·scu \₁an-tə-'nes-(₁)kü\ Ion \'yòn\ 1882–1946 Romanian gen.; dictator (1940–44); Fascist; allied with Germany in war against Russia (1941); overthrown in coup d'état by King Michael (1944); executed as war criminal

An·to·ni·nus \₁an-tə-'nī-nəs\ Marcus Au·re·lius \ò-'rēl-yəs, -'rē-lē-əs\ A.D. 121–180 *nephew, son-in-law, and adopted son of Antoninus Pius* Rom. emp. (161–180); eminent Stoic philosopher, gentle and wise, but opposed Christianity and supported persecutions; wrote *Meditations*, precepts of practical morality

Antoninus Pi·us \-'pī-əs\ A.D. 86–161 Rom. emp. (138–161); reign was generally peaceful; in Britain, Wall of Antonine built by Roman governor from Forth to Clyde to keep out Picts, Scots

An·to·ni·us \-'tō-nē-əs\ Marcus E Mark *or* Marc An·to·ny \'an-tə-nē\ *or* An·tho·ny \'an(t)-thə-nē, *chiefly Brit* 'an-tə-\ *ca* 82–30 B.C. Rom. orator, triumvir, & gen.; went to Asia to punish Cleopatra but succumbed to her charms (41); took East in division of empire (40–36); settled with Cleopatra in Egypt (34); with Cleopatra, defeated by Octavian in naval battle at Actium (31); committed suicide

Apel·les \ə-'pe-lēz\ 4th cent. B.C. Greek painter; court painter of Philip II of Macedon and Alexander the Great; reputedly greatest painter of antiquity

Apol·li·naire \ə-,pä-lə-'nar, -'ner\ Guillaume 1880–1918 orig. *Wilhelm Apollinaris de Kos·tro·witz·ki* \,kös-trə-'vēt-skē\ Fr. poet; often wrote in fantastic or whimsical manner; wrote verse *Calligrams*, etc.; stories *Cubist Paintings* (with the aid of Picasso), play *The Breasts of Teiresias*, for which he coined the term "surrealism"

Ap·ol·lo·ni·us \,a-pə-'lō-nē-əs\ **of Rhodes** 3d cent. B.C. Greek poet; wrote epic *Argonautica* based on legend of Jason, Medea, and the Argonauts — **Ap·ol·lo·nian** \-nē-ən, -nyən\ *adj*

Appius Claudius — see CLAUDIUS

Appleseed Johnny — see John CHAPMAN

Ap·ple·ton \'a-pəl-tən\ Sir Edward 1892–1965 Eng. physicist; awarded 1947 Nobel prize for physics for discovery of electrically charged atmospheric layer (Appleton Layer or F region) that reflects radio waves

Apraks·in or **Aprax·in** \ə-'prak-sən\ Fyodor Matveyevich 1661–1728 Russ. admiral; defeated Swedes (1708), saving St. Petersburg from destruction

Ap·u·le·ius \,a-pə-'lā-əs\ Lucius *ca* A.D. 124–after 170? Rom. philos. & rhetorician; wrote *Metamorphoses, or The Golden Ass*, Latin novel that provided material for many later authors

Aquinas Saint Thomas — see THOMAS AQUINAS

Aqui·no \ə-'kē-nō\ Corazon 1933– pres. of Philippines (1986–92); elected president after husband assassinated

'Ar·a·fāt \är-ə-'fät, 'ar-ə-,fat\ Yāsir 1929– *Raḥmān 'Abd Ar-ra'ūf Al-Qudwah* Palestinian polit. leader; head of Palestinian Liberation Organization (from 1968); awarded (with Yitzhak Rabin and Shimon Peres) 1994 Nobel prize for peace

Ar·am \'ar-əm, 'er-\ Eugene 1704–1759 Eng. philologist & murderer; recognized early the Indo-European affinities of Celtic; subject of romance by Bulwer-Lytton and of ballad by Thomas Hood

Ara·nha \ə-'ran-yə\ Oswaldo 1894–1960 Braz. lawyer & polit.; a leader in Vargas coup d'état (1930); held political positions including ambassador to U.S., pres. of U.N. General Assembly, etc.

Ar·ber \'är-bər\ Werner 1929– Swiss microbiologist; awarded (with Daniel Nathans and Hamilton O. Smith) 1978 Nobel prize in physiology or medicine for their discoveries in molecular genetics

Arblay, d' Madame — see Fanny BURNEY

Ar·buth·not \är-'bəth-nət, 'är-bəth-,nät\ John 1667–1735 Scot. physician & author; friend of Swift, Pope, Gay; founder with them of Scriblerus Club; wrote witty political pamphlets which popularized modern conception of John Bull as typical Englishman

Ar·cher \'är-chər\ Jeffrey Howard 1940– Brit. author, politician; member Parliament (1969–74); author of novels *Not a Penny More, Not a Penny Less, Kane and Abel, A Matter of Honor*, etc.

Archer William 1856–1924 Scot. critic & dram.; wrote *Masks or Faces?* (1888), *Play-Making* (1912), *The Green Goddess* (1923)

Ar·chi·me·des \,är-kə-'mē-dēz\ *ca* 287–212 B.C. Greek math. & inventor; known esp. for work in mechanics; discovered principle of buoyancy; wrote treatises on volumes of spheres and cylinders, value of pi, etc. — **Ar·chi·me·de·an** \-'mē-dē-ən, -mi-'dē-\ *adj*

Ar·chi·pen·ko \,är-kə-'peŋ-(,)kō\ Aleksandr Porfiryevich 1887–1964 Am. (Ukrainian-born) sculptor; worked in cubist and then purely abstract manner; revolutionized sculpture through use of abstract forms in voids and solids

Arendt \ə-'rent\ Hannah 1906–1975 Am. (Ger.-born) political scientist; wrote *The Origins of Totalitarianism* (1951), *Eichmann in Jerusalem* (1963), *On Violence* (1970), etc.

Are·ti·no \,ar-ə-'tē-(,)nō\ Pietro 1492–1556 Ital. satirist; known as "Scourge of Princes" for harsh attacks on powerful contemporaries

Ar·gall \'är-,gȯl, -gəl\ Sir Samuel *ca* 1572–*ca* 1626 Eng. mariner; first to sail northern route direct to Virginia (1609); captured Pocahontas (1613), confined her to Jamestown; broke up French settlements on coasts of Maine, Nova Scotia

Argyll 9th Duke of — see John D.S. CAMPBELL

Ar·i·as Sán·chez \'är-ē-,äs-'sän-chez\ Oscar 1941–   pres. of Costa Rica (1986–90); awarded 1987 Nobel peace prize for developing a plan to end civil wars in Central America

Ari·o·sto \,är-ē-'ȯ-(,)stō\ Ludovico 1474–1533 Ital. poet; wrote *Orlando Furioso;* work generally considered epitome of Italian poetic Renaissance

Ar·is·tar·chus \,ar-ə-'stär-kəs\ of Samothrace *ca* 217–145 B.C. Greek grammarian & critic; chief librarian in Alexandria (from ca. 153 B.C.); first to arrange *Iliad* and *Odyssey* in 24 books

Aristarchus of Samos *fl ca* 270 B.C. Greek astron.; first to hold that earth rotates on axis, revolves around sun; devised method for estimating relative distances of sun and moon from earth

Ar·is·tide \,ar-i-'stēd, ä-rē-stēd\ Jean-Bertrand 1953–   pres. of Haiti (1991; 1994–96)

Ar·is·ti·des or **Ar·is·tei·des** \,ar-ə-'stī-dēz\ *ca* 530–*ca* 468 B.C. *the Just* Athenian statesman; elected chief archon (489–488); temporarily ostracized after opposing Themistocles, but later supported him in naval battle at Salamis

Ar·is·tip·pus \,ar-ə-'sti-pəs\ *ca* 435–366 B.C. Greek philos.; founded school of hedonism at Cyrene which taught that pleasure, regulated by prudence, is chief goal of life

Ar·is·toph·a·nes \,ar-ə-'stä-fə-,nēz\ *ca* 450–*ca* 388 B.C. Athenian dram.; regarded as one of greatest writers of comedy of all time; wrote *The Clouds* (423), *The Birds* (414), *Lysistrate* (411) — **Ar·is·to·phan·ic** \,ar-ə-stə-'fa-nik\ *adj*

Aristophanes of Byzantium *ca* 257–180 B.C. Greek scholar; chief librarian in Alexandria (ca. 195); edited works of Hesiod, Homer, Pindar, Anacreon, Aristophanes, Euripides, Alcaeus

Ar·is·tot·le \'ar-ə-,stä-tᵊl\ 384–322 B.C. Greek philos.; taught in Athens as head of Lyceum (or Peripatetic school (335–323); works include *Poetics, Physics, Metaphysics, Politics*, etc.; wrote on logic, metaphysics, natural science, ethics, politics; one of greatest thinkers in history; principal shaper of western rationalism — **Ar·is·to·te·lian** also **Ar·is·to·te·lean** \,ar-ə-stə-'tēl-yən\ *adj or n*

Ari·us \'ar-ē-əs, 'er-\ *ca* A.D. 250–336 Greek theol.; taught Neoplatonic doctrine that God is unknowable, that Christ is created, not fully divine; teachings declared heresy by Council of Nicaea (325)

Ark·wright \\'ärk-ˌrīt\ Sir Richard 1732–1792 Eng. inventor; invented water-powered spinning frame capable of producing cotton thread firm and hard enough for the warp

Ar·len \\'är-lən\ Harold 1905–1986 Am. composer; wrote "Over the Rainbow," "It's Only a Paper Moon," "That Old Black Magic," etc.

Arlen Michael 1895–1956 orig. *Dik·ran* \\'di-krän\ *Kou·youm·djian* \kü-'yüm-jē-ən\ Brit. (Bulg.-born) nov.; wrote *The London Venture, The Green Hat, Hell!Said the Duchess,* etc.

Ar·min·i·us \är-'mi-nē-əs\ *or* **Ar·min** \är-'mēn\ 18 B.C.?–A.D. 19 sometimes *Her·mann* \\'her-ˌmän\ Ger. hero; led revolt of Cherusci against Roman gov., annihilating three Roman legions (9 A.D.)

Arminius Jacobus 1560–1609 *Jacob Har·men·sen* \\'här-mən-sən\ *or Her·mansz* \\'her-ˌmän(t)s\ Du. theol.; turned against Calvinist doctrine of predestination in favor of conditional election, emphasizing free will and God's grace

Ar·mour \\'är-mər\ Philip Danforth 1832–1901 Am. industrialist; head of Armour & Co. (1875); developed methods of using waste products, refrigeration, preparation of canned meat

Arm·strong \\'ärm-ˌstrȯŋ\ Hamilton Fish 1893–1973 Am. editor; founder, managing editor, edition *Foreign Affairs* (1922–72)

Armstrong Louis 1901–1971 *Satch·mo* \\'sach-ˌmō\ Am. jazz musician; first great jazz virtuoso; invented scat singing; composed "Sister Kate," "Gut Bucket Blues," etc.

Armstrong Neil Alden 1930– Am. astronaut; commander of Apollo 11; first man to walk on the moon (July 1969)

Armstrong William George 1810–1900 Baron *Armstrong of Cragside* Eng. inventor & industrialist; invented high-pressure hydraulic machinery, breech-loading gun, prototype of modern artillery

Arm·strong–Jones \\'ärm-ˌstrȯŋ-'jȯnz\ Antony Charles Robert 1930– Earl of *Snow·don* \\'snō-d°n\ Eng. photographer; known as a portraitist

Arne \\'ärn\ Thomas Augustine 1710–1778 Eng. composer; wrote music for plays of Addison, Fielding, Milton, etc., including "Rise, Glory Rise" (1733), "Rule Britannia" (1740)

Ar·nold \\'är-n°ld\ Benedict 1741–1801 Am. Revolutionary gen. & traitor; infamous for planning to surrender West Point to British (1779–80); from 1781, lived life of disgrace, poverty in England

Arnold Henry Harley 1886–1950 *Hap Arnold* Am. gen.; chief of U.S. Army Air Corps (1938); chief of Army Air Forces (1941); general of the army (1943); of air force (1944)

Arnold Matthew 1822–1888 Eng. poet & critic; considered quintessential Victorian writer; wrote verse, including "Dover Beach" (1867); critical essays, including *Essays in Criticism, Culture and Anarchy* (1869), etc. — **Ar·nold·ian** \är-'nȯl-dē-ən\ *adj*

Arnold Thomas 1795–1842 *father of Matthew* Eng. educ.; headmaster of Rugby (1828–42); introduced mathematics, modern history, modern languages to curriculum; influenced development of modern English public schools

Ar·nold·son \\'är-nəld-sən\ Klas Pontus 1844–1916 Swed. pacifist; awarded (with Fredrik Bajer) 1908 Nobel prize for peace for founding the Swedish Society for Arbitration and Peace

Arou·et \är-we\ François-Marie — see VOLTAIRE

Arp \\'ärp\\ Jean (or Hans) 1887–1966 Fr. artist & poet; a founder of Dada (1916); one of surrealist group of painters in Paris (from 1925)

Ár·pád \\'är-ˌpäd\\ d 907 Hung. national hero; founded first Magyar dynasty of Hungary; led Magyars into Hungary from Black Sea region (ca. 896); took territory from Bulgars, Khazars, etc.

Ar·rau \\ə-'raú\\ Claudio 1903–1991 Am. (Chilean-born) pianist; renowned as interpreter of Bach, Beethoven, Chopin, Schumann, Brahms

Ar·rhe·ni·us \\ə-'rē-nē-əs, -'rā-\\ Svante August 1859–1927 Swed. physicist & chem.; awarded 1903 Nobel prize in chemistry for theory about behavior of electrolytes

Ar·row \\'ar-(ˌ)ō\\ Kenneth Joseph 1921–   Am. econ.; awarded (with Sir John Hicks) 1972 Nobel prize in economics for their contribution to general equilibrium theory and to welfare theory

Ar·son·val, d' \\'där-sᵊn-ˌväl\\ Jacques Arsène 1851–1940 Fr. biophysicist; invented devices to treat diseases through electricity

Ar·ta·xer·xes \\ˌär-tə(g)-'zərk-ˌsēz\\ name of 3 Pers. kings: **I** d 425 B.C. (reigned 465–25); kept Persia neutral during Samian, Peloponnesian wars; allowed practice of Judaism in Jerusalem (458); **II** d 359/58 B.C. (reigned 404–359/58); reign marked by many rebellions; made peace with Sparta (386); restored early gods; **III** d 338 B.C. (reigned 359/58–338); succeeded in subjugating Egypt (343)

Ar·te·vel·de, van \\vän-'är-tə-ˌvel-də\\ Jacob ca 1295–1345; Flemish leader; declared Ghent neutral in Anglo-French disputes (1338); & his son Philip 1340–1382 led unsuccessful revolt of Ghent against count of Flanders (1382)

Ar·thur \\'är-thər\\ Chester Alan 1829–1886 21st pres. of the U.S. (1881–85); supported creation of civil-service commission to regulate government hiring

As·bury \\'az-ˌber-ē, -b(ə-)rē\\ Francis 1745–1816 Methodist bishop; helped found Methodist Episcopal church in U.S. (1770–84)

Asch \\'ash\\ Sho·lem \\'shō-ləm, 'shō-\\ or Sha·lom \\shə-'lōm\\ or Sho·lom \\'shō-ləm, 'shō-\\ 1880–1957 Am. (Pol.-born) Yiddish writer; wrote plays *The God of Vengeance* (1910), etc., fiction *Kiddush Hashem* (1920), *The Mother* (1930), *East River* (1946), etc.

As·cham \\'as-kəm\\ Roger 1515–1568 Eng. scholar & author; tutor, secy. to Queen Elizabeth; wrote *Toxophilus*, treatise on archery (1545), *The Scholemaster*, treatise on practical education

Ashburton Baron — see Alexander BARING

Ash·croft \\'ash-ˌkróft\\ Dame Peggy 1907–1991 Brit. actress; renowned for stage roles of Desdemona (1920), Juliet in John Gielgud's production of *Romeo and Juliet* (1935), for film *A Passage to India*

Ashe \\'ash\\ Arthur Robert 1943–93 Am. tennis player; U.S. Open champion (1968); Australian Open champion (1970); French Open doubles champion (1972); Wimbledon singles champion (1975); Australian Open doubles champion (1977)

Ashton Winifred — see Clemence DANE

Ashur·ba·ni·pal *also* **As·sur·ba·ni·pal** *or* **Asur·ba·ni·pal** \\ä-sər-ˈbä-nə-ˌpäl, ä-shər-\\ king of Assyria (668–627 B.C.); raised Assyria to height of military and cultural power; collected great library of tablets

As·i·mov \\'a-zi-,môf\ Isaac 1920–1992 Am. (Russ.-born) writer; author of nearly 500 books, many of them science fiction novels as *I, Robot* (1951), the *Foundation* trilogy, *Foundation's Edge*, etc.

Aśo·ka *or* **Aço·ka** \ə-'shō-kə, -'sō-\ *d* 238 *or* 232 B.C. king of Magadha, India (*ca* 265–238 *or ca* 273–232 B.C.); converted to Buddhism, made it state religion; tried to rule according to dharma; left Buddhist edicts on rocks, pillars throughout India

As·pa·sia \as-'pā-zh(ē-)ə\ 470?–410 B.C. consort of Pericles noted for beauty, wit, learning

As·quith \'as-,kwith, -kwəth\ Herbert Henry 1852–1928 1st Earl of *Oxford and Asquith* Brit. statesman; prime min. (1908–16); responsible for Parliament Act (1911), limiting power of House of Lords

Assad, al- \al-'ä-,säd\ Hafiz 1928–   pres. of Syria (1971–   ); known as a steadfast opponent of Israel and key player in Mideastern power politics

As·ser \'ä-sər\ Tobias Michael Carel 1838–1913 Du. jurist; promoted establishment of Permanent Court of Arbitration; awarded (with A. H. Fried) 1911 Nobel peace prize

Astaire \ə-'star, -'ster\ Fred 1899–1987 Am. dancer & actor; appeared in many films with Ginger Rogers, including *The Gay Divorcée* (1934), *Top Hat* (1935), *Swing Time* (1936)

As·ton \'as-tən\ Francis William 1877–1945 Eng. physicist; devised mass spectrograph; discovered 212 of 287 natural isotopes; awarded 1922 Nobel prize in chemistry

As·tor \'as-tər\ John Jacob 1763–1848 Am. (Ger.-born) fur trader & capitalist; dominated American fur trade by 1800; controlled fur trade in Mississippi Valley (by 1817), upper Missouri (1822–34)

Astor Nancy Witcher 1879–1964 Viscountess *Astor* 1st woman member of Brit. Parliament (1919–45); succeeded husband in House of Commons when he entered House of Lords; noted hostess at Cliveden, where she hosted the "Cliveden set" in 1930s

As·tu·ri·as \ə-'stúr-ē-əs, -'styúr-\ Miguel Angel 1899–1974 Guatemalan author; wrote novels combining mysticism and social protest, including *Hombres de maíz*; awarded 1967 Nobel prize for literature

Ata·huall·pa *or* **Ata·hual·pa** \,ä-tə-'wäl-pə\ *ca* 1502–1533 last Incan king of Peru; arrested (1532) by Pizarro on refusal to become Christian; executed for complicity in half-brother's death

Ath·a·na·si·us \,a-thə-'nā-zh(ē-)əs, -sh(ē-)əs\ Saint *ca* 293–373 Greek (Egypt.-born) church father; chief defender in battle against Arianism — **Ath·a·na·sian** \-zhən, -shən\ *adj*

Ath·el·stan \'a-thəl-,stan\ *d* 939 Anglo-Saxon ruler; issued several codes of law; established rule over all England

Ath·er·ton \'a-thər-t²n\ Gertrude Franklin 1857–1948 née *Horn* Am. nov.; wrote *The Californians* (1898), *Black Oxen* (1923), *The Horn of Life* (1942), etc.

'At·tār \'a-tär, -,tär\ Farīd od-Dīn Mohammad ebn Ebrāhīm *ca* 1142–*ca* 1220 Pers. mystical poet; wrote *Conference of Birds*, a Şūfi allegory, prose work on early Şūfism, etc.

At·ten·bor·ough \'a-t²n-,bər-ō, -,bə-rō\ Sir Richard 1923–   Brit. actor, producer, director; produced, directed films *Oh! What a Lovely War* (1969), *Gandhi* (1982), etc.

At·ti·la \'a-t²l-ə, ə-'til-ə\ 406?–453 *the Scourge of God* king of the

Huns; one of the greatest barbarian rulers who attacked the Roman Empire; invaded Gaul (451); invaded northern Italy (452) but yielded to Pope Leo I

Att·lee \'at-lē\ Clement Richard 1883–1967 1st Earl *Attlee* Eng. polit.; prime min. (1945–51); directed nationalization of industry, formation of welfare state, granting independence to India, transformation of British Empire into Commonwealth

At·tucks \'a-təks\ Crispus 1723?–1770 Am. patriot; probably mulatto, possibly a runaway slave; in mob of "Boston Massacre" (March 5, 1770), one of three men killed by British fire

At·wood \'at-,wúd\ Margaret Eleanor 1939–   Canad. author; wrote many volumes of poetry, and novels *The Handmaid's Tale* (1985), *Cat's Eye* (1988), etc.

Au·ber \ō-'ber\ Daniel-François-Esprit 1782–1871 Fr. composer; influenced development of opéra comique with *La Bergère châtelaine* (1820), and with Eugène Scribe *Manon Lescaut* (1856), etc.; considered creator of grand opera with *Muette de Portici* (1828)

Au·brey \'ó-brē\ John 1626–1697 Eng. antiquarian; wrote *Lives of Eminent Men* (1813), containing portrayals of Bacon, Milton, Raleigh, Hobbes, etc.

Au·chin·closs \'ó-kən-,kläs\ Louis Stanton 1917–   Am. writer; wrote *Pursuit of the Prodigal* (1960), *The Embezzler* (1966), etc.

Au·den \'ó-dᵊn\ Wystan Hugh 1907–1973 Am. (Eng.-born) poet; wrote *Poems* (1930), *Shield of Achilles* (1955), *City Without Walls* (1969), etc. — **Au·den·esque** \,ó-dᵊn-'esk\ *adj*

Au·du·bon \'ó-də-bən, -,bän\ John James 1785–1851 Am. (Haitian-born) artist & ornithologist; known for drawings and paintings of North American birds; produced *Birds of America* (1827–38), etc.

Au·er·bach \'aú(-ə)r-,bäk, -,bäk\ Berthold 1812–1882 Ger. nov.; known for descriptions of life in Black Forest; wrote fiction *Spinoza* (1837), *Edelweiss* (1861), etc.

Au·gier \ō-'zhä, -'zhyä; ,ō-zhē-'ā\ Émile 1820–1889 Fr. poet & dram.; comedies of manners, satires included *Gabrielle* (1849), *Le Mariage d'Olympe* (1855), *Lions et Kenards* (1869), etc.

Au·gus·tine \'ó-gə-,stēn; ó-'gəs-tən, ə-\ Saint 354–430 church father; bishop of Hippo (396–430); enormously influential throughout Christian world; wrote *Confessions* (ca. 400), *The City of God* (413–26), etc. — **Au·gus·tin·i·an** \,ó-gə-'sti-nē-ən\ *adj or n*

Augustine also **Aus·tin** \'ós-tən, 'äs-\ Saint d 604 *Apostle of the English* 1st archbishop of Canterbury (601–04); sent by Pope Gregory I as missionary to English (596); baptized Aethelbert I, King of Kent (597); established see of London (604)

Au·gus·tus \ó-'gəs-təs, ə-\ 63 B.C.–A.D. 14 orig. *Gaius Oc·ta·vi·us* \äk-'tā-vē-əs\ then *Gaius Julius Caesar* 1st Rom. emp. (27 B.C.–A.D. 14); instituted reforms, imperial administration; added to empire by victories in Spain, Gaul, etc.; promoted agriculture and the arts (golden age of Latin literature) — **Au·gus·tan** \-tən\ *adj or n*

Aung San Suu Kyi \'óŋ-'sän-'sü-'chē\ 1945–   Burmese human rights activist; awarded 1991 Nobel peace prize for her nonviolent struggle for democracy and human rights in Burma (Myanmar)

Aurangzeb — see 'ALAMGIR

Au·re·lian \ò-'rēl-yən\ *ca* A.D. 215–275 *Lucius Domitius Aurelianus* Rom. emp. (270–275); recovered Egypt (273); reconquered Gaul, Britain (274); began fortification walls of Rome

Au·riol \ȯr-ē-'ȯl, -'ȯl\ Vincent 1884–1966 Fr. polit.; 1st pres. of 4th Republic (1947–54)

Au·ro·bin·do \ȯr-ə-'bin-dō\ Sri 1872–1950 orig. *Sri Aurobindo Ghose* \'gōs\ Indian seer, poet, & nationalist; founded ashram to promote his teachings of cosmic salvation; wrote *The Life Divine* (1940), *Synthesis of Yoga* (1948), *Savitri* (1950), etc.

Aus·ten \'ȯs-tən, 'äs-\ Jane 1775–1817 Eng. nov.; considered creator of novel of manners and one of great novelists in English; noted for psychological insight; wrote *Pride and Prejudice* (1813), *Emma* (1815), *Persuasion* (1817), etc.

Aus·tin \'ȯs-tən, 'äs-\ Alfred 1835–1913 Eng. poet; poet laureate (1896–1913); wrote 20 volumes of verse including *The Season* (1861), *The Human Tragedy* (1862), *Savanarola* (1881), etc.

Austin John 1790–1859 Eng. jurist; professor of jurisprudence, University Coll., London (1828–32); wrote *Province of Jurisprudence Determined* (1832), *Lectures on Jurisprudence* (1861–63)

Austin John Langshaw 1911–1960 Eng. philos.; a leader of the 'Oxford Philosophy' movement; concentrated on examining ordinary linguistic usage to resolve philosophical problems

Austin Mary 1868–1934 née *Hunter* Am. nov.; wrote novels, story collections *The Land of Little Rain*, *A Woman of Genius*, etc.

Austin Stephen Fuller 1793–1836 Am. colonizer in Texas; governed colony (1822–32); imprisoned (1833–34) for urging separation from Mexico; secy. of state, Republic of Texas (1936)

Aut·ry \'ȯ-trē\ (Orvon) Gene 1907– Am. actor & singer; starred in 88 musical Western films (1934–53), in 91 half-hour TV movies (1950–55); wrote or co-wrote more than 200 songs, including "Tears on My Pillow," "Here Comes Santa Claus," etc.

Avebury 1st Baron — see LUBBOCK

Avenzoar — see IBN ZUHR

Aver·ro·ës *or* **Aver·rho·ës** \ə-'ver-ə-,wēz, ,a-və-'rō-(,)ēz\ 1126–1198 also *Ibn-Rushd* Span.-Arab philos. & physician; wrote philosophical works (ca. 1179), esp. commentaries on Aristotle, on Plato's *Republic*; chief reconciler of Islamic and Greek thought

Avery \'ā-və-rē, 'äv-rē\ Milton Clark 1885–1965 Am. artist; style reminiscent of Matisse; works included *Mother and Child* (1944), *Moon Path* (1958), *Bathers by the Sea* (1960), etc.

Av·i·cen·na \,a-və-'se-nə\ 980–1037 also *Ibn Sīnā* Islamic (Pers.-born) philos. & scientist; wrote works on science, medicine, language, religion, philosophy, esp. interpretations of Aristotle

Avi·la Ca·ma·cho \'ä-vē-lə-kə-'mä-(,)chō\ Manuel 1897–1955 Mex. soldier & polit.; pres. of Mexico (1940–46); brought stability, moderately progressive legislation

Avo·ga·dro \,a-və-'gä-(,)drō, ,ä-\ Amedeo 1776–1856 Conte *di Quaregna e Ceretto* Ital. chem. & physicist; developed Avogadro's hypothesis (1811) that equal volumes of all gases at same temperature and pressure contain equal numbers of molecules

Avon Earl of — see Anthony EDEN

Ax·el·rod \'ak-səl-,räd\ Julius 1912– Am. biochem.; awarded (with Bernard Katz and Ulf Svante von Euler) 1970 Nobel prize for physiology or medicine, for their discoveries of the role played by certain chemicals in the transmission of nerve impulses

Ay·de·lotte \\'ā-d^əl-ˌät\\ Frank 1880–1956 Am. educ.; pres., Swarthmore Coll. (1921–40), Institute of Advanced Study, Princeton (1939–47)

Ayer \\'ar, 'er\\ Sir Alfred Jules 1910–1989 Eng. philos.; wrote *Language, Truth, and Logic* (1936), examining antimetaphysical doctrines of the Vienna Circle and dismissing moral and religious discourse as not literally significant

Ayl·win Azó·car \\'āl-win-ä-'sō-kär\\ Patricio 1918– pres. of Chile (1990–94)

Aza·ña y Di·az \\ə-'thän-yə-ē-'thē-äth\\ Manuel 1880–1940 Span. polit.; pres. of Spain (1936–39); president until victory of General Franco in civil war drove him into exile in France

B

Ba'al Shem Tov — see ISRAEL BEN ELIEZER

Bab·bitt \\'ba-bət\\ Bruce Edward 1938– U.S. secy. of interior (1993–)

Babbitt Irving 1865–1933 Am. scholar; founder (with Paul Elmer More) of Neohumanistic Movement; wrote *Literature and the American College* (1908), *The New Laokoön* (1910); *On Being Creative* (1932), etc.

Babbitt Milton Byron 1916– Am. composer; works include *Music for the. Mass* (1940), *Philomel* (1964), etc.; a leading proponent of 12-tone and electronic music

Ba·beuf \\bä-'bəf, bá-'bœf\\ François-Noël 1760–1797 Fr. agitator; journalist during French revolution; joined Jacobins and others (1796) to overthrow Directory, reestablish constitution

Bab·ing·ton \\'ba-biŋ-tən\\ Anthony 1561–1586 Eng. conspirator against Queen Elizabeth I; worked with priest John Ballard to lead general Catholic uprising and release Mary, Queen of Scots; executed; his letters to Mary led directly to her trial, execution

Bab·son \\'bab-sən\\ Roger Ward 1875–1967 Am. statistician; founded Babson Business Statistical Organization (1904) and Babson Institute (1919)

Bā·bur \\'bä-bür\\ 1483–1530 *Zahīr-ud-Dīn Muhammad* founder of Mogul dynasty of India; emp. (1526–30); wrote classic biography *Bābur-nāmeh*, verses in Turki

Ba·bu·ren \\bä-'bür-rän, -'bir-ən\\ Dirck van *ca* 1590–1624 Du. painter; leading member of Utrecht school; influenced by Caravaggio; painted *Christ Crowned with Thorns*, etc., genre pieces

Bach \\'bäk, 'bäk\\ Carl Philipp Emanuel 1714–1788 *son of J.S.* Ger. composer; pioneered sonata form; composed many concertos, sonatas, fantasias for clavier and piano, songs, church and chamber music; wrote *The True Art of Clavier Playing* (1753–62)

Bach Johann Christian 1735–1782 *son of J.S.* Ger. organist & composer; "the English Bach"; composed operas, oratorios, arias, cantatas, clavier concertos, chamber music, symphonies, overtures, etc; a leading exponent of Italianate Rococo style

Bach Johann Sebastian 1685–1750 Ger. organist & composer; composed enormous quantity of church, vocal, and instrumental music including *Goldberg Variations, Well-Tempered Clavier,* six *Brandenberg Concertos,* etc.; greatest composer of later German Baroque

Bach Wilhelm Friedemann 1710–1784 *son of J.S.* Ger. organist & composer; the "Halle Bach"; organist at Halle (1747–64); composed concertos, sonatas, fantasias for organ and clavier, an opera, symphonies, etc.

Ba·con \'bā-kən\ Francis 1561–1626 1st Baron *Ver·u·lam* \'ver-(y)ə-ləm\ Viscount *St. Al·bans* \sänt-'ȯl-bənz, sȯnt-\ Eng. philos.; published *Essayes;* wrote philosophical and scientific works including *Novum Organum* (1620), etc. — **Ba·co·ni·an** \bā-'kō-nē-ən\ *adj or n*

Bacon Francis 1909–1992 Brit. (Irish-born) painter; renowned for paintings of terror and angst, figures imprisoned in vague architectural sellings; became famous for *Three Figures at the Base of the Crucifixion* (1945)

Bacon Nathaniel 1647–1676 Am. colonial leader led short-lived uprising in Virginia known as Bacon's Rebellion

Bacon Roger *ca* 1220–1292 Eng. philos. and scientist; Franciscan monk; advocated experimental science; studied alchemy, optics; on request of Pope Clement IV, prepared encyclopedic *Opus Majus* (1268)

Ba·den–Pow·ell \'bā-d³n-'pō-əl\ Robert Stephenson Smyth 1857–1941 1st Baron of *Gilwell* founder of Boy Scout movement; began Boy Scouts (1908) and, with sister Agnes (1858–1945), The Girl Guides (1910); began Wolf Cubs (1916); created baron (1929)

Ba·do·glio \bə-'dōl-(ˌ)yō\ Pietro 1871–1956 Ital. gen.; prime min. (1943–44); as premier succeeding Mussolini, arranged armistice with Allies (1944)

Bae·yer, von \'bā-ər\ Adolf 1835–1917 Ger. chem.; known esp. for synthesis of indigo (1880), phthalein dyes, discovery of uric acid derivatives, etc.; awarded 1905 Nobel prize in chemistry

Baf·fin \'ba-fən\ William *ca* 1584–1622 Eng. navigator; piloted several expeditions searching for Northwest Passage (1612–16); discovered Baffin Bay (1616)

Bage·hot \'ba-jət\ Walter 1826–1877 Eng. econ. & journalist; edited *Economist* (1860–77); wrote *The English Constitution* (1867), *Physics and Politics* (1872), etc.; pioneered application of sociology, evolutionary thought to business, economics

Ba·gra·tion \bä-ˌgrä-tē-'ȯn, -ˌgrät-sē-; ˌbä-grə-'tyȯn\ Prince Pyotr Ivanovich 1765–1812 Russ. gen.; noted for success at Hollabrunn (1805) in Austro-Russian War; fought at Austerlitz (1805), etc.

Ba·hā' Al·lāh *or* **Ba·ha·ul·lah** \bä-'hä-ü-'lä\ Mīrzā Ḥoseyn Alī Nūrī 1817–1892 Pers. founder of the Bahā'ī faith

Bai·ley \'bā-lē\ Francis Lee 1933– Am. lawyer; defense attorney in celebrated trials of Dr. Sam Sheppard, Patty Hearst, O. J. Simpson, etc.

Bailey Liberty Hyde 1858–1954 Am. botanist; established horticulture as applied science; edited *Cyclopedia of American Horticulture, Cyclopedia of American Agriculture,* etc.

Bailey Nathan *or* Nathaniel *d* 1742 Eng. lexicographer; wrote *An Universal Etymological English Dictionary* (1721), the basis of Dr. Johnson's dictionary

Bailey Pearl Mae 1918–1990 Am. singer; starred in Broadway musicals *Carmen Jones, Porgy and Bess, Hello, Dolly!,* etc.

Bail·lie \'bā-lē\ Joanna 1762–1851 Scot. dram. & poet; wrote *Fugitive Verses* (1790), series *Plays on the Passions* (1798, 1802, 1812), dramas including *The Family Legend* (1810)

Bain \'bān\ Alexander 1818–1903 Scot. psychol.; known for applying findings of physiology to psychology and for improving education in Scotland

Baird \'bard, 'berd\ John Logie 1888–1946 *father of television* Scot. inventor; produced first televised picture of moving objects (1926); developed color television (1928)

Bairns·fa·ther \'barnz-,fä-thər, 'bernz-\ Bruce 1888–1959 Eng. cartoonist; created "Old Bill" cartoons (in *Bystander* from 1915); published several collections

Ba·jer \'bī(-ə)r\ Fredrik 1837–1922 Dan. statesman & writer; worked for women's emancipation, international cooperation; a founder (1891), pres. (1891–1907) of International Peace Bureau, Bern; awarded (with Klas Arnoldson) 1908 Nobel peace prize

Ba·ker \'bā-kər\ James Addison 1930–   U.S. secy. of treasury (1985–88); secy. of state (1989–92)

Baker Josephine 1906–1975 Fr. (Am.-born) singer & dancer; achieved fame in Paris first in La Revue Negre and then in the Folies Bergère; worked with French Resistance during WWII

Baker Newton Diehl 1871–1937 Am. statesman; U.S. secy. of war (1916–21)

Baker Ray Stannard 1870–1946 pseud. *David Gray·son* \'grās-ᵊn\ Am. journalist & author; crusader for League of Nations; wrote *Woodrow Wilson: Life and Letters* (1927–39, Pulitzer prize), etc.

Baker Russell Wayne 1925–   Am. journalist & author; wrote for *Baltimore Sun* (1947–64), *N.Y. Times* (1954–   ); *Poor Russell's Almanac* (1972), *Growing Up* (1982), etc.

Baker Sir Samuel White 1821–1893 Eng. explorer in Africa; explored Nile tributaries in Abyssinia (1861–62); discovered Lake Albert (1864); worked to suppress slave trade

Bakst \'bäkst\ Léon 1866–1924 orig. *Lev Samoylovich Rosenberg* Russ. painter; designed scenery at Hermitage court theater (1900); designed sets for Diaghilev's ballet productions (1908 ff.); also designed for Paris Opera, etc.

Ba·ku·nin \bə-'kün-yən, bä-, -'kü-nən\ Mikhail Aleksandrovich 1814–1876 Russ. anarchist and writer; active in European revolutionary movements (1848–49); organized many secret revolutionary societies; quarreled with Karl Marx

Bal·an·chine \,ba-lən-'shēn, 'ba-lən-,\ George 1904–1983 *Georgy Melitonovich Balanchivadze* Am. (Russ.-born) choreographer; established company that became New York City Ballet (1948); choreographed over 90 ballets, musical comedies, films

Bal·bo \'bäl-(,)bō\ Italo 1896–1940 Ital. aviator & polit.; led Fascist Blackshirt militia in march on Rome (1922)

Bal·boa \bal-'bō-ə\ Vasco Núñez de 1475–1519 Span. explorer & conquistador; explored coast of Colombia (1500); sighted Pacific Ocean (1513), claimed possession for Spain

Balch \'bȯlch\ Emily Greene 1867–1961 Am. econ. & sociol.; a founder of Women's International League for Peace and Freedom; awarded (with John R. Mott) 1946 Nobel prize for peace

Bald·win I \'bȯl-dwən\ 1058?–1118 *bro. of Godfrey of Bouillon* king of Jerusalem (1100–18); on First Crusade (1096–99); took Edessa (1098); enlarged kingdom by taking coastal cities

Baldwin James 1924–1987 Am. writer; wrote novels *Go Tell It on the Mountain* (1954), *Giovanni's Room* (1957), etc.; essays *The Fire Next Time*, etc.

Baldwin James Mark 1861–1934 Am. psychol.; specialist in child and social psychology; founded with J. M. Cattell, and edited (1894–1909) *Psychological Reviews;* wrote *Mental Development in the Child and the Race* (1895), *Genetic Logic* (1906–11), etc.

Baldwin Stanley 1867–1947 1st Earl *Baldwin of Bewd·ley* \'byüd-lē\ Eng. statesman; conservative prime min. (1923–24, 1924–29, 1935–37) during general strike (1926), abdication of Edward VIII (1936)

Balfe \'balf\ Michael William 1808–1870 Irish composer & singer; sang Papageno in first English production of *Magic Flute* (1838); best known as composer of opera *The Bohemian Girl* (1843)

Bal·four \'bal-fər, -ˌfȯr, -ˌfȯr\ Arthur James 1848–1930 1st Earl of Balfour; Brit. philos. & statesman; prime min. (1902–05); concluded Anglo-French entente (1904); as foreign secy. (1916–19), made Balfour Declaration (1917) that British government favored establishment in Palestine of national homeland for Jewish people

Ba·liol *or* **Bal·liol** \'bāl-yəl\ John de 1249–1315 king of Scotland (1292–96); crowned at Scone (1292); rebelled against English rule but brought to submission, forced to give up crown by Edward

Ball \'bȯl\ John *d* 1381 Eng. priest & social agitator; excommunicated (ca. 1366) for inflammatory sermons; helped lead Peasant Revolt (Wat Tyler's Rebellion); hanged

Ball Lucille 1911–1989 Am. actress; starred in landmark television comedy series "I Love Lucy" (1951–56), "The Lucy Show" (1962–68), "Here's Lucy" (1968–74)

Bal·lan·tyne \'ba-lən-ˌtīn\ James 1772–1833 Scot. printer; published Walter Scott's works (1802 ff.)

Bal·ti·more \'bȯl-tə-ˌmȯr, -ˌmȯr, -mər\ David 1938–   Am. microbiologist; awarded (with Renato Dulbecco and Howard M. Temin) 1975 Nobel prize in physiology or medicine for research on how certain viruses affect the genes of cancer cells

Baltimore Baron — see George CALVERT

Bal·zac \'bȯl-ˌzak, 'bal-, *F* bál-zák\ Honoré de 1799–1850 Fr. nov.; considered greatest novelist of France; founder of realistic novel in which environment molds personality; wrote *La Comedie Humaine* (from 1842; published posthumously in 47 vols.), *Le Père Goriot,* etc. — **Bal·za·cian** \bȯl-'zā-shən, bal-, -'za-kē-ən\ *adj*

Ban·croft \'ban-ˌkrȯft, 'baŋ-\ George 1800–1891 Am. hist.; established United States Naval Academy, Annapolis (1845–46); published 10 volumes of *History of the United States* (1834–40, 1852–74), etc.

Bancroft Richard 1544–1610 Eng. prelate; archbishop of Canterbury (1604–10); sponsored canons against Puritanism among clergy

Ban·del·lo \ban-'de-(ˌ)lō, bän-\ Matteo 1485–1561 Ital. writer;

known esp. for *Novelle*, 214 stories in 4 volumes (1554–73) which provided material for Shakespeare and other Elizabethan playwrights and for Lope de Vega, Byron, and others

Bangs \'baŋz\ John Kendrick 1862–1922 Am. humorist; wrote *Tiddledywink Tales* (1891), *A Houseboat on the Styx* (1896), etc.

Banks \'baŋ(k)s\ Sir Joseph 1743–1820 Eng. naturalist; accompanied Cook's expedition around the world (1768–71)

Ban·ting \'ban-tiŋ\ Sir Frederick Grant 1891–1941 Canad. physician; discovered (with Charles H. Best) the hormone insulin (1921), specific remedy for diabetes; awarded (with J. R. R. Macleod) the 1923 Nobel prize for physiology or medicine

Ba·ra·nov \bə-'rä-nəf\ Aleksandr Andreyevich 1747–1819 Russ. fur trader; 1st gov. of Russ. America

Bá·rány \'bär-,än-yə\ Robert 1876–1936 Austrian physician; investigated physiology and pathology of balancing apparatus in inner ear; awarded 1914 Nobel prize for physiology or medicine

Barbarossa — see FREDERICK I

Bar·ba·ros·sa \,bär-bə-'rä-sə, -'rò-\ *d* 1546 *Khayr ad-Dīn* Barbary pirate; practiced piracy in the Mediterranean against Spain, Portugal, Italy, and other European countries

Bar·ber \'bär-bər\ Samuel 1910–1981 Am. composer; composed setting for *Dover Beach* (1931), *String Quartet* (1936, including *Adagio for Strings*), opera *Vanessa* (1958, Pulitzer prize), etc.

Bar·bie \'bär-bē\ Klaus 1913–1991 Ger. Nazi leader; known as "the Butcher of Lyon;" sent thousands to Auschwitz while stationed at Lyon

Bar·busse \bär-büs; bär-'büs, -'byüs\ Henri 1873–1935 Fr. author; wrote novel *Le Feu* (1916, Joncourt prize) about his experience in WWI; also wrote poetry, novels *L'Enfer* (1908), etc.

Bar·clay \'bär-klē\ Robert 1648–1690 Scot. Quaker author; received with William Penn and others patent of East Jersey; wrote *Apology* (1678), standard exposition of Quaker doctrine

Bar·clay de Tol·ly \,bär-'klī-də-'tō-lē, -'klä-\ Prince Mikhail 1761–1818 Russ. field marshal; led Russian troops against Napoleon's invasion of Russia; helped capture of Paris (1814) and commanded second invasion of France (1815); created prince (1815)

Bar·deen \bär-'dēn\ John 1908–1991 Am. physicist; awarded (with Walter H. Brattain and William Shockley) 1956 Nobel prize for physics, for inventing the transistor

Ba·rents \'bar-ən(t)s, 'bär-\ Willem *ca* 1550–1597 Du. navigator; led expeditions (1594, 1595) in search for northeast passage to Asia; Barents Island, Barents Sea named for him

Bar·ing \'bar-iŋ\ Alexander 1774–1848 1st Baron *Ash·bur·ton* \'ash-,bər-tᵊn\ Brit. financier & diplomat; head of family banking house; M.P. (1806–35); negotiated boundary between Maine and Canada (in Webster-Ashburton Treaty, 1842)

Baring Evelyn 1841–1917 1st Earl of *Cro·mer* \'krō-mər\ Brit. diplomat; in Egypt (1883–1907); created "Veiled Protectorate" in dominating khedive; created earl (1901)

Bark·la \'bär-klə\ Charles Glover 1877–1944 Eng. physicist; developed X-ray scattering analysis, used to find number of electrons in carbon atom (1906); awarded 1917 Nobel prize for physics

Bark·ley \'bär-klē\ Al·ben \'al-bən\ William 1877–1956 Am. lawyer & polit.; vice pres. of U.S. (1949–53)

Bar·low \'bär-ˌlō\ Joel 1754–1812 Am. poet & diplomat; U.S. consul to Algiers (1795–97); wrote epic poem *The Vision of Columbus* (1787), revised as *The Columbiad* (1807), etc.

Bar·nard \'bär-nərd, -ˌnärd\ Christiaan Neethling 1922– So. African surgeon; performed first successful human heart transplant (1967)

Bar·nard \'bär-nərd\ George Grey 1863–1938 Am. sculptor; chief works include *Struggle of Two Natures in Man* (1894), controversial statue of Abraham Lincoln for Cincinnati (1917), etc.

Barnevelt Jan van Olden — see OLDENBARNEVELT

Bar·num \'bär-nəm\ Phineas Taylor 1810–1891 Am. showman; opened "The Greatest Show on Earth" in Brooklyn in 1871, combined with James A. Bailey (1881) to form Barnum and Bailey Circus — **Bar·num·esque** \ˌbär-nə-'mesk\ *adj*

Ba·ro·ja \bä-'rō-(ˌ)hä\ Pío 1872–1956 Span. writer; wrote nearly 100 novels, including trilogy *La lucha por la vida* (1904–05), *Cèsar o nada* (1911), *Memorias de un hombre de acción,* cycle of 22 novels on 19th-century revolutionary Spain (1913–35), etc.

Barozzi Giacomo — see VIGNOLA

Bar·rès \ba-'res\ Auguste-Maurice 1862–1923 Fr. nov. & polit.; fervent nationalist; wrote trilogy on his own self-analysis, *Le Culte del moi* (1888–91), nationalist trilogy *Le Roman de l'énergie nationale* (1897–1902), etc.

Bar·rie \'bar-ē\ Sir James Matthew 1860–1937 Scot. nov. & dram.; wrote plays *Quality Street* (1901), *Peter Pan* (1904), *Dear Brutus* (1917), etc.

Bar·ros \'bär-üsh\ João de *ca* 1496–1570 Port. hist.; government official in Portuguese Guinea, India; wrote *Décadas da Asia* (1552–1615), history of Portuguese exploration and colonization

Bar·row \'bar-(ˌ)ō\ Isaac 1630–1677 Eng. math. & theol.; translated Euclid (1660); wrote *Lectiones geometricae* (1670), controversial pieces including *Pope's supremacy* (1680), *Sermons*

Bar·ry \bá-rē\ Jeanne Bécu 1743–1793 *Comtesse du Barry* mistress of Louis XV of France; banished to nunnery (1774–76) on accession of Louis XVI; arrested, guillotined by Revolutionary Tribunal

Bar·ry \'bar-ē\ Philip 1896–1949 Am. dram.; wrote *Holiday* (1928), *The Philadelphia Story* (1939), etc.

Bar·ry·more \'bar-i-ˌmōr, -ˌmȯr\ family of Am. actors: Maurice 1847–1905 orig. *Herbert Blythe;* his wife Georgiana Emma 1854–1893 *dau. of John Drew;* their children Lionel 1878–1954; on stage in *The Jest* (1919), etc., and in films *Free Soul* (Academy Award 1931), *Grand Hotel* (1932), *Rasputin and the Empress* (with siblings, 1932), *Captains Courageous* (1937), etc.; Ethel 1879–1959; on stage in *Alice-Sit-by-the-Fire* (1905), etc.; in films *None but the Lonely Heart* (Academy Award 1944), *Spiral Staircase* (1946), etc.; & John Blythe 1882–1942; known as "the Great Profile"; on stage in esp. *Richard III* (1920), *Hamlet* (1922), etc.; in films *Dr. Jekyll and Mr. Hyde* (1920), *Moby Dick* (1930), *Grand Hotel* (1932), etc.

Bart \'bär\ *or* **Barth** \'bärt\ Jean 1650–1702 Fr. naval hero; captured 96-ship wheat convoy (1696) to relieve French famine

Barth \'bärth\ John Simmons 1930– Am. author; wrote novels *The Sot-Weed Factor* (1960), *Giles Great Boy* (1966), *The Tidewater Tales* (1987), etc.

Barth \'bärt, 'bärth\ Karl 1886–1968 Swiss theol.; promoted dialectic theology, opposed liberal rationalism; wrote *The Word of God and Theology* (1924), *Theology and the Church* (1928), *Credo* (1935), etc. — **Barth·ian** \ˈbär-tē-ən, -thē-\ *adj*

Bar·thol·di \bär-ˈtäl-dē, -ˈtȯl-, -ˈthäl-, -ˈthȯl-\ Frédéric-Auguste 1834–1904 Fr. sculptor; known esp. for colossal figures such as *Statue of Liberty* (presented 1885, unveiled 1886)

Bar·thol·o·mew \bär-ˈthä-lə-ˌmyü\ 1940–   archbishop of Constantinople and ecumenical patriarch (1991–   )

Bart·lett \ˈbärt-lət\ John 1820–1905 Am. publisher & editor; compiled *Familiar Quotations* (1855), *Complete Concordance to Shakespeare's Dramatic Works and Poems* (1894)

Bar·tók \ˈbär-ˌtäk, -ˌtȯk\ Béla 1881–1945 Hung. composer; composed symphonic poem *Kossuth* (1903), suites, piano concertos, violin concertos, six string quartets, *Piano Quintet* (1904), sonatas, opera *Duke Bluebeard's Castle* (1918), etc.

Bar·to·lom·meo \ˌbär-ˌtō-lə-ˈmä-(ˌ)ō\ Fra 1472–1517 *Baccio della Porta* Florentine painter; painted *Annunciation* (Volterra cathedral), *Vision of St. Bernard, Mystic Marriage of St. Catherine,* etc.; leading exponent of High Renaissance style

Bar·ton \ˈbär-tᵊn\ Clara 1821–1912 in full *Clarissa Harlow Barton* founder of Am. Red Cross Society (1881)

Barton Sir Derek Harold Richard 1918–   Brit. chem.; awarded (with Odd Hassel) 1969 Nobel prize in chemistry for studies relating chemical reactions to the three-dimensional shape of molecules

Bar·tram \ˈbär-trəm\ John 1699–1777 Am. botanist; exchanged plants with Peter Collinson, English horticulturist, and with Linnaeus

Bartram William 1739–1823 *son of John* Am. naturalist; wrote *Travels* (1791) recounting his travels through southeastern U.S. in search of plant, animal specimens; influenced Romantic writers

Ba·ruch \bə-ˈrük\ Bernard Man·nes \ˈma-nəs\ 1870–1965 Am. businessman & statesman; adviser to President Roosevelt on economic mobilization in WWII; adviser to presidents, popular sage

Ba·rysh·ni·kov \bə-ˈrish-nə-ˌkȯf\ Mikhail 1948–   Am. (Latvian-born) ballet dancer; with American Ballet Theater, then New York City Ballet; artistic director, American Ballet Theater

Bashō — see MATSUO

Ba·sie \ˈbā-sē\ William 1904–1984 *Count* Am. bandleader & composer; known for music in the "Kansas City" style, including distinctive piano technique; composed "One O'Clock Jump," "Jumpin'at the Woodside," etc.

Bas·il \ˈbā-zəl, ˈba-, -səl\ *or* **Ba·sil·i·us** \bə-ˈsi-lē-əs, -ˈzi-\ Saint *ca* 329–379 *the Great* church father; bishop of Caesarea; improved liturgy, organized monastic institutions on basis of work, charitable services, communal life instead of asceticism

Bas·ker·ville \ˈbas-kər-ˌvil\ John 1706–1775 Eng. typographer; pioneer manufacturer of fine printing paper and inks; designed Baskerville type

Ba·sov \ˈbä-ˌsȯf, -ˌsȯv\ Nikolay Gennadiyevich 1922–   Russ. physicist; awarded (with Charles H. Townes and Alexander M. Prokhorov) 1964 Nobel prize for physics, for developing masers and lasers

Bates \\'bāts\ Katharine Lee 1859–1929 Am. poet & educ.; wrote *Rose and Thorn, Hermit Island, Fairy Gold*, etc.; best known for poem "America the Beautiful" (1893; rev. 1904, 1911)

Ba·tis·ta y Zal·dí·var \bə-'tēs-tə-,ē-zäl-'dē-,vär\ Fulgencio 1901–1973 Cuban soldier; pres. of Cuba (1940–44; 1952–59); regime marked by repression, personal embezzlement of huge sums; overthrown by Fidel Castro (1959)

Bat·tā·nī, al- \,al-bə-'tä-nē\ *ca* 858–929 *Al·ba·te·gni* \,al-bə-'tän-yē\ or *Al·ba·te·ni·us* \-'tē-nē-əs\ Arab astron.; calculated improved values for length of year, precession of equinoxes, etc.; best known of Arab astronomers to Europeans in Middle Ages

Battle \\'ba-tᵊl\ Kathleen Deanne 1948–   Am. opera singer; roles included Susanna in *Marriage of Figaro*, Rosina in *Barber of Seville*, Sophie in *Der Rosenkavalier*, etc.

Bau·de·laire \bōd-'lar, -'ler\ Charles-Pierre 1821–1867 Fr. poet; wrote novel *La Fanfarlo* (1847), essays, poems *Les Fleurs du mal* (1857, 1861, 1868); viewed as earliest, finest poet of modernism in French, forerunner of Symbolists — **Bau·de·lair·ean** *also* **Bau·de·lair·ian** \-ē-ən\ *adj*

Bau·douin \bō-'dwaⁿ\ 1930–1993 king of Belgium (1951–93)

Baum \\'bäm\ Lyman Frank 1856–1919 Am. journalist & writer; wrote children's books *Father Goose* (1899), *Wonderful Wizard of Oz* (1900; as musical comedy 1901); 13 more "Oz" books, etc.

Baum \baúm\ Vicki 1888–1960 Am. (Austrian-born) nov.; wrote *Menschen im Hotel* (1929), translated as *Grand Hotel*, best-seller in English and basis of play and film

Bau·mé \bō-'mā\ Antoine 1728–1804 Fr. chem.; improved processes for purifying saltpeter, bleaching, making sal ammoniac, etc.; invented improved hydrometer (1768)

Bax·ter \\'bak-stər\ Richard 1615–1691 Eng. Puritan scholar & writer; imprisoned (1685) on charge of libeling Church of England; wrote *Aphorisms of Justification* (1649), etc.

Ba·yard \\'bī-ərd, 'bā-ərd, *F* bä-yàr\ Pierre Terrail *ca* 1473–1524 *Seigneur de Bayard* Fr. mil. hero; earned fame in Italian campaigns of Charles VIII, Louis XII, Francis I

Bayle \\'bā(ə)l, 'bel\ Pierre 1647–1706 Fr. philos. & critic; defender of religious toleration; compiled (1697) *Dictionnaire historique et critique* critiquing accepted historical and philosophical tenets

Beaconsfield Earl of — see Benjamin DISRAELI

Bea·dle \\'bē-dᵊl\ George Wells 1903–1989 Am. biol.; awarded (with Edward Lawrie Tatum) 1958 Nobel prize for physiology or medicine, for their work in biochemical genetics

Beard \\'bird\ Charles Austin 1874–1948 Am. hist.; wrote influential economic interpretation of U.S. institutions; & his wife Mary née *Ritter* 1876–1958 Am. hist.; active in woman suffrage campaign; collaborated with husband on *History of the United States* (1921), *The Rise of American Civilization* (1927), etc.

Beard Daniel Carter 1850–1941 Am. painter, illustrator, & organizer of Boy Scouts in U.S.; wrote *American Boys' Handy Book* (1882), *Shelters, Shacks, and Shanties* (1914)

Beards·ley \\'birdz-lē\ Aubrey Vincent 1872–1898 Eng. illustrator; a leader in the Aesthetic movement; principal artist in Art Nouveau style; illustrated books *Morte D'Arthur* (1893), Oscar Wilde's *Salome* (1894), etc. — **Beards·ley·esque** \,birdz-lē-'yesk\ *adj*

Be·a·trix \'bā-ə-ˌtriks\ 1938–   queen of the Netherlands (1980–)

Beat·tie \'bē-tē\ James 1735–1803 Scot. poet; wrote *The Minstrel* (1771–74), popular descriptive poem in Spenserian stanzas which influenced the Romantics

Beau·fort \'bō-fərt\ Sir Francis 1774–1857 Brit. admiral; devised "Beaufort's scale" (1805) for indicating wind velocities

Beaufort Henry *ca* 1374–1447 Eng. cardinal & statesman; chancellor under Henry V (1403–04, 13–17, 24–26); in virtual control of government of Henry VI (ca. 1435–43)

Beau·har·nais, de \ˌbō-är-'nā\ Fr. family including: Vicomte Alexandre 1760–1794 gen.; as general in chief, army of the Rhine (1793), made responsible for surrender of Mainz; guillotined; his wife Joséphine 1763–1814 later the *1st wife of Napoleon I*; marriage annulled at request of Napoléon (1810); their son Eugène 1781–1824 prince of Eich·stätt \'ik-ˌshtet\; adopted by Napoléon, made heir apparent to crown of Italy (1806); fought in Austrian (1809) and Russian campaigns (1812); their daughter Hortense \òr-täⁿs\ 1783–1837 *wife of Louis Bonaparte & mother of Napoleon III*; center of Bonapartist intrigue (from 1814)

Beau·mar·chais \ˌbō-mär-'shā\ Pierre-Augustin Caron de 1732–1799 Fr. dram. & businessman; wrote *Le Barbier de Seville* (first performed 1775), *Le Mariage de Figaro* (first performed 1784), inspiration for operas by Rossini, Mozart

Beau·mont \'bō-ˌmänt, -mənt\ Francis 1584–1616 Eng. dram.; with John Fletcher wrote comedies and tragedies, including *The Maides Tragedy, A King and No King*, etc.; wrote *The Knight of the Burning Pestle* alone

Beau·mont \-ˌmänt\ William 1785–1853 Am. surgeon; studied digestion by experiments with Alexis St. Martin, whose stomach was exposed by gunshot wound (1822)

Beau·re·gard \'bōr-ə-ˌgärd, 'bòr-\ Pierre Gustave Toutant 1818–1893 Am. Confed. gen.; in command of bombardment of Ft. Sumter (April 12, 1861); commanded at Bull Run and Shiloh

Beau·voir, de \də-bō-'vwär\ Simone 1908–1986 Fr. author; with a feminist sensibility wrote works *Le Deuxième sexe* (1949, *The Second Sex*), *Les Mandarins* (1954, Prix Goncourt), etc.

Bea·ver·brook \'bē-vər-ˌbrùk\ 1st Baron 1879–1964 *William Maxwell Aitken* Brit. (Canad.-born) newspaper publisher & polit.; member of Winston Churchill's cabinet in WWII

Be·bel \'bā-bəl\ August 1840–1913 Ger. Social Democrat leader & writer; cofounder of Social Democratic Labor party (1869); wrote numerous books on socialism and German society

Beck·er \'be-kər\ Gary Stanley 1930–   Am. econ.; awarded 1992 Nobel Prize for economics for extending economic theory to aspects of behavior previously dealt with by sociology, etc.

Beck·et \'be-kət\ Saint Thomas *ca* 1118–1170 *Thomas à Becket*; chancellor under Henry II (1155–62); archbishop of Canterbury (1162–70); staunch defender of rights of Church against lay power; murdered in Canterbury Cathedral by knights supporting Henry

Beck·ett \'be-kət\ Samuel 1906–1989 Irish author in France; wrote (originally in French) novels *Malloy, Malone Dies*, plays *Waiting for Godot* (1952), *End Game* (1957), etc.; awarded 1969 Nobel prize for literature — **Beck·ett·ian** \be-'ke-tē-ən\ *adj*

Beck·ford \'bek-fərd\ William 1760–1844 Eng. author; best known for classic Gothic novel *Vathek* (1782, in French) and Gothic residence Fonthill Abbey

Bec·que·rel \be-'krel, ˌbe-kə-'rel\ family of Fr. physicists including: Antoine-César 1788–1878; a creator of science of electrochemistry; invented thermoelectric needle for determining internal bodily temperatures; his son Alexandre-Edmond 1820–1891; investigated light, phosphorescence, photochemistry, spectroscopy, magnetism; the latter's son Antoine-Henri 1852–1908; discovered (1896) natural radioactivity; awarded (with Pierre Curie and Marie Curie) 1903 Nobel prize for physics

Bed·does \'be-ˌdōz\ Thomas Lovell 1803–1849 Eng. writer; wrote *The Bride's Tragedy* (1822), *Death's Jest-Book; or, The Fool's Tragedy* (1850)

Bede \'bēd\ *or* **Bae·da** *or* **Be·da** \'bē-də\ Saint *ca* 672–735 *the Venerable Bede* Anglo-Saxon scholar, hist., & theol.; wrote ecclesiastical history of England, scriptural commentaries; introduced custom of dating events from birth of Christ

Bedford Duke of — see JOHN OF LANCASTER

Bed·norz \'bed-ˌnórts\ Johannes Georg 1950– Ger. physicist; awarded (with K. Alex Müller) 1987 Nobel prize for physics for discovery of superconductivity in a ceramic material

Bee·be \'bē-bē\ Charles William 1877–1962 Am. naturalist, explorer & writer; led expeditions to Mexico, etc.; with Otis Barton made Bathysphere descent to record 3028 feet (1934)

Bee·cham \'bē-chəm\ Sir Thomas 1879–1961 Eng. conductor; founded British National Opera Co. (1919), London Symphony Orchestra (1932), Royal Philharmonic Orchestra (1947); a leading interpreter of Mozart, Haydn, Sibelius

Bee·cher \'bē-chər\ Henry Ward 1813–1887 Am. clergyman; powerful, convincing speaker influential throughout country; opposed slavery; advocated women's suffrage, evolutionary theory

Beecher Lyman 1775–1863 *father of H.W. & of Harriet Beecher Stowe* Am. Presbyterian clergyman; president, Lane Theological Seminary, Cincinnati (1832–50)

Beer·bohm \'bir-ˌbōm, -bəm\ Sir Max 1872–1956 Eng. critic & caricaturist; wrote *A Christmas Garland*, parodies of contemporary authors; pictorial caricatures *The Poet's Corner*, etc.

Beer·naert \'ber-ˌnärt\ Auguste Marie François 1829–1912 Belg. statesman; member of International Peace Conference, The Hague (1899, 1907); awarded (with Baron d'Estournelles de Constant) 1909 Nobel peace prize

Bee·tho·ven \'bā-ˌtō-vən\ Ludwig van 1770–1827 Ger. composer; often viewed as greatest composer; developed forms of symphony, quartet, sonata, etc. to new heights; inspired Romantics although himself a classicist; known esp. for symphonies, piano concertos, piano sonatas, string quartets, opera *Fidelio*, etc. — **Bee·tho·ve·nian** \ˌbā-ˌtō-'vē-nyən\ *adj*

Be·gin \'bā-gin\ Me·na·chem \mə-'nä-kəm\ 1913–1992 prime min. of Israel (1977–83); signed peace agreement with Anwar Sadat of Egypt (1979); with him awarded 1978 Nobel prize for peace

Be·han \'bē-ən\ Brendan Francis 1923–1964 Irish dram.; wrote *The Quare Fellow, The Hostage*, memoirs *Borstal Boy* (1958)

Beh·ring \\'ber-iŋ\ Emil von 1854–1917 Ger. bacteriol.; pioneer in immunology; developed diphtheria antitoxin (1892); awarded 1901 Nobel prize for physiology or medicine

Behr·man \\'ber-mən\ Samuel Nathaniel 1893–1973 Am. dram.; wrote plays *No Time for Comedy* (1939), *Fanny* (1954), etc.

Bé·ké·sy \\'bā-kə-shē\ Georg von 1899–1972 Am. (Hung.-born) physicist; studied detection and analysis of sound by human ear; awarded 1961 Nobel prize for physiology or medicine

Be·las·co \bə-'las-(ˌ)kō\ David 1853–1931 Am. dram. & producer; known for success in developing actors and for methods of staging and lighting

Bel·i·sar·i·us \ˌbe-lə-'sar-ē-əs, -'ser-\ *ca* 505–565 Byzantine gen.; subdued Vandals in North Africa and Ostrogoths in Italy, conquered Sicily, southern Italy, and Rome

Bell \\'bel\ Alexander Graham 1847–1922 Am. (Scot.-born) inventor; experimented with electrical and acoustical devices; produced first intelligible telephonic transmission of voice (June 3, 1875) to assistant Thomas A. Watson; patented telephone (1876)

Bel·la·my \\'be-lə-mē\ Edward 1850–1898 Am. author; wrote Utopian romance *Looking Backward* (1888)

Bel·lay, du \ˌdü-bə-'lā, ˌdyü-\ Joachim *ca* 1522–1560 Fr. poet; leader of group The Pléiade; wrote *Defense et illustration de la langue francaise* (1549) to illustrate their beliefs; wrote *Les Antiquites de Rome, Les Regrets* (both 1558); etc.

Bel·li·ni \bə-'lē-nē\ family of Venetian painters including: Jacopo *ca* 1400–*ca* 1470; initiator of Venetian school of painting; painted *Crucifixion*, etc.; left two sketchbooks showing experiments in linear perspective; and his sons Gentile *ca* 1429–1507; introduced oil painting in Venetian mural decoration; known for portraits and scenes of Venice; and Giovanni *ca* 1430–1516; known esp. for altarpieces, other devotional works; master of light; later paintings show greatness of landscape technique

Bellini Vincenzo 1801–1835 Ital. composer; composed melodic operas *La sonnambula* (1831), *Norma* (1831), *I puritani* (1835), etc.; a great composer of bel canto music

Bel·loc \\'be-ˌläk, -lək\ (Joseph-Pierre) Hilaire 1870–1953 Eng. author; wrote essays, verse, novels, history, biography, criticism including *Bad Child's Book of Beasts* (1896), *Danton* (1899), *History of England* (1925–31), etc.; considered a master of prose style

Bel·low \\'be-(ˌ)lō\ Saul 1915– Am. (Canad.-born) writer; wrote *The Adventures of Augie March* (1953), *Herzog* (1964), *Humboldt's Gift* (1975), etc.; awarded 1976 Nobel prize for literature

Bel·lows \\'be-(ˌ)lōz\ George Wesley 1882–1925 Am. painter & lithographer; associated with "Ashcan School"; known for sporting and action scenes, including *42 Kids, Stag at Sharkey's*, etc.

Be·na·cer·raf \be-'na-sə-ˌräf\ Baruj 1920– Am. (Venezuelanborn) pathologist; awarded (with George D. Snell and Jean Dausset) 1980 Nobel prize for physiology or medicine; for their discoveries concerning genetic regulation of the body's immune system

Be·na·ven·te y Mar·tí·nez \ˌbe-nə-'ven-tē-ˌē-mär-'tē-nəs\ Jacinto 1866–1954 Span. dram.; wrote plays noted for realism and social criticism; awarded 1922 Nobel prize for literature

Bench·ley \'bench-lē\ Robert Charles 1889–1945 Am. humorist; drama critic for *New Yorker* (1929–40); member of famous "Algonquin Round Table" at Algonquin Hotel in Manhattan

Ben·e·dict \'be-nə-,dikt\ name of 15 popes: esp. **XIV** (*Prospero Lambertini*) 1675–1758 (pope 1740–58); enlarged Vatican Library, U. of Rome; settled concordats with Savoy and Naples (1741) and with Spain (1753); **XV** (*Giacomo della Chiesa*) 1854–1922 (pope 1914–22); during World War I maintained neutrality, organized relief work, attempted to mediate a peace settlement (1917)

Benedict of Nur·sia \'nər-sh(ē-)ə\ Saint *ca* 480–*ca* 547 Ital. founder of Benedictine order; founded monastery at Monte Cassino, source of European monasticism — **Ben·e·dic·tine** \,be-nə-'dik-tən, -,tēn\ *adj or n*

Benedict Ruth 1887–1948 née *Fulton* Am. anthropol.; studied Pueblo, Apache, Zuñi, other Native American groups, etc.; wrote *Patterns of Culture* (1934), etc.

Be·neš \'be-,nesh\ Edvard 1884–1948 Czech statesman; pres. (1935–38; 1940–48); resigned on German occupation of Sudetenland; president of Czechoslovak government in England (1940–45); resigned again rather than sign Communist constitution

Be·nét \bə-'nā\ Stephen Vincent 1898–1943 *bro.* of *W.R.* Am. poet & novelist; wrote epic poem *John Brown's Body* (1928, Pulitzer prize), short story "The Devil and Daniel Webster" (1937), etc.

Benét William Rose 1886–1950 Am. poet, nov., & editor; wrote verse *Perpetual Light* (1919), *The Dust Which is God* (1941, Pulitzer prize), etc.; novels *The First Person Singular* (1922), etc.

Ben–Gu·rion \,ben-gùr-'yòn, ben-'gùr-ē-ən\ David 1886–1973 Israeli (Pol.-born) statesman; prime min. of Israel (1949–53; 1955–63); member of Knesset (1948–70)

Ben·ja·min \'ben-jə-mən\ Judah Philip 1811–1884 Am. Confed. statesman & lawyer; member of Confederate government (1861–65)

Ben·nett \'be-nət\ (Enoch) Arnold 1867–1931 Eng. nov.; wrote in realist manner, depicting provincial or lower class life; known esp. for novels *Anna of the Five Towns, Old Wives' Tale,* etc.

Bennett James Gordon 1795–1872 Am. (Scot.-born) journalist; started *New York Herald* (1835); pioneered in publishing financial news, society news, using telegraph, European correspondents

Bennett Richard Bedford 1870–1947 *Viscount Bennett* Canad. prime min. (1930–35); leader of Conservative party (1927–38)

Ben·ny \'be-nē\ Jack 1894–1974 orig. *Benjamin Ku·bel·sky* \kə-'bel-skē\ Am. comedian; conducted regular show on radio (1932–55), on television (1950–65); known for air of bemused annoyance, legendary miserliness, and seriocomic violin playing

Be·noît de Sainte–Maure \ben-'wä-də-(,)sa⁼n(t)-'mór\ 12th cent. Fr. trouvère; wrote *Chronique des ducs de Normandie* for patron Henry II of England and *Roman de Troie*

Ben·son \'ben(t)-sən\ Edward White 1829–1896 Brit. prelate; archbishop of Canterbury (1882–96); resolved dispute over proper forms of worship

Ben·tham \'ben(t)-thəm\ Jeremy 1748–1832 Eng. jurist & philos.; expounded doctrine that morality of actions is determined by utility, that the object of all conduct and legislation is "the greatest happiness of the greatest number"

Ben·tinck \\'ben-ti(ŋ)k\\ Lord William Cavendish 1774–1839 *son of W.H.C.* 1st gov.-gen. of India (1833–35)

Bentinck William Henry Cavendish 1738–1809 3d Duke of *Portland* Brit. prime min. (1783; 1807–09)

Bent·ley \\'bent-lē\\ Richard 1662–1742 Eng. clergyman, scholar, & critic; proved spuriousness of *Epistles of Phalaris* in *Dissertation* (1699); known for critical texts of classical authors

Ben·ton \\'ben-t²n\\ Thomas Hart 1782–1858 *Old Bullion* Am. polit.; member, U.S. Senate (1821–51); Democratic leader in Senate; opposed extension of slavery to territories and defeated on this issue; member, U.S. House of Representatives (1853–55)

Benton Thomas Hart 1889–1975 Am. painter; leader of American Regionalist school; painted vigorous realistic portraits of ordinary people, work in Middle West, including *Cotton Pickers, Meal*, etc.

Bent·sen \\'ben(t)-sən\\ Lloyd Millard, Jr. 1921–   U.S. secy. of treasury (1993–   )

Bé·ran·ger \\bā-räⁿ-zhā\\ Pierre-Jean de 1780–1857 Fr. poet; wrote popular chansons expressing liberal, humanitarian sympathies and satirizing Bourbon restoration

Ber·dya·yev \\bərd-'yä-yəf, bər-'jä-\\ Nikolay Aleksandrovich 1874–1948 Russ. philos.; under influence of Kant and Böhme developed Christian Existentialism

Ber·en·son \\'ber-ən-sən\\ Bernard 1865–1959 Am. (Lith.-born) art critic; foremost authority on art of Italian Renaissance; wrote *Venetian Painters of the Renaissance* (1894), *Drawings of the Florentine Painters* (1903), *Italian Painters of the Renaissance* (1952), etc.

Berg \\'berg\\ Alban 1885–1935 Austrian composer; master of atonal style, blending it with classical forms; composed *Piano Sonata* (1908), *String Quartet* (1910), opera *Wozzeck* (1925), etc.

Berg \\'bərg\\ Paul 1926–   Am. chem.; awarded (with Walter Gilbert and Frederick Sanger) 1980 Nobel prize for chemistry, for studies of the chemical structure of nucleic acids

Bergerac, de Cyrano — see CYRANO DE BERGERAC

Ber·gi·us \\'ber-gē-əs\\ Friedrich 1884–1949 Ger. chem.; awarded (with Carl Bosch) 1931 Nobel prize for chemistry, for inventing methods of manufacturing ammonia and liquefying coal

Berg·man \\'bərg-mən, *Sw* 'ber-ē-mån\\ Ingmar 1918–   Swed. film & theater director; explored personal torment in films *The Seventh Seal* (1956), *Wild Strawberries* (1957), *Persona* (1966), etc.

Bergman Ingrid 1915–1982 Swed. actress; starred in films *Intermezzo* (1938), *Casablanca* (1942), *Anastasia* (1956), etc.

Berg·son \\'berg-sən, berk-sōⁿ\\ Henri-Louis 1859–1941 Fr. philos.; developed humanistic philosophy of process to counter positivism; awarded 1928 Nobel prize for literature — **Berg·son·ian** \\berg-'sō-nē-ən, berk-\\ *adj*

Berg·ström \\'berg-strəm, 'bar-ē-strüm\\ K. Sune D. 1916–   Swed. biochem.; awarded (with Bengt I. Samuelsson and John R. Vane) 1982 Nobel prize for physiology or medicine, for discoveries regarding prostaglandins and related substances

Be·ria *or* **Be·ri·ya** \\'ber-ē-ə\\ Lavrenty Pavlovich 1899–1953 Russ. polit.; member of Politburo (from 1946); controlled vast security network, supervised purges of political enemies

Be·ring \\'ber-iŋ, 'bir-\\ Vitus Jonassen 1681–1741 Dan. navigator; sailed for Czar Peter the Great on expeditions (from 1724) to discover whether Asia and North America were connected; sailed through Bering Strait (1728); explored (1741) coast of Alaska

Berke·ley \'bär-klē, 'bər-\ George 1685–1753 Irish bishop & philos.; developed Empiricism which holds that everything except the spiritual exists only insofar as it is perceived by the senses — **Berke·le·ian** *or* **Berke·ley·an** \-klē-ən; bär-', bər-'\ *adj or n*

Berke·ley \'bər-klē\ Sir William 1606–1677 colonial gov. of Virginia (1641–48, 1661–77); his policies provoked Bacon's Rebellion (1676)

Berle \'bərl\ Milton 1908–   orig. surname *Berlinger* Am. comedian; starred in landmark comedy-variety show "Texaco Star Theater" (1948–56); nicknamed "Mr. Television" and credited with popularizing the medium of television

Ber·lich·ing·en \'ber-li-ˌkiŋ-ən\ Götz *or* Gottfried von 1480–1562 Ger. knight; called "Götz of the Iron Hand" after iron hand substituted for right hand lost in battle (1504); his autobiography used by Goethe as source for *Götz von Berlichingen* (1773)

Ber·lin \(ˌ)bər-'lin\ Irving 1888–1989 Am. (Russ.-born) composer; wrote songs "Alexander's Ragtime Band," "God Bless America," "White Christmas," etc., musicals *Annie Get Your Gun* (1946), *Call Me Madam* (1950), etc.

Ber·li·ner \'bər-lə-nər\ Emile 1851–1929 Am. (Ger.-born) inventor; developed improved versions of the telephone, phonograph; invented lightweight internal combustion engine; invented (1925) acoustic tiles and acoustic cells

Ber·li·oz \'ber-lē-ˌōz\ Hector 1803–1869 in full *Louis-Hector Berlioz* Fr. composer; first French Romantic composer; composed *Symphonie fantastique* (1830–31), choral work *Requiem* (1837), etc. — **Ber·li·oz·ian** \ˌber-lē-'ō-zē-ən\ *adj*

Ber·na·dette of Lourdes \ˌbər-nə-'det\ Saint 1844–1879 *Marie-Bernarde Sou·bi·rous* \ˌsü-bē-'rü\ Fr. religious; experienced visions; result was establishment of shrine at Lourdes

Bernadotte Jean Baptiste Jules — see CHARLES XIV JOHN

Ber·nard \ber-'när\ Claude 1813–1878 Fr. physiol.; investigated chemistry of digestion, including role of pancreas and liver; discovered regulation of blood supply by vasometer nerves

Ber·nard of Clair·vaux \bər-'närd-əv-ˌklär-'vō, ber-'när-, -ˌkler-\ Saint 1090–1153 Fr. ecclesiastic; renowned for piety, charity, mystical faith; founder of abbey of Clairvaux (1115); author of epistles, sermons, polemics, etc. — **Ber·nar·dine** \'bər-nə(r)-ˌdēn\ *adj*

Ber·nar·din de Saint–Pierre \ˌber-nər-'daⁿ-də-ˌsänt-pē-'er\ Jacques-Henri 1737–1814 Fr. author; precursor of French romantic movement; wrote *Paul et Virginie* (1788), etc.

Berners Baron — see TYRWHITT-WILSON

Bern·hardt \'bərn-ˌhärt, bər-'när\ Sarah 1844–1923 orig. *Henriette-Rosine Ber·nard* \ber-när\ Fr. actress; after years on stage in Paris, formed company and toured U.S., Europe; known for voice, emotional acting, unconventional personal life

Ber·ni·ni \ber-'nē-nē\ Gian *or* Giovanni Lorenzo 1598–1680 Ital. sculptor, architect, & painter; created Baroque style in sculpture; became architect of St. Peter's

Bern·stein \'bərn-ˌstīn *also* -ˌstēn\ Leonard 1918–1990 Am. conductor & composer; composed three symphonies, an opera *Trouble*

in Tahiti, musicals *On the Town* (1944), *West Side Story* (1957), a mass, a ballet, orchestral works, operetta *Candide* (1956)

Bern·storff \\'bern-,shtôrf\\ Johann-Heinrich 1862–1939 Graf *von Bernstorff* Ger. diplomat; tried to advance Woodrow Wilson's attempts at mediation before U.S. entry into WWI

Ber·ra \\'ber-ə\\ Yogi 1925–   *Lawrence Peter Berra* Am. baseball player and coach; catcher with N.Y. Yankees (1946–63), manager (1964), coach (1975–84), manager (1984–85); coach, N.Y. Mets (1965–72), manager (1972–75); coach, Houston Astros (1986–89)

Ber·ry·man \\'ber-ē-mən\\ John 1914–1972 Am. poet; wrote *Poems* (1942), *Dream Songs* (1964, Pulitzer prize), *Love & Fame* (1970), etc.

Ber·thier \\ber-'tyā\\ Louis-Alexandre 1753–1815 Prince de Neuchâtel; Prince de Wagram Fr. soldier; marshal of France; with Napoléon in Italy and Egypt; min. of war (1800–07)

Ber·til·lon \\,ber-tē-'yōⁿ\\ Alphonse 1853–1914 Fr. criminol.; devised system of identifying criminals by body measurements

Ber·ton \\'bər-tⁿn\\ Pierre 1920–   Canad. writer; author of 37 books, many dealing with Canadian history and land

Ber·ze·li·us \\(,)bər-'zē-lē-əs, ber-'zā-\\ Baron Jöns Jakob 1779–1848 Swed. chem.; discovered the elements cerium, selenium, thorium, and first isolated silicon, zirconium, titanium; introduced modern system of chemical symbols and formulas

Bes·ant \\'be-sⁿnt, -z'nt\\ Annie 1847–1933 née *Wood* Eng. theosophist and Indian political leader; president of Theosophical Society (1907–33); organized India Home Rule League (1916); president, Indian National Congress (1917)

Bes·se·mer \\'be-sə-mər\\ Sir Henry 1813–1898 Eng. engineer; developed Bessemer process for manufacturing steel by decarbonization of melted pig iron by blast of hot air

Best \\'best\\ Charles Herbert 1899–1978 Canad. (Am.-born) physiol.; along with F. G. Banting and others, discovered insulin (1921); introduced use of anticoagulant heparin

Be·tan·court \\,be-,tän-'kúr(t), -tä̱n-\\ Rómulo 1908–1981 Venezuelan pres. (1959–64)

Be·the \\'bā-tə\\ Hans Albrecht 1906–   Am. (Ger.-born) physicist; awarded 1967 Nobel prize for physics for contributions to nuclear theory, especially energy production in stars

Beth·mann—Holl·weg \\'bet-mən-'hôl-,väg, -,mən-\\ Theobald Theodor Friedrich Alfred von 1856–1921 Ger. statesman; chancellor (1909–17)

Be·thune \\bə-'thün, -'thyün\\ Mary 1875–1955 née *McLeod* Am. educ.; pres. of Bethune-Cookman College (1923–42, 1946–47) which she helped found; founded, first pres. of National Council of Negro Women (1935–49)

Bet·je·man \\'be-chə-mən\\ Sir John 1906–1984 Brit. author; poetical works include *Mount Zion* (1933), *New Bats in Old Belfries* (1945), *Collected Poems* (1958), etc.; poet laureate (1972–84)

Bet·tel·heim \\'be-təl-,hīm\\ Bruno 1903–1990 Am. (Austrian-born) psychol.; renowned for work with autistic children; wrote *Love Is Not Enough* (1950), *The Uses of Enchantment* (1976), etc.

Bet·ter·ton \\'be-tər-tⁿn\\ Thomas *ca* 1635–1710 Eng. actor; known for versatility, created more than 130 new roles and played many established ones, including Lear, Macbeth, Othello, etc.

Beuys \'bȯis\ Joseph 1921–1986 Ger. sculptor, performance artist, & political activist; created stationary sculptures and enigmatic performances known as "actions"; founder of several political groups, including the Green Party

Bev·er·idge \'be-və-rij, 'bev-rij\ Albert Jeremiah 1862–1927 Am. polit. & hist.; leader of Progressive Republicans; wrote *The Life of John Marshall* (1916–19, Pulitzer prize)

Beveridge William Henry 1879–1963 1st Baron *Beveridge of Tuggal* \'tə-gəl\ Eng. econ.; produced report which shaped postwar social welfare policies in Great Britain

Bev·in \'be-vən\ Ernest 1881–1951 Brit. labor leader & polit.; union organizer (from 1908); negotiated merger of 14 unions into one (1922); largely responsible for NATO treaty (1949)

Beyle Marie-Henri — see STENDHAL

Bhu·mi·bol Adul·ya·dej \'pü-mē-‚pōn-ä-'dún-lə-‚dät — *sic*\ 1927– king of Thailand (1946–)

Bhut·to \'bü-tō\ Benazir 1953– prime min. of Pakistan (1988–90; 1993–)

Bi·dault \bē-'dō\ Georges 1899–1983 Fr. statesman; prime min. (1946, 1949–50)

Bid·dle \'bi-dᵊl\ John 1615–1662 founder of Eng. Unitarianism; imprisoned several times for publishing *Twelve Arguments Against the Deity of the Holy Ghost* (ca. 1644)

Biddle Nicholas 1786–1844 Am. financier; as director of Bank of the United States, followed policy of stable money supply, restricted credit; focus of attack by Jackson against bank

Bien·ville \bē-'en-‚vil, -vəl; byaⁿ-'vēl\ Jean-Baptiste Le Moyne, sieur de 1680–1768 Fr. colonial gov. of Louisiana; explored Mississippi River; founded New Orleans (1718)

Bierce \'birs\ Ambrose Gwinnett 1842–?1914 Am. author; known for caustic, witty style; wrote *The Fiend's Delight* (1872), *Tales of Soldiers and Civilians* (1891), *Devil's Dictionary* (1906), etc.

Bier·stadt \'bir-‚stat\ Albert 1830–1902 Am. (Ger.-born) painter; one of last of Hudson River school of landscape painters; traveled through West, painted *Rocky Mountains, Estes Park,* etc.

Bing·ham \'biŋ-əm\ George Caleb 1811–1879 Am. painter; painted portraits, genre paintings of frontier, including *Jolly Flatboatmen, Fur Traders Descending the Missouri*

Bin·nig \'bi-nik\ Gerd 1947– Ger. physicist; awarded (with Heinrich Rohrer) 1986 Nobel prize for physics for their invention of the scanning tunnel microscope

Bi·on \'bī-‚än, -ən\ *fl* 100 B.C. Greek bucolic poet; wrote *Bucolica,* extant in fragments, and *Lament for Adonis*

Bird \'bərd\ Larry Joe 1957– Am. basketball player; Boston Celtics (1979–92); helped win three NBA championships, won three MVP awards, won 1992 Olympic gold medal

Birk·beck \'bər(k)-‚bek\ George 1776–1841 Eng. physician; founder, first pres. (1823–41), London Mechanics Institute (later Birkbeck College), pioneering school for workingmen

Bir·ken·head \'bər-kən-‚hed\ 1st Earl of 1872–1930 *Frederick Edwin Smith* Eng. jurist & statesman; responsible for major legal reforms; helped negotiate Anglo-Irish treaty (1921)

Bi·ron \'bē-ˌròn\ Ernst Johann 1690–1772 orig. *Büh·ren* \'büē-rən\ Duke of *Kurland* Ger. polit. in Russia; as lover of Anna Ivanovna, was virtual ruler of Russia during her reign (1730–40)

Bish·op \'bi-shəp\ Elizabeth 1911–1979 Am. poet; wrote *North & South: A Cold Spring* (1955, Pulitzer prize), *Questions of Travel* (1965), etc.

Bishop John Michael 1936–   Am. microbiologist; awarded (with Harold E. Varmus) 1989 Nobel prize for physiology or medicine, for research on cancer-causing genes called oncogenes

Bis·marck \'biz-ˌmärk\ Prince Otto Eduard Leopold von 1815–1898 in full *Bismarck-Schön·hau·sen* \-shōēn-'haù-z°n\ founder & 1st chancellor of Ger. Empire (1871–90); built system of key strategic alliances — **Bis·marck·ian** \biz-'mär-kē-ən\ *adj*

Bi·zet \bē-'zā\ Alexandre-César-Léopold 1838–1875 called *Georges* Fr. composer; composed operas *Carmen* (1875), etc., music for *L'Arlésienne* (1872), *Symphony in C major* (1855), etc.

Bjørn·son \'byərn-sən\ Bjørnstjerne Martinius 1832–1910 Norw. poet, dram., & nov.; wrote poem that is national anthem; epic cycle (1870), novels and tales, plays; prominent public figure; awarded 1903 Nobel prize for literature

Black \'blak\ Hugo LaFayette 1886–1971 Am. jurist & polit.; associate justice, U.S. Supreme Court (1937–71); champion of Bill of Rights and strong constitutionalist

Black Sir James Whyte 1924–   Brit. pharmacologist; awarded (with Gertrude B. Elion and George H. Hitchings) 1988 Nobel prize for physiology or medicine, for discoveries of important principles for drug treatment

Black·ett \'bla-kət\ Patrick Maynard Stuart 1897–1974 Brit. physicist; awarded 1948 Nobel prize in physics for discoveries in cosmic radiation; helped develop the cloud chamber

Black Hawk \'blak-ˌhòk\ 1767–1838 *Ma-ka-ta-i-me-she-kia-kiak* Sauk Indian chief; allied with British in War of 1812; led dissident Sauk and Fox Indians in Black Hawk War of 1812

Black·more \'blak-ˌmōr, -ˌmòr\ Richard Doddridge 1825–1900 Eng. nov.; wrote *Lorna Doone* (1869), *Springhaven* (1887), etc.

Black·mun \'blak-mən\ Harry Andrew 1908–   Am. jurist; associate justice, U.S. Supreme Court (1970–94)

Black·stone \'blak-ˌstōn, *chiefly Brit* -stən\ Sir William 1723–1780 Eng. jurist; gave first lectures at Oxford on English law (1753); lectures gave rise to *Commentaries on the Laws of England* (1765–69), basis for legal education in England and No. America

Black·well \'blak-ˌwel, -wəl\ Elizabeth 1821–1910 Am. physician; first woman doctor of medicine of modern times; opened dispensary (1853) which became New York Infirmary for Women and Children (1857); Woman's Medical Coll. established there (1868)

Black·wood \'blak-ˌwùd\ William 1776–1834 Scot. publisher; founded, edited *Edinburgh Monthly Magazine* (1817), soon called *Blackwood's Magazine*

Blaine \'blān\ James Gillespie 1830–1893 Am. statesman; lost 1884 presidential election to Grover Cleveland

Blair \'blar, 'bler\ Bonnie 1964–   Am. speed skater, won gold medals in three consecutive winter Olympics (1988, 1992, 1994); first American woman to do so

Blake \'blāk\ Eubie 1883–1983 *James Hubert Blake* Am. pianist &

composer; with Noble Sissle wrote many of songs; produced 5 Broadway musicals, which were among the earliest to be written, produced, directed by blacks

Blake Eugene Carson 1906–1985 Am. clergyman; gen. secy., World Council of Churches (1966–72)

Blake Robert 1599–1657 Eng. admiral; commander of navy under Oliver Cromwell; renowned for victories over English Royalist, Dutch, Barbary pirates, Spanish fleets

Blake William 1757–1827 Eng. artist, poet, & mystic; illustrated poems *Songs of Innocence* (1789), *Songs of Experience* (1794); wrote mystical and metaphysical works *Marriage of Heaven and Hell* (1793), etc. — **Blak·ean** \'blā-kē-ən\ *adj*

Blanc \'blaŋk\ Melvin Jerome 1908–1989 *Mel* Am. vocal specialist; voice of many Warner Brothers' Looney Tunes and Merrie Melodies characters, including Porky Pig, Bugs Bunny, Tweetie, Sylvester, Road Runner, Wile E. Coyote, Woody Woodpecker, etc.

Blanda \'blan-də\ George 1927– Am. football player; with Chicago Bears (1949–58), Houston Oilers (1960–66), Oakland Raiders (1967–76); held records for most seasons played (26), most games played (340), most points scored (2,002), etc.

Blas·co Ibá·ñez \'bläs-(,)kō-ē-'bän-(,)yäs\ Vicente 1867–1928 Span. nov.; wrote *Flor de mayo* (1895), *La catedral* (1903), *Mare nostrum* (1917), etc.

Bla·vat·sky \blə-'vat-skē, -'vät-\ Helena Petrovna 1831–1891 née *Hahn* Russ. traveler & theosophist; organized, with Henry Steel Olcott, Theosophical Society (1875); began journal, *The Theosophist* (1879); wrote *The Key to Theosophy* (1889), etc.

Blé·riot \'bler-ē-,ō\ Louis 1872–1936 Fr. engineer & pioneer aviator; first to fly English Channel (July 25, 1909) in heavier-than-air machine, a monoplane of his own manufacture

Bligh \'blī\ William 1754–1817 Eng. naval officer; commanded H.M.S. *Bounty* at the time of famous mutiny (1789)

Bloch \'bläk, 'blōk, 'blȯk\ Ernest 1880–1959 Am. (Swiss-born) composer; composed works on Jewish themes *Trois poèmes juifs* (1913), *Israel* symphony (1916), etc.; symphonic works *Hiver-printemps* (1905), *America* (1926), etc.

Bloch \'bläk\ Felix 1905–1983 Am. physicist; awarded (with Edward Mills Purcell) 1952 Nobel prize for physics, for developing magnetic measurement methods for atomic nuclei

Bloch \'bläk, 'blōk, 'blȯk\ Konrad Emil 1912– Am. (Ger.-born) biochem.; awarded (with Feodor Lynen) 1964 Nobel prize for physiology or medicine, for work on cholesterol, fatty acids

Block \'bläk\ Herbert Lawrence 1909– *Her·block* \'här-,bläk\ Am. editorial cartoonist; with *Washington Post* (from 1946)

Bloem·ber·gen \'blüm-,bər-gən\ Nicolaas 1920– Am. (Du.-born) physicist; awarded (with Arthur L. Schawlow) 1981 Nobel prize for physics, for research on laser spectroscopy

Bloom·er \'blü-mər\ Amelia 1818–1894 née *Jenks* Am. reformer; as advocate of temperance, women's rights, dress reform for women; wore full trousers that came to be called "bloomers"

Bloom·field \'blüm-,fēld\ Leonard 1887–1949 Am. linguist; studied esp. Native American and Polynesian languages; developed behavioristic approach to language; wrote *Language* (1933), etc. — **Bloom·field·ian** \,blüm-'fēl-dē-ən\ *adj*

Blü·cher \\'blü-kər, 'blue̩-kər\\ Gebhard Leberecht von 1742–1819 prince of *Wahlstatt* Pruss. field marshal; defeated Napoléon at Laon and entered Paris (1814); aided in victory at Waterloo

Blum \\'blüm\\ Léon 1872–1950 Fr. polit.; premier (1936–37, 1938); imprisoned by Vichy government (1940–45); provisional pres. (1946–47)

Blum·berg \\'bləm-ˌbərg, 'blüm-\\ Baruch Samuel 1925– Am. virologist; awarded (with D. Carleton Gajdusek) 1976 Nobel prize for physiology or medicine, for discoveries concerning the origin and spread of infectious diseases

Bluntsch·li \\'blünch-lē\\ Johann Kaspar 1808–1881 Swiss legal scholar; a founder of Inst. of International Law, Ghent; wrote *Das modern Kriegsrecht*, etc.

Boabdil — see MUHAMMAD XI

Boadicea — see BOUDICCA

Bo·as \\'bō-ˌaz\\ Franz 1858–1942 Am. (Ger.-born) anthropol. & ethnol.; pioneer in anthropology of 20th century; established dominance of cultural relativism; wrote *The Mind of Primitive Man* (1911), *Race, Language, and Culture* (1940), etc.

Bo·ba·di·lla \\ˌbō-bə-'dē-yə\\ Francisco de *d* 1502 Span. viceroy of Indies after Columbus, whom he arrested (1500) and sent back to Spain in chains; arrested and recalled (1502)

Boc·cac·cio \\bō-'kä-ch(ē-ˌ)ō\\ Giovanni 1313–1375 Ital. author; called father of classic Italian prose because of *Decameron* (pub. 1353); writings used as source by Chaucer, Shakespeare, etc.

Boc·che·ri·ni \\ˌbä-kə-'rē-nē\\ Luigi 1743–1805 Ital. composer; known esp. as composer of chamber works; helped develop form of string quartet; created string quintet, string and piano quintet

Bod·ley \\'bäd-lē\\ Sir Thomas 1545–1613 Eng. diplomat & founder of Bodleian library at Oxford, opened 1602

Bo·do·ni \\bə-'dō-nē\\ Giambattista 1740–1813 Ital. printer & type designer; one of first to design modern typefaces, including Bodoni

Bo·e·thi·us \\bō-'ē-thē-əs\\ Anicius Manlius Severinus *ca* 480–524 Rom. philos.; wrote *De consolatione philosophiae (The Consolation of Philosophy)*; translated, wrote commentaries on several of Aristotle's works; wrote treatises on logic, arithmetic, music, theology

Boh·len \\'bō-lən\\ Charles Eustis 1904–1974 Am. diplomat; ambassador to U.S.S.R. (1953–57), to the Philippines (1957–59), to France (1962–68)

Böh·me \\'bə(r)m-ə, 'bœ̄-mə\\ Jakob \\'yä-ˌkȯp\\ 1575–1624 Ger. mystic; wrote *Mysterium Magnum* (1623), etc.; wrote about problems of evil, dual nature of God; works influenced Idealism, Romanticism, theology esp. of Quakers, Pietists

Bohr \\'bȯr, 'bȯr\\ Aage Niels 1922– *son of Niels* Dan. physicist; awarded (with L. James Rainwater and Ben R. Mottelson) 1975 Nobel prize for physics for work on the structure of atomic nuclei

Bohr Niels Henrik David 1885–1962 Dan. physicist; proposed theory of atomic structure; major contributor to field of quantum physics; awarded 1922 Nobel prize for physics

Bo·iar·do \\bȯi-'är-(ˌ)dō, bō-'yär-\\ Matteo Maria 1441?–1494 Ital. poet; known esp. for incomplete *Orlando Innamorato* (1487) which was source for Ariosto's *Orlando Furioso*

Boi·leau–Des·pré·aux \'bwä-lō-,dā-prē-'ō\ Nicolas 1636–1711 Fr. critic & poet; wrote *L'Art Poétique* (1674), regarded as definitive statement of principles of French verse

Boi·ta·no \bói-'tä-(,)nō\ Brian 1963– Am. figure skater; Olympic gold medalist (1988); won numerous American and world championships

Boj·er \'bói-ər\ Johan \yō-'hän\ 1872–1959 Norw. writer; wrote novels *Et folketog* (1896), *Den siste Viking* (1921), etc.

Bok \'bäk\ Edward William 1863–1930 Am. (Du.-born) editor; editor-in-chief, *Ladies Home Journal* (1889–1919); led campaigns against patent medicines, for public beautification, pure food and drug regulation, public health, etc.

Bo·leyn \bu̇-'lin, -'lēn; 'bu̇-lən\ Anne 1507?–1536 *2d wife of Henry VIII of England & mother of Queen Elizabeth I;* charged with adultery, condemned unanimously by assembly of peers, beheaded

Boles \'bōlz\ Paul 1919–84 Am. writer; wrote novels *The Beggars in the Sun* (1954), *Deadline* (1957), *Parton's Island* (1959), etc.

Bol·ger \'bäl-jər, 'bōl-\ James Brendan 1935– prime min. of New Zealand (1990–)

Bol·ger \'bōl-jər\ Raymond Wallace 1904–1987 *Ray Bolger* Am. actor, singer, & dancer; starred in Broadway musicals *Where's Charley* (1948), etc., in film *The Wizard of Oz* (1939), etc.

Bo·ling·broke \'bä-liŋ-,brùk, 'bù-, *US also* 'bō-liŋ-, -,brōk\ 1st Viscount 1678–1751 *Henry St. John* \'sin-jən, *US also* (,)sänt-jän, sənt-\ Eng. polit. & writer; known as brilliant conversationalist, notorious libertine; a major propagandist in opposition to Whig party led by Robert Walpole; associated with Pope, Swift, Gay

Bo·lí·var Si·món \se̱-,mōn-bə-'lē-,vär; ,sī-mən-'bä-lə-,vär, -vər\ 1783–1830 So. Am. liberator; led revolutions throughout Latin America; made pres. and military dictator of new republic of Colombia (1819); gained independence for Venezuela (1821); freed Peru from Spain, becoming its dictator (1824–27); transformed (1825) upper Peru into new republic of Boliva (named after him)

Böll \'bəl, 'bœl\ Heinrich Theodor 1917–1985 Ger. writer; awarded 1972 Nobel prize for literature

Bo·na·parte \'bō-nə-,pärt\ *It* **Buo·na·par·te** \,bwó-ō-'pär-tē\ Corsican family including Na·po·léon I \nə-'pōl-yən, -'pō-lē-ən\ *(q.v.)* & his bros.: Joseph 1768–1844 king of Naples (1806–08) & Spain (1808–14); Lucien 1775–1840 prince of Ca·ni·no \kə-'nē-(,)nō\ (1814); Louis 1778–1846 *father of Napoléon III* king of Holland (1806–10); Jérôme 1784–1860 king of Westphalia (1807–13)

Bonar Law — see LAW

Bon·a·ven·tu·ra \,bä-nə-,ven-'tùr-ə, -'tyùr-\ *or* **Bon·a·ven·ture** \,bä-nə-'ven-chər, 'bä-nə-,\ Saint *ca* 1217–1274 *the Seraphic Doctor* Ital. philos.; revitalized Franciscan order

Bone \'bōn\ Sir Muirhead 1876–1953 Scot. etcher & painter; known esp. for architectural drawings, including series *Glasgow Fifty Drawings* (1911)

Bon·heur \bä-'nər\ Rosa 1822–1899 *Marie-Rosalie* Fr. painter; known esp. for paintings of animals, including *Tillage in Nivernais, Horse Fair,* etc.

Bon·i·face \'bä-nə-fəs, -,fās\ Saint *ca* 675–754 *Wynfrid* or *Wynfrith* Eng. missionary in Germany; had major role in Christianization of Germany; archbishop (732)

Boniface name of 9 popes: esp. **VIII** (*Benedict Caetani*) *ca* 1235(or 1240)–1303 (pope 1294–1303); issued bulls forbidding collection of taxes on church property and asserting pope's temporal as well as spiritual supremacy

Bon·nard \bȯ-ˈnär\ Pierre 1867–1947 Fr. painter; mature works include Mediterranean landscapes, still lifes, nudes, etc.; seen as brilliant, subtle colorist, master of light

Bon·ner or **Bon·er** \ˈbä-nər\ Edmund *ca* 1500–1569 Eng. prelate; bishop of London (1540); supported Henry VIII's anti-papal measures but rejected imposition of Protestant doctrine during reigns of Edward VI and Elizabeth I

Bon·net \bȯ-ˈnā\ Georges-Étienne 1889–1973 Fr. polit. & diplomat; min. of foreign affairs during Munich conference (1938–39)

Bon·ney \ˈbä-nē\ William orig. *Henry* 1859–1881 *Billy the Kid* Am. outlaw; committed a total of 21 murders

Bon·temps \bän-ˈtäm\ Arna Wendell 1902–1973 Am. writer; depicted lives and struggles of black Americans in novels, including *Black Thunder* (1936), *Drums at Dusk* (1939), etc.; also wrote verse, nonfiction

Boone \ˈbün\ Daniel 1734–1820 Am. pioneer; traveled through Cumberland Gap to Kentucky region (1767, 1769-71); guided settlers to Kentucky (1775); erected fort at Boonesboro

Booth \ˈbüth, *chiefly Brit* ˈbüth\ family of Am. actors: Junius Brutus 1796–1852 *b* in England; chief roles Othello, Iago, Richard III, Shylock; & his sons Edwin Thomas 1833–1893; regarded as greatest Hamlet of his day; & John Wilkes 1838–1865 assassin of Lincoln; successful Shakespearean actor (1860–63); shot, killed Lincoln at Ford's Theater, Washington (April 14, 1865)

Booth William 1829–1912 Eng. founder of Salvation Army (1878) with program of reforms, charities in slums and among paupers and criminals; *father of:* William Bramwell 1856–1929 Salvation Army gen.; Ballington 1857–1940 founder of Volunteers of America; Evangeline Cory 1865–1950 Salvation Army gen.; established servicemen's canteens in World War I

Boothe Clare — see Clare Boothe LUCE

Bo·rah \ˈbȯr-ə, ˈbȯr-\ William Edgar 1865–1940 Am. polit.; U.S. Senator from Idaho (1907–40); maverick Republican, isolationist; opposed World Court, entrance of U.S. into League of Nations

Bor·den \ˈbȯr-dᵊn\ Sir Robert (Laird) 1854–1937 Canad. lawyer & statesman; prime min. (1911–20)

Bor·det \bȯr-ˈdā\ Jules 1870–1961 Belg. bacteriol.; discovered (1895) immunity factors in blood serum; with Octave Gengou, discovered (1906) agent of whooping cough; awarded 1919 Nobel prize for physiology or medicine

Bor·ges \ˈbȯr-ˌhäs\ Jorge Luis 1899–1986 Argentine author; wrote short stories of great fantasy and intricacy, including *Ficciónes* (1944, 1946), *The Aleph and Other Stories, 1933–69, El hacedor* (1960, *Dreamtigers*), etc.

Bor·gia \ˈbȯr-(ˌ)jä, -jə, -zhə\ Cesare 1475(or 1476)–1507 *son of Rodrigo* Ital. cardinal & mil. leader; with papal army began (1499) series of campaigns in Italy, using cruel methods and spreading terror; portrayed favorably by Machiavelli in *The Prince*

Borgia Lucrezia 1480–1519 *dau. of Rodrigo* duchess of Ferrara; set up brilliant court at Ferrara that included Ariosto, Titian, Dosso Dossi, etc.; devoted later life to education, charity

Borgia Rodrigo — see Pope ALEXANDER VI

Bor-glum \'bȯr-gləm\ (John) Gut-zon \'gət-sən\ (de la Mothe) 1867–1941 Am. sculptor; best known for figures of Washington, Jefferson, Lincoln, T. Roosevelt on Mt. Rushmore

Bo-ris III \'bȯr-əs, 'bȯr-, 'bär-\ 1894–1943 czar of Bulgaria (1918–43); ruled as virtual dictator (1938–43)

Bor-laug \'bȯr-ˌlȯg\ Norman Ernest 1914— Am. agronomist; awarded 1970 Nobel peace prize for his role in developing high-yield grains that increased food production in developing countries

Borman \'bȯr-mən\ Frank 1928— Am. astronaut; Command Pilot Gemini VII (1965); Commander Apollo VIII (1968)

Born \'bȯrn\ Max 1882–1970 Ger. physicist; awarded 1954 Nobel prize for physics for research in quantum mechanics

Bo-ro-din \ˌbȯr-ə-'dēn, ˌbär-\ Aleksandr Porfiryevich 1833–1887 Russ. composer & chem.; noted for research on aldehydes; composed opera, symphonies, chamber and vocal music, symphonic poem *In the Steppes of Central Asia* (1880)

Bor-row \'bär-(ˌ)ō\ George Henry 1803–1881 Eng. author; compiled lexicon of Romany (1874); wrote *The Zincali, or the Gypsies in Spain* (1841), *The Bible in Spain* (1843), *Romany Rye* (1857), etc.

Bosch \'bäsh, 'bȯsh\ Carl 1874–1940 Ger. industrial chem.; awarded (with Friedrich Bergius) 1931 Nobel prize for chemistry, for methods of manufacturing ammonia and liquefying coal

Bosch \'bäsh, 'bȯsh, *D* 'bȯs\ Hieronymus *ca* 1450–*ca* 1516 Du. painter; painted religious pictures, using symbols, allegory, representations of devils, etc.; painted *Garden of Earthly Delights*, etc.

Bo-sco \'bäs-kō\ Saint Giovanni Melchior 1815–1888 *Don Bosco* Ital. religious & founder of Society of St. Francis de Sales or Salesian Fathers; founded, with St. Maria Mazzarello, Salesian Sisters

Bose \'bōs, 'bȯs, 'bȯsh\ Sir Ja-ga-dis \ˌjə-gə-'dēs\ Chan-dra \'chən-drə\ 1858–1937 Indian physicist & plant physiol.; invented sensitive instruments to study plant responses to mechanical stimuli

Bos-suet \bȯ-'swä\ Jacques-Bénigne 1627–1704 Fr. bishop; known for funerary orations, classics of French Baroque prose, tracts supporting absolutism

Bos-well \'bäz-ˌwel, -wəl\ James 1740–1795 Scot. biographer & diarist; best known for *Journal of Tour to Hebrides* (1785) and *Life of Samuel Johnson* (1785), a masterpiece of biography — **Bos-well-ian** \bäz-'we-lē-ən\ *adj*

Bo-tha \'bō-tə, 'bü(ə)-\ Louis 1862–1919 Boer gen.; 1st prime min. of Transvaal (1907) & of Union of So. Africa (1910–19); staunch advocate of reconciliation between Boers and Britons

Botha Pieter Willem 1916— prime min. of Republic of So. Africa (1978–89); attempted to introduce constitutional reforms

Bo-the \'bō-tə\ Walther Wilhelm Georg Franz 1891–1957 Ger. physicist; awarded (with Max Born) 1954 Nobel prize in physics for new method of detecting subatomic particles

Bot-ti-cel-li \ˌbä-tə-'che-lē\ Sandro 1445–1510 *Alessandro di Mariano Filipepi* Ital. painter; known for deep, saturated colors, linear rhythms, vividly imagined composition; painted *The Primavera, Adoration of the Magi, Birth of Venus*, etc.

Bou·cher \bü-'shā\ François 1703–1770 Fr. painter; painted in soft colors, generally on frivolous subjects; viewed as height of French Rococo style

Bou·ci·cault \'bü-si-ˌkō\ or **Bour·ci·cault** \'bur-\ Dion 1820(or 1822)–1890 *Dionysius Lardner Boursiquot* Am. (Irish-born) actor & dram.; a leading figure on N.Y. stage (1853–62, 1872–90)

Bou·dic·ca \bü-'di-kə\ also **Bo·a·di·cea** \ˌbō-ə-də-'sē-ə\ d A.D. 60 ancient Brit. queen; upon annexation of her kingtom by Rome, led ferocious revolt before finally being crushed by Roman army

Bou·gain·ville \'bü-gən-ˌvil, bü-gaⁿ-vēl\ Louis-Antoine de 1729–1811 Fr. navigator; commanded first French expedition around the world (1766–69); wrote popular account of voyage

Bou·lan·ger \bü-län-zhā\ Georges-Ernest-Jean-Marie 1837–1891 Fr. gen.; led authoritarian movement that threatened to topple government; called "Man on Horseback" because he appeared thus before crowds; accused of conspiracy and fled abroad

Boulanger Nadia-Juliette 1887–1979 Fr. music teacher & conductor; taught Aaron Copland, Virgil Thomson, Leonard Bernstein

Bou·lez \bü-'lez\ Pierre 1925–   Fr. composer & conductor; conducted New York Philharmonic (1971–77); composed *Le Marteau sans maître* (1955), piano sonatas, orchestral pieces, etc.

Bour·bon \'bür-bən, bür-'bōⁿ\ Charles de 1490–1527 *Duc de Bourbon* Fr. gen.; constable of France; began treasonable negotiations with Henry VIII of England, Emperor Charles V; escaped to Charles V (1523); unsuccessfully invaded France (1524)

Bour·geois \bürzh-'wä, 'bürzh-ˌ\ Léon-Victor-Auguste 1851–1925 Fr. statesman; headed French delegation to Hague Peace Conferences (1899, 1907); helped draft Covenant of League of Nations (1919); awarded 1920 Nobel prize for peace

Bour·geois \bür-'zhwä\ Louise 1911–   Am. (Fr.-born) sculptor; created abstract sculptures with highly symbolic male and female imagery

Bour·get \bür-'zhā\ Paul-Charles-Joseph 1852–1935 Fr. author; wrote several poems set to music by Debussy; novels include *Cruelle énigme, Un Crime d'amour, Un Divorce,* etc.

Bour·gui·ba \bür-'gē-bə\ Habib ibn Ali 1903–   Tunisian pres. (1957–87); deposed by Islamic fundamentalists

Bourke–White \ˌbark-'(h)wīt\ Margaret 1906–71 Am. photographer; on original staff of *Life* magazine (1936–69); first accredited female war correspondent (1942); wrote/photographed *You Have Seen Their Faces* (1937), etc.

Bou·tros–Gha·li \'bü-trōs-'gä-lē\ Boutros 1922–   Egypt. U.N. official; secy.-gen. (1992–   )

Bo·vet \bō-'vā\ Daniele 1907–1992 Ital. (Swiss-born) pharmacologist; awarded 1957 Nobel prize for physiology or medicine for discovering antihistamines

Bow·ditch \'baü-dich\ Nathaniel 1773–1838 Am. math. & astron.; published *The New American Practical Navigator* (1802), etc.

Bow·ell \'bō-əl\ Sir Mackenzie 1823–1917 Canad. polit.; prime min. of Canada (1894–96); member of Senate, leader of Conservative opposition (1896–1906)

Bow·en \'bō-ən\ Elizabeth 1899–1973 Irish author; wrote novels *The Hotel* (1927), *The Death of the Heart* (1938), etc.; story collections *The Demon Lover,* etc.; essay collections *Afterthought,* etc.

Bow·ie \'bü-ē, 'bō-\ James 1796–1836 hero of Texas revolution; killed at the Alamo; credited with inventing the Bowie knife

Bowles \'bōlz\ Chester 1901–1986 Am. econ. & diplomat; director, U.S. office of price administration during WWII; ambassador to India and Nepal (1951–53, 1961–69)

Boy·den \'bȯi-dᵊn\ Seth 1788–1870 Am. inventor; invented process for making patent leather, malleable cast iron, sheet iron, hat-shaping machine; made locomotives, stationary steam engines

Boyd Orr \'bȯid-'ȯr, -'ȯr\ John 1880–1971 Baron *Boyd-Orr of Brechin Mearns* Scot. agriculturist; first dir. of U.N. Food and Agriculture Organization (1945–48); awarded 1949 Nobel peace prize

Boyle \'bȯi(ə)l\ Kay 1902–1992 Am. author; wrote novels *Plagued by the Nightingale, Generation Without Farewell*, short story collections *The White Horses of Vienna and Other Stories,* etc.

Boyle Robert 1627–1691 Brit. physicist & chem.; charter member of the Royal Society; noted for pioneer experiments on properties of gases and early version of modern theory of chemical elements

Brad·bury \'brad-ˌber-ē, -b(ə-)rē\ Ray Douglas 1920–　Am. writer; wrote novel *Fahrenheit 451* (1953), short story collections *The Martian Chronicles* (1950), *The Illustrated Man* (1951), etc.

Brad·dock \'bra-dək\ Edward 1695–1755 Brit. gen. in America; led expedition against Fort Duquesne (1755); ambushed by force of French & Indians (July 9, 1755) and forced to retreat

Brad·ford \'brad-fərd\ Gamaliel 1863–1932 Am. biographer; wrote *Lee the American* (1912), *Portraits of Women* (1916), *Darwin* (1926), etc.

Bradford William 1590–1657 Pilgrim father; 2d gov. of Plymouth colony; wrote *History of Plymouth Plantation* (pub. in full 1856)

Bradford William 1663–1752 Am. printer; produced first New York paper money (1709), first *American Book of Common Prayer* (1710), first newspaper in New York, *New York Gazette* (1727)

Brad·ley \'brad-lē\ Bill 1943–　*William Warren Bradley* Am. politician; played basketball for N.Y. Knickerbockers (1967–77); Democratic senator from New Jersey (1979–　)

Bradley Francis Herbert 1846–1924 Eng. philos.; developed theories of metaphysical system of absolute idealism (*Appearance and Reality,* 1893, and *Essays on Truth and Reality,* 1914) — **Brad·le·ian** *also* **Brad·ley·an** \'brad-lē-ən, brad-'\ *adj*

Bradley Henry 1845–1923 Eng. philologist & lexicographer; editor of *Oxford English Dictionary*

Bradley Omar Nelson 1893–1981 Am. gen.; commanded 12th Army Group in WWII, largest force under field commander; chairman, joint chiefs of staff (1949–53)

Bradley Thomas 1917–　Am. politician; mayor, City of Los Angeles (1973–93)

Brad·shaw \'brad-ˌshȯ\ Terry 1948–　Am. football player; played with Pittsburgh Steelers (1970–84); quarterback on Super Bowl championship team 1974, 75, 78, 79

Brad·street \'brad-ˌstrēt\ Anne *ca* 1612–1672 née *Dudley;* wife of *Simon* Am. poet; her poems published under title *The Tenth Muse Lately Sprung Up in America* (London, 1650); viewed as first American poet

Bradstreet \'brad-strēt\ Simon 1603–1697 colonial gov. of Massachusetts (1679–86, 1689–92)

Bra·dy \'brā-dē\ Mathew B. 1823?–1896 Am. photographer; took photographs of Union Army (1861–65), published *Brady's National Photographic Collection* (1870), pictorial history of the Civil War

Bragg \'brag\ Braxton 1817–1876 Am. Confed. gen.; won battle of Chickamauga (1863); unsuccessfully besieged Chattanooga; military adviser to President Davis (1864–65)

Bragg Sir (William) Lawrence 1890–1971 *son of W.H.* Eng. physicist; discovered Bragg's law describing reflection of electromagnetic waves by atomic planes; awarded (with father Sir William Henry Bragg) 1915 Nobel prize for physics

Bragg Sir William Henry 1862–1942 Eng. physicist; pioneered with son William, the study of crystalline structure using X-rays; awarded (with son) 1915 Nobel prize for physics

Brahe \'brä; 'brä-hē, -hə\ Ty·cho \'tē-(,)kō, 'tī-\ 1546–1601 Dan. astron.; compiled most accurate astronomical records to date in Europe; proved nova (1572) was a star

Brahms \'brämz\ Johannes 1833–1897 Ger. composer & pianist; composed symphonies, overtures, piano concertos, violin and cello concertos, sonatas, trios, quartets, etc., and many works for piano, organ, chorus, etc. — **Brahms·ian** \'bräm-zē-ən\ *adj*

Braille \'brā(ə)l, 'brī\ Louis 1809–1852 Fr. blind teacher of the blind; devised (1829) system of raised-point writing for literature and music (known as *Braille*) used throughout the world

Bra·man·te \brə-'män-tē, -(,)tā\ Donato 1444–1514 orig. *Donato d'Agnolo* or *d'Angelo* Ital. architect; designed Basilica of St. Peter (begun 1506); influenced city plan of Pope Julius II (from ca. 1508); developed High Renaissance style

Bran·cu·si \bran-'kü-sē\ Constantin 1876–1957 Fr. (Romanian-born) sculptor; style emphasized geometrical aspects of forms; a major figure in the development of modern sculpture

Bran·deis \'bran-,dīs, -,dīz\ Louis Dembitz 1856–1941 Am. jurist; associate justice, U.S. Supreme Court (1916–39); noted for devotion to free speech

Bran·des \'brän-dəs\ Georg Morris 1842–1927 Dan. lit. critic; champion of materialism, esp. in literature; accused of radicalism; wrote *Main Currents in 19th Century Literature* (1871–87), etc.

Bran·do \'bran-(,)dō\ Marlon 1924– Am. actor; plays include *A Streetcar Named Desire* (1947), etc.; films include *The Men* (1950), *On the Waterfront* (1954), *The Godfather* (1972), etc.

Brandt \'bränt, 'brant\ Wil·ly \'vi-lē, 'wi-\ 1913–1992 orig. *Herbert Ernst Karl Frahm* W. Ger. polit.; chancellor of West Germany (1969–74); awarded 1971 Nobel prize for peace for efforts to improve relations between communist and noncommunist nations

Brant \'brant\ Joseph 1742–1807 *Thayendanegea* Mohawk Indian chief; fought with British in French and Indian War, American Revolution; responsible for the Cherry Valley massacre (1778); helped Tories ravage Mohawk Valley

Brant Molly 1736–1796 *sister of prec.* Mohawk Tribal leader; married Sir William Johnson, British official responsible for Indian affairs within American colonies; helped persuade Mohawks and most other Iroquois to side with British in American Revolution

Bran·ting \'bran-tin\ Karl Hjal·mar \'yäl-,mär\ 1860–1925 Swed. statesman & socialist leader; prime min. (1920, 1921–25)

Braque \'brak, 'bräk\ Georges 1882–1963 Fr. painter; helped Picasso develop Cubism (ca. 1908); developed personal styles, including white line drawings incised into blackened plaster plaques, series of paintings of mantelpieces, tables, birds, etc.

Brat·tain \'bra-t⁼n\ Walter Houser 1902–1987 Am. physicist; awarded (with John Bardeen and William Shockley) 1956 Nobel prize for physics for inventing the transistor

Brau·chitsch \'braù-kich, -kich\ Heinrich Alfred Hermann Walther von 1881–1948 Ger. gen.; commander in chief of German army (1938); planned and executed German campaigns against Poland, Netherlands, Belgium, France, Balkans, and Russia

Braun \'braùn\ Karl Ferdinand 1850–1918 Ger. physicist; awarded (with Marconi) 1909 Nobel prize for physics for developing the wireless telegraph

Braun Wernher von 1912–1977 Am. (Ger.-born) engineer; pioneer experimenter with rockets; developed V-2 ballistic missile for Germany; after 1945, developed rockets for U.S.

Bream \'brēm\ Julian 1933– Eng. guitarist & lutenist; helped revive interest in Elizabethan lute music

Breas·ted \'bres-təd\ James Henry 1865–1935 Am. orientalist; directed archaeological expeditions to Egypt, Mesopotamia; wrote *A History of Egypt* (1905), *Ancient Times* (1916), etc.

Brecht \'brekt, 'brekt\ Bertolt 1898–1956 Ger. dram.; evolved theater of social criticism; wrote *The Threepenny Opera* (with Kurt Weill, 1928), *Mother Courage and Her Children* (with Paul Dessau, 1941), etc. — **Brecht·ian** \'brek-tē-ən, 'brek-\ *adj*

Breck·in·ridge \'bre-kən-(,)rij\ John Cabell 1821–1875 Am. polit.; vice pres. of the U.S. (1857–61); joined Confederate army (1861); secy. of war, Confederate States of America (1865)

Bren·nan \'bre-nən\ William Joseph, Jr. 1906– Am. jurist; associate justice, U.S. Supreme Court (1956–90)

Bre·ton \brə-tōⁿ\ André 1896–1966 Fr. surrealist poet; member of Dadaist movement (ca. 1916); leader of Surrealists (1922); wrote *Manifesto of Surrealism* (1924), etc.

Brew·ster \'brü-stər\ William 1567–1644 Pilgrim father; leader of church and of Plymouth Colony

Brey·er \'brī-ər\ Stephen Gerald 1938– Am. jurist; associate justice, U.S. Supreme Court (1994–)

Brezh·nev \'brezh-,nef\ Leonid Ilyich 1906–1982 Russ. polit.; pres. of U.S.S.R. (1960–64; 1977–82); 1st secy. of Communist party (1964–82)

Bri·an \'brī-ən, 'brēn\ *also* **Brian Bo·ru** \bə-'rü\ 941–1014 king of Ireland (1002–14); killed while defeating forces of Leinster and Norse Dublin at battle of Clontarf

Bri·and \brē-äⁿ\ Aristide 1862–1932 Fr. statesman; prime min. (1909–10, 1913, 1921–22, 1925–26, 1929); helped develop Kellogg-Briand Pact for renunciation of war (1927–28); awarded (with Gustav Stresemann) 1926 Nobel prize for peace

Brid·ger \'bri-jər\ James 1804–1881 Am. pioneer & scout; first white man known to have visited Great Salt Lake (1824); established Ft. Bridger (1843)

Brid·ges \'bri-jəz\ Robert Seymour 1844–1930 Eng. poet; wrote *Achilles in Scuros* (1890), *Eros and Psyche* (1885), *Spirit of Man* (1916), etc.; poet laureate (1913–30)

Bridg·man \'brij-mən\ Percy Williams 1882–1961 Am. physicist; awarded 1946 Nobel prize for physics for studies of materials at extremely high pressures

Bright \'brīt\ John 1811–1889 Eng. orator & statesman; helped defeat corn laws (1846); agitated for free trade, financial reform, electoral reform, religious freedom, etc.

Brig·it \'bri-jət, 'brē-yit\ *also* **Brid·get** \'bri-jət\ *or* **Brig·id** \'bri-jəd, 'brē-yid\ *or* **Brighid** \'brēd\ Saint *d ca* 524–528 *Bride of Kildare* or *Bride of Ireland* a patron saint of Ireland; founded four monasteries, including one at Kildare

Bril·lat–Sa·va·rin \brē-'yä-,sa-və-'raⁿ, -'sa-və-rən\ Anthelme 1755–1826 Fr. gastronome; wrote *The Physiology of Taste* (1825)

Brit·ten \'bri-tᵊn\ (Edward) Benjamin 1913–1976 Baron *Britten of Aldeburgh* Eng. composer; composed operas *Paul Bunyan* (1941), *Peter Grimes* (1945), *Billy Budd* (1951), etc.; also composed church music, song cycles, instrumental works, concertos, etc.

Brock·house \'bräk-,haůs\ Bertram Neville 1918–   Canad. physicist; awarded (with C. G. Shull) 1994 Nobel prize in physics for work on probing atomic structure using neutron beams

Brod·sky \'bräd-skē\ Joseph 1940–96 Am. (Russ.-born) poet & essayist; wrote *Ostanovka v pustyne* (1970, *A Halt in the Wilderness*), *Uraniia* (1984, *To Urania*), etc.; awarded 1987 Nobel prize for literature

Bro·gan \'brō-gən\ Sir Denis William 1900–1974 Brit. hist.; wrote *The American Political System* (1933), *American Problem* (1944), etc.

Broglie \broĭ\ Louis-Victor-Pierre-Raymond de 1892–1987 Fr. physicist; awarded 1929 Nobel prize for physics for discovering the wave character of electrons

Bron·të \'brän-tē, -(,)tä\ a family of Eng. writers: Charlotte 1816–1855; wrote *Jane Eyre* (1847), *Shirley* (1849), etc.; & her sisters Emily 1818–1848; wrote *Wuthering Heights* (1847); & Anne 1820–1849; wrote *Agnes Grey* (1847), *The Tenant of Wildfell Hall* (1848)

Brook \'brůk\ Peter 1925–   Eng. director & producer; known for daring, innovative productions esp. of Shakespeare; stage productions included *King Lear* (1962), *Marat/Sade* (1964), *A Midsummer Night's Dream* (1970)

Brooke \'brůk\ Sir Alan Francis 1883–1963 1st Viscount *Al·an·brooke* \'a-lən-,brůk\ Brit. field marshal; chief of Imperial General Staff (1941–46)

Brooke Edward William 1919–   Am. polit.; U.S. sen. for Massachusetts (1967–79)

Brooke Rupert 1887–1915 Eng. poet; wrote *Poems* (1911), *1914 and other Poems* (1915), *Letters from America* (1916)

Brooks \'brůks\ Gwendolyn Elizabeth 1917–   Am. poet; won Pulitzer prize for *Annie Allen* (1949); first African-American to win this prize

Brooks Phillips 1835–1893 Am. bishop; wrote hymn "O Little Town of Bethlehem" (1868)

Brooks Van Wyck \van-'wĭk, vən-\ 1886–1963 Am. essayist & critic; wrote *The Ordeal of Mark Twain* (1920), *The Flowering of New England* (1936, Pulitzer prize), etc.

Brow·der \'braú-dər\ Earl 1891–1973 Am. Communist polit.; candidate for president (1936, 1940); expelled from party (1946) for advocating peaceful coexistence

Brown \'braún\ Charles Brockden 1771–1810 Am. nov.; wrote Gothic romances *Wieland* (1798), *Ormond* (1799), etc.; first American novelist with international reputation

Brown Ford Mad·ox \'ma-dəks\ 1821–1893 Eng. painter; allied with Pre-Raphaelite group; known for historical and literary paintings; painted *Work, Last of England*, etc.

Brown Helen Gurley 1922– Am. author & editor; wrote *Sex and the Single Girl* (1962), etc.; editor of *Cosmopolitan* magazine (1965–)

Brown Herbert Charles 1912– Am. (Eng.-born) chem.; awarded (with Georg Wittig) 1979 Nobel prize for chemistry for developing compounds with special bonding characteristics

Brown Jesse 1944– U.S. secy. of veteran affairs (1993–)

Brown Jim 1936– *James Nathaniel Brown* Am. football player; played with Cleveland Browns (1957–65); held records for rushing and for greatest yardage gained in one season

Brown John 1800–1859 *Old Brown of Osa·wat·o·mie* \ˌō-sə-'wä-tə-mē\ Am. abolitionist; seized Harper's Ferry, Va., and government arsenal there (1859) to signal general slave uprising; convicted of treason, hanged; viewed as martyr by abolitionists

Brown John Mason 1900–1969 Am. lit. critic; drama critic, *Saturday Review* (1944 ff.); wrote *Modern Theater in Revolt* (1929), etc.

Brown Michael Stuart 1941– Am. biochemist; awarded (with Joseph L. Goldstein) 1985 Nobel prize for physiology or medicine for explaining how high cholesterol causes heart disease

Brown Ronald Harmon 1941– U.S. secy. of commerce (1993–)

Browne \'braún\ Charles Farrar 1834–1867 pseud. *Ar·te·mus* \'är-tə-məs\ *Ward* Am. humorist; wrote *Artemus Ward, His Book* (1862), *Artemus Ward, His Travels* (1865)

Browne Sir Thomas 1605–1682 Eng. physician & author; wrote *Religio Medici* (1643), *Urne-Buriall* (1658), *The Garden of Cyrus* (1658), etc.

Brow·ning \'braú-nĭŋ\ Elizabeth Barrett 1806–1861 *wife of Robert* Eng. poet; wrote *Sonnets from the Portuguese* (1850), *Aurora Leigh* (1857), etc.

Browning Robert 1812–1889 *husband of Elizabeth* Eng. poet; wrote *Sordello* (1840), *The Ring and the Book* (1868–69); famous for dramatic monologues "My Last Duchess," "Fra Lippo Lippi," "Rabbi Ben Ezra," etc.

Broz Josip — see TITO

Bruce \'brüs\ Sir David 1855–1931 Brit. physician & bacteriol.; demonstrated role of trypanosome and tsetse fly in sleeping sickness (1908–10)

Bruce David Kirkpatrick Este 1898–1977 Am. diplomat; ambassador to France (1949–52), West Germany (1957–59), Britain (1961–69), NATO (1974–76)

Bruce Robert — see ROBERT I the Bruce

Bruce Stanley Melbourne 1883–1967 1st Viscount *Bruce of Melbourne* Austral. statesman; prime min. (1923–29)

Bruck·ner \'brŭk-nər\ Anton 1824–1896 Austrian composer; composed symphonies, quintet, cantatas, sacrad music, etc. — **Bruck·ner·ian** \,brŭk-'ner-ē-ən\ *adj*

Brue·ghel *or* **Breu·ghel** \'brü-gəl, 'broi-, *Dutch* 'brœ̄-kəl\ family of Flem. painters including: Pieter *ca* 1525(or 1530)–1569; created drawings and engravings, paintings of peasant scenes, biblical episodes, fantastic scenes similar to work of Bosch; viewed as greatest Flemish painter of 16th century; & his sons Pieter 1564–1638; called "Hell Breughel" for paintings of grotesques, devils, infernal regions, as well as paintings in his father's style of rural and genre subjects; & Jan 1568–1625; called "Velvet Breughel" and "Flower Breughel" for paintings of flowers and landscapes with biblical or mythological scenes, and of backgrounds for many figure painters, including Rubens

Brum·mell \'brə-məl\ George Bryan 1778–1840 *Beau Brummell* Eng. dandy; leader of fashion in London

Bru·nel·le·schi \,brü-n'l-'es-kē\ *or* **Bru·nel·le·sco** \-(,)kō\ Filippo 1377–1446 Ital. architect; developed theory of perspective; designed and constructed dome of Santa Maria del Fiore, Florence; major architect and engineer of his day; precursor of Renaissance

Bru·ne·tière \,brü-nə-'tyer, ,brēˈ-\ Vincent de Paul-Marie-Ferdinand 1849–1906 Fr. critic; wrote *Le roman naturaliste* (1883), *L'Evolution de la poésie lyrique* (1894), etc.

Brü·ning \'brü-niŋ, 'brē-\ Heinrich 1885–1970 chancellor of Germany (1930–32); governed by emergency decree but forced to resign over failure to ease economic crisis

Bru·no \'brü-(,)nō\ Giordano 1548–1600 Ital. philos.; criticized Aristotelian logic, championed Copernican cosmology, to which he added the idea of infinite universe

Bru·tus \'brü-təs\ Marcus Junius 85–42 B.C. Rom. polit. & conspirator; headed conspiracy against Caesar and helped assassinate him; defeated at Philippi with Cassius (42) by Antony and Octavian

Bry·an \'brī-ən\ William Jennings 1860–1925 Am. lawyer & polit.; candidate for president (1896, 1900, 1908); a prosecutor in celebrated Scopes Trial in which he engaged in courtroom debate with Clarence Darrow

Bry·ant \'brī-ənt\ Paul William 1913–83; *Bear Bryant* Am. football coach; most successful college coach in history of football; coached at the Univ. of Alabama (1958–1983); won 323 games

Bry·ant \'brī-ənt\ William Cullen 1794–1878 Am. poet & editor; co-owner, editor New York *Evening Post* (1829–78); early poems included "Thanatopsis" and "To a Waterfowl"

Bu·ber \'bü-bər\ Martin 1878–1965 Israeli (Austrian-born) philos.; developed philosophy based on encounter with nature, man and God; wrote *I and Thou* (1923), etc.; translated Hebrew Bible into German (1926?–37)

Buch·an \'bə-kən, -kən\ Sir John 1875–1940 1st Baron *Tweedsmuir* \'twēdz-,myŭr\ Scot. author; gov.-gen. of Canada (1935–40); wrote novels of adventure *Prester John* (1910), *Thirty-Nine Steps* (1915), *Greenmantle* (1916), etc.

Bu·chan·an \byü-'ka-nən, bə-\ James 1791–1868 Am. polit. & diplomat; 15th pres. of the U.S. (1857–61); unsuccessful in attempt to find compromise in conflict between North and the South leading to Civil War

Buchanan James McGill 1919–   Am. econ.; awarded 1986 Nobel prize for economics for developing methods of analyzing the decision-making process in government

Buchanan Patrick Joseph 1938–   Am. journalist & polit.; syndicated columnist, newspaper political commentator; wrote *Right from the Beginning* (1988); a leading conservative spokesman

Buch·man \'bük-mən, 'bək-\ Frank Nathan Daniel 1878–1961 Am. evangelist; organized international revivalist movement called Buckmanism and Moral Re-armament

Buch·ner \'bük-nər, 'bük-\ Eduard 1860–1917 Ger. chem.; awarded 1907 Nobel prize for chemistry for research on alcoholic fermentation

Buck \'bək\ Pearl 1892–1973 née Sy·den·strick·er \'sī-d³n-,stri-kər\ Am. nov.; noted for novels of life in China; wrote *The Good Earth* (1931, Pulitzer prize), etc.; awarded 1938 Nobel prize for literature

Buckingham 1st & 2d Dukes of — see VILLIERS

Buck·ley \'bə-klē\ William Frank 1925–   Am. editor & writer; founded conservative journal *National Review* (1955); noted conservative commentator in print and on television

Buck·ner \'bək-nər\ Simon Bolivar 1823–1914 Am. Confed. gen. & polit.; surrendered to Grant at Fort Donelson, Tenn. (1862); gov. of Kentucky (1887–91)

Buckner Simon Bolivar 1886–1945 *son of prec.* Am. gen.; commanded Tenth Army (1944–45); killed in capture of Okinawa

Buddha — see SIDDHĀRTHA GAUTAMA

Bu·den·ny \bü-'dyȯ-nē, bü-'de-\ Semyon Mikhaylovich 1883–1973 Russ. gen.; active in Revolution of 1917; member of Central Committee of Communist party (1939–61)

Buffalo Bill — see William Frederick CODY

Buf·fon \,bə-'fōⁿ, byü-, bᵫ-\ Comte Georges-Louis Leclerc de 1707–1788 Fr. naturalist; director of Jardin du Roi and royal museum (1739); wrote *Discours sur le style*, etc.

Buis·son \bwē-'sōⁿ\ Ferdinand-Edouard 1841–1932 Fr. educ.; helped found (1898) Ligue des Droits de l'Homme; awarded (with Ludwig Quidde) 1927 Nobel peace prize

Bu·kha·rin \bü-'kär-ən\ Nikolay Ivanovich 1888–1938 Russ. Communist leader & editor; edited *Pravda* (1917–29); edited *Izvestia* (1934); arrested, executed with other Bolshevik leaders

Bul·finch \'bùl-,finch\ Charles 1763–1844 Am. architect; first professional architect in U.S.; designed Mass. State House (1795–98); architect of National Capitol (1817–30)

Bul·ga·nin \bùl-'ga-nən\ Nikolay Aleksandrovich 1895–1975 Russ. polit. & marshal; premier of Russian republic (1937–38); premier of Soviet Union (1955–58)

Bull \'bùl\ Ole \'ō-lə\ Bornemann 1810–1880 Norw. violinist; composed solos, concertos, fantasias for violin

Bul·litt \'bù-lət\ William Christian 1891–1967 Am. diplomat; first U.S. ambassador to Russia (1933–36)

Bü·low \'byü-(,)lō, 'bᵫ-\ Bernhard Heinrich Martin Karl 1849–1929 Prince von Bülow Ger. diplomat & statesman; chancellor of Germany (1900–09); forced Europe to accept Austria-Hungary's annexation of Bosnia-Herzegovina (1908)

Bult·mann \'bůlt-ˌmän\ Rudolf Karl 1884–1976 Ger. theol.; used Existentialist philosophy to derive theology that "demythologized" New Testament, recast its message in contemporary terms — **Bult·mann·ian** \-bůlt-'mä-nē-ən\ adj

Bul·wer \'bůl-wər\ William Henry Lytton Earle 1801–1872 bro. of 1st Baron Lytton Brit. diplomat; concluded Clayton-Bulwer Treaty (1850) between U.S. and Great Britain guaranteeing mutual control and protection of Panama canal

Bulwer–Lytton — see LYTTON

Bunche \'bənch\ Ralph Johnson 1904–1971 Am. diplomat; chief U.N. mediator in Palestine (1948); awarded 1950 Nobel prize for peace

Bu·nin \'bün-yən, -ˌyēn; 'bü-nən, -ˌnēn\ Ivan Alekseyevich 1870–1953 Russ. poet & nov.; wrote verse, short stories, novels; awarded 1933 Nobel prize for literature

Bun·ker \'bəŋ-kər\ Ellsworth 1894–1984 Am. diplomat; U.S. ambassador to South Vietnam (1967–73)

Bun·sen \'bün-zən, 'bən(t)-sən\ Robert Wilhelm 1811–1899 Ger. chem.; introduced Bunsen burner (1855); with Gustav Kirchoff pioneered in spectrum analysis (from 1859); discovered elements cesium, rubidium (1860)

Bun·shaft \'bən-ˌshaft\ Gordon 1909–1990 Am. architect; in charge of designing Lever House, N.Y. City; Beinecke Rare Book and Manuscript Library, New Haven, etc.

Bu·ñu·el \ˌbün-yü-'wel\ Luis 1900–83 Span. filmmaker; used satire, irony in films about religion, bourgeois values, etc., including L'Áge d'or (1930), Viridiana (1961), Belle de jour (1967), etc.

Bun·yan \'bən-yən\ John 1628–1688 Eng. preacher & author; wrote immensely popular religious allegory Pilgrim's Progress (1678), etc. — **Bun·yan·esque** \ˌbən-yə-'nesk\ adj

Buonaparte Ital. spelling of BONAPARTE

Bur·bage \'bər-bij\ Richard ca 1567–1619 Eng. actor; first player of many of Shakespeare's leading roles; also played chief parts in plays of Ben Jonson, Thomas Kyd, Beaumont and Fletcher

Bur·bank \'bər-ˌbaŋk\ Luther 1849–1926 Am. horticulturist; developed more and better varieties of cultivated plants

Burch·field \'bərch-ˌfēld\ Charles Ephraim 1893–1967 Am. painter; known for imaginative landscapes, lonely town- and city≠ scapes, highly personal depictions of nature as April Mood, etc.

Bur·ger \'bər-gər\ Warren Earl 1907–1995 Am. jurist; chief justice U.S. Supreme Court (1969–86)

Bür·ger \'bür-gər, 'bir-, 'bür-\ Gottfried August 1747–1794 Ger. poet; a founder of German Romantic ballad literature; wrote ballads Lenore (1773), Leonardo and Blandine, etc.

Bur·gess \'bər-jəs\ Anthony 1917–1993 Brit. writer; wrote novels A Clockwork Orange (1962), Earthly Powers (1980), etc.; also produced critical studies, film scripts, musical compositions

Burgess (Frank) Gelett 1866–1951 Am. humorist & illustrator; author of "Purple Cow" jingle; wrote and illustrated Goops and How to Be Them (1900), Why Men Hate Women (1927), etc.

Burgess Thornton Waldo 1874–1965 Am. writer; wrote nature and animal stories for children, including Old Mother West Wind series (1910–18), Old Briar Patch (1947), "Peter Rabbit" stories

Burghley or **Burleigh** 1st Baron — see William CECIL

Bur·goyne \(ˌ)bər-'gȯin, 'bər-ˌ\ John 1722–1792 Brit. gen. in America; commanded expedition against American colonies (1776); captured Fort Ticonderoga, surrendered at Saratoga (1777)

Burk \'bərk\ Martha Jane 1852?–1903 née *Can·nary* \'ka-nə-rē\ pseud. *Calamity Jane* Am. frontier figure; companion of Wild Bill Hickock (from 1876); romanticized in many dime novels

Burke \'bərk\ Edmund 1729–1797 Brit. statesman & orator; advocated liberal treatment of colonies in *Conciliation with the Colonies* (1775) etc.; champion of tradition and constitutionalism; wrote *Reflections on the French Revolution* (1790), etc. — **Burk·ean** or **Burk·ian** \'bər-kē-ən\ *adj*

Bur·lin·game \'bər-lən-ˌgām\ Anson 1820–1870 Am. diplomat; concluded Burlingame Treaty between U.S. and China (1868) establishing reciprocal rights of citizens of both countries

Burne–Jones \'bərn-'jōnz\ Sir Edward Co·ley \'kō-lē\ 1833–1898 orig. surname *Jones* Eng. painter & designer; painted in late Pre-Raphaelite style; pioneered in Arts and Crafts movement

Bur·net \(ˌ)bər-'net, 'bər-nət\ Sir (Frank) Macfarlane 1899–1985 Austral. physician; awarded (with Peter B. Medawar) 1960 Nobel prize for physiology or medicine

Bur·nett \(ˌ)bər-'net, 'bər-nət\ Frances Eliza 1849–1924 née *Hodg·son* \'häj-sən\ Am. (Eng.-born) writer; wrote *Little Lord Fauntleroy* (1886), *Secret Garden* (1910), etc.

Bur·ney \'bər-nē\ Fanny 1752–1840 orig. *Frances; Madame d'Ar·blay* \'där-ˌblā\ Eng. nov. & diarist; wrote *Evelina* (1778), classic novel of manners

Burns \'bərnz\ James MacGregor 1918– Am. political scientist & historian; wrote *Presidential Government: The Crucible of Leadership* (1966), *Roosevelt: The Soldier of Freedom* (1970), *The Vineyard of Liberty* (1982), etc.

Burns \'bərnz\ Robert 1759–1796 Scot. poet; wrote *Poems, Chiefly in the Scottish Dialect* (1786); songs, original or restored traditional, included "Green Grow the Rushes, O," "Auld Lang Syne," "Comin' thro' the Rye," etc. — **Burns·ian** \'bərn-zē-ən\ *adj*

Burn·side \'bərn-ˌsīd\ Ambrose Everett 1824–1881 Am. gen.; commanded Army of the Potomac, mostly unsuccessfully, during Civil War; sidewhiskers known as "burnsides" named for him

Burr \'bər\ Aaron 1756–1836 3d vice pres. of the U.S. (1801–05); killed Alexander Hamilton in duel (1804); conspired to invade Mexico; arrested, tried for treason, acquitted (1807)

Bur·roughs \'bər-(ˌ)ōz, 'bə-(ˌ)rōz\ Edgar Rice 1875–1950 Am. writer; wrote *Tarzan of the Apes* (1914), more than 30 sequels

Burroughs John 1837–1921 Am. naturalist; wrote *Wake-Robin* (1871), *Winter Sunshine* (1875), etc.

Burroughs William Seward 1914– Am. writer; became spokesman for Beat generation in *The Naked Lunch* (1959), etc.

Bur·ton \'bər-tᵊn\ Harold Hitz 1888–1964 Am. jurist; associate justice, U.S. Supreme Court (1945–58)

Burton Richard 1925–1984 Brit. actor; appeared on stage in *Camelot* (1960), *Hamlet* (1964), etc. and in films *Cleopatra* (1963), *Beckett* (1964), *Who's Afraid of Virginia Woolf?* (1966), etc.

Burton Sir Richard Francis 1821–1890 Brit. explorer & orientalist; visited hitherto forbidden Muslim cities; explored Lake Tanganyika region (1858), etc.; translated *Arabian Nights* (1885–88)

Burton Robert 1577–1640 Eng. clergyman & author; wrote *The Anatomy of Melancholy* (1621), including much miscellaneous information about contemporary thought and Utopian ideas

Bush \'bùsh\ George Herbert Walker 1924– Am. polit.; 41st pres. of the U.S. (1989–93); liberated Kuwait from Iraqi conquest (1991)

Bush Van·ne·var \və-'nē-vər\ 1890–1974 Am. electrical engineer; built differential analyzer, pioneering analog computer (1928)

Bu·so·ni \byü-'zō-nē, bü-\ Ferruccio Benvenuto 1866–1924 Ital. composer & pianist; wrote operas *Turandot* (1917), *Arlecchino* (1917), etc., works for piano and for orchestra

Bu·sta·man·te y Sir·vén \bü-stä-'män-(,)tā-ē-sir-'ven\ Antonio Sán·chez \'sän-(,)chez\ 1865–1951 Cuban jurist; drew up Bustamente Code of international private law (adopted 1928)

Bu·te·nandt \'bü-t°n-,änt\ Adolph Friedrich Johann 1903–1995 Ger. chem.; awarded but declined 1939 Nobel prize for chemistry for studies of sex hormones

But·ler \'bət-lər\ Benjamin Franklin 1818–1893 Am. gen. & polit.; mil. gov. of New Orleans during Civil War; arbitrary rule caused protest, charges of corruption; gov. of Massachusetts (1882–84)

Butler Joseph 1692–1752 Eng. theol.; wrote *The Analogy of Religion* (1736)

Butler Nicholas Murray 1862–1947 Am. educ.; pres., Carnegie Endowment for International Peace (1925–45); awarded (with Jane Addams) 1931 Nobel peace prize

Butler Samuel 1612–1680 Eng. satirical poet; wrote *Hudibras* (1663–78), mock heroic poem satirizing Presbyterians and Independents

Butler Samuel 1835–1902 Eng. nov. & satirist; wrote *Erewhon* (1872), utopian novel, and *The Way of All Flesh* (1903), largely autobiographical novel satirizing contemporary family life

Bux·te·hu·de \,bùk-stə-'hü-də\ Dietrich 1637–1707 Dan. organist & composer; organist in Lübeck (1668–1707); composed church music including cantatas, preludes, fugues, toccatas, chaconnes for organ

Byng \'biŋ\ George 1663–1733 1st Viscount *Torrington* Brit. admiral; commanded taking of Gibraltar (1704); first lord of admiralty (1727–33)

Byng Julian Hedworth George 1862–1935 1st Viscount *Byng of Vimy* Brit. gen.; broke Hindenburg line (1918); gov.-gen. of Canada (1921–26)

Byrd \'bərd\ Richard Evelyn 1888–1957 Am. admiral & polar explorer; flew with Floyd Bennett over North Pole (1926); established Antarctic base, flew over South Pole (1929)

Byrnes \'bərnz\ James Francis 1879–1972 Am. polit. & jurist; U.S. senator from S.C. (1931–41); associate justice, U.S. Supreme Court (1941–42); secy. of state (1945–47); gov. of S.C. (1951–55)

By·ron \'bī-rən\ Lord 1788–1824 in full *George Gordon Byron*, 6th Baron *Byron* Eng. poet; wrote *Childe Harold's Pilgrimage* (1812), "The Prisoner of Chillon" (1816), *Manfred* (1817), *Don Juan* (1819–24), etc.; a leading Romantic; his dashing personality and love affairs made him a public figure — **By·ron·ic** \bī-'rä-nik\ *adj*

C

Ca·ba·lle \kä-'vä-yä, -'väl-yä\ Montserrat 1933–   Span. opera and concert singer; roles include Luisa Miller, Violetta in *La Traviata*, Norma, Tosca, etc.; over 120 roles sung and recorded

Ca·be·za de Va·ca \kə-'bā-zə-də-'vä-kə\ Alvar Núñez *ca* 1490–*ca* 1560 Span. explorer; led expedition to Río de la Plata region of South America (1541–42); published accounts of his adventures in the New World and spread the legend of El Dorado

Ca·ble \'kā-bəl\ George Washington 1844–1925 Am. nov.; wrote *Old Creole Days* (1879), *The Creoles of Louisiana* (1884) and other works in the local-color vein

Cab·ot \'ka-bət\ John *ca* 1450–*ca* 1499 It. *Giovanni Ca·bo·to* \kä-'bō-(,)tō\ Venetian navigator & explorer for England; landed at Labrador, Newfoundland, while searching for route to Asia (1497)

Cabot Sebastian 1476?–1557 *son of John* Eng. navigator & explorer; published engraved map of world (1544); led Spanish expedition to La Plata region (1525–28)

Ca·bral \kə-'bräl\ Pedro Álvares 1467(or 1468)–1520 Port. navigator; landed at, took possession of Brazil for Portugal (1500)

Ca·bril·ho \kə-'brē-(,)yō, -'bri-(,)lō\ João Rodrigues *d* 1543 Sp. *Juan Rodríguez Cabrillo* Span. (Port.-born) explorer in Mexico & California; first European to reach California (1542)

Ca·bri·ni \kə-'brē-nē\ Saint Frances Xavier 1850–1917 *Mother Cabrini* 1st Am. citizen canonized (1946); founded Missionary Sisters of the Sacred Heart (1880)

Cade \'käd\ John *d* 1450 *Jack Cade* Eng. rebel; led bloody revolt of Kentish small property holders (1450) against high taxation

Cad·il·lac \'ka-d°l-,ak, *F* kä-dē-yäk\ Antoine de la Mothe, sieur de 1658–1730 Fr. founder of Detroit (1701); gov. of Louisiana (1710–16 or 1717)

Caed·mon \'kad-mən\ *fl* 658–680 Anglo-Saxon poet; earliest known English Christian poet; paved way for English vernacular poetry; wrote 9-line poem on Creation

Cae·sar \'sē-zər\ Gaius Julius 100–44 B.C. Rom. gen., statesman, & writer; made military reputation in Gaul (58–50); led army across Rubicon (49) in defiance of senate and moved against Pompey; Roman dictator (from 49); murdered by group including Brutus and Cassius on ides of March (March 15, 44); wrote commentaries on the Gallic and civil wars

Cage \'kāj\ John Milton 1912–1992 Am. composer; proponent of musical minimalism, aleatory composition, and improvisational multimedia performance art

Ca·glio·stro \kal-'yö-(,)strō, käl-\ Count Alessandro di 1743–1795 *orig. Giuseppe Bal·sa·mo* \'bäl-sə-,mō\ Ital. adventurer; sold "elixir of long life" in Europe; posed as a soothsayer, etc.

Cag·ney \'kag-(,)nē\ James 1899–1986 Am. film actor; first played screen gangster in *Public Enemy* (1931); appeared in *Yankee Doodle Dandy* (1942), *White Heat* (1949), *Mister Roberts* (1955), etc.

Cain \'kān\ James Mallahan 1892–1977 Am. novelist; wrote *The Postman Always Rings Twice* (1934), *Double Indemnity* (1936), *Mildred Pierce* (1941), etc.

Caine \'kān\ Sir (Thomas Henry) Hall 1853–1931 Eng. nov.; wrote *Shadow of a Crime* (1885), *Son of Hagar* (1886), *Life of Christ* (1938), etc.

Calamity Jane — see Martha Jane BURK

Cal·der \'kȯl-dər\ Alexander 1898–1976 Am. sculptor; developed motor-driven (1931) then freely moving structures dubbed mobiles; made similar non-moving works, called stabiles

Cal·de·ra Rod·ri·guez \käl-'thā-rä-rōth-'rē-gäs\ Rafael 1916– pres. of Venezuela (1969–74; 1993–   )

Cal·de·rón de la Bar·ca \,käl-də-'rōn-dä-lə-'bär-kə\ Pedro 1600–1681 Span. dram. & poet; dramatic works included over 100 comedies, zazuelas, operas, etc.; also wrote sacramental works

Cal·de·rón Sol \,käl-dā-'rȯn-'sōl\ Armando 1949–   pres. of El Salvador (1994–   )

Cal·di·cott \'ka-də-,kät, 'kȯl-, 'käl-\ Helen 1938–   Am. (Austral.-born) physician & social activist; campaigned against nuclear armament and atmospheric testing

Cald·well \'kȯl-,dwel, -dwəl, 'käl-\ Erskine 1903–1987 Am. nov.; wrote *Tobacco Road* (1932), *God's Little Acre* (1933), etc.

Caldwell (Janet) Taylor 1900–1985 Am. (Eng.-born) author; wrote *Dear and Glorious Physician* (1959), *The Captains and the Kings* (1972), etc.

Caldwell Sarah 1924–   Am. opera conductor, producer, and impresario; known for innovative productions of new and/or challenging operas

Cal·houn \kal-'hün\ John Caldwell 1782–1850 Am. polit.; vice pres. of the U.S. (1825–32); resigned vice presidency to enter Senate (1832–43, 1845–50); championed slavery, southern cause

Ca·lig·u·la \kə-'li-gyə-lə\ A.D. 12–41 *Gaius Caesar* Rom. emp. (37–41); at first ruled with moderation, but soon became erratic and cruel; murdered by members of Praetorian guard

Cal·la·ghan \'ka-lə-hən, -,han\ (Leonard) James 1912–   Brit. prime min. (1976–79)

Callaghan Morley Edward 1903–1990 Canad. author; wrote novels *Strange Fugitive* (1928), *The Loved and the Lost* (1951), *A Time for Judas* (1983), etc.

Cal·las \'ka-ləs, 'kä-\ Maria 1923–1977 orig. *Maria Anna Sofia Cecilia Kalogeropoulos* Am. soprano; noted for dramatic force; revived art of coloratura soprano and helped restore bel canto repertoire

Cal·les \'kä-,yäs\ Plutarco Elías 1877–1945 Mex. gen.; pres. of Mexico (1924–28); founded (1929) Partido Nacional Revolucionario and controlled subsequent presidents through it

Cal·lim·a·chus \kə-'li-mə-kəs\ 5th cent. B.C. Greek sculptor; said to have invented the Corinthian capital

Callimachus *ca* 305–*ca* 240 B.C. Greek scholar & Alexandrian librarian; wrote narrative *Aetia* that was the model for Ovid's *Metamorphoses*

Cal·lis·the·nes \kə-'lis-thə-,nēz\ *ca* 360–328 B.C. Greek philos. & hist.; wrote a history of Greece from 386 to 355 B.C. and other historical works, all lost

Cal·lis·tra·tus \kə-'lis-trə-təs\ *d* 355 B.C. Athenian orator & gen.; oratorical skills influenced Demosthenes

Cal·vert \'kal-vərt\ George 1580?–1632 1st Baron *Baltimore* Eng. proprietor in America; acquired territory for present-day Maryland (1632) but died before charter issued

Calvert Leonard 1606–1647 *son of George* gov. of Maryland province (1634–47)

Cal·vin \'kal-vən\ John 1509–1564 orig. *Jean Chau·vin* \shō-vaⁿ\ or *Caul·vin* \kōl-vaⁿ\ Fr. theol. & reformer; major Protestant reformer of 16th century; established reformed church and theocracy in Geneva; his government and writings influenced development of Protestantism throughout Europe — **Cal·vin·ist** \'kal-və-nist\ *adj or n*

Calvin Melvin 1911– Am. chem.; awarded 1961 Nobel prize for chemistry for research on photosynthesis

Camacho Manuel Ávila — see ÁVILA CAMACHO

Cam·ba·cé·rès \ˌkäⁿ-ˌbä-sə-ˈres, -ˌbä-\ Jean-Jacques-Régis de 1753–1824 Duc de *Parme* Fr. jurist; counselor of Napoléon I; instrumental in formulation of Code Napoléon (1804)

Cambridge 1st Baron of — see Edgar Douglas ADRIAN

Cam·by·ses II \kam-ˈbī-(ˌ)sēz\ *d* 522 B.C. *son of Cyrus II the Great* king of Persia (529–22); conquered Egypt (525)

Cam·den \'kam-dən\ William 1551–1623 Eng. antiquarian & hist.; compiled *Britannia*, topographical account in Latin of British Isles from earliest times (pub. 1586)

Cam·er·on of Loch·iel \ˈka-mə-rən-əv-lä-ˈkē(ə)l, ˈkam-rən-, -ˈkē(ə)l\ 1629–1719 Sir *Ewen Cameron* Scot. chieftain; supporter of Charles II and James II; renowned for feats of strength and ferocity in combat

Cameron of Lochiel 1695?–1748 *Donald Cameron; the gentle Lochiel* Scot. chieftain; wounded at Culloden (1746) and escaped with Prince Charles Edward to France

Ca·mões \kə-ˈmȯiⁿsh\ *E* **Ca·mo·ëns** \kə-ˈmō-ənz, ˈka-mə-wənz\ Luiz Vaz de 1524(or 1525)–1580 Port. poet; wrote *Os buisadas* (1572), based on Portugese history, etc.; developed Portuguese lyric to its height; influenced national drama

Camp \'kamp\ Walter Chauncey 1859–1925 Am. football coach; helped define rules of American football; helped select earliest All-American football teams

Camp·bell \'kam-bəl, 'ka-məl\ Alexander 1788–1866 Am. (Irish≈born) founder of Disciples of Christ; founded Bethany Coll., Bethany, W. Va. (1840), pres. (1840-66)

Campbell Ben Nighthorse 1993– Am. polit.; member, U.S. House of Representatives (1987–93), U.S. Senate (1993–); first Native American member of Congress

Campbell Colin 1792–1863 orig. surname *Mac·li·ver* \mə-ˈklē-vər\; Baron *Clyde* Brit. field marshal; commander in chief in India (1857–60); suppressed Sepoy Mutiny (1857–58)

Campbell John 1705–1782 4th Earl of *Lou·doun* \ˈlau̇-dⁿn\ Brit. gen. in America; commander in chief during French and Indian War

Campbell John Douglas Sutherland 1845–1914 9th Duke of *Argyll* gov.-gen. of Canada (1878–83)

Campbell Joseph 1904–1987 Am. comparative mythologist & folklorist; wrote *The Hero with a Thousand Faces*, series *The Masks of God, Historical Atlas of World Mythology*, etc.

Campbell Kim 1947–   orig. *Avril Phaedra Campbell* prime min. of Canada (1993); first woman to hold this office

Campbell Thomas 1777–1844 Brit. poet; renowned for patriotic and battle lyrics "Ye Mariners of England," "Soldier's Dream," etc.

Camp·bell–Ban·ner·man \-'ba-nər-mən\ Sir Henry 1836–1908 Brit. statesman; prime min. (1905–08); ended importing of indentured Chinese labor into South Africa

Cam·pi \'käm-(,)pē\ Ital. family of painters in Cremona including: Galeazzo 1477–1536; painted chiefly religious pictures; & his three sons Giulio 1502–1572; painted high altar in San Abbondio, Cremona (1527), frescoes in Santa Margherita, Cremona (1847), etc.; Antonio 1536–*ca* 1591; known for *Birth of Christ* in San Paolo, Milan, & Vincenzo 1536–1591; painted chiefly portraits, still lifes, genre scenes

Cam·pi·on \'kam-pē-ən\ Thomas 1567–1620 Eng. poet & composer; best known for graceful and musical lyrics published in four *Bookes of Ayres* (1601–17)

Ca·mus \kȧ-mᵫ̇\ Albert 1913–1960 Fr. nov., essayist, & dram.; wrote novels *L'Etranger* (1942, *The Stranger*), *La Peste* (1947, *The Plague*), *La Chute* (1956, *The Fall*), expressing postwar disillusionment; awarded 1957 Nobel prize for literature for his novels

Ca·na·let·to \,kȧ-nᵊl-'e-(,)tō\ orig. *Giovanni Antonio Canal* Ital. painter; leader of Venetian school of topographical painters; painted views of Venice, playing with light, shadow

Can·by \'kan-bē\ Henry Sei·del \'sī-dᵊl\ 1878–1961 Am. editor & author; edited "Literary Review" of N.Y. *Evening Post* (1920–24), *Saturday Review of Literature* (1924–36); wrote *The Short Story in English* (1909), etc.

Can·dolle \käⁿ-dȯl\ Augustin Pyrame de 1778–1841 Swiss botanist; introduced system of classifying plants by structure in *Théorie élémentaire de la botanique* (1813)

Can·dra·gup·ta \,kən-drə-'gúp-tə\ or **Chan·dra·gup·ta** \,chən-\ d *ca* 297 B.C. Indian emp. (*ca* 321–*ca* 297 B.C.); founder of Maurya dynasty

Can·dra Gup·ta II \'kən-drə-'gúp-tə\ *also* **Chan·dra Gup·ta II** \'chən-\ Indian ruler of Gupta dynasty (*ca* 380–*ca* 415)

Ca·net·ti \kə-'ne-tē\ Elias 1905–1994 Brit. (Bulg.-born) author writing in German; awarded 1981 Nobel prize for literature

Canfield Dorothy — see Dorothy Canfield FISHER

Can·ning \'ka-niŋ\ Charles John 1812–1862 Earl *Canning* Brit. gov.-gen. of India (1856–58); 1st viceroy of India (1858–62)

Canning George 1770–1827 *father of C.J.* Brit. statesman; as foreign secretary and leader of House of Commons (1822) advocated nonintervention and fostered liberal and nationalist movements in Europe; prime min. (1827)

Canning Stratford 1786–1880 1st Viscount *Stratford de Red·cliffe* \'red-,klif\ Brit. diplomat; negotiated treaty of Bucharest between Russia and Turkey (1812)

Can·non \'ka-nən\ Joseph Gurney 1836–1926 *Uncle Joe* Am. polit.; Speaker of the House (1903–11) and leader of reactionary Republicans

Ca·no·va \kə-'nō-və, -'nò-\ Antonio 1757–1822 Ital. sculptor; critical influence in development of Neoclassical sculpture; works included *Daedalus and Icarus*, *Napoléon as First Consul*, etc.

Ca·nute \kə-'nüt, -'nyüt\ *d* 1035 *the Great* king of England (1016–35); of Denmark (1018–35); of Norway (1028–35); subject of many legends

Ca·pek \'chä,pek\ Ka·rel \'kär-əl\ 1890–1938 Czech nov. & dram.; wrote plays satirizing science, industrialism, militarism, totalitarianism; also wrote stories

Capet Hugh — see HUGH CAPET

Ca·pone \kə-'pōn\ Alphonse 1899–1947 *Scarface* Am. gangster; ordered St. Valentine's Day Massacre of Bugs Moran gang (1929); convicted of income tax evasion (1931) and imprisoned (1931–39)

Ca·pote \kə-'pō-tē\ Truman 1924–1984 Am. writer; wrote novels *The Grass Harp* (1951), *In Cold Blood* (1966), stories *Breakfast at Tiffany's* (1958), etc.

Capp \'kap\ Al 1909–1979 orig. *Alfred Gerald Caplin* Am. cartoonist; produced (1934–77) comic strip "L'il Abner," concerning hillbilly folk in fictional Dogpatch

Cap·ra \'ka-prə\ Frank 1897–1991 Am. film director & producer; directed *It Happened One Night* (1934), *Mr. Smith Goes to Washington* (1939), *It's a Wonderful Life* (1946), etc. — **Cap·ra·esque** \,ka-prə-'esk\ *adj*

Car·a·cal·la \,kar-ə-'ka-lə\ A.D. 188–217 *Marcus Aurelius Antoninus* orig. *Bas·si·a·nus* \,ba-sē-'ä-nəs\ Rom. emp. (211–217); granted Roman citizenship to all free inhabitants of empire; constructed Baths of Caracalla in Rome

Ca·rat·a·cus \kə-'ra-ti-kəs\ *also* **Ca·rac·ta·cus** \-'rak-ti-\ *W* **Ca·ra·doc** *or* **Ca·ra·dog** \kə-'rä-(,)dòg\ 1st cent. A.D. Brit. chieftain; joint chieftain with brother Togodumnus (from ca. 42); unsuccessfully resisted invasion of Roman Emperor Claudius

Ca·ra·vag·gio \,kar-ə-'vä-j(ē,)ō, -'vä-zhō\ Michelangelo da 1573–1610 *Michelangelo Merisi* Ital. painter; known for startlingly naturalistic depiction of religious figures; master of chiaroscuro; influential figure in Baroque art; works include *Supper at Emmaus*, *Death of the Virgin* — **Ca·ra·vag·gesque** \,kär-ə-,vä-'jesk\ *adj*

Car·ber·ry \'kär,ber-ē, -bə-rē\ John Joseph 1904– Am. cardinal

Cár·de·nas \'kär-d°n-äs, 'kär-thā-,näs\ Lázaro 1895–1970 Mex. gen. & polit.; pres. of Mexico (1934–40); instituted Six-Year Plan to redistribute land, develop industry, renew struggle with Catholic Church, expropriate foreign-owned oil properties

Car·do·so \kár-'dō-(,)zü\ Fernando Henrique 1931– pres. of Brazil (1995–)

Car·do·zo \kär-'dō-(,)zō\ Benjamin Nathan 1870–1938 Am. jurist; associate justice, U.S. Supreme Court (1932–33)

Car·duc·ci \kär-'dü-(,)chē\ Giosuè 1835–1907 Ital. poet; awarded 1906 Nobel prize for literature; promoted use of classical meter in Italian poetry; considered modern Italy's national poet

Ca·rew \kə-'rü; 'kar-ē, 'ker-\ Thomas 1595?–?1640 Eng. poet; wrote chiefly short amatory or occasional lyrics; known as first of Cavalier poets

Car·ey \'kar-ē, 'ker-\ George Leonard 1935– archbishop of Canterbury (1991–)

Carl XVI Gus·taf \\'kärl-'gəs-,täv, -'gùs-, -,täf\\ 1946– king of Sweden (1973–)

Carle·ton \\'kär(-ə)l-tən\\ Sir Guy 1724–1808 1st Baron *Dorchester* Brit. gen. & administrator in America; gov. of Quebec and commander of British forces in Canada (1775–77); repelled attack of Montgomery and Benedict Arnod (1775–76)

Car·los \\'kär-ləs, -,lōs\\ Don 1788–1855 infante & pretender to Span. throne; defeated in Carlist wars (1833–39) and fled to France — **Car·list** \\'kär-list\\ *adj or n*

Carlos de Aus·tria \\-thä-'aù-strē-ə\\ Don 1545–1568 *son of Philip II of Spain* prince of Asturias & heir to Span. throne; imprisoned (1568) for plotting with Dutch leaders against father

Car·lo·ta \\kär-'lō-tə, -'lä-\\ 1840–1927 *Marie-Charlotte-Amélie= Augustine-Victoire-Clémentine-Léopoldine* empress of Mexico (1864–67); became incurably insane after downfall of regime

Car·lyle \\kär-'lī(ə)l, 'kär-\\ Thomas 1795–1881 Scot. essayist & hist.; wrote *Sartor Resartus* (1836), *French Revolution* (1837), *On Heroes, Hero-Worship,* and *the Heroic in History* (1841), etc.; self= styled prophet, a great sage — **Car·lyl·ean** or **Car·lyl·ian** \\kär-'lī-lē-ən\\ *adj*

Car·mo·na \\kär-'mō-nə\\ António Óscar de Fragoso 1869–1951 Port. gen.; pres. of Portugal (1928–51)

Car·nap \\'kär-,nap\\ Rudolf 1891–1970 Am. (Ger.-born) philos.; member of Vienna Circle of logical positivists; wrote works on logic, analysis of language, theory of probability, philosophy of science

Car·ne·gie \\kär-'ne-gē, 'kär-nə-gē\\ Andrew 1835–1919 Am. (Scot.= born) industrialist & philanthropist; retired (1901) after making a fortune in steel; made large contributions for public libraries, public education, international peace

Car·not \\kär-'nō\\ Lazare-Nicolas-Marguerite 1753–1823 Fr. statesman & gen.; opposed making Napoléon consul for life and establishment of empire; min. of interior during Hundred Days (1815)

Carnot Marie-François-Sadi 1837–1894 pres. of France (1887–94); met crises of political agitation (1889) and Panama scandals (1892); assassinated by Italian anarchist

Car·ol II \\'kar-əl\\ 1893–1953 king of Romania (1930–40); during his reign, tried to please both Russia and Germany; established corporatist dictatorship; driven out by German influence

Car·pac·cio \\kär-'pä-ch(ē-,)ō\\ Vittore *ca* 1460–1525(or 1526) Ital. painter of great compositional and narrative power; created series on St. Ursula, on St. Jerome, altarpiece *Presentation in the Temple*

Car·ran·za \\kə-'ran-zə, -'rän-\\ Venustiano 1859–1920 pres. of Mexico (1915–20); after career as revolutionary, first pres. of Mexico; accepted Constitution of 1917 but resisted social reforms

Car·rel \\kə-'rel, 'kar-əl\\ Alexis 1873–1944 Fr. surgeon & biol.; awarded 1912 Nobel prize for physiology or medicine for suturing blood vessels and grafting vessels and organs

Ca·rre·ras \\kä-'rer-äs\\ José 1947– Span. tenor; opera debut in *Lucrezia Borgia,* Barcelona (1970); U.S. debut in *Madame Butterfly,* N.Y.C. (1972); performed in Covent Garden, La Scala, etc.

Car·rère \kə-'rer\ John Merven 1858–1911 Am. architect; with Thomas Hastings, designed U.S. Senate and U.S. House of Representatives office buildings, N.Y. Public Library, etc.

Car·roll \'kar-əl\ Charles 1737–1832 *Carroll of Carrollton* Am. patriot; signed Declaration of Independence; U.S. Senator (1789–92)

Carroll Lewis — see Charles Lutwidge DODGSON — **Car·roll·ian** \ka-'rō-lē-ən\ *adj*

Car·son \'kär-s⁰n\ Christopher 1809–1868 *Kit* \'kit\ *Carson* Am. scout; guide for John C. Frémont's expeditions (1842, 1843, 1845) to California

Carson Rachel Louise 1907–1964 Am. scientist & writer; best known for book *Silent Spring* (1962), warning of the dangers of nuclear testing

Carte, D'Oy·ly \,dȯi-lē-'kärt\ Richard 1844–1901 Eng. opera impresario; specialized in Gilbert and Sullivan operas, etc.; built Savoy Theatre

Car·ter \'kär-tər\ Elliott Cook 1908–   Am. composer; composed works of great intricacy and complexity, including two symphonies, concertos, sonatas, etc.

Carter Howard 1873–1939 Eng. archaeol.; in Egypt (from 1890); discovered tombs of Hatshepsut and Thutmose IV (1902); with Earl of Carnarvon on discovery of tomb of Tutankhamen (1922)

Carter Jimmy 1924–   *James Earl Carter, Jr.* Am. polit.; 39th pres. of the U.S. (1977–81); negotiated Camp David peace agreement between Egypt and Israel

Car·ter·et \,kär-tə-'ret, 'kär-tə-,\ John 1690–1763 Earl *Gran·ville* \'gran-,vil\ Eng. statesman; effective head of administration (1742–44) though officially only secy. of state

Car·tier \kär-'tyā, 'kär-tē-,ā\ George Étienne 1814–1873 Canad. polit.; joint prime min. with Sir John Macdonald (1858–62); brought Quebec into federation (1867)

Cartier Jacques 1491–1557 Fr. navigator & explorer for Francis I; explored Gulf of St. Lawrence (1534), sailed up St. Lawrence River to site of Montreal (1535)

Cart·wright \'kärt-,rīt\ Edmund 1743–1823 Eng. inventor; patented power loom for weaving (1785–87), the direct ancestor of modern looms

Ca·ru·so \kə-'rü-(,)sō, -(,)zō\ En·ri·co \en-'rē-(,)kō\ 1873–1921 orig. *Errico* Ital. tenor; sang on leading stages of U.S. and Europe; had large repertoire of operas, especially *Rigoletto, I Pagliacci, La Bohème;* known for warm lyric tenor voice, emotive power

Car·ver \'kär-vər\ George Washington *ca* 1864–1943 Am. botanist; developed over 300 products derived from peanuts, 118 from sweet potatoes

Carver John 1576–1621 Eng. *Mayflower* pilgrim; 1st gov. of Plymouth colony

Cary \'kar-ē, 'ker-ē\ (Arthur) Joyce (Lunel) 1888–1957 Brit. nov.; wrote *Mister Johnson* (1939), *To Be a Pilgrim* (1942), *Horse's Mouth* (1944), etc.

Cary Henry Francis 1772–1844 Eng. clergyman & translator; translated Dante's *Inferno* (1805), *Purgatorio* and *Paradiso* (1812)

Ca·sals \kə-'sälz, -'zälz\ Pablo 1876–1973 Catalan *Pau* Span.-born cellist, conductor, & composer; known esp. for interpretations of Bach; wrote works for cello and piano, violin and piano, chorus

Ca·sa·no·va \,ka-zə-'nō-və, ,ka-sə-\ Giovanni Giacomo 1725–1798 Chevalier *de Seingalt* Ital. adventurer; became a preacher, gambler, violinist, etc., but always a seducer; wrote witty autobiography

Ca·sau·bon \kə-'sō-bən, ,ka-zō-'bōⁿ\ Isaac 1559–1614 Fr. theol. & scholar; a leading 16th-century classical scholar; theological stance regarded as midway between Puritanism and Romanism

Case·ment \'kās-mənt\ Sir Roger David 1864–1916 Irish rebel; joined Irish Nationalists and helped organize National Volunteers (1913)

Ca·si·mir–Pé·rier \'ka-zə-,mir'per-ē-,ā\ Jean-Paul-Pierre 1847–1907 Fr. statesman; pres. of France (1894–95)

Cas·lon \'kaz-lən\ William 1692–1766 Eng. typefounder; designed "English Arabic" typeface (1720); designed Caslon typeface (1720–26)

Cass \'kas\ Lewis 1782–1866 Am. statesman; opened up territory of Michigan (1813–31); directed Black Hawk and Seminole wars (1831–36)

Cas·satt \kə-'sat\ Mary Stevenson 1845–1926 Am. painter in France; produced oils, pastels, prints, etchings; known for portrayals of mothers and children

Cas·sin \ka-'saⁿ, kä-\ René-Samuel 1887–1976 Fr. statesman; chief author of U.N. Universal Declaration of Human Rights (1948); awarded 1968 Nobel prize peace for promoting human rights

Cas·si·o·do·rus \,ka-sē-ə-'dōr-əs, -'dȯr-\ Flavius Magnus Aurelius *ca* 490–*ca* 585 Rom. statesman & author; founded monasteries where priests copied, translated Greek, Christian, pagan, etc., works to preserve Roman culture

Cas·si·us Lon·gi·nus \'ka-sh(ē-)əs,län-'jī-nəs, -s(ē-)əs-\ Gaius *d* 42 B.C. Rom. gen. & conspirator; headed conspiracy against Caesar (44) and was one of the assassins; defeated at Philippi

Cas·te·lar y Ri·poll \,kas-tə-'lär-ē-rē-'pȯl\ Emilio 1832–1899 Span. statesman & writer; president of republic (1873–74); strengthened army, suppressed revolts, conciliated church; ousted by Republicans and exiled after military coup

Ca·stel·ve·tro \kä-,stel-'ve-(,)trō\ Lodovico *ca* 1505–1571 Ital. critic & philologist; wrote works on Aristotle's *Poetics*, Cicero's *Rhetorics*, Dante, Petrarch

Ca·sti·gli·o·ne \,käs-tēl-'yō-(,)nā\ Baldassare 1478–1529 Ital. writer; known for dialogue on ideal courtly life, *Il cortegiano*

Cas·ti·lho \kash-'tēl-(,)yü, kas-\ António Feliciano de 1800–1875 Port. poet; a leader of Portuguese Romantic Movement; later adhered to traditionalism

Castlereagh Viscount — see Robert STEWART

Cas·tro \'kas-(,)trō, 'käs-\ Cipriano 1858–1924 Venezuelan gen.; led insurrection (1899) and became supreme military leader (1899–1901); pres. of Venezuela (1902–08); administration beset with revolts, despotism

Cas·tro \'käs-(,)trō\ Inés \ē-'nəs\ de 1320?–1355 Span. noblewoman; mistress of Dom Pedro (to become Peter I); murdered on orders from Dom Pedro's father Alfonso IV

Castro (Ruz) \'rüs\ Fi·del \fē-'del\ 1926— Cuban leader (1959—); instituted communist regime; repelled Bay of Pigs invasion (1961) — **Cas·tro·ite** \'kas-(,)trō-,īt\ *n*

Cates·by \'kāts-bē\ Mark 1679?–1749 Eng. naturalist; traveled in America (1712–19, 1722–25) to study flora and fauna; wrote *The Natural History of Carolina, Florida, and the Bahama Islands*

Catesby Robert 1573–1605 Eng. rebel; chief instigator of Gunpowder Plot (1604–05); betrayed and killed resisting arrest

Cath·er \'ka-thər\ Willa Sibert 1873–1947 Am. nov.; wrote novels *O Pioneers!*(1913), *Song of the Lark* (1915), *My Antonia* (1918), etc., and poems, stories, essays

Cath·er·ine \'ka-th(ə-)rən\ name of 1st, 5th, & 6th wives of Henry VIII of England: Catherine of Aragon 1485–1536; abandoned by Henry on pretext of questioning validity of marriage to brother's widow (1531); Catherine Howard 1520?–1542; confessed prenuptial unchastity; beheaded when convicted of adultery; Catherine Parr \'pär\ 1512–1548; married Sir Thomas Seymour after Henry's death

Catherine I 1684–1727 *wife of Peter the Great* empress of Russia (1725–27); relied on Prince Menshikov; founded Russian Academy of Sciences

Catherine II 1729–1796 *the Great* empress of Russia (1762–96); extended territory of empire by large conquests; led country into full participation in political and cultural life of Europe; reorganized administration and law of Russian Empire

Catherine of Bra·gan·za \brə-'gan-zə\ 1638–1705 *queen of Charles II of England;* accused of plot to poison king and of complicity in Popish Plot (1678–80); reconverted Charles to Catholicism on his deathbed (1685)

Cath·er·ine de Mé·di·cis \-də-,mā-dē-'sēs, -'me-də-(,)chē *also* kä-'trēn-\ *It* **Ca·te·ri·na de' Me·di·ci** \,kä-tā-'rē-nä-dā-'me-dē-(,)chē\ 1519–1589 *queen of Henry II of France;* three of four sons became kings of France; exercised increasing influence during reigns and regencies of her sons

Cat·i·line \'ka-tᵊl-,in\ *ca* 108–62 B.C. *Lucius Sergius Cat·i·li·na* \,ka-tᵊl-'ī-nə, -'ē-nə\ Rom. polit. & conspirator; involved in conspiracy to murder consuls, plunder Rome (63)

Cat·lin \'kat-lən\ George 1796–1872 Am. artist; painted series of Indian portraits and sketches

Ca·to \'kā-(,)tō\ Marcus Porcius 234–149 B.C. *the Elder; the Censor* Rom. statesman; championed policy against Carthage that brought on Third Punic War; influential orator and writer

Cato Marcus Porcius 95–46 B.C. *the Younger; great-grandson of prec.* Rom. statesman; leader of conservative Optimate faction; supported Cicero against Catiline, Pompey against Caesar

Catt \'kat\ Carrie Chapman 1859–1947 *née* Lane Am. suffragist; a leader in campaign resulting in adoption of 19th (suffrage) Amendment to U.S. Constitution (1920)

Cat·tell \kə-'tel\ James McKeen 1860–1944 Am. psychol. & editor; known esp. for development of experimental methods in psychology; edited *Psychological Review, Science,* etc.

Cat·ton \'ka-tᵊn\ (Charles) Bruce 1899–1978 Am. journalist & hist.; wrote trilogy *Mr. Lincoln's Army* (1951), *Glory Road* (1952), *A Stillness at Appomattox* (1953, Pulitzer prize), etc.

Ca·tul·lus \kə-'tə-ləs\ Gaius Valerius *ca* 84–*ca* 54 B.C. Rom. poet; wrote 113 to 116 extant poems; including epics, small epics, epithalamia, lyrics; one of greatest Roman lyric poets

Cau·lain·court \ˌkō-ˌlaⁿ-'kür\ Marquis Armand-Augustin-Louis de 1773–1827 Fr. gen. & diplomat; aide-de-camp to Napoléon (1802); min. of foreign affairs (1813–14, Hundred Days)

Ca·vell \'ka-vəl, kə-'vel\ Edith Louisa 1865–1915 Eng. nurse; helped about 200 English, French and Belgian soldiers escape to Dutch border (Nov. 1914–Aug. 1915)

Cav·en·dish \'ka-vən-(ˌ)dish\ Henry 1731–1810 Eng. scientist; discovered composition of water; developed notion of electrical potential; discovered nitric acid; devised Cavendish experiment to determine gravitational constant, density of Earth

Cavendish Spencer Compton 1833–1908 8th Duke of *Devonshire* Eng. statesman; opposed Irish home rule policy in favor of coercion; declined premiership (1880, 1886, 1887); opposed to tariff reform, resigned as president of council under Balfour (1903)

Cavendish Sir William 1505?–1557 Eng. statesman; treasurer of royal chamber under Henry VIII, Edward VI, Mary

Cavendish William 1640–1707 1st Duke of *Devonshire* Eng. statesman; led anticourt, anti-Romanist party in House of Commons (1666–78); deposition of James II (1689)

Ca·vour \kə-'vür, kä-\ Con·te \'kōn-(ˌ)tā\ Camillo Benso di 1810–1861 Ital. statesman; prime min. (1852–59); exploited international rivalries and revolutionary movements to aid Garibaldi in uniting Italy

Ca·xi·as \kə-'shē-əs\ Du·que \'dü-kə\ de 1803–1880 *Luiz Alves de Lima e Silva* Braz. gen. & statesman; min. of war (from 1855); pres. of council of ministers (1866, 1875–78); commanded army in Paraguayan War (1867–70)

Cax·ton \'kak-stən\ William *ca* 1422–1491 1st Eng. printer; issued Earl Rivers's *The Dictes and Sayenges of the Philosophers* (1477), first dated book printed in England

Ceau·șes·cu \chaù-'shes-(ˌ)kü\ Nicolae 1918–1989 pres. of Romania (1974–1989); notorious for his repressive regime

Cech \'chek\ Thomas Robert 1947– Am. biochem.; awarded (with Sidney Altman) 1989 Nobel prize for chemistry for discovering that ribonucleic acid (RNA) assists chemical reactions in cells

Ce·cil \'se-səl, 'si-\ (Edgar Algernon) Robert 1864–1958 1st Viscount *Cecil of Chelwood* \'chel-ˌwüd\ Eng. statesman; helped draft League of Nations covenant (1919); pres. of League of Nations Union (1923–45); awarded 1937 Nobel peace prize

Cecil Lord (Edward Christian) David 1902–1986 Eng. biographer; wrote biographies of Sir Walter Scott, Jane Austen, Thomas Hardy, etc.

Cecil Robert 1563–1612 1st Earl of *Salisbury* & 1st Viscount *Cranborne* \'kran-ˌbórn\ Eng. statesman; secured accession of James I (1603); negotiated end of Spanish War (1604)

Cecil Robert Arthur Talbot Gas·coyne- \'gas-ˌkòin\ 1830–1903 3d Marquis of *Salisbury* \'sòlz-b(ə-)rē, 'sälz-\ Eng. statesman; prime min. and foreign secy. (1885–86, 1886–92, 1895–1902); annexed Burma, opened China; conducted Boer War (1902)

Ce·cil William 1520–1598 1st Baron *Burgh·ley* or *Bur·leigh* \'bər-lē\ Eng. statesman; originated and directed Elizabeth I's policy as secy. of state (1558–72)

Ce·la \'sā-lə\ Camilo José 1916–   Span. writer; wrote *La familia de Pascual Duarte* (1946); established *tremendismo*, a literary style emphasizing violence and grotesque imagery

Cel·li·ni \chə-'lē-nē\ Ben·ve·nu·to \,ben-və-'nü-(,)tō\ 1500–1571 Ital. goldsmith & sculptor; sculpted works included marble *Hyacinth* and *Narcissus*, bronze *Perseus*, etc.; wrote classic autobiography that is lively account of Italian Renaissance life

Cel·sius \'sel-sē-əs, -shəs\ Anders 1701–1744 Swed. astron.; published observations on the Aurora Borealis (1733); first to describe centigrade thermometer (1742), also called Celsius thermometer

Cen·ci \'chen-(,)chē\ Be·a·tri·ce \,bā-ä-'trē-(,)chā\ 1577–1599 Ital. woman executed for parricide; conspired with brother and stepmother to kill cruel, vicious father

Cer·van·tes \sər-'van-,tēz, -'vän-,tās\ Miguel de 1547–1616 full surname *Cervantes Saa·ve·dra* \,sä-(ə-)'vä-drə\ Span. writer; wrote masterpiece *Don Quixote* (part I, 1605; part II, 1615), etc.; most important figure in Spanish literature

Cé·zanne \sā-'zan\ Paul 1839–1906 Fr. painter; one of the greatest of the Postimpressionists; viewed as a founder of modern painting; works include *The Bathers, The Card Players*, self portraits, etc. — **Cé·zann·esque** \,sā-,za-'nesk\ *adj*

Cha·bri·er \,shä-brē-'ā, ,sha-\ (Alexis-) Emmanuel 1841–1894 Fr. composer; composed operas *L'Etoile* (1877), etc., piano works *Trois valses romantiques* (1883), etc., orchestral works *España* (1883), *Suite pastorale* (1888), etc.

Chad·wick \'chad-(,)wik\ Sir James 1891–1974 Eng. physicist; awarded 1935 Nobel prize for physics for discovering the neutron

Cha·gall \shə-'gäl, -'gal\ Marc 1887–1985 Russ. painter in France; painted surrealist, impressionistic figures and objects from his life, dreams, Russian folklore, etc.

Chag·a·tai \,cha-gə-'tī\ or **Jag·a·tai** \ja-\ *d* 1241 2d son of Geng·his Khan Mongol ruler; ruled Kashgaria, most of Transoxania after father's death (1227)

Chain \'chān\ Ernst Boris 1906–1979 Brit. (Ger.-born) biochem.; awarded (with Alexander Fleming and Howard W. Florey) 1945 Nobel prize for physiology or medicine for developing the use of penicillin as an antibiotic

Cha·lia·pin \shəl-'yä-(,)pēn, -pən\ Fyodor Ivanovich 1873–1938 Russ. basso; renowned as bass of great resonance with great acting ability; great roles included *Faust*, Mussorgsky's *Boris Godunov*, Verdi's *Don Carlos*, etc.

Chal·mers \'chal-mərz, 'chä-mərz\ Alexander 1759–1834 Scot. biographer & editor; edited works of Shakespeare, Fielding, Pope, Gibbon, etc.; published *General Biographical Dictionary* (32 vols., 1812–17), etc.

Cham·ber·lain \'chām-bər-lən\ Joseph 1836–1914; & his sons; British statesmen; father advocated expansion and consolidation of British Empire; his sons Sir (Joseph) Austen 1863–1937; arranged for signing of Locarno Pact (1925); awarded (with Charles G. Dawes) 1925 Nobel peace prize; & (Arthur) Neville 1869–1940; prime min. (1937–40); called for avoiding war by appeasement;

agreed to partition Czechoslovakia; declared war on Germany (1939); resigned after military disaster in Norway (1940)

Chamberlain Owen 1920– Am. physicist; awarded (with Emilio Segrè) 1959 Nobel prize for physics for work in demonstrating the existence of the antiproton

Chamberlain Wilton Norman 1936– Am. basketball player; played (1958–73) for Harlem Globetrotters, Philadelphia/San Francisco Warriors, Philadelphia 76ers, Los Angeles Lakers; held NBA record for most points scored in one game: 100

Cham·ber·lin \ˈchäm-bər-lən\ Thomas Chrow·der \ˈkrau̇-dər\ 1843–1928 Am. geologist; formulated, with F. R. Moulton, the planetismal hypothesis of earth's origin

Cham·bers \ˈchäm-bərz\ Robert 1802–1871 Scot. publisher & editor; wrote *Vestiges of the Natural History of Creation* (1844) which proposed a theory of evolution, preparing way for Darwin

Cham·bord \shäⁿ-ˈbȯr\ Comte de 1820–1883 *Henri-Charles-Ferdinand-Marie Dieudonné d'Artois* Duc de Bordeaux Bourbon claimant to Fr. throne; called France to unite under Bourbon restoration after death of Napoléon III (1870)

Cha·mor·ro \chä-ˈmȯr-(ˌ)ō\ Violeta Barrios de 1929– pres. of Nicaragua (1990–)

Cham·plain \ˌsham-ˈplān, shäⁿ-ˈplaⁿ\ Samuel de *ca* 1567–1635 Fr. navigator; explored St. Lawrence River; founded Quebec (1608), explored northern New York, Ottawa River, Great Lakes

Cham·pol·lion \shäⁿ-ˌpȯl-ˈyōⁿ\ Jean-François 1790–1832 Fr. Egyptologist; found clue to hieroglyphics from Rosetta stone (1821–22)

Cham·pol·lion–Fi·geac \-fē-zhák\ Jacques-Joseph 1778–1867 *bro. of prec.* Fr. archaeol.; wrote *L'Egypte ancienne* (1839, *Ancient Egypt*), etc.; edited brother's Egyptian grammar and dictionary

Chan·dra·gup·ta — see CANDRAGUPTA

Chandra Gupta II — see CANDRA GUPTA II

Chan·dra·se·khar \ˌchən-drə-ˈshā-kär\ Subrahmanyan 1910– Am. (Indian-born) physicist; awarded (with William A. Fowler) 1983 Nobel prize for physics for work on the evolution and death of stars

Cha·nel \shə-ˈnel, sha-\ Gabrielle 1883–1971 *Co·co Chanel* \ˈkō-(ˌ)kō-\ Fr. fashion designer & perfumer; pioneered style of casual elegance; introduced (1954) classic Chanel suit; designed accessories and, esp. perfume Chanel No. 5 (from 1922)

Chang Hsüeh–liang \ˈjäŋ-shü-ˈā-lē-ˈäŋ\ *son of Chang Tso-lin* 1898– Chin. gen.

Chang Tso–lin \-ˈ(t)sō-ˈlin\ 1873–1928 Chin. gen.; with Japanese help took control of three Manchurian provinces (1918); occupied northeastern provinces (1926–28)

Chan·ning \ˈcha-niŋ\ William Ellery 1780–1842 Am. clergyman; organizer and leader of American Unitarian Association; influenced social issues through sermons, writings

Chao K'uang–yin \ˈjau̇-ˈkwäŋ-ˈyin\ 927–976 *T'ai Tsu* \ˈtīd-ˈzü\ Chin. emp. (960–976) & founder of Sung dynasty; created bureaucracy based on ability; made legal and fiscal reforms

Chap·lin \ˈcha-plən\ Sir Charles Spencer 1889–1977 Brit. actor & producer; hugely successful as "the tramp"; films include *The Tramp* (1915), *Modern Times* (1936), etc. — **Chap·lin·esque** \ˌcha-plə-ˈnesk\ *adj*

Chap·man \'chap-mən\ Frank Mich·ler \'mi-klər\ 1864–1945 Am. ornithologist; curator, American Museum of Natural History; wrote *Handbook of Birds of Eastern North America*, etc.

Chapman George 1559?–1634 Eng. dram. & translator; translated rhyming version of *Iliad* (1598–1611), *Odyssey* (1614–16), *Homeric Hymns* (1624) that were standard English versions for centuries

Chapman John 1774–1845 *Johnny Ap·ple·seed* \'ap-əl-,sēd\ Am. pioneer; collected apple seeds (from c. 1800), planted them throughout Ohio valley; subject of many legends

Char·cot \shär-'kō, 'shär-,\ Jean-Mar·tin \'zhäⁿ-mär-'taⁿ\ 1825–1893 Fr. neurologist; conducted research on hysteria, hypnotism (influencing his pupil, Sigmund Freud), senile diseases, etc.

Char·din \shär-'daⁿ\ Jean-Baptiste-Siméon 1699–1779 Fr. painter; known for still lifes, family scenes, genre pieces of simplicity; paintings include *La Raie, Le Buffet, Le jeune violiniste*, etc.

Char·le·magne \'shär-lə-,mān\ 742–814 *Charles the Great* or *Charles I* Frankish king (768–814) & emp. of the West (800–814); organized beginnings of Holy Roman Empire; strengthened Christianity, founded schools, encouraged arts, science

Charles I \'chär(-ə)lz\ 1600–1649 *Charles Stuart* king of Great Britain (1625–49); ruled for 11 years without Parliament; engaged in civil war (1642–45) that ended in the annihilation of royal army and later in his trial and execution as a tyrant

Charles II 1630–1685 *son of Charles I* king of Great Britain (1660–85); after fall of Puritan Commonwealth, restored to his father's throne; years of his reign known in English history as Restoration period; attempted to secure religious toleration of English Catholics and Puritans and to strengthen monarchy; made deathbed profession of Catholic faith

Charles 1948– *son of Elizabeth II* prince of Wales

Charles 1771–1847 archduke of Austria; field marshal; commander of Austrian army of the Rhine during Napoleonic wars; modernized Austrian army

Charles I 1887–1922 *Charles Francis Joseph; nephew of Francis Ferdinand* emp. of Austria & (as *Charles IV*) king of Hungary (1916–18); failed in attempts to take Austria-Hungary out of WWI

Charles I *or II* 823–877 *the Bald* king of France as *Charles I* (840–877); reign beset by invading Normans, Bretons; Holy Rom. emp. as *Charles II* (875–877)

Charles IV 1294–1328 *the Fair* king of France (1322–28); last of direct line of Capetian kings; renewed war with England

Charles V 1337–1380 *the Wise* king of France (1364–80); faced mercenary bands, wars with England, Navarre; rule generally wise, moderate; patronized art, literature, collected library at Louvre

Charles VI 1368–1422 *the Mad* or *the Beloved* king of France (1380–1422); ruled well until beset by bouts of insanity (from 1392); defeated by Henry V at Agincourt (1415) resulting in Treaty of Troyes and marriage of Henry V to daughter Catherine

Charles VII 1403–1461 king of France (1422–61); raised siege of Orleans with help of Joan of Arc (1429)

Charles IX 1550–1574 king of France (1560–74); kingdom ruled by mother Catherine de Medici during his minority; reign marked by civil wars between Catholics and Huguenots; ordered St. Bartholomew's Day massacre (1572)

Charles X 1757–1836 king of France (1824–30); led ultraroyalists after Restoration; deposed by revolution, reaction to increasing absolutism

Charles V 1500–1558 Holy Rom. emp. (1519–56); king of Spain as *Charles I* (1516–56); summoned Diet of Worms (1521); made Peace of Augsburg (1555) with Lutheran states; took Rome, imprisoned pope (1527); last emperor crowned by a pope (1530)

Charles XII 1682–1718 king of Sweden (1697–1718); achieved peace with Denmark, Poland, Russia; defeated Peter the Great (1707–08) but unable to reach Moscow

Charles Prince 1903–1983 *bro. of King Leopold* regent of Belgium (1944–50)

Charles XIV John 1763–1844 *orig.* Jean-Baptiste-Jules Ber·na·dotte \ber-nà-dòt\ French gen.; served under Napoléon; elected crown prince of Sweden (1810); allied with Russia (1812); led army against Napoléon (1813); king of Sweden & Norway (1818–44)

Charles Edward 1720–1788 *the Young Pretender; (Bonnie) Prince Charlie* Brit. prince; head of Jacobite faction; raised army in Scotland and led uprising (1745); defeated by Duke of Cumberland at Culloden (April 16, 1746); fled to France

Charles Mar·tel \-mär-ˈtel\ *ca* 688–741 *grandfather of Charlemagne* Frankish ruler (719–741); defeated caliph's army at Tours after Arab invasion of southern France (732)

Charlotte Empress of Mexico — see CARLOTA

Char·pak \shär-ˈpäk\ Georges 1924–　　Fr. (Pol.-born) physicist; awarded 1992 Nobel prize for physics for inventing devices that detect subatomic particles in particle accelerators

Chase \ˈchās\ Mary Ellen 1887–1973 Am educ. & author; wrote *Uplands* (1927), *Mary Peters* (1934), *Silas Crockett* (1935), etc.

Chase Sal·mon \ˈsa-mən, ˈsal-\ Portland 1808–1873 Am. statesman; chief justice U.S. Supreme Court (1864–73)

Cha·teau·bri·and \(,)sha-ˌtō-brē-ˈäⁿ\ Vi·comte \vē-ˈkōⁿt\ François-Auguste-René de 1768–1848 Fr. author; wrote *Essai sur les révolutions* (1794), *Atala* (1801), *René* (1805), *Mémoires* (1849–50), etc.

Chatham 1st Earl of — see William PITT

Chatrian Alexandre — see ERCKMANN-CHATRIAN

Chat·ter·jee \ˈcha-tər-jē\ Ban·kim \ˈbòn-kim\ Chan·dra \ˈchən-(,)dra\ 1838–1894 Indian nov.; created Indian school of fiction; made Bengali prose a literary language; wrote *Durgesnandini* (1864), *Indira* (1873), etc.

Chat·ter·ton \ˈcha-tər-tᵊn\ Thomas 1752–1770 Eng. poet; famed as boy poet who initiated a Gothic literary revival and was a precursor of the Romantics; early death by suicide brought fame

Chau·cer \ˈchò-sər\ Geoffrey *ca* 1342–1400 Eng. poet; regarded as greatest English poet before Shakespeare; his *Canterbury Tales* ranks as one of the greatest poetic works in English; also wrote *Book of the Duchesse, The Parlement of Fooles, Troilus and Criseyde*, etc. — **Chau·ce·ri·an** \chò-ˈsir-ē-ən\ *adj*

Chau·temps \shō-ˈtäⁿ\ Camille 1885–1963 Fr. lawyer & polit.; premier (1930; 1933–34; 1937–38)

Chavannes, de — see PUVIS DE CHAVANNES

Chá·vez \ˈchä-vəs, -ˌvez\ Carlos 1899–1978 Mex. conductor & composer; used folk melodies and rhythms in his compositions;

works included ballets *El fuego nuevo* (1921), etc., concertos, symphonies, choral and vocal works

Chee·ver \'chē-vər\ John 1912–1982 Am. writer; wrote urbane, ironic, stylistically refined stories of upper-middle-class America, including novels *The Wapshot Chronicle* (1957), *Bullet Park* (1969), *Falconer* (1977), etc., novella, and short-story collections

Che·khov *also* **Che·kov** \'che-ˌkôf, -ˌkóv\ Anton Pavlovich 1860–1904 Russ. dram. & writer; works include *Uncle Vanya* (1897), *The Seagull* (1898), *The Three Sisters* (1901), *The Cherry Orchard* (1904), etc. — **Che·kho·vi·an** \che-'kō-vē-ən\ *adj*

Ché·nier \shän-'yä\ André-Marie de 1762–1794 Fr. poet; guillotined for protesting Reign of Terror; generally considered greatest French poet of 18th cent.

Chen·nault \sha-'nólt\ Claire Lee 1890–1958 Am. gen.; formed "Flying Tigers" air squadron to help Chiang Kai-shek (1941); protected Burma Road against Japanese (1941–42)

Cheops — see KHUFU

Che·ren·kov \chə-'reŋ-kəf\ Pavel Alekseyevich 1904–1990 Russ. physicist; awarded (with Ilya M. Frank and Igor Y. Tamm) the 1958 Nobel prize for physics for studies of high-energy particles

Cher·nen·ko \cher-'nʸeŋ-kō\ Konstantin Ustinovich 1911–1985 Soviet polit.; pres. U.S.S.R. (1984–85); 1st secy. of Communist party (1984–85)

Cher·ny·shev·sky \ˌcher-ni-'shef-skē, -'shev-\ Nikolay Gavrilovich 1829–1889 Russ. revolutionary & author; imprisoned (1862–64) and exiled to Siberia (1864–88); wrote a classic of the revolutionary movement, *Shto delat?* (1863, *What Is to Be Done?*)

Che·ru·bi·ni \ˌker-ə-'bē-nē, ˌkā-rü-\ (Maria) Lu·i·gi \lü-'ē-(ˌ)jē\ Carlo Zenobio Salvatore 1760–1842 Ital. composer; composed 29 operas in Italian and French, helping advance form; composed much sacred music; considered a forerunner of Romanticism

Ches·ter·field \'ches-tər-ˌfēld\ 4th Earl of 1694–1773 *Philip Dormer Stan·hope* \'sta-nəp\ Eng. statesman & author; best known as writer of *Letters to His Son* (1732–68) and *Letters to His Godson*

Ches·ter·ton \'ches-tər-tʸn\ Gilbert Keith 1874–1936 Eng. journalist & author; wrote verse, essays, literary criticism, religious works, fiction *Napoleon of Notting Hill* (1904), *The Man Who Was Thursday* (1908), and detective series featuring Father Brown — **Ches·ter·to·nian** \ˌches-tər-'tō-nē-ən, -nyən\ *adj*

Che·va·lier \sha-'val-(ˌ)yā\ Mau·rice \mò-'rēs\ 1888–1972 Fr. entertainer; successful café singer and music hall entertainer; appeared in films *Merry Widow* (1934), *Gigi* (1958), *Can-Can* (1960), etc.

Chiang Kai-shek \jē-'äŋ-'kī-'shek, 'chaŋ-\ 1887–1975 pinyin *Jiang Jie-shī* \jē-'äŋ-jē-'ä-'she\ Chin. gen. & polit.; leader of Chinese Nationalist independence movement, pres. of Nationalist government in China (1928–49); waged civil war with Communists (1946–49); pres. of Nationalist government in exile on Taiwan, 1950–75)

Chi·ca·go \shə-'kä-(ˌ)gō, -'kò-, -gə\ Judy 1939–   orig. surname *Cohen* Am. artist; best known for feminist constructions, esp. *The Dinner Party*

Ch'ien-lung \chē-'en-'lùŋ\ 1711–1799 Chin. emp. (1736–96) of the Ch'ing dynasty and among ablest Manchu rulers; extended empire to its widest limit, eliminated threats from Turks and Mongols

Chi-ka-ma-tsu \,chē-kə-'mät-(,)sü\ Monzaemon 1653–1724 Jp. dram.; wrote more than 160 plays, most for the Bunraku or puppet theater; works generally dealt with historical romances and domestic tragedies

Child \'chī(ə)ld\ Francis James 1825–1896 Am. philologist & ballad editor; wrote *English and Scottish Ballads* (1857–58), *English and Scottish Popular Ballads* (1883–98), etc.

Child Julia 1912– née *McWilliams* Am. cooking expert; with Simone Beck and Louisette Bertholle wrote *Mastering the Art of French Cooking* (1961); hosted several TV series, beginning with "The French Chef" (1962)

Childe \'chī(ə)ld\ Vere Gordon 1892–1957 Brit. anthropol. & archaeol.; wrote *The Dawn of European Civilization* (1925), *What Happened in History* (1942), etc.

Chil-ders \'chil-dərz\ Erskine Hamilton 1905–1974 Irish (Eng.-born) polit.; pres. of Ireland (1973–74)

Ch'in Shih Huang Ti \'chin-'shir-'hwäŋ-'dē\ *ca* 259–210 B.C. prename *Cheng* \'jeŋ\ Chin. emp. (221–210 B.C.); created Ch'in dynasty; constructed the Great Wall of China; quarrel with Confucian scholars led to Burning of the Books

Chip-pen-dale \'chi-pən-,dāl\ Thomas 1718–1779 Eng. cabinetmaker; collected and published *The Gentleman and Cabinet Maker's Director* (1754), summary of English Rococo style

Chi-rac \shē-räk\ Jacques-René 1932– prime min. of France (1974–76; 1986–88); pres. (1995–)

Chi-ri-co, De \'kir-i-,kō, 'kē-ri-\ Gior·gio \'jōr-(,)jō\ 1888–1978 Ital. painter; style marked by light and shadow, full color, eerie juxtaposition of architecture, classical figures, deserted plazas; created *Enigma of an Autumn Afternoon, The Seer,* etc

Choate \'chōt\ Joseph Hodges 1832–1917 Am. lawyer & diplomat; counsel in Tweed Ring prosecution, Tilden will contest, Standard Oil antitrust cases, etc.; U.S. ambassador to Britain (1899–1905)

Choate Rufus 1799–1859 Am. lawyer; leading trial lawyer of his day

Choi-seul \shwä-'zəl, -'zər(-ə)l, -'zōēl\ Étienne-François de 1719–1785 Duc *de Choiseul* Fr. statesman; directed French policy through Seven Years' War (1758–63)

Chom-sky \'chäm(p)-skē\ (Avram) Noam 1928– Am. linguist; wrote *Syntactic Structures* (1957), introducing his theory of transformational generative grammar — **Chom-sky-an** *also* **Chom-ski-an** \-skē-ən\ *adj*

Cho-pin \'shō-,pan, -,paⁿ\ Frédéric François 1810–1849 Pol. pianist & composer; composed mainly for piano emotionally expressive pieces; composed polonaises, mazurkas, nocturnes, études, sonatas, ballades, scherzos, etc.

Chou En-lai \'jō-'en-'lī\ 1898–1976 pinyin *Zhou Enlai* Chin. Communist polit. premier of People's Republic of China (1949–76); skilled in negotiating and in intra-party struggles

Chré-tien \krā-tyaⁿ\ (Joseph Jacques) Jean 1934– prime min. of Canada (1993–)

Chré·tien de Troyes \krā-tya^n-də-trwä\ *fl* 1170 Fr. trouvère; composed Arthurian romances, *Erec, Lancelot, Yvain, ou Le Chevalier au lion,* etc.

Christ Jesus — see JESUS

Chris·tian X \'kris-chən, 'krish-\ 1870–1947 king of Denmark (1912–47); granted Iceland a form of independence (1918); symbol of Danish resistance to Germans in World War II (1943–45)

Chris·tie \'kris-tē\ Dame Agatha 1890–1976 *née Miller* Eng. writer; created detectives Hercule Poirot and Jane Marple; wrote detective novels, plays *The Mousetrap* (1952), *Witness for the Prosecution* (1953)

Chris·ti·na \kris-'tē-nə\ 1626–1689 *dau. of Gustav II Adolphus* queen of Sweden (1632–54); abdicated but tried to gain throne of Naples (1656), of Poland (1667); died at Rome

Chris·tine de Pi·san \krēs-tēn-də-pē-zä^n\ 1364–*ca* 1430 Fr. poet; wrote love ballads, rondeaux, lays, etc.; also wrote biography of Charles V (1404), several works championing women

Chris·tophe \krē-stóf\ Henri 1767–1820; revolutionist against French (1791); became provisional chief of Northern Haiti (1806); proclaimed himself king of Haiti (1811–20)

Chris·to·pher \'kris-tə-fər\ Warren Minor 1925–   U.S. secy. of state (1993–)

Chris·ty \'kris-tē\ Howard Chandler 1873–1952 Am. artist; developed the "Christy Girl" in illustrations for *Cosmopolitan,* etc.

Chry·sos·tom \'kri-səs-təm, kri-'säs-təm\ Saint John *ca* 347–407 church father & patriarch of Constantinople; composed influential homilies, commentaries, letters

Chu Hsi \'jü-'shē\ 1130–1200 Chin. philos.; government official, teacher, public moralist; developed system of Neo-Confucianism; commentaries on Confucian Classics, *Ssu shu,* became required reading for civil service applicants

Chun Doo-Hwan \'jün-'dō-'hwän\ 1931–   pres. of So. Korea (1980–88); imposed authoritarian regime

Chung \'chən\ Connie 1946–   *Constance Yu-Hwa Chung* Am. broadcast journalist; TV news correspondent and anchor (1969–); coanchor *CBS Evening News* (1992–95)

Church \'chərch\ Frederic Edwin 1826–1900 Am. painter; known for landscapes, scenes of grandeur; works included *Falls of Tecemdama, Heart of the Andes, Niagara,* etc.

Chur·chill \'chər-,chil, 'chərch-,hil\ John 1650–1722 1st Duke of *Marl·bor·ough* \'märl-,bər-ə, 'mól-, -,bə-rə, -b(ə-)rə\ Eng. gen.; one of England's greatest generals; led British armies to important victories over France; dismissed on charge of embezzlement (1711); restored to military post under George I (1714)

Churchill Randolph Henry Spencer 1849–1895 Lord *Randolph Churchill* Brit. statesman; developed a progressive conservatism known as Tory democracy

Churchill Sir Winston Leonard Spencer 1874–1965 *son of Lord Randolph* Brit. statesman; prime min. (1940–45; 1951–55); rallied the British people during WWII; pursued a successful global war strategy against Axis powers in concert with U.S. Pres. Roosevelt; voted out of power after war; wrote numerous works including *While England Slept* (1938), *The Second World War* (1948–54), etc.; awarded 1953 Nobel prize for literature — **Chur·chill·ian** \,chər-'chi-lē-ən, 'chorch-'hi-\ *adj*

Chu Teh \'jü-'də\ 1886–1976 Chin. gen.; helped overthrow Ch'ing dynasty (1911); helped found Red Army (1927); commanded Communist forces against Japan (1937–45); in civil war (1946–49); commander of People's Liberation Army (1949–54)

Cia·no \'chä-(,)nō\ Galeazzo 1903–1944 Conte *di Cortellazzo* Ital. statesman; member of Fascist Supreme Council; helped send Italy into WWII (1940); helped force Mussolini's resignation (1943)

Ciar·di \'chär-dē\ John 1916–1986 Am. poet; wrote textbook *How Does a Poem Mean?* (1959)

Cib·ber \'si-bər\ Col·ley \'kä-lē\ 1671–1757 Eng. dram. & actor; poet laureate (1730–57); ridiculed in revised version of Pope's *The Dunciad* (1743)

Cic·ero \'si-sə-,rō\ Marcus Tullius 106–43 B.C. Rom. statesman, lawyer, orator, & author; one of the greatest Roman orators; innovator of Ciceronian rhetoric; staunch defender of republican principles; writings include books of rhetoric, orations, philosophical and political treatises, and letters — **Cic·ero·nian** \,si-sə-'rō-nyən, -nē-ən\ *adj*

Cid, El \'sid\ *ca* 1043–1099 *Rodrigo Díaz de Vivar* \'dē-,äs-də-vē-'vär, -,äz-\ Span. soldier & hero; besieged Valencia (1093–94), assumed control of its Muslim government, began Christianizing it; became national hero of Castile, subject of legends, epics, etc.

Çil·ler \chi-'lesh\ Tan·su \tän-'sü\ 1946–   prime min. of Turkey (1993–   ); first woman to hold this position

Ci·ma·bue \,chē-mə-'bü-(,)ā\ Giovanni *ca* 1251–1302 orig. *Bencivieni di Pepo* Florentine painter; considered greatest artist of Byzantine medieval style; works include *Crucifix*, *Four Evangelists*, scenes from life of Virgin, etc.

Ci·mon \'sī-mən, -,män\ *ca* 570–*ca* 451 B.C. Athenian gen. & statesman; defeated and scattered Persian fleet at mouth of Eurymedon River (c. 467); defeated the land forces on the same day

Cin·cin·na·tus \,sin(t)-sə-'na-təs, -'nä-\ Lucius Quinctius *b ca* 519 B.C. Rom. gen. & statesman; according to legend, during crisis made dictator by Senate (458); eased crisis and resigned in 16 days; viewed as model of simplicity, ability, republican virtue

Cis·ne·ros \sis-'ner-(,)ōs\ Henry Gabriel 1947–   U.S. secy. of housing & urban development (1993–   )

Clare \'klar, 'kler\ John 1793–1864 Eng. poet; called the "Northamptonshire peasant poet"; wrote *Poems Descriptive of Rural Life and Scenery* (1820); died in lunatic asylum

Clare of Assisi Saint 1194–1253 Ital. religious; founded order of Poor Clares with St. Francis (1212); known for piety, devotion to Eucharist; canonized (1255)

Clarendon Earl of — see Edward HYDE

Clark \'klärk\ Champ \'champ\ 1850–1921 *James Beau·champ* \'bē-chəm\ *Clark* Am. polit.; speaker of U.S. House of Representatives (1911–19)

Clark George Rogers 1752–1818 Am. soldier & frontiersman; leader in defense of western frontier against Indian raids during American Revolution

Clark Joe 1939–   *Charles Joseph* Canad. polit.; prime min. (1979–80)

Clark Kenneth Bancroft 1914–   Am. psychol.; wrote *Desegregation: An Appraisal of the Evidence, Prejudice and Your Child*, etc.

Clark Kenneth Mackenzie 1903–1983 Baron *Clark of Saltwood* Brit. art hist.; wrote *Leonardo da Vinci* (1939), *Landscape Into Art* (1949), *The Nude* (1956), etc.

Clark Mark Wayne 1896–1984 Am. gen.; commander of U.S. 5th Army during WWII

Clark Tom Campbell 1899–1977 Am. jurist; associate justice, U.S. Supreme Court (1949–67)

Clark William 1770–1838 *bro. of G.R.* Am. explorer; joined Capt. Meriwether Lewis on expedition (1804–06) to explore Louisiana Purchase, find route to Pacific Ocean

Clarke \'klärk\ Charles Cow·den \'kaủ-d³n\ 1787–1877 & his wife Mary Victoria Cowden-Clarke 1809–1898 Eng. Shakespearean scholars; wrote *The Shakespeare Key* (1879); *The Complete Concordance to Shakespeare* (1845) compiled by her alone

Claude \'klōd\ Albert 1898–1983 Belg. physiol. in U.S.; awarded (with Christian de Duve and George E. Palade) 1974 Nobel prize for physiology or medicine for pioneer work in cell biology

Claude Lor·rain \klōd-lō-raⁿ\ 1600–1682 pseud. of *Claude Gel·lée* \zhə-lā\ Fr. painter; renowned for idyllic landscapes, seascapes and for mastery of light; first to use sun in painting as source of illumination; also had command of atmospheric effects, recession

Clau·di·us \'klȯ-dē-əs\ Rom. gens including: **Ap·pi·us** \'a-pē-əs\ **Claudius Cras·sus** \'kra-səs\ consul (471 & 451 B.C.) & decemvir (451–450 B.C.); instituted reign of terror that caused plebeian revolt; **Appius Claudius Cae·cus** \'sē-kəs\ censor (312–307 B.C.), consul (307 & 296 B.C.), & dictator; instituted reforms that benefited plebeians; built first aqueduct and Via Appia highway

Claudius I 10 B.C.–A.D. 54 *Tiberius Claudius Drusus Ne·ro* \'nē-(,)rō, 'nir-(,)ō\ *Germanicus* Rom. emp. (41–54); fought wars in Britain, Germany, Syria, Mauretania; annexed Mauretania, Lycia, Thrace

Claudius II A.D. 214–270 *Marcus Aurelius Claudius Gothicus* Rom. emp. (268–270); defeated Alamanni in northern Italy (268), Goths in Moesia (269)

Clau·se·witz \'klaủ-zə-,vits\ Carl von 1780–1831 Pruss. gen. & military strategist; wrote on science of war, especially *Vom Kriege* (1833) — **Clau·se·witz·ian** \,klaủ-zə-'vit-sē-ən\ *adj*

Clay \'klā\ Henry 1777–1852 Am. statesman & orator; called "Great Pacificator" for success in Missouri Compromise (1820); sought to avoid civil war through Compromise of 1850

Clay Lucius Du Bi·gnon \dü-'bin-yən\ 1897–1978 Am. gen.; oversaw Berlin airlift (1948)

Cle·an·thes \klē-'an-,thēz\ 331(or 330)–232(or 231) B.C. Greek Stoic philos.; head of Stoic school after Zeno (263–232 B.C.)

Cle·ar·chus \klē-'är-kəs\ 5th cent. B.C. Spartan soldier; gov. of Byzantium (408 B.C.); his severe policies caused the people to surrender to Athens in his absence

Cleis·the·nes \'klīs-thə-,nēz\ *or* **Clis·the·nes** \'klis-\ *ca* 570–after 508 B.C. Athenian statesman; founded new political system based on locality rather than clan; called founder of Athenian democracy

Cle·men·ceau \,kle-mən-'sō, klä-män-sō\ Georges 1841–1929 Fr. statesman; premier (1906–09, 1917–20); led France during WWI; chief of French delegation to Paris Peace Conference (1919)

Clem·ens \'kle-mənz\ Samuel Langhorne 1835–1910 pseud. *Mark Twain* \'twān\ Am. writer; wrote *The Adventures of Tom Sawyer* (1876), *Adventures of Huckleberry Finn* (1884), etc.

Clem·ent \'kle-mənt\ name of 14 popes: esp. **VII** (*Giulio de'Medici* \'me-də-(,)chē\) 1478–1534 (pope 1523–34); refused to sanction divorce of Henry VIII from Catherine of Aragon (1533); patron of Raphael, Michelangelo

Cle·men·ti \klə-'men-tē\ Muzio 1752–1832 Ital. pianist & composer in England; led modern school of piano technique; composed symphonies, sonatas, piano studies

Clement of Alexandria Saint *ca* 150–between 211 and 215 *Titus Flavius Cle·mens* \'kle-,menz\ Greek Christian theol. & church father; greatest of the 2nd-century Christian Apologists; prepared for melding of Christian and Hellenistic thought

Cle·om·e·nes \klē-'ä-mə-,nēz\ name of 3 kings of Sparta: esp. **III** (reigned 235–222 B.C.); tried to institute social reforms redistributing land, remitting debt, etc.

Cle·o·pa·tra \,klē-ə-'pa-trə, -'pä-\ 69–30 B.C. queen of Egypt (51–30); famed for her liaisons with Julius Caesar and Mark Antony; allied with Mark Antony against Octavian in decisive battle at Actium (31); killed herself when unable to influence Octavian

Cleve·land \'klēv-lənd\ (Stephen) Grover 1837–1908 22d & 24th pres. of the U.S. (1885–89; 1893–97); advocated civil service reform, lower tariff; sent troops to end Chicago Pullman strike (1894)

Cli·burn \'klī-bərn\ Van 1934–   *Harvey Lavan Cliburn* Am. pianist; first American to win Tchaikovsky competition (1958)

Clin·ton \'klin-tᵊn\ De Witt 1769–1828 Am. statesman; governor of New York (1817–23, 1825–28); chief promoter of Erie Canal

Clinton George 1739–1812 vice pres. of the U.S. (1805–12)

Clinton Sir Henry 1738–1795 Eng. gen. in America; became commander of British forces in North America (1778); captured Charleston (1780); resigned (1781) after quarrel with Cornwallis

Clinton William Jefferson 1946–   Am. polit.; 42d pres. of the U.S. (1993–   )

Clive \'klīv\ Robert 1725–1774 Baron *Clive of Plassey* Brit. gen. & founder of the empire of Brit. India; in India (1743–53, 1755–60, 1764–67); defeated French and Dutch colonizing attempts

Cloots \'klōts\ Baron de 1755–1794 *Jean-Baptiste du Val-de-Grâce*; known as *An·a·char·sis* \a-nə-'kär-səs\ Cloots Pruss.-Fr. revolutionary; leading advocate of French expansionism in Europe

Close \'klōs\ Glenn 1947–   Am. actress; starred on stage in *The Real Thing* (1984), musical *Sunset Boulevard* (1994), and in films *Fatal Attraction* (1987), *Dangerous Liaisons* (1988), etc.

Clough \'kləf\ Arthur Hugh 1819–1861 Eng. poet; subject of Matthew Arnold's elegy "Thyrsis"

Clo·vis I \'klō-vəs\ *G Chlod·wig* \'klōt-(,)vik\ *ca* 466–511 king of the Salian Franks (481–511); converted to Christianity (496); united northern Franks but divided realm among his sons

Clur·man \'klər-mən\ Harold 1901–1980 Am. theater director & critic; helped found Group Theatre (1931); directed on Broadway *Member of the Wedding* (1950), etc.; drama critic for *New Republic* (1948–52), *The Nation* (from 1953)

Clyde Baron — see Colin CAMPBELL

Cnut

Cnut \kə-ˈnüt, -ˈnyüt\ *var of* CANUTE

Coase \ˈkōz\ Ronald Harry 1910–   Am. (Brit.-born) econ.; awarded 1991 Nobel prize for economics for his theories regarding property rights and the costs of business transactions

Coates \ˈkōts\ Joseph Gordon 1878–1943 N. Z. statesman; prime min. (1925–28)

Cobb \ˈkäb\ Tyrus Raymond 1886–1961 *Ty* Am. baseball player; played (1905–26) for and managed (1921–26) Detroit Tigers; played (1926–28) for Philadelphia Athletics; considered outstanding offensive player of all time

Cob·bett \ˈkä-bət\ William 1763–1835 pseud. *Peter Porcupine* Eng. polit. writer; took up cause of dispossessed rural laborers, flogged militiamen

Cob·den \ˈkäb-dən\ Richard 1804–1865 Eng. statesman & econ.; member of Parliament (1840–57, 1859–65); best known for successful fight for repeal of Corn Laws (1846) and his defense of free trade

Cobham Lord — see Sir John OLDCASTLE

Co·chise \kō-ˈchēs\ 1812?–1874 Chiricahua Apache Indian chief; warred with U.S. Army and white settlers in Arizona; eventually settled on reservation occupying ancestral Chiricahua lands

Cock·croft \ˈkä(k)-ˌkróft\ Sir John Douglas 1897–1967 Brit. physicist; awarded (with Ernest T.S. Walton) 1951 Nobel prize for physics for pioneering use of particle accelerators in studying the atomic·nucleus

Coc·teau \käk-ˈtō, kók-\ Jean 1889–1963 Fr. author & artist; known for wide variety of forms in which he worked, including poetry, fiction, ballet, motion pictures, painting; best known works include play *La Machine infernale* (1934), films *La Belle et la bête* (1945), *Orphée* (1950)

Co·dy \ˈkō-dē\ William Frederick 1846–1917 *Buffalo Bill* Am. scout & showman; rider for Pony Express (1860); scout for U.S. Cavalry (1868–76); with Buffalo Bill's Wild West Show from 1883

Coen \ˈkün\ Jan Pieterszoon 1587–1629 Du. colonial gov. & founder of Du. East Indian empire; secured Dutch monopolies in various spices

Coeur de Lion — see RICHARD I of England

Cof·fin \ˈkó-fən, ˈkä-\ Robert Peter Tristram 1892–1955 Am. author; wrote verse *Strange Holiness* (1935, Pulitzer prize), etc.

Cog·gan \ˈkä-gən\ Frederick Donald 1909–   archbishop of Canterbury (1974–80)

Co·han \ˈkō-ˌhan\ George Michael 1878–1942 Am. actor, dram., & producer; composed numerous songs, including "You're a Grand Old Flag," "Give My Regards to Broadway," "I'm a Yankee Doodle Dandy," "Over There"

Co·hen \ˈkō-ən\ Stanley 1922–   Am. biochem.; awarded (with Rita Levi-Montalcini) 1986 Nobel prize for physiology or medicine for research on cell and organ growth

Cohn \ˈkōn\ Ferdinand Julius 1828–1898 Ger. botanist; demonstrated that bacteria are plants; helped disprove notion of spontaneous generation

Coke \ˈkük, ˈkōk\ Sir Edward 1552–1634 *Lord Coke* Eng. jurist; decided that king's proclamation cannot change the law; best known for his legal compendia *Reports* and *Institutes*

Col·bert \kȯl-'ber, 'kōl-,\ Jean-Baptiste 1619–1683 Fr. statesman & financier; created French navy; reformed administration and collection of taxes and greatly increased state revenues

Cole \'kōl\ Thomas 1801–1848 Am. (Eng.-born) painter; founder of Hudson River school

Cole·pep·er *or* **Cul·pep·er** \'kəl-,pe-pər\ Thomas 1635–1689 2d Baron *Colepeper* Eng. colonial administrator; gov. of Virginia; taxed and punished tobacco growers with intolerable severity

Cole·ridge \'kōl-rij, 'kō-lə-rij\ Samuel Taylor 1772–1834 Eng. poet; associate of Wordsworth; wrote "Rime of the Ancient Mariner," "Kublai Khan," "Christabel," etc. — **Cole·ridg·ean** *also* **Cole·ridg·ian** \,kȯl-'ri-jē-ən, ,kō-lə-\ *adj*

Col·et \'kä-lət\ John 1466(or 1467)–1519 Eng. theol. & scholar; preached against sale of bishoprics, church lawyers, etc.; founded and endowed St. Paul's School

Co·lette \kȯ-'let\ Sidonie-Gabrielle 1873–1954 Fr. author; wrote novels of exquisite sensitivity including *Chéri* (1920), *La Chatte* (1933), *Gigi* (1944)

Col·fax \'kōl-,faks\ Schuyler \'skī-lər\ 1823–1885 vice pres. of the U.S. (1869–73)

Co·li·gny \,kō-lēn-'yē, kə-'lēn-yē\ Gaspard II de 1519–1572 *Seigneur de Châtillon* Fr. admiral & Huguenot leader; aided Huguenots by sending colonies to New World

Col·lier \'käl-yər, 'kä-lē-ər\ Jeremy 1650–1726 Eng. clergyman; imprisoned for Jacobin sympathies; attacked for his *Short View of the Immorality and Profaneness of the English Stage*

Collier John Payne 1789–1883 Eng. editor; brought out texts of Shakespeare based on forged *Notes and Emendations to Shakespeare*, but exposed

Collier Peter Fen·e·lon \'fe-nᵊl-ən\ 1849–1909 Am. publisher; founded *Collier's Weekly*

Col·lins \'kä-lənz\ Michael 1890–1922 Irish revolutionary; negotiated peace treaty with Great Britain after declaration of Irish independence

Collins Michael 1930–   Am. astronaut; in command module during Apollo 11 landing on the moon

Collins William 1721–1759 Eng. poet; wrote *Odes*, etc., in Neoclassical forms but was forerunner of Romantics

Collins (William) Wilkie 1824–1889 Eng. nov.; author of mystery novels with skillful plots including *The Moonstone* (1868)

Col·lor de Mel·lo \kō-'lȯr-də-'me-lü\ Fernando Affonso 1949–   pres. of Brazil (1990–92)

Col·man \'kōl-mən\ George 1732–1794 Eng. dram.; won fame with *The Jealous Wife*, based in part on Fielding's *Tom Jones*; edited plays of Beaumont & Fletcher

Col·um \'kä-ləm\ Pad·raic \'pȯth-rig\ 1881–1972 Am. (Irish-born) writer; author of verse, plays, volumes of folktales from Ireland, Hawaii, etc.

Co·lum·ba \kə-'ləm-bə\ *Ir* **Col·um** \'kə-ləm\ *or* **Col·um·cille** \'kə-ləm-,kil\ Saint *ca* 521–597 Irish missionary in Scotland; with 12 disciples established monastery on island of Iona

Co·lum·bus \kə-'ləm-bəs\ Christopher *It* Christoforo **Co·lom·bo** \kə-'lȯm-(,)bō\ *Sp* Cristóbal **Co·lón** \kə-'lōn\ 1451–1506 Genoese navigator & explorer for Spain; with *Santa María*, *Niña*, and *Pinta*

sailed from Spain and landed (Oct. 12) at island in the Bahamas; made additional voyages in 1493, 1498, and 1502; explored Caribbean islands, coast of Central America, South America

Co·me·ni·us \kə-'mē-nē-əs\ John Amos *Czech* Jan Amos **Ko·men·ský** \'kó-mən-skē\ 1592–1670 Czech theol. & educ.; developed new philosophy of education and new methods, esp. for teaching languages

Com·ma·ger \'kä-mi-jər\ Henry Steele 1902–   Am. hist.; wrote (with Samuel Eliot Morison) *The Growth of the American Republic* (1930), etc.

Com·mo·dus \'kä-mə-dəs\ Lucius Aelius Aurelius A.D. 161–192 Rom. emp. (180–192); known as violent, prodigal, self-indulgent

Com·mo·ner \'kä-mə-nər\ Barry 1917–   Am. biol. & educ.; wrote *Science and Survival, The Politics of Energy*, etc.

Com·mynes *or* **Co·mines** *or* **Com·mines** \kò-'mēn\ Philippe *de ca* 1447–1511 Fr. polit. & chronicler; adviser to monarchs of Burgundy and France; his *Mémoires* (1524) are valued chronicle of times

Comp·ton \'käm(p)-tən\ Arthur Holly 1892–1962 Am. physicist; awarded (with C.T.R. Wilson) 1927 Nobel prize for physics for discovering the effect on X-rays colliding with electrons; directed development of first nuclear reactor (1942–45)

Compton Karl Taylor 1887–1954 *bro. of A.H.* Am. physicist & educator; as pres. of Mass. Inst. of Technology (1930–48), broadened and modernized curriculum; played important role in development of atomic bomb

Com·stock \'käm-,stäk *also* 'kəm-\ Anthony 1844–1915 Am. reformer; led crusades against obscenity — **Com·stock·ian** \käm-'stä-kē-ən, ,kəm-\ *adj*

Comte \'kōⁿ(n)t\ Auguste 1798–1857 *in full Isidore-Auguste-Marie= François-Xavier* Fr. math. & philos.; founded positivism, a scientific system of thought and knowledge — **Comt·ian** *or* **Comt·ean** \'käm(p)-tē-ən, 'kōⁿ(n)t-ē-\ *adj or n* — **Comt·ist** \'käm(p)-tist, 'kōⁿ(n)-\ *adj or n*

Conan Doyle — *see* DOYLE

Co·nant \'kō-nənt\ James Bryant 1893–1978 Am. chem. & educ.; wrote *Chemistry of Organic Compounds* (1933), *Education and Liberty* (1953), *Slums and Suburbs* (1961), etc.

Con·dé \kōⁿ-dā\ Prince de 1621–1686 *Louis II de Bour·bon* \'bùr-bən, bùr-'bōⁿ\; *Duc d'En·ghien* \däⁿ-gaⁿ\ Fr. gen.; leader of last of a series of aristocratic uprisings in France known as the Fronde (1648–53); later one of Louis XIV's greatest generals

Con·don \'kän-dən\ Edward Uhler 1902–1974 Am. physicist; involved in atomic bomb project (1943–45)

Con·dor·cet \kōⁿ-dòr-sā\ Marquis de 1743–1794 *Marie-Jean= Antoine-Nicholas de Ca·ri·tat* \,kar-ə-'tä\ Fr. philos. & polit.; advocate of educational reform, idea of perfectability of mankind

Con·fu·cius \kən-'fyü-shəs\ *Chin* **K'ung–Fu–tzu** \'kùŋ-'fü-'dzü\ *or* **K'ung–tzu** \kùŋ-'dzü\ 551–479 B.C. Chin. teacher & philos.; became the most revered person in Chinese history; his teachings form basis of Confucianism — **Con·fu·cian** \kən-'fyü-shən\ *adj or n* — **Con·fu·cian·ist** \-shə-nist\ *adj or n*

Con·greve \'kän-,grēv, 'käŋ-\ William 1670–1729 Eng. dram.; won fame with *Old Bachelour* (1693), *Love for Love* (1695), etc.

Con·ing·ham \'kə-niŋ-,ham, *chiefly Brit* -niŋ-əm\ Sir Arthur 1895–1948 Brit. air marshal; commanded RAF in Libya, Tunisia (1940–43), in Mediterranean (1943–44), in Normandy (1944)

Con·nors \'kä-nərz\ James Scott 1952–   *Jimmy* Am. tennis player; won Australian Open (1974), Wimbledon (1974, 1982), U.S. Open (1974, 1976, 1978, 1982, 1983), etc.

Con·rad \'kän-,rad\ Joseph 1857–1924 orig. *Józef Teodor Konrad Korze·niow·ski* \,kô-zhən-'yóf-skē, -'yóv-\ Brit. (Ukrainian-born of Pol. parents) nov.; a master of English prose in novels and short stories including *Lord Jim* (1900), "Heart of Darkness" (1902)

Con·sta·ble \'kən(t)-stə-bəl, 'kän(t)-\ John 1776–1837 Eng. painter; painted realistic landscapes, scenes of rustic life, esp. of his native Suffolk; known for *The White Horse, The Hay Wain,* etc.

Con·stant de Re·becque \kôⁿ-'stäⁿ-də-rə-'bek\ Benjamin 1767–1830 Fr. writer & polit.; wrote psychological novels *Adolphe, Cécile;* also wrote on theology, journals, etc.

Con·stan·tine \'kän(t)-stən-,tēn, -,tīn\ name of 2 kings of Greece: **I** 1868–1923 (reigned 1913–17; 1920–22); lost disastrously to Turks in Anatolia, suffered military revolt, abdicated in favor of son George II; **II** 1940–   (reigned 1964–73; deposed)

Constantine I *d* 337 *the Great* Rom. emp. (306–337); adopted Christianity; issued Edict of Milan (313) extending rights to Christians; renamed Byzantium Constantinople (330); convened Council of Nicea (325) at which Nicene Creed was adopted

Con·ta·ri·ni \,kän-tə-'rē-nē\ Venetian family including esp. Gasparo 1483–1542 cardinal & diplomat; tried to reconcile Protestants and Catholics at Diet of Ratisbon

Con·ti \'kôn-tē, 'kän-\ Niccolò de' *ca* 1395–1469 Venetian traveler; traveled throughout southern Asia (1414–44); related story of his wanderings

Cook \'kúk\ James 1728–1779 Eng. navigator & explorer; explored coasts of Canada, Pacific Ocean from Antarctic region to Bering Strait, Australia, New Zealand, New Guinea

Cooke \'kúk\ (Alfred) Al·is·tair \'a-lə-stər\ 1908–   Am. (Brit.=born) essayist & journalist; best known for television series *America* (1972–73) and introductions to televised adaptations on *Masterpiece Theater*

Cooke Terence James 1921–1983 Am. cardinal

Coo·lidge \'kü-lij\ (John) Calvin 1872–1933 30th pres. of the U.S. (1923–29)

Cooper Anthony Ashley — see SHAFTESBURY

Coo·per \'kü-pər, 'kú-\ Gary 1901–61 Am. film actor; played roles that projected quiet determination, courage; starred in *Sergeant York* (1941), *High Noon* (1952), *Friendly Persuasion* (1956), etc.

Cooper James Fen·i·more \'fen-ə-,mór, -,mòr\ 1789–1851 Am. nov.; wrote *The Pioneers* (1823), first of Leatherstocking series, *The Last of the Mohicans* (1826), *The Deerslayer* (1841), etc.

Cooper Leon N. 1930–   Am. physicist; awarded (with John Bardeen and John Robert Schrieffer) 1972 Nobel prize for physics for their work on superconductivity

Cooper Peter 1791–1883 Am. manufacturer & philanthropist; designed, built *Tom Thumb,* first American locomotive (1830); promoted and backed laying of Atlantic cable; invented washing machine, etc.; founded Cooper Union, New York City (1859)

Co·per·ni·cus \kō-'pər-ni-kəs\ Nicolaus *Pol* Mikołaj **Ko·per·nik** \kȯ-'per-nēk\ *or* Niklas **Kop·per·nigk** \'kä-pər-,nik\ 1473–1543 Pol. astron.; developed view that Earth rotates on an axis and revolves around a stationary Sun

Cop·land \'kō-plənd\ Aaron 1900–1990 Am. composer; incorporated American folk music and jazz in his classical compositions; composed ballets *Appalachian Spring*, *Billy the Kid*, operas, symphonies, film scores

Cop·ley \'kä-plē\ John Sin·gle·ton \'siŋ-gəl-tən\ 1738–1815 Am. portrait painter; painted Samuel Adams, John Hancock, Paul Revere, and other Colonial figures

Cop·po·la \'kō-pə-lə\ Francis Ford 1939–   Am. film director, writer, & producer; directed the *Godfather* trilogy (1972, 1974, 1990), *Apocalypse Now* (1979), *Bram Stoker's Dracula* (1992), etc.

Co·que·lin \,kȯk-'laⁿ, ,kȯ-kə-\ Benoît-Constant 1841–1909 Fr. actor; with Comédie-Française (1860–92); wrote *L'Art et le comédien* (1880), etc.

Cor·bu·sier, Le \lə-kȯr-büē-'yā\ 1887–1965 orig. *Charles-Édouard Jean·ne·ret* \zhän-'re\ Fr. (Swiss-born) architect, painter, & sculptor; developed personal version of International style, combining the functionalism of the modern movement with bold sculptural expressionism

Cor·day \kȯr-'dā, 'kȯr-,\ Charlotte 1768–1793 *Marie-Anne-Charlotte Corday d'Ar·mont* \där-'mōⁿ\ Fr. patriot; revolutionist, but horrified by excesses of Reign of Terror; stabbed leader of Terrorists, Marat, to death (1793); executed

Co·rel·li \kə-'re-lē\ Arcangelo 1653–1713 Ital. violinist & composer; developed a style of virtuoso playing of violin and created form of concerto grosso; composed *12 Sonatas for Violin and Violone or Harpsichord* (1700), *Concerti grossi* (1714), etc.

Co·rey \'kȯr-ē, 'kȯr-\ Elias James 1928–   Am. chem.; awarded 1990 Nobel prize for chemistry for developing techniques for artificially duplicating natural substances for use as drugs

Co·ri \'kȯr-ē, 'kȯr-\ Carl Ferdinand 1896–1984 & his wife Ger·ty \'ger-tē\ Theresa 1896–1957 née *Rad·nitz* \'räd-,nits\ Am. (Czech-born) biochemists; awarded (with Bernardo Houssay) 1947 Nobel prize for physiology or medicine for their work on insulin

Cor·mack \'kȯr-mək\ Allan MacLeod 1924–   Am. (So. African-born) physicist; awarded (with G.N. Hounsfield) 1979 Nobel prize for physiology or medicine for contributing to the development of the computerized axial tomography (CAT)

Cor·neille \kȯr-'nā\ Pierre 1606–1684 Fr. dram.; known especially for tragedies *Médée* (1635), *Le Cid* (1636 or 37), *Andromède* (1650), etc.; viewed as creator of French classical tragedy and one of France's greatest tragic poets

Cor·ne·lia \kȯr-'nēl-yə, -'nē-lē-ə\ 2d cent. B.C. *Mother of the Gracchi* Rom. matron; famed for replying, "These [her children] are my jewels" to a request to see her jewels

Cornelia d 67? B.C. *wife of Julius Caesar*

Cor·ne·lius \kȯr-'nāl-yəs, -'nā-lē-əs\ Pe·ter \'pā-tər\ von 1783–1867 Ger. painter; known for frescoes; inspired a national German school of painting and revived interest in murals

Cor·nell \kȯr-'nel\ Ezra 1807–1874 Am. financier & philanthropist; organized Western Union Co. (1856); helped found and endow Cornell U. (opened 1868), Ithaca, N.Y.

Cornell Katharine 1893–1974 Am. actress; played prominent roles in *The Green Hat, The Age of Innocence, The Barretts of Wimpole Street*, etc.

Corn·forth \'kȯrn-fȯrth, -ˌfȯrth, -ˌfȯrth\ John Warcup 1917– Brit. (Austral.-born) chem.; awarded (with Vladimir Prelog) 1975 Nobel prize for chemistry for work on the chemical synthesis of important organic compounds

Corn·wal·lis \kȯrn-'wä-ləs\ 1st Marquis 1738–1805 *Charles Cornwallis* Brit. gen. & statesman; during U.S. War of Independence, won many victories but forced to yield at Yorktown (1781); gov.⹀ gen. of India (1768–93, 1805); viceroy of Ireland (1798–1801)

Co·ro·na·do \ˌkȯr-ə-'nä-(ˌ)dō, ˌkär-\ Francisco Vásquez de *ca* 1510–1554 Span. explorer & conquistador; to Mexico (1535); commanded expedition searching for Seven Cities of Cibola (1540); explored Grand Canyon, mouth of Colorado River

Co·rot \kə-'rō, kȯ-\ Jean-Baptiste-Camille 1796–1875 Fr. painter; member of Barbizon school; anticipated Impressionists; works include *La Campagne de Rome, La Danse des nymphes*, etc.

Cor·reg·gio \kə-'re-j(ē-,)ō\ 1494–1534 *Antonio Allegri da Correggio* Ital. painter; works include *Mystic Marriage of St. Catherine*, frescoes at Parma, etc.; influenced Baroque artists through sensuous use of color, space

Cor·ri·gan \'kȯr-i-gən\ Mairead 1944– Irish peace worker; awarded (with Betty Williams) 1976 Nobel peace prize for efforts to end Protestant-Catholic fighting in Northern Ireland

Cor·tés \kȯr-'tez, 'kȯr-ˌ\ Hernán *or* Hernando 1485–1547 Span. conquistador; conquered Aztec Empire for Spain (1519–21); made gov. of Mexico (1523)

Cos·by \'käz-bē\ Bill 1927– Am. actor; starred in numerous TV series, esp. *The Cosby Show* (1984–92); also created comedy act for night clubs and monologues for numerous comedy records

Cos·grave \'käz-ˌgräv\ Liam 1920– prime min. of Ireland (1973–77)

Cosgrave William Thomas 1880–1965 *father of Liam* Irish statesman; first pres. of executive council of Irish Free State (1922–32); leader of Fine Gael party (1922–44)

Cos·ta Ca·bral \ˌkȯsh-tə-kə-'bräl, ˌkȯs-\ António Bernardo da 1803–1889 *Conde de Thomar* Port. statesman; fomented rebellion (1842) and took dictatorial control of government; deposed (1846) but again prime min. (1849–51)

Cos·tel·lo \'käs-tə-ˌlō\ John Aloysius 1891–1976 prime min. of Ireland (1948–51; 1954–57); took Ireland out of British Commonwealth of Nations (1949)

Cot·ton \'kä-tᵊn\ Charles 1630–1687 Eng. author & translator; wrote humorous *Voyage to Ireland* (1670), etc., and standard translation of Montaigne's *Essays* (1685)

Cotton John 1585–1652 Am. (Eng.-born) Puritan clergyman known as "The Patriarch of New England"; head of Congregationalism in America; opposed to democratic institutions and to separation of church and state

Co·ty \kȯ-'tē, kō-\ René-Jules-Gustave 1882–1962 Fr. lawyer; 2d and last pres. of 4th Republic (1954–59)

Cou·lomb \kü-lōⁿ; 'kü-,läm, -,lōm, kü-'\ Charles-Augustin de 1736–1806 Fr. physicist; developed Coulomb's law relating electrical charge and attraction or repulsion; coulomb, unit of electrical charge, named for him

Cou·pe·rin \,kü-'praⁿ, ,kü-pə-\ François 1668–1733 Fr. composer; director of court music (1717–30); works included sacred and secular vocal music, chamber music, harpsichord music

Cou·pe·rus \kü-'pā-rəs, -'per-əs\ Louis Marie Anne 1863–1923 Du. nov.; wrote *Eline vere* (1889), *Van oude menschen, de dingen, die voorbijgaan* (1906)

Cour·bet \kür-'bā\ Gustave 1819–1877 Fr. painter; leader of Realist school; works include *Un Enterrement à Ornans* (1849), *L'Atelier du peintre* (1855)

Cour·nand \kür-'näⁿ\ André Frédéric 1895–1988 Am. (Fr.-born) physiol.; winner (with D.W. Richards, Jr., and Werner Forssmann) of 1956 Nobel prize for physiology or medicine for using a catheter to chart the interior of the heart

Court \'kōrt, 'kȯrt\ Margaret 1942– Austral. tennis player; won Australian Open (1960–66, 1969–71, 1973), French Open (1962, 1964, 1969–70, 1973), Wimbledon (1963, 1965, 1970), etc.; holder of more major tennis titles than anyone

Cou·sin \kü-zaⁿ\ Victor 1792–1867 Fr. philos.; viewed as leader of Eclectic school and first to formulate this method; wrote *Fragments philosophiques* (1826), etc.

Cous·ins \'kə-zᵊnz\ Norman 1912–1990 Am. editor & essayist; as editor of *Saturday Review* known for connecting literature and current events

Cous·teau \kü-'stō\ Jacques-Yves 1910– Fr. marine explorer; invented the Aqualung diving apparatus and a process of underwater television; commander of oceanographic research ship *Calypso*

Co·var·ru·bias \,kō-və-'rü-bē-əs\ Miguel 1904–1957 Mex. artist; wrote and illustrated *The Island of Bali* (1937), *Mexico South* (1946), etc., showing interest in anthropology

Cov·er·dale \'kə-vər-,dāl\ Miles 1488?–1569 Eng. Bible translator; published (1535, Zurich) first translation of entire Bible, with Apocrypha, into English

Cow·ard \'kaů-(ə)rd\ Sir Noël Peirce 1899–1973 Eng. actor & dram.; wrote plays *Private Lives* (1930), *Blithe Spirit* (1941), screenplays *In Which We Serve* (1942), *Brief Encounter* (1946), etc.

Cow·ell \'kaů-(ə)l\ Henry Dixon 1887–1965 Am. composer; developed such innovations as tone clusters, playing directly on piano strings, etc.

Cow·en \'kaů-ən, 'kō-\ Sir Zelman 1919– gov.-gen. of Australia (1977–82)

Cowl \'kaů(ə)l\ Jane 1883–1950 orig. *Cowles* Am. actress; starred in *Lilac Time* (1917), *Smilin'Through* (1919), *Romeo and Juliet*, etc.

Cow·ley \'kaů-lē\ Abraham 1618–1667 Eng. poet; wrote *Pindarique Odes* (1656), *Verses upon Several Occasions* (1663), etc.

Cowley Malcolm 1898–1989 Am. lit. critic; literary editor of *New Republic* (1929–44); edited anthology *The Portable Faulkner* (1946)

Cow·per \'kü-pər, 'kú-, 'kaü-\ William 1731–1800 Eng. poet; works include *Olney Hymns* (1779, with John Newton), *The Task* (1785), etc.; brought new directness to 18th-cent. nature poetry

Cox·ey \'käk-sē\ Jacob Sechler 1854–1951 Am. polit. reformer; led "Coxey's army" of unemployed to Washington (1894) to protest, demand legislation to provide jobs for unemployed

Coz·zens \'kə-z°nz\ James Gould 1903–1978 Am. author; wrote *Confusion* (1924), *Cockpit* (1928), *Guard of Honor* (1948, Pulitzer prize), etc.

Crabbe \'krab\ George 1754–1832 Eng. poet; wrote *The Library* (1781), *The Village* (1783); noted for simplicity of diction, realistic detail of everyday life

Craig·av·on \krā-'ga-vən\ 1st Viscount 1871–1940 *James Craig* Brit. statesman; 1st prime min. of Northern Ireland (1921–40); signed agreement with Great Britain and Irish Free State preserving Irish frontier (1925)

Crai·gie \'krā-gē\ Sir William Alexander 1867–1957 Brit. philologist & lexicographer; joint editor of *Oxford English Dictionary* (1901–33); edited *A Dictionary of the Older Scottish Tongue* (1931 ff.), *A Historical Dictionary of American English* (1936–43)

Cram \'kram\ Donald James 1919– Am. chem.; awarded (with Jean-Marie Lehn and Charles J. Pedersen) 1987 Nobel prize for chemistry for the development of and work with artificial molecules that function like natural organic molecules

Cram Ralph Adams 1863–1942 Am. architect & author; promoted Gothic Revival; designed rebuilding of U.S. Military Academy (1903), Rice Institute (1910), etc.

Cra·nach \'krä-,näk\ Lucas 1472–1553 Ger. painter & engraver; works include altarpieces, portraits, biblical paintings, woodcuts, book illustrations, designs for coins, tapestries, etc.; highly influential originator of Protestant religious painting

Cranborne Viscount — see Robert CECIL

Crane \'krān\ (Harold) Hart 1899–1932 Am. poet; wrote *White Buildings* (1926), *The Bridge* (1930)

Crane Stephen 1871–1900 Am. writer; wrote *Maggie: A Girl of the Streets* (1893), *Red Badge of Courage* (1895), many short stories, verse; style often realistic or impressionistic

Crane Walter 1845–1915 Eng. artist; led, with William Morris, Arts and Crafts movement in Eng.; best known for humorous book illustrations, including *Stories from Grimm* (1882), etc.

Cran·mer \'kran-mər\ Thomas 1489–1556 Eng. reformer; first Protestant archbishop of Canterbury (1533–56); adviser to Henry VIII and Edward VI; composed litany for Church of England (1545); compiled Edward VI's first Prayer Book (1549, revised 1552)

Cras·sus \'kra-səs\ Marcus Licinius 115?–53 B.C. *Di·ves* \'dī-(,)vēz\ Rom. polit.; joined Pompey and Caesar in First Triumvirate (60); defeated by Parthians, captured, executed

Craw·ford \'krò-fərd\ Joan 1908–1977 Am. film actress; portrayed stong-willed career women, vamps, society women, etc. in over 80 films, including *The Women* (1939), *Mildred Pierce* (1945), *Whatever Happened to Baby Jane?* (1962)

Crazy Horse \'krā-zē-,hòrs\ 1842–1877 *Ta-sunko-witko* or *Ta-shunca-Uitco* Sioux Indian chief; leader in Sioux resistance in northern Great Plains; won battles (1876) at Rosebud Creek and Little Bighorn; killed while resisting imprisonment

Cré·bil·lon \ˌkrā-bē-ˈyōⁿ\ 1674–1762 pseud. of *Prosper Jolyot* Fr. dram.; considered rival of Voltaire; wrote *Idoménée* (1705), *Électre* (1708), *Xerxès* (1714), etc.

Cre·mer \ˈkrē-mər\ Sir William Randal 1838–1908 Eng. pacifist; advocated international arbitration as secy. of Workmen's Peace Association (1871–1908); awarded 1903 Nobel prize for peace

Cres·ton \ˈkres-tən\ Paul 1906–1985 orig. *Giuseppe Guttoveggio* Am. composer; composer of *Fantasies* for trombone and orchestra, sonatas for saxophone, *Choric Dances*, songs, etc.

Crève·coeur \krev-ˈkər, krēv-, -ˈkür\ Michel-Guillaume-Jean de 1735–1813 pseud. *J. Hector St. John* Am. (Fr.-born) essayist; wrote *Letters from an American Farmer* (1782), giving a farmer's reactions to the life and issues of the day

Crich·ton \ˈkrī-tᵊn\ James 1560–1582 *the Admirable Crichton* Scot. man of letters; reputed to have argued on scientific questions in twelve languages; exposed faulty mathematics of professors in Padua and disputed their interpretation of Aristotle (1581)

Crichton (John) Michael 1942– Am. writer & film director; wrote *The Andromeda Strain* (1969), *Jurassic Park* (1990), *Disclosure* (1994); directed film *The Great Train Robbery* (1978), etc.

Crick \ˈkrik\ Francis Harry Compton 1916– Brit. biophysicist; awarded (with James D. Watson and Maurice H. F. Wilkins) 1962 Nobel prize for physiology or medicine for determining molecular structure of DNA

Crile \ˈkrī(ə)l\ George Washington 1864–1943 Am. surgeon; conducted pioneering research into shock, trauma, resuscitation, etc.

Cripps \ˈkrips\ Sir (Richard) Stafford 1889–1952 Brit. statesman; min. of aircraft production (1942–45); chancellor of exchequer (1947–50)

Cri·spi \ˈkris-pē, ˈkrēs-\ Francesco 1819–1901 Ital. statesman; premier (1887–91; 1893–96); advocated Triple Alliance (Germany, Italy, Austria); deposed after Italian defeat in Ethiopia

Cris·ti·ani \ˌkris-tē-ˈä-nē\ Alfredo 1947– pres. of El Salvador (1989–1994)

Cro·ce \ˈkrō-(ˌ)chā\ Benedetto 1866–1952 Ital. philos. & statesman; wrote *Filosofia dello spirito* in 4 volumes (1902–17), etc.; foremost Italian philosopher of first half of 20th cent.

Crock·ett \ˈkrä-kət\ David 1786–1836 *Davy* Am. frontiersman & polit.; active on frontier in western Tennessee; humorist and crack shot; killed at Alamo with Texas forces

Croe·sus \ˈkrē-səs\ *d ca* 546 B.C. king of Lydia (*ca* 560–546); extremely wealthy; subject of many legends

Cro·ker \ˈkrō-kər\ John Wilson 1780–1857 Brit. essayist & editor; one of chief writers for *Quarterly Review*, including scathing reviews of Keats's *Endymion* and works of Tennyson, Macaulay; edited Boswell's *Life of Johnson* (1831), etc.

Cromer 1st Earl of — see Evelyn BARING

Cromp·ton \ˈkräm(p)-tən\ Samuel 1753–1827 Eng. inventor; invented spinning mule (1779)

Crom·well \ˈkräm-ˌwel, ˈkrəm-, -wəl\ Oliver 1599–1658 Eng. gen. & statesman; during English Civil War led Roundhead army to victory against King Charles I and Royalists; played major role in abolition of the monarchy; lord protector of England (1653–58) —

Crom·well·ian \kräm-ˈwe-lē-ən, ˌkrəm-\ *adj*

Cromwell Richard 1626–1712 *son of Oliver* lord protector (1658–59); named successor by his father; dismissed by Rump Parliament

Cromwell Thomas 1485?–1540 Earl of *Essex* Eng. statesman; principal adviser to Henry VIII (1532–40); drafted most of Reformation acts (1532–39); put into effect suppression of monasteries (1536–39); accused of treason, beheaded

Cro·nin \ˈkrō-nən\ Archibald Joseph 1896–1981 Eng. physician & nov.; practiced medicine in Glasgow, Wales, London; wrote *The Citadel* (1937), *Keys of the Kingdom* (1942), etc.

Cro·nyn \ˈkrō-nən\ Hume 1911– Am. (Canad.-born) actor & director; with wife Jessica Tandy starred on stage in *The Fourposter* (1951), *A Delicate Balance* (1966), *The Gin Game* (1977) and in films *Cocoon* (1985), etc.

Cronin James Watson 1931– Am. physicist; awarded (with Val L. Fitch) 1980 Nobel prize for physics for research on subatomic particles

Cron·jé \krön-ˈyā\ Piet Arnoldus *ca* 1835–1911 Boer leader & gen.; began Transvaal rebellion (1880) to protest taxes; in Boer War of 1899 commanded western frontier

Crookes \ˈkrůks\ Sir William 1832–1919 Eng. physicist & chem.; discovered thallium (1861); invented radiometer (1875); invented Crookes tube, producing X-rays

Cros·by \ˈkräz-bē\ Bing 1904–1977 *Harry Lillis Crosby* Am. singer & actor; best known for easygoing stage manner and "crooner" singing style; teamed with Bob Hope in series of "Road" films; other films included *Going My Way* (1944), *White Christmas* (1954), etc.

Cross \ˈkrös\ Wilbur Lucius 1862–1948 Am. educ. & polit.; dean of Yale Graduate School (1916–30); governor of Connecticut (1931–39)

Crouse \ˈkraůs\ Russel 1893–1966 Am. journalist & dram.; worked with Howard Lindsay on *Anything Goes* (1934), *Life with Father* (1939), *State of the Union* (1946, Pulitzer prize), etc.

Cru·den \ˈkrü-dᵊn\ Alexander 1701–1770 Scot. compiler of a biblical concordance

Cruik·shank \ˈkrůk-ˌshaŋk\ George 1792–1878 Eng. caricaturist & illustrator; illustrated Charles Dickens's *Sketches by "Boz"* (1836–37), *Oliver Twist* (1838), Ainsworth's *Rookwood* (1836), etc.

Cruz \ˈkrüs\ Juana Inés de la 1651–1695 orig. *Juana Inés de Asbaje* Mex. religious & poet; wrote many lyric poems, as in *Inundación castálida* (1689), etc.

Cud·worth \ˈkəd-(ˌ)wərth\ Ralph 1617–1688 Eng. philos.; chief of Cambridge Platonists; sought to refute determinism, to justify moral ideas, to establish free will

Cu·kor \ˈkü-(ˌ)kòr\ George Dewey 1899–1983 Am. film director; known for witty, sophisticated films featuring award-winning performances; directed *Dinner at Eight* (1933), *The Philadelphia Story* (1940), *My Fair Lady* (1964), etc.

Cul·pep·er \ˈkəl-ˌpe-pər\ *var of* COLEPEPER

Cum·mings \\'kə-miŋz\ Edward Estlin 1894–1962 known as *e. e. cummings* Am. poet; used experimental diction, unorthodox typography and punctuation

Cu·nha \\'kün-yə\ Tristão da \\,tris-tən-də-'kü-nə, trēsh-,taún-də-'kün-yə, trēs-\ 1460–1540 Port. navigator & explorer; discovered islands named after him on voyage to India

Cun·ning·ham \\'kə-niŋ-,ham, *chiefly Brit* -niŋ-əm\ Allan 1784–1842 Scot. author; edited works of Burns (1834) wrote novels, biographies, dramatic and lyric poems and songs

Cunningham Merce 1919?– Am. choreographer; with Martha Graham (1939–45); ran own school (from 1959); choreographed *The Seasons* (1947), *Nocturnes* (1956), *Rune* (1959), etc.

Cu·rie \\kyú-'rē, 'kyúr-(,)ē\ Eve 1904– *dau. of Marie & Pierre* Am. (Fr.-born) author; wrote *Madame Curie* (1937), *Journey Among Warriors* (1943)

Curie Marie 1867–1934 née *Maria Skłodowska* \\sklə-'dóf-skə, -'dóv-\ Fr. (Pol.-born) chem.; distinguished types of radiation in radioactivity (a term she coined in 1898); discovered (1898) polonium and radium; awarded 1911 Nobel prize for chemistry for this discovery and for isolation of pure radium

Curie Pierre 1859–1906 *husband of Marie* Fr. chem.; conducted research on various forms of magnetism; awarded (with Marie Curie and A. H. Becquerel) 1903 Nobel prize for physics for work on radioactivity

Curie Joliot — see JOLIOT-CURIE

Cur·ley \\'kər-lē\ James Michael 1874–1958 Am. polit.; mayor of Boston (1914–18, 1922–26, 1930–34, 1946–50); governor of Massachusetts (1935–37); considered the perfect urban political boss

Cur·ri·er \\'kər-ē-ər, 'kə-rē-\ Nathaniel 1813–1888 Am. lithographer; issued (in partnership with James Merritt Ives from 1857) series of lithographs portraying scenes, events of the U.S.

Cur·ry \\'kər-ē, 'kə-rē\ John Steuart 1897–1946 Am. painter; member of the Regionalist school; painted *Tornado, State Fair, Hogs Killing a Rattlesnake,* etc.

Cur·tin \\'kər-tᵊn\ John 1885–1945 Austral. polit.; prim. min. and minister of defense (1941–45)

Cur·tis \\'kər-təs\ Charles 1860–1936 vice pres. of the U.S. (1929–33)

Curtis Cyrus Hermann Kotzschmar 1850–1933 Am. publisher; head (1890–1933) of Curtis Publishing Co., publishers of *Ladies Home Journal, Saturday Evening Post,* etc.; bought N.Y. *Evening Post* (1924), *Philadelphia Inquirer* (1930), etc.

Curtis George Ticknor 1812–1894 Am. lawyer & writer; argued Dred Scott case before Supreme Court (1857); wrote books on patent law, U.S. Constitution, *Life of Daniel Webster* (1870), etc.

Curtis George William 1824–1892 Am. author & editor; editor of *Harper's Weekly* (from 1863); wrote *Lotus-Eating* (1852), *Potiphar Papers* (1853), etc.

Cur·tiss \\'kər-təs\ Glenn Hammond 1878–1930 Am. aviator & inventor; won trophy for first public airplane flight of a kilometer in U.S. (1908); developed JN-4 "Jenny" flying boat that made first Atlantic crossing (1919), etc.

Cur·ti·us \\'kürt-sē-əs\ Ernst 1814–1896 Ger. hist. & archaeol.; directed excavation of Olympia, Greece (1875–81)

Cur·wen \\'kər-wən\\ John 1816–1880 Eng. music teacher; adapted system of Sarah Ann Glover to develop tonic sol-fa system of notation

Cur·zon \\'kər-zᵊn\\ George Nathaniel 1859–1925 1st Baron & 1st Marquis *Curzon of Ked·le·ston* \\'ke-dᵊl-stən\\ Eng. statesman; viceroy of India (1899–1905); reduced salt tax, carried out reforms

Cush·ing \\'ku̇-shiŋ\\ Caleb 1800–1879 Am. lawyer & diplomat; negotiated Treaty of Wanghia (1944) opening five Chinese ports to American trade and establishing principle of extranationality

Cushing Harvey 1869–1939 Am. surgeon; wrote *The Pituitary Body and Its Disorders* (1912), *The Life of Sir William Osler* (1925, Pulitzer prize), etc.

Cushing Richard James 1895–1970 Am. cardinal

Cush·man \\'ku̇sh-mən\\ Charlotte Saunders 1816–1876 Am. actress; known for powerful emotional portrayals in Shakespearean roles, including as males, as Lady Macbeth, Bianca, Hamlet, etc.

Cus·ter \\'kəs-tər\\ George Armstrong 1839–1876 Am. gen.; involved in fighting Indians (1867–76); killed with all his immediate command in battle of Little Bighorn against Crazy Horse (1876)

Cuth·bert \\'kəth-bərt\\ Saint 635?–687 Eng. monk; retired to hermit's cell on island of Inner Farne; body, believed to perform miracles, transferred to Durham cathedral

Cu·vier \\'kü-vē-ˌā, 'kyü-, kü̅-vyä\\ Baron Georges 1769–1832 orig. *Jean-Léopold-Nicolas-Frédéric Cuvier* Fr. naturalist; considered founder of comparative anatomy and of paleontology

Cuyp *or* **Cuijp** \\'kı̄p\\ Aelbert Jacobsz 1620–1691 Du. painter; works include *Herdsman with Cows by a River, Castle by a River Bank, Piper with Cows*, etc.; known for landscapes

Cyn·e·wulf \\'kı̄-nə-ˌwu̇lf\\ *or* **Cyn·wulf** \\'kin-ˌwu̇lf\\ 9th cent. Anglo-Saxon poet; wrote four poems preserved in 10th-century manuscripts

Cyp·ri·an \\'si-prē-ən\\ Saint *d* 258 *Thascius Caecilius Cyprianus* Christian martyr; bishop of Carthage (*ca* 248–258); established principle of church's power to remit deadly sin

Cy·ran·kie·wicz \\ˌ(t)sir-ən-'kyä-vich\\ Józef 1911–1989 Pol. polit.; prime min. (1947–52; 1954–70)

Cy·ra·no de Ber·ge·rac \\'sir-ə-ˌnō-də-'ber-zhə-ˌrak\\ Savinien de 1619–1655 Fr. poet, dramatist & soldier; famous as a duelist; works combine political satire and science fantasy

Cyr·il \\'sir-əl\\ Saint *ca* 827–869 *Constantine* apostle to the Slavs; credited with invention of the Cyrillic alphabet which he and his brother Methodius used to translate gospels and liturgies

Cy·rus II \\'sī-rəs\\ *ca* 585–*ca* 529 B.C. *the Great* or *the Elder* king of Persia (*ca* 550–529); conquered Babylon (539) and delivered Jews from captivity; empire extended from Aegean Sea to Indus River

Cyrus 424?–401 B.C. *the Younger* Persian prince & satrap; led army into Babylonia against his brother, Artaxerxes II; defeated and killed at Cunaxa

Czer·ny \\'cher-nē, 'chər-\\ Carl 1791–1857 Austrian pianist & composer; best known for piano exercises *The School of Fingering, The School of Velocity, The School of Virtuosity*

D

D' \d-\, **De** \də-, di-; *in Dutch names* dē-\, **Du** \dü, dyü-, də-\, etc. for many names beginning with these elements see the specific family names

Da·guerre \də-ˈger\ Louis-Jacques-Mandé 1789–1851 Fr. painter & inventor; invented the daguerrotype (1839), the obtaining of permanent pictures on metal plates by the action of sunlight

Daim·ler \ˈdīm-lər\ Gottlieb Wilhelm 1834–1900 Ger. automotive manuf.; invented a high-speed internal combustion engine (1885) and a carburetor to use gasoline as fuel; manufactured Mercedes automobile (from 1899)

Da·kin \ˈdā-kən\ Henry Drysdale 1880–1952 Eng. chem.; helped develop Carrel-Dakin solution used for treating wounds in WWI; conducted research on enzymes

Da·la·dier \də-ˈlä-dē-ˌā, ˌda-lə-ˈdyä\ Édouard 1884–1970 Fr. statesman; premier of France (1933, 1934, 1938–40); signed Munich Pact (1938), allowing Germany to seize Sudetenland

Da·lai La·ma \ˈdä-ˌlī-ˈlä-mə\ 1935–   *Tenzin Gyatso* Tibetan religious & political leader; awarded 1989 Nobel prize for peace for his nonviolent struggle to end China's rule of Tibet

D' Al·bert \ˈdal-bərt\ Eugen Francis Charles 1864–1932 Scot. pianist & composer; court pianist at Weimar (1885); composed operas *Tiefland* (1903), string quartets, piano concertos, etc.

Dalcroze Emile Jaques — see Émile JAQUES-DALCROZE

Dale \ˈdā(ə)l\ Sir Henry Hallett 1875–1968 Eng. physiol.; discovered acetylcholine; awarded (with Otto Loewi) 1936 Nobel prize for physiology or medicine for work relating to chemical transmission of nerve impulses

Dale Sir Thomas *d* 1619 Eng. colonial administrator in Virginia; placed colonists under martial law to make them work harder

Da·lén \də-ˈlān\ Nils Gustaf 1869–1937 Swed. inventor; improved hot-air turbines; awarded 1912 Nobel prize for physics for inventing the valve used to regulate gaslights in unmanned beacons

Da·ley \ˈdā-lē\ Richard Joseph 1902–1976 Am. polit.; mayor of Chicago (1955–76); known as last of the big-city bosses

Dalhousie Earl & Marquis of — see RAMSAY

Da·lí \ˈdä-lē, *by himself* dä-ˈlē\ Salvador 1904–1989 Span. surrealistic painter; depicted dream world in which commonplace objects appear deformed or bizarrely juxtaposed; religious scenes; painted *The Persistence of Memory* (1931), *Christ of St. John of the Cross* (1951), etc. — **Da·li·esque** \ˌdä-lē-ˈesk\ *adj*

Dal·las \ˈda-ləs, -lis\ George Mifflin 1792–1864 vice pres. of the U.S. (1845–49); Dallas, Texas, was named after him

Dal·rym·ple \dal-ˈrim-pəl, ˈdal-,\ Sir James 1619–1695 1st Viscount *Stair* \ˈster\ Scot. jurist; wrote *The Institutions of the Law of Scotland* (1681)

Dalrymple Sir John 1673–1747 2d Earl of *Stair* Brit. gen. & diplomat; as ambassador to France counteracted schemes for reinstatement of James Edward, the Old Pretender

Dal·ton \ˈdȯl-tᵊn\ Baron 1887–1962 *Hugh Dalton* Brit. polit.; oversaw nationalization of Bank of England as chancellor of the exchequer (1945–47)

Dalton John 1766–1844 Eng. chem. & physicist; formulated Charles's law of relation of temperature and volume of bodies of gas; arranged table of atomic weights (1803) and first gave clear statement of atomic theory (1803–07)

Da·ly \'dā-lē\ (John) Augustin 1838–1899 Am. dram. & theater manager; presented revivals of Old English comedies and his own plays *Divorce* (1871), *The Dark City* (1877), etc.

Dam \'dam, 'däm\ (Carl Peter) Henrik 1895–1976 Dan. biochem.; awarded (with E. A. Doisy) 1943 Nobel prize for physiology or medicine for discovery of vitamin K

Da·mien \'dā-mē-ən, ˌdä-mē-'aⁿ\ Father 1840–1889 orig. *Joseph de Veuster* Belg. R.C. missionary in Hawaiian islands; improved lot of lepers in colony on Molokai

Dam·pi·er \'dam-pē-ər\ William 1652–1715 Eng. buccaneer & navigator; plundered Peruvian coast (1679); explored coasts of Chile, Peru, Mexico (1683); explored coasts of Australia, New Guinea, New Britain for British Admiralty (1699)

Dam·rosch \'dam-ˌräsh\ Walter Johannes 1862–1950 Am. (Ger.-born) musician & conductor; champion of Wagnerian opera; presented first U.S. performances of symphonies of Brahms and Tchaikovsky

Da·na \'dā-nə\ Charles Anderson 1819–1897 Am. newspaper editor; associated with New York *Tribune* (1847–62), *New American Cyclopaedia* (1857–63), New York *Sun* (1868–97)

Dana James Dwight 1813–1895 Am. geologist; leading American gemologist of the day; wrote *A System of Mineralogy* (1st ed. 1837), *Manual of Mineralogy* (1848), *Manual of Geology* (1864), etc.

Dana Richard Henry 1815–1882 Am. lawyer & author; wrote *Two Years Before the Mast* (1840) about his sail from Boston to California via Cape Horn (1834–36)

Dane \'dān\ Clemence 1888–1965 pseud. of *Winifred Ash·ton* \'ash-tən\ Eng. nov.; wrote novels *Regiment of Women* (1919), *Legend* (1919), etc., plays *Bill of Divorcement* (1921), *Will Shakespeare* (1921), etc.

Dan·iel \'dan-yəl\ Samuel 1562?–1619 Eng. poet; wrote sonnets *Delia* (1592), romance *The Complaint of Rosamond* (1592), verse history *The Civile Warres* (1595–1609), *Defence of Rime* (1603)

Dan·iels \'dan-yəlz\ Josephus 1862–1948 Am. journalist & statesman; U.S. secy. of navy (1913–21)

Da·ni·lo·va \də-'nē-lə-və\ Aleksandra 1903?–   Am. (Russ.-born) choreographer & dancer; worked with Sergei Diaghilev (1924–29), Ballet Russe (1933–38), Ballet Russe de Monte Carlo (1938–52); formed her own company (1954–56)

D'An·nun·zio \dä-'nün(t)-sē-ˌō\ Gabriele 1863–1938 Ital. author & soldier; leading Italian writer of his day; wrote poetry *Laudi del cielo, del mare, della terra, e degli eroi* (1899), etc., short stories, dramas *La figlia di Iorio* (1904), etc., erotic novels

Dan·te \'dän-(ˌ)tā, 'dan-, -(ˌ)tē\ 1265–1321 *Dante* or *Durante Alighie·ri* \ˌä-lə-'gyer-ē\ Ital. poet; known for *Divine Comedy* (begun ca. 1308, finished 1321) in three parts, *Inferno, Purgatorio, Paradiso*); also wrote sonnets in the *dolce stil nuovo* (sweet new style), etc. — **Dan·te·an** \'dan-tē-ən, 'dän-\ or **Dan·tes·can** \dan-'tes-kən, dän-\ or **Dan·tesque** \-'tesk\ *adj*

Dan·ton \dän-tōⁿ\ Georges-Jacques 1759–1794 Fr. revolutionary;

minister of justice following fall of monarchy (1792); gradually identified as leader of moderates; overpowered by Robespierre and leaders of the Reign of Terror; guillotined

Dare \'dar, 'der\ Virginia 1587–? 1st child born in America of Eng. parents

Da·ri·us \də-'rī-əs\ name of 3 kings of Persia: esp. **I** 550–486 B.C. (reigned 522–486) *Darius Hys·tas·pes* \his-'tas-pəs\; *the Great;* noted for administrative genius, great building projects; sent two expeditions to conquer Greece, both of which failed, the second by defeat at Marathon (490)

Dar·lan \där-'län\ Jean-Louis-Xavier-François 1881–1942 Fr. admiral; during Vichy regime foreign min. and min. of defense (1941–42)

Darn·ley \'därn-lē\ Lord 1545–1567 Henry Stewart or Stuart; *husband of Mary, Queen of Scots;* in conspiracy (1566) to murder Mary's secy.; strangled, perhaps with Mary's knowledge

Dar·row \'dar-(,)ō\ Clarence Seward 1857–1938 Am. lawyer; defense counsel in dramatic trials, as for Eugene V. Debs, Socialist leader (1894), John T. Scopes (1925), etc.

Dar·win \'där-wən\ Charles Robert 1809–1882 Eng. naturalist; renowned for his theories of evolution and natural selection; published *On the Origin of Species by Means of Natural Selection* (1859) to controversy, *The Descent of Man and Selection in Relation to Sex* (1871), etc. — **Dar·win·i·an** \där-'winē-ən\ *adj or n*

Darwin Erasmus 1731–1802 *grandfather of C. R.* Eng. physiol. & poet; wrote *The Botanic Garden* (verse, 1794–95), *Zoonomia or the Laws of Organic Life* (1794–96), etc.

Dau·bi·gny \,dō-bēn-'yē, dō-'bē-nyē\ Charles-François 1817–1878 Fr. landscape painter; concerned with careful observation of nature; use of light influenced Impressionists

Dau·det \dō-'dā\ Alphonse 1840–1897 Fr. nov.; worked often in naturalist manner; wrote novels and stories *Lettres de mon moulin* (1869), *Contes du lundi* (1873), *Le Nabab* (1877), etc.

Daudet Léon 1867–1942 *son of Alphonse* Fr. journalist & writer; wrote novels *L'Astre noir* (1893), *Le Voyage de Shakespeare* (1896), etc., political works, literary criticism, reminiscence

Dau·mier \dō-myā, 'dō-mē-,ā\ Honoré 1808–1879 Fr. caricaturist & painter; caricatured bourgeois society; also painted in Impressionist manner and sculpted

Daus·set \dō-se, -sā\ Jean-Baptiste-Gabriel 1916–   Fr. physician; awarded (with Baruj Benacerraf and George D. Snell) 1980 Nobel prize for physiology or medicine for discoveries concerning genetic regulation of the body's immune system

Dav·e·nant or **D'Av·e·nant** \'dav-nənt, 'da-və-\ Sir William 1606–1668 Eng. poet & dram.; wrote comedy *The Witts* (1634), masques, poetry *Madagascar* (1638); poet laureate (1638–68)

Dav·en·port \'da-vən-,pōrt, 'da-vᵐ-, -,pȯrt\ John 1597–1670 Am. (Eng.-born) clergyman & founder of New Haven colony

Dav·id \'dā-vəd\ *d* 962 B.C. second king of Judah and Israel; reputed author of many Psalms

David I *ca* 1082–1153 king of Scotland (1124–53); unsuccessfully invaded England (1149); introduced Norman aristocracy, furthered feudalization of Scotland

Da·vid \\'dä-vət\\ Gerard *ca* 1460–1523 Du. painter; last master of the school of Bruges; works include *Christ Nailed to the Cross, Madonna Triptych, Judgment of Cambyses*, etc.

Da·vid \\dä-'vēd\\ Jacques-Louis 1748–1825 Fr. painter; founder of French Neoclassical school; court painter to Napoléon (1804); works include *Oath of the Horatii, The Sabine Women*

Da·vid d'An·gers \\dä-'zhä\\ Pierre-Jean 1788–1856 Fr. sculptor; executed statues of Condé, Cuvier, etc., busts of Goethe, Bentham, Victor Hugo, etc., medallions of Bonaparte, Ney, Rossini, etc.

Da·vid·son \\'dä-vəd-sən\\ Jo 1883–1952 Am. sculptor; created Woodrow Wilson, Anatole France, Marshal Foch, Will Rogers, etc.

Davidson Randall Thomas 1848–1930 archbishop of Canterbury (1903–28); a leader of ecumenical movement

Da·vies \\'dä-vēz\\ Arthur Bowen 1862–1928 Am. painter; painted Arcadian pastoral scenes, allegorical neo-Romantic compositions; works include *The Girdle of Ares, Leda and the Dioscuri*, etc.

Davies (William) Robertson 1913–   Canad. author; wrote 'The Deptford Trilogy' (1970–75; *Fifth Business, The Manticore, World of Wonders*), etc.

Dá·vi·la Pa·di·lla \\'dä-vi-lə-pä-'dē-yə\\ Agustín 1562–1604 Mex. monk & hist. called "Chronicler of the Indies"

Da·vis \\'dä-vəs\\ Bet·te \\'be-tē\\ 1908–1989 orig. *Ruth Elizabeth Davis* Am. actress; noted for emotional honesty; won Academy awards for *Dangerous* (1935), *Jezebel* (1938)

Davis Dwight Filley 1879–1945 Am. statesman; secy. of war (1925–29); gov. gen. of Philippines (1929–32); donated Davis Cup (1900)

Davis Elmer Holmes 1890–1958 Am. radio broadcaster & news commentator; headed Office of War Information (1942–45); ABC news broadcaster (1945–53); outspoken critic of Joseph McCarthy

Davis Harold Le·noir \\lə-'nȯr, -'nȯr\\ 1896–1960 Am. writer; wrote realistically about the American West; wrote *Honey in the Horn* (1935, Pulitzer prize), *Beulah Land* (1945), etc.

Davis Jefferson 1808–1889 Am. statesman; pres. of Confed. states (1861–65); imprisoned for two years after Civil War, indicted for treason but never tried

Davis Miles 1926–1991 Am. jazz composer & musician; a preeminent jazz trumpeter; compositions included "Nardis," "Milestones," "So What"

Da·vis·son \\'dä-və-sən\\ Clinton Joseph 1881–1958 Am. physicist; awarded (with George Thomson) 1937 Nobel prize for physics for discovering the diffraction of electrons by crystals

Da·vout \\dä-'vü\\ Louis-Nicolas 1770–1823 Duc *d'Au·er·städt* \\'daú(-ə)r-,stet\\ & Prince *d'Eck·mühl* \\'dek-,myül\\ marshal of France (1804); minister of war during Hundred Days (1815)

Da·vy \\'dä-vē\\ Sir Humphry 1778–1829 Eng. chem.; discovered several elements, including sodium and potassium; invented miner's safety lamp

Dawes \\'dȯz\\ Charles Gates 1865–1951 Am. lawyer & financier; devised The Dawes Plan to manage Germany's payment of reparations after WWI; awarded (with Sir Austen Chamberlain) 1925 Nobel prize for peace; vice pres. of U.S. (1925–29)

Daw·son \'do̊-s⁊n\ Sir John William 1820–1899 Canad. geologist; discovered fossil remains of *Psilophyton*, then earliest known land plant, and *Dendrepeton*, air-breathing reptile

Day \'dā\ Clarence Shepard, Jr. 1874–1935 Am. author; wrote *Life with Father* (1935), *Life with Mother* (1937), etc.

Day Dorothy 1897–1980 Am. social activist; with Peter Maurin founded (1933) *Catholic Worker* to promote "Green Revolution," combining direct action for social justice and nonviolent resistance

Day Thomas 1748–1789 Eng. philanthropist; admired Rousseau's doctrines; attempted moral and social reform; wrote *History of Sandford and Merton* (1783–89), attempt in fiction to reconcile naturalism of Rousseau with convention

Day William Rufus 1849–1923 Am. statesman & jurist; associate justice, U.S. Supreme Court (1903–22)

Da·yan \dī-'än\ Moshe 1915–1981 Israeli soldier & polit.; credited with Israeli success in Gaza and Sinai in Suez War (1956); planned and commanded Six-Day War (1967)

Day–Le·wis \'dā-'lü-əs\ Cecil 1904–1972 pseud. *Nicholas Blake* Brit. writer; associated with W. H. Auden in 1930s; later used more traditional lyric forms; wrote *Transitional Poem* (1929), etc.

De·ák \'dā-äk\ Fe·renc \'fer-,en(t)s\ 1803–1876 Hung. statesman; leader in movement to emancipate Hungary; his negotiations with Austria led to restoration of Hungarian constitution, establishment of dual monarchy of Austria-Hungary (1867)

Dean \'dēn\ Sir Patrick 1909–1994 Brit. diplomat; permanent representative to U.N. (1960–64)

Deane \'dēn\ Silas 1737–1789 Am. lawyer & diplomat; sent to France to secure supplies, aid (1776–78); enlisted Lafayette, Steuben, Pulaski, etc.

De·bierne \də-'byern\ André-Louis 1874–1949 Fr. chem.; discovered actinium (1899); helped Marie Curie isolate pure radium (1910)

De·breu \də-'brœ\ Gerard 1921–   Am. (Fr.-born) econ.; awarded 1983 Nobel prize for economics for development of a mathematical model that proved the theory of supply and demand

Debs \'debz\ Eugene Victor 1855–1926 Am. socialist; a founder of American Railway Union (1893); organized Social Democratic party of America (1897); ran as Socialist candidate for pres. of U.S. (1900, 1904, 1908, 1912, 1920)

De·bus·sy \,de-byü-'sē, ,dä-; də-'byü-sē\ (Achille-) Claude 1862–1918 Fr. composer; evolved inventive approach to harmony; composed *Clair de lune, Prélude à l'après-midi d'un Faune* (1894), *La Mer* (1905), etc. — **De·bus·sy·an** \,de-byü-'sē-ən, ,dä-; də-'byü-sē-ən\ *adj*

De·bye \də-'bī\ Peter Joseph William 1884–1966 Am. (Du.-born) physicist; awarded 1936 Nobel prize for chemistry for studies on dipole moments, the diffractions of electrons, and X-rays in gases

De·ca·tur \di-'kā-tər\ Stephen 1779–1820 Am. naval officer; won victories in War of 1812; successfully fought Barbary states

De·cazes \də-käz\ Duc Élie 1780–1860 Fr. statesman; leader of moderate royalists in Chamber of Deputies during Bourbon restoration (1815–20); premier (1819–20)

De·cius \'dē-sh(ē-)əs\ Gaius Messius Quintus Trajanus *ca* 201–251 Rom. emp. (249–51); conducted first systematic persecution of Christians

Dee·ping \'dē-piŋ\ (George) Warwick 1877–1950 Eng. nov.; wrote *Unrest* (1916), *Valour* (1918), *Laughing House* (1947), etc.

Deer \'dir\ Ada Elizabeth 1935–   Am. polit.; member of Menominee tribe; head of Bureau of Indian Affairs (1933–); first woman to hold this position

Deere John 1804–1886 Am. inventor; designed and manufactured steel plows for use on Great Plains

Def·fand, du \dä-fäⁿ\ Marquise 1697–1780 née *Marie de Vichy=Cham·rond* \də-vē-shē-shäⁿ-rōⁿ\ Fr. woman of letters; established salon frequented by Fontenelle, Voltaire, etc.; known for correspondence with Voltaire, Horace Walpole, duchesse de Choiseul

De·foe \di-'fō\ Daniel 1660–1731 Eng. journalist & nov.; one of the creators of the English novel; wrote *Robinson Crusoe* (1719), *Moll Flanders* (1722), *A Journal of the Plague Year* (1722), etc.

De For·est \di-'fôr-əst, -'fär-\ Lee 1873–1961 Am. inventor; known as "the father of radio"; patented over 300 inventions in wireless telegraphy, radio telephone, talking pictures, facsimile transmission, television, radiotherapy, radar, etc.

De·gas \də-gä\ (Hilaire-Germain-) Edgar 1834–1917 Fr. artist; associated with Impressionists; known for figure groups in theatrical, orchestral, or racecourse settings

de Gaulle Charles — see GAULLE

De Gennes \də-zhen\ Pierre-Gilles 1932–   Fr. physicist; awarded 1991 Nobel prize for analyses of segments and other orderly arrangements of molecules in certain substances

Deh·melt \'dā-məlt\ Hans Georg 1922–   Am. (Ger.-born) physicist; awarded (with Wolfgang Paul) 1989 Nobel prize for physics for isolating and measuring single atoms

Dei·sen·hof·er \'dī-zən-₊hō-fər\ Johann 1943–   Ger. biochem.; awarded (with Robert Huber and Hartmut Michel) 1988 Nobel prize for chemistry for revealing the structure of proteins that are essential to photosynthesis

Dek·ker \'de-kər\ Thomas 1572?–?1632 Eng. dram.; collaborated with Ben Jonson, John Webster, etc.; wrote or helped with at least 42 plays, including *The Shoemaker's Holiday*

de Klerk \də-'klärk, -'klerk\ Frederik Willem 1936–   pres. of Republic of So. Africa (1989–94); vice pres. (1994–); awarded (with Nelson Mandela) 1993 Nobel prize for peace for working to end apartheid in South Africa

de Koo·ning \də-'kō-niŋ\ Willem 1904–   Am. (Du.-born) painter; a dominant figure in the Abstract Expressionist school

de Kruif \də-'krīf\ Paul Henry 1890–1971 Am. bacteriol. & author; wrote *Microbe Hunters* (1926), *Health is Wealth* (1940), etc.

De·la·croix \₊de-lə-'k(r)wä\ (Ferdinand-Victor-) Eugène 1798–1863 Fr. painter; known for color, modeling; developed style anticipating Impressionists; works included *Dante and Virgil in Hell, Massacre at Chios, The Death of Sardanapalus*, etc.

de la Mare \₊de-lə-'mar, -'mer\ Walter John 1873–1956 Eng. poet & nov.; wrote novels *Memoirs of a Midget* (1921), etc.; published anthology *Come Hither* (1923)

De·land \də-'land\ Margaret 1857–1945 née *Margaretta Wade Campbell* Am. nov.; known for tales of "Old Chester" around the character "Dr. Lavendar," including *Old Chester Tales* (1899), etc.

De La Rey \de-la-'rī, -'rā\ Jacobus Hercules 1847–1914 Boer gen. & statesman; leader in South African War (1899–1902)

De·la·roche \də-lə-'rōsh, -'rosh\ (Hippolyte-) Paul 1797–1859 Fr. painter; known esp. for historical scenes; combined classical and romantic elements; works include *Les Enfants d'Edouard*, etc.

De·la·vigne \də-lə-'vēnʸ, -'vēn-ya\ Jean-François-Casimir 1793–1843 Fr. poet & dram.; published elegies *Les Messéniennes* (1818) after fall of Napoléon

De La Warr \də-lə-,war, -,wer\ Baron 1577–1618 *Thomas West; Lord Delaware* Eng. colonial administrator in America; gov. of Virginia (from 1610); Delaware named for him

Del·brück \'del-,brük, -,brúk\ Max 1906–1981 Am. (Ger.-born) biol.; awarded (with Alfred Hersey and Salvador Luria) 1969 Nobel prize for physiology or medicine for work with bacteriophages; discovered (1946) recombination of viral DNA

De·led·da \dā-'le-də, də-\ Grazia 1875–1936 Ital. author; known esp. for depictions of Sardinian peasantry; wrote *Dopo il divorzio* (1902), *Cenere* (1904), *La madre* (1920), etc.; awarded 1926 Nobel prize for literature

De·libes \də-'lēb\ (Clément-Philibert-) Léo 1836–1891 Fr. composer; composed operas *Le Roi l'a dit* (1873), *Lakmé* (1883), etc.; first to compose seriously for ballets, as in *Coppélia* (1870), etc.

De·lius \'dē-lē-əs, 'dēl-yəs\ Frederick 1862–1934 Eng. composer; works include orchestral pieces *Dance Rhapsodies* (1908, 1916), etc., choral works, concerti, sonatas, songs

Del·la Rob·bia \,de-lə-'rä-bē-ə, -'rō-\ Luca 1399 (or 1400)–1482 orig. *Luca di Simone de Marco* Florentine sculptor; a pioneer of Florentine Renaissance style; developed technique of enameling terra-cotta figures or reliefs

De Long \də-'lóŋ\ George Washington 1844–1881 Am. naval officer & explorer; led Arctic expedition (1879–81); ship crushed in ice; died seeking rescue in Siberia

De·lorme *or* **de l'Orme** \de-'lórm\ Philibert 1515?–1570 Fr. architect; directed work at Fontainebleau (1548–58)

de Mille \də-'mil\ Agnes George 1905–1993 Am. dancer & choreographer; choreographed musicals *Oklahoma!*, *Carousel*, etc.

De·Mille \də-'mil\ Cecil \'se-səl\ Blount \'blənt\ 1881–1959 Am. film director & producer; produced *Ten Commandments* (1923), *Cleopatra* (1934), *Greatest Show on Earth* (1952, Academy award), etc.; noted for spectacular productions

De·moc·ri·tus \di-'mä-krə-təs\ *ca* 460–*ca* 370 B.C. *the Laughing Philosopher* Greek philos.; important early advocate of the atomic theory of the universe

De Mor·gan \di-'mór-gən\ William Frend 1839–1917 Eng. artist & nov.; produced ceramic tiles, pottery with brilliant blue and green glazes (1871–1905); wrote novels *Joseph Vance* (1906), *Alice-for-Short* (1907), etc.

De·mos·the·nes \di-'mäs-thə-,nēz\ 384–322 B.C. Athenian orator & statesman; viewed as greatest Greek orator; attacked Philip of Macedon in series of "Philippics" (from 351)

Demp·sey \'dem(p)-sē\ William Harrison 1895–1983 *Jack* Am. boxer; world heavyweight champion (1919–26); lifetime record included 60 wins, 7 losses, 7 draws, with 49 knockouts

Deng Xiaoping — see TENG HSIAO-P'ING

De·ni·ker \,dä-nē-'ker\ Joseph 1852–1918 Fr. anthropol.; in *Les Races de l'Europe* (1908), presented ethnologic classification of Europeans by stature, cranial index, hair color

De·Niro \də-'nir-(,)ō\ Robert 1943–   Am. actor; films include *The Godfather, Part II* (1974), *Raging Bull* (1980), *Cape Fear* (1990), etc.

De·nis *or* **De·nys** \'de-nəs, də-nē\ Saint *d* 258? 1st bishop of Paris & patron saint of France; martyred by decapitation under Emperor Valerian's persecution

Dent \'dent\ Joseph Mal·a·by \'ma-lə-bē\ 1849–1926 Eng. publisher; published "Temple" edition of Shakespeare (1893), "Temple Classics," and "Everyman's Library" series

De·par·dieu \,də-pär-'d(y)ü, -d'dy'\ Gérard 1948–   Fr. actor; able to project both sensitivity and great physicability on screen; films include *The Return of Martin Guerre* (1981), *Jean de Florette* (1986), *Cyrano de Bergerac* (1990)

De·pew \di-'pyü\ Chauncey Mitchell 1834–1928 Am. lawyer & polit.; U.S. Senator (1899–1911); famous as speaker and wit

De Quin·cey \di-'kwin(t)-sē, -'kwin-zē\ Thomas 1785–1859 Eng. author; lifelong opium addict; published *Confessions of an English Opium-Eater* (1822)

De·rain \də-raⁿ\ André 1880–1954 Fr. painter; a leader of Postimpressionists and a Fauvist; created illustrations and theatrical designs, esp. for Ballets Russes

Der·ri·da \de-rē-dä\ Jacques 1930–   Fr. philos. & critic; founder of controversial deconstructionist school of criticism

Der·sho·witz \'dər-shə-(,)wits\ Alan Morton 1938–   Am. lawyer; professor of law, Harvard U. (1967–   ); defended Claus von Bülow in his retrial on murder charges; wrote *Reversal of Fortune: Inside the von Bülow Case* (1986), etc.

Der·zha·vin \der-'zhä-vən\ Gavrila Romanovich 1743–1816 Russ. poet; works included *Felitsa* (1782), *Bog* (1784), *Vodopad* (1794), etc.; viewed as greatest Russian poet before Pushkin

De·sai \de-'sī\ Morarji Ranchhodji 1896–1995 prime min. of India (1977–79)

De·saix de Vey·goux \də-'sā-də-(,)vā-'gü\ Louis-Charles-Antoine 1768–1800 Fr. gen.; fought in battle of the Pyramids (1798), conquered Upper Egypt (1798–99)

De·sargues \dā-'zärg\ Gérard *or* Girard 1591–1661 Fr. math.; published Desargues's theorem on the perspective of two triangles (1636), a key to development in projective geometry

Des·cartes \dā-'kärt\ René 1596–1650 L. *Renatus Cartesius* Fr. math. & philos.; wrote *Discours de la méthode* (1637), an attempt to unify all knowledge as the product of clear reasoning from self-evident premises — **Car·te·sian** \kär-'tē-zhən\ *adj or n*

Des·cha·nel \,dā-shə-'nel\ Paul-Eugène-Louis 1855–1922 Fr. statesman; pres. of France (1920)

De Se·ver·sky \də-sə-'ver-skē\ Alexander Procofieff 1894–1974 Am. (Russ.-born) aeronautical engineer; invented various airplane devices, including a bombsight

Des·mou·lins \dā-mü-laⁿ\ Camille 1760–1794 *Lucie-Simplice-Camille-Benoît Desmoulins* Fr. revolutionary; helped incite crowds that began French Revolution (1789); published pamphlets and journals

de Soto Hernando — see SOTO, DE

Des Prez Josquin — see JOSQUIN DES PREZ

Des·saix \də-'sā\ Comte Joseph-Marie 1764–1834 Fr. gen.; dubbed "l'Intrépide" by Napoléon after battle of Wagram (1809)

Des·sa·lines \,dā-sə-'lēn, ,de-\ Jean-Jacques 1758?–1806 emp. as *Jacques I* \zhäk\ of Haiti (1804–06); confiscated white-owned lands and instigated massacres of whites; assassinated

De Si·ca \dā-'sē-kä\ Vittorio 1901–1974 Ital. film director; a leader of the post-WWII neorealism; films include *Shoeshine* (1946), *Bicycle Thief* (1948), *Umberto D* (1952)

De·taille \də-'tī\ (Jean-Baptiste-) Édouard 1848–1912 Fr. painter; best known for battle scenes and paintings of soldiers

Deus Ra·mos \dā-əsh-'ra-(,)müsh\ João 'zhwäuⁿ\ de 1830–1896 Port. poet; foremost Portuguese poet of his time; wrote *Flores do campo* (1868), *Ramode flores* (1875), *Folhas Sôltas* (1876), etc.

De Va·le·ra \,de-və-'ler-ə, -'lir-ə\ Ea·mon \'ā-mən\ 1882–1975 Irish polit.; leader in Irish nationalist uprising (1916); prime min. of Ireland (1937–48; 1951–54; 1957–59); pres. (1959–73)

De Vere \də-'vir\ Aubrey Thomas 1814–1902 Irish poet; wrote *The Waldenses and Other Poems* (1842), *English Misrule and Irish Misdeeds* (1848), *Inisfail* (1862), etc.

Dev·er·eux \'de-və-,rüks, -,rü\ Robert 1566–1601 2d Earl of *Essex* Eng. soldier & courtier; favorite of Elizabeth I after death of Leicester; raised unsuccessful revolt against queen (1601)

Devonshire dukes of — see CAVENDISH

De Vo·to \di-'vō-(,)tō\ Bernard Augustine 1897–1955 Am. author; wrote *Across the Wide Missouri* (1947, Pulitzer prize), etc.

De Vries Hugo — see VRIES, DE

Dew·ar \'dü-ər, 'dyü-\ Sir James 1842–1923 Scot. chem. & physicist; produced liquid hydrogen, solid hydrogen; invented Dewar vessel (vacuum bottle); invented cordite (with F. A. Abel)

De Wet Christiaan Rudolph — see WET, DE

Dew·ey \'dü-ē, 'dyü-\ George 1837–1917 Am. admiral; destroyed Spanish fleet in battle of Manila Bay (1898); helped army capture Manila

Dewey John 1859–1952 Am. philos. & educ.; helped C. S. Pierce, William James develop philosophy of Pragmatism; helped found New School for Social Research (1919) — **Dew·ey·an** \-ən\ *adj*

Dewey Melvil 1851–1931 Am. librarian; originated decimal classification system (1876)

Dewey Thomas Edmund 1902–1971 Am. lawyer & polit.; gov., New York (1943–55); Republican candidate for pres. of U.S. (1944, 1948)

De Witt Johan — see WITT, DE

De Witte Emanuel — see WITT, DE

Dia·ghi·lev \dē-'ä-gə-,lef\ Sergey Pavlovich 1872–1929 Russ. ballet producer; organized Ballets Russes (1909); enlisted dancers Nijinsky, Pavlova, etc.; produced Stravinsky's *Firebird*, *Sacre du printemps*, etc.

Di·as \'dē-ˌäsh\ Bartholomeu *ca* 1450–1500 Port. navigator; sailed beyond tip of Africa (1488); sighted Cape of Good Hope

Dí·az \'dē-ˌäts\ Armando 1861–1928 Duca *della Vittoria* Ital. gen.; defeated Austrians at Vittorio Veneto (1918); marshal of Italy

Dí·az \'dē-ˌäs, -ˌäz\ Porfirio 1830–1915 *José de la Cruz Porfirio* Mex. gen.; pres. of Mexico (1877–80; 1884–1911); administration marked by dictatorial methods and little benefit for the masses

Díaz de Vivar — see CID

Dí·az Or·daz \'dē-ˌäs-ȯr-'däz\ Gustavo 1911–1979 pres. of Mexico (1964–70)

Dick \'dik\ George Frederick 1881–1967 & Gladys Henry 1881–1963 Am. physicians; isolated bacterium of and developed serum for scarlet fever; devised Dick test to determine susceptibility to the disease

Dick·ens \'di-kənz\ Charles John Huffam 1812–1870 pseud. *Boz* \'bäz, 'bōz\ Eng. nov.; generally considered the greatest novelist of Victorian period; major works include *Oliver Twist* (1837–39), *Nicholas Nickleby* (1838–39), *A Christmas Carol* (1843), etc. — **Dick·en·si·an** \di-'ken-zē-ən, -sē-\ *adj*

Dick·ey James Lafayette 1923– Am. writer; best known for novel *Deliverance* (1970) and for lyrical, mystical poems collected in *Into the Stone* (1960), *The Whole Motion* (1992)

Dick·in·son \'di-kən-sən\ Emily Elizabeth 1830–1886 Am. poet; led reclusive life in family home; six volumes of verse published after her death established her as one of greatest American poets

Dickinson John 1732–1808 Am. statesman; wrote *Letters from a Farmer in Pennsylvania, to the Inhabitants of the British Colonies* (1767–68); helped draft Articles of Confederation (1776)

Di·de·rot \dē-'drō, 'dē-də-ˌrō\ Denis 1713–1784 Fr. encyclopedist; contributed innumerable articles to grand *Encyclopédie, ou Dictionnaire Raisonné des Sciences, des Arts, et des Métiers* (28 volumes, 1751–72), a major influence during the Enlightenment

Die·ben·korn \'dē-bən-ˌkȯrn\ Richard Clifford Jr. 1922–1993 Am. painter; best known for his expressionistic California landscapes featuring broad vistas shimmering with sunlight

Die·fen·ba·ker \'dē-fən-ˌbā-kər\ John George 1895–1979 prime min. of Canada (1957–63)

Diels \'dē(ə)lz, 'dē(ə)ls\ Otto Paul Hermann 1876–1954 Ger. chem.; awarded (with Kurt Alder) 1950 Nobel prize for chemistry for developing a method of synthesizing organic compounds

Die·sel \'dē-zəl, -səl\ Rudolf 1858–1913 Ger. mechanical engineer; built the first successful Diesel engine, a pressure-ignited internal combustion engine (1896)

Die·trich \'dē-trik, -trik\ Marlene 1901?–1992 Am. (Ger.-born) actress & singer; appeared as glamorous woman in *The Blue Angel* (1930), *Morocco* (1930), *Blond Venus* (1932), etc.

Dietz \'dēts\ Howard 1896–1983 Am. lyricist; wrote lyrics to over 500 songs, including "Dancing in the Dark," "That's Entertainment," etc.

Diez \'dēts\ Friedrich Christian 1794–1876 Ger. philologist; founded Romance philology; wrote *Grammatik der romanischen Sprachen* (1836–43), etc.

Dig·by \'dig-bē\ Sir Ken·elm \'ke-ˌnelm\ 1603–1665 Eng. naval commander, diplomat, & author; supported king's cause during

Civil War; banished (1649–54); spent time in literary, scientific pursuits

Dill \'dil\ Sir John Greer 1881–1944 Brit. gen.; chief British representative on Anglo-American board of strategy (1941–44)

Dil·lon \'di-lən\ John 1851–1927 Irish nationalist polit.; imprisoned several times for violent attacks on government

Di·Mag·gio \də-'mä-zhē-(,)ō, -'ma-jē-(,)ō, -'ma-jō\ Joseph Paul 1914– Am. baseball player; with New York Yankees his entire career (1936–51); holds record of hits in 56 consecutive games

Di·mi·tri·os I \thē-'mē-trē-ŏs; də-'mē-trē-əs\ 1914–1991 archbishop of Constantinople and ecumenical patriarch (1972–91)

Di·ne·sen \'dē-nə-sən, 'di-\ Isak \'ē-,säk\ 1885–1962 pseud. of *Karen Christence Dinesen*, Baroness *Blixen-Finecke* Dan. author; wrote *Out of Africa* (1937), *Winter's Tales* (1942), etc.

Din·wid·die \din-'wi-dē\ Robert 1693–1770 Eng. colonial administrator in America; sent George Washington and troops to protect Ohio region from French (1754)

Di·o·cle·tian \,dī-ə-'klē-shən\ 245(or 248)–313(or 316) *Gaius Aurelius Valerius Diocletianus* Rom. emp. (284–305); reorganized administration, finances, military forces of empire; reign noted for last great persecution of Christians

Di·og·e·nes \dī-'ä-jə-,nēz\ *d ca* 320 B.C. Greek Cynic philos.; advocated asceticism, self-sufficiency, freedom from convention, moral zeal

Di·o·ny·sius \,dī-ə-'ni-shē-əs, -sē-əs, -shəs; -'nī-sē-əs\ *ca* 430–367 B.C. *the Elder* Greek tyrant of Syracuse (405–367); made Syracuse a major power

Dionysius *the Younger* tyrant of Syracuse (367–356; 354–343 B.C.); brought Plato to Syracuse as his tutor; ousted for despotism

Dionysius Ex·ig·u·us \eg-'zi-gyə-wəs\ *ca* 500–*ca* 560 Christian monk; introduced modern method of reckoning Christian era with birth of Christ as starting point

Dionysius of Alexandria Saint *ca* 200–*ca* 265 theol. & bishop of Alexandria (247); succeeded Origen as head of catechetical school in Alexandria

Dionysius of Hal·i·car·nas·sus \,ha-lə-(,)kär-'na-səs\ *fl ca* 20 B.C. Greek scholar; wrote history of Rome

Di·rac \di-'rak\ Paul Adrien Maurice 1902–1984 Eng. physicist; awarded (with Erwin Schrödinger) 1933 Nobel prize for physics for discovering new forms of atomic theory

Dirk·sen \'dərk-sən\ Everett McKinley 1896–1969 Am. polit.; member of Congress (1933–69); known for magniloquent oratory

Dis·ney \'diz-nē\ Walter Elias 1901–1966 Am. film producer; created animated cartoons featuring Mickey Mouse, Donald Duck, etc.; produced animated films *Snow White* (1937), *Pinocchio* (1940), *Fantasia* (1940), etc.; built Disneyland amusement parks

Dis·rae·li \diz-'rā-lē\ Benjamin 1804–1881 1st Earl of *Bea·cons·field* \'bē-kənz-,fēld\ Brit. polit. & author; prime min. (1868; 1874–80); established Tory policies of strong foreign policy, consolidation of empire, social reform; wrote novels *Coningsby*, etc.

Dit·mars \'dit-,märz\ Raymond Lee 1876–1942 Am. naturalist; wrote *The Reptile Book, Strange Animals I Have Known*, etc.

Dix \'diks\ Dorothea Lynde 1802–1887 Am. social reformer; brought about reforms in treatment of insane in prisons, alms houses, houses of correction in Mass. and elsewhere

Dix Dorothy — see Elizabeth Meriwether GILMER

Dix·on \'dik-sən\ Jeremiah *d* 1777 Eng. surveyor in America; helped Charles Mason determine boundary between Maryland and Pennsylvania (1763–68), since known as Mason-Dixon line

Dmow·ski \də-'mȯf-skē, -'mȯv-\ Roman 1864–1939 Pol. statesman; leader of Poland's struggle for national liberation; supported cooperation with Russia as means toward that goal

Dö·be·rei·ner \'də(r)-bə-ˌrī-nər, 'dœ-\ Johann Wolfgang 1780–1849 Ger. chem.; recognized relationship between properties of elements and their atomic weights, basis of periodic table

Do·bie \'dō-bē\ James Frank 1888–1964 Am. folklorist; wrote *A Vaquero of the Brush Country* (1929), *Coronado's Children* (1931), *Apache Gold and Yaqui Silver* (1939), etc.

Do·brée \'dō-ˌbrā\ Bon·a·my \'bä-nə-mē\ 1891–1974 Eng. scholar; authority on Restoration drama; wrote *Restoration Comedy* (1924), *Restoration Tragedy* (1929), *English Revolts* (1937), etc.

Dob·son \'däb-sən\ (Henry) Austin 1840–1921 Eng. poet & essayist; wrote *Vignettes in Rhyme* (1873), *At the Sign of the Lyre* (1885), etc., and prose works including critical essays, biographies, etc.

Dodge \'däj\ Mary Elizabeth 1831–1905 née Mapes \'māps\ Am. author; edited *St. Nicholas Magazine* (1873–1905); wrote *Hans Brinker, or the Silver Skates* (1865), etc.

Dodg·son \'däd-sən, 'däj-\ Charles Lut·widge \'lət-wij\ 1832–1898 pseud. Lewis Car·roll \'kar-əl\ Eng. math. & writer; wrote *Alice's Adventures in Wonderland* (1865), *Through the Looking Glass* (1872), etc.

Dods·ley \'dädz-lē\ Robert 1703–1764 Eng. author & bookseller; edited *Olds Plays* (12 vols., 1744) and *A Collection of Poems By Several Hands* (3 vols., 1748)

Doi·sy \'dȯi-zē\ Edward Adelbert 1893–1986 Am. biochem.; awarded (with Henrik Dam who discovered vitamin K) 1943 Nobel prize for physiology or medicine for synthesizing vitamin K

Dole \'dōl\ Robert Joseph 1923–   Am. polit.; U.S. senate majority leader (1985–86; 1989–)

Dole Sanford Ballard 1844–1926 Am. jurist; pres. (1894–1900) & gov. (1900–03) of Hawaii

Doll·fuss \'dȯl-ˌfüs\ Engelbert 1892–1934 Austrian statesman; as chancellor (1932–34) abolished political parties, established himself as dictator; assassinated by Austrian Nazi rebels

Do·magk \'dō-ˌmäk\ Gerhard 1895–1964 Ger. bacteriol.; awarded 1939 Nobel prize for physiology or medicine for discovery of and work on sulfonamide drugs

Do·me·ni·chi·no \(ˌ)dō-ˌmā-nə-'kē-(ˌ)nō\ 1581–1641 *Domenico Zam·pie·ri* \ˌtsäm-pē-'er-ē, ˌzäm-\ Ital. painter; a leader of Baroque eclectic school; works include *The Hunt of Diana*, frescoes, etc.

Do·min·go \dō-'miŋ-gō\ Placido 1941–   Span. tenor; a leading lyric-dramatic tenor of accomplished vocal and acting technique, esp. in works by Puccini, Verdi

Dom·i·nic \'dä-mə-(ˌ)nik\ Saint *ca* 1170–1221 *Domingo de Guzmán* \güz-'män, güs-\ Span.-born founder of the Dominican order of friars; directed order toward university teaching

Do·mi·tian \də-'mi-shən\ A.D. 51–96 *Titus Flavius Domitianus* Rom. emp. (81–96); noted for severity, esp. in reign of terror (93–96) and personal ostentation

Don·a·tel·lo \,dä-nə-'te-(,)lō\ 1386?–1466 *Donato de Betto di Bardi* Florentine sculptor; a leading innovator and exponent of new Renaissance style; greatest sculptor of his century; works include *St. George, David, Magdalen*, etc.

Dong·en \'dòn-ən\ Kees van 1877–1968 orig. *Cornelis Theodorus Maria Dongen* Fr. (Du.-born) painter; early associated with Fauve, Die Brücke movements; later known esp. for fashionable portraits

Dö·nitz \'də(r)-nəts, 'dœ-\ Karl 1891–1980 Ger. admiral; conducted effective "Battle of the Atlantic"; commanded German navy (1943–45); named by Hitler to succeed him as head of state (1945); surrendered to Allies, tried as war criminal, imprisoned

Don·i·zet·ti \,dä-nə(d)-'ze-tē, ,dō-\ Gaetano 1797–1848 Ital. composer; wrote 75 operas; influenced Verdi; operas include *Lucia di Lammermoor* (1835), etc. — **Don·i·zet·ti·an** \-'ze-tē-ən\ *adj*

Donne \'dən *also* 'dän\ John 1572–1631 Eng. poet & clergyman; leading Metaphysical poet; noted for love poetry, religious verse and treatises, sermons; works include "A Valediction: Forbidding Mourning," "The Canonization," "Death Be Not Proud," "Batter My Heart," etc. — **Donn·ean** *or* **Donn·ian** \'dä-nē-ən, 'dä-\ *adj*

Don·o·van \'dä-nə-vən, 'də-\ William Joseph 1883–1959 *Wild Bill* Am. lawyer & gen.; head of Office of Strategic Services (1942–45)

Doo·lit·tle \'dü-,li-t°l\ James Harold 1896–1993 Am. aviator & gen.; commanded B-52 raid on Tokyo (1942)

Dopp·ler \'dä-plər\ Christian Johann 1803–1853 Austrian physicist; published work on the Doppler effect (1842), stating that observed frequency of light and sound is affected by relative motion of the source and the observer

Do·ra·ti \də-'rä-tē\ An·tal \'än-,täl\ 1906–1988 Am. (Hung.-born) conductor; worked with Budapest Royal Opera, Dresden Opera, American Ballet Theater, etc.

Do·ré \dó-'rā, də-\ (Paul-) Gustave 1832–1883 Fr. illustrator & painter; known for fantastic imagination; illustrated books, including *Dante's Inferno* (1861), *Don Quichotte* (1863), the Bible (1866)

Dor·ge·les \,dòr-zhə-'les\ Roland 1886–1973 Fr. nov.; wrote *Les Croix de Bois* (1919), *Le Réveil des Morts* (1923), *Tout est a vendre* (1956), etc.

Dor·nier \'dòrn-,yā\ Claudius 1884–1969 Ger. airplane builder; designed first all-metal airplane (1911); bombers, seaplanes, 12-engine "Do-X," largest aircraft of its time

Dorr \'dòr\ Thomas Wilson 1805–1854 Am. lawyer & polit.; led "Dorr's Rebellion" in Rhode Island to force adoption of new state constitution; tried for treason, convicted, jailed for a year

Dorset 1st Earl of — see Thomas SACKVILLE

Dos Pas·sos \däs-'pa-səs\ John Roderigo 1896–1970 Am. writer; wrote trilogy *U.S.A.* comprising *The 42nd Parallel* (1930), *1919* (1932), *Big Money* (1936), etc.

Dos·to·yev·sky \,däs-tə-'yef-skē, -'yev-\ Fyodor Mikhaylovich 1821–1881 Russ. nov.; wrote *Notes from the Underground* (1864), *Crime and Punishment* (1866), *Brothers Karamazov* (1879–80), etc., powerful studies of peoples' search for faith, meaning, truth — **Dos·to·yev·ski·an** *or* **Dos·to·ev·ski·an** \-skē-ən\ *adj*

Dou or **Douw** \'daủ\ Gerrit or Gerard 1613–1675 Du. painter; studied under Rembrandt; headed school of Leiden after Rembrandt; known for highly refined genre scenes, portraits

Dou·ble·day \'də-bəl-,dā\ Abner 1819–1893 Am. soldier & reputed inventor of baseball; claims to the invention and naming of baseball disproved in modern times

Dough·ty \'daủ-tē\ Charles Montagu 1843–1926 Eng. poet & traveler; traveled through Arabia disguised as Arab (1876–78); published observations in *Travels in Arabia Deserta* (1888)

Doug·las \'də-gləs\ John Shol·to \'shôl-(,)tō\ 1844–1900 8th Marquis & Earl of *Queens·ber·ry* \'kwěnz-,ber-ē, -b(ə-)rē\ Scot. boxing patron; promoter of Marquis of Queensbury Rules (1867)

Douglas Stephen Arnold 1813–1861 Am. polit.; debated Abraham Lincoln on slavery in senatorial campaign of 1858; defeated by Lincoln for Democratic presidential nomination (1860)

Douglas William Orville 1898–1980 Am. jurist; associate justice, U.S. Supreme Court (1939–75)

Douglas–Home — see HOME

Douglas of Kir·tle·side \'kər-t'l-,sīd\ 1st Baron 1893–1969 *William Sholto Douglas* Brit. air marshal; commander, Fighter Command (1940–42), Middle East Command (1943–44), Coastal Command (1944–45)

Doug·lass \'də-gləs\ Frederick 1817–1895 orig. *Frederick Augustus Washington Bailey* Am. abolitionist; born a slave; escaped (1838); wrote *Narrative of the Life of Frederick Douglass* (1845); famous for oratorical skills

Dou·mer \dü-'mer\ Paul 1857–1932 pres. of France (1931–32); assassinated by French anarchist

Dou·mergue \dü-'merg\ Gaston 1863–1937 Fr. statesman; pres. of France (1924–31); term marked by constant political instability

Dow·den \'daủ-d'n\ Edward 1843–1913 Irish lit. critic; wrote *Shakespeare: His Mind and Art* (1875), *Life of Shelley* (1886), etc.

Dow·ie \'daủ-ē\ John Alexander 1847–1907 Am. (Scot.-born) religious leader; organized sect known as Christian Catholic Church; founded Zion City, Illinois, with himself as sole owner and gov.

Dow·son \'daủ-s'n\ Ernest Christopher 1867–1900 Eng. lyric poet; wrote polished verse in *Verses* (1896), *Decorations* (1899); author of phrase, "I have been faithful to thee, Cynara, in my fashion"

Dox·ia·dis \,dòk-sē-'ä-thēs\ Konstantinos Apostolos 1913–1975 Greek architect and city planner; wrote *Urban Renewal and the Future of the American City* (1966)

Doyle \'dòi(ə)l\ Sir Arthur Co·nan \'kō-nən\ 1859–1930 Brit. physician, nov., & detective-story writer; best known for Sherlock Holmes detective stories, including *A Study in Scarlet* (1887), *The Hound of the Baskervilles* (1902), etc.

D'Oyly Carte — see CARTE

Drab·ble \'dra-bəl\ Margaret 1939–   Eng. nov.; wrote *A Summer Bird-cage* (1962), *The Needle's Eye* (1972), *The Middle Ground* (1980), etc.

Drach·mann \'dräk-mən\ Holger Henrik Herholdt 1846–1908 Dan. author; one of foremost modernist poets in Denmark; also wrote novels *Forskrevet* (1890), etc., plays *Dar var engang* (1885)

Dra·co \'drā-(,)kō\ late 7th cent. B.C. Athenian lawgiver; prepared prob. first comprehensive written law code for Athens (ca. 621 B.C.), prescribing death for most offenses, whence the word *draconian*

Drake \'drāk\ Sir Francis 1540(or 1543)–1596 Eng. navigator & buccaneer; first English commander to see Pacific Ocean (1572); circumnavigated globe (1577–1580) in attempt to find Northwest Passage in *Golden Hind*

Dra·per \'drā-pər\ Henry 1837–1882 Am. astron.; obtained first photograph of spectrum of a star (Vega, 1872), also first photograph of a nebula

Dray·ton \'drā-tⁿn\ Michael 1563–1631 Eng. poet; published eclogues, sonnets, love letters, Horatian odes, etc.; wrote masterpiece *Poly-Olbion* (1612, 1622), description of England in verse

Drei·ser \'drī-sər, -zər\ Theodore 1871–1945 Am. editor & nov.; edited various magazines (1906–10); wrote *Sister Carrie* (1900), *An American Tragedy* (1925), *The Stoic* (1947), etc. — **Drei·ser·ian** \,drī-'ser-ē-ən, -'zər-\ *adj*

Drew \'drü\ John 1827–1862 Am. (Irish-born) actor; successful in portraying Irish roles in comedies, as Sir Lucius O'Trigger in Sheridan's *Rivals*

Drew John 1853–1927 *son of prec.* Am. actor; noted for roles in Shakespearean comedy, society drama, light comedies

Drey·fus \'drī-fəs, 'drā-; dre-fū̄s\ Alfred 1859–1935 Fr. army officer; convicted of treason and imprisoned (1895); case provoked political upheaval amid charges of anti-Semitism in France — **Drey·fu·sard** \,drī-f(y)ə-'sär(d), ,drā-, zär(d)\ *n*

Driesch \'drēsh\ Hans Adolf Eduard 1867–1941 Ger. biol. & philos.; pioneer experimenter in embryology; last important exponent of vitalism

Drink·wa·ter \'driŋk-,wȯ-tər, -,wä-\ John 1882–1937 Eng. writer; wrote *Swords and Plowshares* (1915), *Collected Poems* (1923), autobiographies, plays *Rebellion* (1914), *Abraham Lincoln* (1918), etc.

Drou·et \drü-'e, -'ā\ Jean-Baptiste 1765–1844 Comte *d'Er·lon* \der-'lōⁿ\ Fr. gen.; served under Napoléon in several engagements including Waterloo; marshal of France (1843)

Drum·mond \'drə-mənd\ Henry 1851–1897 Scot. clergyman & writer; tried to reconcile evangelical Christianity and evolution in *Natural Law in the Spiritual World* (1883)

Drummond William Henry 1854–1907 Canad. (Irish-born) poet; portrayed French-Canadian character and culture in patois in *The Habitant* (1897), *Johnny Courteau* (1901), etc.

Drummond of Haw·thorn·den \'hȯ-,thȯrn-dən\ William 1585–1649 Scot. poet; wrote sonnets and songs in memory of bride who died on eve of their marriage

Dru·sus \'drü-səs\ 38–9 B.C. *Ne·ro* \'nē-(,)rō, 'nir-(,)ō\ *Claudius Drusus Ger·man·i·cus* \(,)jər-'ma-ni-kəs\ Rom. gen.; helped brother Tiberius (later emperor) subdue tribes of Gaul, Germany

Dry·den \'drī-dⁿn\ John 1631–1700 Eng. poet & dram.; poet laureate (1668–88); dominated the literary scene of his day; works include comedy *Marriage-à-la Mode* (1672), verse satire *Absalom and Achitophel* (1681), *Mac Flecknoe* (1682) — **Dry·de·ni·an** \,drī-'dē-nē-ən, -'dē-\ *adj*

Du Barry Comtesse — see Jeanne BARRY

Du·bois \dü-'bwä, dyü-; düē-bwä\ Paul 1829–1905 Fr. sculptor; works include busts of Pasteur, Gounod, etc., equestrian statue of Joan of Arc, etc.

Dubois (François-Clément-) Théodore 1837–1924 Fr. composer; composed operas, oratorios, Masses, chamber music, organ and piano pieces, songs

DuBois \dü-'bóis, dyü-\ William Edward Burghardt 1868–1963 Am. educ. & writer; helped create National Association for the Advancement of Colored People (1909); wrote *The Souls of Black Folk* (1903), *John Brown* (1909), *The World and Africa* (1947), etc.

Du·buf·fet \dü-bə-'fā, dyü-; dūē-būē-fe\ Jean 1901–1985 Fr. artist; developed Art Brut, using trash to depict images; viewed as precursor of Pop Art, Dada-like styles of '60s

Du Cange \dü-'känzh, dyü-\ Sieur Charles Du Fresne 1610–1688 Fr. scholar & glossarist; wrote *Histoire de L'empire de Constantinople sous les empereurs français* (1657); compiled glossaries of Latin (1678) and Greek (1688); pioneered historical study of language

Du Chail·lu \də-'shal-(,)yü, -'shī-(,)ü\ Paul Belloni 1831–1903 Am. (Fr.-born) explorer in Africa; brought back animal specimens including first gorillas ever seen in America

Du·champ \dü-'shän, dyü-\ Marcel 1887–1968 Fr. painter; created famous *Nude Descending a Staircase, No. 2* (1912); invented medium of "ready mades," e.g. *Bicycle Wheel* (1913); associated with Dadaists, Surrealists — **Du·champ·ian** \-'shäm-pē-ən\ adj

Du·com·mun \dü-kə-'mœⁿ, ,dyü-\ Elie 1833–1906 Swiss journalist; awarded (with Charles Albert Gobat) 1902 Nobel Prize for peace for organizing International Bureau of Peace, Bern

Dudevant Aurore — see George SAND

Dud·ley \'dəd-lē\ Robert 1532 (or 1533)–1588 1st Earl of *Leicester* Eng. courtier; sometime favorite and suitor of Queen Elizabeth I; given command of armies to resist Spanish Armada

Dudley Thomas 1576–1653 colonial administrator in Massachusetts Bay Colony; gov. (1634, 1640, 1645, 1650); one of first overseers at Harvard

Duf·fer·in and Ava \,də-fə-rin-ən(d)-'ä-və\ 1st Marquis of 1826–1902 *Frederick Temple Hamilton-Temple-Blackwood* Brit. diplomat; gov.-gen. of Canada (1872–78), of India (1884–88)

Duff–Gor·don \'dəf-'gór-dᵊn\ Lady Lucie 1821–1869 Eng. author; known for translations from German, historical works; wrote *Letters from the Cape* (1862–63), *Letters from Egypt* (1865), etc.

Duf·fy \'də-fē\ Sir Charles Gavan 1816–1903 Irish nationalist & Austral. polit.; organized Young Ireland party; imprisoned (1848–49) for suspected part in abortive insurrection; to Australia (1855); prime min. (1871–72)

Du·fy \dü-'fē, dyü-\ Raoul 1877–1953 Fr. painter; Impressionist and Fauvist; worked with bright colors, bold composition; ran factories for printed fabrics, etc.; created theatrical designs, etc.

Du Gard Roger Martin — see MARTIN DU GARD

Du Guesclin Bertrand — see GUESCLIN

Du·ha·mel \,dü-ä-'mel, ,dyü-; dūē-â-mel\ Georges 1884–1966 Fr. writer; most noted for two novel cycles *Vie et aventures de Salavin* (1920–32), *Chronique des Pasquier* (1933–44)

Du·ka·kis \dü-'kä-kis\ Michael Stanley 1933– Am. polit.; 1988 Democratic presidential candidate

Duke \dük, 'dyük\ Benjamin Newton 1855–1929 & his bro. James Buchanan 1856–1925 Am. tobacco industrialists; built American Tobacco Co; benefactors of Trinity College, Durham, renamed Duke Univ. in their honor (1924)

Dul·bec·co \(,)dəl-'be-(,)kō\ Renato 1914– Am. (Ital.-born) virologist; awarded (with David Baltimore, Howard M. Temin) 1975 Nobel prize for physiology or medicine for research on how certain viruses affect the genes of cancer cells

Dul·les \'də-ləs\ John Foster 1888–1959 Am. diplomat; secy. of state (1953–59); chief architect of SEATO pact (1954), Baghdad Pact (1955), Eisenhower Doctrine (1957)

Du·mas \dü-'mä, dyü-; 'd(y)ü-,\ Alexandre 1802–1870 *Dumas père* \'per\ Fr. nov. & dram.; wrote historical novels *Les trois mousquetaires* (1844, *The Three Musketeers*), *Comte de Monte Cristo* (1844, *The Count of Monte Cristo*), etc.

Dumas Alexandre 1824–1895 *Dumas fils* \'fēs\ Fr. nov. & dram.; wrote plays *La Dame aux camélias* (novel 1848, play 1852), *Le Demi-Monde* (1855), *Le Fils naturel* (1858), etc.

du Mau·rier \dü-'mȯr-ē-,ā, dyü-\ Dame Daphne 1907–1989 Brit. writer; wrote novels *Jamaica Inn* (1936), *Rebecca* (1938), *The Flight of the Falcon* (1965), etc.

du Maurier George Louis Palmella Busson 1834–1896 *grandfather of prec.* Brit. artist & nov.; illustrations appeared in *Punch;* wrote and illustrated three novels including *Trilby* (1894), etc.

Du·mou·riez \dú-'mür-ē-,ā, dyü-\ Charles-François du Périer 1739–1823 Fr. gen.; won victories for French Revolution (1792–93); traitorously deserted to Austrians

Du·nant \dü-'nä, dyü-\ Jean-Henri 1828–1910 Swiss philanthropist & founder of the Red Cross; awarded (with Frédéric Passy) 1901 Nobel prize for peace

Dun·bar \'dən-,bär\ Paul Laurence 1872–1906 Am. poet & nov.; one of first black writers in U.S. to attain national prominence; wrote *Lyrics of Lowly Life* (1896), *The Sport of the Gods* (1902), etc.

Dunbar \'dən-,bär, ,dən-'\ William 1460?–?1530 Scot. poet; poet attached to court of James IV; one of the dominant courtly poets in golden age of Scottish poetry

Dun·can \'dən-kən\ Isadora 1877–1927 Am. dancer; acclaimed in London, Paris, Germany, Budapest, Vienna; established schools of dance for children near Berlin (1904), in Moscow (1921)

Dun·das \,dən-'das\ Henry 1742–1811 1st Viscount *Melville* & Baron *Dun·ira* \,də-'nir-ə\ Brit. statesman; advocated belligerent policy against American colonies; know as "Starvation Dundas" for promoting restrictive trade measures against colonies

Dun·lop \,dən-'läp, 'dən-,\ John Boyd 1840–1921 Scot. inventor; credited with invention of pneumatic tire (1888), basis of Dunlop Rubber Co.

Dunne \'dən\ Finley Peter 1867–1936 Am. humorist; created Irish saloon keeper-philosopher "Mr Dooley," as in *Mr. Dooley in Peace and War* (1898), *Mr. Dooley Says* (1910), etc.

Du·nois \dün-'wä\ Comte de 1403–1468 *Jean d'Orléans; the bastard of Orléans* Fr. gen.; adviser and chamberlain of dauphin Charles (from 1420); defended Orléans against siege of Joan of Arc

Dun·sa·ny \ˌdən-'sā-nē\ 18th Baron 1878–1957 *Edward John Moreton Drax Plunkett* Irish poet & dram.; wrote verse *Fifty Poems* (1929), etc.; plays *The Glittering Gate* (1909), etc.

Duns Sco·tus \'dənz-'skō-təs\ John 1266?–1308 Scot. scholastic theol.; founded Scotism, upholding separability and independence of rational soul from body

Dun·stan \'dən(t)-stən\ Saint 924–988 archbishop of Canterbury (959–988); chief adviser to kings of Wessex; best known for major monastic reforms

Du·pleix \dü-'pleks, dyü-\ Marquis Joseph-François 1697–1763 Fr. colonial administrator in India; worked unsuccessfully to destroy British East India Co.

Duplessis–Mornay — see Philippe de MORNAY

Du Pont \dü-'pänt, dyü-; 'd(y)ü-,\ Éleuthère Irénée 1771–1834 *son of P.S. Du Pont de Nemours* Am. (Fr.-born) industrialist; established gunpowder plant (1802), the beginning of E.I. Du Pont de Nemours & Co.

Du Pont de Ne·mours \-də-nə-'múr\ Pierre-Samuel 1739–1817 Fr. econ. & statesman; writings devoted to spreading tenets of physiocratic school; helped England negotiate treaty giving independence to United States (1783)

Du·quesne \dü-'kän, dyü-\ Marquis Abraham 1610–1688 Fr. naval officer; defeated combined fleets of Holland and Spain (1676)

Du·rant \dü-'rant, dyü-\ William James 1885–1981 Am. educ. & writer; collaborated with wife Ida Kaufman, called Ariel Durant, on 11-volume series, "Story of Civilization," (1935–75)

Du·ran·te \də-'ran-tē\ Jimmy 1893–1980 *James Francis Durante* Am. comedian; starred in night clubs, vaudeville, Broadway productions, films, radio, and television; famous for his gravel-voiced singing, malapropisms, mispronunciations, and outsized nose

Dü·rer \'dúr-ər, 'dyúr-, 'dǖr-\ Albrecht 1471–1528 Ger. painter & engraver; viewed as foremost German artist of the Renaissance; worked in painting, woodblock, copper- and iron-engraving — **Dü·rer·esque** \ˌdúr-ər-'esk, dyúr-, ˌdǖr-\ *adj*

D'Ur·fey \'dər-fē\ Thomas 1653–1723 Eng. songwriter & dram.; wrote popular comedies *The Fond Husband* (1676), *Madame Fickle* (1677), etc.; songs of wit and satire collected as *Wit and Mirth or Pills to Purge Melancholy* (1719–20)

Durk·heim \dúr-'kem\ Émile 1858–1917 Fr. sociol.; established methodology and theory of rigorous social science — **Durk·heim·ian** \-'ke-mē-ən\ *adj*

Du·roc \dü-'räk, dyü-\ Géraud-Christophe-Michel 1772–1813 Duc de Fri·oul \frē-ül\ Fr. gen. under Napoleon; undertook diplomatic missions; at Austerlitz, Essling, Wagram

Du·ro·cher \də-'rō-shər\ Leo Ernest 1905–1991 Am. baseball player & manager; played for several major league teams (1928–48); managed N.Y. Giants (1948–55), etc.; famous for remark "Nice guys finish last"

Dur·rell \'dər-əl, 'də-rəl\ Lawrence 1912–1990 Eng. nov. & poet; wrote the "Alexandria Quartet," *Justine, Balthazar, Mountolive, Clea* (1957–60), etc., and poems, stories, travel books

Dür·ren·matt \'dúr-ən-ˌmät, 'dür-\ Friedrich 1921–1990 Swiss author; wrote plays esp. *Der Besuch der alten Dame* (1956; *The Visit*, 1958) and novels, stories, essays, radio dramas

Du·ruy \dür-'wē, dǖe-rwē\ Victor 1811–1894 Fr. hist.; wrote *Histoire des Romains* (1879–85, *History of the Romans*), etc.

Du·se \'dü-(,)zā\ Eleonora 1858–1924 Ital. actress; appeared in works of Dumas fils, Verga, Ibsen, etc.; associated with D'Annunzio (1894–99)

Du·tra \'dü-trə\ Eurico Gaspar 1885–1974 Braz. gen.; pres. of Brazil (1946–51)

Du·va·lier \dü-'val-(,)yā, dyü-\ François 1907–1971 *Papa Doc* pres. of Haiti (1957–71); held power through regime of terror

Du·ve \'dü-və\ Christian René Marie Joseph de 1917–ㅤㅤBelg. (Eng.-born) physiol.; awarded (with Albert Claude and George E. Palade) 1974 Nobel prize for physiology or medicine for pioneer work in cell biology

Du Vi·gneaud \dü-'vēn-(,)yō, dyü-\ Vincent 1901–1978 Am. biochem.; awarded 1955 Nobel prize for chemistry for synthesis of two pituitary hormones

Dvo·řák \(də-)'vȯr-,zhäk\ Antonín 1841–1904 Bohemian composer; adapted folk motifs to serious romantic music; wrote operas, 9 symphonies including No. 9 *From the New World* (1893), symphonic poems, overtures, rhapsodies, nocturnes, concertos, etc.

Dwig·gins \'dwi-ganz\ William Addison 1880–1956 Am. type designer; designed typefaces Metro (1929), Electra (1935), Caledonia (1939), etc.

Dwight \'dwīt\ Timothy 1752–1817 Am. clergyman; pres. Yale U. (1795–1817); wrote *Greenfield Hill* (1794), *The Conquest of Canaan* (1785), etc.

Dwight Timothy 1828–1916 *grandson of prec.* Am. clergyman; pres. Yale U. (1886–99)

Dwyfor Earl of — see LLOYD GEORGE

Dyce \'dīs\ Alexander 1798–1869 Scot. editor; produced edition of Shakespeare (1857, 1864–67), notes on Shakespeare and on Collier's edition of Shakespeare

Dy·er \'dī(-ə)r\ John 1699–1757 Brit. poet; wrote "Grongar Hill" (1726); known for natural description and precision of phrase

Dyer Mary *d* 1660 Am. Quaker martyr; condemned in Boston for sedition and hanged after being arrested and banished

E

Eads \'ēdz\ James Buchanan 1820–1887 Am. engineer & inventor; best known for building first bridge across Mississippi, at St. Louis (1867–74, Eads Bridge)

Ea·kins \'ā-kənz\ Thomas 1844–1916 Am. artist; master of draftsmanship and anatomy; painted *Max Schmitt in a Single Scull, The Gross Clinic, Agnew Clinic*, etc.

Ear·hart \'er-,härt, 'ir-\ Amelia 1897–1937 Am. aviator; first woman to cross Atlantic in airplane (1928) and first woman to fly Atlantic solo (1932); lost while attempting to fly around the world

Ear·ly \\'ər-lē\\ Ju·bal \\'jü-bəl\\ Anderson 1816–1894 Am. Confed. gen.; defeated by Sheridan on march down Shenandoah Valley toward Washington (1865)

Earp \\'ərp\\ Wyatt 1848–1929 Am. lawman; at Dodge City, Kans. (1876, 1878–79) and Tombstone, Ariz. (1881) on occasion of "Gunfight at O.K. Corral"

East·man \\'ēst-mən\\ George 1854–1932 Am. inventor & industrialist; developed processes for making photographic plates, flexible film; invented Kodak box camera; organized Eastman Kodak Co.

Eastman Max Forrester 1883–1969 Am. editor & writer; roving editor, *Reader's Digest* (from 1941); wrote *Enjoyment of Poetry* (1913), *Since Lenin Died* (1925), *Love and Revolution* (1965), etc.

East·wood \\'ēst-ˌwud\\ Clinton Jr. 1930–   Am. film actor & dir.; achieved fame as laconic cowboy hero in TV series *Rawhide* and in Spanish-Italian western *A Fistful of Dollars* (1964), etc.; directed and starred in *Unforgiven* (1992), etc.

Ea·ton \\'ēt-ᵊn\\ Theophilus 1590–1658 Eng. colonial administrator in America; gov. of New Haven colony (1638–58)

Ebert \\'ā-bərt\\ Friedrich 1871–1925 pres. of Germany (1919–25); suppressed Kapp Putsch (1920) and Hitler's attempt to establish dictatorship in Bavaria (1923)

Ec·cles \\'e-kəlz\\ Sir John Carew 1903–   Brit. physiol.; awarded (with Alan Lloyd Hodgkin) 1963 Nobel prize for physiology or medicine for research on the transmission of nerve impulses

Eccles Marriner Stoddard 1890–1977 Am. banker & econ.; member (1936–48), board of governors of Federal Reserve System

Eche·ga·ray y Ei·za·guir·re \\ˌā-chə-gə-ˈrī-ˌē-ˌā-thə-ˈgwir-(ˌ)ā, -sə-ˈgwir\\ José 1832–1916 Span. dram.; wrote plays *El libro talonario* (1874), etc.; awarded 1904 Nobel prize for literature

Eche·ver·ría Al·va·rez \\ˌā-chə-və-ˈrē-ə-ˈal-və-ˌrez, ˌe-chə-\\ Luis 1922–   pres. of Mexico (1970–76)

Eck \\'ek\\ Johann 1486–1543 orig. *Maier* Ger. R.C. theol.; disputed with Luther (1519) and procured papal bull against him (1520); debated Melanchthon at convocation at Worms (1540)

Ecke·hart \\'ek-ə-ˌhärt\\ *or* **Eck·art** *or* **Eck·hart** \\'ek-ˌhärt, 'e-ˌkärt\\ Johannes 1260?–?1327 *Meister Eckehart* Ger. mystic; charged with heresy for mystical doctrine (1327); viewed as founder of German idealism, Romanticism, Protestantism

Eck·er·mann \\'e-kər-ˌmän, -mən\\ Johann Peter 1792–1854 Ger. writer; wrote *Conversations with Goethe in the Last Years of His Life* (1836–48)

Ed·ding·ton \\'e-diŋ-tən\\ Sir Arthur Stanley 1882–1944 Eng. astron.; known for research on the motion, internal constitution, and evolution of stars, cosmology; explicated theory of relativity

Ed·dy \\'e-dē\\ Mary Morse 1821–1910 née *Baker* Am. founder of the Christian Science Church; wrote *Science and Health* (1875) explaining system; chartered "Church of Christ Scientist" (1879) and founded "Mother Church," Boston (1895)

Ed·el·man \\'e-dᵊl-mən\\ Gerald Maurice 1929–   Am. biochem.; awarded (with Rodney R. Porter) 1972 Nobel prize for physiology or medicine for discovering chemical structure of antibodies

Eden \\'ē-dᵊn\\ (Robert) Anthony 1897–1977 Earl of *Avon* \\'ā-vən\\ Eng. statesman; prime min. (1955–57); resigned after failed Anglo-French efforts to prevent Suez Canal nationalization (1956)

Edge·worth \'ej-(,)wərth\ Maria 1767–1849 Brit. nov.; wrote novels portraying Irish life and local color, including *Castle Rackrent* (1800), *Belinda* (1801), etc.

Edinburgh Duke of — see PHILIP

Ed·i·son \'e-də-sən\ Thomas Alva 1847–1931 Am. inventor; inventions include phonograph (1877), incandescent electric lamp (1879), etc.; produced talking motion pictures (1913)

Ed·mund or **Ead·mund** II \'ed-mənd\ *ca* 993–1016 *Ironside* king of the English (1016)

Ed·ward \'ed-wərd\ name of 8 post-Norman Eng. (Brit.) kings: **I** 1239–1307 (reigned 1272–1307); made administrative reforms weakening feudalism and establishing parliamentary system; **II** 1284–1327 (reigned 1307–27); defeated by Robert Bruce at Bannockburn (1314); was captured, forced to resign throne (1327), tortured, and murdered; **III** 1312–1377 (reigned 1327–77); became involved in Hundred Years' War; **IV** 1442–1483 (reigned 1461–70; 1471–83); leading participant in the Yorkist-Lancastrian conflict known as the War of the Roses; **V** 1470–1483 (reigned 1483); deposed and probably murdered with his brother, Duke of York, in Tower of London by order of uncle Richard, Duke of Gloucester; **VI** 1537–1553 (reigned 1547–53) *son of Henry VIII & Jane Seymour;* **VII** 1841–1910 (reigned 1901–10) *Albert Edward, son of Victoria;* immensely popular sovereign and leader of society; **VIII** 1894–1972 (reigned 1936) Duke of *Windsor, son of George V;* abdicated to marry American divorcee Wallace Warfield Simpson — **Ed·war·di·an** \e-'dwär-dē-ən, -'dwôr-\ *adj or n*

Edward 1330–1376 *the Black Prince; son of Edward III* prince of Wales; helped arrange treaty of Brétigny (1360); received lands of Aquitane and Gascony (1362)

Edward or **Ead·ward** \'ed-\ 1003?–1066 *the Confessor* king of the English (1042–66); last of Anglo-Saxon line; entrusted administration to Norman or court favorites

Ed·wards \'ed-wərdz\ Jonathan 1703–1758 Am. theol.; known widely as powerful preacher; led influential revivals in Connecticut Valley; considered greatest theologian of American Puritanism — **Ed·ward·ean** \ed-'wär-dē-ən, -'wôr-\ *adj*

Ed·win or **Ead·wine** \'ed-wən\ 585?–633 king of Northumbria (616–633); converted to Christianity by Paulinus; made archbishop of York (627)

Egas Mo·niz \'ā-gäs-mō-'nēz\ António Caetano de Abreu Freire 1874–1955 Port. neurologist & polit.; awarded (with Walter Hess) 1949 Nobel prize for physiology or medicine for originating prefrontal lobotomy

Eg·bert \'eg-bərt\ *d* 839 king of the West Saxons (802–839) & 1st king of the English (828–839)

Eg·gle·ston \'e-gəl-stən\ Edward 1837–1902 Am. writer; wrote novels *The Hoosier Schoolmaster* (1871), *Roxy* (1878), etc.

Eggleston George Cary 1839–1911 *bro. of Edward* Am. writer; wrote Big Brother Series (1875–82), *Strange Stories from History* (1886); novels *A Man of Honor* (1873), *Evelyn Byrd* (1904), etc.

Eg·mond \'eg-,mänt\ or **Eg·mont** Lamoraal 1522–1568 Graaf *van Egmond* Flem. gen. & statesman; refused to join plan to overthrow Spanish regime; arrested nonetheless by Duke of Alba, condemned to death; theme of Goethe's drama *Egmont* (1788)

Eh·ren·burg \\'er-ən-ˌbu̇rg, -ˌbu̇rk\\ Ilya Grigoryevich 1891–1967 Russ. writer; wrote poems, stories, novels including *Padenie Parizha* (*Fall of Paris*, 1941), *Burya* (*The Storm*, 1948), etc.

Ehr·lich \\'er-lik\\ Paul 1854–1915 Ger. bacteriol.; awarded (with E. Metchnikoff) 1908 Nobel prize for physiology or medicine for work on immunity; discovered remedy for syphilis, yaws, etc.

Ehr·lich \\'ər-lik\\ Paul Ralph 1932– Am. biol.; wrote *The Population Bomb* (1968) advocating zero population growth

Eif·fel \\'ī-fəl, e-fel\\ Alexandre-Gustave 1832–1923 Fr. engineer; built framework for Statue of Liberty, Eiffel Tower (1887–89), etc.

Ei·gen \\'ī-gən\\ Manfred 1927– Ger. chem.; awarded (with Ronald G.W. Norrish, George Porter) 1967 Nobel prize for chemistry for developing techniques for measuring chemical reactions

Eijk·man \\'īk-ˌmän, 'āk-\\ Christiaan 1858–1930 Du. pathologist; awarded (with Frederick Hopkins) 1929 Nobel prize for physiology or medicine for discovering vitamins that prevent beriberi

Ein·stein \\'īn-ˌstīn\\ Albert 1879–1955 Am. (Ger.-born) physicist; enunciated theory of relativity; discovered equivalence of mass and energy ($E = mc^2$), etc.; awarded 1921 Nobel prize for physics for contributing to theoretical physics and his photoelectric law — **Ein·stein·ian** \\īn-'stī-nē-ən\\ *adj*

Eint·ho·ven \\'īnt-ˌhō-vən, 'änt-\\ Willem 1860–1927 Du. physiol.; awarded 1924 Nobel prize for physiology or medicine for discovering the way in which electrocardiography works

Ei·sen·how·er \\'ī-zᵊn-ˌhau̇(-ə)r\\ Dwight David 1890–1969 Am. gen.; planned and commanded liberation of Europe (1944–45); 34th pres. of the U.S. (1953–61); administration noted for truce ending Korean War (1953), sending troops to Little Rock, Ark., to support integration (1957), etc.

Ei·sen·stein \\'ī-zᵊn-ˌstīn\\ Sergey Mikhaylovich 1898–1948 Soviet (Russ.-born) film director; major contributor to development of cinematic art and criticism; films included *Potemkin* (1925), *Aleksandr Nevsky* (1938), *Ivan the Terrible* (1944–46), etc.

El·a·gab·a·lus \\ˌe-lə-'ga-bə-ləs\\ *Gk* **He·li·o·gab·a·lus** \\ˌhē-lē-ō-'ga-bə-ləs\\ 204–222 Rom. emp. (218–222); imposed worship of Baal; executed generals; lived debauched life

El·ders \\'el-dərz\\ (Minnie) Joycelyn 1933– U.S. surgeon general (1993–94)

El·don \\'el-dən\\ 1st Earl of 1751–1838 *John Scott* Eng. jurist; instituted rigorous prosecution for libel and constructive treason and suspension of habeas corpus during period of French revolution

El·ea·nor \\'e-lə-nər, -ˌnȯr\\ **of Aquitaine** 1122?–1204 *queen of Louis VII of France (divorced 1152) & of Henry II of England;* supported rebellion of sons against Henry; confined (1174–89); secured succession of Richard I; administered realm during his crusading

Eleanor of Castile 1246–1290 *queen of Edward I of England*

Eleanor of Provence 1223–1291 *queen of Henry III of England;* governor of England with king's brother (1253); entered nunnery on accession of son Edward I (1272)

El·gar \\'el-ˌgär, -gər\\ Sir Edward 1857–1934 Eng. composer; compositions included *Enigma Variations* (1896), oratorio *Lux Christi* (1896), *Pomp and Circumstance* marches (1901–07, 1930), etc.

Eli·jah \i-'lī-jə\ 9th cent. B.C. Hebrew prophet; championed worship of Jehovah as against Baal

El·i·on \'e-lē-ən\ Gertrude Belle 1918– Am. biochem.; awarded (with George H. Hitchings and Sir James Black) 1988 Nobel prize for physiology or medicine for developing drugs to treat several major diseases

Eli·ot \'e-lē-ət, 'el-yət\ Charles William 1834–1926 Am. educ.; pres. Harvard U. (1869–1909); promoted sciences in undergraduate curriculum; eliminated required courses; raised admission standards

Eliot George 1819–1880 pseud. of *Mary Ann (or Marian) Evans* Eng. nov.; wrote novels *Adam Bede* (1859), *The Mill on the Floss* (1860), *Silas Marner* (1861), *Middlemarch* (1871–72), etc.

Eliot Sir John 1592–1632 Eng. statesman; Puritan; urged free speech, enforcement of laws against Roman Catholics

Eliot John 1604–1690 *apostle to the Indians* Am. clergyman; produced Indian translation of the Bible (1661, 1663), first Bible printed in North America

Eliot Thomas Stearns 1888–1965 Brit. (Am.-born) poet & critic; wrote *Prufrock and Other Observations* (1917), *The Waste Land* (1922), *Four Quartets* (1943), etc.; awarded 1948 Nobel prize for literature — **El·i·ot·ian** \,e-lē-'ō-tē-ən, -'ō-sh(ē-)ən\ *adj* — **Eli·ot·ic** \,e-lē-'ä-tik\ *adj*

Eli·sha \i-'lī-shə\ 9th cent. B.C. Hebrew prophet; disciple and successor of Elijah

Eliz·a·beth \i-'li-zə-bəth\ name of 2 Eng. (Brit.) queens: **I** 1533–1603 *dau. of Henry VIII & Anne Boleyn* (reigned 1558–1603); reign marked by England's growth as major European power in politics, commerce, arts; had Mary, Queen of Scots executed (1587); defeated Spanish Armada (1588); **II** 1926– *Elizabeth Alexandra Mary; dau. of George VI* (reigned 1952–   ) — **Eliz·a·be·than** \i-,li-zə-'bē-thən\ *adj or n*

Elizabeth *also* **Elizabeth Stu·art** \-'stü-ərt, -'styü-; 'stü-(ə)rt, 'styü-(ə)rt\ 1596–1662 *queen of Frederick V of Bohemia;* in exile after husband routed by Catholic League (1620)

Elizabeth 1900–   *Elizabeth Angela Marguerite Bowes-Ly·on* \'bōz-'lī-ən\ *queen of George VI of Great Britain*

Elizabeth 1843–1916 pseud. of *Car·men Syl·va* \'kär-mən-'sil-və\ queen of Romania & writer; wrote *Pensées d'une reine* (1882), *Astra* (1886), *The Bard of Dimbovitza* (1891), etc.

Elizabeth Pe·trov·na \pə-'trȯv-nə\ 1709–1762 empress of Russia (1741–62); annexed part of Finland (1743); followed pro-Austria, anti-Prussian foreign policy; founded Univ. of Moscow (1755), Academy of Fine Arts of St. Petersburg (1758)

Ellenborough 1st Baron — see LAW

El·ling·ton \'e-liŋ-tən\ Edward Kennedy 1899–1974 *Duke Ellington* Am. bandleader & composer; composed suites *Black, Brown, and Beige* (1943), *Harlem* (1950), etc.; film scores, songs, including "Mood Indigo," "In My Solitude," etc.

El·liott \'e-lē-ət, 'el-yət\ Maxine 1868–1940 pseud. of *Jessie Dermot* Am. actress

El·lis \'e-ləs\ Alexander John 1814–1890 orig. surname *Sharpe* Eng. philologist; first in England to develop phonetic science

El·lis (Henry) Have·lock \'hav-,läk, -lək\ 1859–1939 Eng. psychol. & writer; produced 7-volume series *Studies in the Psychology of Sex* (1897–1928), etc.

El·li·son \'e-lə-sən\ Ralph Waldo 1914–1994 Am. writer; best known for novel *Invisible Man* (1952)

Ells·worth \'elz-(,)wərth\ Lincoln 1880–1951 Am. explorer; led first transarctic (1926) and transantarctic (1935) air crossings; on Wilkens'transarctic submarine expedition (1931)

Ellsworth Oliver 1745–1807 Am. jurist; chief justice U.S. Supreme Court (1796–1800); co-author (with Roger Sherman) of Connecticut Compromise (1787), concerning representation in two houses of Congress

El·man \'el-mən\ Mi·scha \'mē-shə\ 1891–1967 Am. (Ukraine‐born) violinist; noted for virtuosity and warm tone

El·phin·stone \'el-fən-,stōn, *chiefly Brit* -stən\ Mount·stu·art \maùnt-'st(y)ü-ərt\ 1779–1859 Brit. statesman in India; organized Territory of Poona; governor of Bombay (1819–27)

Elphinstone William 1431–1514 Scot. bishop & statesman; founded King's Coll. (1494); facilitated introduction of first printing press into Scotland (1507)

El·yot \'e-lē-ət, 'el-yət\ Sir Thomas 1490?–1546 Eng. scholar & diplomat; championed increased use of English language; wrote treatise on education (1531), first Latin-English dictionary (1538)

El·y·tis \'e-lē-(,)tēs\ Odysseus 1911–   *pseudonym of Odysseus Alepoudhelis* Greek poet; awarded 1979 Nobel prize for literature for his poems, including *To axion esti* (1959)

El·ze·vir *or* **El·ze·vier** \'el-zə-,vir\ family of Du. printers including esp. Lodewijk *or* Louis 1546?–1617, his son Bonaventura 1583–1652, & his grandson Abraham 1592–1652

Em·er·son \'e-mər-sən\ Ralph Waldo 1803–1882 Am. essayist & poet; developed Transcendental philosophy, first delineated in *Nature* (1836); published two vols. of *Essays* (1841, 1844), including "Self-Reliance" (1841) — **Em·er·so·nian** \,e-mər-'sō-nē-ən, -nyən\ *adj*

Em·met \'e-mət\ Robert 1778–1803 Irish nationalist & rebel; led unsuccessful uprising (1803)

Em·ped·o·cles \em-'pe-də-,klēz\ *ca* 490–430 B.C. Greek philos. & statesman; disciple of Parmenides; proposed that physical world was comprised of four elements; reputed founder of rhetoric

Endara (Galimany) \en-'där-ə-,gä-lē-'mä-nē\ Guillermo 1936–   pres. of Panama (1989–94)

En·de·cott *or* **En·di·cott** \'en-di-kət, -də-,kät\ John 1588–1665 colonial gov. of Massachusetts (1644, 1649, 1651–53, 1655–64)

En·ders \'en-dərz\ John Franklin 1897–1985 Am. bacteriol.; awarded (with Thomas H. Weller and Frederick C. Robbins) 1954 Nobel prize for physiology or medicine for discovering a simple method of growing polio virus in test tubes

Enes·cu \ə-'nes-(,)kü\ Gheorghe *or* George *Fr* **Enes·co** \-(,)kō\ Georges 1881–1955 Romanian composer; composed opera *Oedipe* (1936), piano sonatas, chamber works, symphonies, etc.

Eng·els \'eŋ-gəlz, -əlz, *G* 'eŋ-əls\ Friedrich 1820–1895 Ger. socialist; with Karl Marx, published *The Communist Manifesto* (1848); completed vols. 2, 3 of *Das Kapital* after Marx's death

En·ver Pa·şa \en-,ver-'pä-shə, -'pä-shə, -pə-'shä\ 1881–1922

Turk. soldier & polit.; led coup of Jan. 1913; member of ruling triumvirate and min. of war (1914–18); allied Turkey with Germany in WWI

Epam·i·non·das \i-,pa-mə-'nän-dəs\ *ca* 410–362 B.C. Theban gen. & statesman; defeated Spartans at Leuctra (371 B.C.); contained Spartan power by invading Peloponnesus (370–369)

Ep·ic·te·tus \e-pik-'tē-təs\ *ca* A.D. 55–*ca* 135 Greek Stoic philos. in Rome; philosophy known through *Discourses, Encheiridion* of pupil Flavius Arrian — **Ep·ic·te·tian** \-'tē-shən\ *adj*

Ep·i·cu·rus \e-pi-'kyur-əs\ 341–270 B.C. Greek philos.; taught that pleasure is the only good and the end of all morality, through a life of simplicity, prudence, honor, justice — **Ep·i·cu·re·an** \,e-pi-kyu-'rē-ən, -'kyur-ē-\ *adj or n*

Ep·stein \'ep-,stīn\ Sir Jacob 1880–1959 Brit. (Am.-born) sculptor; created controversy with nude *Strand Statues* (1907–08) and tomb of Oscar Wilde (1912); created allegorical works, large bronzes, bronze portraits, etc.

Eras·mus \i-'raz-məs\ Desiderius 1466?–1536 Du. scholar; edited Greek New Testament (1516); wrote *Encomium moriae* (1509, *The Praise of Folly*), etc.; viewed as leader in northern European renaissance — **Eras·mi·an** \-mē-ən\ *adj*

Er·a·tos·the·nes \,er-ə-'täs-thə-,nēz\ *ca* 276–*ca* 194 B.C. Greek astron.; headed library at Alexandria (from ca. 255); calculated circumference of Earth; devised "sieve of Eratosthenes" for finding prime numbers

Erck·mann—Cha·tri·an \'erk-,män-,shä-trē-'äⁿ, -,sha-\ joint pseud. of *Émile Erckmann* 1822–1899 & *Alexandre Chatrian* 1826–1890 Fr. authors; wrote *Waterloo* (1865), etc.

Er·hard \'er-härt\ Ludwig 1897–1977 chancellor of West Germany (1963–66)

Er·ics·son \'er-ik-sən\ John 1803–1889 Am. (Swed.-born) engineer & inventor; designed first warship with screw propellers (1844); designed and built ironclad *Monitor* (1862)

Erig·e·na \i-'ri-jə-nə\ John Sco·tus \'skō-təs\ *ca* 810–*ca* 877 Scot. (Irish-born) philos. & theol.; attempted to reconcile Neoplatonism and Christian creationism

Er·ik \'er-ik\ *the Red* 10th cent. Norw. navigator & explorer; explored southwest coast of Greenland (982–985), naming it "Greenland" to attract colonists

Eriksson Leif — see LEIF ERIKSSON

Er·lan·der \er-'län-dər\ Tage Frithiof 1901–1985 Swed. polit.

Er·lang·er \'ər-,laŋ-ər\ Joseph 1874–1965 Am. physiol.; awarded (with Herbert Gasser) 1944 Nobel prize for physiology or medicine for work on nerve fibers and the transmission of nerve impulses

Er·len·mey·er \'ər-lən-,mī(-ə)r, 'er-\ Richard August Carl Emil 1825–1909 Ger. chem.; helped develop modern structural notation; originated (1861) the conical gas flask named after him

Ernst \'ern(t)st, 'ərn(t)st\ Max 1891–1976 Ger. painter; cofounded Dadaist group in Cologne (1919); worked with collage, photomontage; helped found Surrealist group in Paris (1931)

Ernst Richard Robert 1933– Swiss chem.; awarded 1991 Nobel prize for chemistry for improvements in the use of nuclear magnetic resonance (NMR) to analyze chemicals

Er·skine \'ər-skən\ John 1879–1951 Am. educ. & writer; taught at

Columbia U. (1909–37); pres. of Juilliard School of Music (1928–37); wrote novel *The Private Life of Helen of Troy* (1925), etc.

Erskine of Car·nock \'kär-nək\ John 1695–1768 Scot. jurist; presented connected interpretation of Scots law in *Principles of the law of Scotland* (1754)

Er·vine \'ər-vən\ St. John \sänt-'jän, sənt-; 'sin-jən\ Greer 1883–1971 Irish dram. & nov.; wrote plays *Mixed Marriage* (1910), *Jane Clegg* (1913), *John Ferguson* (1915), etc., novels, biographies

Erz·ber·ger \'erts-,ber-gər\ Matthias 1875–1921 Ger. statesman; during WWI advocated negotiated peace; signed armistice ending war (1918); briefly chancellor (1919); assassinated by nationalist partisans

Es·a·ki \ə-'sä-kē\ Leo 1925– Jp. physicist; awarded (with Ivar Giaever and Brian Josephson) 1973 Nobel prize for physics for discoveries regarding semi- and superconductor materials

Esch·er \'e-shər, 'es-kər\ Maurits Cornelis 1898–1972 Du. graphic artist; known for lithographs and woodcuts incorporating illusions, transformations, geometric distortions, etc.

Esh·kol \esh-'kōl\ Levi 1895–1969 prime min. of Israel (1963–69)

Es·par·te·ro \,es-pər-'ter-(,)ō\ Baldomero 1793–1879 Conde *de Luchana* Span. gen. & statesman; pres. of provisional govt. (1840–41) and regent (1841–43); prime min. (1854–56)

Es·po·si·to \,es-pə-'zē-(,)tō\ Philip Anthony 1942– Am. (Canad.-born) hockey player; played with Chicago Black Hawks (1963–67), Boston Bruins (1967–75), N.Y. Rangers (1975–78)

Es·qui·vel \,ä-skē-'vel\ Adolfo Pérez 1931– Argentine sculptor and dissident; awarded 1980 Nobel prize for peace for his role in promoting human rights

Es·sen \'e-sᵊn\ Count Hans Henrik von 1755–1824 Swed. field marshal & statesman; commanded army sent against Norway; gov. of Norway (1814–16)

Essex 2d Earl of — see DEVEREUX

Es·taing, d' \des-taⁿ\ Comte Jean-Baptiste-Charles-Henri-Hector 1729–1794 Fr. admiral; commanded first French squadron sent to aid American Revolution (1778)

Este \'es-(,)tā\ Ital. princely family beginning with *Alberto Az·zo II* \'äd-(,)zō\ 996–1097 & ending with *Er·co·le III* \'er-kə-,lā\ *Rinaldo* 1727–1803

Es·ter·ha·zy \'es-tər-,hä-zē\ Marie-Charles-Ferdinand-Walsin 1847–1923 Fr. army officer; confessed (1899) that as German spy he had forged the chief piece of evidence against Dreyfus

Es·tienne \ä-'tyen\ or **Étienne** Fr. family of printers & booksellers including esp.: Henri I *ca* 1470–1520; his son Robert 1503–1559; & Robert's son Henri II 1528–1598; known for their editions of Greek and Latin classics

Es·tra·da Pal·ma \ä-'strä-thə-'päl-mə\ Tomás 1835–1908; Cuban revolutionary; in exile in Honduras and U.S. (1878–1902); 1st pres. of Cuba (1902–06)

Ethelbert — see AETHELBERHT

Ethelred — see AETHELRED

Eth·er·ege \'e-th(ə-)rij\ Sir George 1635?–1692 Eng. dram.; began Restoration comedy with *Love in a Tub* (1664), *The Man of the Mode* (1676), etc.

Euck·en \\'òi-kən\\ Rudolf Christoph 1846–1926 Ger. philos.; wrote works on philosophy, including Aristotle, religion, his own ethical activism; awarded 1908 Nobel prize for literature for his writings

Eu·clid \\'yü-kləd\\ *fl ca* 300 B.C. Greek geometer; founded a school in Alexandria; wrote *Stoicheia (Elements)*, which remained definitive source of geometrical reasoning and methods until 19th cent. — **Eu·clid·e·an** *also* **Eu·clid·i·an** \\yü-'kli-dē-ən\\ *adj*

Eu·gene \\yü-'jēn, 'yü-,\\ *F* œ̄-zhen\\ 1663–1736 *François-Eugène de Savoie-Carignan* prince of Savoy & Austrian gen.; fought in Italy in War of Spanish Succession (1701–03), etc.; viewed as one of history's greatest generals

Eu·gé·nie \\'yü-jə-,nē; yü-'jā-nē, -'jē-; *F* œ̄-zhā-nē\\ 1826–1920 *Eugénia Maria de Montijo de Guzmán; wife of Napoleon III* empress of the French (1853–71); influenced husband in policies toward church, opposition to liberal ideas, foreign policy

Eu·ler \\'òi-lər\\ Leonhard 1707–1783 Swiss math. & physicist; made contributions in geometry, calculus, number theory; developed problem-solving methods in astronomy, applications of mathematics in technology

Eu·ler–Chel·pin \\'òi-lər-'kel-pən\\ Hans Karl August Simon von 1873–1964 Swed. (Ger.-born) chem.; awarded (with Arthur Harden) 1929 Nobel prize for chemistry for research on the fermentation of sugar and coenzyme action

Eu·rip·i·des \\yú-'ri-pə-,dēz\\ *ca* 484–406 B.C. Greek dram.; with Aeschylus and Sophocles, greatest of Greek tragic poets; extant plays include *Medea, Hippolytus, Bacchae,* etc. — **Eu·rip·i·de·an** \\-,ri-pə-'dē-ən\\ *adj*

Eus·den \\'yüz-dən\\ Laurence 1688–1730 Eng. poet; poet laureate (1718–30); object of Pope's satire; "L.E." of Pope and Swift's treatise on bathos

Eu·se·bi·us of Caesarea \\yü-'sē-bē-əs\\ *ca* 260–*ca* 339 theol. & church hist.; wrote a history of the church to 324, an epitome of universal history to 303, etc.

Eu·sta·chio \\eü-'stä-kē-,ō\\ Bartolomeo 1520–1574 *L. Eu·sta·chius* \\yü-'stā-kē-əs, -'stä-sh(ē-)əs\\ Ital. anatomist; a founder of modern anatomy; described Eustachian tube in the ear

Ev·ans \\'e-vənz\\ Sir Arthur John 1851–1941 Eng. archaeol.; excavated prehistoric palace of Knossos on Crete; named culture Minoan; published *The Palace of Minos* (1921–36), etc.

Evans Herbert McLean 1882–1971 Am. anatomist & embryologist; discovered 48 chromosomes in humans (1918) and vitamin E (1922); investigated pituitary hormones

Evans Maurice 1901–1929 Am. (Eng.-born) actor; appeared mainly in Shakespeare, Shaw, other classics

Evans Rudulph 1878–1960 Am. sculptor; created sculpture of Thomas Jefferson for Jefferson Memorial

Evans Walker 1903–1975 Am. photographer; known esp. for architectural photographs and portrayal of Great Depression, as in *Let Us Now Praise Famous Men* (with James Agee, 1941)

Ev·arts \\'e-vərts\\ William Maxwell 1818–1901 Am. lawyer & statesman; chief defense counsel for Andrew Johnson in impeachment proceedings (1868); led movements for law reform in New York against "Tweed Ring" etc.

Ev·att \'e-vət\ Herbert Vere 1894–1965 Austral. jurist & statesman; pres. of U.N. General Assembly (1948)

Eve·lyn \'ēv-lən, 'ev-\ John 1620–1706 Eng. diarist; recorded his travels and contemporary events in his *Diary* (1640–1706, pub. 1818)

Ev·er·ett \'ev-rət, 'e-və-\ Edward 1794–1865 Am. clergyman, orator, & statesman; gov. of Massachusetts (1836–40); min. to Great Britain (1841–45); pres. of Harvard (1846–49), etc.; brilliant orator

Ev·ert \'e-vərt\ Christine Marie 1954–   Am. tennis player; won total of 18 Grand Slam titles between 1975 and 1986; including U.S. Open, Wimbledon, French Open

Ewald \'ī-,väl\ Johannes 1743–1781 Dan. poet & dram.; wrote *Rolf Krage* (1770), opera *Fiskerne* (1779) containing Danish national anthem, etc.; drew on national myths and legends

Ew·ell \'yü-əl\ Richard Stoddert 1817–1872 Am. Confed. gen.; under "Stonewall" Jackson in Shenandoah Valley campaign; succeeded to his command and cleared Union forces from the valley

Ew·ing \'yü-iŋ\ Patrick Aloysius 1962–   Am. (Jamaican-born) basketball player; played with N.Y. Knickerbockers (1985–   )

Eyck, van \van-'īk\ Hubert *or* Huybrecht *ca* 1370–1426 & his bro. Jan before 1395–1441 Flem. painters; founders of Flemish school; reputed originators of oil painting with drying varnish; Jan helped develop techniques of light, texture, etc., to produce new realism

Eze·kiel \i-'zēk-yəl\ 6th cent. B.C. Hebrew priest & prophet; subject and author, in part, of Old Testament book of Ezekiel

Ezekiel Moses Jacob 1844–1917 Am. sculptor; works include *Virginia Mourning Her Dead*, Lexington, Va.; monument to the Confederate dead, Arlington National Cemetery

Ez·ra \'ez-rə\ 5th cent. B.C. Hebrew scribe, priest & reformer; instituted many reforms of Judaism based on Pentateuchal law

F

Fa·bio·la \,fa-bē-'ō-lə, fə-'byō-\ 1928–   *queen of King Baudouin I of Belgium*

Fa·bi·us \'fā-bē-əs\ *d* 203 B.C. *Quintus Fabius Maximus Verrucosus Cunc·ta·tor* \,kəŋk-'tā-tər\ Rom. gen. against Hannibal; used strategy of harassing enemy while avoiding decisive conflict

Fa·bre \fäbr°\ Jean-Henri 1823–1915 Fr. entomologist; studied habits of insects, spiders, etc., by direct observation; work cited by Darwin

Fad·den \'fa-d°n\ Sir Arthur William 1895–1973 Austral. statesman; prime min. (1941) and acting prime min. on ten other occasions

Fahd \'fäd\ 1923–   *Fahd ibn 'Abd al-'Azīz as-Sa'ūd* king of Saudi Arabia (1982–   )

Fah·ren·heit \'far-ən-,hīt, 'fär-\ Daniel Gabriel 1686–1736 Ger. physicist; invented alcohol thermometer (1709), mercury thermometer (1714); introduced Fahrenheit scale

Fair·banks \\'far-ˌbaŋ(k)s, 'fer-\ Charles Warren 1852–1918 Am. lawyer & polit.; vice pres. of U.S. (1905–09)

Fairbanks Douglas Elton 1883–1939 Am. actor; starred in films *The Mark of Zorro* (1920), *The Three Musketeers* (1921), *Robin Hood* (1922), etc.

Fair·child \\'far-ˌchīld, 'fer-\ David Grandison 1869–1954 Am. botanist; supervised introduction of thousands of plants into U.S.

Fair·fax \\'far-ˌfaks, 'fer-\ Baron Thomas 1612–1671 Eng. gen.; commander in chief Parliamentary forces (1645–50); defeated Charles I at Naseby (1645) and Royalist forces at Maidstone (1647)

Fairfax Baron Thomas 1692–1782 proprietor in Virginia; employed George Washington as surveyor in Shenandoah Valley (1748)

Fai·sal \\'fī-səl, 'fā-\ *ca* 1906–1975 king of Saudi Arabia (1964–75)

Fai·sal I *Ar* **Fay·sal** \\'fī-səl, 'fā-\ 1885–1933; leader of Arab revolt against Ottoman rule (1916); with British captured Jerusalem (1917), Damascus (1918); king of Syria (1920), of Iraq (1921–1933)

Faisal II *Ar* **Fay·sal** 1935–1958 king of Iraq (1939–58); under regency (1939–53); executed during overthrow of monarchy

Fa·lier \fal-'yer\ *or* **Fa·lie·ro** \-(ˌ)ō\ Marino 1274–1355 doge of Venice (1354–55); executed for conspiracy to murder Venetian patricians and make himself prince; story often dramatized

Fal·ken·hau·sen \\'fäl-kən-ˌhau̇-z°n, 'fal-\ Ludwig 1844–1936 Freiherr *von* Falkenhausen Ger. gen.; served in Austro-Prussian War (1866), Franco-Prussian War (1870–71), WWI (1914–18)

Fal·ken·hayn \\'fäl-kən-ˌhīn, 'fal-\ Erich *von* 1861–1922 Ger. gen.; helped plan offensives against Russia, Serbia, Verdun (1914–16)

Falkner William — see FAULKNER

Fal·la \\'fä-yə, 'fäl-\ Manuel de 1876–1946 Span. composer; composed operas, ballets *El amor brujo* (1915), *El sombrero de tres picos* (1919), suite *Noches èn los jardines de España* (1916), etc.

Fal·lières \fal-'yer\ Clément-Armand 1841–1931 Fr. statesman; pres. of France (1906–13)

Fal·well \\'fȯl-ˌwel, -wəl\ Jerry L. 1933–   Am. clergyman; ordained Baptist minister; founder and pres. Moral Majority Inc./Liberty Federation (1979–89)

Fan·euil \\'fan-yəl, 'fa-n°l, 'fan-yə-wəl\ Peter 1700–1743 Am. merchant; amassed fortune in Boston and gave city building since known as Faneuil Hall

Far·a·day \\'far-ə-ˌdā, -dē\ Michael 1791–1867 Eng. chem. & physicist; first to liquefy chlorine, etc.; discovered electromagnetic rotation (1821), and induction (1831), laws of electrolysis (1833)

Fa·ri·na \fə-'rē-nə\ Salvatore 1846–1918 Ital. nov.; wrote *Mio figlio* (1877, *My Son*), *Il Signor Io* (1882), etc.

Far·ley \\'fär-lē\ James Aloysius 1888–1976 Am. polit.; played key role in F.D. Roosevelt's 1932 and 1936 presidential campaigns

Far·man \\'fär-ˌmäⁿ, 'fär-mən\ Henri 1874–1958 & his bro. Maurice 1877–1964 Fr. pioneer aviators and airplane manufacturers; built first long-distance passenger plane (1917) for London-Paris runs

Far·mer \\'fär-mər\ Fannie Merritt 1857–1915 Am. cookery expert; established Miss Farmer's School of Cookery (1902) to train housewives; edited *The Boston Cooking School Cookbook* (1896)

Farmer James Leonard 1920–   Am. civil rights leader; founded the Committee on Racial Equality (CORE, 1942), a loose coalition of civil rights groups

Far·ne·se \fär-'nā-zē, -sē\ Alessandro 1545–1592 Duke of *Parma* Ital. gen. in Span. service; responsible for maintaining Spanish control in Netherlands

Fa·rouk I \fə-'rük\ *Ar* **Fā·rūq al–Aw·wal** \fär-'ük-al-'a-wal\ 1920–1965 king of Egypt (1936–52; abdicated)

Far·quhar \'fär-kər, -kwər\ George 1678–1707 Brit. dram.; wrote comedies *The Constant Couple* (1700), *The Beaux' Strategem* (1707), etc.

Far·ra·gut \'far-ə-gət\ David Glasgow 1801–1870 Am. admiral; commander in Union navy during Civil War; took control of Mobile Bay, running blockade of "torpedoes" (i.e., mines), about which he reputedly said, "Damn the torpedoes! Full speed ahead"

Far·rar \'far-ər\ Frederic William 1831–1903 Eng. clergyman & writer; dean of Canterbury (1895–1903); wrote novels *Eric* (1858), *St. Winifred's* (1862); also wrote *Life of Christ* (1874), etc.

Far·rar \fə-'rär\ Geraldine 1882–1967 Am. soprano; member of Metropolitan Opera, N.Y. (1906–22); roles included Carmen, Madame Butterfly, Manon, Mignon, Tosca, etc.

Far·rell \'far-əl, 'fer-\ Eileen 1920–   Am. soprano; sang with N.Y. Philharmonic Orchestra (1960); made debut with Metropolitan Opera (1960) in Gluck's *Alcestis*

Farrell James Thomas 1904–1979 Am. nov.; wrote about lower middle class Irish life in Chicago, including *Studs Lonigan* trilogy (1932-34), etc.

Farrell Suzanne 1945–   Am. dancer; with New York City Ballet, Maurice Bejart's Ballet of the 20th Century; starred in works created by Balanchine, including *Union Jack* (1976)

Fa·ruk *var of* FAROUK

Fāt·i·mah \fa-tə-mə\ *ca* 606–633 *az-Zahrā* ('Shining One') dau. of Muhammad; source of Fāṭimid dynasty of northern Africa

Faulk·ner \'fók-nər\ William Cuthbert 1897–1962 orig. *Falkner* Am. nov.; wrote *The Sound and the Fury* (1929), *As I Lay Dying* (1930), *Light in August* (1932), etc.; awarded 1949 Nobel prize for literature — **Faulk·ner·ian** \fók-'nir-ē-ən, -'ner-\ *adj*

Faure \'fór, 'for\ François-Félix 1841–1899 Fr. statesman; pres. of France (1895–99); term marked by Fashoda conflict with Britain in the Sudan (1898), rapprochement with Russia

Fau·ré \fó-'rā\ Gabriel-Urbain 1845–1924 Fr. composer; composed nocturnes, barcaroles, impromptus for piano, chamber music, incidental music for plays

Faus·ta \'fö-stə, 'faú-\ 289–326 *Flavia Maximiana Fausta; wife of Constantine the Great* Rom. empress

Fawkes \'fóks\ Guy 1570–1606 Eng. conspirator; involved in Gunpowder Plot (1604–05) to blow up Houses of Parliament to avenge laws against Catholics

Fech·ner \'fek-nər, 'feḵ-\ Gustav Theodor 1801–1887 Ger. physicist & psychol.; a founder of psychophysics, the study of the relationship between sensations and stimuli

Feif·fer \'fī-fər\ Jules 1929–   Am. cartoonist and writer; known for satirical comment on contemporary mores; also wrote revues, plays, screenplays, novels

Fei·ning·er \'fī-niŋ-ər\ Lyonel Charles Adrian 1871–1956 Am. painter; influenced by Cubism; painted architectural subjects, townscapes, seascapes, sailing ships, etc.

Feke \'fēk\ Robert *ca* 1705–*ca* 1750 Am. painter; known for portraits of leading citizens, including *The Bowdoin Family* (ca. 1749)

Fel·li·ni \fə-'lē-nē\ Federico 1920–1993 Ital. film director; made highly individual films from his own scripts, including *La strada* (1954), *Amarcord* (1973), *La dolce vita* (1960), etc. — **Fel·li·ni·esque** \-,lē-nē-'esk\ *adj*

Fell·tham \'fel-thəm\ Owen 1602?–1668 Eng. writer; wrote collections of essays *Resolves Divine, Morall and Politicall* (1623), etc.

Fé·ne·lon \,fā-n°l-'ō⁾n, fen-'lō⁾n\ François de Salignac de La Mothe- 1651–1715 Fr. prelate & writer; wrote *Traité de L'education des filles* (1687), for liberalization of women's education; wrote *Les Aventures de Telemaque* (1699), etc.

Feng Yü–hsiang \'fəŋ-'yü-shē-'äŋ\ 1882–1948 Chin. gen.; "the Christian general"; initially supported Kuomintang and Chiang Kai-shek, later opposed them; defeated, driven into exile (1930)

Fer·ber \'fər-bər\ Edna 1887–1968 Am. writer; wrote novels and short stories, including *So Big* (1924, Pulitzer prize), *Show Boat* (1926), *Giant* (1952), etc., plays (with George S. Kaufman) *Dinner at Eight* (1932), *Stage Door* (1936), etc.

Fer·di·nand I \'fər-d°n-,and\ 1503–1564 Holy Rom. emp. (1558–64); negotiated uneasy peace with Turks (1562) by agreeing to pay tribute for Austria's share of Hungary

Ferdinand II 1578–1637 king of Bohemia (1617–19; 1620–27) & of Hungary (1618–25); Holy Rom. emp. (1619–37); championed Catholic Counter-Reformation; waged war against Protestants Thirty Years' War; signed Peace of Prague (1635)

Ferdinand III 1608–1657 king of Hungary (1625–47); Holy Rom. emp. (1637–57); signed Peace of Westphalia (1648) ending Thirty Years'War

Ferdinand I 1861–1948 king of Bulgaria (1908–18); invaded Serbia (1915) as ally of Central Powers in World War I; forced to abdicate

Ferdinand I 1016 (or 1018)–1065 *the Great* king of Castile (1035–65); of León (1037–65); reclaimed territory from Moors (1058–65); established power over Toledo, Saragossa, Seville

Ferdinand II of Aragon *or* **V** of Castile 1452–1516 *the Catholic; husband of Isabella I* king of Castile (1474–1504); of Aragon (1479–1516); of Naples (1504–16); founder of the Span. monarchy; established Inquisition (1478); warred with Moors (1482–92), conquering Granada (1492); expelled Jews (1492); aided Columbus' voyages to Americas

Ferdinand VII 1784–1833 king of Spain (1808; 1814–33); imprisoned by Napoléon (1808–14); during his reign, Spain lost all American colonies except Cuba, lost power in Europe

Fer·mat \fer-'mä\ Pierre de 1601–1665 Fr. math.; founder of modern theory of numbers, inventor of differential calculus and (with Pascal) of theory of probability; discovered analytic geometry (independent of Descartes); discovered Fermat's last theorem

Fer·mi \'fer-(,)mē\ Enrico 1901–1954 Am. (Ital.-born) physicist; with Manhattan Project (1942–45); awarded 1938 Nobel prize for physics for discovery of neutron-induced nuclear reactions (1934–37); directed first controlled nuclear reaction (1942)

Fer·nán·dez \fər-'nan-,dez\ Juan *ca* 1536–*ca* 1604 Span. navigator; discovered (1563–74) Juan Fernandez Islands

Fernández de Cór·do·ba \-thä-'kȯr-də-bə, -və\ Gon·za·lo \gȯn-'zä-lō\ 1453–1515 *El Gran Capitán* Span. soldier & statesman; renowned for military exploits in Italy (1495–1503)

Fer·re·ro \fə-'rer-(,)ō\ Guglielmo 1871–1943 Ital. hist. & author; wrote *Grandezza e decadenza di Roma* (1902–1907), *La ruine de la civilisation antique* (1921), etc.

Fes·sen·den \'fe-sᵊn-dən\ William Pitt 1806–1869 Am. polit.; a founder of the Republican party (1856); secy. of the treasury (1864–65)

Fes·tus \'fes-təs\ Porcius *d ca* A.D. 62 Rom. procurator of Judea (58 or 60–62); St. Paul made his "appeal unto Caesar" before him

Feucht·wang·er \'fȯikt-,väŋ-ər, 'fȯikt-\ Li·on \'lē-,ȯn\ 1884–1958 Ger. nov. & dram.; wrote novels *Josephus-Trilogie* (1932–45), *Der falsche Nero* (1936), *Jefta und sein Tochter* (1957), etc.

Feuil·let \,fə-'yā\ Octave 1821–1890 Fr. nov. & dram.; wrote novels *La petite comtesse* (1857), *Monsieur de Camours* (1867), *La Morte* (1886), etc.; plays *Le Sphinx* (1874), etc.

Feyn·man \'fīn-mən\ Richard Phillips 1918–1988 Am. physicist; awarded (with Shinichiro Tomonaga and Julian S. Schwinger) 1965 Nobel prize for physics for basic work in quantum electrodynamics

Fi·bi·ger \'fē-bē-gər\ Johannes Andreas Grib 1867–1928 Dan. pathologist; awarded 1926 Nobel prize in physiology or medicine for discovery of a parasite that causes cancer

Fich·te \'fik-tə, 'fik-\ Johann Gottlieb 1762–1814 Ger. philos.; espoused system of transcendental idealism, setting forth a perfected Kantian system — **Fich·te·an** \-tē-ən\ *adj*

Fied·ler \'fēd-lər\ Arthur 1894–1979 Am. conductor; founded free outdoor Esplanade Concerts in Boston (1929); conducted Boston Pops Orchestra (1930–79)

Field \'fē(ə)ld\ Cyrus West 1819–1892 Am. financier; chiefly responsible for laying of first submarine telegraph cable from America to Europe (1887–66)

Field Eugene 1850–1895 Am. poet & journalist; poems include "Wynken, Blynken, and Nod" and "Little Boy Blue"

Field Marshall 1834–1906 Am. merchant; developed largest wholesale and retail drygoods establishment in world; gave land for U. of Chicago, funds for Field Museum of Natural History

Field·ing \'fē(ə)l-diŋ\ Henry 1707–1754 Eng. nov.; wrote realistic novels *Joseph Andrews* (1742), *Tom Jones* (1749), *Amelia* (1751), etc., parody *Shamela* (1741)

Fields \'fē(ə)l(d)z\ Dorothy 1905–1974 Am. songwriter; wrote lyrics for songs "On the Sunny Side of the Street," "I'm in the Mood for Love," etc. and for Broadway musicals

Fields \'fē(ə)ldz\ W.C. 1880–1946 orig. *William Claude Dukenfield* Am. actor; starred in films *David Copperfield* (1935), *The Bank Dick* (1940), *My Little Chickadee* (1940), etc.

Figl \'fē-gəl\ Leopold 1902–1965 Austrian polit.; president of National Assembly (1959–62)

Fi·guei·re·do \,fē-ge-'rā-(,)dü\ João Baptista de Oliveira 1918– pres. of Brazil (1979–85)

Fi·gue·roa \,fē-gə-'rō-ə\ Francisco de *ca* 1536–*ca* 1620 Span. poet; master of blank verse; wrote an eclogue *Tirsi*, sonnets, elegies, canzoni

Fill·more \'fil-,mōr, -,mȯr\ Millard 1800–1874 13th pres. of the U.S. (1850–53); supported compromise on slavery issue; signed Fugitive Slave Law; encouraged expansion in the Pacific; sent Matthew Perry to Japan (1853)

Fin·lay \fin-'lī\ Carlos Juan 1833–1915 Cuban physician & biol.; identified mosquito as transmitter of yellow fever (1881)

Finn·bo·ga·dot·tir \'fin-,bō-gə-,dȯ·tər\ Vigdis 1930–   pres. of Iceland (1980–   ); first woman in history to be elected head of state

Fin·sen \'fin(t)-sən\ Niels Ryberg 1860–1904 Dan. physician; awarded 1903 Nobel prize for physics for treating diseases, esp. lupus vulgaris, with concentrated light rays

Fir·bank \'fər-,baŋk\ (Arthur Annesley) Ronald 1886–1926 Eng. author; wrote comic novels of manners including *Vainglory* (1915), *Inclinations* (1916), *The Flower Beneath the Foot* (1923), etc. — **Fir·bank·ian** \,fər-'baŋ-kē-ən\ *adj*

Fir·daw·sī *or* **Fer·dow·sī** \fər-'dau̇-sē, -'dȯ-\ *or* **Fir·du·si** \-'dü-\ *or* **Fir·dou·si** \-'dau̇-, -'dȯ-\ *ca* 935–*ca* 1020 (or 1026) orig. *Abū ol-Qāsem Mansūr* Pers. poet; wrote great epic, *Shah-nameh* (Book of Kings), first published 1010

Fire·stone \'fīr-,stōn\ Harvey Samuel 1868–1938 Am. industrialist; organized Firestone Tire & Rubber Co. (1900); pioneered manufacture of nonskid tire treads, low-pressure balloon tires, etc.

Fi·scher \'fi-shər\ Edmond Henri 1920–   Am. (Chin.-born of Fr. parents) biochem.; awarded (with Edwin Krebs) 1992 Nobel prize for physiology or medicine for discovering a chemical process in cells that is linked to cancer and to organ rejection

Fischer Emil 1852–1919 Ger. chem.; awarded 1902 Nobel prize for chemistry for synthesizing sugars, purine derivatives, and peptides

Fischer Ernst Otto 1918–   Ger. chem.; awarded (with Geoffrey Wilkinson) 1973 Nobel prize for chemistry for work on substances consisting of organic compounds and metal atoms

Fischer Hans 1881–1945 Ger. chem.; awarded 1930 Nobel prize for chemistry for studying the coloring matter of blood and leaves and for synthesizing hemin

Fi·scher \'fi-shər\ Bobby 1943–   *Robert James Fischer* Am. chess master; youngest player ever to attain rank of grand master (1958); first American to be Chess Champion of the World (1972)

Fi·scher–Dies·kau \'fi-shər-'dēs-,kau̇\ Dietrich 1925–   Ger. baritone; a foremost interpreter of German lieder; known for vast repertory including classic and modern operatic roles, choral works

Fish \'fish\ Hamilton 1808–1893 Am. statesman; U.S. secy. of state (1869–77); negotiated settlement of "Alabama Claims" (1871) and settlement from Spain for seizure of *Virginia* (1873)

Fish·bein \'fish-,bīn\ Morris 1889–1976 Am. physician & editor; editor (1924–49) *Journal of the American Medical Assn.;* wrote *Medical Follies* (1925), *Fads and Quackery in Healing* (1933), etc.

Fish·er \'fi-shər\ Dorothy 1879–1958 *Dorothea Frances* née *Canfield* \'kan-ˌfēld\ Am. nov.; wrote *The Squirrel-Cage* (1912), *The Bent Twig* (1915), *The Deepening Stream* (1930), etc.

Fisher Irving 1867–1947 Am. econ.; developed concept of relationship between changes in money supply and general level of prices

Fisher John Arbuthnot 1841–1920 1st Baron *Fisher of Kil·ver·stone* \'kil-vər-stən\ Brit. admiral; largely responsible for preparing British navy for efficient action in WWI

Fisher Mary Frances Kennedy 1908–1992 Am. writer; created the food essay, writing with style and wit about food as a cultural metaphor

Fiske \'fisk\ John 1842–1901 orig. *Edmund Fisk Green* Am. philos. & hist.; applied theory of evolution to his optimistic theory of inevitable historical progress

Fitch \'fich\ (William) Clyde 1865–1909 Am. dram.; excelled in society drama, including *Beau Brummel* (1890), etc.

Fitch John 1743–1798 Am. inventor; pioneer of steamboat transportation in U.S.; began steamboat service between Philadelphia and Burlington, N.J. (1787)

Fitch Val Logsdon 1923–　 Am. physicist; awarded (with James W. Cronin) 1980 Nobel prize for physics for research on subatomic particles

Fitz·ger·ald \fits-'jer-əld\ Ella 1918–　 Am. singer; top jazz and popular singer; hits include "A-tisket A-tasket" (1938), etc.; recorded "songbooks" of popular songs of American composers

Fitzgerald Francis Scott Key 1896–1940 Am. writer; chronicler of the Jazz Age; wrote novels *This Side of Paradise* (1920), *The Great Gatsby* (1925), *Tender Is the Night* (1934), etc.

FitzGerald Edward 1809–1883 Eng. poet & translator; best known for his *The Rubáiyát of Omar Khayyám* (1859)

FitzGerald Garret 1926–　 prime min. of Ireland (1981–87)

Fitz·her·bert \fits-'hər-bərt\ Maria Anne 1756–1837 née *Smythe*; *wife of George IV of England*

Flagg \'flag\ James Montgomery 1877–1960 Am. illustrator; created WWI recruiting poster of Uncle Sam saying "I Want You"

Flag·stad \'flag-ˌstad, *Norw* 'fläg-ˌstä\ Kir·sten \'kish-tən, 'kir-stən\ 1895–1962 Norw. soprano; best known for interpretation of Wagnerian roles, such as Sieglinde in *Die Walküre* (1935)

Fla·min·i·us \flə-'mi-nē-əs\ Gaius *d* 217 B.C. Rom. gen. & statesman; while censor built Circus Flaminius and Via Flamina from Rome to Ariminum (Rimini)

Flam·ma·rion \flə-ˌmar-ē-'ō̃\ (Nicolas-) Camille 1842–1925 Fr. astron. & writer; founded French Astronomical Society (1887); studied moon, Mars, double stars; popularized study of astronomy

Flan·a·gan \'fla-ni-gən\ Edward Joseph 1886–1948 Am. (Irishborn) R. C. priest & founder of Boys Town (1917) in Omaha

Flan·din \flä̃-da̅n\ Pierre-Étienne 1889–1958 Fr. polit.; premier (1934–35); min. of foreign affairs (1936, 1940–41 in Vichy regime)

Flau·bert \flō-'ber\ Gustave 1821–1880 Fr. nov.; pioneer and master of realist style of French literature; tried but acquitted on charges of immorality for *Madame Bovary* (1857); also wrote *La Tentation de Saint Antoine* (1874), *L'Education sentimentale* (1869), etc. — **Flau·ber·tian** \-'bər-shən, -'ber-tē-ən\ *adj*

Flax·man \\'flaks-mən\\ John 1755–1826 Eng. sculptor; leading Neoclassical artist in England; sculpted monuments of Nelson in St. Paul's, statue of Burns in Westminster Abbey, etc.

Fleet·wood \\'flēt-ˌwu̇d\\ Charles *d* 1692 Eng. gen.; supporter of Oliver Cromwell; a commander at Naseby (1645); fought at Dunbar (1650), Worcester (1651); helped depose Richard Cromwell (1659)

Flem·ing \\'fle-miŋ\\ Sir Alexander 1881–1955 Brit. bacteriol.; awarded (with Howard W. Florey and Ernst B. Chain) 1945 Nobel prize for physiology or medicine for discovering penicillin

Fleming Ian Lancaster 1908–1964 Brit. writer; wrote popular James Bond novels of espionage, including *Casino Royale* (1953), *From Russia with Love* (1957), *Goldfinger* (1959), etc.

Fleming Sir John Ambrose 1849–1945 Eng. electrical engineer; invented two-electrode radio rectifier (pat. 1904)

Fletch·er \\'fle-chər\\ John 1579–1625 Eng. dram.; collaborated with Francis Beaumont (ca. 1606–13) on ten comedies and tragedies, with Philip Massinger (1619–25), with Shakespeare on *Henry VIII* (1613), etc.

Fleu·ry \\ˌflər-'ē\\ André-Hercule de 1653–1743 Fr. cardinal & statesman; tutor of young Louis XV (1715); held influence over him (1715–43); virtually prime min. (1726–43)

Fleury Claude 1640–1723 Fr. ecclesiastical hist.; wrote *Histoire ecclésiastique* (1690–1720), first large history of the Catholic church (to 1414)

Flint \\'flint\\ Austin 1812–1886 Am. physician; popularized binaural stethoscope in U.S.; discovered Austin Flint heart murmur (1862); wrote classic *Treatise on the Principles and Practice of Medicine* (1866)

Flo·res \\'flȯr-ˌās, 'flȯr-\\ Juan José 1800–1864 Ecuadorian soldier; proclaimed Ecuadoran independence (1830); pres. of Ecuador (1830–35; 1839–45)

Flo·rey \\'flȯr-ē, 'flȯr-\\ Sir Howard Walter 1898–1968 Brit. pathologist; awarded (with Ernst B. Chain and Alexander Fleming) 1945 Nobel prize for physiology or medicine for developing use of penicillin as an antibiotic

Flo·rio \\'flȯr-ē-ˌō, 'flȯr-\\ John *ca* 1553–*ca* 1625 Eng. lexicographer & translator; compiled Italian-English dictionaries (1598), (1611); translated Montaigne's *Essays* (1603, rev. 1613)

Flo·ry \\'flȯr-ē, 'flȯr-\\ Paul John 1910–85 Am. chem.; awarded 1975 Nobel prize for chemistry for work in polymer chemistry

Flo·tow \\'flō-(ˌ)tō\\ Friedrich 1812–1883 Freiherr *von Flotow* Ger. composer; composed operas *Alessandro Stradella* (1844), *Martha* (1847), *L'Ombre* (1869), etc.

Foch \\'fȯsh, 'fäsh\\ Ferdinand 1851–1929 Fr. gen.; supreme commander of Allied armies (1918); marshal of France (from 1918); led Allied offensive to victory

Fo·gel \\'fō-gəl\\ Robert William 1926– Am. econ.; awarded (with Douglass C. North) 1993 Nobel prize for economics for work in economic history

Fo·kine \\'fȯ-ˌkēn, fȯ-'\\ Michel 1880–1942 Am (Russ.-born) choreographer; chief choreographer of Diaghilev's Ballets Russes (1909–14); created *L'Oiseau de feu* (1910) and *Petrushka* (1911)

Fok·ker \\'fä-kər, 'fō-\\ Anthony Herman Gerard 1890–1939 Am.

(Du.-born) aircraft designer & builder; made German pursuit planes during WWI, invented device making it possible to shoot through field of airplane propeller

Fol·ger \'fōl-jər\ Henry Clay 1857–1930 Am. bibliophile; collected great Shakespearean library; founded (1928) and endowed Folger Shakespeare Library, Washington, D.C., to house it

Fon·da \'fän-də\ Henry Jaynes 1905–1982 Am. actor; known for portrayals of honest, decent men in some 80 films, including *Young Mr. Lincoln* (1939), *Mister Roberts* (1955), *On Golden Pond* (1981, Academy Award)

Fon·tanne \fän-'tan, 'fän-,\ Lynn 1887?–1983 *wife of Alfred Lunt* Am. (Eng.-born) actress; from 1924, popular team with husband; known esp. for appearances in plays of Noel Coward

Fon·teyn \fän-'tān, 'fän-,\ Dame Margot 1919–1991 orig. *Margot Hook·ham* \'hu̇-kəm\ Eng. ballerina; one of the 20th century's greatest ballerinas; famed partner of Rudolf Nureyev in 1960s

Foote \'fu̇t\ Andrew Hull 1806–1863 Am. admiral; known esp. for service during Civil War

Foote \'fu̇t\ Horton 1916–   Am. playwright & screenwriter; works include play *The Trip to Bountiful* (1953, filmed 1985), films *To Kill A Mockingbird* (1962), *Tender Mercies* (1983), etc.

Foote Samuel 1720–1777 Eng. actor & playwright; plays include *The Knights* (1749), *The Minor* (1760), *The Nabob* (1772), etc.

Foote Shelby 1916–   Am. hist. & nov.; known for works about the Civil War and the American South; works include novel *Follow Me Down* (1950) and three-volume nonfiction *The Civil War: A Narrative* (1958–74)

Forbes–Rob·ert·son \'fȯrbz-'rä-bərt-sən\ Sir Johnston 1853–1937 Eng. actor; known as finest Hamlet of his time; appeared in *Othello* and *Hamlet* (1898), Shaw's *Caesar and Cleopatra* (1906), etc.

Ford \'fȯrd, 'fȯrd\ Ford Mad·ox \'ma-dəks\ 1873–1939 orig. *Huef·fer* \'hu̇-fər; 'hwe-fər, 'we-\ Eng. author; collaborated with Joseph Conrad in novels *The Inheritors* (1901), *Romance* (1903); wrote *The Good Soldier* (1915), tetralogy *Parade's End* (1924–26)

Ford Gerald Rudolph 1913–   Am. polit.; 38th pres. of the U.S. (1974–77); granted full pardon to Nixon (1974)

Ford Henry 1863–1947 Am. automobile manuf.; formed Ford Motor Co. (1903); used assembly-line method for production of Model T Ford (1913); introduced Model A (1928), V8 engine (1932)

Ford John 1586?–1639 Eng. dram.; wrote *'Tis Pity She's a Whore* (1633), *The Broken Heart* (1633), etc.

Ford John 1895–1973 orig. *Sean Aloysius O'Fearna* Am. film director; known esp. for westerns, including *Stagecoach* (1939), *My Darling Clementine* (1946), *The Searchers* (1956)

Fore·man \'fōr-mən, 'fȯr-\ George 1948–   Am. boxer; world heavyweight champion (1973–74, 1994–   ); oldest title holder in boxing history

For·es·ter \'fȯr-əs-tər, 'fär-\ Cecil Scott 1899–1966 Brit. writer; wrote *The African Queen* (1935), etc., and series of Horatio Hornblower novels

For·rest \'fȯr-əst, 'fär-\ Edwin 1806–1872 Am. actor; at height of success as Othello, Lear, Coriolanus, Richard III, etc.

Forrest Nathan Bedford 1821–1877 Am. Confed. gen.; fought at Shiloh, Chickamauga; massacred 300 blacks at surrender of Ft. Pillow, Tenn. (1864)

For·res·tal \ˈfȯr-əs-tᵊl, ˈfär-, -ˌtȯl\ James Vincent 1892–1949 Am. banker; 1st secy. of defense (1947–49)

Forss·mann \ˈfȯrs-ˌmän\ Werner Theodor Otto 1904–1979 Ger. surgeon; awarded (with Andre F. Cournand and Dickinson W. Richards, Jr.) 1956 Nobel prize for physiology or medicine for using a catheter to chart the interior of the heart

For·ster \ˈfȯr-stər\ Edward Morgan 1879–1970 Brit. nov.; wrote *A Room With a View* (1908), *Howard's End* (1910), *A Passage to India* (1924), etc., and criticism *Aspects of the Novel* (1927), essays — **For·ste·ri·an** \fȯr-ˈstir-ē-ən\ *adj*

For·syth \ˈfȯr-ˌsīth, fər-\ John 1780–1841 Am. statesman; U.S. min. to Spain (1819–23); gained Spanish king's ratification of treaty of 1819 ceding Florida to the U.S.; U.S. secy. of state (1834–41)

For·tas \ˈfȯr-təs\ Abe 1910–1982 Am. jurist; associate justice, U.S. Supreme Court (1965–69)

Fos·dick \ˈfäz-(ˌ)dik\ Harry Emerson 1878–1969 Am. clergyman; advocated liberal Protestant theology, pastoral counseling, etc.; wrote *The Second Mile* (1908), *As I See Religion* (1932), etc.

Fos·sey \ˈfȯ-sē, ˈfä-\ Dian 1932–1985 Am. ethologist; extensively studied and endeavored to save mountain gorillas of Rwanda

Fos·ter \ˈfȯs-tər, ˈfäs-\ Stephen Collins 1826–1864 Am. songwriter; wrote many minstrel songs, including "My Old Kentucky Home," "O Susanna," "Jeanie with the Light Brown Hair," etc.

Foster William Zebulon 1881–1961 Am. Communist; Communist party candidate for president of U.S. (1924, 1928, 1932)

Fou·cault \fü-ˈkō\ Jean-Bernard-Léon 1819–1868 Fr. physicist; measured the speed of light with extreme accuracy (1850); demonstrated the axial rotation of the earth with a pendulum (1851)

Fou·qué \fü-ˈkā\ Friedrich Heinrich Karl de la Motte \ˈmȯt\ 1777–1843 Freiherr *Fouqué* Ger. author; wrote often on chivalric themes; wrote *Undine* (1811), trilogy *Der Held des Nordens* (1808–10), modern version of Niebelung story

Fou·quet *or* **Fouc·quet** \fü-ˈkā\ Nicolas 1615–1680 Fr. govt. official; confidential agent of Cardinal Mazarin; superintendent of finance (from 1653); imprisoned for embezzlement

Fou·quier–Tin·ville \fü-kyä-taⁿ-ˈvēl\ Antoine-Quentin 1746–1795 Fr. polit.; public prosecutor of the Revolutionary Tribunal during Reign of Terror (1793–94)

Four·dri·nier \ˌfȯr-drə-ˈnir, ˌfȯr-; ˈfu̇r-ˈdri-nē-ər, fȯr-, fȯr-\ Henry 1766–1854 & his bro. Sealy *d* 1847 Eng. papermakers & inventors; invented (with Brian Donkin) machine for making a continuous sheet of paper from wood pulp

Fou·ri·er \ˈfu̇r-ē-ˌā\ (François-Marie-) Charles 1772–1837 Fr. sociol. & reformer; advocated reconstruction of society based on cooperative agricultural communities

Fowl·er \ˈfau̇-lər\ Henry Watson 1858–1933 Eng. lexicographer; wrote (with brother Francis George Fowler) *The King's English* (1906), *The Concise Oxford Dictionary of Current English* (1911)

Fowler William Alfred 1911–1995 Am. physicist; awarded (with Subrahmanyan Chandrasekhar) 1983 Nobel prize for physics for work on the evolution and death of stars

Fox \\'fäks\\ Charles James 1749–1806 Eng. statesman & orator; led opposition to coercive measures against American colonies, including tea duty (1774)

Fox George 1624–1691 Eng. preacher & founder of Society of Friends; preached supiority of God-given inspiration (inward light); made missionary journeys to North America, etc.

Fox Henry 1705–1774 1st Baron *Hol·land* \\'hä-lənd\\ Brit. statesman; carried Treaty of Paris (1763)

Foxe \\'fäks\\ John 1516–1587 Eng. martyrologist; fled reign of Queen Mary I (1554–59); wrote *Rerum in ecclesia gestarum . . . commentarii* (1559) in English as *The Book of Martyrs* (1563)

Foxe *or* **Fox** Richard *ca* 1448–1528 Eng. prelate & statesman; in service of Henry VII before and after his accession to English throne (1485); negotiated treaties, executed financial policies, etc.

Foyt \\'fȯit\\ Anthony Joseph Jr. 1935– Am. automobile racer; won Indianapolis 500 (1961, 1964, 1967, 1977), Le Mans (1967); won record seven national championships

Fra·go·nard \\,fra-gə-'när\\ Jean-Honoré 1732–1806 Fr. painter & engraver; moved from Rococo style and manner to Neoclassical

France \\'fran(t)s, fräs\\ Anatole 1844–1924 pseud. of *Jacques-Anatole-François Thibault* Fr. nov. & satirist; supported Alfred Dreyfus; expressed social and political concerns in play *Crainquebille* (1903), novels; awarded 1921 Nobel prize for literature

Francesca Piero della — SEE PIERO DELLA FRANCESCA

Francesca da Rimini — SEE POLENTA

Fran·cis I \\'fran(t)-səs\\ 1494–1547 king of France (1515–47); waged war against Holy League; began series of wars with Holy Roman Empire; reign marked by Renaissance in France

Francis II 1768–1835 last Holy Rom. emp. (1792–1806); emp. of Austria (as *Francis I*) 1804–35; guided by Metternich (1815–35) in policy of reaction; revived power of Roman Catholic church

Francis Fer·di·nand \\'fǝr-də-,nand, ,fer-dē-,nänt\\ 1863–1914 archduke of Austria; heir apparent to crown; assassinated (1914) by Serbian nationalist at Sarajevo, Bosnia, immediate cause of WWI

Francis Jo·seph I \\'jō-səf, 'yō-sef\\ 1830–1916 emp. of Austria (1848–1916); precipitated WWI with ultimatum to Serbia (1914)

Francis of Assisi Saint 1181(or 1182)–1226 in full *Francesco di Pietro di Bernardone* Ital. friar; founder of Franciscan order and order of Poor Clares; led movements to reform the church

Francis of Sales \\'sä(ə)lz\\ Saint 1567–1622 Fr. R. C. bishop of Geneva; helped found Visitation of Holy Mary (1610)

Franck \\'fräŋk\\ César Auguste 1822–1890 Fr. (Belg.-born) organist & composer; noted for strongly Romantic works, Symphony in D Minor (1889), *Variations symphoniques* (1885), etc.

Franck James 1882–1964 Am. (Ger.-born) physicist; awarded (with Gustav Hertz) 1925 Nobel prize for physics for stating laws on the collision of an electron with an atom

Francke \\'fräŋ-kə\\ Kuno 1855–1930 Am. (Ger.-born) hist. & educ.; founder, curator of Germanic Museum, Harvard (1903–17);

wrote *A History of German Literature as Determined by Social Forces* (1901), etc.

Fran·co \'frän-(,)kō, 'fr48\ Francisco 1892–1975 *Francisco Paulino Hermenegildo Teódulo Franco Bahamonde* Span. gen. & head of Span. state (1936–75); defeated Republican army in Spanish Civil War; ruled with dictatorial powers; noted anti-Communist

Frank \'fraŋk, 'fräŋk\ Anne 1929–1945 Ger.-born diarist during the Holocaust; wrote celebrated diary of her family's life of hiding in an Amsterdam attic for two years

Frank Ilya Mikhaylovich 1908–1990 Russ. physicist; awarded (with P. A. Cherenkov and I. Y. Tamm) the 1958 Nobel prize for physics for explaining the Cherenkov effect, that light is emitted by high-speed charged particles

Frank·en·thal·er \'fraŋ-kən-,tä-lər, -,thä-\ Helen 1928– Am. artist; abstract expressionist known for brilliantly colored canvas

Frank·furt·er \'fraŋk-fə(r)-tər, -,fər-\ Felix 1882–1965 Am. (Austrian-born) jurist; helped found American Civil Liberties Union (1920); associate justice, U.S. Supreme Court (1939–62); exponent of doctrine of judicial self-restraint

Frank·lin \'fraŋk-lən\ Aretha 1942– Am. gospel and blues singer; one of first African-American performers of "soul music" to achieve popularity with white audiences

Franklin Benjamin 1706–1790 Am. statesman & philos.; printer (from 1729) in Philadelphia; published *Poor Richards Almanack* (1732–57); helped found U. of Penna. (1751); invented Franklin stove, bifocal spectacles, lightning rod; helped draft Declaration of Independence, negotiate peace with Great Britain (1781, 1783)

Franklin Sir John 1786–1847 Eng. arctic explorer; led three expeditions into Arctic; on last expedition (1845–45), lost all members but proved existence of Northwest Passage

Franklin Rosalind Elsie 1920–1958 Eng. biophysicist; studied X-ray diffraction and helped bring about discovery (1953) of molecular structure of DNA

Franks \'fraŋks\ Oliver Shewell 1905–1992 *Baron Franks of Headington* Eng. philos. & diplomat; as chair of Falkland Islands Review Committee (1982) exonerated British of any negligence

Fra·ser \'frā-zər, -,zhər\ James Earle 1876–1953 Am. sculptor; executed busts of Ulysses S. Grant, Saint-Gaudens, Theodore Roosevelt, etc. and equestrian statue *The End of the Trail* (1896), etc.

Fraser (John) Malcolm 1930– prime min. of Australia (1975–83)

Fraser Peter 1884–1950 N.Z. statesman; prime min. (1940–49); proved strong leader during WWII; helped plan U.N. (1945)

Fraun·ho·fer \'fraún-,hō-fər\ Joseph von 1787–1826 Bavarian optician & physicist; observed and mapped dark lines (Fraunhofer lines) in solar spectrum; invented diffraction grating to measure wave lengths of light, etc.

Fra·zer \'frā-zər, -,zhər\ Sir James George 1854–1941 Scot. anthropol.; produced *The Golden Bough*, a study of cults, myths, rites, etc., their origins and importance

Fré·chette \frā-'shet\ Louis-Honoré 1839–1908 Canad. poet; author of patriotic poems in French, including *Mes loisirs*, *Les Oiseaux de niege*, *Les Fleurs boréales*, etc.

Fred·er·ick I \'fre-d(ə-)rik\ *ca* 1123–1190 *Frederick Bar·ba·ros·sa*

\,bär-bə-'rä-sə, -'rȯ-\ Holy Rom. emp. (1152–90); enlarged empire, advanced learning, maintained internal peace, encouraged development of towns, cities

Frederick II 1194–1250 Holy Rom. emp. (1215–50); king of Sicily (1198–1250); noted for his varied talents and learning; patron of literature and science

Frederick I 1657–1713 king of Prussia (1701–13); freed Prussia from imperial control, increased its territory, revenues, industry

Frederick II 1712–1786 *the Great* king of Prussia (1740–86); skillful administrator of economy; began codification of new law code; instituted social reforms; improved army

Frederick IX 1899–1972 king of Denmark (1947–72); encouraged Danish resistance to German occupation; provided for female succession to throne

Frederick Pauline 1906–1990 Am. journalist; trailblazing woman news correspondent for radio and television; gained prominence on television as NBC's U.N. correspondent (1953–74)

Frederick William 1620–1688 *the Great Elector* elector of Brandenburg (1640–88); greatly aided education, improved finances and commerce, developed strong army

Frederick William name of 4 kings of Prussia: **I** 1688–1740 (reigned 1713–40); spent most of reign improving kingdom internally; **II** 1744–1797 (reigned 1786–97); his court noted for cultural activities; expanded territory, issued religious edict and law code; **III** 1770–1840 (reigned 1797–1840); liberated Prussia from Napoléon and restored power; Prussia declined during last 25 years; **IV** 1795–1861 (reigned 1840–61); his conservative politics helped spark the Revolution of 1848

Free·man \'frē-mən\ Douglas Sou·thall \'saȯ-ˌthȯl, -ˌthȯl\ 1886–1953 Am. editor & hist.; author of *R.E. Lee, George Washington* (both Pulitzer prizes), etc.

Freeman Mary Eleanor 1852–1930 née *Wilkins* Am. writer; wrote novels chiefly of frustrated lives in New England villages, including novels *Pembroke*, etc., stories *Edgewater People*, etc.

Fre·ge \'frā-gə\ (Friedrich Ludwig) Gottlob 1848–1925 Ger. math. & philos.; founder of modern mathematical logic

Frei Ru·iz-Ta·gle \'frā-rü-ˈēs-ˈtä-glä\ Eduardo 1941–   pres. of Chile (1994–)

Fre·ling·huy·sen \'frē-liŋ-ˌhī-zᵊn\ Frederick Theodore 1817–1885 Am. statesman; U.S. senator (1866–69, 1871–77); secy. of state (1881–85); obtained Pearl Harbor as naval base

Fré·mont \'frē-ˌmänt\ John Charles 1813–1890 Am. gen. & explorer; mapped Oregon Trail, helped conquer California in Mexican War; one of first two senators from Calif. and first Republican presidential candidate (1856)

French \'french\ Daniel Chester 1850–1931 Am. sculptor; created *The Minute Man* (Concord, Mass.), the seated Lincoln in Lincoln Memorial, Washington, D.C.

Fre·neau \fri-'nō\ Philip Morin 1752–1832 Am. poet; known as the Poet of the American Revolution

Fres·co·bal·di \,fres-kə-'bäl-dē, -'bȯl-\ Girolamo 1583–1643 Ital. composer; strongly influenced German Baroque school; work characterized by dramatic inventiveness, chromaticism

Fres·nel \frä-'nel\ Augustin-Jean 1788–1827 Fr. physicist; instrumental in establishing the wave theory of light; pioneered in use of compound lenses in lighthouses

Freud \'froid\ Sigmund 1856–1939 Austrian neurol.; founder of psychoanalysis; developed theories based on repressed and forgotten memories; examined infantile sexuality and dreams; developed concept of id, ego, superego — **Freud·ian** \'froi-dē-ən\ adj or n

Frey·berg \'frī-,bȯrg\ 1st Baron 1889–1963 Bernard Cyril Freyberg N.Z. gen.; gov.-gen. of New Zealand (1946–52)

Frey·tag \'frī-,täk, -,täg\ Gustav 1816–1895 Ger. author; champion of German liberalism and middle class in plays, esp. comedies, and novels

Frick \'frik\ Henry Clay 1849–1919 Am. industrialist; important in formation of United States Steel Corp.; bequeathed art-filled home in New York City as public museum

Fried \'frēt, 'frēd\ Alfred Hermann 1864–1921 Austrian pacifist; founded German Peace Society (1892); awarded (with Tobias Asser) 1911 Nobel prize for peace

Frie·dan \fri-'dan, frē-\ Betty Naomi 1921–   née Goldstein Am. feminist; wrote The Feminine Mystique (1963), etc.; founded National Organization for Women (1966)

Fried·man \'frēd-mən\ Jerome Isaac 1930–   Am. physicist; awarded (with Henry Kendall and Richard Taylor) 1990 Nobel prize for physics for proving the existence of quarks

Friedman Milton 1912–   Am. econ.; awarded 1976 Nobel prize for economics for work in the fields of economic consumption, monetary history and theory, and prize stabilization policy

Frie·drich \'frē-drik\ Caspar David 1774–1840 Ger. painter; created vast land- and seascapes with sense of desolation; helped establish pessimism and the sublime as themes of German Romanticism; works include The Cross in the Mountains (1807), etc.

Frisch \'frish\ Karl von 1886–1982 Austrian zool.; awarded (with Nikolaas Tinbergen and Konrad Lorenz) 1973 Nobel prize for physiology or medicine for studies of animal behavior

Frisch Ragnar 1895–1973 Norw. econ.; awarded (with Jan Tinbergen) 1969 Nobel prize for economics for work on econometrics

Fro·bi·sher \'frō-bi-shər\ Sir Martin 1535?–1594 Eng. navigator; discovered Frobisher Bay while in search for Northwest Passage

Froe·bel or **Frö·bel** \'frä-bəl, 'frē-, 'frœ-\ Friedrich Wilhelm August 1782–1852 Ger. educ.; founded kindergarten system

Froh·man \'frō-mən\ Charles 1860–1915 Am. theater manager; leader among group known as The Theatrical Syndicate

Frois·sart \'froi-,särt, frwä-'sär\ Jean 1333?–ca 1405 Fr. chronicler; 4 vols. of Chroniques give information on period of Hundred Years' War, 1325–1400

Fromm \'frȯm, 'främ\ Erich 1900–1980 Am. (Ger.-born) psychoanalyst; explored influence of economic and social factors on human behavior; advocated use of psychoanalytic principles in solving social, cultural problems

Fron·di·zi \frän-'dē-zē, -sē\ Arturo 1908–1995 Argentine pres. (1958–62)

Fron·te·nac et Pal·lu·au \frōⁿ-tə-nák-ā-pá-lwȯ\ Comte de 1622–1698 Louis de Buade \'bwȧd\ Fr. gen. & colonial administrator in America; encouraged exploration, fur trade in West; defended Quebec (1690); subdued Iroquois (1696)

Frost \\'fròst\ Robert Lee 1874–1963 Am. poet; used colloquial language, apparently easy verse forms, symbols from common experience, esp. from rural New England — **Frost·ian** \\'fròs-tē-ən, -chən\ *adj*

Froude \\'früd\ James Anthony 1818–1894 Eng. hist.; wrote *History of England from the Fall of Wolsey to the Defeat of the Spanish Armada* (1856–70), etc.

Fry \\'frī\ Christopher 1907–   Eng. dram.; wrote plays in free verse with religious and mystic themes; including *The Lady's Not for Burning* (1949), etc.

Frye \\'frī\ (Herman) Northrop 1912–1991 Canad. lit. critic; known for literary theories of grammar of mythic form, biblical symbolism

Fu·ʾād I \\fü-'äd\ 1868–1936 sultan (1917–22) & king (1922–36) of Egypt; opposed British attempts at control but himself opposed by ultranationalist Wafd party; promulgated constitution (1923)

Fu·en·tes \\fü-'en-ˌtäs\ Carlos 1928–   Mex. author; wrote *La Muerte de Artemio Cruz* (1962, *The Death of Artemio Cruz*), *Terra Nostra* (1975), *The Hydra Head* (1978), essays

Fuer·tes \\'fyür-(ˌ)tēz\ Louis Agassiz 1874–1927 Am. illustrator; illustrated *Song Birds and Water Fowl* (1897), *Handbook of Birds of the Eastern United States* (1902), etc.

Fu·gard \\fü-'gärd\ Athol 1932–   So. African playwright; wrote *Blood Knot* (1969), *Boesman and Lena* (1969), etc.

Fu·ji·mo·ri \\ˌfü-jē-'mò-rē\ Alberto 1938–   pres. of Peru (1990–)

Fu·kui \\'fü-kü-ē, fü-'kü-ē\ Kenichi 1918–   Jp. chem.; awarded (with Roald Hoffmann) 1981 Nobel prize for chemistry for using quantum mechanics to predict the course of chemical reactions

Ful·bright \\'fúl-ˌbrīt\ (James) William 1905–1995 Am. polit.; U.S. senator (1945–74); major critic of Vietnam War; introduced Fulbright scholarship program of international exchange

Ful·ler \\'fü-lər\ Melville Weston 1833–1910 Am. jurist; chief justice U.S. Supreme Court (1888–1910)

Fuller (Richard) Buckminster 1895–1983 Am. engineer; developed geodesic dome; famous for asserting that all human needs could be met through technology and planning

Fuller (Sarah) Margaret 1810–1850 Marchioness *Os·so·li* \\'ò-sə-(ˌ)lē\ Am. critic & reformer; edited *The Dial* (1840–42), organ of Transcendentalists; known as one of ablest critics in America

Fuller Thomas 1608–1661 Eng. divine & author; Royalist chaplain during Civil War; chaplain to Charles II (1660); wrote *The Holy State and the Profane State* (1642), etc.

Ful·ton \\'fúl-tᵊn\ Robert 1765–1815 Am. engineer & inventor; invented submarine while in France (1797–1806); developed steamboat into commercial success (1801); designed first steam warship (1814)

Funk \\'fuŋk, 'fəŋk\ Casimir 1884–1967 Am. (Pol.-born) biochem.; identified and named vitamins (1912)

Funk \\'fəŋk\ Isaac Kauffman 1839–1912 Am. editor & publisher; founded, with Adam Wagnalls, company that later became Funk and Wagnalls Co. (1877); edited *Standard Dictionary of the English Language* (1890–93)

Fun·ston \ˈfən(t)-stən\ Frederick 1865–1917 Am. gen.; fought with insurrectionists in Cuba (1896–98), in Spanish-American War, in Philippines

Fur·ness \ˈfər-nəs, -ˌnes\ Horace Howard: father 1833–1912 & son 1865–1930 Am. Shakespeare scholars; prepared and published *Variorum Shakespeare* (from 1871)

Fur·ni·vall \ˈfər-nə-vəl\ Frederick James 1825–1910 Eng. philologist; conceived (1857) and helped produce *New English Dictionary*

Furt·wäng·ler \ˈfu̇rt-ˌveŋ-lər\ (Gustav Heinrich Ernst Martin) Wilhelm 1886–1954 Ger. conductor; known for passion, romantic style, interpretations of romantic music, esp. Beethoven and Wagner; composed symphonies, choral works, chamber music, songs

G

Ga·ble \ˈgā-bəl\ (William) Clark 1901–1960 Am. actor; portrayed rough, masterful, romantic heroes; appeared in over 70 films, including *It Happened One Night* (1934, Academy award), *Mutiny on the Bounty* (1935), *Gone with the Wind* (1939), etc.

Ga·bo \ˈgä-(ˌ)bō\ Naum 1890–1977 orig. *Naum Pevs·ner* \ˈpevz-nər\ Am. (Russ.-born) sculptor; founder and leader of Constructivist school; works included *Spiral Theme, Number 4*, etc.

Ga·bor \ˈgä-(ˌ)bȯr, gə-ˈbȯr\ Dennis 1900–1979 Brit. (Hung.-born) physicist; awarded 1971 Nobel prize for physics for his invention of holography

Ga·bo·riau \gə-ˈbȯr-ē-ˌō\ Émile 1832(or 1833 or 1835)–*ca* 1873 Fr. writer; known as the father of the *roman policier* (detective novel); wrote *Monsieur Lecoq* (1868), *La Vie infernale* (1870), etc.

Ga·bri·eli \ˌgä-brē-ˈe-lē\ Giovanni *ca* 1556–1612 Ital. composer; master of dialog-and echo-madrigal; composed more than 85 pieces of sacred and secular music

Gad·ha·fi \gə-ˈdä-fē, kə-, -ˈda-\ Muʾammar Muḥammad al- 1942– Libyan leader (1969–)

Gads·den \ˈgadz-dən\ James 1788–1858 Am. army officer & diplomat; negotiated treaty (1854) for purchase of land (Gadsden Purchase) in what is New Mexico and Arizona

Ga·ga·rin \gə-ˈgär-ən\ Yu·ry \ˈyu̇r-ē\ Alekseyevich 1934–1968 Russ. astronaut; first man to travel in space (1961)

Gage \ˈgāj\ Thomas 1721–1787 Brit. gen. & colonial gov. in America; precipitated battles of Lexington and Bunker Hill (1775); last royal gov. of Massachusetts

Gail·lard \gil-ˈyärd\ David DuBose \dü-ˈbōz, dyü-\ 1859–1913 Am. army officer & engineer; in charge of excavating Panama Canal (1907) and Culebra Cut (1908, renamed Gaillard Cut)

Gaines \ˈgānz\ Edmund Pendleton 1777–1849 Am. gen.; defended Fort Erie in War of 1812

Gains·bor·ough \\'gānz-ˌbər-ə, -ˌbə-rə, -b(ə-)rə\\ Thomas 1727–1788 Eng. painter; excelled in portraits; painted *The Blue Boy* (ca. 1770), *The Morning Walk* (1785); etc.

Gait·skell \\'gāt-skəl\\ Hugh Todd Naylor 1906–1963 Eng. polit.

Ga·ius \\'gā-əs, 'gī-əs\\ *fl* A.D. 130–180 Rom. jurist; wrote *Institutiones* (ca. 161) which served as basis for Institutes of Justinian

Gaj·du·sek \\'gī-də-ˌshek\\ D(aniel) Carleton 1923–   Am. virologist; awarded (with Baruch S. Blumberg) 1976 Nobel prize for physiology or medicine for research into infectious diseases

Gal·ba \\'gal-bə, 'gȯl-\\ Servius Sulpicius 3 B.C.–A.D. 69 Rom. emp. (68–69); made emperor on Nero's death, then executed many who had put him on throne; killed by Praetorians

Gal·braith \\'gal-ˌbrāth\\ John Kenneth 1908–   Am. (Canad.=born) econ.; advisor to Presidents Kennedy and Johnson; wrote *The Affluent Society* (1958), *The Age of Uncertainty* (1977), etc. — **Gal·braith·ian** \\ˌgal-'brā-thē-ən, -'brāth-yən\\ *adj*

Gale \\'gā(ə)l\\ Zona 1874–1938 Am. nov.; wrote *Romance Island* (1906), *Mothers to Men* (1911), *Birth* (1918), etc.

Ga·len \\'gā-lən\\ A.D. 129–*ca* 199 Greek physician & writer; considered founder of experimental physiology; works long accepted by Greeks, Romans, Arabs; showed that arteries carry blood — **Ga·len·ic** \\gə-'le-nik\\ *or* **Ga·len·i·cal** \\-ni-kəl\\ *adj*

Ga·le·ri·us \\gə-'lir-ē-əs\\ *d* 311 *Gaius Galerius Valerius Maximianus* Rom. emp. (305–311); became emperor in East on abdication of Diocletian; notorious for persecution of Christians

Gal·i·leo \\ˌga-lə-'lē-(ˌ)ō, -'lā-\\ 1564–1642 in full *Galileo Galilei* Ital. astron. & physicist; discovered law of uniform acceleration of falling bodies; discovered that moon shines with reflected light; denounced for advocating Copernican system; was later tried by Inquisition (1632) and forced to recant

Gall \\'gȯl, 'gȯl\\ *ca* 1840–1894 Hunkpapa Sioux war chief; one of the leading Sioux warriors at Battle of Little Big Horn (1876)

Gal·land \\gä-'läⁿ\\ Antoine 1646–1715 Fr. orientalist & translator; made first translation of *Mille et une nuits* (1704–17, *Arabian Nights' Entertainment*)

Gal·la·tin \\'ga-lə-t²n\\ (Abraham Alphonse) Albert 1761–1849 Am. (Swiss-born) financier & statesman; helped negotiate peace with Great Britain (1814)

Gal·lau·det \\ˌga-lə-'det\\ Thomas Hopkins 1787–1851 Am. teacher of the hearing- and speech-impaired; established first free American school for the deaf (1817)

Gal·le·gos Frei·re \\gä-'yā-ə-(ˌ)gōs-'frā-(ˌ)rā\\ Rómulo 1884–1969 Venezuelan nov.; pres. of Venezuela (1948)

Gal·li–Cur·ci \\ˌga-li-'kúr-chē, ˌgä-, -'kər-\\ Amelita 1889–1963 née *Galli* Am. (Ital.-born) soprano; known for florid coloratura singing, including Violetta in *La Traviata*, Mimi in *La Bohème*, etc.

Gal·lie·ni \\ˌgal-yā-'nē, gal-'yā-nē\\ Joseph-Simon 1849–1916 Fr. gen. & colonial administrator; pacified French Sudan (1886–88) and Madagascar (1896–1905)

Gal·lie·nus \\ˌga-lē-'ē-nəs, -'ā-nəs\\ Publius Licinius Valerianus Egnatius *d* 268 Rom. emp. (253–268); lost much territory, finally controlling only Italy and the Balkans

Gal·lup \\'ga-ləp\\ George Horace 1901–1984 Am. statistician; developed Gallup poll for testing public opinion

Ga·lois \gal-'wä\ Évariste 1811–1832 Fr. math.; made important contributions to aspect of higher algebra known as group theory

Gals·wor·thy \'gȯlz-ˌwər-thē\ John 1867–1933 Eng. nov. & dram.; known for series of novels about Forsyte family, including *The Forsyte Saga* trilogy, *A Modern Comedy* trilogy, etc.; plays include *Loyalties* (1922), etc.; awarded 1932 Nobel prize for literature

Galt \'gȯlt\ John 1779–1839 Scot. nov.; wrote novels depicting Scottish country and small-town life including *The Ayrshire Legatees* (1820), *The Provost* (1822), etc.

Gal·ton \'gȯl-tᵊn\ Sir Francis 1822–1911 Eng. scientist; best known for work in anthropology, heredity, study of human intelligence; founded eugenics — **Gal·to·nian** \gȯl-'tō-nē-ən, -nyən\ *adj*

Gal·va·ni \gal-'vä-nē, gäl-\ Luigi 1737–1798 Ital. physician & physicist; conducted experiments (1794) establishing presence of bioelectric forces in animal tissue

Gál·vez \'gäl-ˌves\ José 1729–1787 Marqués *de la Sonora* Span. jurist & colonial administrator; in New Spain (1765–71); began settlements in Upper California; in Indies (1776)

Ga·ma, da \dä-'ga-mə, -'gä-\ Vas·co \'vas-kō, 'väs-\ *ca* 1460–1524 Port. navigator & explorer; made first voyage from Western Europe around Africa to the East (1497–98); helped establish Portugal as a power in Africa, Asia

Ga·mar·ra \gə-'mär-ə\ Augustín 1785–1841 Peruvian gen.; pres. of Peru (1829–33; 1839–41)

Gam·bet·ta \gam-'be-tə, ˌgän-bə-'tä\ Léon-Michel 1838–1882 Fr. lawyer & statesman; helped proclaim Third Republic and form provisional government (1870–71); premier (1881–82)

Ga·me·lin \ˌgam-'lⁿ, ˌga-mə-\ Maurice-Gustave 1872–1958 Fr. gen.; commander in chief of Allied forces in France (1939); defeated by German attack (1940) leading to French collapse

Gan·dhi \'gän-dē, 'gan-\ In·di·ra \in-'dir-ə, 'in-də-rə\ Nehru 1917–1984 *dau. of Jawaharlal Nehru* prime min. of India (1966–77; 1980–84); renowned as leader of developing nations; assassinated by Sikh extremist bodyguards

Gandhi Mohandas Karamchand 1869–1948 *Ma·hat·ma* \mə-'hät-mə, -'hat-\ Indian nationalist leader; considered the father of his country; used nonviolence to achieve ends against British; president of Indian National Congress (1925–34); negotiated for autonomous Indian state (1947); assassinated by Hindu extremist — **Gan·dhi·an** \-ən\ *adj*

Gandhi Ra·jiv \rä-'jēv\ Ratna 1944–1991 *son of Indira* prime min. of India (1984–89); assassinated while campaigning for reelection

Gar·a·mond \'gar-ə-ˌmänd, ˌgar-ə-'mōⁿ\ *or* **Gar·a·mont** \-ˌmänt, -'mōⁿ\ Claude *ca* 1480–1561 Fr. typefounder; perfected design of Roman type and introduced it (from 1531) to replace Gothic

Ga·rand \gə-'rand, 'gar-ənd\ John Cantius 1888–1974 Am. (Canad.-born) inventor; invented semiautomatic Garand rifle that became standard (1936) shoulder weapon (M-1) for U.S. army

Gar·bo \'gär-(ˌ)bō\ Greta 1905–1990 orig. *Greta Lovisa Gustafsson* Am. (Swed.-born) actress; starred in *Anna Christie* (1930), *Anna Karenina* (1935), *Ninotchka* (1939), etc.; retired in 1941 and remained a recluse — **Gar·bo·esque** \ˌgär-bō-'wesk\ *adj*

Gar·cí·a Gu·tiér·rez \gär-'sē-ə-gü-'tyer-əs\ Antonio 1813–1884 Span. dram.; wrote in Romantic style; known esp. for play *El trovador* (1836), adapted by Verdi to opera *Il trovatore*

García Íñi·guez \-'ēn-yi-ˌgäs\ Calixto 1839–1898 Cuban revolutionary; led Cuban force in Spanish-American War (1898); subject of Elbert Hubbard's essay "A Message to Garcia"

García Lor·ca \-'lòr-kə\ Federico 1898–1936 Span. poet & dram.; noted for poems of death *Llanto por Ignacio Sanchez Mejítas* (1935; *Lament for the Death of a Bullfighter*), etc. and dramatic trilogy based on themes of violence and frustration

García Már·quez \-'mär-ˌkäs\ Gabriel 1928– Colombian author; proponent of style of magic realism; wrote *One Hundred Years of Solitude* (1967), *Love in the Time of Cholera* (1985), etc.; awarded 1982 Nobel prize for literature

García Mo·re·no \-mə-'rā-(ˌ)nō\ Gabriel 1821–1875 Ecuadorian journalist; pres. of Ecuador (1861–65; 1869–75); centralized government, established Roman Catholic church as state church

Gar·ci·la·so de la Ve·ga \ˌgär-si-'lä-sō-ˌdä-lə-'vä-gə\ 1539–1616 *El Inca* Peruvian hist.; wrote *La Florida del Ynca* (1605, account of de Soto's expedition) and a two-part history of Peru (1609, 1617)

Gar·den \'gär-d°n\ Mary 1874–1967 Am. (Scot.-born) soprano; chosen by Debussy to sing part of Mélisande in opera *Pelléas et Mélisande* (1902); chief roles included Marguerite, Salome, etc.

Gar·di·ner \'gärd-nər\ Samuel Rawson 1829–1902 Eng. hist.; wrote books about English Civil Wars

Gardiner Stephen *ca* 1482–1555 Eng. prelate & statesman; helped Henry VIII obtain divorce from Catherine of Aragon; later supported Queen Mary's persecution of Protestants

Gard·ner \'gärd-nər\ Erle Stanley 1889–1970 Am. writer; wrote more than 80 detective novels featuring Perry Mason

Gar·field \'gär-ˌfēld\ James Abram 1831–1881 20th pres. of the U.S. (1881)

Gar·i·bal·di \ˌgar-ə-'bòl-dē\ Giuseppe 1807–1882 Ital. patriot; led fight for Italian freedom; led Redshirts and defeated Kingdom of the Two Sicilies (1860); united Two Sicilies with Sardinia into single kingdom (1861) — **Gar·i·bal·di·an** \-dē-ən\ *adj*

Gar·land \'gär-lənd\ (Hannibal) Hamlin 1860–1940 Am. nov.; wrote *Prairie Folks* (1892), *A Daughter of the Middle Border* (1921, Pulitzer prize), *The Trail-Makers* (1926), etc.

Garland Judy 1922–1969 orig. *Frances Gumm* Am. actress & singer; starred in films musicals *The Wizard of Oz* (1939), *Meet Me in St. Louis* (1944), *Easter Parade* (1948), etc.

Gar·ner \'gär-nər\ John Nance 1868–1967 Am. polit.; vice pres. of the U.S. (1933–41)

Gar·nett \'gär-nət\ Constance 1862–1946 née *Black* Eng. translator; first to translate Russian authors Dostoyevsky, Chekhov, Turgenev, Gogol, and Tolstoy

Gar·rick \'gar-ik\ David 1717–1779 Eng. actor; known for acting in *Richard III* (1741); rewrote, acted in many Shakespeare plays

Gar·ri·son \'gar-ə-sən\ William Lloyd 1805–1879 Am. abolitionist; opposed Compromise of 1850; urged separation between North and South

Gar·shin \\'gär-shən\\ Vsevolod Mikhaylovich 1855–1888 Russ. writer; wrote psychological works dealing with madness, war, moral issues, including *Krasny tsvetok* (1883), etc.

Gar·vey \\'gär-vē\\ Marcus Moziah 1887–1940 Jamaican black leader; founded Universal Negro Improvement Assoc. (UNIA, 1914); preached pride of race, economic self-sufficiency as key to dignity and civil rights; conceived "Back to Africa" movement

Gary \\'gar-ē, 'ger-ē\\ Elbert Henry 1846–1927 Am. industrialist; instrumental in organizing United States Steel Corp.; Gary, Ind., named for him

Gas·coigne \\'gas-ˌkȯin\\ George ca 1525–1577 Eng. poet; produced play *Jocasta* (1566), first translation from Greek on English stage; published sonnets in *A Hundreth Sundrie Flowres* (1573)

Gas·kell \\'gas-kəl\\ Elizabeth Cleghorn 1810–1865 née *Stevenson* Eng. nov.; novels, set in industrial Midlands, include *Mary Barton* (1848), *Cranford* (1853), etc.; wrote *Life of Charlotte Brontë*

Gas·ser \\'ga-sər\\ Herbert Spencer 1888–1963 Am. physiol.; awarded (with Joseph Erlanger) 1944 Nobel prize for physiology or medicine for work on nerve fibers

Gates \\'gāts\\ Horatio ca 1728–1806 Am. gen. in Revolution; forced Burgoyne to surrender at Saratoga (1777), turning tide of victory to Americans

Gates William Henry III 1955–   Am. computer software manuf.; cofounder, Microsoft Corp. (1976)

Gau·guin \\gō-gaⁿ\\ (Eugène-Henri-) Paul 1848–1903 Fr. painter; leading French painter of Post-Impressionism; developed conceptual method of representation, using pure color, strong lines, two-dimensional patterns; lived (from 1891) in Tahiti, elsewhere in South Pacific — **Gau·guin·esque** \\(ˌ)gō-ˌga-'nesk\\ *adj*

Gaulle, de \\di-'gōl, -'gȯl\\ Charles-André-Marie-Joseph 1890–1970 Fr. gen. & polit.; led Free French Forces during WWII; pres. of Fifth Republic (1958–69); granted independence to 12 African territories; ended Algerian War (1962); devised independent foreign policy; restored power, reputation of France

Gauss \\'gau̇s\\ Carl Friedrich 1777–1855 Ger. math. & astron.; developed technique for calculating orbits of asteroids; introduced Gaussian error curve; considered founder of mathematical theory of electricity; magnetic unit, the gauss, named for him

Gautama Buddha — see SIDDHĀRTHA GAUTAMA

Gau·tier \\gō-tyā\\ Théophile 1811–1872 Fr. author; a leader of the Parnassians advocating art for art's sake; wrote verse, novels, short stories, literary criticism; ballet *Giselle* (coauthor, 1841); plays

Gay \\'gā\\ John 1685–1732 Eng. poet & dram.; wrote verse, plays including *The Beggar's Opera* (1728, music by J. C. Pepush), etc.

Gay–Lus·sac \\gā-lə-'sak\\ Joseph-Louis 1778–1850 Fr. chem. & physicist; pioneer investigator of behavior of gases, techniques of chemical analysis; one of the founders of meteorology

Geber — see JĀBIR IBN ḤAYYĀN

Ged·des \\'ge-dēz\\ Norman Bel 1893–1958 Am. designer; designed, produced, or directed more than 200 operas, films, plays, musicals; also designed furniture, buildings, etc.; popularized streamlining

Geh·rig \\'ger-ig\\ Lou 1903–1941 *Henry Louis Gehrig* Am. baseball player; known as the "Iron Horse," played a then-record 2130

consecutive games with New York Yankees (1925–39); retired because of neurological disease now called Lou Gehrig's disease

Gei·kie \'gē-kē\ Sir Archibald 1835–1924 Scot. geologist; directed geological survey of Scotland (1867 ff.) and United Kingdom

Gei·sel \'gī-zəl\ Theodor Seuss 1904–1991 pseud. *Dr. Seuss* \'süs\ Am. writer & illustrator; wrote books *The Cat in the Hat (1958)*, *Green Eggs and Ham* (1960), *Oh, The Places You'll Go* (1990), etc.

Gellée Claude — see CLAUDE LORRAIN

Gell–Mann \'gel-,män\ Murray 1929–   Am. physicist; awarded 1969 Nobel prize for physics for discoveries concerning nuclear particles; proposed existence of quarks

Ge·net \zhə-'nā\ Edmond-Charles-Édouard 1763–1834 Fr. diplomat in U.S.; tried to draw U.S. into France's war with Great Britain, Spain by use of privateers and intrigue

Genet Jean 1910–1986 Fr. dram. & nov.; portrayed criminal world and seamy side of society in plays and novels

Gen·ghis Khan \jeŋ-gəs-'kän, ,gen-\ *ca* 1162–1227 Mongol conqueror; consolidated nomadic tribes into a unified Mongolia; created an empire extending from China to Europe's Adriatic Sea

Gen·ser·ic \'gen(t)-sə-rik, 'jen(t)-\ *or* **Gai·se·ric** \'gī-zə-(,)rik, -sə-\ *d* 477 king of the Vandals (428–477); invaded Africa (429); defeated Roman army sent after him; sacked Rome (455)

Gen·ti·le da Fa·bri·a·no \jen-'tē-lē-də-,fä-brē-'ä-(,)nō\ *ca* 1370–1427 orig. *Niccolo di Giovanni di Massio* Ital. painter; first great representative of Umbrian school; worked in International Gothic style; painted masterpiece *Adoration of the Magi* (1423), etc.

Gen·ti·les·chi \,jen-t³l-'es-kē\ Orazio Lomi *ca* 1562–*ca* 1647 & his dau. Artemisia *ca* 1597–after 1651 Ital. painters; father adopted Caravaggio's realism, chiaruscuro style with own lyrical, light, color elements; works included *The Annunciation* (1623), etc.; daughter added more graceful, colorful elements to style; painted many portraits, gruesome biblical subjects, etc.

Geof·frey of Mon·mouth \'jef-rē-əv-'män-məth\ *ca* 1100–1154 Brit. ecclesiastic & chronicler; wrote largely fictional *Historia regum Britanniae* (ca. 1135–39), introducing figure of Arthur

George \'jȯrj\ Saint 3d cent. Christian martyr & patron saint of England; subject of legends of his rescue of a maiden from a dragon

George name of 6 kings of Great Britain: **I** 1660–1727 (reigned 1714–27); early reign troubled by Jacobite plots; strengthened position by forming Triple Alliance (1717, with France, Holland); **II** 1683–1760 (reigned 1727–60); suppressed Jacobite rebellion in Scotland at battle of Culloden Moor (1746); **III** 1738–1820 (reigned 1760–1820); suffered attacks of mental illness; provoked war with and lost American colonies; **IV** 1762–1830 (reigned 1820–30); Catholic Emancipation Act passed (1829) during his reign; **V** 1865–1936 (reigned 1910–36); forged agreement with Irish Free State (1921); **VI** 1895–1952 (reigned 1936–52); succeeded on abdication of brother Edward VIII; selected Winston Churchill prime min. (1940); oversaw evolution of Commonwealth of Nations, British welfare state — **Geor·gian** *adj or n*

George name of 2 kings of Greece: **I** 1845–1913 (reigned 1863–1913); involved in First Balkan War (1912–13); assassinated at Salonika; **II** 1890–1947 (reigned 1922–23; 1935–47); first reign ended by military coup; recalled by plebiscite

George David Lloyd — see David LLOYD GEORGE

George Henry 1839–1897 Am. econ.; developed single-tax theory

Ge·rard \jə-ˈrärd, ˈjer-ärd\ Charles 1618?–1694 1st Baron *Gerard of Bran·don* \ˈbran-dən\; Viscount *Brandon* Eng. royalist commander

Gé·rard \zhā-ˈrär\ Comte Étienne-Maurice 1773–1852 Fr. Napoleonic gen.; marshal of France

Ger·hard·sen \ˈger-ˌhär-sᵊn\ Einar Henry 1897–1987 Norw. polit.; prime min. of Norway (1945–51, 1955–63, 1963–65)

Gé·ri·cault \ˌzhā-ri-ˈkō\ (Jean-Louis-André-) Théodore 1791–1824 Fr. painter; used unorthodox coloring, bold designs; helped usher in the Romantic movement in French art

Ger·man·i·cus Cae·sar \jər-ˌma-ni-kə(s)-ˈsē-zər\ 15 B.C.–A.D. 19 Rom. gen.; as consul, commanded armies that inflicted defeats on Germanic tribes; later, supreme commander of eastern provinces

Gé·rôme \zhā-ˈrōm\ Jean-Léon 1824–1904 Fr. painter; known for anecdotal, erotic, photographic-like paintings

Ge·ron·i·mo \jə-ˈrä-nə-ˌmō\ 1829–1909 *Goyathlay* Chiricahua Apache leader; led campaigns against whites; famed for courage, determination, skill in resisting capture by U.S. military

Ger·ry \ˈger-ē\ Elbridge 1744–1814 Am. polit.; signed Declaration of Independence, Articles of Confederation; redistricting of Mass. to insure Republican control produced term "gerrymander"; vice pres. of the U.S. (1813–14)

Gersh·win \ˈgər-shwən\ George 1898–1937 orig. *Jacob Gershvin* Am. composer; wrote song "Swanee" (1919), score (lyrics by brother Ira) for *Of Thee I Sing* (1931, Pulitzer prize), etc.; composed orchestral works with jazz elements *Rhapsody in Blue* (1924), *An American in Paris* (1928), opera *Porgy and Bess* (1935)

Ge·sell \gə-ˈzel\ Arnold Lucius 1880–1961 Am. psychol. & pediatrician; pioneer in study of normal infants and children

Ges·ner \ˈges-nər\ Conrad 1516–1565 Swiss naturalist; his *Historiae animalium* (1551–87) considered basis of modern zoology; one of first to write about mountaineering

Get·ty \ˈge-tē\ Jean Paul 1892–1976 Am. business executive; amassed fortune through control of Pacific Western Oil Corp. (renamed Getty Oil Co.) and other oil interests

Getz \ˈgets\ Stan 1927–1991 orig. *Stanley Gayetzby* Am. jazz saxophone player; known for his mellow, "cool" style of playing; popularized bossa nova in 1960s

Gha·zā·lī, al- \ˌal-gə-ˈza-lē\ 1058–1111 *Abu Hāmid Muhammad ibn Muhammad at-Tūsī al-Ghazālī* Islamic jurist, theol., & mystic; wrote *The Revival of the Religious Sciences*, establishing mysticism as acceptable part of orthodox Islam

Ghi·ber·ti \gē-ˈber-tē\ Lorenzo *ca* 1378–1455 Florentine goldsmith, painter, & sculptor; created bronze doors for Baptistry of Florence Cathedral, masterpiece of Italian Renaissance art

Ghir·lan·da·jo or **Ghir·lan·da·io** \ˌgir-lən-ˈdä-(ˌ)yō\ Domenico 1449–1494 orig. *Domenico di Tommaso Bigordi* Florentine painter; known for frescoes, often with portraits of contemporaries

Ghose Sri Aurobindo — see AUROBINDO

Gia·co·met·ti \jä-kə-′me-tē\ Alberto 1901–1966 Swiss artist; produced abstract sculpture; developed (from 1935) more realistic, skeletal style to sculpt attenuated, solitary figures

Glae·ver \′yā-vər\ Ivar 1929–   Am. (Norw.-born) physicist; awarded (with Leo Esaki and Brian Josephson) 1973 Nobel prize for physics for work on semi- and superconductor materials

Gi·auque \jē-′ók\ William Francis 1895–1982 Am. chem.; awarded 1949 Nobel prize for chemistry for studying reactions to extreme cold

Gib·bon \′gi-bən\ Edward 1737–1794 Eng. hist.; chiefly known for *The History of the Decline and Fall of the Roman Empire* (1776–88) — **Gib·bon·ian** \gi-′bō-nē-ən\ *adj*

Gib·bons \′gi-bənz\ James 1834–1921 Am. cardinal; induced growth in church in U.S. through sermons, writings

Gibbons Orlando 1538–1625 Eng. organist & composer; organist of Chapel Royal and Westminster Abbey; composed anthems, keyboard music, madrigals, motets, fantasies

Gibbs \′gibz\ James 1682–1754 Brit. architect; designed St.-Martin-in-the-Fields Church, London (1722–26), etc.

Gibbs Josiah Willard 1839–1903 Am. math. & physicist; through his investigations, established basic theory for physical chemistry

Gib·ran *or* **Jib·ran** \jə-′brän\ Kahlil 1883–1931 *Jubrān Khalil Jubrān* Lebanese nov., poet, & artist in U.S.; wrote religious, mystical works, esp. *The Prophet* (1923)

Gib·son \′gib-sən\ Charles Dana 1867–1944 Am. illustrator; master of black-and-white drawing; created "Gibson girl" drawings depicting feminine ideal

Gibson William 1914–   Am. dram.; best known for stageplay about Helen Keller *The Miracle Worker* (1959)

Gide \′zhēd\ André 1869–1951 Fr. nov., critic, & essayist; awarded 1947 Nobel prize for literature for his novels, stories including *L'Immoraliste* (1902), *La Porte étroite* (1909), *Thésée* (1946), etc.

Giel·gud \′gil-₁gùd, ′gēl-\ Sir (Arthur) John 1904–   Eng. actor; became leading Shakespearean actor, known esp. for Hamlet

Gie·rek \′gyer-ək\ Edward 1913–   1st secy. of Polish Communist party (1970–80); focus of strikes led by Solidarity free trade union movement, forced to resign

Gie·se·king \′gē-zə-kiŋ\ Walter Wilhelm 1895–1956 Ger. (Fr.-born) pianist; known for interpretation of Debussy, Ravel, Beethoven, Prokofiev, Domenico Scarlatti

Gil·bert \′gil-bərt\ Cass 1859–1934 Am. architect; designed Woolworth Building, N.Y. (1908–13), U.S. Supreme Court Building, Washington, D.C. (1935), etc.

Gilbert Sir Humphrey *ca* 1539–1583 Eng. navigator; established first British colony in North America at St. John's, Newfoundland

Gilbert Walter 1932–   Am. biochem.; awarded (with Paul Berg and Frederick Sanger) 1980 Nobel prize for chemistry for studies of the chemical structure of nucleic acids

Gilbert William 1540–1603 Eng. physician & physicist; called "father of electricity" for experiments in magnetism, use of terms electric force, electric attraction, magnetic pole

Gilbert Sir William Schwenck 1836–1911 Eng. librettist & poet; collaborated with Arthur Sullivan to create comic operas, including *HMS Pinafore* (1878), *The Pirates of Penzance* (1879), *The Mikado* (1885), etc. — **Gil·bert·ian** \\,gil-ʹbər-tē-ən\ *adj*

Gil·les·pie \gə-ʹles-pē\ John Birks 1917–1993 *Dizzy* Am. jazz musician; developed bebop style

Gil·lette \jə-ʹlet\ King Camp 1855–1932 Am. inventor & manuf.; invented safety razor, organized and headed Gillette Safety Razor Co. (1901–32)

Gillette William Hooker 1855–1937 Am. actor; best known for title role (1899) in Conan Doyle's *Sherlock Holmes*

Gil·man \ʹgil-mən\ Alfred Goodman 1941–   Am. biochem.; awarded (with Martin Rodbell) 1994 Nobel prize for physiology or medicine for discovery of G-proteins

Gilman Daniel Coit \ʹkȯit\ 1831–1908 Am. educ.; pres. Johns Hopkins U. (1875–1901)

Gil·mer \ʹgil-mər\ Elizabeth 1870–1951 née *Mer·i·weth·er* \ʹmer-ə-,we-thər\ pseud. *Dorothy Dix* \ʹdiks\ Am. journalist; wrote widely syndicated advice to the lovelorn column

Gil·pin \ʹgil-pən\ Charles Sidney 1878–1930 Am. actor; one of first black actors to gain wide following on American stage; appeared in O'Neill's *Emperor Jones* (1920–24), etc.

Gi·na·ste·ra \,hē-nə-ʹster-ə\ Alberto Evaristo 1916–1983 Argentine composer; composed operas, ballets, orchestral works, choral works, etc.

Gin·grich \ʹgiŋ-(,)grich\ Newton Leroy 1943–   Am. polit.; speaker of the U.S. House of Representatives (1995–   )

Gins·berg \ʹginz-,bərg\ Allen 1926–   Am. poet; member of Beat movement with friends Jack Kerouac, William Burroughs, etc.; wrote *Howl* (1956), *Kaddish and other Poems* (1961), etc.

Gins·burg \ʹginz-,bərg\ Ruth Bader 1933–   Am. jurist; associate justice, U.S. Supreme Court (1993–   )

Gior·gio·ne \(,)jȯr-ʹjō-nē\ *ca.* 1477–1511 *Giorgione da Castelfranco* Venetian painter; chief master of Venetian school; influenced Titian, etc.; painted *Holy Family* (ca. 1508), etc.

Giot·to \ʹjȯ(t)-(,)tō, jē-ʹä-(,)tō\ 1266/67(or 1276)–1337 *Giotto di Bondone* Florentine painter, architect, & sculptor; chief Italian pre-Renaissance painter; painted fresco pieces *Life of Christ*, *Life of the Virgin*, etc.; architect of the Duomo, Florence

Gi·rard \zhē-ʹrär\ Jean-Baptiste 1765–1850 Swiss Franciscan & educ.; emphasized moral and religious aspects of education; wrote works outlining his philosophy of education

Gi·rard \jə-ʹrärd\ Stephen 1750–1831 Am. (Fr.-born) financier & philanthropist; helped government finance War of 1812; bequeathed funds to found Girard College, Philadelphia

Gi·raud \zhē-ʹrō\ Henri-Honoré 1879–1949 Fr. gen.; commanded French force in North Africa (1942–43)

Gi·rau·doux \,zhē-rō-ʹdü\ (Hyppolyte-) Jean 1882–1944 Fr. writer; emphasized dialogue, style; wrote plays *Judith* (1931), *La Guerre de Troie n'aura pas lieu* (1935), etc.

Gir·tin \ʹgər-tᵊn\ Thomas 1775–1802 Eng. painter; considered founder of art of modern watercolor painting

Gis·card d'Es·taing \zhis-kär-des-taⁿ, -,kär-des-ʹtaⁿ\ Valéry 1926–   pres. of France (1974–81)

Gish \\'gish\\ Lillian Diana 1893–1993 Am. actress; starred in films (1912–87) including *Birth of a Nation* (1915), *Intolerance* (1916), *Way Down East* (1920)

Gis·sing \\'gi-siŋ\\ George Robert 1857–1903 Eng. nov.; depicted realistically middle-class life in England, esp. degrading effect of poverty on character; wrote *New Grub Street* (1891), etc.

Giu·lio Ro·ma·no \\,jül-yō-rə-'mä-(,)nō\\ *ca* 1499–1546 *Giulio di Pietro di Filippo de' Gianuzzi* Ital. painter & architect; an initiator of the Mannerist style; as architect, designed and built Reggia dei Gonzaga, etc., in Mantua

Gjel·le·rup \\'ge-lə-,rúp\\ Karl 1857–1919 Dan. writer; wrote novels *En Idealist* (1878), etc., plays *Brynhilde* (1884), etc., verse; awarded 1917 Nobel prize for literature

Glad·stone \\'glad-,stōn, *chiefly Brit* -stən\\ William Ewart 1809–1898 Brit. statesman; prime min. (1868–74; 1880–85; 1886; 1892–94); leader of Liberal party (from 1867); responsible for many social and political reforms — **Glad·ston·ian** \\,glad-'stō-nē-ən\\ *adj*

Gla·ser \\'glā-zər\\ Donald Arthur 1926–   Am. physicist; awarded 1960 Nobel prize for physics for inventing the bubble chamber to study subatomic particles

Glas·gow \\'glas-(,)kō, -(,)gō; 'glaz-(,)gō\\ Ellen Anderson Gholson 1873–1945 Am. nov.; wrote *The Descendant* (1897), *They Stooped to Folly* (1929), *In This Our Life* (1941, Pulitzer prize), etc.

Glash·ow \\'gla-(,)shō\\ Sheldon Lee 1932–   Am. physicist; awarded (with Steven Weinberg and Abdus Salam) 1979 Nobel prize for physics for research on elementary particles

Glas·pell \\'glas-,pel\\ Susan 1882–1948 Am. nov. & dram.; wrote novels *The Visioning* (1911), *Norma Ashe* (1940), etc.; plays *Alison's House* (1930), etc.

Glass \\'glas\\ Carter 1858–1946 Am. statesman; U.S. senator from Virginia (1920–46); influential foe of New Deal legislation

Glass Philip 1937–   Am. composer; studied western and eastern musical traditions; composed operas *Einstein on the Beach* (1976), *Satyagraha* (1980), etc.

Gla·zu·nov \\'gla-zə-,nòf, -,nóv, ,glä-zù-'\\ Aleksandr Konstantinovich 1865–1936 Russ. composer; composed 8 symphonies, ballets, violin concerto, piano concertos, serenades, fantasies, etc.

Glea·son \\'glē-s°n\\ Jackie 1916–1987 *Herbert John Gleason* Am. comedian; starred in "The Jackie Gleason Show" (1952 ff.) esp. as comic character Ralph Kramden, who was later spun off into hit series "The Honeymooners"

Glen·dow·er \\glen-'daù(-ə)r\\ Owen *ca* 1359–*ca* 1416 Welsh rebel; led unsuccessful Welsh rebellion against Henry IV

Glenn \\'glen\\ John Herschel 1921–   Am. astronaut & polit.; first American to orbit the earth; U.S. senator from Ohio (1975–   )

Glick·man \\'glik-mən\\ Daniel Robert 1941–   U.S. secy. of agriculture (1995–   )

Glin·ka \\'glin-kə\\ Mikhail Ivanovich 1804–1857 Russ. composer; composed *A Life for the Czar* (1836), symphonies, songs, suites, etc.; considered founder of Russian national school

Gloucester Duke of — see HUMPHREY

Glov·er \'glə-vər\ John 1732–1797 Am. gen. in Revolution; led advance on Trenton (Dec. 25, 1776)

Glover Sarah Ann 1785–1867 Eng. music teacher; invented (ca. 1812) tonic sol-fa system of notation

Gluck \'glük\ Alma 1884–1938 née (*Reba*) *Fiersohn* Am. (Romanian-born) soprano; known esp. as concert and recording artist

Gluck Christoph Willibald 1714–1787 Ger. composer; revolutionized opera by putting music at service of drama through expressiveness and simplicity

Go·bat \gō-'bä\ Charles Albert 1834–1914 Swiss statesman; awarded 1902 Nobel prize for peace for his work with the International Peace Bureau (shared with Elie Ducommun)

God·dard \'gä-dərd\ Robert Hutchings 1882–1945 Am. physicist; pioneer experimenter with rockets (from 1908); tested first liquid-fueled rocket (1926), etc.

God·frey of Bouillon \'gäd-frē\ *F* **Gode·froy de Bouillon** \gȯt-frwä\ *ca* 1060–1100 Fr. crusader; named "protector of the Holy Sepulchre" (1099); idealized in legends as perfect Christian knight

Go·dol·phin \gə-'däl-fən\ Sidney 1645–1712 1st Earl of *Godolphin* Eng. statesman; helped arrange union with Scotland (1706–07); dismissed by Anne (1710)

Go·doy \gō-'dȯi\ Manuel de 1767–1851 Span. statesman; prime min. (1792–98); disastrous foreign policy led to abdication of Charles IV, occupation of Spain by armies of Napoléon

Go·du·nov \'gō-dºn-,ȯf, 'gȯ-, 'gä-\ Boris Fyodorovich *ca* 1551–1605 czar of Russia (1598–1605); reformed legal system, encouraged education; died in struggle with rival boyars

God·win \'gäd-wən\ *or* **God·wine** \-gäd-(,)wi-na\ *d* 1053 earl of Wessex; helped place Edward the Confessor on throne (1042)

Godwin William 1756–1836 Eng. philos. & nov.; atheist and radical; wrote *Enquiry Concerning Political Justice* (1793), etc. — **God·win·ian** \gäd-'wi-nē-ən\ *adj*

Godwin–Aus·ten \-'ȯs-tən, -'äs-\ Henry Haversham 1834–1923 Eng. explorer & geologist; surveyed in northern India, Assam, Tibet, Bhutan, etc. (1856–77)

Goeb·bels \'gə(r)-bəlz, 'gœ-bəls\ (Paul) Joseph 1897–1945 Ger. Nazi propagandist; named by Hitler to succeed him as chancellor; took own life in Hitler's bunker

Goe·ring *var of* GÖRING

Goes \'güs\ Hugo van der *ca* 1440–1482 Flemish painter; noted for ability to convey emotion and profound spirituality

Goe·thals \'gō-thəlz\ George Washington 1858–1928 Am. gen. & engineer; supervised building of Panama Canal (1907–14)

Goe·the \'gə(r)-tə, 'gœ̄-tə\ Johann Wolfgang von 1749–1832 Ger. poet & dram.; greatest figure of German Romantic period; contributed to *Sturm und Drang* movement; wrote *Die Lieden des jungen Werthers* (1774, *The Sorrows of Young Werther*), masterpiece *Faust* (1808–32) — **Goe·the·an** \-tē-ən\ *adj*

Gogh, van \van-'gō, -'gäk, -'kȯk, *Brit also* -'gəf\ Vincent Willem 1853–1890 Du. painter; developed unique style of broad, expressive brushwork, heightened colors and contoured forms; influenced Expressionist and Symbolist schools

Go·gol \'gȯ-gəl, 'gō-ˌgȯl\ Nikolay Vasilyevich 1809–1852 Russ. writer; called father of Russian Realism; wrote masterpiece *Dead Souls* (1842), etc. — **Go·gol·ian** \gȯ-'gōl-yən, gō-'gȯl-\ *adj*

Gold·berg \'gō(d)-ˌbərg\ Arthur Joseph 1908–1990 Am. lawyer and jurist; associate justice, U.S. Supreme Court (1962–65); U.S. ambassador to U.N. (1965–68)

Goldberg Whoopi 1955–　　orig. *Caryn Johnson* Am. actress; starred in solo Broadway show *Whoopi Goldberg on Broadway* (1984–85) and in films *The Color Purple* (1985), *Ghost* (1990), etc.

Gol·den \'gōl-dən\ Harry Lewis 1902–1981 Am. journalist; founded and edited (1941–68) *Carolina Israelite* newspaper; leader in campaign against racial segregation

Gol·den·wei·ser \'gōl-dən-ˌwī-zər\ Alexander Alexandrovich 1880–1940 Am. (Russ.-born) anthropol. & sociol.; wrote *Totemism* (1910), *Sex in Civilization* (1929), etc.

Gol·ding \'gōl-diŋ\ William Gerald 1911–1993 Eng. author; wrote novels *Lord of the Flies* (1954), *Pincher Martin* (1956), etc.; awarded 1983 Nobel prize for literature

Gold·man \'gōl(d)-mən\ Emma 1869–1940 Am. (Lith.-born) anarchist; conducted leftist activities in U.S. (ca. 1890–1917); deported (1919) to U.S.S.R. but left disillusioned

Gol·do·ni \gäl-'dō-nē, gōl-\ Carlo 1707–1793 Ital. dram.; created modern Italian comedy in style of Molière; wrote about 50 comedies, including *La putta onorata* (1759), etc.

Gold·smith \'gōl(d)-ˌsmith\ Oliver 1730–1774 Brit. author; wrote novel *The Vicar of Wakefield* (1766), drama *She Stoops to Conquer* (1773), poem *Retaliation* (1774), etc.

Gold·stein \'gōl(d)-ˌstīn\ Joseph Leonard 1940–　　Am. medical geneticist; awarded (with Michael S. Brown) 1985 Nobel prize for physiology or medicine for explaining how high cholesterol causes heart disease

Gold·wa·ter \'gōld-ˌwȯ-tər, -ˌwä-\ Barry Morris 1909–　　Am. polit.; U.S. senator from Arizona (1952–64; 1969–87); Republican candidate for president (1964)

Gold·wyn \'gōl-dwən\ Samuel 1879?–1974 orig. *Schmuel Gelbfisz* Am. (Pol.-born) motion-picture producer; produced *All Quiet on the Western Front* (1930), *Best Years of Our Lives* (1946, Academy award), etc.

Gol·gi \'gȯl-(ˌ)jē\ Camillo \kä-'mēl-(ˌ)lō\ 1843(or 1844)–1926 Ital. physician; awarded (with Santiago Ramón y Cajal) 1906 Nobel prize for physiology or medicine for studies of nerve tissue

Gol·lancz \gə-'lan(t)s\ Sir Hermann 1852–1930 Eng. Semitic scholar; knighted (1923), first British rabbi so honored

Gó·mez \'gō-ˌmez\ Juan Vicente 1864–1935 Venezuelan gen. & polit.; dictator (1908–35); eliminated foreign debt, developed oil industry

Gom·pers \'gäm-pərz\ Samuel 1850–1924 Am. (Brit.-born) labor leader; helped found precursor of American Federation of Labor (1886)

Go·muł·ka \gō-'mu̇l-kə, -'məl-\ Władysław 1905–1982 Pol. polit.; first secretary of Communist party (1954–71)

Gon·çal·ves Di·as \gən-'säl-vəs-ˌdē-əs\ Antônio 1823–1864 Braz. poet; considered national poet of Brazil; wrote collections of lyric poems, unfinished Indian epic, etc.

Gon·cha·ro·va \gən-'chär-ə-və\ Nathalie 1883–1962 Russ. artist; original member of Rayonist movement, reducing forms to rays of light; designed sets for Ballets Russes

Gon·court \gōⁿ-'kùr\ Edmond-Louis-Antoine Huot de 1822–1896 & his bro. Jules-Alfred Huot de 1830–1870 Fr. nov. & collaborators on social histories, art criticism, novels in Naturalistic manner

Gon·do·mar \ˌgän-də-'mär\ Conde de 1567–1626 *Diego Sarmiento de Acuña* Span. diplomat; one of the most influential people at the court of James I of England

Gon·za·ga \gən-'zä-gə, gän-, -'za-\ Saint Aloysius 1568–1591 Ital. Jesuit; ministered to victims of pestilence and famine in Rome

Gon·zá·lez \gən-'zä-ləs\ Manuel 1833–1893 Mex. gen.; pres. of Mexico (1880–84)

Gon·za·lo de Cór·do·ba — see FERNÁNDEZ DE CÓRDOBA

Goo·dall \'gù-(ˌ)dòl, -(ˌ)däl\ Jane 1934–   Brit. ethologist; studied chimpanzees in Tanzania

Good·hue \'gùd-(ˌ)hyü, -(ˌ)yü\ Bertram Grosvenor 1869–1924 Am. architect; designed U.S. Military Academy, West Point, Academy of Sciences, Washington, D.C., etc.

Good·man \'gùd-mən\ Benjamin David 1909–1986 *Benny Goodman* Am. musician and bandleader; noted clarinetist; formed own jazz band (1934); dubbed "King of Swing"

Good·rich \'gùd-(ˌ)rich\ Samuel Griswold 1793–1860 pseud. *Peter Parley* \'pär-lē\ Am. writer; published over a hundred "Peter Parley" books

Good·year \'gùd-ˌyir\ Charles 1800–1860 Am. inventor; developed vulcanization process for rubber (1839)

Gor·ba·chev \ˌgòr-bə-'chóf, -'chef; 'gòr-bə-ˌ\ Mikhail Sergeyevich 1931–   Soviet polit.; 1st secy. of communist party (1985–91); pres. of U.S.S.R. (1990–91); reformed economic and political system; aimed for more peaceful relations with West; resigned when Communist party dissolved, Soviet Union disbanded

Gor·cha·kov \ˌgòr-chə-'kóf, -'kóv\ Prince Aleksandr Mikhaylovich 1798–1883 Russ. statesman & diplomat; chancellor (1866–82); worked to restore Russia as European power

Gor·di·mer \'gòr-də-mər\ Nadine 1923–   So. African writer; wrote *A Guest of Honour* (1970), *Burger's Daughter* (1979), *A Sport of Nature* (1987), etc.; awarded 1991 Nobel prize for literature

Gor·din \'gòr-dⁿ\ Jacob 1853–1909 Am. (Russ.-born) Yiddish dram.; leading Yiddish playwright of New York City

Gor·don \'gòr-dⁿ\ Charles George 1833–1885 *Chinese Gordon, Gordon Pasha* Brit. soldier; known for exploits in China, ill-fated defense of Khartoum against Sudanese rebels

Gordon Charles William 1860–1937 pseud. *Ralph Connor* Canad. clergyman & nov.; wrote *Black Rock* (1898), *The Rock and the River* (1931), *The Girl from Glengarry* (1933), etc.

Gordon Lord George 1751–1793 Eng. polit. agitator; precipitated No-Popery (Gordon) Riots (1780)

Gore \'gòr, 'gòr\ Albert, Jr. 1948–   Am. polit.; vice pres. of the U.S. (1993–)

Go·re·my·kin \ˌgòr-ə-'mē-kən\ Ivan Logginovich 1839–1917 Russ. statesman; prime min. (1906; 1914–16); arrested after Revolution (1917); imprisoned and murdered in Caucasus by Bolsheviks

Gor·ey \'gòr-ē, 'gòr-\ Edward St. John 1925–   Am. writer &

illustrator; wrote and illustrated many volumes of macabrely humorous stories, including *The Doubtful Guest* (1957), *The Hapless Child* (1961), and *The Deranged Cousins: or, Whatever* (1969)

Gor·gas \\'gór-gas\ William Crawford 1854–1920 Am. army surgeon & sanitation expert; suppressed yellow fever, malaria during digging of Panama Canal

Gö·ring \\'gor-iŋ, 'ger-, 'gœr-\ Hermann 1893–1946 Ger. Nazi polit.; built up German air force; directed war economy (from 1937); convicted of war crimes by Nürnberg tribunal (1946)

Gor·ky \\'gór-kē\ Maksim 1868–1936 pseud. of *Aleksey Maksimovich Pesh·kov* \\'pesh-,kóf, -,kóv\ Russ. writer; helped develop Socialist Realism; wrote stories, novels, plays, etc.

Gor·ky \\'gòr-kē\ Arshile 1905–1948 Am. (Armenian-born) artist; influenced by Surrealism, developed style that led to Abstract Expressionism

Gort Viscount — see VEREKER

Gosse \\'gäs\ Sir Edmund William 1849–1928 Eng. poet & critic; known for literary criticism and for introducing Scandinavian literature to English readers

Gott·schalk \\'gä-,chók, 'gät-,shók\ Louis Moreau 1829–1869 Am. composer; first American composer to become popular in Europe

Gou·dy \\'gaù-dē\ Frederic William 1865–1947 Am. type designer; designed over 90 type faces, including Goudy, Garamond, etc.

Gough \\'gäf\ Hugh 1779–1869 1st Viscount *Gough* Eng. field marshal; in command in China during Opium War (1839–42)

Gould \\'güld\ Glenn Herbert 1932–1982 Canad. pianist; pioneered the highly engineered recording; stretched the technological possibilities of recorded music in 65 albums of classical works

Gould Jay 1836–1892 orig. *Jason Gould* Am. financier; with James Fisk caused panic of Black Friday (Sept. 24, 1869) by attempting to corner the gold market

Gould Stephen Jay 1941–   Am. paleontologist & evolutionary biologist; with Niles Eldredge developed (1972) theory of punctuated equilibria, according to which evolutionary change occurs in rapid bursts followed by long periods of stability

Gou·nod \\gü-'nō; 'gü-,nō\ Charles-François 1818–1893 Fr. composer; composed operas, church music, oratorios, songs including "Ave Maria" based on Bach's Prelude in C Major

Gour·mont \\gùr-'mōⁿ\ Remy de 1858–1915 Fr. writer; wrote novels, critical, philosophical works, verse, and plays; major disseminator of Symbolist aesthetic

Gove \\'gōv\ Philip Babcock 1902–1972 Am. lexicographer; editor in chief, *Webster's Third New International Dictionary* (1961)

Gow·er \\'gaù-(-)r, 'gō-(-)r, 'gó-(-)r\ John 1330?–1408 Eng. poet; wrote *Speculum meditantis* (in French), *Vox clamantis* (in Latin), *Confessio amantis* (in English)

Go·ya y Lu·cien·tes \\'gói-ə-,ē-,lü-sē-'en-,tās\ Francisco José de 1746–1828 Span. painter; painted many portraits, historical and allegorical works, including *Naked Maja*, *Clothed Maja*, etc. — **Go·ya·esque** \\,gói-ə-'esk\ or **Go·yesque** \\gói-'yesk\ *adj*

Goy·en or **Goij·en, van** \\van-'gói-ən, 'kói-\ Jan Josephszoon 1596–1656 Du. painter; known esp. for landscapes and river scenes, often in muted tones

Grac·chus \'gra-kəs\ Gaius Sempronius 153–121 B.C. & his bro. Tiberius Sempronius 163–133 B.C. *the Grac·chi* \'gra-ˌkī\ Rom. statesmen; attempted agrarian and civil reforms

Gra·ham \'grā-əm, 'gra(-ə)m\ John 1648–1689 *Graham of Claverhouse; Bonny Dundee;* 1st Viscount of *Dundee* Scot. Jacobite; led armies in support of England's King James II and against William of Orange during Revolution of 1688

Graham Martha 1893–1991 Am. choreographer & dancer; created *Appalachian Spring* (1944), *Clytemnestra* (1958), etc., employing psychological drama; her methods widely used in teaching

Graham Thomas 1805–1869 Scot. chem.; formulated Graham's law of diffusion of gases (1833); discovered and named dialysis; worked toward concept of polybasic acids

Graham William Franklin 1918– *Billy Graham* Am. evangelist; conducted widely televised international revival crusades

Gra·hame \'grā-əm, 'gra(-ə)m\ Kenneth 1859–1932 Brit. writer; wrote classic children's story *The Wind in the Willows* (1908), etc.

Gramme \'gram\ Zénobe Théophile 1826–1901 Belg. engineer; invented (1869) direct-current dynamo

Gra·na·dos \grə-'nä-(ˌ)dōs, -(ˌ)thōs\ Enrique 1867–1916 Span. composer; a leader of nationalist movement in Spanish music

Gran·di \'grän-(ˌ)dē\ Dino 1895–1988 Conte *di Mordano* Ital. Fascist polit.; presented motion resulting in Mussolini's resignation (1943)

Grange \'gränj\ Red 1903–1991 *Harold Edward Grange* Am. football player; running back for Chicago Bears (1925–26, 1929–34); played in 141 games, carried the ball for 8,151 yards and scored 87 touchdowns

Gra·nit \'grä-ˌnēt\ Ragnar Arthur 1900–1991 Swed. (Finn.-born) physiol.; awarded (with H. Keffer Hartline and George Wald) 1967 Nobel prize for physiology or medicine for findings about the chemical and physiological processes in the eye

Grant \'grant\ Cary 1904–1986 orig. *Archibald Alexander Leach* Am. (Brit.-born) actor; played debonair, witty sophisticate in films, including *Bringing Up Baby* (1938), *The Philadelphia Story* (1940), *North by Northwest* (1959)

Grant Ulysses 1822–1885 orig. *Hiram Ulysses Grant* Am. gen.; commander in chief of the Union armies during the late years (1864–65) of the American Civil War; 18th pres. of the U.S. (1869–77); administration marred by scandals and corruption

Gran·ville–Bar·ker \'gran-ˌvil-'bär-kər\ Harley Granville 1877–1946 Eng. actor, manager, & dram.; noted for stress on natural acting, esp. in Shakespeare; wrote plays, books on drama

Grass \'gräs\ Günter Wilhelm 1927– Ger. writer; wrote *The Tin Drum* (1959), *Cat and Mouse* (1961), *The Flounder* (1992), etc.; considered Germany's foremost post-war novelist

Grasse \'gras, 'gräs\ François-Joseph-Paul 1722–1788 Comte *de Grasse* & Marquis *de Grasse-Tilly* \-tē-'yē\ Fr. naval officer; commanded fleet in Chesapeake Bay which prevented English from reaching Cornwallis at Yorktown (1781)

Gras·so \'gra-(ˌ)sō\ Ella Rosa Giovanna Oliva 1919–1981 *née Tambussi* Am. polit.; governor of Connecticut (1975–81); first woman to hold a U.S. state governorship in her own right

Gra·tian \\'grā-sh(ē-)ən\\ *L Flavius Gratianus* 359–383 Rom. emp. (367–383); ruled as emperor in the West; fought Goths, Alamanni, etc.

Grat·tan \\'gra-tᵊn\\ Henry 1746–1820 Irish orator & statesman; brilliant orator, in Irish Parliament, British Parliament; championed Catholic emancipation; unsuccessfully opposed union with England

Grau San Mar·tín \\'graù-ˌsan-(ˌ)mär-'tēn, -ˌsän-\\ Ramón 1887–1969 Cuban physician & polit.; pres. of Cuba (1944–48)

Graves \\'grāvz\\ Robert Ranke 1895–1985 Brit. author; wrote novel *I Claudius* (1934), etc.; analyzed Greek and Roman myths, translated classical works; published *Collected Poems* (1975)

Gray \\'grā\\ Asa 1810–1888 Am. botanist; assembled large botanical library, herbarium at Harvard Univ. (1842–73)

Gray Thomas 1716–1771 Eng. poet; known esp. for "Elegy Written in a Country Churchyard"

Grayson David — see Ray Stannard BAKER

Gra·zia·ni \\ˌgrät-sē-'ä-nē\\ Rodolfo 1882–1955 Marchese *di Neghelli* Ital. marshal & colonial administrator; commander of forces in North Africa during WWII; defeated in Egypt by British

Gre·co, El \\el-'gre-(ˌ)kō *also* -'grā-\\ 1541–1614 *Doménikos Theotokópoulos* Span. (Cretan-born) painter; one of greatest Spanish artists; works, chiefly religious in subject matter, known for Mannerist style, contrast of colors, shadowy settings, elongated figures

Gree·ley \\'grē-lē\\ Horace 1811–1872 Am. journalist & polit.; founded New York *Tribune* (1841), important in molding northern thought; Liberal Republican candidate for president (1872)

Gree·ly \\'grē-lē\\ Adolphus Washington 1844–1935 Am. gen. & arctic explorer; attained most northerly point reached to time (1881), 83° 24′ N, on expedition to Ellesmere Island

Green \\'grēn\\ John Richard 1837–1883 Eng. hist.; wrote standard *Short History of the English People* (1874), etc.

Green Julien 1900– Fr. nov.; wrote novels about neurotic, obsessive French provincials; influenced by American Southern gothic; works include *Mont-Cinere* (1926), *Adrienne Mesurat* (1927)

Green William 1873–1952 Am. labor leader; president (1924–52) American Federation of Labor

Gree·na·way \\'grē-nə-ˌwā\\ Catherine 1846–1901 *Kate* Eng. artist; published *Under the Window* (1879), *Kate Greenaway's Birthday Book* (1880), *Mother Goose* (1886), etc.

Greene \\'grēn\\ Graham 1904–1991 Brit. nov.; incorporated religious issues in novels as *Brighton Rock* (1938), *The End of the Affair* (1951), *A Burnt-Out Case* (1961), etc.

Greene Nathanael 1742–1786 Am. gen. in Revolution; forced British out of Georgia, Carolinas (1781); besieged Charleston (1781–82)

Greene Robert 1558?–1592 Eng. poet & dram.; best known for *The Honorable Historie of frier Bacon and frier Bongay* (acted 1594); famous for calling Shakespeare "upstart crow"

Gree·nough \\'grē-ˌnō\\ Horatio 1805–1852 Am. sculptor; best known for toga-clad statue of George Washington

Greg·o·ry \'gre-g(ə-)rē\ Saint 240–332 *the Illuminator* apostle & founder of the Armenian Church

Gregory name of 16 popes: esp. **I** Saint *ca* 540–604 *the Great* (pope 590–604); created papal system that lasted through Middle Ages; may have arranged Gregorian chant; **VII** Saint orig. *Hil·de·brand* \'hil-də-,brand\ *ca* 1020–1085 (pope 1073–85); worked to establish supremacy of papacy; excommunicated Henry IV of Germany (1076, 1080); ultimately driven from Rome by Henry; **XIII** orig. *Ugo Buon·com·pa·gni* \'ü-gō-bwôn-kōm-'pän-yē\ 1502–1585 (pope 1572–85); produced (1582) Gregorian calendar still in use — **Gre·go·ri·an** \gri-'gōr-ē-ən, -'gȯr-\ *adj or n*

Gregory Isabella Augusta 1852–1932 *Lady Gregory* née *Persse* Irish dram.; helped W.B. Yeats, etc., found Irish Literary Theater (1899); wrote plays on peasant themes; translated, arranged Irish legends and sagas, etc.

Gregory of Nys·sa \'ni-sə\ Saint *ca* 335–*ca* 394 Eastern church father; chief orthodox theologian in Asia Minor; wrote works in which he balanced Platonic and Christian traditions

Gregory of Tours Saint 538–594 Frankish ecclesiastic & hist.; wrote *Historia Francorum*, history of Merovingian kingdom to 591, also lives of saints, books of miracles

Gren·fell \'gren-,fel, -fəl\ Sir Wilfred Thomason 1865–1940 Eng. medical missionary; built hospitals, schools, industrial centers, etc., in Labrador (from 1892)

Gren·ville \'gren-,vil, -vəl\ George 1712–1770 Eng. statesman; prime min. (1763–65); enacted Stamp Act (1765)

Grenville *or* **Greyn·ville** \'grän-\ Sir Richard 1542–1591 Brit. naval commander; commanded fleet for colonization of Virginia (1585); mortally wounded, captured in battle with Spanish

Gresh·am \'gre-shəm\ Sir Thomas 1519–1579 Eng. financier; traditionally but mistakenly credited with "Gresham's law" regarding hoarding of coins if each other have intrinsic value

Gretz·ky \'gret-(,)skē\ Wayne 1961– *The Great Gretzky* Canad. ice-hockey player; played with Edmonton Oilers (1979–88), Los Angeles Kings (1988–); awarded MVP trophy eight consecutive years; held NHL all-time scoring record

Greuze \'grœz, 'grœz\ Jean-Baptiste 1725–1805 Fr. painter; popular for moralistic or sentimental genre works

Gré·vy \grā-'vē\ (François-Paul-) Jules 1807–1891 Fr. lawyer; 3d pres. of the Republic (1879–87); term confirmed the establishment of Third Republic

Grey \'grā\ 2d Earl 1764–1845 *Charles Grey* Eng. statesman; prime min. (1830–34); carried Reform Bill (1832), providing reform of electoral system and suffrage

Grey Edward 1862–1933 Viscount *Grey of Fal·lo·don* \'fa-lə-d'n\ Eng. polit.; won over divided cabinet to declaration of war (1914); negotiated treaty (1915) bringing Italy into war on Allied side

Grey Lady Jane 1537–1554 titular queen of England for 9 days; beheaded, with husband Lord Guildford Dudley, after father's participation in Wyatt's Rebellion

Grey Zane 1875–1939 Am. nov.; wrote many western novels including *Riders of the Purple Sage* (1912), *Wild Horse Mesa* (1928), *Code of the West* (1934), etc.

Grieg \\'grēg\\ Edvard Hagerup 1843–1907 Norw. composer; considered founder of Norwegian national school of composition; composed music for Ibsen's *Peer Gynt* (1876), etc.

Grieve Christopher Murray — see Hugh MACDIARMID

Grif·fin \\'gri-fən\\ Walter Burley 1876–1937 Am. architect; designed federal capital at Canberra, Australia (1912)

Grif·fith \\'gri-fəth\\ Arthur 1872–1922 Irish journalist & nationalist; organized group that became Sinn Fein; negotiated treaty with England (1921); elected president of Irish Free State (1922)

Griffith David Lewelyn Wark 1875–1948 Am. motion-picture producer & director; helped develop many basic techniques of filmmaking; produced epics *Birth of a Nation* (1915), *Intolerance* (1916)

Gri·gnard \\grēn-'yär\\ (François-Auguste-) Victor 1871–1935 Fr. chem.; discovered (1900) Gignard reagent; awarded (with Paul Sabatier) 1912 Nobel prize for chemistry

Grill·par·zer \\'gril-ˌpärt-sər\\ Franz 1791–1872 Austrian dram. & poet; wrote *Sappho* (1818), trilogy *Das Goldene Vlies* (1818–22, *The Golden Fleece*), etc.

Grimm \\'grim\\ Jacob 1785–1863 & his bro. Wilhelm 1786–1859 Ger. philologists & folklorists; collected German folk tales, published them (1812–15) as *Grimm's Fairy Tales*, etc.; Jacob wrote *Deutsche Grammatik* (1819–37), viewed as foundation of German philology and containing formulation of Grimm's law

Gris \\'grēs\\ Juan 1887–1927 *José Victoriano González* Span. painter in France; associated with Picasso, Braque in Paris; developed more disciplined, severely classical Synthetic Cubism

Gro·fé \\'grō-ˌfā\\ Fer·de \\'fər-dē\\ 1892–1972 Am. conductor & composer; composed *Grand Canyon Suite* (1931), *Café Society* (1938), etc.

Gro·lier de Ser·vières \\ˌgrōl-'yā-də-ˌser-vē-'er, 'grōl-yər-\\ Jean 1479–1565 Vicomte *d'Aguisy* Fr. bibliophile; his library of some 3,000 books was among finest of its time

Gro·my·ko \\grə-'me-(ˌ)kō, grō-\\ Andrey Andreyevich 1909–1989 Russ. econ. & diplomat; as foreign min. (1957–85), conducted relations with West during Cold War; pres. of U.S.S.R. (1985–88)

Groo·te \\'grō-tə\\ Gerhard 1340–1384 *Ge·rar·dus Mag·nus* \\jə-ˌrär-dəs-'mag-nəs\\ Du. religious reformer; founded Brothers of the Common Life, teaching order that influenced education

Gro·pi·us \\'grō-pē-əs\\ Walter 1883–1969 Am. (Ger.-born) architect; founded (1919) Bauhaus school in Weimar; formed The Architects Collaborative (1946) in Cambridge, Mass.

Grop·per \\'grä-pər\\ William 1897–1977 Am. artist; painted in social protest manner; executed mural for U.S. Department of the Interior building in Washington, D.C.

Gros·ve·nor \\'grōv-nər, 'grō-və-\\ Gilbert Hovey 1875–1966 Am. geographer and editor; director (from 1899), National Geographic Society; sponsored numerous expeditions, scientific projects

Grosz \\'grōs\\ George 1893–1959 Am. (Ger.-born) painter; developed style of caricature and painting showing hatred of bourgeoisie, militarism, capitalism

Grote \\'grōt\\ George 1794–1871 Eng. hist.; best known for *History of Greece* (1846–56)

Gro·tius \\'grō-sh(ē-)əs\\ Hugo 1583–1645 *Huigh de Groot* \\də-

'grŏt\ Du. jurist & statesman; wrote essay *Mare liberum* (1609) on freedom of seas and *De jure belli ac Pacis* (1625), a fundamental work on international law

Grou·chy \grü-'shē\ Emmanuel 1766–1847 Marquis de Grouchy Fr. gen.; failed to aid Napoléon or stop opposition at Waterloo (1815); exiled

Grove \'grōv\ Sir George 1820–1900 Eng. musicologist; edited musical dictionary (1876–79)

Groves \'grōvz\ Leslie Richard 1896–1970 Am. gen.; commanded atomic bomb project (1942–47)

Grü·ne·wald \'grü-nə-‚wōld, 'grüe-nə-‚vält\ Matthias *ca* 1455–1528 Ger. painter; known through few works as one of greatest painters of his day

Gryph·i·us \'gri-fē-əs\ Andreas 1616–1664 *G* Greif \'grīf\ Ger. poet & dram.; wrote lyric verse, much of it pessimistic and melancholic

Guar·ne·ri \gwär-'ner-ē\ *L* Guar·ne·ri·us \gwär-'nir-ē-əs, -'ner-\ family of Ital. violin makers: esp. Giuseppe Antonio 1687–1745; produced variety of instruments of markedly robust tone

Gu·de·ri·an \gü-'der-ē-ən\ Heinz Wilhelm 1888–1954 Ger. gen.; a leading tactical theorist of armored warfare before WWII

Gue·dal·la \gwi-'da-lə\ Philip 1889–1944 Eng. writer; wrote popular histories *The Second Empire* (1922), *The Duke* (1931), etc.

Gue·rin \'ger-ən\ Jules 1866–1946 Am. painter; best known for murals in Lincoln Memorial, Washington, D.C., Penn Station, N.Y., etc.

Gues·clin \ges-'klaⁿ\ Bertrand du *ca* 1320–1380 Fr. soldier; recovered provinces of Poitou, Guienne, Auvergne from English, seized Brittany (1373); died on seige

Guesde \ged\ Jules 1845–1922 *Mathieu Basile* Fr. socialist; early organizer of Marxist wing of French labor movement

Guest \'gest\ Edgar Albert 1881–1959 Am. journalist & poet; wrote many volumes of popular verse, as *Just Folks* (1917), etc.

Gue·va·ra \ge-'vär-ə, gä-\ Ernesto 1928–1967 *Che* Latin-Am. (Argentine-born) revolutionary leader; fought in Cuban revolution (1956–59), in guerilla movements in Congo and Latin America (1965–67); killed in Bolivia

Gug·gen·heim \'gü-g°n-‚hīm\ Peggy 1898–1979 *Marguerite Guggenheim* Am. art patron; major patron of the New York school of artists; bequeathed her Venice palazzo and its collection of post-1910 paintings and sculpture as an art museum

Gui·do of Arezzo \'gwē-(‚)dō\ *or* Guido Are·ti·nus \‚ar-ə-'tē-nəs\ *ca* 991–1050 Benedictine monk & music reformer; devised four-line staff that made possible precise notation of pitch

Guil·laume \gē-'yōm\ Charles Édouard 1861–1938 Fr. physicist; awarded 1920 Nobel prize for physics for discovering invar (nickel-steel alloys)

Guille·min \gē-(ə-)'maⁿ\ Roger Charles Louis 1924– Am. (Fr.-born) physiol.; awarded (with Andrew Schally and Rosalyn Yallow) 1977 Nobel prize for physiology or medicine for research concerning the role of hormones in the body's chemistry

Guin·ness \'gi-nis, -nəs\ Sir Alec 1914– Brit. actor; played a wide variety of roles on stage and screen; gave especially notable performances in stage *Hamlet*, film *Kind Hearts and Coronets* (1949), *The Bridge on the River Kwai* (1957, Academy Award)

Guiscard Robert — see ROBERT GUISCARD

Guise \'gēz *also* 'gwēz\ 2d Duc de 1519–1563 *François de Lorraine* Fr. soldier & polit.; brought about Treaty of Chateau Cambrésis (1559) with English

Guise 3d Duc de 1550–1588 *Henri I de Lorraine* Fr. soldier & polit.; helped contrive massacre of St. Bartholomew's day (1572); led Holy League against Bourbons; assassinated

Gui·te·ras \gē-'ter-əs\ Juan 1852–1925 Cuban physician; involved with William Gorgas and Walter Reed in study of yellow fever

Gui·zot \gē-'zō\ François-Pierre-Guillaume 1787–1874 Fr. hist. & statesman; proponent of constitutional monarchy; premier (1847–48)

Gull·strand \'gəl-‚strand\ Allvar 1862–1930 Swed. ophthalmologist; awarded 1911 Nobel prize for medicine or physiology for research on the refraction of light through the eye

Gun·nars·son \'gə-nər-sən\ Gunnar 1889–1975 Icelandic writer; wrote *Af Borgslægtens historie* (1912–14, *From the Annals of the House of Borg*) in Danish

Gun·ter \'gən-tər\ Edmund 1581–1626 Eng. math.; invented Gunter chain, line, quadrant, and scale and first used terms *cosine* and *cotangent* (1620)

Gus·tav \'gús-‚täv\ *or* **Gus·ta·vus** \(‚)gə-'stä-vəs, -'stä-\ name of 6 kings of Sweden, the first 4 of the Vasa dynasty: **I** (*Gustav Eriksson*) 1496?–1560 (reigned 1523–60); led successful revolt against Danes (1521–23), had throne declared hereditary; **II** (*Gustav Adolph*) 1594–1632 (reigned 1611–32); sought cooperation of all classes in resolving domestic and foreign troubles; instituted major reforms; **III** 1746–1792 (reigned 1771–92); introduced reforms but assassinated by conspiracy of nobles; **IV** (*Gustav Adolph*) 1778–1837 (reigned 1792–1809); entered coalition against Napoléon; lost many possessions; dethroned (1809); **V** 1858–1950 (reigned 1907–50); kept Sweden neutral in WWI, WWII; **VI** (*Gustav Adolph*) 1882–1973 (reigned 1950–73); last Swedish monarch with real political power, following constitutional reforms (1971)

Gu·ten·berg \'gü-t⁸n-‚bərg\ Johannes *ca* 1390–1468 Ger. inventor of printing from movable type; printed 42-line Bible

Guth·rie \'gə-thrē\ Woodrow Wilson 1912–1967 *Woody* Am. folksinger; composed "So Long (It's Been Good to Know Ya)," "This Land is Your Land," "Hard Times," etc.

Gutz·kow \'gúts-‚kō\ Karl Ferdinand 1811–1878 Ger. journalist, nov., & dram.; a leader of Young Germany movement; wrote satirical, skeptical novels

Guz·mán Blan·co \güs-‚män-'bläŋ-(‚)kō\ Antonio 1829–1899 Venezuelan soldier & statesman; dictator of Venezuela (1870–89); encouraged education, public works, economic growth, diminished power of church; ousted in coup

Gwin·nett \gwi-'net\ Button *ca* 1735–1777 Am. Revolutionary leader; signed Declaration of Independence

Gwyn *or* **Gwynn** *or* **Gwynne** \'gwin\ Eleanor 1650–1687 *Nell* Eng. actress *mistress of Charles II*; bore him two sons, Charles Beauclerk (duke of St. Albans) and James, Lord Beauclerk

H

Haa·kon VII \\'hȯ-kən, -ˌkän\\ 1872–1957 king of Norway (1905–57); strengthened resistance to German occupation by refusal to abdicate

Haa·vel·mo \\'hȯ-vəl-ˌmō\\ Trygve 1911– Norw. econ.; awarded 1989 Nobel prize for economics for developing statistical techniques necessary for making economic predictions

Ha·bak·kuk \\'ha-bə-ˌkək, hə-'ba-kək\\ 7th cent. B.C. Hebrew prophet; author of biblical book of Habakkuk

Ha·ber \\'hä-bər\\ Fritz 1868–1934 Ger. chem.; awarded 1918 Nobel prize for chemistry for synthesis of ammonia; during WWI helped develop poison gas

Há·cha \\'hä-(ˌ)kä\\ Emil 1872–1945 Czech jurist & statesman; third pres. of Czechoslovakia (1938–39) and of Bohemia and Moravia (1939–45); died awaiting trial for war crimes

Had·field \\'had-ˌfēld\\ Sir Robert Abbott 1858–1940 Eng. metallurgist; invented manganese steel, silicon steel, other steel alloys

Had·ley \\'had-lē\\ Henry Kimball 1871–1937 Am. composer; composed Romantic works including operas, symphonies, suites, chamber music, choral works, songs

Had·ow \\'ha-(ˌ)dō\\ Sir (William) Henry 1859–1937 Eng. educ. & musicologist; advocated reform of elementary education and creation of modern secondary schools

Ha·dri·an \\'hā-drē-ən\\ *var of* ADRIAN

Hadrian A.D. 76–138 Rom. emp. (117–138); constructed Hadrian's Wall in Britain from Solway Firth to mouth of Tyne; constructed many great buildings in Rome, including Tivoli villa

Haeck·el \\'he-kəl\\ Ernst Heinrich 1834–1919 Ger. biol. & philos.; first German adherent of Darwin's theory of evolution; formulated principle "ontogeny recapitulates phylogeny"

Hā·fez \\hä-'fez\\ 1325(or 1326)–1389(or 1390) *Mohammad Shams od-Din Hāfez* Pers. poet; master of simple musical language conveying levels of meaning; considered greatest Persian lyric poet

Hag·gai \\'ha-gē-ˌi, 'ha-ˌgi\\ 6th cent. B.C. Hebrew prophet; advocated that Temple in Jerusalem be rebuilt; presumed author of biblical book of Haggai

Hag·gard \\'ha-gərd\\ Sir (Henry) Rider 1856–1925 Eng. nov.; known for novels written against South African background, including *She* (1887)

Hahn \\'hän\\ Otto 1879–1968 Ger. physical chem.; awarded 1944 Nobel award for chemistry for discoveries in fission

Hah·ne·mann \\'hä-nə-mən\\ (Christian Friedrich) Samuel 1755–1843 Ger. physician; formulated homeopathic principle that a disease could be cured by a drug that produced similar symptoms in a healthy person

Haider Ali — see HYDER ALI

Haig \\'hāg\\ 1st Earl 1861–1928 *Douglas Haig* Brit. field marshal; commander in chief of British force in France, Flanders (1915–19); developed controversial strategy of attrition (1916–17)

Hai·le Se·las·sie \\'hī-lē-sə-'la-sē, -'lä-\\ 1892–1975 Ras *Tafari* emp. of Ethiopia (1930–36; 1941–74); fostered education and modernization; driven out by Italian occupation (1936–41)

Hak·luyt \'hak-ˌlüt\ Richard *ca* 1552–1616 Eng. geographer & hist.; publicist of exploration and colonization, esp. by Virginia Company, Northwest Passage Company

Hal·dane \'hȯl-ˌdān, -dən\ John Burdon Sanderson 1892–1964 *son of J.S.* Brit. biol.; noted as Marxist, researcher, popularizer of science

Haldane John Scott 1860–1936 Brit. physiol.; studied breathing mechanism and disorders; developed decompression technique to prevent caisson disease (bends)

Haldane Richard Burdon 1856–1928 Viscount *Haldane of Cloan* \'klōn\; *bro. of J.S.* Brit. lawyer, philos., & statesman; reorganized British army

Hal·der \'häl-dər\ Franz 1884–1972 Ger. gen.; dismissed for opposing Hitler's Russian strategy; in concentration camp (1944–45)

Hale \'hā(ə)l\ Edward Everett 1822–1909 Am. Unitarian clergyman & writer; pastor, South Congregational Church, Boston (1856–1901); wrote stories, esp. "Man Without a Country"

Hale George Ellery 1868–1938 Am. astron.; conducted important research in solar and stellar spectroscopy

Hale Sir Matthew 1609–1676 Eng. jurist; took leading part in reform of legal system; defended Royalists and promoted Restoration

Hale Nathan 1755–1776 Am. Revolutionary hero; hanged as spy by British; last words supposedly, "I regret that I have but one life to lose for my country"

Ha·lé·vy \ˌ(h)a-lā-'vē, ˌ(h)ä-\ (Jacques-François-) Fromental (-Elie) 1799–1862 pseud. of *Elie Lévy* \lā-'vē\ Fr. composer; taught Gounod, Bizet, etc.; composed many operas

Halévy Ludovic 1834–1908 *nephew of prec.* Fr. dram. & nov.; helped write libretti for many Offenbach operas, comedies, novels

Hal·i·fax \'ha-lə-ˌfaks\ Earl of 1881–1959 *Edward Frederick Lindley Wood* Eng. statesman & diplomat; British viceroy of India (1925–31), foreign secretary (1938–40), ambassador to the U.S. (1941–46)

Hall \'hȯl\ Charles Francis 1821–1871 Am. arctic explorer; led three arctic expeditions, including searches for survivors of Franklin expedition and 1871 attempt to reach North Pole

Hall Charles Martin 1863–1914 Am. chem. & manuf.; invented, simultaneously with Paul Héroult, electrolytic process of making aluminum; set up company to produce aluminum (1888)

Hall Granville Stanley 1844–1924 Am. psychol. & educ.; considered founder of child psychology, educational psychology, scientific psychology in U.S.

Hall James Norman 1887–1951 Am. nov.; wrote (with Charles B. Nordhoff) trilogy on ship Bounty, including *Mutiny on the Bounty* (1932), etc.

Hal·lam \'ha-ləm\ Henry 1777–1859 Eng. hist.; wrote *Europe During the Middle Ages* (1818), *Introduction to the Literature of Europe* (1837–39), etc.

Hal·leck \'ha-lək, -lik\ Fitz-Greene 1790–1867 Am. poet; wrote "Green be the turf above thee," "Burns," "Young America," etc.

Halleck Henry Wager 1815–1872 Am. gen.; effective in training, mobilizing but not in tactics or strategy in Civil War

Hal·ley \'ha-lē *also* 'hā-lē\ Edmond *or* Edmund 1656–1742 Eng.

astron.; studied comets, predicting accurately the return in 1758 of comet observed in 1531, 1607, 1682, and subsequently known as Halley's comet

Hals \'hälz, 'häls\ Frans *ca* 1581–1666 Du. painter; among greatest portraitists; master of character depiction, subtle color, expressive brushwork

Hal·sey \'hól-sē, -zē\ William Frederick 1882–1959 Am. admiral; commander of Allied naval forces in South Pacific (1942–44); defeated Japanese in battle off Solomon Islands (Nov. 1942)

Hal·sted \'hól-stəd, -,sted\ William Stewart 1852–1922 Am. surgeon; administered perhaps first blood transfusion in U.S. (1881); emphasized aseptic procedures

Ham·bro \'häm-,brō\ Carl Joachim 1885–1964 Norw. statesman; delegate to League of Nations, pres. of Assembly (1939–46); delegate to U.N. (1945–57)

Ha·mil·car Bar·ca \hə-'mil-,kär-'bär-kə, 'ha-məl-\ *or* **Bar·cas** \'bär-kəs\ 270?–229 (or 228) B.C. *father of Hannibal* Carthaginian gen.; forced to make peace with Rome (241), led campaign to take Spain (237–228)

Ham·il·ton \'ha-məl-tən, -t'n\ Alexander 1755–1804 Am. statesman; U.S. secy. of the treasury (1789–95); planned and initiated national fiscal system, strong central government, increased trade, industry, etc. — **Ham·il·to·ni·an** \,ha-məl-'tō-nē-ən\ *adj*

Hamilton Edith 1867–1963 Am. classicist; wrote *The Greek Way* (1930), *The Roman Way* (1932), *Mythology* (1942); effective in popularizing classical culture

Hamilton Lady Emma 1765–1815 née *Amy Lyon* mistress of Lord Nelson

Ham·lin \'ham-lən\ Hannibal 1809–1891 Am. polit.; vice pres. of the U.S. (1861–65); prominent anti-slavery advocate

Ham·mar·skjöld \'ha-mər-,shóld, 'häm-, -,shüld, -,shēld\ Dag \'däg\ Hjalmar Agne Carl 1905–1961 Swed. U.N. official; secy.-gen. (1953–61); helped settle crises in Suez, Lebanon, Congo

Ham·mer·stein \'ha-mər-,stīn, -,stēn\ Oscar 1846–1919 Am. (Ger.-born) theater impresario; leased or built many theaters in New York, Philadelphia, London

Hammerstein Oscar 1895–1960 *grandson of prec.* Am. lyricist & librettist; one of greatest lyricists in American musical theater; wrote lyrics for *Oklahoma!, South Pacific, Sound of Music*

Ham·mett \'ha-met\ (Samuel) Dashiell 1894–1961 Am. writer; created "hard-boiled" school of detective fiction in *The Maltese Falcon* (1930), *The Thin Man* (1932), etc.

Ham·mond \'ha-mənd\ John Hays 1855–1936 Am. mining engineer; a leader in Transvaal reform movement in South Africa (1895–96)

Hammond John Hays 1888–1965 *son of prec.* Am. electrical engineer & inventor; invented radio-controlled torpedo, variable pitch ship propeller, remote-control devices

Hammond Laurens 1895–1973 Am. inventor; developed electric organ (Hammond electronic organ) and Hammond Novachord producing sounds like orchestral instruments

Ham·mu·ra·bi \,ha-mə-'rä-bē\ *or* **Ham·mu·ra·pi** \-'rä-pē\ *d* 1750 B.C. king of Babylon (1792–50); known for code of laws, once thought to be oldest existing

Hamp·den \\'ham(p)-dən\\ John 1594–1643 Eng. statesman; led opposition to Charles I on tax issue

Hampden Walter 1879–1955 stage name of *W. H. Dougherty* Am. actor; known esp. for Shakespearean roles, *Cyrano de Bergerac*, *Richelieu*, etc.

Hamp·ton \\'ham(p)-tən\\ Wade 1751?–1835 Am. gen.; held responsible for failure of expedition against Montréal (1813)

Hampton Wade 1818–1902 *grandson of prec.* Am. polit. & Confed. gen.; served at Bull Run (1861), Gettysburg, in the Wilderness; gov., South Carolina (1876–79), senator (1879–91)

Ham·sun \\'häm-sən\\ Knut 1859–1952 pseud. of *Knut Pedersen* Norw. writer; wrote Neo-Romantic novels stressing individualism; reputation damaged by support of Quisling regime

Han·cock \\'han-ˌkäk\\ John 1737–1793 Am. statesman in Revolution; first signer of Declaration of Independence, first gov. of state of Massachusetts

Hancock Winfield Scott 1824–1886 Am. gen. & polit.; played key role in Battle of Gettysburg (1863); unsuccessful Democratic candidate for president (1880)

Hand \\'hand\\ (Billings) Learned 1872–1961 Am. jurist; compiled record tenure on federal bench (1909–61); considered one of greatest jurists of his day

Han·del \\'han-dᵊl\\ George Frideric 1685–1759 Brit. (Ger.-born) composer; composed many operas, oratorios, esp. *Messiah* (1742), concerti for oboe and for organ, *Water Music* (1717), *Fireworks Music* (1749), overtures, harpsichord works, chamber works — **Han·de·li·an** \\han-ˈdē-lē-ən\\ *adj*

Han·dy \\'han-dē\\ William Christopher 1873–1958 Am. blues musician; first to codify and publish songs in mode known as blues; composed "St. Louis Blues," "Careless Love," etc.

Han·na \\'ha-nə\\ Marcus Alonzo 1837–1904 *Mark* Am. businessman & polit.; instrumental in forging alliance of Republican party and business interests

Han·nay \\'ha-ˌnā, 'ha-nē\\ James Owen 1865–1950 Irish clergyman & nov.; wrote *Spanish Gold* (1908), *Lady Bountiful* (1921), etc.

Han·ni·bal \\'ha-nə-bəl\\ 247–183 B.C. *son of Hamilcar Barca* Carthaginian gen.; crossed Alps (218) on elephants from Spain into Italy in Second Punic War (218–201)

Han·no \\'ha-(ˌ)nō\\ 3d cent. B.C. *the Great* Carthaginian statesman; opposed Hannibal by advocating peace with Rome during Second Punic War (218–201)

Ha·no·taux \\ˌa-nə-ˈtō, ˌä-\\ (Albert-Auguste-) Gabriel 1853–1944 Fr. hist. & statesman; directed colonial expansion in Africa; wrote histories of French Revolution, WWI, etc.

Han·sard \\'han-ˌsärd, 'han(t)-sərd\\ Luke 1752–1828 Eng. printer; printed House of Commons' journals (from 1774), reports still known as *Hansards*

Han·son \\'han(t)-sən\\ Howard 1896–1981 Am. composer; established annual festival to promote American composers and founded (1958) Eastman Philharmonic

Hans·son \\'han(t)-sən\\ Per Albin 1885–1946 Swed. statesman; prime min. (1932–46); secured much social legislation; maintained Swedish neutrality in WWII

Han Wu Ti \'hän-'wü-'dē\ 156–87 B.C. orig. *Liu Ch'e* often called *Wu Ti* Chin. emp. (140–87); expanded Chinese empire (133–101); reorganized government; made Confucianism the state religion

Han Yü \'hän-'yü\ 768–824 *Han Wen-kung* Chin. poet, essayist, & philos.; laid foundation of Neo-Confucianism; advocated simple prose style, unorthodox forms

Har·bach \'här-,bäk\ Otto Abels 1873–1963 Am. dram. & librettist; collaborator in *No! No! Nanette* (1924), *The Desert Song* (1926), etc.

Har·de·ca·nute or **Har·di·ca·nute** \,här-di-kə-'nüt, -'nyüt\ *ca* 1019–1042 king of Denmark (1028–42) and of England (1040–42); unpopular with English subjects

Har·den \'här-dᵊn\ Sir Arthur 1865–1940 Eng. chem.; awarded (with Hans von Euler-Chelpin) 1929 Nobel prize for chemistry for research on sugar fermentation and enzymes

Harden Maximilian 1861–1927 orig. *Felix Ernst Witkowski* Ger. writer; advocated war as nationalist campaign but became pacifist in WWI and then radical socialist

Har·den·berg \'här-dᵊn-,bȯrg, -,berk\ Prince Karl August von 1750–1822 Pruss. statesman; advocate of constitutionalism and chief architect of Prussian independence

Har·ding \'här-diŋ\ Warren Gamaliel 1865–1923 29th pres. of the U.S. (1921–23); called for "return to normalcy" but administration suffered from corruption of officials appointed by him

Har·dy \'här-dē\ Thomas 1840–1928 Eng. nov. & poet; wrote novels noted for stoical pessimism, mastery of dialect and folkways, including *The Return of the Native* (1878), *Tess of the D'Urbervilles* (1891), etc. — **Har·dy·esque** \,här-dē-'esk\ *adj*

Har·greaves \'här-,grēvz\ James *d* 1778 Eng. inventor; invented the spinning jenny (ca. 1764, pat. 1770)

Har·ing·ton or **Har·ring·ton** \'har-iŋ-tən\ Sir John 1561–1612 Eng. writer & translator; translated Ariosto's *Orlando Furioso* (1591), wrote barbed epigrams, a satire (1596) on his invention of the flush toilet

Ḥa·ri·ri, al- \,al-hə-'rir-ē\ 1054–1122 Arab scholar & poet; known esp. for *Marquāmāt*, collection of humorous tales in refined style

Har·lan \'här-lən\ John Marshall 1833–1911 & his grandson 1899–1971 Am. jurists; grandfather was associate justice, U.S. Supreme Court (1877–1911); declared constitution "color-blind"; grandson was associate justice, U.S. Supreme Court (1955–71)

Har·ley \'här-lē\ Robert 1661–1724 1st Earl of *Oxford* Eng. statesman; engaged in much political intrigue until forced from office (1715) and imprisoned (1715–17)

Harms·worth \'härmz-(,)wȯrth\ Alfred Charles William 1865–1922 Viscount *North·cliffe* \'nȯrth-,klif\ Eng. publisher & polit.; published several newspapers; in WWI advocated vigorous conduct of war, directed propaganda

Harmsworth Harold Sidney 1868–1940 1st Viscount *Roth·er·mere* \'rä-thər-mir\ *bro. of A.C.W.* Eng. publisher & polit.; endowed two chairs at Cambridge, one at Oxford

Har·old \'har-əld\ name of 2 kings of the English: **I** *d* 1040 *Harold Hare·foot* \'har-,fút, 'her-\ (reigned 1035–40); illegitimate son of Canute, elected king by the witan (1037); **II** *ca* 1022–1066 (reigned

1066); defeated and killed in Battle of Hastings (Oct. 14, 1066) by William of Normandy

Harold name of 3 kings of Norway: esp. **III** Hard·raa·de \'hȯr-ˌrȯ-də\ 1015–1066 (reigned 1045–66); killed at battle of Stanford Bridge while helping Harold II of England conquer that land

Har·ri·man \'har-ə-mən\ William Aver·ell \'āv-rəl, 'ā-və-\ 1891–1986 Am. businessman, diplomat, & polit.; negotiated U.S.-U.S.S.R. partial nuclear test-ban treaty (1963)

Har·ring·ton \'har-iŋ-tən\ (Edward) Michael 1928–1989 Am. writer; wrote *The Other America: Poverty in the United States* (1962) which examined a "culture of poverty" and prompted expansion of social security, food stamps, public housing, medical programs, etc.

Har·ris \'har-əs\ Barbara Clementine 1930–   Am. bishop; first woman to be consecrated bishop in the Episcopal Church

Harris Frank 1856–1931 Am. (Irish-born) writer; works provoked hostile criticism because of their sexual frankness; wrote biography *Oscar Wilde* (1916), autobiography, novels, stories, plays

Harris Joel Chandler 1848–1908 Am. writer; famed for creation of Uncle Remus, Brer Rabbit, Brer Fox, and other characters

Harris Roy 1898–1979 Am. composer; composed 14 symphonies, notably No. 3 (1937) and choral *Folksong Symphony* No. 4 (1940), other orchestral, choral, chamber, vocal pieces

Harris William Torrey 1835–1909 Am. philos. & educ.; leading American interpreter of German philosophical thought, esp. of Hegel

Har·ri·son \'har-ə-sən\ Benjamin 1833–1901 *grandson of W. H. Harrison* 23d pres. of the U.S. (1889–93)

Harrison Frederic 1831–1923 Eng. writer & philos.; a leader in the positivist movement and the Church of Humanity in England

Harrison Sir Rex 1908–1990 orig. Reginald Carey Harrison Brit. actor; known for charming, blasé style in comedy parts in *Blithe Spirit* (1945), *My Fair Lady* (1964, Academy award), etc.

Harrison William Henry 1773–1841 9th pres. of the U.S. (1841); elected on slogan "Tippecanoe and Tyler too" referring to his victorious campaigns against Indians; died after one month in office

Har·san·yi \här-'shä-nē\ John Charles 1920–   Am. (Hung.-born) econ.; awarded (with John F. Nash and Reinhard Selten) 1994 Nobel prize for economics for pioneering work in game theory

Hart \'härt\ Albert Bushnell 1854–1943 Am. hist. & editor; edited several series of histories, as *The American Nation* (1903–18)

Hart Basil Henry Liddell — see LIDDELL HART

Hart Lorenz 1895–1943 Am. lyricist; with Richard Rogers wrote songs for Broadway shows *A Connecticut Yankee* (1927), *Pal Joey* (1940), etc., songs "Where or When," "Blue Moon," etc.

Hart Moss 1904–1961 Am. librettist & dram.; collaborated with Irving Berlin, Cole Porter, esp. George S. Kaufman on *You Can't Take It With You* (1936, Pulitzer prize), etc., movie scripts; directed *My Fair Lady* (1956), *Camelot* (1960), etc.

Hart Sir Robert 1835–1911 Brit. diplomat; played important role in Anglo-Chinese affairs

Hart William Surrey 1872–1946 Am. actor; famous world-wide as hero in movie westerns

Harte \'härt\ Francis Brett 1836–1902 *Bret Harte* Am. writer; wrote popular tales of California mining camps as "Outcasts of Poker Flat," etc.

Hart·line \'härt-ˌlīn\ Haldan Keffer 1903–1983 Am. biophysicist; awarded (with Ragnar Granit and George Wald) 1967 Nobel prize for physiology or medicine for their findings about the eye

Har·tung \'här-ˌtůŋ\ Hans 1904–1989 Fr. (Ger.-born) painter; among foremost French abstract painters, his brushwork shows influence of Chinese calligraphy

Hā·rūn ar–Ra·shīd \ha-ˈrün-är-rə-ˈshēd\ 763(or 766)–809 *Hārūn ar-Rashīd ibn Muḥammad al-Mahdī ibn al-Manṣūr al-'Abbāsī* caliph of Baghdad (786–809); led Eastern caliphate to greatest power and extent; made Baghdad the center of Arabic culture

Har·vard \'här-vərd\ John 1607–1638 Am. clergyman & benefactor; left his library and half his estate to college at "New Towne" (later Cambridge); college named in his honor in 1639

Har·vey \'här-vē\ George Brinton McClellan 1864–1928 Am. journalist & diplomat; editor, *North American Review* (1899–1926), *Harper's Weekly* (1901–13)

Harvey Sir John Martin 1863–1944 Eng. actor & producer; achieved great success in *The Only Way* (1899) and *Oedipus Rex* (1912)

Harvey William 1578–1657 Eng. physician & anatomist; developed theory of circulation of the blood (1628), including explanation of heart valves, pulse, pulmonary circulation, etc.

Has·dru·bal \'haz-ˌdrü-bəl, haz-'\ *d* 207 B.C. *bro. of Hannibal* Carthaginian gen.; commanded Carthaginian army in Spain after Hannibal crossed into Italy (218); crossed Alps (207) and met defeat

Ha·shi·mo·to \ˌhä-shē-ˈmō(ˌ)tō\ Ryutaro 1937–   prime min. of Japan (1996–   )

Has·sam \'ha-səm\ (Frederick) Childe 1859–1935 Am. artist; a foremost exponent of Impressionism in America; known for scenes emphasizing light, atmosphere

Has·sel \'hä-səl\ Odd 1897–1981 Norw. chem.; awarded (with Derek H.R. Barton) 1969 Nobel prize for chemistry for studies tying chemical reactions to the shape of molecules

Hass·ler \'häs-lər\ Hans Leo 1564–1612 Ger. composer; composed much church music and secular songs

Has·tings \'häs-tiŋz\ 1st Marquess of 1754–1826 *Francis Rawdon-Hastings* \'rȯd-ⁿn-\ Brit. gen. & colonial administrator; fought against Americans at Bunker Hill, Camden, Hobkirk's Hill; established British supremacy in central India

Hastings Warren 1732–1818 Eng. statesman & administrator in India; credited with establishing political and judicial organization in India, and the method of governmental administration

Haugh·ey \'hȯ-hē\ Charles James 1925–   prime min. of Ireland (1979–81; 1982; 1987–92); tried and acquitted for arms conspiracy (1970); resigned (1992) after wire-tapping scandal

Haupt·man \'haůpt-mən\ Herbert Aaron 1917–   Am. biophysicist; awarded (with Jerome Karle) 1985 Nobel prize for chemistry for techniques to determine the chemical structure of molecules

Haupt·mann \'haůpt-ˌmän\ Gerhart 1862–1946 Ger. writer; awarded 1912 Nobel prize for literature for naturalistic, realistic, proletarian plays and novels

Haus·ho·fer \'haús-,hō-fər\ Karl Ernst 1869–1946 Ger. gen. &
geographer; evolved theory and discipline of geopolitics

Hauss·mann \ōs-'män, 'haús-mən\ Baron Georges-Eugène
1809–1891 Fr. administrator; inaugurated boulevard system, land-
scaping of parks and gardens, etc., in Paris

Ha·vel \'hä-vel, -vəl\ Václav \'vät-,släf\ 1936–   Czech writer &
polit.; imprisoned (1979–83, 1989) for plays judged subversive;
pres. of Czechoslovakia (1989–92), Czech Republic (1993–   )

Have·lock \'hav-,läk, -lək\ Sir Henry 1795–1857 Brit. gen.; fought
during Sepoy Mutiny (1857) in India and in other British conflicts
in Far East

Hawke \'hȯk\ 1st Baron 1705–1781 *Edward Hawke* Eng. admiral;
defeated French in Quiberon Bay (1759), preventing invasion of
England

Hawke Robert James Lee 1929–   prime min. of Australia
(1983–91); adept at handling industrial disputes

Haw·king \'hȯ-kiŋ\ Stephen William 1942–   Brit. physicist;
concerned with cosmological research in black holes, singularities,
"big bang" theory, etc.

Haw·kins \'hȯ-kənz\ Sir Anthony Hope 1863–1933 pseud.
Anthony Hope Eng. nov. & dram.; author of novels *The Prisoner of
Zenda* (1894), *Little Tiger* (1925), etc., and plays

Hawkins Erick 1909–1994 Am. dancer & choreographer; founded
Erick Hawkins Dance Company (1958); created free-flowing, idio-
syncratic, plotless dances that were often celebrations of the human body and its place in the natural world

Hawkins or **Haw·kyns** Sir John 1532–1595 Eng. admiral; engaged in slave trade (1562–67); exposed Ridolfi plot to depose
Elizabeth (1571)

Hawks \'hȯks\ Howard Winchester 1896–1977 Am. film director;
in career that spanned over four decads directed *Bringing Up Baby*
(1938), *His Girl Friday* (1940), *Red River* (1948), etc.

Haw·orth \'haú-ərth\ Sir (Walter) Norman 1883–1950 Eng.
chem.; awarded (with Paul Karrer) 1937 Nobel prize for physics
for research on carbohydrates and vitamin C

Haw·thorne \'hȯ-,thȯrn\ Nathaniel 1804–1864 Am. author; wrote
The Scarlet Letter (1850), *The House of the Seven Gables* (1851),
etc., and many stories

Hay \'hā\ John Milton 1838–1905 Am. statesman; promoted Open
Door policy toward China (1899–1900) and negotiated treaty providing for Panama Canal (1901)

Hay·den \'hā-dⁿn\ Carl Trumbull 1877–1972 Am. polit.; served a
record 56 years in Congress

Haydn \'hī-dⁿn\ (Franz) Joseph 1732–1809 Austrian composer;
regarded as first great master of symphony and quartet, composed
106 symphonies, 79 quartets, 54 piano sonatas, etc.

Hay·ek \'hī-ak\ Friedrich August von 1899–1992 Brit. (Austrian-
born) econ.; awarded (with Gunnar Myrdal) 1974 Nobel prize for
economics for work on the theory of money and economic change
and the relationship between economic and social factors

Hayes \'hāz\ Helen 1900–1993 *Helen Hayes Brown* Am. actress;
celebrated as "first lady" of the American theater; stage roles include Queen Victoria in *Victoria Regina* (1935–36); starred in films

The Sin of Madelon Claudet (1931, Academy Award), *Airport* (1970, Academy Award), etc.

Hayes Isaac Israel 1832–1881 Am. arctic explorer; led expedition to prove the existence of open sea around North Pole (1860–61)

Hayes Roland 1887–1977 Am. tenor; internationally known for renditions of spirituals and classics

Hayes Rutherford Birchard 1822–1893 19th pres. of the U.S. (1877–81); as Republican victor in disputed presidential election, placated Southern Democrats by ending Reconstruction

Haynes \ˈhānz\ Elwood 1857–1925 Am. inventor; built one of first horseless carriages (1893–94), discovered various alloys including stainless steel

Hays \ˈhāz\ Will Harrison 1879–1954 Am. lawyer & polit.; instituted Production Code for motion pictures (1930) and made further efforts on behalf of film censorship

Ha·zard \ä-ˈzär\ Paul-Gustave-Marie-Camille 1878–1944 Fr. lit. hist.; author of *La Crise de la conscience européenne, 1680–1715* (1935)

Haz·litt \ˈhaz-lət, ˈhāz-\ William 1778–1830 Eng. essayist; famous for critical essays on art and literature in *Table Talk* (1821), *The Plain Speaker* (1826)

Head \ˈhed\ Edith 1898?–1981 Am. costume designer; her more than 1000 films include *All About Eve* (1950), *Sabrina* (1954), *The Sting* (1973)

Hea·ly \ˈhē-lē\ Timothy Michael 1855–1931 Irish statesman; first gov.-gen. of Irish Free State (1922–28)

Hearn \ˈhärn\ Laf·ca·dio \laf-ˈkä-dē-ˌō\ 1850–1904 Jp. *Yakumo Koizumi* Am. (Greek-born) writer in Japan; introduced literature and culture of Japan to the West

Hearst \ˈhərst\ William Randolph 1863–1951 Am. newspaper publisher; built circulation with sensational reportage, color comics, etc.; popularized "yellow journalism"

Heath \ˈhēth\ Edward 1916–   Brit. prime min. (1970–74); chief negotiator for Britain's entry into Europe's common market

Heav·i·side \ˈhe-vē-ˌsīd\ Oliver 1850–1925 Eng. physicist; made important contributions to theory of electrical communications

Heb·bel \ˈhe-bəl\ (Christian) Friedrich 1813–1863 Ger. dram.; wrote realistic, psychological tragedies involving Hegelian concepts of history and moral values

He·ber \ˈhē-bər\ Reginald 1783–1826 Eng. prelate & hymn writer; among best known hymns were "From Greenland's Icy Mountains," "Holy, Holy, Holy"

Hé·bert \ā-ˈber\ Jacques-René 1757–1794 Fr. radical journalist; helped plan overthrow of monarchy (1792), pressed Jacobins to radical measures; guillotined

He·din \hä-ˈdēn\ Sven Anders 1865–1952 Swed. explorer; traveled through Persia, Mesopotamia, Khurāsān, Turkistan, to Peking, Gobi Desert, Tibet (1885–1908)

Heem \ˈhām\ Jan Davidsz de 1606–1683 (or 1684) Du. painter; regarded as perhaps the finest of Dutch still life painters

He·gel \ˈhā-gəl\ Georg Wilhelm Friedrich 1770–1831 Ger. philos.; his dialectic process for reconciling opposites influenced Existentialists, Marx, etc. — **He·ge·li·an** \ˈhā-ˈgā-lē-ən, hi-\ *adj or n*

Hei·deg·ger \\'hī-,de-gər, 'hī-di-gər\\ Martin 1889–1976 Ger. philos.; one of the main exponents of 20th-century Existentialism — **Hei·deg·ger·ian** \\,hī-di-'gar-ē-ən, -'ger-\\ adj

Hei·den·stam \\'hā-d²n-,stam, -,stäm\\ (Carl Gustaf) Verner von 1859–1940 Swed. writer; began literary renaissance in Sweden with his poetry

Hei·fetz \\'hī-fəts\\ Ja·scha \\'yä-shə\\ 1901–1987 Am. (Russ.-born) violinist; toured widely, commissioned works from leading contemporary composers

Hei·ne \\'hī-nə also -nē\\ Heinrich 1797–1856 Ger. poet & critic; author of some of best-loved German lyrics, many set to music by Schumann, Schubert, etc.

Hei·sen·berg \\'hī-z²n-,bərg, -,berk\\ Werner Karl 1901–1976 Ger. physicist; awarded 1932 Nobel prize for physics for development of quantum mechanics

Heliogabalus — see ELAGABALUS

Hel·ler \\'he-lər\\ Joseph 1923– Am. nov.; best known for novel *Catch 22* (1961), a term since used of any double bind

Hell·man \\'hel-mən\\ Lillian 1905–1984 Am. dram.; left-wing activist; author of *The Children's Hour, The Little Foxes*, etc.

Helm·holtz \\'helm-,hōlts\\ Hermann Ludwig Ferdinand von 1821–1894 Ger. physicist, anatomist, & physiol.; a founder of the principle of the conservation of energy, developer of the theory of electricity, etc.

Helms \\'helms\\ Jesse 1921– Am. polit.; U.S. senator (1973–); noted leader of conservative causes

Hé·lo·ïse \\'ā-lə-,wēz, 'e-lə-\\ ca 1098–1164 *wife of Abelard* Fr. abbess; entered convent after marriage to Abelard exposed

Hel·vé·tius \\hel-'vā-sh(ē-)əs, -'vē-; ,(h)el-,vās-'yüs, -'yüēs\\ Claude=Adrien 1715–1771 Fr. philos.; a Philosophe; evolved sensationalist philosophy, explication of which was condemned and burned

He·mans \\'he-mənz, 'hē-\\ Felicia Dorothea 1793–1835 née *Browne* Eng. poet; known for light Romantic lyrics, including "Landing of the Pilgrims"

Hem·inge *or* **Hem·minge** \\'he-miŋ\\ John ca 1556–1630 Eng. actor; closely associated with Shakespeare and editor with Condell of First Folio of Shakespeare

Hem·ing·way \\'he-miŋ-,wā\\ Ernest Miller 1899–1961 Am. writer & journalist; awarded 1954 Nobel prize for literature for novels and stories, including *A Farewell to Arms*, (1929), *For Whom the Bell Tolls* (1940), *The Old Man and the Sea*, (1952), etc. — **Hem·ing·way·esque** \\,he-miŋ-,wā-'esk\\ adj

Hench \\'hench\\ Philip Showalter 1896–1965 Am. physician; awarded (with E.C. Kendall and T. Reichstein) 1950 Nobel prize for physiology or medicine for research on adrenal hormones

Hen·der·son \\'hen-dər-sən\\ Arthur 1863–1935 Brit. labor leader & statesman; awarded 1934 Nobel prize for peace

Henderson Sir Nev·ile \\'ne-vəl\\ Meyrick 1882–1942 Brit. diplomat; ambassador to Germany (1937–39)

Hen·dricks \\'hen-driks\\ Thomas Andrews 1819–1885 Am. polit.; vice pres. of the U.S. (1885)

Hen·gist *or* **Hen·gest** \\'heŋ-gəst, -,gist\\ & *his bro.* **Hor·sa** \\'hôr-sa\\ 5th cent. Jute invaders of Britain; Hengest reputedly founded line of kings of Kent

Hen·ley \'hen-lē\ William Ernest 1849–1903 Eng. editor & author; best known for poem "Invictus"

Hen·ne·pin \'he-nə-pən, ˌe-nə-'pan\ Louis 1626–after 1701 Belg. friar & explorer in America; explored Great Lakes with La Salle and upper Mississippi region

Hen·ri \'hen-rē\ Robert 1865–1929 Am. painter; with others formed The Eight, or Ashcan School of realism

Hen·ry \'hen-rē\ name of 8 kings of England: **I** 1068–1135 (reigned 1100–35); elected king by witan; conquered and defended Normandy; **II** 1133–1189 (reigned 1154–89); first Plantagenet king, conquered Welsh and increased authority over barons; instituted judicial, financial reforms; **III** 1207–1272 (reigned 1216–72); showed preference toward foreigners, leading to Baron's War; **IV** 1366–1413 (reigned 1399–1413); when banished, invaded England and defeated Richard II; **V** 1387–1422 (reigned 1413–22); invaded France and won battle of Agincourt (Oct. 25, 1415); **VI** 1421–1471 (reigned 1422–61 & 1470–71); reign marked by periods of mental derangement, economic unrest, struggle between Lancaster and York leading to Wars of Roses; **VII** 1457–1509 (reigned 1485–1509); defeated and killed Richard III to regain throne; increased royal power and fortune; **VIII** 1491–1547 (reigned 1509–47); obtained Act of Supremacy to resolve conflict with pope over marriage to six wives; united Wales and England

Henry name of 4 kings of France: **I** ca 1008–1060 (reigned 1031–60); quashed rebellions, subdued nobles, defeated by Duke of Normandy; **II** 1519–1559 (reigned 1547–59); laid groundwork for continuing persecution of Protestants in France; **III** 1551–1589 (reigned 1574–89); conspired in St. Bartholomew Day massacre; after continuous civil conflicts between Catholics and Huguenots, finally sided with the latter; **IV** (Henry III of Navarre) 1553–1610 (reigned 1589–1610); after wars of early years, his final years marked by recovery, prosperity, and, generally, peace

Henry 1394–1460 *the Navigator* Port. prince; directed voyages of discovery along African coast; improved compass and shipbuilding

Henry Joseph 1797–1878 Am. physicist; built first electric motor; observed electrical induction

Henry O. — see William Sydney PORTER

Henry Patrick 1736–1799 Am. statesman & orator; made speech advocating strong colonial opposition to British tyranny with words "Give me liberty, or give me death"

Hens·lowe \'henz-(ˌ)lō\ Philip ca 1550–1616 Eng. theater manager; his company chief rival of Shakespeare's; his records a valuable source for study of drama of period

Hen·son \'hen-sən\ Jim 1936–1990 *James Maury Henson* Am. puppeteer; created the Muppets, first introduced (1969) on the television show "Sesame Street"; later produced "The Muppet Show," reportedly the most watched show in television history

Hep·burn \'hep-(ˌ)bərn\ Katharine 1907– Am. actress; famed as strong character actress in *Woman of the Year, African Queen, On Golden Pond,* etc.

Hep·ple·white \'he-pəl-ˌhwit, -ˌwit\ George d 1786 Eng. cabinetmaker and designer; produced elegant, delicate neoclassical designs in furniture

Hep·worth \'hep-(ₐ)wərth\ Dame Barbara 1903–1975 Brit. sculptor; works in abstract, formal manner were noted for mastery of texture, interplay of mass and interior space

Her·a·clei·tus or **Her·a·cli·tus** \ₐher-ə-'klī-təs\ ca 540–ca 480 B.C. Greek philos.; evolved cosmology in which fire is principle element of orderly universe — **Her·a·cli·te·an** \-'klī-tē-ən, -klī-'tē-\ adj

He·ra·cli·us \her-ə-'klī-əs, hi-'ra-klē-\ ca 575–641 Byzantine emp. (610–641); fought Slavs, Avars, Persians, Muslims and lost much territory while instituting system of defense by peasants

Her·bart \'her-ₐbärt\ Johann Friedrich 1776–1841 Ger. philos. & educ.; led renewed 19th-cent. interest in Realism; considered a founder of modern scientific pedagogy

Her·bert \'hər-bərt\ George 1593–1633 Eng. divine & poet; one of the Metaphysical poets; wrote 160 religious poems of ingenious imagery and metrical inventiveness

Herbert Victor 1859–1924 Am. (Irish-born) composer & conductor; composer of light operas *Babes in Toyland, The Red Mill,* etc.

Herbert William 1580–1630 3d Earl of *Pembroke* Eng. statesman & poet; patron of literature, colonial companies, and object of inscription in First Folio of Shakespeare

Herblock — see Herbert Lawrence BLOCK

Her·der \'her-dər\ Johann Gottfried von 1744–1803 Ger. philos. & writer; helped lay basis of German Romanticism

He·re·dia \ā-rā-'dyä, (ₐ)ā-'rā-dē-ə\ José María de 1842–1905 Fr. (Cuban-born) poet; a leading representative of French Parnassians and a master of the French sonnet

Her·ford \'her-fərd\ Oliver 1863–1935 Eng. writer & illustrator; wrote humorous verse and prose illustrated by himself

He·ring \'her-iŋ, 'hā-riŋ\ Ewald 1834–1918 Ger. physiol. & psychol.; investigated respiration and visual space perception

Her·ki·mer \'hər-kə-mər\ Nicholas 1728–1777 Am. gen. in Revolution; mortally wounded when troops attempting to relieve Fort Stanwix, N.Y., ambushed and defeated

Her·man \'hər-mən\ Woodrow Charles 1913–1987 *Woody Herman* Am. musician & bandleader; played jazz clarinet and saxophone; hits by his Thundering Herd band included "Woodchoppers' Ball"

Hern·don \'hərn-dən\ William Henry 1818–1891 Am. lawyer; partner of Abraham Lincoln (from 1844)

He·ro \'hē-(ₐ)rō, 'hir-(ₐ)ō\ or **He·ron** \'hē-ₐrän\ 1st cent. A.D. Greek scientist; derived Hero's formula for area of triangle; invented aeolipile, first steam-powered engine

Her·od \'her-əd\ 73–4 B.C. *the Great* Rom. king of Judea (37–4); middle period of reign marked by building of cities and public buildings and beginning of rebuilding of Great Temple at Jerusalem; later reign marked by intrigue, mental instability

Herod An·ti·pas \'an-tə-pəs, -ₐpas\ 21 B.C.–A.D. 39 *son of prec.* Rom. tetrarch of Galilee (4 B.C.–A.D. 39); had John the Baptist beheaded; declined to pass judgment on Jesus of Nazareth

He·rod·o·tus \hi-'rä-də-təs\ ca 484–between 430 and 420 B.C. Greek hist.; systematic treatment of Greco-Persian wars from 500 to 479 B.C. earned him title "Father of History"— **He·rod·o·te·an** \-ₐrä-də-'tē-ən\ adj

Her·re·ra \(h)ə-'rer-ə\ Francisco de 1576–*ca* 1656 *el Viejo* Span. painter; regarded as founder of national style of Spain, marking transition from Mannerism to the Baroque

Her·rick \'her-ik\ Robert 1591–1674 Eng. poet; author of epigrams and classically elegant lyrics

Her·riot \er-ē-'ō\ Édouard 1872–1957 Fr. statesman

Hersch·bach \'harsh-,bäk\ Dudley Robert 1932– Am. chem.; awarded (with Yuan T. Lee and John C. Polanyi) 1986 Nobel prize for chemistry for research on basic chemical reactions

Her·schel \'hər-shəl\ Sir John Frederick William 1792–1871 & his father Sir William 1738–1822 Eng. astronomers; son discovered (1819) solvent power of sodium hyposulphite on silver salts; first to use "positive" and "negative" of photographic images; father discovered planet Uranus and its satellites, etc.; regarded as virtual founder of sidereal science

Her·sey \'hər-sē\ John Richard 1914–1993 Am. nov.; mastered art of fictionalizing historical fact, as in *A Bell for Adano* (1944, Pulitzer prize), *Hiroshima* (1946), etc.

Her·shey \'hər-shē\ Alfred Day 1908– Am. geneticist; awarded (with Max Delbrück and Salvador Luria) 1969 Nobel prize for physiology or medicine for work with bacteriophages

Her·ter \'hər-tər\ Christian Archibald 1895–1966 Am. diplomat; secy. of state (1959–61)

Hertz \'herts, 'hərts\ Gustav Ludwig 1887–1975 Ger. physicist; awarded (with James Franck) 1925 Nobel prize for physics for stating laws on the collision of an electron with an atom

Hertz Heinrich Rudolf 1857–1894 Ger. physicist; conducted research on electromagnetic waves that demonstrated their existence and led to development of wireless telegraphy

Hert·zog \'hert-,sȯk\ James Barry Munnik 1866–1942 So. African gen.; organized (1914) Afrikaner Nationalist party demanding complete independence from Britain; prime min. (1924–39)

Herz·berg \'hərts-,bərg\ Gerhard 1904– Canad. (Ger.-born) physical chemist; awarded 1971 Nobel prize for chemistry for research in the structure of molecules, particularly free radicals

Herzl \'hert-s³l\ Theodor 1860–1904 Austrian (Hung.-born) Zionist; considered founder of organized Zionist movement

He·si·od \'hē-sē-əd, 'hes-\ *fl ca* 800 B.C. Greek poet; wrote epics *Works and Days*, with experiences of daily life, and *Theogony*, both full of precepts, fables, allegories, myths

Hess \'hes\ Dame Myra 1890–1965 Eng. pianist; known esp. as interpreter of Bach, Beethoven, Mozart, Schumann

Hess (Walther Richard) Rudolf 1894–1987 Ger. Nazi polit.; Hitler's deputy; tried to negotiate Anglo-German peace (1941) and imprisoned in England; held in Spandau prison until his death

Hess Victor Franz 1883–1964 Austrian physicist; awarded (with C.D. Anderson) 1936 Nobel prize for physics for discovering cosmic rays

Hess Walter Rudolf 1881–1973 Swiss physiol.; awarded (with A.F. Moniz) 1949 Nobel prize for physiology or medicine for discovering how certain parts of the brain control organs of the body

Hes·se \'he-sə\ Hermann 1877–1962 Ger. author; wrote novels and stories of search for spiritual fulfillment, often with Oriental and mystical themes, including *Siddhartha* (1922), etc.; awarded 1946 Nobel prize for literature

He·ve·sy \'he-və-shē, -ve-shē\ Georg Karl 1885–1966 Hung. chem.; awarded 1943 Nobel prize for chemistry for using isotopes as indicators

Hew·ish \'hyü-ish\ Antony 1924–   Brit. astron.; awarded (with Martin Ryle) 1974 Nobel prize for physics for his role in the discovery of pulsars

Hey·drich \'hī-drik, -drik\ Reinhard 1904–1942 *the Hangman* Ger. Nazi administrator; deputy to Himmler; "protector" of Bohemia and Moravia (1941–42); his assassination provoked destruction of Lidice, Czech., and its male population

Hey·er·dahl \'hā-ər-,däl\ Thor 1914–   Norw. explorer & writer; known for nautical and archaeological adventures in Polynesia, Easter Island, West Indies, Middle East

Hey·mans \ā-'män(t)s, -'man(t)s\ Corneille-Jean-François 1892–1968 Belg. physiol.; awarded 1938 Nobel prize for physiology or medicine for discoveries concerning respiration

Hey·rov·ský \'hā-,róf-skē, -,róv-\ Jaroslav 1890–1967 Czech chem.; awarded 1959 Nobel prize for chemistry for discovery and development of instrumental method of chemical analysis

Hey·se \'hī-zə\ Paul Johann Ludwig von 1830–1914 Ger. writer; leader of traditionalist Munich circle and author of stories and plays; awarded 1910 Nobel prize for literature

Hey·ward \'hā-wərd\ (Edwin) Du·Bose \dü-'bōz, dyü-\ 1885–1940 Am. author; wrote verse, novels, plays; produced dramatized version of his novel *Porgy* (1927) that was basis of Gershwin opera *Porgy and Bess*

Hey·wood \'hā-,wúd\ John 1497?–?1580 Eng. author; wrote epigrams, proverbs, ballads, and interludes that in the individualized representation of characters were forerunners of English comedy

Heywood Thomas 1574?–1641 Eng. dram.; claimed to have written or collaborated on 220 plays, including *A Woman Kilde with Kindnesse* (1607), *The Rape of Lucrece* (1608)

Hick·ok \'hi-,käk\ James Butler 1837–1876 *Wild Bill* Am. scout & U.S. marshal; reputation as fighter and crack shot inspired many legends and dime novels; murdered in Dakota Territory

Hicks \'hiks\ Edward 1780–1849 Am. painter; known for naive scenes of rural Pennsylvania and New York and for many versions of allegorical *The Peaceable Kingdom*

Hicks Sir John Richard 1904–1989 Brit. econ.; awarded (with Kenneth J. Arrow) 1972 Nobel prize for economics for their contribution to general equilibrium and welfare theories

Hi·ero I \'hī-ə-,rō\ *or* **Hi·er·on** \-,rän\ *d* 467(or 466) B.C. tyrant of Syracuse (478–467 or 466); gained supreme control of Sicily; patron of poets and philosophers

Hieronymus Saint Eusebius — see JEROME

Hig·gin·son \'hi-gən-sən\ Thomas Wentworth Storrow 1823–1911 Am. clergyman & writer; active in antislavery and women's rights movements; colonel of first Negro regiment in Union army

Hil·bert \'hil-bərt\ David 1862–1943 Ger. math.; made advances in number theory, geometry, theory of gases, and theory of radiation

Hildebrand — see Pope GREGORY VII

Hill \\'hil\\ Ambrose Powell 1825–1865 Am. Confed. gen.; initiated attack that began Battle of Gettysburg (July 1, 1863)

Hill Archibald Vivian 1886–1977 Eng. physiol.; awarded (with Otto Meyerhof) 1922 Nobel prize for physiology or medicine for discoveries on heat production in muscles

Hill James Jerome 1838–1916 Am. financier; his battle for control of Northern Pacific Railroad caused financial panic of 1901

Hill Sir Rowland 1795–1879 Eng. postal reformer; advocated uniform low rates, prepayment through postage stamps

Hil·la·ry \\'hi-lə-rē\\ Sir Edmund Percival 1919–   N.Z. mountaineer & explorer; with Sherpa Tenzing Norgay reached summit of Mt. Everest (1953)

Hil·lel \\'hi-ləl, -ˌlel\\ 1st cent. B.C.–1st cent. A.D. Jewish teacher; revered as leader of exemplary virtue who strongly affected Jewish life and outlook

Hil·liard \\'hil-yərd\\ Nicholas 1547–1619 Eng. painter; founded English school of miniature painting

Hill·man \\'hil-mən\\ Sidney 1887–1946 Am. labor leader; organizer among textile workers

Hil·ton \\'hil-t²n\\ Conrad Nicholson 1887–1979 Am. hotelier; built or acquired hotels across the U.S. and then around the world

Hilton James 1900–1954 Eng. nov.; author of *Goodbye, Mr. Chips* (1934), etc.

Himm·ler \\'him-lər\\ Heinrich 1900–1945 Ger. Nazi polit.; in charge of establishment of concentration camps and internment of Jews and others and of extermination campaign (1941–45)

Hin·de·mith \\'hin-də-ˌmit, -ˌmith, -mət, -ˌməth\\ Paul 1895–1963 Am. (Ger.-born) violist & composer; sought to revive tonality and to develop idea of pieces composed for ordinary occasions

Hin·den·burg \\'hin-dən-ˌbərg, -ˌbûrg\\ Paul von 1847–1934 *Paul Ludwig Hans Anton von Beneckendorff und von Hindenburg* Ger. field marshal; pres. of Germany (1925–34); defeated Hitler at polls (1932) but forced to appoint him chancellor (1933)

Hin·shel·wood \\'hin(t)-shəl-ˌwûd\\ Sir Cyril Norman 1897–1967 Brit. chem.; awarded (with N. Semenov) 1956 Nobel prize for chemistry for research on reaction rates and mechanisms, esp. oxygen-hydrogen reaction

Hip·par·chus \\hi-'pär-kəs\\ d 514 B.C. tyrant of Athens (527–514); assassinated by Harmodius and Aristogiton

Hipparchus *or* **Hip·par·chos** \\hi-'pär-kəs\\ fl 146–127 B.C. Greek astron.; great astronomer of antiquity; devised latitude and longitude, trigonometry; discovered precession of equinoxes

Hip·pi·as \\'hi-pē-əs\\ d 490 B.C. *bro. of Hipparchus* tyrant of Athens; ruled with great severity after assassination of brother until forced into exile (510)

Hip·poc·ra·tes \\hi-'pä-krə-ˌtēz\\ ca 460–ca 377 B.C. *father of medicine* Greek physician; traditionally but incorrectly credited with Hippocratic oath administered to graduate physicians

Hi·ro·hi·to \\ˌhir-ō-'hē-(ˌ)tō\\ 1901–1989 emp. of Japan (1926–89); democratic constitutional monarch after WWII

Hi·ro·shi·ge \\ˌhir-ə-'shē-gä\\ Ando 1797–1858 Jp. painter; last great master of Ukiyo-e color woodblock print; known for landscapes

Hitch·cock \\'hich-ˌkäk\\ Sir Alfred Joseph 1899–1980 Brit. film director; known as master of suspense and film technique with *Vertigo* (1958), *Psycho* (1960), etc. — **Hitch·cock·ian** \hich-'kä-kē-ən\ *adj*

Hitchcock Edward 1793–1864 Am. geologist; conducted geological survey of Massachusetts, including investigation of dinosaur tracks in Connecticut Valley sandstone

Hitch·ings \'hi-chiŋz\ George Herbert 1905– Am. biochem.; awarded (with Gertrude B. Elion and Sir James Black) 1988 Nobel prize for physiology or medicine for discoveries of important principles for drug treatment

Hit·ler \'hit-lər\ Adolf 1889–1945 Ger. chancellor & führer; with associates Göring, Goebbels, Himmler, Streicher, etc., conducted regime of terror based on belief in superiority of Aryan race, infallibility of Führer, and inferiority of all others, especially Jews; brought on WWII — **Hit·ler·ian** \hit-'lir-ē-ən, -'ler-\ *adj*

Hit·ti \'hi-tē\ Philip Khuri 1886–1978 Am. (Lebanese-born) orientalist; wrote *The Near East in History* (1961), *History of the Arabs* (1967), etc.

Hit·torf \'hi-ˌtȯrf\ Johann Wilhelm 1824–1914 Ger. physicist; pioneer in electrochemical research on rarefied gases, cathode rays

Hoare \'hȯr, 'hȯr\ Sir Samuel John Gurney 1880–1959 Viscount *Templewood* Eng. statesman; attempted to settle Italian claims in Ethiopia with Hoare-Laval plan (1935)

Ho·bart \'hō-ˌbärt, -bart\ Garret Augustus 1844–1899 Am. polit.; vice pres. of the U.S. (1897–99)

Hob·be·ma \'hä-bə-mə\ Mein·dert *or* Meyn·dert \'mīn-ˌdert\ 1638–1709 Du. painter; one of leading Baroque landscape painters of his day

Hobbes \'häbz\ Thomas 1588–1679 Eng. philos.; best known for political philosophy based on idea of social contract for security of individual and absolute authority of sovereign — **Hobbes·ian** \'häb-zē-ən\ *adj* — **Hob·bist** \'hä-bist\ *adj or n*

Hoc·cleve \'häk-ˌlēv\ *or* **Oc·cleve** \'äk-\ Thomas 1368 (or 1369)–ca 1450 Eng. poet; wrote mediocre verse of considerable historical value

Ho Chi Minh \'hō-'chē-'min, -'shē-\ 1890–1969 orig. *Nguyen That Thanh* pres. of No. Vietnam (1945–69); presided over successful war with French (1946–54), with South and U.S. (1959–69)

Hock·ing \'hä-kiŋ\ William Ernest 1873–1966 Am. philos.; concerned with spiritual dimension of human experience

Hodg·kin \'häj-kin\ Sir Alan Lloyd 1914– Brit. physiol.; awarded (with A.F. Huxley and J.C. Eccles) 1963 Nobel prize for physiology or medicine for describing the behavior of nerve impulses

Hodgkin Dorothy Mary Crowfoot 1910–1994 Brit. physicist; awarded 1964 Nobel prize for chemistry for X-ray studies of compounds such as vitamin B_{12}, insulin, penicillin

Hoe \'hō\ Richard March 1812–1886 *son of Robert* Am. inventor; invented rotary press (1847), web press (ca. 1847), web perfecting press (1871) that made large-circulation daily newspaper possible

Hoe Robert 1784–1833 Am. (Eng.-born) printing-press manuf.; produced Samuel Rust's iron-framed "Washington" press

Ho·fer \\'hō-fər\\ Andreas 1767–1810 Tyrolese patriot; established independence of Tyrol (1809) but defeated by French and Bavarian forces

Hof·fa \\'hä-fə\\ James Riddle 1913–?1975 Am. labor leader; pres., International Brotherhood of Teamsters (1957–71); imprisoned for mail fraud, financial irregularities (1967–71); disappeared

Hoff·man \\'häf-mən, 'hóf-\\ Mal·vi·na \\mal-'vē-nə\\ 1887–1966 Am. sculptor; executed portrait busts of Paderewski, Pavlova, John Muir, etc.

Hoff·mann \\'häf-mən, 'hóf-, -ˌmän\\ August Heinrich 1798–1874 Ger. poet, philologist, & hist.; wrote lyric, patriotic verse including "Deutschland, Deutschland über Alles" (1841), used as national hymn (from 1922)

Hoffmann Ernst Theodor Wilhelm 1776–1822 known as *Ernst Theodor Amadeus Hoffmann* Ger. composer, writer, & illustrator; composed operas, tales of supernatural that inspired operas and ballets by Offenbach, Delibes, Hindemith, etc.

Hoffmann Roald 1937– Am. (Pol.-born) chem.; awarded (with Kenichi Fukui) 1981 Nobel prize for chemistry for using quantum mechanics to predict the course of chemical reactions

Hof·mann \\'häf-mən, 'hóf-, -ˌmän\\ August Wilhelm von 1818–1892 Ger. chem.; known for researches in organic chemistry, esp. on coal-tar products

Hofmann Hans 1880–1966 Am. (Ger.-born) painter; a founder and leading exponent of Abstract Expressionism

Hofmann Josef Casimir 1876–1957 Am. (Pol.-born) pianist; child prodigy; studied with Anton Rubenstein; composed under name Michel Dvor·sky \\'dvór-skē\\

Hof·manns·thal \\'häf-mənz-ˌtäl, 'hóf-\\ Hugo von 1874–1929 Austrian poet & dram.; wrote libretti for Strauss's operas *Der Rosenkavalier* (1911), *Ariadne auf Naxos* (1912), etc.

Hof·stadt·er \\'hóf-ˌsta-tər\\ Robert 1915–1990 Am. physicist; awarded (with R.L. Mössbauer) 1961 Nobel prize for physics for study of nucleons

Ho·garth \\'hō-ˌgärth\\ William 1697–1764 Eng. painter & engraver; remembered for satirical narrative pictures — **Ho·garth·ian** \\hō-'gär-thē-ən\\ *adj*

Hog·ben \\'hóg-bən, 'häg-\\ Lancelot Thomas 1895–1975 Eng. scientist; developed theories of social biology in *Nature and Nurture* (1933), etc.

Hogg \\'hóg, 'häg\\ James 1770–1835 *the Ettrick Shepherd* Scot. poet; wrote ballads that were popular during the ballad revival of the Romantic movement

Ho·hen·zol·lern \\hō-ənt-'só-lərn\\ Michael — see MICHAEL

Ho·ku·sai \\'hō-kú-ˌsī, ˌhō-kú-'\\ Katsushika 1760–1849 Jp. artist; a leader of Ukiyo-e woodblock school; developed landscape art to new level of simple grandeur and influenced European artists

Hol·bein \\'hōl-ˌbīn, 'hól-\\ Hans 1465?–1524 *the Elder* & Hans 1497?–1543 *the Younger* Ger. painters; the Elder is known for religious works; the Younger is known for vivid, psychologically penetrating portraits esp. of the court of England's Henry VIII

Hol·berg \\'hōl-ˌberg\\ Baron 1684–1754 *Ludvig Holberg* Dan. (Norw.-born) author; considered founder of Norwegian and Danish literature

Hol·i·day \'hä-lə-‚dā\ Eleanora 1915–1959 *Billie Holiday* Am. jazz singer; considered supreme jazz singer of her day, with intensely dramatic style of phrasing and diction

Hol·in·shed \'hä-lən-‚shed\ *or* **Hol·lings·head** \-liŋz-‚hed\ Raphael *d ca* 1580 Eng. chronicler; published *Chronicles of England, Scotlande, and Irelande* (1577) that gave Shakespeare data for historical plays, Macbeth, King Lear, etc.

Hol·land \'hä-lənd\ John Philip 1840–1914 Am. (Irish-born) inventor; invented submarine with both internal-combustion and electric motors, purchased by U.S. government

Holland Sir Sidney George 1893–1961 prime min. of New Zealand (1945–57); secured abolition of Legislative Council (1950)

Hol·ley \'hä-lē\ Robert William 1922–1993 Am. biochem.; awarded (with H. Gobind Khorana and Marshall W. Nirenberg) 1968 Nobel prize for physiology or medicine for explaining how genes determine the function of cells

Holm \'hōm\ Hanya 1898–1992 *orig. Johanna Kantze née Eckert* Am. dancer & choreographer; best known for choreographing Broadway musicals, including *My Fair Lady* (1956), *Camelot* (1960)

Holman–Hunt William — see Holman HUNT

Holmes \'hōmz, 'hōlmz\ Oliver Wendell 1809–1894 Am. physician & author; wrote poems "Old Ironsides," "The Chambered Nautilus," etc., and light, witty verse, novels, essays

Holmes Oliver Wendell 1841–1935 *son of prec.* Am. jurist; associate justice, U.S. Supreme Court (1902–32); narrow constructionist; promulgated "clear and present danger" test for freedom of speech

Holst \'hōlst\ Gustav Theodore 1874–1934 Eng. composer; influenced by English folk music, Hindu literature, Stravinsky, etc.

Holt \'hōlt\ Harold Edward 1908–1967 Austral. polit.; prime min. (1966–67)

Holt Luther Emmett 1855–1924 Am. pediatrician; a founder (1898) and first pres., American Pediatric Society

Hol·yoake \'hōl-‚yōk, 'hō-lē-‚ōk\ Sir Keith Jacka 1904–1983 prime min. of New Zealand (1960–72); governor-general (1977–80), first politician to hold post

Home \'hyüm, 'hōm\ Sir Alec Douglas- 1903–1995 Brit. prime min. (1963–64); renounced peerage to fight by-election (1964)

Home William Douglas- 1912–1992 Brit. dram.; known chiefly for light drawing-room comedies, as *The Secretary Bird*, etc.

Ho·mer \'hō-mər\ 9th–8th? cent. B.C. Greek epic poet; traditional name of author or authors of epics *Iliad* and *Odyssey*, among greatest poet(s) of history

Homer Winslow 1836–1910 Am. artist; painted American genre scenes, seascapes, landscapes, esp. in watercolor

Ho·neck·er \'hō-nə-kər\ Erich 1912–1994 gen. secy. of East German Communist party (1971–89); dismissed with German reunification

Ho·neg·ger \‚ȯ-nā-'ger, '(h)ä-ni-gər\ Arthur 1892–1955 Fr. composer; associated with modern movement in French music in first half of 20th cent.; composed operas, ballets, orchestral works, 5 symphonies, concertos, film scores, etc.

Ho·no·ri·us \hə-ˈnōr-ē-əs, -ˈnȯr-\ Flavius 384–423 Rom. emp. of the West (395–423); ruled while Visigoths ravaged Italy, sacked Rome (410); lost several provinces and much power

Hont·horst \ˈhȯnt-ˌhȯrst\ Gerrit van 1590–1656 Du. painter; known as portrait and figure painter, often of night scenes; influenced by Caravaggio

Hooch or **Hoogh** \ˈhōk\ Pieter de 1629–after 1684 Du. painter; member of Delft baroque school, known for genre paintings marked by striking use of light

Hood \ˈhu̇d\ John Bell 1831–1879 Am. Confed. gen.; defended Atlanta against Sherman

Hood Samuel 1724–1816 1st Viscount *Hood* Brit. admiral; defeated French in West Indies during American Revolution and later directed operations in Gulf of Lyon

Hood Thomas 1799–1845 Eng. poet; produced series of *Comic Annuals* treating current events with caricature

Hooke \ˈhu̇k\ Robert 1635–1703 Eng. scientist; discovered phenomenon of diffraction, propounded wave theory of light, suggested kinetic theory of gases, etc.

Hook·er \ˈhu̇-kər\ Joseph 1814–1879 Am. gen.; known as "Fighting Joe" for service at Williamsburg (May, 1862) and wounded at Antietam

Hooker Sir Joseph Dalton 1817–1911 Eng. botanist; friend of Darwin and supporter of his theory of evolution

Hooker Richard 1554–1600 Eng. theol.; staunch Anglican, opposed to Calvinist, Roman Catholic, Puritan positions

Hooker Thomas 1586?–1647 Eng. Puritan clergyman & founder of Connecticut; helped frame and secure adoption of "Fundamental Orders," Connecticut's constitution

Hoo·ton \ˈhü-tᵊn\ Earnest Albert 1887–1954 Am. anthropol.; known for studies of human evolution, racial types, somatotypes, criminality

Hoo·ver \ˈhü-vər\ Herbert Clark 1874–1964 31st pres. of the U.S. (1929–33); engineered creation of Federal Farm Board, Reconstruction Finance Corp. in response to financial distress

Hoover John Edgar 1895–1972 Am. criminologist; F.B.I. director (1924–72)

Hope \ˈhōp\ Anthony — see Sir Anthony Hope HAWKINS

Hope Bob 1903–   *Leslie Townes Hope* Am. (Brit.-born) comedian; starred in many films, most notably with Bing Crosby in several "Road" (*Road to Singapore* etc.) pictures; also known for entertaining American troops in every foreign conflict since WWII

Hope Victor Alexander John 1887–1951 8th Earl of *Hope·toun* \ˈhōp-tən\ & 2d Marquis of *Lin·lith·gow* \lin-ˈlith-(ˌ)gō\ Brit. soldier; viceroy of India (1936–43)

Hop·kins \ˈhäp-kənz\ Sir Frederick Gow·land \ˈgau̇-lənd\ 1861–1947 Eng. biochem.; awarded (with Christiaan Eijkmans) 1929 Nobel prize for physiology or medicine for finding vitamins that aid growth

Hopkins Gerard Manley 1844–1889 Eng. poet; notable for extraordinary prosodic and technical innovations as in "Carrion Comfort," "Pied Beauty," etc.

Hopkins Harry Lloyd 1890–1946 Am. polit. & administrator; head of Federal Emergency Relief Administration, Works Progress (later Projects) Administration, Lend-Lease Administration

Hopkins Johns \\'jänz\\ 1795–1873 Am. financier; left endowment to found hospital and university named in his honor

Hopkins Mark 1802–1887 Am. educ.; inspired teacher and lecturer and author of books on moral, religious subjects

Hop·kin·son \\'häp-kən-sən\\ Francis 1737–1791 Am. lawyer & satirist; active in pre-Revolutionary activity; signer of Declaration of Independence; helped design American flag

Hop·pe \\'hä-pē\\ William Frederick 1887–1959 Am. billiard player; many-time world champion at 18.1 and 18.2 balkline games and at three-cushion game

Hop·per \\'hä-pər\\ Edward 1882–1967 Am. artist; known for starkly realistic scenes of contemporary life, often with sense of lonely isolation, and marked by a mastery of light

Hopper Grace 1906–1992 Am. admiral, math., & computer scientist; notable for her contributions to the invention of COBOL and computer science; coined the term "bug" to refer to computer error

Hopper (William) DeWolf 1858–1935 Am. actor; starred in Gilbert and Sullivan productions; popularized poem "Casey at the Bat"

Hop·wood \\'häp-,wu̇d\\ (James) Avery 1882–1928 Am. dram.; best known for mystery melodramas and for clever, often risqué, comedies

Hor·ace \\'hȯr-əs, 'här-\\ 65–8 B.C. *Quintus Horatius Flaccus* Rom. poet & satirist; wrote satires, many odes, epodes, verse epistles, treatise on poetry — **Ho·ra·tian** \\hə-'rā-shən\\ *adj*

Hore–Be·li·sha \\'hȯr-bə-'lē-shə, 'hȯr-\\ Leslie 1893–1957 Eng. polit.; originator of Belisha beacons used at pedestrian crossings

Hor·na·day \\'hȯr-nə-,dā\\ William Temple 1854–1937 Am. zool.; promoted game preserves and laws for the protection of wildlife

Horne \\'hȯrn\\ Lena Calhoun 1917–   Am. singer & actress; starred in Broadway musical, films; had long career in nightclubs and concert halls; noted civil rights activist

Horne Marilyn 1934–   Am. opera singer; noted for the exceptional range and flexibility of her mezzo-soprano voice, esp. in roles by Rossini and Handel

Hor·ney \\'hȯr-,nī\\ Karen 1885–1952 née *Danielsen* Am. (Ger.-born) psychoanalyst & author; published critique of Freudian practices; founded Assn. for the Advancement of Psychoanalysis and Amer. Inst. for Psychoanalysis

Hor·nung \\'hȯr-,nəŋ\\ Paul 1935–   Am. football player; quarterback, Greenbay Packers (1956–63, 1964–67); led Packers to 1961 NFL championship

Ho·ro·witz \\'hȯr-ə-,wits, 'här-\\ Vladimir 1903–1989 Am. (Russ.-born) pianist; widely regarded as one of the preeminent pianists of the 20th century; known for exquisite interpretations of music of the Romantics and flawless technique

Horsa — see HENGIST

Hortense de Beauharnais — see BEAUHARNAIS

Hor·thy de Nagy·bán·ya \\'hȯr-tē-dā-'näj-,bán-yə\\ Miklós 1868–1957 Hung. admiral; combated communist regime of Béla Kun (1919); regent of Hungary (1920–44)

Ho·sea \hō-'zā-ə, -'ze-\ 8th cent. B.C. Hebrew prophet

Hou·di·ni \hü-'dē-nē\ Harry 1874–1926 orig. *Erik Weisz* Am. (Hung.-born) magician; known for ability to extricate himself from handcuffs, locked and sealed containers, etc.

Hou·don \'hü-ˌdän, ü-dō⁼\ Jean-Antoine 1741–1828 Fr. sculptor; leading exponent of Rococo style in sculpture with mythological figures, portrait busts

Houns·field \'haúnz-ˌfē(ə)ld\ Godfrey Newbold 1919–   Brit. engineer & inventor; awarded (with A. M. Cormack) 1979 Nobel prize for physiology or medicine for contributions to the development of the computerized axial tomographic (CAT) scanner

House \'haús\ Edward Mandell 1858–1938 *Colonel House* Am. diplomat; acted for U.S. in negotiating armistice with Central Powers; helped negotiate peace (1918–19); helped frame covenant of League of Nations

House·man \'haús-mən\ John 1902–1988 orig. *Jacques Haussmann* Am. (Rom.-born) actor, producer, & director; with Orson Welles founded Mercury Theatre, produced "The War of the Worlds" (1938); produced and/or directed many plays and films

Hous·man \'haús-mən\ Alfred Edward 1859–1936 Eng. classical scholar & poet; edited works of Manilius, Juvenal, Lucan; wrote Romantic yet impeccably classical verse such as "A Shropshire Lad," etc.

Housman Laurence 1865–1959 *bro. of prec.* Eng. writer & illustrator; author of *The Writings of William Blake, The House of Joy,* etc.

Hous·say \ü-'sī\ Bernardo Alberto 1887–1971 Argentine physiol.; awarded (with C.F. and Gerty Cori) 1947 Nobel prize for physiology or medicine for studying the pancreas and pituitary gland

Hous·ton \'hyü-stən, 'yü-\ Samuel 1793–1863 Am. gen.; worked on behalf of Cherokee Nation; defeated Mexican troops; pres. of the Republic of Texas (1836–38, 1841–44); U.S. senator (1846–59); gov. of state of Texas (1859–61)

How·ard \'haú(-ə)rd\ Catherine — see CATHERINE

Howard Henry 1517?–1547 Earl of *Surrey* Eng. soldier & poet; convicted of treason on flimsy evidence and beheaded; helped Wyatt introduce sonnet into English

Howard Oliver Otis 1830–1909 Am. gen. & educ.; served in Sherman's march to the sea; founder & president, Howard Univ.

Howard Sidney Coe 1891–1939 Am. dram.; wrote plays and screenplay for *Gone With the Wind*

Howe \'haú\ Ed 1853–1937 *Edgar Watson* Am. journalist; gained reputation for homely wisdom and nickname "Sage of Potato Hill"

Howe Elias 1819–1867 Am. inventor; patented (1846) design for a sewing machine

Howe Gordon 1928–   Am. (Canad.-born) ice hockey player; played with Detroit Red Wings (1946–71), Houston Aeros (1971–77), New England Whalers (1978–80); scored a then-record career total of 1850 points in NHL

Howe Irving 1920–1993 Am. critic & educator; noted for probing discussion of social and political opinions in literary criticism; wrote *World of Our Fathers* (1976) about emigration of European Jews to U.S.

Howe James Wong 1899–1976 orig. *Wong Tung Jim* Am. (Chin.-born) cinematographer; pioneered in use of wide-angle lens, deep focus, ceilinged sets, hand-held shooting, etc.; one of the greatest cinematographers in film history; filmed *Hud* (1963) etc.

Howe Julia 1819–1910 née *Ward* Am. suffragist & reformer; author of "Battle Hymn of the Republic"; first woman elected to Amer. Academy of Arts and Letters

Howe Richard 1726–1799 *Earl Howe* Eng. admiral; commanded Channel fleet in great victory over the French (1794)

Howe William 1729–1814 5th Viscount *Howe; bro. of prec.* Eng. gen. in America; during Amer. Revolution captured N.Y. City; won victories at White Plains and Brandywine; occupied Phila.

How·ells \ˈhau̇-əlz\ William Dean 1837–1920 Am. author; conducted "Easy Chair" column, *Harper's*, etc.; considered dean of American letters; forwarded careers of Mark Twain, Henry James, Bret Harte, Stephen Crane, etc.

Hr·dlič·ka \ˈhərd-lich-ˌkä\ Aleš \ˈä-ˌlesh\ 1869–1943 Am. (Bohemian-born) anthropol.; known for studies of early man in America, theory that American Indians have Asian origin

Hsüan–t'ung \shü-ˈän-ˈtüŋ\ — see PʻU-I

Hua Kuo–feng \ˈhwä-ˈgwō-ˈfəŋ\ 1920–   pinyin *Hua Guofeng* Chin. premier (1976–80); promoted more pragmatic domestic and foreign policy, encouraging industry and education and closer ties to the West and to developing nations

Huás·car \ˈwäs-ˌkär\ *d* 1532 Inca prince; struggled for sole control of realm with half-brother Atahualpa, who finally captured and assassinated him

Hub·bard \ˈhə-bərd\ Elbert Green 1856–1915 Am. writer; founded Roycroft shop to revive esp. artistic printing; published chiefly biographical sketches

Hub·ble \ˈhə-bəl\ Edwin Powell 1889–1953 Am. astron.; discovered "red shift" that demonstrates galaxies are moving away from ours; deduced Hubble constant

Hu·bel \ˈhyü-bəl, ˈyü-\ David Hunter 1926–   Am. (Canad.-born) neurobiologist; awarded (with R. W. Sperry and T. N. Wiesel) 1981 Nobel prize for physiology or medicine for research on the organization of the brain

Hu·ber \ˈhü-bər, ˈhyü-\ Robert 1937–   Ger. biochem.; awarded (with J. Diesenhofer and H. Michel) 1988 Nobel prize for chemistry for revealing the structure of proteins essential to photosynthesis

Hud·son \ˈhəd-sən\ Henry *d* 1611 Eng. navigator & explorer; in ship *Half Moon* discovered (1609) Hudson River and sailed up it as far as Albany; in the *Discovery* reached Hudson Bay (1610–11)

Hudson Manley Ottmer 1886–1960 Am. jurist; served League of Nations, Permanent Court of Arbitration, Permanent Court of International Justice

Hudson William Henry 1841–1922 Eng. naturalist & writer; author of *The Purple Land that England Lost* (1885), *Green Mansions* (1904); also wrote ornithological studies

Huer·ta \ˈwer-tə, ü-ˈer-\ Victoriano 1854–1916 Mex. gen.; provisional pres. of Mexico (1913–14); not recognized by U.S.; faced with revolts of Caranza, Obregon, Villa, Zapata, resigned

Hug·gins \ˈhə-gənz\ Charles Brenton 1901–   Am. (Canad.-born) physician; awarded (with F.P. Rous) 1966 Nobel prize for physiology or medicine for discovering the use of hormones in treating cancer

Huggins Sir William 1824–1910 Eng. astron.; helped invent stellar spectroscope; studied nebulae; determined velocity of stars, etc.

Hugh Ca·pet \\'hyü-'kā-pət, -'ka-, -ka-'pä\\ *ca* 938–996 king of France (987–996); founded Capetian line through intrigue and use of power against rivals

Hughes \\'hyüz *also* 'yüz\\ Charles Evans 1862–1948 Am. jurist; chief justice U.S. Supreme Court (1930–41)

Hughes Howard Robard 1905–1976 Am. businessman & aviator; set many flight records; built and flew wooden "Spruce Goose;" lived as recluse from 1950 on

Hughes (James) Langston 1902–1967 Am. writer; wrote stories *The Ways of White Folks,* poems *Shakespeare in Harlem, Fields of Wonder,* etc.

Hughes Ted 1930–   Brit. poet; poet laureate (1984–); best known for animal poems *The Hawk in the Rain, Lupercal,* etc., and children's poems

Hughes Thomas 1822–1896 Eng. jurist, reformer, & writer; best known for *Tom Brown's School Days* and *Tom Brown at Oxford*

Hughes William Morris 1864–1952 Austral. statesman; prime min. of Australia (1915–23)

Hu·go \\'hyü-(,)gō, 'yü-\\ Victor-Marie 1802–1885 Fr. poet, nov., & dram.; leader of the Romantic movement in France; author of novels *Notre-Dame de Paris, Les Misérables,* satirical poems *Les Châtiments,* etc. — **Hu·go·esque** \\,hyü-(,)gō-'esk, ,yü-\\ *adj*

Hui·zin·ga \\'hī-zin-gə\\ Johan 1872–1945 Du. hist.; wrote *Der Herfsttij der middeleeuwen* (*The Waning of the Middle Ages*), *Erasmus, Homo Ludens,* etc.

Hü·le·gü \\hü-'lā-(,)gü\\ *ca* 1217–*ca* 1265 grandson of Genghis Khan Mongol ruler; overthrew 'Abbāsid caliphate; broke Seljuq power in Persia, invaded Syria but defeated by sultan of Egypt

Hull \\'həl\\ Cordell 1871–1955 Am. statesman; author of federal income tax and inheritance laws; secy. of state (1933–44); awarded 1945 Nobel prize for peace

Hull Isaac 1773–1843 Am. naval officer; in command of the *Constitution* ("Old Ironsides") in its defeat of British *Guerrière*

Hull Robert Marvin 1939–   *Bobby Hull* Am. (Canad.-born) ice hockey player; played (1957–81) with Chicago Black Hawks, Winnipeg Jets, Hartford Whalers; known for swinging slap shot

Hull William 1753–1825 Am. gen.; convicted of cowardice and neglect of duty and sentenced to death for surrender of Detroit during War of 1812; reprieved by Madison

Hulse \\'həls\\ Russell Alan 1950–   Am. physicist; awarded (with J. H. Taylor, Jr.) 1993 Nobel prize for physics for discovery of binary pulsars

Hu·mā·yūn \\hü-'mä-,yün\\ 1508–1556 Mogul emp. of India (1530–56); driven out of India, once to Persia and once to Afghan kingdom; returned both times to reclaim part of territory

Hum·boldt \\'həm-,bōlt, 'hüm-\\ (Friedrich Wilhelm Karl Heinrich) Alexander von 1769–1859 Ger. naturalist, traveler, & statesman; founded comparative climatology, studied origin of tropical storms, intensity of earth's magnetic field, volcanoes, etc.

Humboldt (Karl) Wilhelm von 1767–1835 *bro. of prec.* Ger. philologist & diplomat; pioneer in the study of the interrelationship of language and culture

Hume \'hyüm *also* 'yüm\ David 1711–1776 Scot. philos. & hist.; known esp. for philosophical skepticism; great influence on later metaphysical thought — **Hum·ean** *or* **Hum·ian** \'(h)yü-mē-ən\ *adj*

Hum·per·dinck \'hùm-pər-,diŋk, 'həm-\ Engelbert 1854–1921 Ger. composer; best known as composer of opera *Hansel und Gretel*

Hum·phrey \'həm(p)-frē\ 1391–1447 *son of Henry IV* Duke of *Gloucester* (*the Good Duke*) & Earl of *Pembroke* Eng. statesman & book collector; popular leader of war party hostile to France; gave first books for library at Oxford, later part of Bodleian

Humphrey Hubert Horatio 1911–1978 Am. polit.; vice pres. of the U.S. (1965–69); Democratic candidate for pres. (1968)

Hun·e·ker \'hə-ni-kər\ James Gibbons 1860–1921 Am. critic; wrote *Mezzotints in Modern Music, Melomaniacs, Overtones,* etc.

Hung–wu \'hùŋ-'wü\ *Chu Yüan-chang* \'jü-'yü-'än-'jäŋ\ Chin. emp. (1368–98); founder of Ming dynasty; ruled despotically but established schools, reformed civil service, extended rule beyond China

Hunt \'hənt\ (James Henry) Leigh 1784–1859 Eng. writer; published and defended verse of Shelley, Keats, etc., and championed Romanticism; wrote *The Story of Rimini, Foliage,* etc.

Hunt (William) Hol·man \'hōl-mən\ 1827–1910 Eng. painter; a founder of Pre-Raphaelite Brotherhood, with Millais, Rossetti

Hun·ter \'hən-tər\ Alberta 1895–1984 Am. blues singer; a leading singer in 1920s, 1930s; composed "Workin' Man," "Downhearted Blues," etc.; resumed career in 1977

Hunter John 1728–1793 Brit. anatomist & surgeon; investigated descent of testes in fetus, course of olfactory nerves, function of lymphatics, etc.

Hun·ting·ton \'hən-tiŋ-tən\ Collis Potter 1821–1900 Am. railroad builder; involved in building of transcontinental railroad

Huntington Ellsworth 1876–1947 Am. geographer & explorer; explored canyons of Euphrates River, Russian Turkestan

Huntington Henry Edwards 1850–1927 Am. bibliophile; left library at San Marino, Calif., for public benefit

Huntington Samuel 1731–1796 Am. Revolutionary polit.; signed Declaration of Independence

Hun·tzi·ger \,(h)ənt-sē-'zher\ Charles-Léon-Clément 1880–1941 Fr. gen.; headed delegation that signed peace terms with Germany in 1940 and part of Pétain regime

Hu·nya·di \'hùn-,yä-dē, -,yò-\ Já·nos \'yä-(,)nòsh\ 1407?–1456 Hung. soldier & hero; broke Ottoman hold on Bosnia, Hercegovina, Serbia, Bulgaria, Albania, but later defeated

Hur·ley \'hər-lē\ Patrick Jay 1883–1963 Am. lawyer & diplomat; U.S. ambassador to China (1944–45) charged with reconciling Kuomintang and Communists

Hurst \'hərst\ Sir Cecil James Barrington 1870–1963 Eng. jurist; judge of Permanent Court of International Justice at the Hague (1929–46)

Hurst Fannie 1889–1968 Am. writer; author of novels *Stardust, A President Is Born, Anywoman,* etc., plays, screenplays

Hus \'həs, 'hús\ Jan 1372 (or 1373)–1415 Bohemian religious reformer; excommunicated, tried for heresy, burned at the stake — **Huss·ite** \'həs-, sit, 'hú-\ *adj or n*

Hu·sák \'hü-(,)säk, 'hyü-\ Gustav 1913–1991 pres. of Czechoslovakia (1975–87); fall from power was part of general collapse of communism in Eastern Europe

Ḥu·sayn ibn 'Alī \hü-'sän-,i-bən-ä-'lē\ *ca* 1854–1931 1st king of the Hejaz (1916–24)

Hu Shih \'hü-'shir\ 1891–1962 Chin. philos.; one of leading liberals in China and opponent of communists

Hus·sein I \hü-'sān\ 1935–   king of Jordan (1952–   ); active in promoting peace in the Middle East

Hussein Saddam al-Tikriti 1937–   pres. of Iraq (1979–   ); invaded Kuwait and provoked Persian Gulf war (1991)

Hus·serl \'hú-sə-rəl\ Edmund 1859–1938 Ger. philos.; developed phenomenological method — **Hus·serl·ian** \'hú-'sər-lē-ən\ *adj*

Hus·ton \'hyü-stən, 'yü-\ John 1906–1987 Am. motion-picture director, writer, & actor; directed *The Maltese Falcon* (1941), *The African Queen* (1951), etc.; noted for action, use of color

Hu·szár \'hú-,sär\ Károly 1882–1941 Hung. journalist & polit.; imprisoned during communist dictatorship (1919); prime min. (1919–20)

Hutch·ins \'hə-chənz\ Robert Maynard 1899–1977 Am. educ.; introduced "Great Books" undergraduate program and abolished football at U. of Chicago (1929–51)

Hutch·in·son \'hə-chə(n)-sən\ Anne 1591–1643 née *Marbury* Am. (Eng.-born) religious dissident; preached salvation by individual intuition of God's grace and moral laws; banished from Mass. Bay Colony; one of the founders of Rhode Island

Hutchinson Thomas 1711–1780 Am. colonial administrator; as chief justice of Mass. (1760–69) upheld legality of Stamp Act; as royal governor (1771–74) staunchly upheld British authority

Hut·ten \'hú-t ʰn\ Ulrich von 1488–1523 Ger. humanist & supporter of Luther; known in literature as a bitter satirist; wrote Latin pamphlets on Luther's behalf

Hux·ley \'həks-lē\ Al·dous \'ól-dəs\ Leonard 1894–1963 *bro. of J.S.* Eng. nov. & critic; best known for novel *Brave New World* (1932) — **Hux·lei·an** \,həks-'lē-ən, 'həks-lē-\ *or* **Hux·ley·an** \'həks-lē-ən\ *adj*

Huxley Andrew Fielding 1917–   Brit. physiol. & educ.; awarded (with A. L. Hodgkin and J.C. Eccles) 1963 Nobel prize for physiology or medicine for work on the behavior of nerve impulses

Huxley Sir Julian Sorell 1887–1975 *grandson of T.H.* Eng. biol.; developed pragmatic ethical system based on natural selection

Huxley Thomas Henry 1825–1895 Eng. biol.; foremost advocate in England of Darwin's theory of evolution

Huy·gens \'hī-gənz, 'hòi-\ Christiaan 1629–1695 Du. math., physicist, & astron.; enunciated Huygen's principle for determining the surface constituting a wave front, etc.

Huys·mans \wē-'smäⁿs\ Camille 1871–1968 Belg. polit.; helped form Socialist party (1933), prime min. (1946–47)

Huysmans Joris-Karl 1848–1907 orig. *Georges-Charles* Fr. nov.; novels notable for realism, later for anti-materialism; aesthetic views influenced Oscar Wilde

Hwang \'hwaŋ\ David Henry 1957–   Am. playwright & screenwriter; best known for Broadway play *M. Butterfly* (1988)

Hy·att \'hī-ət\ Alpheus 1838–1902 Am. naturalist; founded new school of invertebrate paleontology

Hyde \'hīd\ Douglas 1860–1949 pseud. *An Craoibhín Aoibhinn* Irish author; identified with Irish nationalist movement from its inception; pres. of Republic of Ireland (1938–45)

Hyde Edward 1609–1674 1st Earl of *Clar·en·don* \'klar-ən-dən, 'kler\ Eng. statesman & hist.; virtual head of government under Charles II, enforcing repressive laws and measures; banished

Hy·der Ali *or* **Hai·dar Ali** \'hī-dər-ä-'lē\ 1722–1782 Indian ruler & soldier; successfully expanded Mysore territory at expense of British until defeated by them (1781)

Hy·mans \'hī-ˌmän(t)s, ē-'mäⁿs\ Paul 1865–1941 Belg. statesman; represented Belgium at Paris Peace Conference and League of Nations

Hy·pse·lan·tes \ˌēp-sə-'län-dēs\ *var of* YPSILANTIS

I

Ibáñez Vicente Blasco- — see BLASCO IBÁÑEZ

Iber·ville \'ē-bər-ˌvil, -ˌvēl; 'ī-bər-ˌvil\ Sieur d' 1661–1706 *Pierre Le Moyne* \'mwän\ Fr.-Canad. explorer & founder of Louisiana; explored the Mississippi; discovered Lake Pontchartrain

Ibn–Khal·dūn \ˌi-bən-ˌkal-'dün, -ˌkal-\ 1332–1406 Arab hist.; wrote *Muqaddimah* (a masterly theory of history and pioneering work in sociology) and a definitive history of Muslim North Africa

Ibn–Rushd \ˌi-bən-'rüsht\ — see AVERROËS

Ibn Sa·ʿūd \ˌi-bən-sä-'üd, -'saúd\ *ca* 1880–1953 king of Saudi Arabia (1932–53); Muslim leader and founder of Saudi Arabia; granted first oil concession to a U.S. company in 1933

Ibn Zuhr \ˌi-bən-'zúr\ *L* **Av·en·zo·ar** \ˌa-vən-'zō-ər, -zō-'är\ *or* **Abu·me·ron** \ˌa-byü-'mer-ˌän\ *ca* 1090–1162 Muslim physician; described pericarditis, cataract surgery, kidney stones, etc.

Ibrā·him Pa·sha \i-ˌbrä-'him-'pä-shə, -'pa-shə, -pə-'shä\ 1789–1848 Egypt. gen. & viceroy; reformed administration; repressed revolts; defeated invading Ottoman army

Ib·sen \'ib-sən, 'ip-\ Henrik 1828–1906 Norw. poet & dram.; plays including *Peer Gynt* (1867), *A Doll's House* (1879), *Hedda Gabler* (1890), etc., noted for psychological insight, symbolism, social criticism — **Ib·se·ni·an** \ib-'sē-nē-ən, ip-, -'se-nē-\ *or* **Ib·sen·esque** \ˌib-sə-'nesk, ˌip-\ *adj* — **Ib·sen·ite** \'ib-sə-ˌnit\ *adj or n*

Ick·es \'i-kəs\ Harold LeClair 1874–1952 Am. polit.; U.S. secy. of the interior (1933–46); head of Public Works Administration (1933–39)

Ic·ti·nus \ik-'tī-nəs\ 5th cent. B.C. Greek architect; chief designer (with Callicrates) of Parthenon at Athens

Ig·na·tius \ig-'nā-sh(ē-)əs\ Saint *d ca* A.D. 110 *Theophorus* bishop of Antioch & church father; martyred at Rome under Trajan

Ignatius of Loyola Saint 1491–1556 orig. *Iñigo de Oñaz y Loyola* Span. religious & founder of Society of Jesus; directed order toward worldwide apostolate and education of youth — **Ig·na·tian** \-sh(ē)ən\ *adj*

Ike·da \ē-'kä-də, -'ke\ Hayato 1899–1965 Jp. polit.; prime min. (1960–64); a chief architect of Japan's postwar economic growth and development

Ikhnaton — see AKHENATON

Il·ies·cu \i-lē-'es-(,)kü, il-'yes-\ Ion 1930–   pres. of Romania (1989–   )

Im·mel·mann \'i-məl-,män, -mən\ Max 1890–1916 Ger. aviator; regarded as a founder of German technique of air combat; developed the "Immelmann turn"

In·di·ana \,in-dē-'a-nə\ Robert 1928–   orig. surname *Clarke* Am. painter & designer; part of pop art movement; best known for compositions based on the word *love*

In·dy, d' \'dan-dē; dan-'dē, daⁿ-\ (Paul-Marie-Théodore-) Vincent 1851–1931 Fr. composer; a leader of radical modern French school; revived interest in Gregorian plainchant

Inés de Castro — see CASTRO

Inge \'inj\ William 1913–1973 Am. playwright; wrote *Come Back, Little Sheba, Picnic* (1953, Pulitzer prize), *Bus Stop*, etc.

Inge \'in\ William Ralph 1860–1954 Eng. prelate & author; "the Gloomy Dean," wrote works on mysticism, modern ethical dilemmas

In·ger·soll \'in-gər-,sól, -səl\ Robert Green 1833–1899 Am. orator; noted agnostic lecturer who attacked popular Christian beliefs

In·gres \'aⁿ(n)grᵊ\ Jean-Auguste-Dominique 1780–1867 Fr. painter; leader among the Classicists; known for portraits, mythological and historical paintings, and scenes celebrating Napoléon

In·ness \'i-nəs\ George: father 1825–1894 & son 1854–1926 Am. painters; father was landscapist who showed influence of Hudson River School, the Dutch, and the Barbizon school

In·no·cent \'i-nə-sənt\ name of 13 popes: esp. **II** *d* 1143 (pope 1130–43); drafted Concordat of Worms; **III** 1160 (or 1161)–1216 (pope 1198–1216); brought papal power to its highest point; **IV** *d* 1254 (pope 1243–54); carried on struggle with Holy Roman Emperor Frederick II and his sons; **XI** 1611–1689 (pope 1676–89); engaged in long struggle with France's Louis XIV and joined Holy League

Inö·nü \,i-nə-'nü, -'nyü\ İsmet \is-'met\ 1884–1973 Turk. statesman; pres. of Turkey (1938–50); premier (1961–65); in large measure responsible for transformation of Turkey into modern state

In·sull \'in(t)-səl\ Samuel 1859–1938 Am. (Eng.-born) financier; private secretary to Thomas Edison; creator, pres. of several large electric companies

Io·nes·cu \,ē-ə-'nes-(,)kō\ Eugène 1909–1994 Fr. (Rom.-born) dram.; leading exponent of Theatre of the Absurd with *The Bald Soprano* (1949), *Rhinoceros* (1959), etc.

Ipa·tieff \i-'pä-tē-,ef, -'pä-chəf\ Vladimir Nikolayevich 1867–1952

Am. (Russ.-born) chem.; authority on high-pressure catalytic reactions important in refining of petroleum and synthesizing hydrocarbons

Ire·dell \'ir-,del\ James 1751–1799 Am. jurist; associate justice, U.S. Supreme Court (1790–99)

Ire·ton \'ir-t°n\ Henry 1611–1651 Eng. soldier & polit.; presented "Heads of Proposals" scheme for constitutional monarchy; signed warrant for execution of Charles I

Iri·go·yen \,ir-i-'gō-,yen\ Hi·pó·li·to \ē-'pó-lē-,tō\ 1852–1933 pres. of Argentina (1916–22; 1928–30); forced out by military coup

Iron·side \'i(-ə)rn-,sīd\ William Edmund 1880–1959 1st Baron *Ironside* Brit. field marshal; served in Boer War, WWI, and in Persia, India, and Middle East; commander of Home Defense Forces (1940)

Ir·ving \'ər-viŋ\ Sir Henry 1838–1905 orig. *John Henry Brodribb* Eng. actor; noted for sumptuous, meticulously detailed productions; first actor to be knighted

Irving Washington 1783–1859 Am. essayist, nov., & hist.; wrote "Rip Van Winkle," "Legend of Sleepy Hollow," *A History of the Conquest of Granada, The Alhambra, Life of Washington,* etc.

Ir·win \'ər-wən\ William Henry 1873–1948 *Will Irwin* Am. journalist; war correspondent for *Saturday Evening Post,* author of *Men, Women, and War, Propaganda and the News,* etc.

Isaacs \'i-ziks, -zəks\ Sir Isaac Alfred 1855–1948 Austral. jurist & statesman; gov.-gen. of Australia (1931–36)

Isaacs Rufus Daniel — see Marquis of READING

Is·a·bel·la I \,i-zə-'be-lə\ 1451–1504 *wife of Ferdinand V of Castile* queen of Castile (1474–1504) & of Aragon (1479–1504); aided Columbus; interested in reform of clergy and religious orders

Isa·iah \i-'zā-ə\ 8th cent. B.C. Hebrew prophet; considered author of first 39 chapters of Old Testament book of Isaiah

Ish·er·wood \'i-shər-,wud\ Christopher William Bradshaw 1904–1986 Am. (Brit.-born) writer; best known for *Mr. Norris Changes Trains* and *Goodbye to Berlin,* novels republished as *The Berlin Stories* (1956) and later dramatized as play *I Am a Camera* and musical *Cabaret*

Ishii \'ē-shē-,ē, 'i-\ Viscount Kikujiro 1866–1945 Jp. diplomat; negotiated agreement (1917) by which U.S. recognized Japan's interests in China

Is·i·dore of Seville \'i-zə-,dōr, -,dòr\ Saint *ca* 560–636 L. *Isidorus Hispalensis* Span. prelate & scholar; considered most learned man of his time; last of the Latin church fathers, his *Etymologiae* was for centuries a popular reference work

Iskander Bey — see SKANDERBEG

Is·mā·'īl Pa·sha \is-'mä-,ēl-'pä-shə, -'pa-shə, -pə-'shä\ 1830–1895 viceroy of Egypt (1863–79); rebuilt Cairo; improved Alexandria; encouraged Suez Canal project

Isoc·ra·tes \i-'sä-krə-,tēz\ 436–338 B.C. Athenian orator; founder of school in Athens; a leader of conservative, Panhellenic opinion

Is·ra·el ben Eli·ezer \'iz-rē-əl,ben-,e-lē-'ā-zər\ *ca* 1700–1760 *Ba'al Shem Tov* \'bä(-ə)l-'shem-'tòv\ Pol.-Jewish religious leader; founder of Hasidism, emphasizing joyful spirituality

Ito \ˈē-(ˌ)tō\ Prince Hirobumi 1841–1909 Jp. statesman; strong supporter of Western ideas; drafted Meiji Constitution (adopted 1889); credited with creating National Diet (1890)

Itur·bi \i-ˈtur-bē\ José 1895–1980 Span.-born pianist & conductor; musical director, Rochester Philharmonic Orchestra (1936–44)

Itur·bi·de \ˌē-ˌtur-ˈbē-(ˌ)thā\ Agustín de 1783–1824 Mex. soldier; emp. of Mexico (1822–23); harsh regime led to revolution by Santa Anna, Guérrero, etc., abdication, exile, execution

Ivan III \ē-ˈvän, ˈī-vən\ **Va·si·lye·vich** \və-ˈsil-yə-ˌvich\ 1440–1505 *the Great* grand prince of Russia (1462–1505); strengthened leadership of Moscow; threw off Tatars; expanded territory

Ivan IV Vasilyevich 1530–1584 *the Terrible* ruler of Russia (1533–84); instituted new legal code, but waged campaign of terror against boyars; killed own son in anger

Ives \ˈīvz\ Charles Edward 1874–1954 Am. composer; known for innovative use of dissonance, polytonal harmonies, unusual rhythms — **Ives·ian** \ˈīv-zē-ən\ *adj*

Ives James Merritt 1824–1895 Am. lithographer; with Nathaniel Currier, issued series of individually hand-colored prints showing manners, picturesque scenes, events, persons of the U.S.

Iyeyasu *or* **Ieyasu** — see TOKUGAWA

J

Jā·bir ibn Ḥay·yān \ˈja-ˌbir-ˌi-bən-hī-ˈyan\ Abū Mūsā *ca* 721–*ca* 851 L. *Ge·ber* \ˈja-ˌbir, ˈga-, ˈge-\ Arab alchemist & mystic; author of highly influential works on alchemy and metaphysics

Jack·son \ˈjak-sən\ Andrew 1767–1845 Am. gen.; 7th pres. of the U.S. (1829–37); introduced spoils system; vetoed charter renewal of U.S. Bank; encouraged Western expansion; paid off national debt — **Jack·son·ian** \jak-ˈsō-nē-ən\ *adj*

Jackson Helen Maria Hunt 1830–1885 née *Fiske* Am. nov.; wrote novel *Ramona*, etc., and nonfictional *A Century of Dishonor* resulting in her appointment to investigate Indian conditions

Jackson Jesse Louis 1941– Am. clergyman & polit. activist; active in civil rights movement; first African-American to become serious candidate for U.S. president

Jackson Mahalia 1911–1972 Am. gospel singer; acknowledged as finest gospel singer of her day

Jackson Michael Joseph 1958– Am. singer; began singing with brothers in The Jackson Five; as solo performer made several hugely successful albums, including *Thriller*, the best-selling album in recording history

Jackson Reggie 1946– *Reginald Martinez Jackson* Am. baseball player; played (1968–87) with Oakland Athletics, Baltimore Orioles, New York Yankees, California Angels; from 1973 played mostly as a designated hitter

Jackson Robert Hough·wout \\'haủ-ət\\ 1892–1954 Am. jurist; associate justice, U.S. Supreme Court (1941–54); chief prosecutor for U.S. at Nürnberg war crimes tribunal

Jackson Thomas Jonathan 1824–1863 *Stone·wall* \\'stōn-ˌwȯl\\ *Jackson* Am. Confed. gen.; led Shenandoah Valley campaign; gave invaluable aid to Lee in Maryland campaign and elsewhere

Ja·cob \\zhä-kȯb\\ François 1920–   Fr. geneticist; awarded (with A. Lwoff and J. Monod) 1965 Nobel prize for physiology or medicine for discoveries concerning genetic control of enzyme and virus synthesis

Ja·co·po del·la Quer·cia \\yä-'kō-(ˌ)pō-ˌdä-lə-'kwer-chä\\ *ca* 1374–1438 Ital. sculptor; one of the most original Italian sculptors of the 15th century

Jac·quard \\zha-'kär, 'ja-ˌkärd\\ Joseph-Marie 1752–1834 Fr. inventor; invented Jacquard loom, first to include all weaving motions and weave figured patterns

Jacques I — see Jean-Jacques DESSALINES

Jag·a·tai — see CHAGATAI

Ja·hän·gir \\jə-'hän-ˌgir\\ 1569–1627 emp. of India (1605–27); visited by first English envoys, Capt. William Hawkins, Sir Thomas Roe

Ja·lāl ad–Dīn ar–Rū·mī \\jə-'lä-lə-'dē-när-'rü-mē\\ *ca* 1207–1273 Pers. poet; influenced by music and natural rhythms; often danced while reciting; disciples became Mawlawīyah (Whirling Dervishes)

James \\'jāmz\\ Saint *d ca* 44 A.D. Christian apostle; son of Zebedee

James Saint 1st cent. A.D. Christian apostle; son of Alphaeus

James Saint *d ca* 62 A.D. Christian leader; believed variously to be brother, stepbrother, or cousin of Jesus; reputed author of New Testament Epistle of James

James name of 6 kings of Scotland & 2 kings of Great Britain: esp. **VI** 1566–1625 of Scotland (reigned 1567–1603) *or* **I** of Great Britain (reigned 1603–25); alienated various Protestant sects; his severity toward Roman Catholics provoked Gunpowder Plot; King James Bible prepared during his reign; **II** 1633–1701 (reigned 1685–88); published Declaration of Indulgence, giving liberty of conscience to all religious denominations; defeated by William of Orange at battle of the Boyne

James Henry 1811–1882 Am. philos.; influenced by Swedenborgianism and Fourierism; author of *Society the Redeemed Form of Man,* etc.

James Henry 1843–1916 *son of prec.* Brit. (Am.-born) writer; author of novels *The Europeans, Daisy Miller, The Bostonians,* etc., shorter works *The Turn of the Screw,* etc., and essays, criticisms, autobiographies, etc. — **James·ian** \\'jām-zē-ən\\ *adj*

James Jesse Woodson 1847–1882 Am. outlaw; led gang comprising brother Frank, the Younger brothers, etc., in train and bank robberies until murdered by gang member for reward

James Phyllis Dorothy 1920–   Brit. writer; author of psychological detective novels *Shroud for a Nightingale, Innocent Blood,* etc., and futuristic *The Children of Men*

James William 1842–1910 *bro. of Henry* Am. psychol. & philos.; a founder of pragmatism; author of *The Varieties of Religious Experience,* etc. — **James·ian** \\'jām-zē-ən\\ *adj*

James Edward 1688–1766 *James Francis Edward Stuart; the Old Pretender* Eng. prince; failed in two attempts to land in Scotland to claim throne

Jame·son \'jām-sən, 'je-mə-sən\ Sir Leander Starr 1853–1917 *Doctor Jameson* Scot. physician & administrator in So. Africa; made unsuccessful attempt to overthrow Boer government of Transvaal; prime min. of Cape Colony; founder, leader of Unionist party

Jā·mī \'jä-mē\ 1414–1492 Pers. poet & mystic; gained great reputation as Sūfī scholar and mystic

Jamison \'jä-mə-sən\ Judith 1943–   Am. dancer & choreographer; with Alvin Ailey's American Dance Theater as dancer (1965–80), as artistic director (1990–); choreographed many works, including *Divining Hymn* for Alvin Ailey

Ja·ná·ček \'yä-nə-ˌchek\ Leoš 1854–1928 Czech composer; a leading exponent of musical nationalism, deeply influenced by Moravian folk music in operas, ballets, etc.

Jan·sen \'jan(t)-sən, 'yän(t)-\ Cor·ne·lis \kȯr-'nā-ləs\ 1585–1638 L. *Cornelius Jansenius* Du. R.C. theol.; maintained that teaching of St. Augustine on grace, free will, predestination was opposed to Jesuit teachings — **Jan·sen·ist** \'jan(t)-sə-nist\ *n* — **Jan·sen·is·tic** \ˌjan(t)-sə-'nis-tik\ *adj*

Jaques–Dal·croze \'zhäk-ˌdal-'krōz, 'zhak-\ Émile 1865–1950 Swiss composer & creator of eurythmics; developed system of rhythmic training of the whole body

Ja·rīr \jə-'rir\ *ca* 650–*ca* 729 Arab poet; known esp. for satirical verse and poems insulting rivals; contender in famous poetic duels

Jar·rell \jə-'rel, ja-\ Randall 1914–1965 Am. writer; author of verse *Blood for a Stranger*, etc., novel, criticism

Ja·ru·zel·ski \ˌyär-ü-'zel-skē\ Wo·jciech \'vȯi-ˌchek\ Witold 1923– gen.; 1st secy. of the communist party in Poland (1981–89); pres. (1989–90)

Jas·pers \'yäs-pərs\ Karl Theodor 1883–1969 Ger. philos.; one of the most important Existentialist philosophers in Germany; worked on a "world philosophy" for the postwar era

Jauregg Julius Wagner von — see WAGNER VON JAUREGG

Jau·rès \zhō-res\ Jean-Joseph-Marie-Auguste 1859–1914 Fr. socialist; a founder of Parti Socialiste Français; fought militaristic legislation on eve of WWI

Jay \'jā\ John 1745–1829 Am. jurist & statesman; 1st chief justice U.S. Supreme Court (1789–95); negotiated Jay's Treaty with Great Britain settling outstanding disputes (1794–95)

Jeanne d'Arc — see JOAN OF ARC

Jeans \'jēnz\ Sir James Hopwood 1877–1946 Eng. physicist, astron., & author; worked esp. on kinetic theory of gases, radiation, multiple star systems, etc.; wrote scholarly and popular works

Jebb \'jeb\ Sir Richard Claverhouse 1841–1905 Scot. scholar; author of *Attic Orators*, etc.; editor and translator of Sophocles

Jef·fers \'je-fərz\ (John) Robinson 1887–1962 Am. poet; author of lyrics expressing bitter contempt of humanity and love of harsh eternal beauties of nature

Jef·fer·son \'je-fər-sən\ Thomas 1743–1826 Am. statesman; chief author of Declaration of Independence (1776); 3d pres. of the U.S.

(1801–09); purchased Louisiana from France, sent Lewis and Clark to explore it; prohibited importation of slaves; instrumental in founding U. of Virginia (1819) — **Jef·fer·so·nian** \je-fər-'sō-nē-ən, -nyən\ *adj*

Jef·frey \'je-frē\ Lord Francis 1773–1850 Scot. critic & jurist; influential but sometimes harsh critic, esp. of Romantics

Jef·freys \'je-frēz\ George 1645–1689 1st Baron *Jeffreys of Wem* Eng. jurist; notorious for injustice and brutality, esp. in "Bloody Assizes"

Je·hosh·a·phat \ji-'hä-sə-ˌfat, -shə-\ *d ca* 849 B.C. king of Judah; brought Judah into an alliance with northern kingdom of Israel

Jel·li·coe \'je-li-ˌkō\ 1st Earl 1859–1935 *John Rushworth Jellicoe* Brit. admiral; relieved Beijing in Boxer Rebellion; fought battle of Jutland (1916); admiral of the fleet (1919)

Jen·ner \'je-nər\ Edward 1749–1823 Eng. physician; discovered vaccination for smallpox (1798) — **Jen·ne·ri·an** \je-'nir-ē-ən\ *adj*

Jenner Sir William 1815–1898 Eng. physician; established separate identities of typhus and typhoid fevers

Jen·sen \'yen-zən\ (Johannes) Hans Daniel 1907–1973 Ger. physicist; awarded (with M.G. Mayer and E.P. Wagner) 1963 Nobel prize for physics for research on nuclear shell structure

Jen·sen \'yen(t)-sən, 'jen(t)-\ Johannes Vilhelm 1873–1950 Dan. poet & nov.; best known for series of six novels known as *Den lange rejse* (1908–22, *The Long Journey*) retracing human history; awarded 1944 Nobel prize for literature

Jen·son \'jen-sən, zhän-'sōⁿ\ Nicolas *ca* 1420–1480 Fr. printer & engraver in Venice; perfected Roman type

Jer·e·mi·ah \ˌjer-ə-'mī-ə\ 650?–*ca* 570 B.C. Hebrew prophet; author of Old Testament book of Jeremiah

Jerne \'yer-ne\ Niels Kai 1911–1994 Dan. (Eng.-born) immunologist; awarded (with G.F.J. Köhler, C. Milstein) 1984 Nobel prize for physiology or medicine for discoveries in immunology

Je·rome \jə-'rōm *also* 'jer-əm\ Saint *ca* 347–419 (or 420) L. *Eusebius Hi·eron·y·mus* \ˌhī-ə-'rä-nə-məs, hi-\ church father; published Latin version of the Bible known as the Vulgate

Jer·vis \'jär-vəs, 'jär-\ John 1735–1823 Earl of *St. Vincent* Brit. admiral; averted mutiny and neutralized sedition in Channel fleet; eliminated corruption in dockyards; reformed naval administration

Jes·per·sen \'yes-pər-sən\ (Jens) Otto Harry 1860–1943 Dan. philologist; helped revolutionize teaching of languages in Europe; proposed international language, Novial; published *A Modern English Grammar on Historical Principles* (1909–49), etc.

Je·sus \'jē-zəs, -zəz\ *or* **Jesus Christ** \'krīst\ *or* **Christ Jesus** *ca* 6 B.C.–*ca* A.D. 30 *Jesus of Nazareth; the Son of Mary* source of the Christian religion & Savior in the Christian faith; believed to be miraculously conceived by his Mother; received as great teacher by disciples and common people; preached redeeming love of God for every person; suspected of revolutionary aims as Messiah; seized by Romans but turned over to and crucified by Jewish authorities; believed by followers to have been miraculously resurrected; proclaimed by disciples and believers as Messiah and savior of all

Jev·ons \'je-vənz\ William Stanley 1835–1882 Eng. econ.; developed marginal utility theory of value

Jew·ett \\'jü-ət\\ Sarah Orne 1849–1909 Am. writer; author of sketches and tales of New England; important in the "local color" school

Jez·e·bel \\'je-zə-‚bel\\ *d ca* 843 B.C. Phoenician princess; wife of Ahab, king of Israel; introduced worship of Baal into Israel, persecuted prophets of Jehovah, esp. Elijah

Ji·ang Ze·min \\jē-'äŋ-zə-'min\\ 1926– gen. secy. of Chin. communist party (1989–); pres. of China (1993–); became powerful following pro-democracy Tiananmen Square massacre; promoted continued 'open door' economic policy

Ji·mé·nez \\hē-'mä-nəs\\ Juan Ramón 1881–1958 Span. poet; awarded 1956 Nobel prize for literature for his poems

Jiménez de Cis·ne·ros \\-‚dā-sis-'ner-əs\\ Francisco 1436–1517 Span. prelate & statesman; instigated forced conversion of Moors of Granada, leading to revolt (1499–1500); inquisitor general of Castile and Léon

Jin·nah \\'ji-(‚)nä, 'ji-nə\\ Mohammed Ali 1876–1948 Indian polit.; initially worked for Hindu-Muslim unity in India, but gradually came to oppose Hindu ideology and methods; 1st gov.-gen. of dominion of Pakistan (1947–48)

Jo·achim \\yō-'ä-kim, -kim; 'yō-ə-‚kim, -‚kim\\ Joseph 1831–1907 Hung. violinist; known esp. for emphasizing aesthetic over technical aspects in interpretations of Bach, Mozart, Beethoven

Joan of Arc \\‚jōn-əv-'ärk\\ *F* **Jeanne d'Arc** \\zhän-därk\\ Saint *ca* 1412–1431 *the Maid of Orleans* Fr. national heroine; forced English to abandon siege of Orléans; later tried by English for witchcraft, heresy and burned at the stake

Jobs \\'jäbz\\ Steven Paul 1955– Am. inventor & entrepreneur; cofounder of Apple Computer Co. (1975); credited with bringing about widespread use of personal computers

Jodl \\'yō-d'l\\ Alfred 1890–1946 Ger. gen.; principal adviser of Hitler; signed act of surrender; hanged as war criminal

Jof·fre \\zhȯfrᵊ\\ Joseph-Jacques-Césaire 1852–1931 Fr. field marshal; marshal of France; planned and directed victory in the battle of the Marne

Jof·frey \\'jäf-rē\\ Robert 1930–1988 orig. *Abdullah Jaffa Bey Khan* Am. dancer & choreographer; founder of Joffrey Ballet (1956); his company notable for an eclectic repertoire that included classics, new works, and fusions of modern dance and ballet

John \\'jän\\ Saint 1st cent. A.D. *John the Baptist* Jewish prophet; preached the coming of a messiah; baptized Jesus

John Saint 1st cent. A.D. Christian apostle; traditionally held to be the author of fourth Gospel, three epistles, book of Revelations in the New Testament

John name of 21 popes: esp. **XXIII** (*Angelo Giuseppe Roncalli*) 1881–1963 (pope 1958–63); notably interested in ecumenism and in peace; convoked 2d Vatican Council (1962)

John 1167–1216 *John Lack·land* \\'lak-‚land\\ king of England (1199–1216); forced by barons at Runnymede to sign Magna Carta, basis of English political and personal liberty

John I 1357–1433 *the Great* king of Portugal (1385–1433); captured Ceuta from Moors, setting off great age of exploration, conquest, colonization

John Augustus Edwin 1878–1961 Brit. painter & etcher; known esp. for portraits, for landscapes with Symbolist tendencies, vigorous brush work and superb draftsmanship

John of Austria 1547–1578 Don *John* Span. gen.; led Holy League fleet in defeat of Turks at Lepanto (1571); later tried to subdue revolt in the Netherlands against Spanish authority

John of Gaunt \'gónt, 'gänt\ 1340–1399 Duke of *Lancaster; son of Edward III of England;* fought with Black Prince in Spain, France; supported Wycliffe to resist prelates in England; failed to gain Spanish throne or control over Aquitaine; supported Richard II

John of Lancaster 1389–1435 Duke of *Bedford; son of Henry IV of England;* forced by Joan of Arc to lift siege of Orléans; later allowed her to be burnt as witch

John of Leiden ca 1509–1536 Du. Anabaptist; led Protestant rebellion in Münster and ruled briefly (1534–35); reign marked by lawlessness and pomp until deposed and executed

John of Salisbury 1115 (or 1120)–1180 Eng. ecclesiastic; supporter of Becket and present at his murder at Canterbury (1170)

John of the Cross 1542–1591 *Juan de Yepes y Álvarez* Span. mystic & poet; a founder of ascetic order of Discalced Carmelites; author of lyrical poems schematizing steps of mystical ascent to union of soul and God

John Paul \'pól\ name of 2 popes: esp. **II** (Karol Wojtyla) 1920– (pope 1978–); advocate of economic justice, rights of church under communism, moral conservatism

John III So·bies·ki \sō-'byes-kē, ˌsō-bē-'es-\ 1629–1696 king of Poland (1674–96); relieved siege of Vienna and ejected Ottomans from Hungary; recovered much of Ukraine

Johns \'jänz\ Jasper 1930–   Am. painter & graphic artist; a pioneer of pop art; raised commonplace subjects (as numbers, letters, flags) to status of icons by rendering them in simple colors and with purposeful, ironic banality

John·son \'jän(t)-sən\ Andrew 1808–1875 17th pres. of the U.S. (1865–69); acquitted during impeachment proceedings provoked by Reconstruction policies — **John·so·nian** \jän-'sō-nē-ən, -nyən\ *adj*

Johnson (Jonathan) Eastman 1824–1906 Am. painter; known for genre scenes and portraits of J.Q. Adams, Daniel Webster, Longfellow, etc.

John·son \'yün-sòn\ Eyvind 1900–1976 Swed. author; wrote novels with protagonists overcome by feelings of frustration; awarded (with H. Mortinson) 1974 Nobel prize for literature

John·son \'jänt)-sən\ James Weldon 1871–1938 Am. author; wrote *The Autobiography of an Ex-Colored Man, The Book of American Negro Poetry,* etc.

Johnson Lyndon Baines 1908–1973 Am. polit.; 36th pres. of the U.S. (1963–69); adopted several "Great Society" welfare measures; administration marked by escalation of U.S. involvement in Vietnam — **John·so·nian** \jän-'sō-nē-ən, -nyən\ *adj*

Johnson Magic 1959–   *Earvin Johnson* Am. basketball player; played with L.A. Lakers (1979–91, 1996–); held NBA record for most career assists; named Most Valuable Player of NBA (1987, 1989, 1990)

Johnson Philip Cortelyou 1906–   Am. architect; an exponent of the International Style and principle of space unification; later designed in a postmodernist style

Johnson Richard Mentor 1780–1850 vice pres. of the U.S. (1837–41); only vice pres. elected by vote of U.S. Senate

Johnson Samuel 1709–1784 *Dr. Johnson* Eng. lexicographer & author; leading figure in 18th cent. literary life; published critical edition of Shakespeare, English dictionary (1755), *Lives of the Poets*, verse, etc. — **John·so·nian** \jän-ˈsō-nē-ən, -nyən\ *adj*

Johnson Sir William 1715–1774 Brit. administrator in America; successful in dealing with esp. Indians of the Six Nations

John·ston \ˈjän(t)-stən, -sən\ Albert Sidney 1803–1862 Am. Confed. gen.; defeated Union army and Grant at Shiloh, but killed in action

Johnston Joseph Eggleston 1807–1891 Am. Confed. gen.; notable for never suffering a direct defeat during the Civil War; often at odds with Jefferson Davis

Join·ville \zhwaⁿ-ˈvē(ə)l\ Jean de *ca* 1224–1317 Fr. chronicler; author of invaluable record of the Seventh Crusade, *Histoire de Saint-Louis*

Jó·kai \ˈyō-ˌkȯi\ Mór 1825–1904 Hung. nov. & dram.; author of popular novels and plays

Jo·liot–Cu·rie \zhȯl-ˌyō-kyü-ˈrē, -ˈkyür-(ˌ)ē\ (Jean-) Frédéric 1900–1958 *orig.* Joliot Fr. physicist; awarded (with wife Irène Curie) 1935 Nobel prize for chemistry for synthesizing new radioactive elements

Joliot–Curie Irène 1897–1956 *formerly Irène Curie-Joliot, dau. of Marie & Pierre Curie & wife of prec.* Fr. physicist; awarded (with husband Frédéric Joliot-Curie) 1935 Nobel prize for chemistry for synthesizing new radioactive elements

Jol·liet *or* **Jo·liet** \zhȯl-ˈyä\ Louis 1645–1700 Fr. explorer; discovered Mississippi River, floating down it to modern-day Arkansas

Jo·mi·ni \zhō-mə-ˈnē\ Henri de 1779–1869 Swiss-born soldier & mil. strategist; author of influential works on conduct of war

Jones \ˈjōnz\ Anson 1798–1858 pres. of the Republic of Texas (1844–46); last pres. before Texas joined the U.S.

Jones Daniel 1881–1967 Eng. phonetician; author of *English Pronouncing Dictionary* based on Southern British speech, etc.

Jones Howard Mumford 1892–1980 Am. educ. & critic; wrote *Ideas in America, O Strange New World* (Pulitzer prize), etc.

Jones In·i·go \ˈi-ni-ˌgō\ 1573–1652 Eng. architect; influenced by Palladio and considered founder of English classical architecture

Jones James Earl 1931–   Am. actor; best known for his appearances on Broadway in *The Great White Hope, Paul Robeson,* and *Othello*

Jones John Paul 1747–1792 *orig. in full John Paul* Am. (Scot.-born) naval officer; said "I have not yet begun to fight" aboard *Bonhomme Richard* in battle against British (1779)

Jones Thomas Hudson 1892–1969 Am. sculptor; created sculpture for Tomb of the Unknown Soldier in Arlington National Cemetery, bust of U.S. Grant in Hall of Fame, N.Y. City, etc.

Jon·son \ˈjän(t)-sən\ Benjamin 1572–1637 *Ben Jonson* Eng. dram.; wrote plays *Volpone* (1605), *The Alchemist* (1610), etc., poems, songs including "Drink to me only with thine eyes," etc. — **Jon·so·nian** \jän-'sō-nē-ən, -nyən\ *adj*

Jop·lin \'jä-plən\ Scott 1868–1917 Am. pianist & composer; composed "Maple Leaf Rag," "The Entertainer," ragtime opera *Treemonisha*, etc.

Jor·daens \'yòr-dän(t)s\ Jacob 1593–1678 Flem. painter; known for vigorous, colorful scenes of Flemish life, historical, religious, and mythological subjects; murals, portraits, tapestry designs, etc.

Jor·dan \'jòr-d°n\ Barbara Charline 1936–1996 Am. polit.; member from Texas, U.S. House of Representatives (1972–78); first black congresswoman elected from the Deep South; noted orator

Jor·dan David Starr 1851–1931 Am. biol. & educ.; regarded as foremost American ichthyologist of his time; also wrote on issues of world peace, war, economics, etc.

Jordan Michael Jeffrey 1963–   Am. basketball player; played with Chicago Bulls (1984–93, 95–   ); instrumental in the 1991–93 Bulls winning three consecutive league championships; generally regarded as greatest player in history of basketball

Jordan Vernon 1935–   Am. civil rights activist; exerted considerable influence through positions with Southern Regional Council, National Urban League, etc.

Jo·seph \'jō-zəf *also* -səf\ Saint 1st cent. B.C.–1st cent. A.D. husband of Mary, mother of Jesus

Joseph *ca* 1840–1904 *In-mut-too-yah-lat-lat* Nez Percé Indian chief; led people in Nez Percé War resisting white encroachment

Joseph II 1741–1790 Holy Rom. emp. (1765–90); had many schemes for territorial expansion but his despotism only alienated other nations, his own ministers

Jo·se·phine \'jō-zə-ˌfēn\ Empress — see BEAUHARNAIS

Jo·seph·son \'jō-zəf-sən *also* -səf-\ Brian David 1940–   Brit. physicist; awarded (with I. Giaever and L. Esaki) 1973 Nobel prize for physics for work on semiconductor and superconductor materials

Jo·se·phus \jō-'sē-fəs\ Flavius *ca* A.D. 37–*ca* 100 Jewish hist.; under patronage of emperors Vespasian, Titus, and Domitian, wrote *History of the Jewish War, Antiquities of the Jews*, etc.

Jos·quin des Prez \zhó-'skaⁿ-de-'prā\ *or* **Des·prez** \de-'prā\ *ca* 1440–1521 Fr. composer; considered greatest composer of the Renaissance, introducing new ideas in formal structure, expressiveness; composed masses, motets, and many secular chansons

Jou·bert \zhü-'ber\ Joseph 1754–1824 Fr. essayist & moralist; associate of Chateaubriand and Bonald, author of *Pensées*

Joubert \yü-'ber, yō-\ Petrus Jacobus 1834–1900 known as *Piet Joubert* Boer gen. & statesman; acting president of South African Republic (1875); opposed British annexation of the Transvaal

Jou·haux \zhü-ō\ Léon 1879–1954 Fr. trade-union leader; awarded 1951 Nobel prize for peace

Joule \'jül\ James Prescott 1818–1889 Eng. physicist; formulated Joule's law describing the rate at which heat is produced by an electric current; the joule, unit of work or energy, is named for him

Jour·dan \zhúr-'däⁿ\ Comte Jean-Baptiste 1762–1833 Fr. soldier; marshal of France; served in Revolutionary army; twice a member of the Five Hundred; supported Louis XVIII

Jo·vi·an \'jō-vē-ən\ *ca* 331–364 Flavius Jovianus Rom. emp. (363–364); gave up Roman provinces beyond Tigris; restored privileges to Christians; supported Nicene Creed

Jow·ett \'jaù-ət, 'jō-\ Benjamin 1817–1893 Eng. Greek scholar; considered one of the century's greatest teachers; known for translations of *The Dialogues of Plato, Thucydides,* etc.

Joyce \'jòis\ James Augustine 1882–1941 Irish writer; developed techniques of interior monologue and stream-of-consciousness narrative in *Portrait of the Artist as a Young Man* (1916), *Ulysses* (1922), *Finnegan's Wake* (1939), etc. — **Joyc·ean** \'jòi-sē-ən\ *adj*

Juan Car·los \'(h)wän-'kär-ˌlōs\ 1938– king of Spain (1975–); instituted democracy in Spain; defeated military coup (1981); became constitutional monarch

Juan Manuel Don — see MANUEL

Juá·rez \'hwär-əs, 'wär-\ Benito Pablo 1806–1872 Mex. lawyer; pres. of Mexico (1861–65; 1867–72); administration marked by many reforms; last years clouded by attempted revolutions

Judas Maccabaeus — see MACCABEES

Ju·gur·tha \jü-'gər-thə\ *or* **Iu·gur·tha** \yü-\ *ca* 160–104 B.C. king of Numidia (118–105 B.C.); defeated by Quintus Metellus in Jugurthine War against Rome; executed at Rome

Ju·lian \'jül-yən\ *ca* 331–363 Flavius Claudius Julianus, the Apostate Rom. emp. (361–363); made paganism the state religion while maintaining toleration of Christianity

Ju·li·ana \ˌjü-lē-'a-nə\ 1909– dau. of Wilhelmina queen of the Netherlands (1948–80)

Jung \'yùn\ Carl Gustav 1875–1961 Swiss psychol.; founded analytic psychology; developed theory of collective unconscious and archetypes, etc.

Ju·nius \'jü-nyəs, -nē-əs\ Franciscus 1589–1677 Eng. (Ger.-born) philologist; work on large collection of manuscripts greatly stimulated interest in Anglo-Saxon and other Germanic languages

Jun·kers \'yùn-kərz, -kərs\ Hugo 1859–1935 Ger. airplane designer & builder; instrumental in establishing one of first regular mail and passenger lines

Ju·not \zhē-'nō\ Andoche 1771–1813 Duc d'Abran·tès \ˌda-brän-'tès\ Fr. gen.; aide-de-camp to Napoléon; served in Italian and Egyptian campaigns; captured Portugal but driven out by British

Jus·se·rand \zhūs-rän, zhū·sə-\ Jean-(Adrien-Antoine-) Jules 1855–1932 Fr. scholar & diplomat; student of English literature and history; author of *En Amérique jadis et maintenant* (1916, *In America Yesterday and Today,* Pulitzer prize)

Jus·tin \'jəs-tən\ Saint *ca* 100–*ca* 165 Justin (the) Martyr church father; opened first Christian school at Rome; scourged and martyred at Rome

Jus·tin·i·an I \ˌjə-'sti-nē-ən\ 483–565 the Great Byzantine emp. (527–565); oversaw most brilliant reign of Eastern Empire; collected imperial laws, issued Code of laws, digest, textbook which with new laws formed foundation of civil law in most of Europe

Ju·ve·nal \'jü-və-nᵊl\ A.D. 55 to 60–*ca* 127 Decimus Junius Juvenalis Rom. poet & satirist; wrote 16 satirical poems, in 5 books, attacking with brutal frankness vices of imperial Rome — **Ju·ve·na·lian** \ˌjü-və-'näl-yən\ *adj*

K

Ká·dár \'kä-ˌdár\ János 1912–1989 1st secy. of Hung. communist party (1956–88); formed government that helped repress 1956 uprising

Kaf·ka \'käf-kə, 'kaf-\ Franz 1883–1924 Czech-born author writing in German; expressed 20th century anxiety and alienation in his visionary, metaphorical, psychological fiction such as novels *The Trial* (1925), *The Castle* (1926), *Amerika* (1927)

Ka·ga·wa \kä-'gä-wə\ Toyohiko 1888–1960 Jp. social reformer; tried to avert WWII; later a leader in woman suffrage and adaptation of democratic institutions

Kahane \kə-'hä-ˌnä\ Meir 1932–1990 orig. *Martin David Kahane* Israeli (Am.-born) polit. & rabbi; founded (1968) paramilitary Jewish Defense League in N.Y. City; in Israel formed (1971) extremist Kach political party

Kai·fu \'kī-(ˌ)fü\ Toshiki 1931–   prime min. of Japan (1989–91)

Kai·ser \'kī-zər\ Henry John 1882–1967 Am. industrialist; owner of construction, cement, shipbuilding, steel, aluminum, automobile companies; established (1942) foundation to provide health services to workers and later to public

Kalb \'kälp, 'kalb\ Johann 1721–1780 Baron *de Kalb* \di-'kalb\ Ger. gen. in Amer. Revolution; present with Washington during trying winter at Valley Forge; mortally wounded in battle at Camden, S.C.

Kā·li·dā·sa \ˌkä-li-'dä-sə\ 5th cent. A.D. Indian dram. & poet; master of Sanskrit; viewed as greatest Indian writer

Ka·li·nin \kə-'lē-nyən, -nyən\ Mikhail Ivanovich 1875–1946 Russ. polit.; formal head of Soviet state (1919–46); active in revolutionary planning and founder of newspaper *Pravda*

Ka·me·ha·me·ha I \kə-ˌmä-ə-'mä-(ˌ)hä\ 1758?–1819 *the Great* king of Hawaii (1795–1819); organized government; allowed foreign traders to settle, ended human sacrifice during autocratic rule

Ka·me·nev \'käm-yə-ˌnef, 'kam-; 'kä-mə-, 'ka-\ Lev Borisovich 1883–1936 Russ. communist leader; opposed by Stalin; imprisoned during purge (1934); executed

Ka·mer·lingh On·nes \ˌkä-mər-liŋ-'ón-əs\ Heike 1853–1926 Du. physicist; awarded 1913 Nobel prize for physics for experimenting with low temperatures and liquefying helium

Kan·din·sky \kan-'din(t)-skē\ Wassily 1866–1944 Russ. painter; usually credited with executing first pure abstraction in painting, using bright colors, geometrical forms

Kane \'kän\ Elisha Kent 1820–1857 Am. arctic explorer; searched with Grinnell for Sir John Franklin; later reached undiscovered territory

K'ang-hsi \'käŋ-'shē\ 1654–1722 Chin. emp. (1661–1722); reign marked by internal peace, construction of public works, low taxes, opening of four ports to foreign trade

Kant \'kant, 'känt\ Immanuel 1724–1804 Ger. philos.; developed critical philosophy determining nature and limits of knowledge, categories of consciousness and their ethical and aesthetic consequences

Kan·to·ro·vich \ˌkän-tə-'ró-vich\ Leonid Vitalyevich 1912–1986

Russ. econ.; awarded (with T. C. Koopmans) 1975 Nobel prize for economics for work on how economic resources should be distributed and used

Ka·pit·sa \'kä-pyit-sə\ Pyotr Leonidovich 1894–1984 Russ. physicist; awarded (with A. Penzias and R. Wilson) 1978 Nobel prize for physics for research in low-temperature physics

Kar·a·george \,kar-ə-'jòrj\ 1762–1817 orig. *George Petrović Karageorge* Serbian nationalist & founder of Kar·a·geor·ge·vić \-'jòr-jə-,vich\ dynasty; led revolt against Turkey; decisively defeated (1813); murdered by rival while preparing second revolt

Ka·ra·jan \'kär-ə-,yän\ Herbert von 1908–1989 Austrian conductor; conductor of Berlin Philharmonic (1955–89), Salzburg Festival (1956–60), etc.; his musical interpretations notable for their precision and clarity

Ka·ra·man·lis \,kär-ə-,män-'lēs, -'män-\ Konstantinos 1907– prime min. (1974–80) & pres. (1980–85; 1990–) of Greece; oversaw restoration of popular rule after military government ousted (1974)

Karle \'kärl\ Jerome 1918– Am. physical chem.; awarded (with H. A. Hauptmann) 1985 Nobel prize for chemistry for developing techniques for quickly determining the chemical structure of molecules vital to life

Karl·feldt \'kär(ə)l-,felt\ Erik Axel 1864–1931 Swed. poet; wrote poems dealing chiefly with nature and peasant life; awarded 1931 Nobel prize for literature posthumously after refusing it earlier

Ká·ro·lyi \'kär-əl-yē, 'kär-\ Count Mihály 1875–1955 Hung. polit.; prime min. (1918–19) and pres. (1919) of the Hungarian Democratic Republic; supplanted by Hungarian Soviet Republic

Kar·rer \'kär-ər\ Paul 1889–1971 Swiss chem.; awarded (with W. N. Haworth) 1931 Nobel prize for chemistry for work on carotenoids, flavins, vitamins A and B_2

Kar·sa·vi·na \kär-'sä-və-nə, -'sa-\ Tamara 1885–1978 Russ. dancer; a partner of Nijinsky in Ballets Russes; later coached Margot Fonteyn

Kast·ler \kàst-ler\ Alfred 1902–1984 Fr. physicist; awarded 1966 Nobel prize for physics for work on the energy levels of atoms

Kastrioti George — see SKANDERBEG

Katz \'kats\ Sir Bernhard 1911– Brit. (Ger.-born) biophysicist; awarded (with J. Axelrod and U. S. von Euler) 1970 Nobel prize for physiology or medicine for discoveries in the role of certain chemicals in transmitting nerve impulses

Kauf·man \'kòf-mən\ George Simon 1889–1961 Am. dram.; collaborated with Moss Hart on *You Can't Take It with You* (1936, Pulitzer prize), *The Man Who Came to Dinner*, etc.

Kau·nitz \'kaú-nəts\ Wenzel Anton von 1711–1794 Prince *von Kaunitz-Rietberg* Austrian statesman; organized and centralized administration of many Hapsburg domains; influenced Maria Theresa, Joseph II, Leopold II

Kaut·sky \'kaút-skē\ Karl Johann 1854–1938 Ger. socialist writer; private secretary of Friedrich Engels but opposed Bolshevism and Russian Revolution

Ka·wa·ba·ta \,kä-wə-'bä-tə, kə-'wä-bə-,tä\ Yasunari 1899–1972 Jp. writer; author of *Yukiguni* (1948, *Snow Country*), etc.; awarded 1968 Nobel prize for literature

Kaye–Smith \\'kā-'smith\ Sheila 1887–1956 Eng. nov.; known esp. for tales set in Sussex, including *Sussex Gorse*, *The Village Doctor*, etc.

Ka·zan·tza·kis \ˌkä-zᵊn-'tsä-kēs, -'chä-\ Nikos 1885–1957 Greek poet, nov., & translator; best known for his epic *Odysseia* (1938) and translations of Dante's *Divine Comedy* and Goethe's *Faust*

Kean \'kēn\ Edmund 1789–1833 Eng. actor; reintroduced a naturalistic style of acting in roles of Shylock, Hamlet, Othello, Iago, Macbeth, Lear, Richard III and became unrivaled as a tragedian

Kear·ny \'kär-nē\ Philip 1814–1862 Am. gen.; brigadier general of volunteers, Union army; killed on reconnoitering expedition

Keat·ing \'kē-tiŋ\ Paul John 1944–   prime min. of Australia (1991–   ); instrumental in deregulating financial markets; won reelection to office (1993) against enormous odds

Keats \'kēts\ John 1795–1821 Eng. poet; wrote poetry, including "On First Looking into Chapman's Homer," *Endymion*, "The Eve of St. Agnes," "Ode on a Grecian Urn," etc., of vivid imagery, sensuous appeal, classical themes — **Keats·ian** \'kēt-sē-ən\ *adj*

Ke·ble \'kē-bəl\ John 1792–1866 Eng. clergyman & poet; initiated Oxford Movement with sermon "National Apostasy"; wrote hymns

Ke·fau·ver \'kē-ˌfȯ-vər\ (Carey) Estes 1903–1963 Am. polit.; conducted televised Senate investigation of organized crime (1950–51); unsuccessful candidate for U.S. pres. (1956)

Kei·tel \'kī-tᵊl\ Wilhelm 1882–1946 Ger. field marshal; channel for Hitler's command of armed forces; signed act of military surrender; hanged as war criminal

Kek·ko·nen \'ke-kə-nən, -ˌnen\ Urho Kaleva 1900–1986 pres. of Finland (1956–81); through policy of neutrality, enjoyed friendship of Soviet Union and Scandinavian countries

Kel·ler \'ke-lər\ Helen Adams 1880–1968 Am. deaf & blind lecturer; worked on behalf of the blind at home and abroad

Kel·logg \'ke-ˌlȯg, -ˌläg\ Frank Billings 1856–1937 Am. statesman; awarded 1929 Nobel prize for peace for negotiating pact to outlaw war as a national policy

Kel·ly \'kel-ē\ Gene 1912–1996 Am. dancer, actor, & director; as a dancer combined classical ballet technique with natural athleticism; starred in film musicals *The Pirate* (1948), *An American in Paris* (1951), *Singin' in the Rain* (1952), etc.

Kelly Grace 1929–1982 Princess Grace of Monaco Am. actress; known for patrician beauty and cool elegance; starred in *The Country Girl* (1954), *Rear Window* (1954), *To Catch a Thief* (1955), etc.; retired from films to marry Prince Rainier of Monaco

Kel·vin \'kel-vən\ 1st Baron 1824–1907 *William Thomson* Brit. math. & physicist; best known for proposing the absolute, or Kelvin, temperature scale

Ke·mal Ata·türk \kə-'mal-'a-tə-ˌtərk, -'ä-\ 1881–1938 orig. *Mustafa Kemal* \mü-stä-'fä-kä-'mäl\ Turk. gen.; pres. of Turkey (1923–38); proclaimed and secured recognition of Turkish independence and instituted many reforms

Kem·ble \'kem-bəl\ Frances Anne 1809–1893 *Fanny* Eng. actress; known for roles as Lady Teazle in *School for Scandal*, in Shakespeare, as Julia in *The Hunchback*

Kemble John Philip 1757–1823 Eng. actor; regarded as chief founder of declamatory school of acting

Kempis Thomas à — see THOMAS À KEMPIS

Ken *or* **Kenn** \'ken\ Thomas 1637–1711 Eng. prelate & hymn writer; author of hymns "Praise God, From Whom All Blessings Flow," "Glory to Thee, My God, This Night," etc.

Ken·dall \'ken-d'l\ Edward Calvin 1886–1972 Am. biochem.; awarded (with P. S. Hench and T. Reichstein) 1950 Nobel prize for physiology or medicine for isolating cortisone and for other work on hormones and the adrenal cortex

Kendall Henry Way 1926– Am. physicist; awarded (with J. Friedman and R. Taylor) 1990 Nobel prize for physics for experiments that proved the existence of quarks

Ken·drew \'ken-(,)drü\ Sir John Cowdery 1917– Brit. chem.; awarded (with M. F. Perutz) 1962 Nobel prize for chemistry for studies on globular proteins

Ken·nan \'ke-nən\ George Frost 1904– Am. hist. & diplomat; first called for containment of Soviet Union, then for U.S. disengagement from Europe

Ken·ne·dy \'ke-nə-dē\ Anthony M. 1936– Am. jurist; assoc. justice, U.S. Supreme Court (1988–)

Kennedy John Fitzgerald 1917–1963 Am. polit.; 35th pres. of the U.S. (1961–63); forced Soviet Union to remove missiles from Cuba (1962); with Great Britain and Soviet Union signed Nuclear Test₌ Ban Treaty (1963) — **Ken·ne·dy·esque** \,ke-nə-dē-'esk\ *adj*

Kennedy Joseph Patrick 1888–1969 *father of J. F. & R. F.* Am. businessman & diplomat; made fortune in banking, stock market, shipbuilding, motion pictures; ambassador to Great Britain (1937–40)

Kennedy Robert Francis 1925–1968 Am. polit.; atty. gen. (1961–64); member from New York, U.S. Senate (1964–68)

Ken·nel·ly \'ke-n'l-ē\ Arthur Edwin 1861–1939 Am. engineer; developed analytic methods in electronics; announced probable existence of ionosphere (Kennelly-Heavyside layer)

Ken·ny \'ke-nē\ Elizabeth 1880–1952 *Sister Kenny* Austral. nurse & physiotherapist; developed technique of rehabilitating victims of paralytic diseases

Kent \'kent\ James 1763–1847 Am. jurist; did much to create American system of equity jurisdiction based on English principles

Kent Rockwell 1882–1971 Am. painter & illustrator; known for landscape and figure painting using rhythmically silhouetted shapes, symbolism

Ken·yon \'ken-yən\ John Samuel 1874–1959 Am. phonetician; author of *American Pronunciation–A Textbook of Phonetics*, co₌ author (with Thomas A. Knott) of *A Pronouncing Dictionary of American English*

Ke·o·kuk \'kē-ə-,kək\ 1790?–1848? Sauk tribal leader; counseled accommodation to advancing white settlers and the concession of Indian lands; for opposing Black Hawk and his resistance movement, rewarded by U.S. government with leadership of Sauk nation

Kep·ler \'ke-plər\ Johannes 1571–1630 Ger. astron.; considered founder of modern optics by postulation of ray theory of light to

explain vision; discovered Kepler's laws of planetary motion —
Kep·ler·ian \ke-ˈplir-ē-ən, -ˈpler-\ *adj*

Kep·pel \ˈke-pəl\ 1st Viscount 1725–1786 *Augustus Keppel* Brit. admiral; served through Seven Years' War (1756–63); commander in chief of grand fleet (1778–79)

Ker \ˈker, ˈkər, ˈkär\ William Paton 1855–1923 Brit. scholar; author of *Epic and Romance, The Dark Ages,* etc.

Ke·ren·sky \ˈker-ən-skē, ke-ˈren-\ Aleksandr Fyodorovich 1881–1970 Russ. revolutionary; overthrown as prime min. by Bolshevik Revolution because of moderate policies and indecision

Kern \ˈkərn\ Jerome David 1885–1945 Am. composer; best known for scores of musical comedies *Show Boat, Sweet Adeline,* etc., and for songs "Smoke Gets in Your Eyes," "Ol' Man River," "A Fine Romance," etc.

Ker·ou·ac \ˈker-ə-ˌwak\ Jack 1922–1969 *Jean-Louis* Am. writer; with *On the Road* (1957) became leader and spokesman of the Beat generation; wrote in unedited, nonconformist style

Ker·tész \ˈkər-tezh\ André 1894–1985 Am. (Hung.-born) photographer; known for capturing on film the cultural milieu of Paris in the 1920s and '30s; afterwards worked in N.Y. City as a highly influential commercial (largely fashion) photographer

Kes·sel·ring \ˈke-səl-riŋ\ Albert 1885–1960 Ger. field marshal; helped Rommel direct North Africa campaign; led brilliant defense in Italy; surrendered southern half of German forces

Ket·ter·ing \ˈke-tə-riŋ\ Charles Franklin 1876–1958 Am. electrical engineer & inventor; invented automotive ignition and lighting systems, high-speed diesel engine, leaded gasoline, variable-speed transmissions, etc.

Key \ˈkē\ Francis Scott 1779–1843 Am. lawyer & author of "The Star-Spangled Banner" adopted as U.S. national anthem (1931)

Keynes \ˈkānz\ John Maynard 1883–1946 1st Baron *Keynes of Tilton* Eng. econ.; known for revolutionary economic theory that recovery from a recession is best achieved by policy of full employment — **Keynes·ian** \ˈkān-zē-ən\ *n or adj*

Key·ser·ling \ˈkī-zər-liŋ\ Hermann Alexander 1880–1946 Graf *Keyserling* Ger. philos. & writer; developed philosophy centered on theme of spiritual regeneration

Kha·cha·tu·ri·an \ˌkä-chə-ˈtūr-ē-ən, ˌka-\ Aram Ilich 1903–1978 Soviet (Armenian-born) composer; wrote three symphonies, ballets (including famous "Sabre Dance"), concertos, etc., and some 25 film scores

Kha·da·fy — see GADHAFI

Khā·lid \ka-lid, ˈkä-\ in full *Khālid ibn ʿAbd al-ʿAzīz ibn ʿAbd ar-Raḥmān al-Saʿūd* 1913–1982 king of Saudi Arabia (1975–82); made improvements in education, medical care, housing, etc.

Kha·me·nei \ˌkä-ˈmä-nā\ Hojatolislam Sayyed Ali 1939– religious leader of Iran (1989–)

Khayyám Omar — see OMAR KHAYYÁM

Khe·ra·skov \kə-ˈräs-kəf\ Mikhail Matveyevich 1733–1807 Russ. poet; wrote epic poems *Rossiyada* (1771–79) and *Vladimir vozrozhdyonny* (1785); influential representative of Russian classicism

Kho·mei·ni \kō-ˈmā-nē, kō-, hō-\ Ayatollah Ruholla Mussaui 1900–1989 religious leader of Iran (1979–89); led Iran in return to strict Muslim practices and tradition

Kho·ra·na \kō-'rä-nə\ Har Gobind 1922– Am. (Indian-born) biochem.; awarded (with R. W. Holley, M. W. Nirenberg) 1968 Nobel prize for physiology or medicine for explaining how genes determine cell function

Khru·shchev \krúsh-'chóf, -'chóv; 'krüsh-,; krü-'shóf, -'shóv; 'krü-,; *also with* e *for* ò\ Ni·ki·ta \nə-'kē-tə\ Sergeyevich 1894–1971 Soviet polit.; premier of Soviet Union (1958–64); led destalinization movement; crushed Hungarian revolution (1956); forced by U.S. to remove missiles from Cuba; removed from office for China policy, failed agricultural policy — **Khru·shchev·ian** \krüsh-'chó-vē-ən, -'chō- *also* -'che-; krú-'shó-, -'shō- *also* -'she-\ *adj* — **Khru·shchev·ite** \krüsh-'chó-,vīt, -'che-,vīt, krüsh-,; krú-'shó-, -'she-, krü-,\ *adj*

Khu·fu \'kü-(,)fü\ *Gk* **Che·ops** \'kē-,äps\ 26th cent. B.C. king of Egypt & pyramid builder; erected Great Pyramid at Giza

Khwā·riz·mī, al– \al-'kwär-əz-mē, -'kwär-\ *ca* 780–*ca* 850 Muḥammad ibn Mūsā al-Khwārizmī Islamic (Persian-born) math. & astron.; one of the greatest scientific minds of Islam; source of much of mathematical knowledge of medieval Europe

Kidd \'kid\ William *ca* 1645–1701 *Captain Kidd* Scot. pirate; originally a shipowner who took up pirating in Indian Ocean and later in West Indies; plunder rumored buried along American coast

Kie·ran \'kir-ən\ John Francis 1892–1981 Am. journalist; sportswriter, *New York Times* (1915–43); regular panelist on "Information Please" radio program

Kier·ke·gaard \'kir-kə-,gär(d), -,gör\ Søren Aabye 1813–1855 Dan. philos. & theol.; regarded as founder of Existentialist philosophy; wrote *Either/Or* (1843), etc. — **Kier·ke·gaard·ian** \,kir-kə-'gär-dē-ən, -'gör-\ *adj*

Kie·sing·er \'kē-ziŋ-ər\ Kurt Georg 1904–1988 chancellor of West Germany (1966–69); continued to work for European unity under a coalition government

Kil·lian \'kil-ē-ən, 'kil-yən\ James Rhyne 1904–1988 Am. educ.; pres., Mass. Inst. of Technology (1948–59); laid groundwork for creation of NASA; oversaw development of government-supported public television network

Kil·mer \'kil-mər\ (Alfred) Joyce 1886–1918 Am. poet; best known for poem "Trees"

Kim Il Sung \'kim-'il-'səŋ, -'sùŋ\ 1912–1994 No. Korean communist leader (1948–94) and pres. (1972–94); fostered isolationist political and economic stance

Kim·mel \'ki-məl\ Husband Edward 1882–1968 Am. admiral; commander in chief of combined U.S. fleet; relieved of command of U.S. fleet after Japanese attack on Pearl Harbor

Kim Young Sam \'kim-'yəŋ-'säm, -'sam\ 1927– pres. of So. Korea (1993–)

Kin·di, al– \al-'kin-dē\ *d ca* 870 Arab philos.; one of first Arab students of Greek philosophers; tried to develop system combining views of Plato and Aristotle

King \'kiŋ\ Billie Jean 1943– née *Moffitt* Am. tennis player; during 1960s and '70s captured a record 20 Wimbledon titles, also U.S., French, Australian titles; championed the rights of women players; awarding of prize money equal to that given men

King Ernest Joseph 1878–1956 Am. admiral; chief of naval operations (1942–45); admiral of the fleet (1944)

King Martin Luther, Jr. 1929–1968 Am. clergyman & civil rights leader; awarded 1964 Nobel prize for peace for leading the black struggle for equality in the U.S. through nonviolent means; assassinated

King Rufus 1755–1827 Am. polit. & diplomat; helped frame Constitution and instrumental in securing its ratification in Massachusetts

King Stephen Edward 1947–   Am. writer; author of novels combining horror, fantasy, science fiction; wrote *Carrie, The Shining, Misery,* etc.

King William Lyon Mackenzie 1874–1950 Canad. statesman; prime min. (1921–26; 1926–30; 1935–48); helped preserve unity of English and French populations

King William Rufus de Vane 1786–1853 Am. polit.; vice pres. of the U.S. (1853)

Kings·ley \'kiŋz-lē\ Charles 1819–1875 Eng. clergyman & nov.; controversy with Cardinal Newman provoked Newman's *Apologia pro Vita Sua;* wrote novel *Westward Ho!,* children's story *Water Babies,* etc.

Kings·ton \'kiŋz-tən, 'kiŋ-stən\ Maxine Hong 1940–   orig. surname *Hong* Am. writer; in novels and nonfiction explored the cultural life of Chinese and American families; wrote *The Woman Warrior: Memoirs of a Girlhood Among Ghosts* (1976), etc.

Kin·kaid \kin-'kād\ Thomas Cassin 1888–1972 Am. admiral; fought battle of Philippine Sea (or Leyte Gulf)

Kin·sey \'kin-zē\ Alfred Charles 1894–1956 Am. sexologist; conducted and published extensive surveys of sexual behavior and opinions of Americans

Kip·ling \'kip-liŋ\ (Joseph) Rud·yard \'rəd-yərd, 'rə-jərd\ 1865–1936 Eng. author; awarded 1907 Nobel prize for literature for stories, novels, and poems, including *The Light That Failed, The Jungle Book, Captains Courageous,* etc. — **Kip·ling·esque** \,kip-liŋ-'esk\ *adj*

Kir·by–Smith \,kər-bē-'smith\ Edmund 1824–1893 orig. surname *Smith* Am. Confed. gen.; last Confederate commander to surrender (May 26, 1865)

Kirch·hoff \'kir-,kóf\ Gustav Robert 1824–1887 Ger. physicist; formulated (1845) Kirchhoff's laws used in mathematically analyzing an electrical network; announced (1859) Kirchhoff's radiation law, etc.

Kirch·ner \'kirk-nər, 'kirk-\ Ernst Ludwig 1880–1938 Ger. painter; influenced by Dürer, African and Polynesian art, and Cubism; developed a style noted for psychological tension, eroticism, sharp colors

Kirkpatrick \kərk-'pa-trik\ Jeane Duane Jordan 1926–   Am. public official & political scientist; U.S. permanent representative to U.N. (1981–85); staunch anticommunist spokesperson; strongly influenced foreign policy of Reagan administration

Ki·rov \'kē-,róf, -,róv\ Sergey Mironovich 1886–1934 Soviet polit.; one of Stalin's chief aids; his assassination instigated Stalin's Great Purge

Kirsten \'kər-stən\ Dorothy 1910–1992 Am. opera singer; in a 30-year career at New York's Metropolitan Opera sang most of the important Puccini soprano roles; sang title roles in *Manon Lescaut, Tosca, Madame Butterfly,* etc.

Kir·wan \'kər-wən\ Richard 1733–1812 Irish chem.; wrote first English treatise on mineralogy, *Elements of Mineralogy*

Kis·sin·ger \'ki-sⁿn-jər\ Henry Alfred 1923–   Am. (Ger.-born) scholar & govt. official; secy. of state (1973–77); awarded (with Le Duc Tho) 1973 Nobel prize for peace for work in negotiating the Vietnam ceasefire

Kitch·e·ner \'kich-nər, 'ki-chə-\ Horatio Herbert 1850–1916 1st Earl *Kitchener of Khartoum and of Broome* Brit. field marshal; known for military achievements in Sudan and South Africa, and for organizing British forces for WWI

Kit·tredge \'ki-trij\ George Lyman 1860–1941 Am. educ.; authority on Shakespeare and medieval English literature

Klee \'klā\ Paul 1879–1940 Swiss painter; developed inventive pictorial language and symbolism to express the subconscious and fantasy in art

Klein \'klīn\ Lawrence Robert 1920–   Am. econ.; awarded 1980 Nobel prize for economics for using econometric models to analyze economic policies and the rise and fall in business activity

Kleist \'klīst\ (Bernd) Heinrich Wilhelm von 1777–1811 Ger. dram.; considered first great dramatist of the 19th century; wrote play *Prinz Friedrich von Homburg,* novella *The Marquise of O*

Kleist \'klīst\ (Paul Ludwig) Ewald von 1881–1954 Ger. field marshal; advanced through Ukraine into Caucasus until forced to withdraw by defeats of Russian winter offensive

Klem·per·er \'klem-pər-ər\ Otto 1885–1973 Ger. conductor; known esp. for interpretations of German Romantic composers; conductor, Philharmonic Orchestra of London (1955–72)

Kles·til \'kles-,til\ Thomas 1932–   pres. of Austria (1992–)

Klitz·ing \'klit-siŋ\ Klaus von 1943–   Ger. physicist; awarded 1985 Nobel prize for physics for developing a precise way to measure electrical resistance

Klop·stock \'kläp-,stäk, 'klóp-,shtók\ Friedrich Gottlieb 1724–1803 Ger. poet; achieved sensational success with first 3 cantos of his religious epic *Der Messias*

Klug \'klüg\ Aaron 1926–   So. African (Lith.-born) molecular biol.; awarded 1982 Nobel prize for chemistry for work with electron microscope and for research into the structure of nucleic acid-protein compounds

Knel·ler \'ne-lər, 'kne-\ Sir Godfrey 1646 (or 1649)–1723 orig. *Gottfried Kniller* Eng. (Ger.-born) painter; painted equestrian portrait of William III and portraits of nine other reigning monarchs and of many other celebrities

Knox \'näks\ Henry 1750–1806 Am. gen. in Revolution; close friend, adviser of Washington who fought in all notable engagements; U.S. secy. of war (1785–94)

Knox John *ca* 1514–1572 Scot. religious reformer; foremost Scottish reformer who set austere moral tone and shaped democratic form of government of church

Knox Philander Chase 1853–1921 Am. statesman; initiated "dollar diplomacy" but opposed League of Nations

Knud·sen \'nüd-sən, 'knüd-\ William Signius 1879–1948 Am. (Dan.-born) industrialist & administrator; automobile executive who took charge of production for national defense and for War Department (1942–45)

Knut \'knüt, 'knyüt\ *var of* CANUTE

Koch \'kȯk, 'kȯk, *or with* ō *or* ä *for* ȯ\ Robert 1843–1910 Ger. bacteriol.; awarded 1905 Nobel prize for physiology or medicine for research on tuberculosis

Ko·cher \'kȯ-kər, -kər\ Emil Theodor 1841–1917 Swiss surgeon; first to excise thyroid gland in treatment of goiter

Kock \'kȯk\ Charles-Paul de 1793–1871 Fr. nov. & dram.; best known for his discreetly pornographic novels about Parisian life

Ko·dály \'kō-,dī\ Zoltán 1882–1967 Hung. composer; collected and published Hungarian folk songs and created a style based on these, contemporary French music, Italian Renaissance religious music

Koest·ler \'kes(t)-lər\ Arthur 1905–1983 Brit. (Hung.-born) writer; best known for political novel *Darkness at Noon* (1940) and for nonfiction works on politics, creativity, parapsychology

Kohl \'kōl\ Helmut 1930–   chancellor of West Germany (1982–90) chancellor of Germany (1990–   ); played a key role in German reunification

Koh·ler \'kō-lər\ Foy David 1908–1990 Am. diplomat; ambassador to Soviet Union (1962–66)

Köhler \'kœ-lər\ Georges J. F. 1946–   Ger. immunologist; awarded (with N. J. Jerne and C. Milstein) 1984 Nobel prize for physiology or medicine for discoveries in immunology

Koi·so \'kȯi-(,)sō, 'kō-ē-(,)sō\ Kuniaki 1880–1950 Jp. gen.; commander in chief in Korea (1935–38); prime min. (1944–45); sentenced as war criminal to life imprisonment

Kokh·ba \'kȯk-bä\ Bar *d* A.D. 135 orig. *Sim·e·on bar Ko·zi·ba* \'si-mē-ən-bär-'kō-zē-,bä\ Jewish leader in Palestine; led unsuccessful revolt against Roman domination; killed in battle

Ko·kosch·ka \kə-'kȯsh-kə\ Oskar 1886–1980 Brit. (Austrian-born) painter; a leading exponent of Expressionism; known for psychological portraits, lyric landscapes, panoramic cityscapes, allegorical compositions

Kol·chak \kȯl-'chäk\ Aleksandr Vasilyevich 1873–1920 Russ. admiral & counterrevolutionary; led coup against Bolsheviks and became head of White army; eventually defeated, captured, shot

Koll·lon·tay \,kä-lən-'ti\ Aleksandra Mikhaylovna 1872–1952 Russ. diplomat; world's first woman ambassador (1943)

Koll·witz \'kōl-,wits, 'kȯl-,vits\ Käthe 1867–1945 Ger. artist; works represented life among the poor and the proletariat

Kol·mo·go·rov \kəl-mə-'gȯ-rəf\ Andrey Nikolayevich 1903–1987 Soviet math.; best known for developing the axiomatic theory of probability, for work in theoretical and applied mathematics

Kol·tsov \kȯlt-'sȯf, -'sȯv\ Aleksey Vasilyevich 1808–1842 Russ. poet; known for lyrics of Russian peasant life

Ko·mu·ra \kō-'mu̇-ä, 'kō-mə-,rä\ Marquis Jutarō 1855–1911 Jp. diplomat; negotiated Treaty of Portsmouth and second Anglo-Japanese alliance (1905)

Kon·di·lis \kȯn-'dē-ləs, -lēs\ Geórgios 1879–1936 Greek gen. & polit.; became prime min. by coup d'état (1926) and later (1935) by coup d'état helped restore monarchy and return of George II

Ko·nev \'kȯn-yef, -ˌyev, -yəf\ Ivan Stepanovich 1897–1973 Soviet gen.; in WWII; commander in chief of Soviet army (1946–60)

Ko·noe \kə-'nō-(ˌ)ā\ Prince Fumimaro 1891–1945 Jp. statesman; tried unsuccessfully to keep war with China from becoming world conflict; helped bring down Tōjō cabinet (1944)

Koo \'kü\ Vi Kyuin Wel·ling·ton \'we-liŋ-tən\ 1888–1985 orig. *Ku Wei-chün* Chin. statesman & diplomat; adviser to U.S. (1946–56); adviser to Chiang Kai-shek

Koop·mans \'küp-mənz, 'kōp-ˌmänz\ Tjalling Charles 1910–1985 Am. (Du.-born) econ.; awarded (with L. M. Kantorovich) 1975 Nobel prize for economics for work on the distribution and use of economic resources

Kopernik *or* **Koppernigk** — see COPERNICUS

Korn·berg \'kȯrn-ˌbərg\ Arthur 1918– Am. biochem.; awarded (with S. Ochoa) 1959 Nobel prize for physiology or medicine for producing nucleic acid by artificial means

Korn·gold \'kȯrn-ˌgōld, -ˌgȯlt\ Erich Wolfgang 1897–1957 Am. (Austrian-born) composer, conductor, & pianist; composed operas, orchestral works, chamber music, scores for 19 films including *Anthony Adverse, The Adventures of Robin Hood* (Academy awards for both), etc.

Kor·ni·lov \kȯr-'nē-ləf\ Lavr Georgiyevich 1870–1918 Russ. gen. & counterrevolutionary; attempted to make himself dictator after Revolution and killed in action at head of Cossack force

Ko·ro·len·ko \ˌkȯr-ə-'leŋ-(ˌ)kō, ˌkär-\ Vladimir Galaktionovich 1853–1921 Russ. nov.; represented older literary traditions, but exiled to Siberia (1879–84) for advanced social ideas

Kor·zyb·ski \kə-'zhip-skē, kȯr-'zib-\ Alfred Habdank Skarbek 1879–1950 Am. (Pol.-born) scientist & writer; originator of general semantics, based on human capacity to transmit ideas from generation to generation

Koś·ciusz·ko \ˌkȯsh-'chüsh-(ˌ)kō, ˌkä-sē-'əs-ˌkō\ Tadeusz Andrzej Bonawentura 1746–1817 Pol. patriot & soldier in Am. Revolution; appointed colonel of engineers in Continental army; in charge of constructing fortifications at West Point

Kos·sel \'kȯ-səl\ Albrecht 1853–1927 Ger. biochem.; awarded 1910 Nobel prize for physiology or medicine for studying cell chemistry, proteins, and nucleic substances

Kos·suth \'kä-ˌsüth, kä-'; 'kȯ-ˌshùt\ La·jos \'lȯi-ˌōsh\ 1802–1894 Hung. patriot & statesman; headed Hungarian insurrection (1848–49) and convinced assembly to declare Hungarian independence; fled abroad after rebellion was crushed

Ko·sy·gin \kə-'sē-gən\ Aleksey Nikolayevich 1904–1980 Soviet polit.; premier of Soviet Union (1964–80); exerted moderating influence on other Soviet leaders but overshadowed by Leonid Brezhnev

Kot·ze·bue \'kät-sə-ˌbü, 'kȯt-\ August Friedrich Ferdinand von 1761–1819 Ger. dram.; widely influential in popularizing poetic drama, infusing it with melodramatic sensationalism and sentimental philosophizing

Kou·fax \'kō-faks\ Sanford 1935– *Sandy Koufax* Am. baseball player; pitched for the Brooklyn (later Los Angeles) Dodgers (1955–66); struck out 2,396 batters in 2,324 innings; ranked among the greatest pitchers in baseball history

Kous·se·vitz·ky \\,kü-sə-'vit-skē\\ Serge \\'sərj, 'serzh\\ 1874–1951 *Sergey Aleksandrovich Kusevitsky* Am. (Russ.-born) conductor; a champion of modern music; commissioned works by Ravel, Prokofiev, Gershwin, Stravinsky

Krafft–Ebing \\'kräft-'ā-biŋ, 'kraft-\\ Richard 1840–1902 Freiherr *von Krafft-Ebing* Ger. neurologist; made studies in sexual psychopathology; identified relationship between syphilis and paralysis

Krebs \\'krebz\\ Edwin Gerhard 1918–   Am. biochem.; awarded (with E. Fischer) 1992 Nobel prize for physiology or medicine for demonstrating basic biochemical mechanisms

Krebs Sir Hans Adolf 1900–1981 Brit. (Ger.-born) biochem.; awarded (with F. Lipmann) 1953 Nobel prize for physiology or medicine for discovering the urea cycle and the citric acid cycle (called the Krebs cycle)

Kreis·ky \\'krī-skē\\ Bruno 1911–1990 chancellor of Austria (1970–83)

Kreis·ler \\'krīs-lər\\ Fritz 1875–1962 Am. (Austrian-born) violinist; composer of many original violin pieces

Krim \\'krim\\ Mathilde 1926–   née *Galland* Am. (Ital.-born) geneticist & virologist; founded (1983) American Foundation for AIDS Research; a leading AIDS researcher and educator

Krogh \\'krŏg\\ (Schack) August Steenberg 1874–1949 Dan. physiol.; awarded 1920 Nobel prize for physiology or medicine for discovering the regulation of the motor mechanism of capillaries

Kro·pot·kin \\krə-'pät-kən\\ Pyotr Alekseyevich 1842–1921 Russ. geographer & revolutionary; explored Siberia, Finland, Manchuria; as leader of anarchist movement, developed theory of "anarchist communism"

Kru·ger \\'krü-gər *Afrik* 'krœ̄-ər\\ Paul 1825–1904 *Stephanus Johannes Paulus* So. African statesman; a founder of Transvaal state; a leader of Boer rebellion, a negotiator of peace in 1881; president of Transvaal (1883–1900)

Krupp \\'krŭp, 'krəp\\ family of Ger. munition makers: including Friedrich 1787–1826; founder of Krupp Works at Essen (1811); his son Alfred 1812–1887; perfected process of making cast steel and supplied arms to more than 46 nations; Alfred's son Friedrich Alfred 1854–1902; manufactured machinery as well as arms; Friedrich Alfred's daughter Bertha 1886–1957; works managed by her husband Gustav; & Bertha's son Alfried 1907–1967; ran factories using inmates of concentration camps as slave labor

Krup·ska·ya \\'krüp-skə-yə\\ Nadezhda Konstantinovna 1869–1939 *wife of Lenin* Russ. revolutionary; held posts in education commissariat

Krutch \\'krüch\\ Joseph Wood 1893–1970 Am. author & critic; wrote *The Great Chain of Life, Edgar Allan Poe, The Modern Temper,* etc.

Ku·bi·tschek de Oli·vei·ra \\'kü-bə-,chek-dā-ȯ-lē-'vä-rə\\ Juscelino 1902–1976 pres. of Brazil (1956–61); administration fostered rapid economic growth, building of new capital, Brasilia

Ku·blai Khan \\'kü-,blə-'kän, -,blī-\\ 1215–1294; overlord of all Mongol dominions in Europe and Asia; founder of Mongol dynasty in China; completed subjugation and organization of China; visited by Marco Polo

Ku·brick \\'kü-brik, 'kyü-\\ Stanley 1928–   Am. film director, writer, & producer; directed *Lolita* (1962), *Dr. Strangelove* (1964), *2001: A Space Odyssey* (1968), etc.

Kuhn \\'kün\\ Richard 1900–1967 Austrian chem.; awarded 1938 Nobel prize for chemistry for work on carotenoids and vitamins

Kuhn Thomas Samuel 1922–   Am. philos. & scientist; best known for his book *The Structure of Scientific Revolutions* questioning linear, gradual scientific progress — **Kuhn·ian** \\'kü-nē-ən\\ *adj*

Kun \\'kün\\ Bé·la \\'bā-lə\\ 1885–1937 Hung. communist; organized brief communist revolution in 1919 and later attempted revolutions in Austria, Germany; liquidated in Stalinist purge

Kung \\'gün\\ Prince 1833–1898 Manchu statesman; advocated governmental reforms and adoption of esp. Western military methods and techniques

K'ung \\'kün\\ H. H. 1881–1967 orig. *K'ung Hsiang-hsi* Chin. statesman; gave support and aid to Sun Yat-sen and to Chiang Kai-shek, both his wife's brothers-in-law

Ku·ro·pat·kin \\,kůr-ə-'pat-kən, -'pät-\\ Aleksey Nikolayevich 1848–1921 Russ. gen.; in command of Russian forces in Far East but opposed to war with Japan

Ku·ro·sa·wa \\,kůr-ə-'saů-ə\\ Akira 1910–   Jp. filmmaker; regarded as greatest of all Japanese filmmakers; developed innovative style in *Rashomon* (1950), *The Seven Samurai* (1954), *Ran* (1985), etc.

Kusch \\'kůsh\\ Polykarp 1911–1993 Am. (Ger.-born) physicist; awarded (with W. E. Lamb) 1955 Nobel prize for physics for determining that the magnetic moment of the electron is greater than its theoretical value

Ku·tu·zov \\kə-'tü-,zóf, -,zóv\\ Mikhail Illarionovich 1745–1813 Prince of *Smolensk* Russ. field marshal; commander in wars against Napoléon, Turks; pursued French into Poland and Prussia

Kuz·nets \\'kəz-(,)nets\\ Simon 1901–1985 Am. (Ukrainian-born) econ.; awarded 1971 Nobel prize for economics for his interpretation of economic growth

Kyd *or* **Kid** \\'kid\\ Thomas 1558–1594 Eng. dram.; initiated the Elizabethan revenge play with *The Spanish Tragedie* (ca. 1592) and may have written an earlier *Hamlet*

Kynewulf *var of* CYNEWULF

L

La Bru·yère \\,lä-brü-'yer, -brē-'er\\ Jean de 1645–1696 Fr. moralist; author of satiric masterpiece *The Characters of Theophrastus translated from Greek, with the Character and Customs of this Century*

La·chaise \\lə-'shāz\\ Gaston 1882–1935 Am. (Fr.-born) sculptor; known for sculptures of massively proportioned female nudes and for portrait busts

La Farge \lə-ˈfärzh, -ˈfärj\ John 1835–1910 Am. artist; painted chiefly landscapes and flowers, church murals; developed opalescent glass and worked with stained glass

La Farge Oliver Hazard Perry 1901–1963 Am. writer & anthropol.; wrote *Laughing Boy* (1929, Pulitzer prize), *The Door in the Wall*, etc.

La·fa·yette \ˌlä-fē-ˈet, ˌla-\ Marquis de 1757–1834 *Marie-Joseph-Paul-Yves-Roch-Gilbert du Motier* Fr. gen. & statesman; served in American Revolutionary War, helping defeat Cornwallis at Yorktown

Laf·fite *or* **La·fitte** \lə-ˈfēt, la-\ Jean *ca* 1780–*ca* 1826 Fr. pirate in America; helped Americans, esp. at New Orleans, in War of 1812, then returned to piracy

La Fol·lette \lə-ˈfä-lət\ Robert Marion 1855–1925 Am. polit.; leader of Progressive Movement in the U.S.; supported reform legislation; opposed U.S. entry into WWI, League of Nations, World Court

La·fon·taine \ˌlä-ˌfōⁿ-ˈten\ Henri 1854–1943 Belg. lawyer & statesman; helped bring about Hague peace conferences (1899, 1907)

La Fon·taine \ˌlä-ˌfōⁿ-\ Jean de 1621–1695 Fr. poet; known for his wit, charm, easy morals, absentmindedness; author of *Fables* based on traditional fables

La·ger·kvist \ˈlä-gər-ˌkvist, -ˌkwist\ Pär Fabian 1891–1974 Swed. dram., poet, & nov.; awarded 1951 Nobel prize for literature for his plays, poems, and novels

La·ger·löf \ˈlä-gər-ˌlœf\ Selma Ottiliana Lovisa 1858–1940 Swed. nov. & poet; awarded 1909 Nobel prize for literature for her novels

La·grange \lə-ˈgränj, -ˈgränzh\ Joseph-Louis 1736–1813 Comte *de Lagrange* Fr. math.; published works on celestial mechanics, differential and variable calculus, theory of numbers, etc.

La Guar·dia \lə-ˈgwär-dē-ə\ Fi·o·rel·lo \ˌfē-ə-ˈre-(ˌ)lō\ Henry 1882–1947 Am. polit.; as mayor of New York (1934–45), fought corruption, revised city charter, fostered civic improvements

Laing \ˈlaŋ\ Ronald David 1927–1989 Brit. psychiatrist; known for studies of schizophrenia and approach known as "anti-psychiatry"— **Laing·ian** \-ē-ən\ *adj*

Lake \ˈlāk\ Simon 1866–1945 Am. naval architect; inventor of even-keel type of submarine

La·marck \lə-ˈmärk\ Jean-Baptiste de Monet de 1744–1829 Chevalier *de Lamarck* Fr. naturalist; forerunner of Darwin in evolutionary theory and responsible for classification of animals into vertebrates and invertebrates — **La·marck·ian** \lə-ˈmär-kē-ən\ *adj*

La·mar·tine \ˌlä-ˌmär-ˈtēn, ˌla-mər-\ Alphonse-Marie-Louis de Prat de 1790–1869 Fr. poet; best known for *Méditations poetiques* which strongly influenced Romantic movement in French literature

Lamas Carlos Saavedra — see Carlos SAAVEDRA LAMAS

Lamb \ˈlam\ Charles 1775–1834 Eng. essayist & critic; contributed *Essays of Elia* to *London Magazine*, wrote children's stories and poems, many great letters, etc.

Lamb William 1779–1848 2d Viscount *Melbourne* Eng. statesman; tactful political adviser to Queen Victoria

Lamb Willis Eugene 1913–   Am. physicist; awarded (with P. Kusch) 1955 Nobel prize for physics for discoveries on the structure of the hydrogen spectrum

Lam·bert \'lam-bərt\ John 1619–1683 Eng. gen.; helped Cromwell gain victory and his chief aide for a time; later became virtual leader of country and finally imprisoned

Lam·masch \'lä-ˌmäsh\ Heinrich 1853–1920 Austrian jurist; favored peace by agreement in WWI and a league of nations

La Motte–Fouqué — see FOUQUÉ

L'Amour \lä-'mȯr, -'mu̇r\ Louis Dearborn 1908–1988 Am. writer; known for Western novels, of which he wrote more than 80

Lan·cas·ter \'lan-ˌkas-tər, 'laŋ-\ Burton Stephen 1913–1994 Am. actor; starred in films *From Here to Eternity, Elmer Gantry* (Academy award), *Birdman of Alcatraz,* etc.

Land \'land\ Edwin Herbert 1909–1991 Am. inventor & industrialist; invented Polaroid Land camera with self-developing system of instant photography (1948)

Lan·dau \län-'daů\ Lev Davidovich 1908–1968 Russ. physicist; awarded 1962 Nobel prize for physics for theories on condensed matter, esp. liquid helium

Lan·dis \'lan-dəs\ Ken·e·saw \'ke-nə-ˌsȯ\ Mountain 1866–1944 Am. jurist & baseball commissioner; first commissioner of baseball; noted for efforts to preserve game's integrity

Lan·don \'lan-dən\ Alfred Mossman 1887–1987 Am. polit.; governor of Kansas (1933–37); unsuccessful Republican candidate for president (1936)

Lan·dor \'lan-ˌdȯr\ Walter Savage 1775–1864 Eng. author; known for verse, dramas, and esp. prose works as *Imaginary Conversations* (5 vols.), *Pericles and Aspasia, The Pentameron*

Lan·dow·ska \lan-'dȯf-ska, -'dȯv-\ Wanda Louise 1879–1959 Pol. pianist; initiated 20th-century revival of the harpsichord

Land·seer \'lan(d)-ˌsir\ Sir Edwin Henry 1802–1873 Eng. painter; extremely popular esp. for animal paintings

Land·stei·ner \'lan(d)-ˌstī-nər, 'länt-ˌshtī-\ Karl 1868–1943 Am. (Austrian-born) pathologist; awarded 1930 Nobel prize for physiology or medicine for developing system of blood typing

Lane \'lān\ Edward William 1801–1876 Eng. orientalist; author of first accurate version of *A Thousand and One Nights;* compiled an Arabic thesaurus

Lan·franc \'lan-ˌfraŋk\ 1005?–1089 Ital.-born prelate in England; as archbishop of Canterbury, rebuilt cathedral, reformed English church, created separate ecclesiastical courts; helped William II secure crown

Lang \'laŋ\ Andrew 1844–1912 Scot. scholar & author; proved folklore the foundation of literary mythology

Lang William Cosmo Gordon 1864–1945 Brit. prelate; archbishop of Canterbury (1928–42); cleared of suspicion of having conspired to achieve abdication of George VI (1936)

Lange \'läŋ-ə\ Christian Louis 1869–1938 Norw. pacifist & hist.; awarded (with K.H. Branting) 1921 Nobel prize for peace

Lange \'lȯŋ-ē\ David Russell 1942–   prime min. of New Zealand (1984–89); promulgated non-nuclear policy

Lang·er \'laŋ-ər\ Susanne Knauth 1895–1985 Am. philos. & educ.; developed philosophy of aesthetics, esp. as based in language

Lang·land \\'laŋ-lənd\\ William *ca* 1330–*ca* 1400 Eng. poet; presumed author of the allegorical poem *The Vision of William concerning Piers the Plowman (Piers Plowman)*

Lang·ley \\'laŋ-lē\\ Samuel Pierpont 1834–1906 Am. astron. & airplane pioneer; studied solar radiation; achieved first flights of mechanically propelled heavier-than-air machines

Lang·muir \\'laŋ-ˌmyu̇r\\ Irving 1881–1957 Am. chem.; awarded 1932 Nobel prize for chemistry for his work in surface chemistry

Lang·ton \\'laŋ(k)-tən\\ Stephen *d* 1228 Eng. prelate; played important role in creation and reissue of Magna Carta and in constitutions of English ecclesiastical courts

Lang·try \\'laŋ(k)-trē\\ Lillie 1853–1929 née (*Emilie Charlotte*) *Le Breton; the Jersey Lily* Brit. actress; celebrated for her beauty and for role as Rosalind in *As You Like It*

La·nier \\lə-'nir\\ Sidney 1842–1881 Am. poet; known for "The Symphony," "Corn," "The Song of the Chattahoochee," etc.

Lan·kes·ter \\'laŋ-kəs-tər; 'lan-ˌkes-, 'laŋ-\\ Sir Edwin Ray 1847–1929 Eng. zool.; contributed to comparative anatomy, embryology, parasitology, anthropology

Lannes \\'län, 'lan\\ Jean 1769–1809 *Duc de Montebello* Fr. soldier; took part in coup d'état which brought Napoléon to power; fought in many important battles

Lan·sing \\'lan(t)-siŋ\\ Robert 1864–1928 Am. lawyer & statesman; arranged purchase of what are now Virgin Islands; advised Wilson to secure peace treaties rather than form League of Nations

Lao·tzu \\'lau̇d-'zə\\ orig. *Li Erh* \\'lē-'er\\ 6th cent. B.C. Chin. philos.; considered founder of Taoism and traditionally author of *Tao-te Ching*

La Pé·rouse \\ˌlä-pā-'rüz, -pə-\\ Comte de 1741–1788 *Jean-François de Galoup* Fr. navigator & explorer; explored coasts of Alaska, California, China, Russia, Samoa, southeastern Australia

La·place \\lə-'pläs\\ Pierre-Simon 1749–1827 *Marquis de Laplace* Fr. astron. & math.; made discoveries about planetary motion, gravity, respiration, moon's acceleration, La Place transform for solving partial differential equations, etc.

Lard·ner \\'lärd-nər\\ Ring 1885–1933 in full *Ringgold Wilmer Lardner* Am. writer; author of humorous, satirical short stories and plays

La·re·do Brú \\lə-'rā-dō-'brü\\ Federico 1875–1946 Cuban soldier; pres. of Cuba (1936–40); led revolutionary movement against Pres. Zayas (1920–24)

Lar·kin \\'lär-kən\\ Philip Arthur 1922–1985 Brit. poet; considered by some the most gifted English poet of his time; author of collected verse *The Less Deceived, The Whitsun Weddings*, etc.

La   Roche·fou·cauld   \\ˌlä-ˌrōsh-fü-'kō,   -ˌrōsh-\\   François 1613–1680 *Duc de La Rochefoucauld* Fr. writer & moralist; known for his *Réflexions ou sentences et maximes morales (Reflections or Statements and Maxims on Morals)*

La·rousse \\lä-'rüs\\ Pierre-Athanase 1817–1875 Fr. grammarian & lexicographer; best known for his *Grand Dictionnaire universel de XIXᵉ siècle* (1866–76, *Great Universal Dictionary of the 19th century*)

Lar·tet \\lär-'tā\\ Édouard-Armand-Isidore-Hippolyte 1801–1871 Fr. archaeol.; credited with discovering earliest human art and with establishing a date for the upper Paleolithic period of the Stone Age

La Salle \lə-'sal\ Sieur de 1643–1687 *René-Robert Cavelier* Fr. explorer in America; claimed Mississippi valley for Louis XIV, naming it Louisiana

Las Ca·sas \läs-'kä-səs\ Bartolomé de 1474–1566 Span. Dominican missionary & hist.; secured passage of laws to protect Indians from slavery; wrote several works on America

Lasch \'lash\ Christopher 1932–1994 Am. hist. & social critic; best known for *The Culture of Narcissism,* which saw pathologically self-absorbed, easily manipulated individuals without moral values as a pervasive element within contemporary society

Las·ki \'las-kē\ Harold Joseph 1893–1950 Eng. polit. scientist; became a Marxist in 1930s in effort to explain Britain's "crisis in democracy"

Las·salle \lə-'sal, -'säl\ Ferdinand 1825–1864 Ger. socialist; worked to change Germany from state based on private property to democratic constitutional state

Lat·i·mer \'la-tə-mər\ Hugh *ca* 1485–1555 Eng. religious reformer; established principles of Reformation in popular mind but refused to accept the Six Articles; burned at stake under Mary for heresy

La Tour \lə-'tùr\ Georges de 1593–1652 Fr. painter; known chiefly for candlelight subjects as *The Mocking of Job,* etc.

La Tour Maurice-Quentin de 1704–1788 Fr. painter; best known for pastel portraits of Diderot, Voltaire, Louis XV, Mme de Pompadour, Jean-Jacques Rousseau, etc.

La·trobe \lə-'trōb\ Benjamin Henry 1764–1820 Am. (Eng.-born) architect & engineer; designed and built Philadelphia city water supply system, first in America; introduced Greek Revival architecture to U.S.

Lat·ti·more \'la-tə-ˌmōr, -ˌmòr\ Owen 1900–1989 Am. orientalist; political adviser to Chiang Kai-shek and director of Pacific operations in the office of war information; wrongly named as high communist agent by Sen. Joseph McCarthy

Lattimore Richmond 1906–1984 Am. poet & translator; best known for translations of Homer's *Iliad* and *Odyssey,* Pindar's *Odes,* etc.

Lau·bach \'laù-ˌbäk\ Frank Charles 1884–1970 Am. educator & missionary; developed an effective way to combat illiteracy among the Moro people of the Philippines, which was then used elsewhere

Laud \'lòd\ William 1573–1645 Eng. prelate; archbishop of Canterbury (1633–45); efforts to eliminate Presbyterianism and Calvinism led to war, Long Parliament, and his beheading for treason —
Laud·ian \'lò-dē-ən\ *adj*

Lau·der \'lò-dər\ Estée 1908?– née *Ment·zer* \'ment-sər\ Am. businesswoman; founded (1946) cosmetics firm Estée Lauder, Inc.

Lauder Sir Harry Maclennan 1870–1950 Scot. singer; popular for his rendition of Scottish songs and ballads, many of his own composition

Laue \'laù-ə\ Max von 1879–1960 Ger. physicist; awarded 1914 Nobel prize for physics for work on measuring X rays and analyzing crystals

Laugh·ton \'lò-t²n\ Charles 1899–1962 Am. (Eng.-born) actor; known for appearances in motion pictures including *The Private*

Life of Henry VIII (Academy award), *The Hunchback of Notre Dame,* etc.

Lau·rence \ˈlȯr-ən(t)s, ˈlär-\ (Jean) Margaret 1926–1987 née *Wemyss* Can. author; best known for Manawaka series of novels including *The Stone Angel, A Jest of God,* etc.

Lau·ren·cin \lȯ-räⁿ-saⁿ\ Marie 1885–1956 Fr. painter; painted esp. delicate, idyllic pastels of young girls and designed costumes for Comédie française and Diaghilev's Ballets Russes

Lau·ri·er \ˈlȯr-ē-ā, ˈlär-\ Sir Wilfrid 1841–1919 Canad. statesman; prime min. (1896–1911); worked for unrestricted reciprocity with U.S., protection of industry, effective transportation system, development of western territories

Lautrec — see TOULOUSE-LAUTREC

La·val \lə-ˈval, -ˈväl\ Pierre 1883–1945 Fr. polit.; pursued policy of collaboration with Germany; executed for treason

La Val·lière \ˌlä-val-ˈyer\ Duchesse de 1644–1710 *Françoise-Louise de La Baume Le Blanc* mistress of Louis XIV of France

La·ve·ran \ˌlä-və-ˈräⁿ\ Charles-Louis-Alphonse 1845–1922 Fr. physiol. & bacteriol.; awarded 1907 Nobel prize for physiology or medicine for work on protozoan disease agents

La Vé·ren·drye \lä-ˌver-ən-ˈdrē, -ˈver-ən-ˌdri\ Sieur de 1685–1749 *Pierre Gaultier de Varennes* Canad. explorer in America; explored westward to upper Missouri River; sons discovered Manitoba, the Dakotas, western Minnesota, Montana, western Canada

La·very \ˈlā-və-rē, ˈla-; ˈläv-rē, ˈlav-\ Sir John 1856–1941 Brit. painter; known for portraits, interiors, and landscapes

La·voi·sier \ləv-ˈwä-zē-ā\ Antoine-Laurent 1743–1794 Fr. chem.; founder of modern chemistry through explanation of combustion including naming of oxygen, experiments on various compounds, help in devising system of chemical nomenclature

Law \ˈlȯ\ (Andrew) Bon·ar \ˈbä-nər\ 1858–1923 Brit. (Canad.-born) statesman; Conservative party leader (from 1911) and prime min. (1922–25)

Law Edward 1750–1818 1st Baron El·len·bor·ough \ˈe-lən-ˌbər-ə, -ˌbə-rə, -brə\ Eng. jurist; lord chief justice of England (1802–18)

Law John 1671–1729 Scot. financier & speculator; founded Banque Générale to test banking reforms; failed in Mississippi scheme to develop lower Mississippi valley

Law William 1686–1761 Eng. writer; wrote influential works on Christian ethics and mysticism including *Serious Call to a Devout and Holy Life*

Lawes \ˈlȯz\ Henry 1596–1662 Eng. composer; composed music for Milton's *Comus,* Sandys version of *Psalms,* three volumes of airs; best known for continuo songs

Lawes Lewis Edward 1883–1947 Am. penologist; warden of Sing Sing Prison, N.Y. (1920–41) and author of works on prisons and penology

Law·rence \ˈlȯr-ən(t)s, ˈlär-\ David 1888–1973 Am. journalist; founded *U.S. News* (1933), became *U.S. News and World Report,* and wrote syndicated news column

Lawrence David Herbert 1885–1930 Eng. nov.; author of novels that analyzed the ills of industrial society and the role of sex in human conduct, including *Sons and Lovers* (1913), *Lady Chatterly's*

Lover (1923), etc. — **Law·renc·ian** \lȯ-ˈren(t)-sē-ən\ *or* **Law·ren·tian** *or* **Lau·ren·tian** \-sh(ē-)ən\ *adj*

Lawrence Ernest Orlando 1901–1958 Am. physicist; awarded 1939 Nobel prize for physics for inventing the cyclotron and working on artificial radioactivity

Lawrence Gertrude 1898–1952 orig. *Gertrud Alexandra Dagmar Lawrence Klasen* Eng. actress; known for roles opposite Noel Coward in *Private Lives, Tonight at Eight-Thirty* and for *The King and I*, etc.

Lawrence James 1781–1813 Am. naval officer; raided British shipping during War of 1812; cried "Don't give up the ship," as he was carried below with mortal wound

Lawrence Sir Thomas 1769–1830 Eng. painter; known for portraits of courtliness and social elegance; instrumental in founding National Gallery

Lawrence Thomas Edward 1888–1935 *Lawrence of Arabia* later surname *Shaw* Brit. archaeol., soldier, & writer; leader of the Arab revolt against the Turks, described in *The Seven Pillars of Wisdom*

Lax·ness \ˈläks-ˌnes\ Halldór Kiljan 1902– Icelandic writer; awarded 1955 Nobel prize for literature for his novels

Lay·a·mon \ˈlī-ə-mən, ˈlä-\ *fl* 1200 Eng. poet; wrote the *Brut*, outstanding literary product of the 12th-cent. revival of English literature

Lay·ard \ˈlā-ˌärd, -ərd\ Sir Austen Henry 1817–1894 Eng. archaeol. & diplomat; at Nineveh, discovered palace of Sennacherib, much artwork, many cuneiform tablets

Lea·cock \ˈlē-ˌkäk\ Stephen Butler 1869–1944 Canad. econ. & humorist; author of *Elements of Political Science* and of many humorous publications

Leadbelly — see Huddie LEDBETTER

Lea·hy \ˈlā-(ˌ)hē\ William Daniel 1875–1959 Am. admiral; served in Spanish-American War, Philippine insurrection, Boxer Rebellion, WWI, as chief of staff to Presidents Roosevelt and Truman

Lea·key \ˈlē-kē\ Louis Seymour Bazett 1903–1972 Brit. paleontologist; through discoveries at Olduvai Gorge, Tanzania, proved that human evolution was centered in Africa

Leakey Mary Douglas 1913– *wife of prec.* Brit. paleontologist; known for discoveries of bones and footprints of hominids in Africa

Lean \ˈlēn\ Sir David 1908–1991 Brit. film director; won Academy awards for *The Bridge on the River Kwai* and *Lawrence of Arabia* and also directed *Dr. Zhivago, A Passage to India*, etc.

Lear \ˈlir\ Edward 1812–1888 Eng. painter & nonsense poet; published illustrated travel books; created large oil paintings influenced by Pre-Raphaelite style; wrote volumes of nonsense stories, songs, and verse

Lea·vis \ˈlē-vəs\ Frank Raymond 1895–1978 Eng. critic; maintained that literature should be a criticism of life and that criticism should be based on an author's moral position — **Lea·vis·ian** \lē-ˈvi-zh(ē-)ən\ *adj* — **Lea·vis·ite** \ˈlē-və-ˌsīt\ *adj*

Le·brun \lə-ˈbrœⁿ(n), -ˈbrœⁿ\ Albert 1871–1950 Fr. statesman; pres. of France (1932–40); attempted to preserve unity but failed to provide leadership

Lebrun Mme. Vigée— — see VIGÉE-LEBRUN

Le Brun or **Le·brun** \lə-'brœⁿ(n), -'brœn\ Charles 1619–1690 Fr. painter; decorated palace at Versailles; created or supervised art commissioned by French government for three decades

Le Car·ré \lə-kä-'rā\ John 1931–   pseud. of *David Corn·well* \'kȯrn-ˌwel\ Eng. nov.; author of Cold War spy novels *The Spy Who Came In from the Cold* (1963), *Tinker, Tailor, Soldier, Spy* (1974), *The Russia House* (1989), etc.

Lecky \'le-kē\ William Edward Hartpole 1838–1903 Irish hist.; author of *History of Rationalism in Europe, History of European Morals,* etc.

Le·conte de Lisle \lə-ˌkōⁿ(n)t-də-'lē(ə)l\ Charles-Marie 1818–1894 orig. *Leconte* Fr. poet; identified with modern Parnassian school; considered a poet of disillusionment and skepticism

Le Corbusier — see CORBUSIER

Led·bet·ter \'led-ˌbe-tər\ Huddie 1888–1949 *Lead·bel·ly* \'led-ˌbe-lē\ Am. blues singer; one of greatest blues singers; composed "Rock Island Line," "Good Night, Irene," etc.

Le·der·berg \'lā-dər-ˌbərg\ Joshua 1925–   Am. geneticist; awarded (with G.W. Beadle and E.L. Tatum) 1958 Nobel prize for physiology or medicine for studies of genetics in bacteria

Led·er·man \'lā-dər-mən\ Leon Max 1922–   Am. physicist; awarded (with M. Schwartz, J. Steinberger) 1988 Nobel prize for physics for work on subatomic neutrinos

Le Duc Tho \'lā-'dək-'tō\ 1911–1990 Vietnamese diplomat; awarded (with H. Kissinger) 1973 Nobel prize for peace for actions at the Paris Conference on Indochina, but declined it

Lee \'lē\ Ann 1736–1784 Am. (Eng.-born) Shaker; founder of Shaker society in U.S., preaching frugality and celibacy and claiming she embodied the female half of God's dual nature

Lee Charles 1731–1782 Am. (Eng.-born) gen.; criticized Washington and betrayed American army to Gen. Howe

Lee Fitzhugh 1835–1905 *nephew of R. E. Lee* Am. gen.; served notably in Civil War on Confederate side and in Spanish-American War

Lee Francis Lightfoot 1734–1797 Am. statesman in Revolution; a signer of the Declaration of Independence

Lee Henry 1756–1818 *Light-Horse Harry* Am. gen.; gave eulogy of Washington that included words, "First in war, first in peace, and first in the hearts of his countrymen"

Lee Richard Henry 1732–1794 Am. statesman in Revolution; moved resolution (adopted July 2, 1776) that led directly to the writing of the Declaration of Independence, which he signed

Lee Robert Edward 1807–1870 Am. Confed. gen.; commanded army of Northern Virginia and later all Confederate armies; surrendered to Grant at Appomattox Court House (April 9, 1865)

Lee Sir Sidney 1859–1926 Eng. editor & scholar; helped edit *Dictionary of National Biography;* prepared facsimile edition of First Folio of Shakespeare; wrote scholarly works on Shakespeare

Lee Yuan Tseh 1936–   Am. (Taiwanese-born) chem.; awarded (with D.R. Herschbach, J.C. Polanyi) 1986 Nobel prize for chemistry for pioneering research on basic chemical reactions

Lee Tsung-Dao \'lē-'dzùŋ-'daú\ 1926–   Chin. physicist; awarded (with C.N. Yang) 1957 Nobel prize for physics for disproving the law of conservation of parity

Leeu·wen·hoek \'lā-vən-ˌhúk\ Antonie van 1632–1723 Du. naturalist; made microscopes through which he observed red blood corpuscles, spermatozoa, blood capillaries, striated muscle fibers, etc.; disproved doctrine of spontaneous generation

Le·feb·vre \lə-'fevrʳ\ François-Joseph 1755–1820 Duc *de Dantzig* Fr. gen.; marshal of France; supported coup d'état of 1799 bringing Napoléon to power and joined him again during the Hundred Days

Le Gal·lienne \lə-'gal-yən\ Eva 1899–1991 Am. (Eng.-born) actress; founded American Repertory Theater Company; known as actress in serious dramas and as director and producer

Le Gallienne Richard 1866–1947 Eng. writer; author of prose and verse, including *Quest of the Golden Girl, The Romantic Nineties,* etc.

Le·gen·dre \lə-'zhäⁿdrʳ\ Adrien-Marie 1752–1833 Fr. math.; made important researches in the theory of elliptic functions, theory of numbers, attraction of ellipsoids, method of least squares

Lé·ger \lā-'zhā\ Alexis Saint-Léger 1887–1975 pseud. *St. John Perse* \saⁿ-ˌjòn-'pers\ Fr. diplomat & poet; author of poetry marked by precision and purity of language, liturgical meter, exotic vocabulary; awarded 1960 Nobel prize for literature

Léger Fernand 1881–1955 Fr. painter; under influence of Cézanne, Cubism, and industrial technology, developed a "machine art" of monumental mechanistic forms in bold colors in highly disciplined compositions

Le·guía y Sal·ce·do \lə-ˌgē-ə-ˌē-säl-'sā-(ˌ)dō, -(ˌ)thō\ Augusto Bernardino 1863–1932 Peruvian banker; pres. of Peru (1908–12, 1919–30); introduced various reforms but ruled dictatorially and overthrown by military revolt

Le Guin \lə-'gwin\ Ursula K. 1929–   orig. surname *Kroe·ber* \'krō-bər\ Am. author; best known for tales of science fiction and fantasy distinctive for their character development and use of language, including *The Left Hand of Darkness, The Dispossessed,* etc.

Le·hár \'lā-ˌhär\ Franz 1870–1948 Hung. composer; composed operettas *The Merry Widow, The Land of Smiles,* etc., symphonic poems, sonatas, marches, dances, etc.

Leh·man \'lē-mən\ Herbert Henry 1878–1963 Am. banker & polit.; gov. of New York (1932–42); U.S. sen. (1949–57); known for philanthropic activities

Leh·mann \'lā-ˌmän\ Lot·te \'lò-tə\ 1888–1976 Ger. soprano; eminent lyric-dramatic soprano known esp. for interpretations of Mozart, Beethoven's Leonore, Wagner, etc.

Lehn \'lān\ Jean-Marie 1939–   Fr. chem.; awarded (with D.J. Cram, C.J. Pedersen) 1987 Nobel prize for chemistry for development of and work with artificial molecules that function like natural organic molecules

Leib·niz \'līb-nəts, *G* 'līp-nits\ Gottfried Wilhelm 1646–1716 Ger. philos. & math.; published work on foundations of integral and differential calculus before Newton, causing long controversy; developed rationalistic theory of metaphysics, etc. — **Leib·niz·ian** \līb-'nit-sē-ən, līp-\ *adj*

Lei·bo·vitz \'lē-bō-ˌvits\ Annie 1949–   Am. photographer; known for her brash, often shocking portraits of celebrities

Leicester 1st Earl of — see Robert DUDLEY; see also de MONT-
FORT

Leif Er·iks·son \ˌlāv-ˈer-ik-sən, ˌlēf-\ or **Er·ics·son** \same\ *fl* 1000
son of Erik the Red Norw. explorer; visited what may be Labrador,
Newfoundland, and Nova Scotia (Helluland, Markland, Vinland)
sailing west from Greenland

Leigh \ˈlē\ Vivian 1913–1967 orig. *Vivian Mary Hartley* Eng. actress; best known for her portrayals of American Southern belles in
films *Gone With the Wind*, *A Streetcar Named Desire* (both Academy awards)

Leigh·ton \ˈlā-tᵊn\ Frederick 1830–1896 Baron *Leighton of Stret-
ton* Eng. painter; excelled in draftsmanship, as in *Hercules Wres-
tling with Death*, *Venus Disrobing for the Bath*, etc.

Leins·dorf \ˈlīnz-ˌdȯrf, ˈlīn(t)s-\ Erich 1912–1993 Am. (Austrian-
born) conductor; notable esp. for his interpretation of Wagner

Le·jeune \lə-ˈjün\ John Archer 1867–1942 Am. marine-corps gen.;
served in Spanish-American War, Philippine Islands, at capture of
Vera Cruz, in WWI; in command of U.S. Marine Corps (1920–29)

Le·land \ˈlē-lənd\ John 1506?–1552 Eng. antiquarian; traveled
through England and Wales searching for manuscripts, records,
relics of antiquity

Leloir \lā-ˈlwär\ Luis Federico 1906–1987 Argentine biochem.;
awarded 1970 Nobel prize for chemistry for his discovery of chemical compounds that affect the storage of energy in living things

Le·ly \ˈlē-lē\ Sir Peter 1618–1680 orig. *Pieter Van der Faes* Brit.
(Westphalian-born) painter; known esp. for his portraits of the
English aristocracy, including the royal family

Le·maî·tre \lə-ˈmetrᵊ\ (François-Elie) Jules 1853–1914 Fr. writer;
wrote literary and dramatic criticism, plays, stories

Lemaître (Abbé) Georges Henri 1894–1966 Belg. astrophysicist;
formulated modern "big-bang" theory of origin of universe (1927)

Le·mieux \lə-ˈmyü\ Mario 1965–   Am. (Canad.-born) ice
hockey player; with Pittsburgh Penguins (1984–   ); All-Star game
MVP (1985, 1988, 1990); NHL player of the year (1992–93)

Le Moyne Pierre — see IBERVILLE

Le·nard \ˈlā-ˌnärt\ Philipp 1862–1947 Ger. physicist; awarded
1905 Nobel prize for physics for studying the properties of cathode
rays

Len·clos \läⁿ-klō\ Anne de 1620–1705 *Ninon de Lenclos* Fr. cour-
tesan; attracted Richelieu, La Rochefoucauld, Condé, Sévigné,
etc., by her beauty and wit; later held fashionable salon

L'En·fant \läⁿ-ˌfäⁿt, läⁿ-fäⁿ\ Pierre-Charles 1754–1825 Am. (Fr.-
born) architect & engineer; designed plan for new national capital
of Washington, D.C.

Le·nin \ˈle-nən\ 1870–1924 orig. *Vladimir Ilyich Ul·ya·nov* \ül-ˈyä-
nəf, -ˌnȯf, -ˌnȯv\ Russ. communist leader; founder of the Russian
communist party (Bolsheviks); guiding light of the Bolshevik Revolution (1917); first head of new U.S.S.R. (1917–24) — **Le·nin·ist**
\-nə-nist\ *adj or n* — **Le·nin·ite** \-ˌnīt\ *adj or n*

Len·non \ˈle-nən\ John Winston 1940–1980 Brit. singer & songwriter; founder (1956), guitarist, and singer with the Quarrymen,
later known as the Beatles, most successful rock-and-roll group of
1960s

Leo \ˈlē-(ˌ)ō\ name of 13 popes: esp. **I** Saint *d* 461 (pope 440–61);

held that papal power was passed on from St. Peter and sought to drive out all heresy; **III** Saint *d* 816 (pope 795–816); crowned Charlemagne emperor, establishing temporal sovereignty of pope and causing schism between Eastern and Western empires; **XIII** 1810–1903 (pope 1878–1903); wrote important encyclicals on marriage, Bible study, education, modern Socialism, etc.

Leon·ard \'le-nərd\ Ray Charles 1956–   *Sugar Ray* Am. boxer; holder of several world titles in welterweight, middleweight, light heavyweight, and super middleweight divisions; fought 36 professional fights, won 33, lost 2, drew 1

Leonard William Ellery 1876–1944 Am. educ. & poet; author of *The Lynching Bee, The Locomotive-God,* etc., and a translation of Lucretius

Le·o·nar·do da Vin·ci \,lē-ə-'när-(,)dō-də-'vin-chē, ,lā-, -'vēn-\ 1452–1519 It. painter, sculptor, architect, & engineer; famed for the breadth of his genius, covering anatomy, architecture, hydraulics, hydrology, geology, meteorology, mechanics, machinery, weaponry, flight, optics, mathematics, botany, etc. — **Le·o·nar·desque** \,lē-ə-,när-'desk, ,lā-\ *adj*

Le·on·ca·val·lo \,lā-,ōn-kə-'vä-(,)lō\ Ruggiero 1858–1919 Ital. composer & librettist; remembered esp. for verismo style opera *Pagliacci*

Le·on·i·das \lē-'ä-nə-dəs\ *d* 480 B.C. Greek hero; king of Sparta (490?–480); famous for his valiant but vain defense of the pass at Thermopylae against a vast Persian army

Le·on·tief \lē-'ònt-yəf, lyē-\ Wassily 1906–   Am. (Russ.-born) econ.; awarded 1973 Nobel prize for economics for development of the input-output method of economic analysis

Le·o·par·di \,lā-ə-'pär-dē\ Giacomo 1798–1837 Ital. poet; leading Italian lyric poet of pessimism

Le·o·pold I \'lē-ə-,pōld\ 1640–1705 king of Hungary (1655–1705) & Holy Rom. emp. (1658–1705); his reign characterized by increasingly absolute monarchy and centralized administration

Leopold II 1747–1792 Holy Rom. emp. (1790–92); formed alliance with Prussia against revolutionary France but died before war declared

Leopold I 1790–1865 king of Belgium (1831–65); first king of independent Belgium; oversaw peaceful development of state

Leopold II 1835–1909 king of Belgium (1865–1909); financed expedition of Stanley to Congo and annexed Congo Free State to Belgium

Leopold III 1901–1983 king of Belgium (1934–51); ordered capitulation of Belgian army to Germany in 1940; forced to abdicate in 1951

Lep·i·dus \'le-pə-dəs\ Marcus Aemilius *d* 13 (or 12) B.C. Rom. triumvir with Marc Antony and Octavian; tried to incite revolt against Octavian in Sicily

Ler·mon·tov \'ler-mən-,tóf, -,tòv\ Mikhail Yuryevich 1814–1841 Russ. poet & nov.; considered foremost Russian Romantic poet and second only to Pushkin among all Russian poets

Ler·ner \'lər-nər\ Alan Jay 1918–1986 Am. dram. & librettist; collaborated with composer Frederick Loewe on Broadway musicals *Brigadoon, My Fair Lady;* alone, film *Gigi,* etc.

Le·sage \lə-ˈsäzh\ Alain-René 1668–1747 Fr. nov. & dram.; author of picaresque masterpiece *L'Histoire de Gil Blas de Santillane*, lesser novels, plays

Le·sche·tiz·ky \ˌle-shə-ˈtit-skē\ Theodor 1830–1915 Pol. pianist & composer; one of greatest pianists and teachers of his time, pupils included Paderewski, Schnabel, etc.

Les·seps \lā-ˈseps, ˈle-səps\ Ferdinand-Marie de 1805–1894 Vicomte *de Lesseps* Fr. diplomat & promoter of Suez Canal; began project but gave it up for financial and political reasons

Les·sing \ˈle-siŋ\ Gotthold Ephraim 1729–1781 Ger. critic & dram.; author of comedies, classic German drama *Minna von Barnhelm* (1763), tragedies in prose, poems, theology, criticism, including *Laokoon* (1766), etc.

L'Es·trange \lə-ˈstrānj\ Sir Roger 1616–1704 Eng. journalist & translator; attacked Milton, Whigs, Titus Oates, dissenters, etc.; translated Quevedo, Seneca, Cicero, Aesop, Josephus

Leu·tze \ˈlöit-sə\ Emanuel 1816–1868 Am. (Ger.-born) painter; known for historical paintings, esp. *Washington Crossing the Delaware* (1851)

Le·ver \ˈlē-vər\ Charles James 1806–1872 Brit. nov.; author of lighthearted, rollicking novels, many on Irish life and characters

Le·vi-Mon·tal·ci·ni \ˈlä-vē-ˌmön-täl-ˈchē-nē\ Rita 1909–   Am. (Ital.-born) neurologist; awarded (with S. Cohen) 1986 Nobel prize for physiology or medicine for research on cell and organ growth

Lé·vi-Strauss \ˈlä-vē-ˈstraús, ˈle-vē-\ Claude 1908–   Fr. (Belg.-born) social anthropol.; developed structural method for analyzing kinship, ritual, myth, etc., through cultural codes of expression —
Lé·vi-Strauss·i·an \-ˈstraú-sē-ən\ *adj*

Lewes \ˈlü-əs\ George Henry 1817–1878 Eng. philos. & critic; author of biographical classic, *Life of Goethe*, and popularizer of science, esp. physiology and psychology

Lew·is \ˈlü-əs\ Sir (William) Arthur 1915–1991 Brit. econ.; awarded (with T.W. Schultz) 1979 Nobel prize for economics for research into the economic problems of developing countries

Lewis Carl 1961–   *Frederick Carlton Lewis* Am. athlete; won four gold medals in track-and-field events at Olympic Games (1984)

Lewis Cecil Day — see DAY-LEWIS

Lewis Clive Staples 1898–1963 Eng. nov. & essayist; known for fantasy tales for children, *Chronicles of Narnia*, works of Christian apologetics, science fiction allegories

Lewis Isaac Newton 1858–1931 Am. army officer & inventor; invented Lewis machine gun and originated modern artillery corps organization

Lewis John Llewellyn 1880–1969 Am. labor leader; organized Congress of Industrial Organizations (CIO) in competition with American Federation of Labor (AFL)

Lewis Matthew Gregory 1775–1818 *Monk Lewis* Eng. author; best known for Gothic romance *Ambrosio, or the Monk*

Lewis Meriwether 1774–1809 Am. explorer; with William Clark, explored and reported on Louisiana territory to the Pacific Ocean

Lewis (Harry) Sinclair 1885–1951 Am. nov.; awarded 1930 Nobel prize for literature for his novels (first American to win this award)

Lewis (Percy) Wyndham 1882–1957 Brit. painter & author; founder of Vorticist movement, relating art to industrial process

Ley \'lī\ Robert 1890–1945 Ger. Nazi leader; ruthlessly enforced obedience in labor ranks; committed suicide awaiting trial as war criminal

Lib·by \'li-bē\ Willard Frank 1908–1980 Am. chem.; awarded 1960 Nobel prize for chemistry for developing a method of radiocarbon dating

Lib·e·ra·ce \,li-bə-'rä-chē\ 1919–1987 in full *Wladziu Valentino Liberace* Am. pianist; flamboyant showman known for his florid renditions of popular and classical favorites, extravagant costumes, and sentimental patter

Lich·ten·stein \'lik-tən-,stīn, -,stēn\ Roy 1923–   Am. artist; creator of American Pop Art images often in comic-book style

Li·cin·i·us \lə-'si-nē-əs\ *d* 325 *Valerius Licinianus Licinius* Rom. emp. (308–324); issued Edict of Milan jointly with Constantine establishing religious tolerance

Lid·dell Hart \'li-d°l-'härt\ Sir Basil Henry 1895–1970 Eng. mil. scientist; author of official *Infantry Training* manual for army; early advocate of air power and mechanized tank warfare

Lie \'lē\ Jonas 1833–1908 Norw. nov. & dram.; author of novels, fairy tales, plays, and verse

Lie Trygve Halvdan 1896–1968 Norw. lawyer; first secy.-gen. of U.N. (1946–52)

Lie·big \'lē-big\ Justus von 1803–1873 Freiherr *von Liebig* Ger. chem.; considered founder of agricultural chemistry; experimented with artificial soil fertilizers

Lieb·knecht \'lēp-,knekt, -,nekt\ Karl 1871–1919 Ger. socialist leader; violently opposed Germany's policy leading to WWI and involved in later Spartacus insurrection (Jan. 1919); arrested and murdered

Li·far \'lē-,fär, lē-'\ Serge 1905–1986 Fr. (Russ.-born) choreographer & dancer; choreographer for Paris Opéra (1929–58)

Li Hung–chang \'lē-'hùŋ-'jäŋ\ 1823–1901 Chin. statesman; promoted Western ideas and modernizing projects; founded Chinese navy

Lil·ien·thal \'lil-yən-,täl, -,thôl\ Otto 1848–1896 Ger. aeronautical engineer; demonstrated advantages of curved surfaces over flat ones for wings

Li·li·u·o·ka·la·ni \li-,lē-ə-(,)wō-kə-'lä-nē\ 1838–1917 *Lydia Paki Liliuokalani; Liliu Kamakaeha* queen of the Hawaiian Islands (1891–93); attempted to restore authority of monarchy and fought annexation, but deposed; wrote song "Aloha Oe"

Lil·lo \'li-(,)lō\ George 1693–1739 Eng. dram.; one of the first to introduce middle-class characters on English stage

Li·món \li-'mōn\ José Arcadio 1908–1972 Am. (Mex.-born) dancer & choreographer; works included *The Moor's Pavane, Emperor Jones, Missa Brevis,* etc.

Lin·a·cre \'li-ni-kər\ Thomas *ca* 1460–1524 Eng. humanist & physician; one of first propagators of the New Learning in England; taught Erasmus and Sir Thomas More

Lin·coln \'liŋ-kən\ Abraham 1809–1865 16th pres. of the U.S. (1861–65); successfully preserved the Union during the American Civil War; issued Emancipation Proclamation freeing all slaves in rebelling states; made famous address dedicating cemetery at Gettysburg; assassinated five days after end of Civil War — **Lin·coln·esque** \\ˌliŋ-kə-'nesk\\ *or* **Lin·coln·ian** \\liŋ-'kō-nē-ən\\ *adj*

Lincoln Benjamin 1733–1810 Am. gen. in Revolution; captured with his army in Charleston, S.C.; later commanded force suppressing Shay's Rebellion

Lind \\'lind\\ Jenny 1820–1887 *orig. Johanna Maria; the Swedish Nightingale* Swed. soprano; unrivaled master of coloratura

Lind·bergh \\'lin(d)-ˌbərg\\ Anne Spencer 1906–   née *Morrow; wife of C. A.* Am. author; known for published letters and diaries and for works including *North to the Orient, Dearly Beloved,* etc.

Lindbergh Charles Augustus 1902–1974 Am. aviator; made (1927) first solo nonstop transatlantic flight, New York to Paris, in *The Spirit of St. Louis*

Lind·ley \\'lin(d)-lē\\ John 1799–1865 Eng. botanist; campaigned for classification system of de Jussieu over that of Linnaeus — **Lind·ley·an** \\-ən\\ *adj*

Lind·say \\'lin-zē\\ Howard 1889–1968 Am. dram. & actor; co-author (with Russel Crouse) of musical comedies *Anything Goes, Sound of Music,* etc.

Lindsay (Nicholas) Va·chel \\'vā-chəl, 'va-\\ 1879–1931 Am. poet; lectured and chanted his verses through the U.S. in attempt to revive poetry as oral art form among common people

Link·la·ter \\'liŋk-ˌlā-tər, -lə-tər\\ Eric 1899–1974 Brit. writer; author of *Mary Queen of Scots, Robert the Bruce,* etc., and autobiographies

Linlithgow Marquis of — see HOPE

Lin·nae·us \\lə-'nē-əs, -'nā-\\ Carolus 1707–1778 Sw. *Carl von Linné* \\lə-'nā\\ Swed. botanist; a father of modern systematic botany and of modern system of nomenclature — **Lin·nae·an** *or* **Lin·ne·an** \\lə-'nē-ən, -'nā-; 'li-nē-\\ *adj*

Lin Yü–t'ang \\'lin-'yᵫ-'täŋ\\ 1895–1976 Chin. author & philologist; wrote wide variety of works in Chinese and English; founded several Chinese magazines specializing in social satire, Western-style journalism

Li·o·tard \\ˌlē-ō-'tär\\ Jean-Étienne 1702–1789 Swiss painter; produced notable pastel portraits of famous people of the day and graceful pastel drawings, genre scenes, enamels, etc.

Lip·chitz \\'lip-shits\\ Jacques 1891–1973 Am. (Latvian-born) sculptor; one of first to produce Cubist sculpture, later often with spiritual content on biblical or mythological themes

Li Peng \\'lē-'pəŋ, -'peŋ\\ 1928–   Chin. communist leader (1987–   ); favored softened relations with the Soviet Union and harsh repression of the student-based pro-democracy movement

Lip·mann \\'lip-mən\\ Fritz Albert 1899–1986 Am. (Ger.-born) biochem.; awarded (with H.A. Krebs) 1953 Nobel prize for physiology or medicine for discoveries in biosynthesis and metabolism

Li Po \\'lē-'bō, -'pō\\ 701–762 Chin. poet; probably the greatest Chinese poet, famous for exquisite imagery, rich language, allusions, cadence of his lyrics

Lip·pi \\'li-pē\\ Fra Filippo *ca* 1406–1469 Florentine painter; works included frescoes *Life of St. John the Baptist* and *Life of St. Stephen* (Prato cathedral), paintings *Annunciation,* etc.

Lippi Filippo *or* Filippino *ca* 1457–1504 *son of prec.* Florentine painter; apprenticed to Botticelli; produced frescoes in churches and in villa of Lorenzo de' Medici, altarpiece, canvases

Lipp·mann \lēp-'män, -'man\ Gabriel 1845–1921 Fr. physicist; awarded 1908 Nobel prize for physics for his method of color photography

Lipp·mann \'lip-mən\ Walter 1889–1974 Am. journalist & author; a founder and associate editor of *New Republic*

Lips·comb \'lips-kəm\ William Nunn, Jr. 1919– Am. chem.; awarded 1976 Nobel prize for chemistry for studies on the structure and bonding mechanisms of boranes

Lip·ton \'lip-tən\ Sir Thomas Johnstone 1850–1931 Eng. merchant & yachtsman; built chain of grocery stores throughout Great Britain; competed for America's Cup with series of yachts named *Shamrock*

Li Shih–min — see T'ANG T'AI TSUNG

Lisle, de — see LECONTE DE LISLE, ROUGET DE LISLE

Lis·ter \'lis-tər\ Joseph 1827–1912 1st Baron *Lister of Lyme Regis* Eng. surgeon; founder of antiseptic surgery, demonstrating conclusively that his method of asepsis reduced danger from surgery

Liszt \'list\ Franz 1811–1886 Hung. pianist & composer; revolutionized technique of piano playing; as composer invented the symphonic poem and the method of transformation of themes — **Liszt·ian** \'lis-tē-ən\ *adj*

Lit·tle·ton *or* **Lyt·tel·ton** \'li-t²l-tən\ *or* **Lut·tel·ton** \'lə-\ Sir Thomas 1422–1481 Eng. jurist; known for his treatise *Tenures* on English land law, one of earliest books printed in England and the earliest treatise on English law printed

Lit·tré \li-'trā\ Maximilien-Paul-Émile 1801–1881 Fr. lexicographer; disciple of Comte and publicist for his Positivist philosophy; produced *Dictionnaire de la langue française*

Lit·vi·nov \lit-'vē-,nóf, -,nóv, -,nəf\ Maksim Maksimovich 1876–1951 Soviet diplomat; headed Russian delegations at disarmament commissions and signed Kellogg Pact (1928); ambassador to U.S. (1941–43)

Liu Shao–ch'i \lē-'ü-'shaú-'chē\ 1898–1974 Chin. communist polit.; denounced during the Cultural Revolution and banished; posthumously reinstated

Liv·ing·ston \'li-viŋ-stən\ Robert R. 1746–1813 Am. statesman; helped draw up Declaration of Independence; administered oath of office to Washington

Liv·ing·stone \'li-viŋ-stən\ David 1813–1873 Scot. missionary & explorer in Africa; sighted Lake Ngami, Zambezi River, Victoria Falls, sources of the Nile, etc.; rescued near death at Ujiji on Lake Tanganyika by Henry M. Stanley

Livy \'li-vē\ 59 B.C.–A.D. 17 *Titus Livius* Rom. hist.; wrote *The Annals of the Roman People* (142 books), covering period from Rome's founding to 9 B.C.

Lloyd George \'lóid-'jórj\ David 1863–1945 1st Earl of *Dwy·for* \'dü-ē-,vòr\ Brit. statesman; prime min. (1916–22); as virtual dictator, directed Britain's policies to victory in WWI and in peace settlement

Lloyd Web·ber \-'we-bər\ Sir Andrew 1948– Brit. composer; wrote music for stage musicals *Jesus Christ Superstar, Evita, Cats,*

The Phantom of the Opera, etc. that blended pop, rock, and classical forms

Llull \'lyül'\ Ramon *ca* 1235–1316 *Raymond Lul·ly* \'lù-lē\ Catalan mystic & poet; attempted to encompass all knowledge in a Neoplatonic schema and to resolve all religious differences in the hope of a peaceful world

Lo·ba·chev·sky \,lō-bə-'chef-skē, ,läb-, -'chev-\ Nikolay Ivanovich 1792–1856 Russ. math.; a founder, with János Bolyai, of non-Euclidean geometry

Lo·ben·gu·la \,lō-bən-'gü-lə, -'gyü-\ *ca* 1836–1894 Zulu king of the Matabele; granted farming and mineral concessions to British South African Company; defeated decisively in attempt to keep whites out

Locke \'läk\ John 1632–1704 Eng. philos.; developed theory of knowledge in *An Essay Concerning Human Understanding* (1689), liberal constitutionalist ideas on government in *Two Treatises on Government* (1698) — **Lock·ean** *also* **Locke·ian** \'lä-kē-ən\ *adj*

Lock·hart \'lä-kərt, -,kärt; 'läk-,härt\ John Gibson 1794–1854 Scot. nov. & biographer; author of novels *Adam Blair, Reginald Dalton,* etc., biography *Life of Sir Walter Scott* in 7 volumes

Lock·yer \'lä-kyər\ Sir Joseph Norman 1836–1920 Eng. astron.; discovered (in sun's atmosphere) and named the element helium

Lodge \'läj\ Henry Cabot 1850–1924 Am. statesman & author; led congressional opposition to U.S. participation in the League of Nations (1919)

Lodge Henry Cabot 1902–1985 *grandson of prec.* Am. polit. & diplomat; Republican vice pres. nominee (1960), ambassador to South Vietnam (1963–64, 1965–67)

Lodge Sir Oliver Joseph 1851–1940 Eng. physicist; first to suggest (1894) the sun might be a source of radio waves

Lodge Thomas 1558–1625 Eng. poet & dram.; one of founders of English drama; wrote prose romance *Rosalynde,* source of Shakespeare's *As You Like It*

Loeb \'lōb\ Jacques 1859–1924 Am. (Ger.-born) physiol.; did pioneer work in analysis of egg fertilization, physiology of the brain, regeneration of tissue, duration of life, etc.

Loewe \'lō\ Frederick 1901–1988 Am. (Austrian-born) composer; composed music for Broadway musicals *Brigadoon, My Fair Lady, Camelot,* film *Gigi*

Loewi \'lō-ē\ Otto 1873–1961 Am. (Ger.-born) pharmacologist; awarded (with H.H. Dale) 1936 Nobel prize for physiology or medicine for discoveries on the chemical transmission of nerve impulses

Löff·ler \'le-flər\ Friedrich August Johannes 1852–1915 Ger. bacteriol.; first isolated diphtheria bacillus and developed protective serum against foot-and-mouth disease

Lo·max \'lō-,maks\ John Avery 1867–1948 and his son Alan 1915– Am. folklorists; collected American folksongs and ballads, recording over 10,000 for Library of Congress

Lombard Peter — see PETER LOMBARD

Lom·bar·di \läm-'bär-dē, läm-\ Vincent Thomas 1913–1970 *Vince Lombardi* Am. football coach; coached Green Bay Packers (1959–67) to five league championships and two Super Bowls

Lom·bro·so \lòm-'brō-(,)sō\ Ce·sa·re \'chā-zä-,rä\ 1836–1909 Ital.

physician & psychiatrist; held that a criminal represents a distinct anthropological type and is the product of heredity, regression, and degeneracy

Lon·don \'lən-dən\ John Griffith 1876–1916 *Jack London* Am. writer; best known for tales of wilderness adventure *The Call of the Wild* (1903), *White Fang* (1906), etc.

Long \'lȯŋ\ Crawford Williamson 1815–1878 Am. surgeon; first to use ether as an anesthetic in surgery

Long Hu·ey \'hyü-ē\ Pierce 1893–1935 Am. polit.; noted for demagoguery, radical Share-the-Wealth program (slogan: "Every man a king"), and dictatorial control over Louisiana through his political machine

Long Stephen Harriman 1784–1864 Am. army officer & explorer; explored upper Mississippi, Rocky Mountain region; discovered Long's Peak, Colo.

Long·fel·low \'lȯŋ-fe-(,)lō\ Henry Wads·worth \'wädz-(,)wərth\ 1807–1882 Am. poet; known for poems *Evangeline*, *Song of Hiawatha*, "The Wreck of the Hesperus," "The Village Blacksmith," etc.

Lon·gi·nus \län-'jī-nəs\ 1st cent. A.D. Greek critic; name generally assigned to author of *On the Sublime*, seminal work of literary criticism and style

Long·street \'lȯŋ-,strēt\ James 1821–1904 Am. Confed. gen.; held responsible for Confederate defeat at Gettysburg

Lönn·rot \'lœn-,rüt\ Elias 1802–1884 Finn. folklorist; one of the founders of modern Finnish literature; collected and edited Finnish epic songs into great national epic *Kalevala*

Lons·dale \'länz-,dāl\ Frederick 1881–1954 Brit. dram.; author of musical comedies and comedies of manners *The Best People*, *Once Is Enough*, etc.

Ló·pez \'lō-,pez\ Carlos Antonio 1790–1862 pres. of Paraguay (1844–62); extremely corrupt; ended Paraguay's isolation and tried to modernize economy and society

López Francisco Solano 1827–1870 *son of prec.* pres. of Paraguay (1862–70); plan to dominate South America led to war with Brazil, Argentina, Uruguay and to utter defeat and death

López Ma·te·os \-mə-'tā-əs, -(,)ōs\ Adolfo 1910–1969 pres. of Mexico (1958–64); increased industrialization; extended agrarian reform laws; began literacy campaign

López Por·til·lo \-pȯr-'tē-yō\ José 1920–   pres. of Mexico (1976–82)

Lorca Federico García — see Federico GARCÍA LORCA

Lo·rentz \'lȯr-,en(t)s, 'lȯr-\ Hendrik Antoon 1853–1928 Du. physicist; awarded (with P. Zeeman) 1902 Nobel prize for physics for discovering the Zeeman effect of magnetism on light

Lo·renz \'lȯr-,en(t)s, 'lȯr-\ Konrad 1903–1989 Ger. (Austrianborn) ethologist; awarded (with N. Tinbergen and K. von Frisch) 1973 Nobel prize for physiology or medicine for studies on animal behavior

Lorrain Claude — see CLAUDE LORRAIN

Lo·thair I \lō-'tar, -'ter, -'thar, -'ther, 'lō-,\ 795–855 Holy Rom. emp. (840–855); by Treaty of Verdun with brothers Pepin and Louis the German given title of emperor and sovereignty over Northern Italy and Lorraine

Lothair II (*or* **III**) 1075–1137 king of Germany & Holy Rom. emp. (1125–37); rebelled against Henry V; waged war with Hohenstaufens; invaded Italy

Lo-ti \lō-'tē, lȯ-\ Pierre 1850–1923 pseud. of *Louis-Marie-Julien Viaud* Fr. naval officer & nov.; author of *Aziyadé, Le Mariage de Loti*, etc.

Lou-bet \lü-'bā\ Émile-François 1838–1929 Fr. statesman; pres. of France (1899–1906); administration marked by Dreyfus crises, signing of Entente Cordiale, separation of church and state

Loudoun 4th Earl of — see John CAMPBELL

Lou-ga-nis \lü-'gä-nəs\ Gregory 1960–   Am. diver; holder of many titles in platform and springboard diving; won total of four gold medals at Olympic Games (1984, 1988)

Lou-is \'lü-ē, lü-'ē\ name of 18 kings of France: esp. **I** 778–840 (reigned 814–840); reign marked by quarrels with sons and various changes in plans for succession; twice deposed by sons; **V** (*le Fainéant*) 967–987 (reigned—last Carolingian—986–987); led frivolous life; **IX** (*Saint*) 1214–1270 (reigned 1226–70); had relatively peaceful reign, led Seventh Crusade and another to Tunisia; ceded Aquitaine to Henry III; **XI** 1423–1483 (reigned 1461–83); founded absolute monarchy of France by destroying power of the princes; **XII** 1462–1515 (reigned 1498–1515); popular ruler who made wide reforms in finance and justice; **XIII** 1601–1643 (reigned 1610–43); timid and in poor health for much of reign and under influence of Richelieu; **XIV** 1638–1715 (reigned 1643–1715); "le Grand" or "le Roi Soleil" (the Sun King); increased monarchical authority and used it despotically; his reign longest in European history; France reached its zenith in power, in prestige, and arts and letters; **XV** 1710–1774 (reigned 1715–74); financial situation worsened; discontent and hatred of king increased; lost Canada and India in Seven Years' War; **XVI** 1754–1793 (reigned 1774–92; guillotined); target of French revolution for taxes and extravagance; **XVII** 1785–1795 (nominally reigned 1793–95); died in prison; later, many claimants as real Louis XVII arose; **XVIII** 1755–1824 (reigned 1814–15, 1815–24); general policy prudent and sensible although controlled by Villèle and ultraroyalists in late years

Louis IV 1283?–1347 Duke of *Bavaria* king of Germany & Holy Rom. emp. (1314–47); in conflict with papacy, seized Rome and set up antipope

Louis II de Bourbon — see CONDÉ

Lou-is \'lü-əs\ Joe 1914–1981 orig. *Joseph Louis Bar-row* \'bar-(,)ō\ Am. boxer; won world's heavyweight championship (1937); defended title 25 times, winning all bouts, 21 by knockouts

Louis–Napoléon — see NAPOLÉON III

Louis Phi-lippe \'lü-ē-fi-lēp, lü-'ē-\ 1773–1850 *the Citizen King* king of the French (1830–48); power weakened by attempts to restore monarchy and inability to win over industrial classes; overthrown by revolution

L'Ouverture — see Pierre Dominique TOUSSAINT LOUVERTURE

Louÿs \lü-'ē\ Pierre 1870–1925 Fr. writer; sought in his verse to combine pagan sensuality with stylistic perfection

Love·lace \'lǝv-ˌlās\ Richard 1618–1657 Eng. poet; prototype of the perfect Cavalier for his graceful lyrics and dashing military career

Lov·ell \'lǝ-vǝl\ Sir (Alfred Charles) Bernard 1913–   Brit. astron.; author of several books on radio astronomy and its importance to contemporary life

Lov·er \'lǝ-vǝr\ Samuel 1797–1868 Irish nov.; author of popular novels *Rory O'More, Handy Andy*, etc., and of songs

Low \'lō\ Sir David Alexander Cecil 1891–1963 Brit. cartoonist; famous for political cartoons and for creation of Colonel Blimp

Low·ell \'lō-ǝl\ Amy 1874–1925 Am. poet & critic; a leading member of Imagist school; wrote much in vers libre and in polyphonic prose

Lowell James Russell 1819–1891 Am. poet, essayist, & dram.; best known for satirical poems collected as *Biglow Papers*, long poem *The Vision of Sir Launfal*, and verse satire *A Fable for Critics*

Lowell Percival 1855–1916 *bro. of Amy* Am. astron.; best known for studies of Mars and for mathematical work predicting the discovery of Pluto

Lowell Robert Traill Spence 1917–1977 Am. poet; author of poetry volumes *Lord Weary's Castle* (1946, Pulitzer prize), *Life Studies*, dramatic trilogy *The Old Glory*, translations, etc.

Lowes \'lōz\ John Livingston 1867–1945 Am. educ.; author of *Essays in Appreciation, The Art of Geoffrey Chaucer*, etc.

Lowndes \'laún(d)z\ William Thomas 1798–1843 Eng. bibliographer; compiled *The Bibliographer's Manual of English Literature*

Low·ry \'laú-(ǝ)r-ē\ (Clarence) Malcolm 1909–1957 Brit. writer; wrote novels *Under the Volcano, Ultramarine*, etc., short stories, poems

Loyola Saint Ignatius — see IGNATIUS OF LOYOLA

Lub·bock \'lǝ-bǝk\ Sir John 1834–1913 1st Baron *Ave·bury* \'āv-b(ǝ-)rē, 'ä-\ *son of Sir J. W.* Eng. financier & author; promulgated banking reforms, etc.; wrote popular science books esp. in archaeology and entomology

Lubbock Sir John William 1803–1865 Eng. astron. & math.; gave uniform method for calculation of orbits of comets and planets; demonstrated stability of solar system

Luc·an \'lü-kǝn\ A.D. 39–65 *Marcus Annaeus Lucanus* Rom. poet; author of *Pharsalia* about civil war between Caesar and Pompey

Luce \'lüs\ Clare 1903–1987 née *Boothe* \'büth\ *wife of H. R.* Am. dram., polit., & diplomat; author of Broadway play *The Women*, etc.; powerful figure in Republican party; ambassador to Italy

Luce Henry Robinson 1898–1967 Am. editor & publisher; founder, editor, and publisher of *Time, Fortune, Life, Sports Illustrated* magazines

Lu·cre·tius \lü-'krē-sh(ē-)ǝs\ *ca* 96–*ca* 55 B.C. *Titus Lucretius Carus* Rom. poet & philos.; created *De rerum natura*, didactic and philosophical poem based on Epicurean doctrine — **Lu·cre·tian** \-shǝn\ *adj*

Lu·cul·lus \lü-'kǝ-lǝs\ Lucius Licinius *ca* 117–58 (or 56) B.C. Rom. gen. & epicure; defeated Mithradates; lived in great luxury and enjoyed the company of leading poets, artists, philosophers

Lu·den·dorff \'lü-dᵊn-ˌdórf\ Erich Friedrich Wilhelm 1865–1937 Ger. gen.; almost crushed Allies on Western Front (1918); involved in unsuccessful coups d'état (1920, 1923); led crusades against Jews, Christians, Freemasons until he deserted Hitler for pacifism

Lu Hsün \'lü-'shuen\ 1881–1936 pseud. of *Chou Shu-Jen* Chin. writer; established reputation with short stories in western manner

Lu·i·gi Ame·deo \lə-'wē-jē-,ä-mə-'dā-(,)ō\ 1873–1933 Duca *D'A·bruz·zi* \dä-'brüt-tsē\ & Prince of *Savoy-Aosta* Ital. explorer & naval officer; reached (1899) record 86° 34' N in Arctic; first to scale Ruwenzori peaks, Africa; reached 20,000 feet on K2 (1909)

Luke \'lük\ Saint 1st cent. A.D. Christian apostle; traditionally regarded as author of third Gospel and the Acts of the Apostles in the New Testament

Lul·ly \lü-'lē\ Jean-Baptiste 1632–1687 Fr. (Ital.-born) composer; called founder of national French opera; his style of composition for court music widely imitated throughout Europe

Lully Raymond — see Ramon LLULL

Lunt \'lənt\ Alfred 1893–1977 *husband of Lynn Fontanne* Am. actor; starred with Fontanne in *The Guardsman, Pygmalion, Design for Living,* etc.

Lu·ria \'lür-ē-ə\ Salvador Edward 1912–1991 Am. (Ital.-born) microbiologist; awarded (with M. Delbrück and A. Hershey) 1969 Nobel prize for physiology or medicine for work with bacteriophages

Lu·ther \'lü-thər\ Martin 1483–1546 Ger. Reformation leader; founder of the Reformation and Protestantism, beginning with his 95 theses — **Lu·ther·an** \-th(ə-)rən\ *adj or n*

Lu·thu·li \lü-'tü-lē, -'thü-\ Albert John 1898–1967 So. African reformer; leader of nonviolent struggle against the government's discriminatory racial policies; awarded 1960 Nobel prize for peace

Lux·em·burg \'lək-səm-,bərg, 'lük-səm-,bùrk\ Rosa 1870–1919 Ger. socialist leader; helped found Polish Social Democratic party; a leader of the Spartacus insurrection; killed en route to prison

Lwoff \'lwòf\ André-Michael 1902–1995 Fr. microbiologist; awarded (with F. Jacob and J. Monod) 1965 Nobel prize for physiology or medicine for discoveries concerning genetic control of enzyme and virus synthesis

Lyau·tey \lē-,ō-'tā\ Louis-Hubert-Gonzalve 1854–1934 Fr. soldier & colonial administrator; conquered Madagascar and pacified Morocco

Ly·cur·gus \lī-'kər-gəs\ 9th cent. B.C. Spartan lawgiver; traditional founder of institutions designed to produce tough, able warriors

Lyd·gate \'lid-,gāt, -gət\ John *ca* 1370–*ca* 1450 Eng. poet; court poet at courts of Henry IV, V, VI; author of tributes to Chaucer (*Troy Book*), descriptions of London manners, allegorical poems, etc.

Ly·ell \'lī-əl\ Sir Charles 1797–1875 Brit. geologist; proponent of theory of uniformitarianism; regarded as father of modern geology

Lyly \'li-lē\ John 1554?–1606 Eng. author; known chiefly for didactic romances, *Euphues, the Anatomy of Wit* and *Euphues and His England,* aiming at reform of education and manners, both in affected style

Lynd \'lind\ Robert Staugh·ton \'stò-t³n\ 1892–1970 & his wife Helen née *Merrell* 1896–1982 Am. sociologists; made study of

Muncie, Ind., and published results in *Middletown: A Study in Contemporary American Culture*, etc.

Ly·nen \'lē-nən\ Feodor Felix Konrad 1911–1979 Ger. biochem.; awarded (with K. Bloch) 1964 Nobel prize for physiology or medicine for work on the metabolism of cholesterol and fatty acids

Ly·on \'lī-ən\ Mary 1797–1849 Am. educ.; pioneer in providing advanced education for women and founder of what became Mount Holyoke College

Ly·ons \'lī-ənz\ Joseph Aloysius 1879–1939 Austral. statesman; prime min. (1931–39)

Ly·san·der \lī-'san-dər\ *d* 395 B.C. Spartan commander; won sea battles off Notium and Aegospotami and captured Athens, ending Peloponnesian War

Ly·sen·ko \lə-'seŋ-(,)kō\ Trofim Denisovich 1898–1976 Soviet biol.; developed doctrine of genetics denying existence of genes and hormones and applied it, greatly harming Soviet agricultural practices, scientific research, and education

Lys·i·as \'li-sē-əs\ *ca* 445–after 380 B.C. Athenian orator; known for speech impeaching Eratosthenes, one of Thirty Tyrants

Ly·sim·a·chus \lī-'si-mə-kəs\ *ca* 355–*ca* 281 B.C. Macedonian gen. under Alexander the Great; king of Thrace (306); defeated by Seleucus Nicator in attempt to control Asia Minor

Ly·sip·pus \lī-'si-pəs\ 4th cent. B.C. Greek sculptor; credited with developing new system of bodily proportions with smaller head and longer legs

Lyt·ton \'li-tᵊn\ 1st Baron 1803–1873 *Edward George Earle Bulwer-Lytton* \'bùl-wər-\; *bro. of Sir Henry Bulwer* Eng. author; author of poems, short stories introducing the occult, historical and romantic novels including *Rienzi* (basis of Wagner's opera), etc.

Lytton 1st Earl of 1831–1891 *(Edward) Robert Bulwer-Lytton; pseud. Owen Meredith; son of prec.* Brit. statesman & poet; as viceroy of India, failed to avert Second Afghan War despite reforms; author of verse, long romances, fantastic epic *King Poppy*

M

Ma \'mä\ Yo-Yo 1955–   Am. (Fr.-born) cellist; noted for warmth of interpretation, impeccable technique, and range of repertoire

Mac·Ar·thur \mə-'kär-thər\ Arthur 1845–1912 Am. gen.; served in Civil War and Spanish-American War; defeated Philippine insurgent forces

MacArthur Charles 1895–1956 Am. dram.; collaborated with Ben Hecht on plays *The Front Page* (1928), *Twentieth Century* (1932), etc.

MacArthur Douglas 1880–1964 *son of Arthur* Am. gen.; commanded Southwest Pacific Theatre in WWII; carried out occupation of postwar Japan; dismissed as commander of Korean War for publicly advocating invasion of China

Ma·cau·lay \mə-'kò-lē\ Dame Rose 1881–1958 Eng. nov.; author of *Told by an Idiot, Going Abroad, The Towers of Trebizond*, etc.

Macaulay Thomas Babington 1800–1859 1st Baron *Macaulay* Eng. hist., author, & statesman; on supreme court of India, secy. of war, etc.; author of *History of England* (1849–61), *Lays of Ancient Rome*, essays, etc.

Mac·beth \mək-'beth\ d 1057 king of Scotland (1040–57); killed cousin Duncan and seized kingdom; defeated and slain by Malcolm III

Mac·Bride \mək-'brīd\ Seán 1904–1988 Irish statesman; co-founder (1961) and chairman (1961–75), Amnesty International; winner of 1974 Nobel prize for peace

Mac·ca·bees \'ma-kə-,bēz\ Judas *or* Judah d 161 B.C. surname *Mac·ca·ba·eus* \,ma-kə-'bē-əs\ Jewish patriot; purified Temple of Jerusalem and restored Jewish worship (165/164 B.C.) as commemorated by Hanukkah

Mac·Di·ar·mid \mək-'dər-məd, -mət\ Hugh 1892–1978 pseud. of *Christopher Murray Grieve* \'grēv\ Scot. poet; advocated Scottish literary revival; preeminent Scottish poet of first half of 20th century; poems collected in *Sangschaw, Penny Wheep*, etc.

Mac·don·ald \mək-'dä-nᵊld\ George 1824–1905 Scot. nov. & poet; author of volumes of verse, books for children *At The Back of the North Wind, The Princess and Curdie*, etc.

Macdonald Sir John Alexander 1815–1891 Canad. statesman; 1st prime min. of Dominion of Canada (1867–73; 1878–91); regarded as organizer of Dominion of Canada

Mac·Don·ald \mək-'dä-nᵊld\ (James) Ramsay 1866–1937 Brit. statesman; opposed England's involvement in WWI; organized first Labour Ministry in Britain

Mac·don·ough \mək-'dä-nə, -'də-\ Thomas 1783–1825 Am. naval officer; defeated and captured British squadron in battle of Plattsburg on Lake Champlain

Mac·Dow·ell \mək-'daú(-ə)l\ Edward Alexander 1860–1908 Am. composer; best known for piano pieces *Woodland Sketches, New England Idylls, Fireside Tales*, etc.

Mach \'mäk, 'mäk\ Ernst 1838–1916 Austrian physicist & philos.; studied flight of projectiles, for which his name was given to ratio of speed of an object to local speed of sound

Ma·cha·do y Mo·ra·les \mä-'chä-dō-,ē-mə-'rä-les\ Gerardo 1871–1939 pres. of Cuba (1925–33); instituted program of public works after liberation from Spain; later deposed for dictatorial behavior

Ma·chi·a·vel·li \,ma-kē-ə-'ve-lē\ Niccolò 1469–1527 Ital. polit. philos.; best known for his work *Il principe* (The Prince) detailing his theory of government and maxims of practical statecraft — **Ma·chi·a·vel·lian** \-lē-ən, -'vel-yən\ *adj or n*

Mac·Kaye \mə-'kī\ Percy 1875–1956 Am. poet & dram.; author of *Fenris the Wolf, Sappho and Phaon*, folk opera *Rip Van Winkle*, etc.

Mack·en·sen \'mä-kən-zən\ August von 1849–1945 Ger. field marshal; commanded forces invading Poland (1914–15) and Romania (1916); defeated Russians at Brest-Litovsk and Pinsk

Mac·ken·zie \mə-'ken-zē\ Alexander 1822–1892 Canad. (Scot.-born) statesman; first Liberal prime min. (1873–78)

Mackenzie Sir Alexander Campbell 1847–1935 Brit. composer & conductor; composed cantatas, choral works, operas, orchestral works *La Belle Dame Sans Merci, Scottish Rhapsodies,* etc.

Mackenzie Sir Compton 1883–1972 Eng. nov.; author of *Carnival, Extraordinary Women, Whisky Galore,* etc.

Mackenzie William Lyon 1795–1861 Canad. (Scot.-born) insurgent leader; succeeded in drawing attention of home government to colonial abuses

Mac·kin·der \mə-'kin-dər\ Sir Halford John 1861–1947 Eng. geographer; developed theory of Eurasia as natural seat of geopolitical power

Maclaren Ian — see John WATSON

Mac·Leish \mə-'klēsh\ Archibald 1892–1982 Am. poet & administrator; known for public verse concerned with social issues, esp. threat from fascism, as *Conquistador, America War Promises,* etc.

Mac·Len·nan \mə-'kle-nən\ (John) Hugh 1907–1990 Canad. nov.; author of novels portraying Canadian national and regional character and tensions

Mac·leod \mə-'klaüd\ John James Rickard 1876–1935 Scot. physiol.; awarded (with F.G. Banting) 1923 Nobel prize for physiology or medicine for discovery of insulin

Mac–Ma·hon \,mäk-,mä-'ōⁿ; mək-'ma-(ə)n, -'män\ Marie-Edme-Patrice-Maurice 1808–1893 Comte *de Mac-Mahon;* duc *de Magenta* marshal (1859) & pres. (1873–79) of France; lost constitutional confrontation with parliament, making presidency largely honorific

Mac·mil·lan \mək-'mil-ən\ (Maurice) Harold 1894–1986 Brit. prime min. (1957–63); popular for enthusiasm, domestic improvements, clarity of foreign policy

Mac·Mil·lan \mək-'mil-ən\ Donald Baxter 1874–1970 Am. explorer; with Peary on north polar expedition (1908–09); led further expeditions to Arctic lands

Mac·Neice \mək-'nēs\ Louis 1907–1963 Irish poet; known for low-keyed, socially committed topical verse and radio plays esp. *The Dark Tower*

Mac·pher·son \mək-'fər-sⁿn\ James 1736–1796 Scot. writer; published (1760) *Fragments of Ancient Poetry Collected in the Highlands of Scotland and Translated from the Gallic or Erse Language,* claiming that they were written by 3rd century Gaelic poet Ossian

Mac·rea·dy \mə-'krē-dē\ William Charles 1793–1873 Eng. actor; confronted in America by mob rioting in support of rival actor Edwin Forrest

Ma·da·ria·ga y Ro·jo \,mä-də-rē-'ä-gə-(,)ē-'rō-(,)hō\ Salvador 1886–1978 Span. writer & diplomat; author of *Shelley and Calderón, The Genius of Spain,* etc.

Ma·de·ro \mə-'der-(,)ō\ Francisco Indalecio 1873–1913 pres. of Mexico (1911–13); overthrew presidency of Díaz but was himself overthrown by Huerta

Mad·i·son \'ma-də-sən\ Dolley 1768–1849 née *(Dorothea) Payne; wife of James* Am. socialite; famous Washington hostess while husband was secy. of state, pres.

Madison James 1751–1836 4th pres. of the U.S. (1809–17); called "father of the U.S. Constitution;" sponsored Bill of Rights — **Mad·i·so·nian** \,ma-də-'sō-nē-ən, -nyən\ *adj*

Mae·ce·nas \mi-ˈsē-nəs\ Gaius *ca* 70–8 B.C. Rom. statesman & patron of literature; close friend, adviser, benefactor of Horace, Virgil, Emperor Augustus

Maes \ˈmäs\ Nicolaes 1634–1693 also called *Nicolas Maas* Du. painter; studied under Rembrandt; known esp. for genre pictures and portraits

Mae·ter·linck \ˈmā-tər-ˌliŋk *also* ˈme-, ˈma-\ Maurice-Polydore-Marie-Bernard 1862–1949 Belg. poet, dram., & essayist; known for Symbolist verse, drama, works on philosophy and nature — **Mae·ter·linck·ian** \ˌmā-tər-ˈliŋ-kē-ən, ˌme-, ˌma-\ *adj*

Ma·gel·lan \mə-ˈje-lən, *chiefly Brit* -ˈge-\ Ferdinand *ca* 1480–1521 Pg. *Fernão de Magalhães* Port. navigator & explorer; sailed from Spain to Philippines (where he died) around tip of So. America; ships continued to Spain in first circumnavigation of globe

Ma·gi·not \ˌma-zhə-ˈnō, ˌma-jə-\ André 1877–1932 Fr. polit.; principal creator of defensive Maginot line, named for him

Ma·gritte \mə-ˈgrēt\ René-François-Ghislain 1898–1967 Belg. painter; one of foremost Surrealist painters; used spatial manipulation, metamorphic themes, iconographic images

Mag·say·say \mäg-ˈsī-ˌsī, -ˌsī-ˈsī\ Ramon 1907–1957 pres. of Philippines (1953–57); crushed the communist Hukbalahap (Huk) rebellion

Mah·fouz \ˈmäk-füz\ Naguib 1911– Egypt. writer; awarded 1988 Nobel prize for literature for his novels; first Arabic writer so honored

Mah·ler \ˈmä-lər\ Gustav 1860–1911 Austrian composer; composer of ten symphonies, cantata, song cycles, six songs with orchestra *Das Lied von der Erde*, etc. — **Mah·ler·ian** \mä-ˈlir-ē-ən, -ˈler-\ *adj*

Mah·mud II \mä-ˈmüd\ 1785–1839 Ottoman sultan (1808–39); forced to accept Greek independence (1830); introduced Western reforms

Mai·ler \ˈmā-lər\ Norman 1923– Am. author; author of *The Naked and the Dead, Armies of the Night* (Pulitzer prize), *Ancient Evenings*, etc.

Mail·lol \mä-ˈyȯl, -ˈyōl\ Aristide 1861–1944 Fr. sculptor; known for large, emotionally restrained statues in style of classical Greece and Rome

Mai·mon·i·des \mī-ˈmä-nə-ˌdēz\ Moses 1135–1204 Heb. *Moses ben Maimon* Jewish philos., jurist, & physician; foremost intellectual figure of medieval Judaism; attempted to reconcile rabbinic Judaism with Aristotelianism modified by Arabic interpretation

Maine \ˈmān\ Sir Henry James Sumner 1822–1888 Eng. jurist; pioneered in study of comparative law, esp. primitive law and anthropological jurisprudence

Main·te·non \ˌmaⁿ(n)-tᵊn-ˈōⁿ, maⁿ(n)t-ˈnōⁿ\ Marquise de 1635–1719 *Françoise d'Aubigné; consort of Louis XIV;* secretly married Louis (1683 or 1697); accused of wielding great influence over king

Mait·land \ˈmāt-lənd\ Frederic William 1850–1906 Eng. hist.; helped write *History of English Law Before the Time of Edward I*, standard authority on the subject

Ma·jor \ˈmā-jər\ John 1943– Brit. prime min. (1990–)

Mal·a·mud \\'ma-lə-(,)məd\\ Bernard 1914–1986 Am. writer; author of novels *The Assistant*, *The Fixer*, etc., based on Jewish life

Ma·lan \\mə-'lan, -'län\\ Daniel François 1874–1959 So. African editor; prime min. (1948–54); instituted policy of apartheid; paved way for establishment of republic

Mal·colm X \\'mal-kəm-'eks\\ 1925–1965 orig. *Malcolm Little* Am. civil rights leader; brilliant orator; preached black separatism and nationalism and pride in race and racial achievements

Male·branche \\,mal-'bräⁿsh, ,mäl-; ,ma-lə-, ,mä-\\ Nicolas de 1638–1715 Fr. philos.; attempted to synthesize Cartesianism, Neoplatonism, and thought of St. Augustine into single philosophy

Ma·len·kov \\mə-'len-,kȯf, -,kȯv, -'leŋ-kəf; ,ma-lən-'kȯf, -'kȯv\\ Georgy Maksimilianovich 1902–1988 Soviet polit.; involved in collectivization of agriculture and purges under Stalin; prime min. (1953–55)

Mal·herbe \\ma-'lerb, mä-\\ François de 1555–1628 Fr. poet; emphasis on strict form, restraint, purity of diction prepared way for French classicism

Ma·li·nov·sky \\,ma-lə-'nȯf-skē, ,mä-, -'nȯv-\\ Rodion Yakovlevich 1898–1967 Soviet gen.; commanded at Battle of Stalingrad, southwestern front in WWII

Ma·li·now·ski \\,ma-lə-'nȯf-skē, ,mä-, -'nȯv-\\ Bronislaw Kasper 1884–1942 Am. (Pol.-born) anthropol.; founder of social anthropology

Mal·lar·mé \\,ma-,lär-'mā\\ Stéphane 1842–1898 Fr. poet; a leader of the Symbolist movement

Ma·lone \\mə-'lōn\\ Edmond 1741–1812 Irish scholar; proposed order of Shakespeare's plays still largely accepted; detected Rowley forgeries of Chatterton, Ireland forgeries of Shakespeare

Mal·o·ry \\'ma-lə-rē, 'mal-rē\\ Sir Thomas *fl* 1470 Eng. author; author of English prose epic *Morte d'Arthur*

Mal·pi·ghi \\mal-'pē-gē, -'pi-\\ Marcello 1628–1694 Ital. anatomist; called father of microscopic anatomy — **Mal·pi·ghi·an** \\-ən\\ *adj*

Mal·raux \\mal-'rō\\ André 1901–1976 Fr. writer & art historian; in French Resistance during WWII; min. of cultural affairs (1958–69); author of *La Condition humaine*, *L'Espoir*, etc.

Mal·thus \\'mal-thəs\\ Thomas Robert 1766–1834 Eng. econ.; aroused controversy with argument about necessity of preventive checks on population growth — **Mal·thu·sian** \\mal-'thü-zhən, mȯl-, -'thyü-\\ *adj or n*

Mam·et \\'ma-mət\\ David Alan 1947– Am. dram.; works include *Sexual Perversity in Chicago*, *American Buffalo*, *Glengarry Glen Ross*

Man·ci·ni \\man-'sē-(,)nē\\ Henry 1924–1994 Am. composer; best known for film scores for *Breakfast at Tiffany's* ("Moon River"), *Days of Wine and Roses*, *The Pink Panther*, etc.

Man·del \\män(n)-'del\\ Georges 1885–1944 orig. *Louis-Georges Rothschild* Fr. polit.; cabinet min. staunchly opposed to Nazi Germany; arrested and eventually executed by French Vichy government

Man·dela \\man-'de-lə\\ Nelson Rolihlahla 1918– So. African black political leader; pres. of So. Africa (1994–); awarded (with F.W. deKlerk) 1993 Nobel prize for peace for efforts to end apartheid

Man·del·brot \\'man-dəl-ˌbröt\\ Benoit 1924–   Am. (Pol.-born) math. & scientist; a leader in the development of fractal theory and in the potential application of fractals to nature

Man·de·ville \\'man-də-ˌvil\\ Bernard de 1670–1733 Brit. (Du.-born) satirist & philos.; author of *The Fable of the Bees, or Private Vices, Public Benefits*, a political satire claiming that every virtue is at bottom some form of selfishness

Mandeville Sir John *fl* 1356 pseud. of an unidentified travel writer; writings described journeys in the East, combining geography and romance and very likely borrowed from works of others

Ma·net \\ma-'nā, mä-\\ Édouard 1832–1883 Fr. painter; developed style combining realism and impressionistic technique that was important precursor of Impressionism

Ma·nil·i·us \\mə-'ni-lē-əs\\ Gaius 1st cent. B.C. Rom. polit.; sponsored law designed to extend power of Pompey over all the East

Man·kie·wicz \\'man-ki-ˌwitz, 'maŋ-\\ Joseph Leo 1909–1993 Am. film director, writer, & producer; known for films marked by witty, sophisticated dialogue; directed *A Letter to Three Wives, All About Eve* (1950, Academy award), *Sleuth*, etc.

Man·kill·er \\'man-ˌki-lər\\ Wilma Pearl 1945–   Cherokee tribal leader; became (1985) first woman principal chief of the Cherokee Nation of Oklahoma

Mann \\'man\\ Horace 1796–1859 Am. educ.; considered father of American public education

Mann \\'män, 'man\\ Thomas 1875–1955 Am. (Ger.-born) author; works include *Buddenbrooks* (1901), *Tonio Kröger* (1903), *Der Tod in Venedig* (1912; *Death in Venice*), *Joseph und seine Brüder* (1933; *Joseph and His Brothers*), etc.; awarded 1929 Nobel prize for literature

Man·ner·heim \\'mä-nər-ˌhäm, 'ma-, -ˌhīm\\ Baron Carl Gustaf Emil von 1867–1951 Finn. gen. & statesman; suppressed Finnish Bolsheviks (1918); planned and constructed Mannerheim defensive line against Russia (1939–40)

Man·ning \\'ma-niŋ\\ Henry Edward 1808–1892 Eng. cardinal; vigorous builder of Catholic schools and institutions

Mans·field \\'manz-ˌfēld, 'manz-\\ Katherine 1888–1923 pseud. of Kathleen Mansfield Beau·champ \\'bē-chəm\\ Brit. (N.Z.-born) writer; wrote short stories collected in *Prelude, Bliss*, etc., and poems, journals, letters

Man·son \\'man(t)-sən\\ Sir Patrick 1844–1922 Brit. parasitologist; first to suggest that the mosquito was host of malarial parasite and an agent in spreading malaria

Man·stein \\'män-shtīn\\ Fritz Erich von 1887–1973 orig. surname von Lewinski Ger. field marshal; planned assault against France in WWII; imprisoned for war crimes

Man·sūr, al- \\al-ˌman-'sür\\ 709 (to 714)–775 in full Abū Ja'far al-Mansūr or al-Mansūr al-'Abbāsī Arab caliph (754–775) & founder of Baghdad; encouraged translation of Greek and Latin classics into Arabic

Man·te·gna \\män-'tān-yə\\ Andrea 1431–1506 Ital. painter & engraver; chief master of Paduan school; his invention of total spatial illusionism by the manipulation of perspective and foreshortening greatly influenced ceiling decoration

Man·tle \'man-tᵊl\ Mickey Charles 1931–1995 Am. baseball player; with New York Yankees (1951–68); as powerful switch-hitter had career total of 536 home runs

Man·uel \män-'wel\ Don Juan 1282–1349 Span. nobleman & writer; involved in political intrigues and in fighting Moors; author of *El libro del conde Lucanor*, 51 moral tales, etc.

Man·zo·ni \män(d)-'zō-nē\ Alessandro Francesco Tommaso Antonio 1785–1873 Ital. nov. & poet; leader of Italian Romantic school; known esp. for novel *I promessi sposi*, a model of modern Italian prose

Mao Tse-tung \maú-(')(d)zə-'dúŋ, -(')tsə-\ 1893–1976 pinyin *Mao Ze-dong* Chin. communist; leader of People's Republic of China (1949–76); instituted Rectification Campaign, the Great Leap Forward, the Cultural Revolution to attempt to implement his policies — **Mao-ist** \'maú-ist\ *adj or n*

Map \'map\ Walter *ca* 1140–*ca* 1209 Eng. writer; author of *Courtiers' Triflings*, but perhaps not (as he is credited) of *Lancelot du Lac, Mort Artus,* or *Queste del Saint Graal*

Map·ple·thorpe \'mā-pəl-,thòrp, 'ma-\ Robert 1946–1989 Am. photographer; known for his classically composed, often austere photographs esp. of flowers and male nudes

Ma·rat \mə-'rä\ Jean-Paul 1743–1793 Fr. (Swiss-born) revolutionary; identified with radical Jacobins; later assassinated by Charlotte Corday in his bath

Mar·cel·lus \mär-'se-ləs\ Marcus Claudius 268?–208 B.C. Rom. gen.; subjugated whole of Sicily; fought Hannibal

March 1st Earl of — see Roger de MORTIMER

Mar·ci·a·no \mär-sē-'ä-(,)nō\ Rocky 1923–1969 orig. *Rocco Francis Marchegiano* Am. boxer; won world heavyweight championship (1952); successfully defended title six times; had career record of 49 victories (43 by knockouts) and no defeats

Mar·co·ni \mär-'kō-nē\ Guglielmo 1874–1937 Ital. physicist & inventor; carried out successful experiments with wireless telegraphy, eventually sending signal across the Atlantic; made numerous improvements in wireless capabilities

Marco Polo — see POLO

Mar·cos \'mär-(,)kōs\ Ferdinand Edralin 1917–1989 pres. of the Philippines (1965–86); tenure marked by increasing repression and corruption; overthrown by movement led by Corazon Aquino, wife of assassinated opponent

Mar·cus \'mär-kəs\ Rudolph Arthur 1923–   Am. (Canad.-born) chem.; awarded the 1992 Nobel prize for chemistry for analyzing the transfer of electrons between molecules

Marcus Aurelius — see Marcus Aurelius ANTONINUS

Mar·cu·se \mär-'kü-zə\ Herbert 1898–1979 Am. (Ger.-born) social & political philos.; known for studies of repressive nature of contemporary society and advocacy of revolutionary reforms

Mar·ga·ret \'mär-g(ə-)rət\ **of Angoulême** 1492–1549 *queen of Henry of Navarre* & writer; friend of literature; supporter of Protestantism, protector of Humanist Reformers; author of tales, dramatic and religious poems

Margaret of Anjou 1430–1482 *queen of Henry VI of England;* a key member of Lancastrian party on behalf of Henry VI in Wars of the Roses

Margaret of Valois or **Margaret of France** 1553–1615 *queen consort of Henry of Navarre;* noted for loose living and for involvement in conspiracies

Margaret Rose \'rōz\ 1930–   *princess of Great Britain; sister of Queen Elizabeth II*

Mar·gre·the II \mär-'grā-tə\ 1940–   queen of Denmark (1972–   )

Ma·ria The·re·sa \mə-'rē-ə-tə-'rā-sə, -'rā-zə\ 1717–1780 *wife of Holy Rom. Emp. Francis I* archduchess of Austria & queen of Hungary & Bohemia; obtained imperial crown for her husband; strengthened Austria's resources; brought on Seven Years' War

Ma·rie \mə-'rē\ 1875–1938 queen of Romania (1914–27); queen dowager (1927–38); showed great courage in working for Red Cross and her people after surrender of Romania to Germany (1917–18)

Marie An·toi·nette \,an-twə-'net, -tə-\ 1755–1793 *dau. of Maria Theresa & wife of Louis XVI of France;* disliked for extravagance, resistance to reforms; tried and convicted of treason and guillotined

Ma·rie–Lou·ise \mə-'rē-lə-'wēz, -'lwēz\ 1791–1847 *dau. of Francis II of Austria & 2d wife of Napoléon I;* ruled as duchess of Parma, Piacenza, and Guastalla but politically naive

Ma·rie de Mé·di·cis \mə-'rē-də-'me-də-(,)chē, -,mā-də-'sē(s)\ 1573–1642 *2d wife of Henry IV of France* regent for Louis XIII; squandered state revenues and vainly opposed Richelieu

Mar·in \'mar-ən\ John Cheri 1870–1953 Am. painter; known esp. for expressionistic watercolor seascapes and views of Manhattan

Ma·ri·net·ti \,mar-ə-'ne-tē, ,mär-\ (Emilio) Filippo Tommaso 1876–1944 Ital. poet; founded Futuristic movement; joined Fascist party

Ma·ri·ni \mə-'rē-nē\ or **Ma·ri·no** \-(,)nō\ Giambattista 1569–1625 Ital. poet; notable as leading exponent of use of complicated wordplay and elaborate conceits in Italian 17th-century literature

Ma·ri·no \mə-'rē-(,)nō\ Daniel Constantine, Jr. 1961–   Am. football player; with Miami Dolphins (1983–); as quarterback, held several NFL records for passing, including career record for most games (10) with 400 or more yards

Mar·i·on \'mer-ē-ən, 'mar-ē-\ Francis 1732?–1795 *the Swamp Fox* Am. gen. in Revolution; in South Carolina, harassed British forces and escaped into swamps and forests

Ma·ri·otte \mar·yót\ Edme *ca* 1620–1684 Fr. physicist; introduced experimental physics into France; independently stated Boyle's law

Mar·is \'mar-əs, 'mer-\ Roger Eugene 1934–1985 Am. baseball player; with New York Yankees (1960–66); hit (1961) 61 home runs, breaking Babe Ruth's record for home runs in a single season

Ma·ri·tain \,mar-ə-'ta[n]\ Jacques 1882–1973 Fr. philos. & diplomat; known as interpreter of thought of St. Thomas Aquinas and for own philosophy based on Aristotelianism and Thomism

Mar·i·us \'mer-ē-əs, 'mar-\ Gaius *ca* 157–86 B.C. Rom. gen.; rivalry with Sulla led to civil war and to his capture of Rome

Ma·ri·vaux \,mar-ə-'vō\ Pierre Carlet de Chamblain de 1688–1763 Fr. dram. & nov.; author of chiefly satirical and love comedies

Mark \\'märk\\ Saint 1st cent. A.D. *John Mark* Christian apostle; traditionally regarded as author of the second Gospel in the New Testament

Mark Antony *or* **Anthony** — see Marcus ANTONIUS

Mark·ham \\'mär-kəm\\ Beryl 1902–1986 Brit. aviator; made historic transatlantic solo flight (1936) from Britain to Canada, which she recounted in *West with the Night*

Markham Edwin 1852–1940 *orig. Charles Edward Anson Markham* Am. poet; achieved sensational success with poem of social protest "The Man with the Hoe"

Mar·ko·va \\mär-'kō-və\\ Dame Ali·cia \\ə-'lē-sē-ə\\ 1910– *orig. Lilian Alicia Marks* Eng. dancer; with Anton Dolin, renowned for interpretation of *Giselle*

Mar·ko·witz \\'mär-kə-,wits\\ Harry M. 1927– Am. econ.; awarded (with M.H. Miller and W.F. Sharpe) 1990 Nobel prize for physics for theories in corporate finance

Marlborough 1st Duke of — see John CHURCHILL

Mar·lowe \\'mär-,lō\\ Christopher 1564–1593 Eng. dram.; first dramatist to discover vigor and variety of blank verse; works include *Doctor Faustus, Edward II, The Jew of Malta* — **Mar·lo·vi·an** \\mär-'lō-vē-ən, -vyən\\ *adj*

Marlowe Julia 1866–1950 *orig. Sarah Frances Frost* Am. (Eng.-born) actress; with Edward Hugh Sothern, leading team of Shakespearean actors of the day

Mar·mont \\mär-'mōⁿ\\ Auguste-Frédéric-Louis Viesse de 1774–1852 Duc *de Raguse* Fr. gen.; marshal of France; surrendered Paris and deserted to Allied side, precipitating Napoléon's abdication; tried unsuccessfully to suppress Revolution of 1830

Mar·mon·tel \\,mär-(,)mōⁿ-'tel\\ Jean-François 1723–1799 Fr. author; wrote tragedies; contributed to *Encyclopédie;* royal historiographer; wrote also fables, philosophical romances, opera librettos

Ma·rot \\ma-'rō\\ Clément 1496?–1544 Fr. poet; among first French poets to use Petrarchan sonnet form; introduced elegy, eclogue, epigram, epithalamium, *strambotto* into France

Mar·quand \\mär-'kwänd\\ John Phillips 1893–1960 Am. nov.; author of detective novels around the character Mr. Moto, including *The Late George Apley* (Pulitzer prize)

Mar·quette \\mär-'ket\\ Jacques 1637–1675 *Père* \\,pir, ,per\\ *Marquette* Fr.-born Jesuit missionary & explorer in America; with Jolliet on voyage down Wisconsin and Mississippi rivers and back up the Illinois River; journal of voyage published 1681

Mar·quis \\'mär-kwəs\\ Donald Robert Perry 1878–1937 Am. humorist; conducted column "The Sun Dial" in New York *Sun* featuring mehitabel the cat, archy the cockroach, the Old Soak, etc.

Mar·ry·at \\'mar-ē-ət\\ Frederick 1792–1848 Eng. naval commander & nov.; author of novels on sea life largely based on his own experiences

Marsh \\'märsh\\ Dame (Edith) Ngaio \\'nī-(,)ō\\ 1899–1982 N.Z. writer; author of mystery novels centering around Inspector Roderick Alleyn of Scotland Yard

Mar·shall \\'mär-shəl\\ Alfred 1842–1924 Eng. econ.; a founder of school of neoclassical economists

Marshall George Catlett 1880–1959 Am. gen. & statesman; chief of staff, U.S. army (1939–45); secy. of state (1947–49); originated

(1947) European Recovery Program (Marshall Plan); secy. of defense (1950–51); awarded 1953 Nobel prize for peace

Marshall John 1755–1835 Am. jurist; chief justice U.S. Supreme Court (1801–35); principal founder of American system of constitutional law, including judicial review

Marshall Thomas Riley 1854–1925 vice pres. of the U.S. (1913–21); advocated neutrality before WWI; supported League of Nations; opposed woman suffrage and prohibition

Marshall Thurgood 1908–1993 Am. jurist; won case of Brown v. Board of Education of Topeka declaring racial segregation in public schools unconstitutional; associate justice, U.S. Supreme Court (1967–91)

Mar·sil·i·us **mär-'si-lē-əs\ **of Padua ca 1280–ca 1343 Ital. scholar; wrote treatise against temporal power of pope; helped Louis IV of Bavaria conquer Rome

**Mar·ston **'mär-stən\ John 1576–1634 Eng. dram.; best known for *The Malcontent* (1604) in which he rails against the iniquities of a lascivious court

Martel Charles — see CHARLES MARTEL

**Mar·tens **'mär-tᵊnz\ Fyodor Fyodorovich 1845–1909 Russ. jurist; authority on international law and representative of Russia in international arbitration proceedings

Martens Wilfried 1936–   prime min. of Belgium (1979–92)

**Mar·tial **'mär-shəl\ ca A.D. 40–ca 103 *Marcus Valerius Martialis* Rom. epigrammatist; published eleven books of epigrams depicting, acutely and often obscenely, aspects of contemporary Roman life; published twelfth book in Spain

**Mar·tin **'mär-tᵊn, mär-taⁿ\ Saint ca 316–397 *Martin of Tours* patron saint of France; founded first monastery in Gaul; patron of publicans and innkeepers

**Mar·tin **'mär-tᵊn\ Archer John Porter 1910–   Brit. chem.; awarded (with R. Synge) 1952 Nobel prize for chemistry for developing the partition chromatography process

Martin Glenn Luther 1886–1955 Am. airplane manuf.; established early airplane factory in U.S.; built aircraft for U.S. army

Martin Homer Dodge 1836–1897 Am. painter; combined elements of Hudson River school and Impressionism in landscapes of spacious design, brilliant color, emotional tone

Martin Joseph William 1884–1968 Am. publisher & polit.; member, U.S. House of Representatives (1925–67)

Martin Mary 1913–1990 Am. actress; starred in Broadway musicals *South Pacific, Peter Pan, The Sound of Music,* etc.

**Mar·tin du Gard **már-taⁿ-dū̄-gár\ Roger 1881–1958 Fr. author; awarded 1937 Nobel prize for literature for his novels

**Mar·ti·neau **'mär-tᵊn-ˌō\ Harriet 1802–1876 Eng. nov. & econ.; author or *Illustrations of Political Economy;* expounded philosophic atheism; wrote novels and tales for children

Martineau James 1805–1900 *bro. of Harriet* Eng. theol. & philos.; author of influential philosophical works as *Types of Ethical Theory,* etc.

**Mar·ti·ni **mär-'tē-nē\ Simone ca 1284–1344 Ital. painter; a leading representative of Sienese school

Mar·tins \'mär-t°nz\ Peter 1946– Am. (Dan.-born) dancer & choreographer; with New York City Ballet as principal dancer (1969), choreographer (1977), ballet master-in-chief (1989–)

Mar·tin·son \'mär-tēn-(,)són\ Harry Edmund 1904–1978 Swed. author; awarded (with E. Johnson) 1974 Nobel prize for literature for poems, novels, essays

Mar·vell \'mär-vəl\ Andrew 1621–1678 Eng. poet & satirist; opposed Restoration government in verse and prose satires; one of the greatest metaphysical poets; known esp. for "To His Coy Mistress"

Marx \'märks\ Groucho 1890–1977 *Julius Henry Marx* Am. comedian; most famous of the Marx Brothers who starred on stage, screen, and radio; master of the leer, wisecrack, and non sequitur

Marx Karl Heinrich 1818–1883 Ger. polit. philos. & socialist; author of *The Communist Manifesto* (1848) and *Das Kapital* (1867, 1885, 1894; completed by F. Engels); founder of historical materialism (Marxism); worked for social reforms and spread of Socialism — **Marx·ist** \'märk-sist\ *adj or n*

Mary \'mer-ē, 'mar-ē, 'ma-rē\ 1st cent. B.C.–1st cent. A.D. mother of Jesus; married to Joseph

Mary I 1516–1558 *Mary Tudor; Bloody Mary* queen of England (1553–58); briefly reestablished Roman Catholicism in England; persecuted Protestants

Mary II 1662–1694 joint Brit. sovereign with William III; *daughter of James II*

Mary Stuart 1542–1587 *Mary, Queen of Scots* queen of Scotland (1542–67); set out to make herself absolute monarch and to impose Roman Catholicism; involvement in intrigues and rebellions resulted in imprisonment by Elizabeth I and eventually to beheading

Ma·sac·cio \mə-'zä-ch(ē-,)ō\ 1401–1428 orig. *Tommaso di Giovanni di Simone Guidi* Ital. painter; member of Florentine school; first to paint in Renaissance style, using central light source and innovations in perspective

Ma·sa·ryk \'mä-sə-(,)rik, 'ma-\ Jan \'yän, 'yan\ Gar·rigue \gə-'rēg\ 1886–1948 *son of T. G.* Czech diplomat & polit.; foreign minister in exile during WWII and after return to Prague in 1945

Masaryk To·máš \'tò-,mäsh, 'tä-məs\ Garrigue 1850–1937 Czech philos. & statesman; 1st pres. of Czechoslovakia (1918–35)

Ma·sca·gni \mä-'skän-yē, ma-\ Pietro 1863–1945 Ital. composer; best known as composer of one-act opera *Cavalleria rusticana*, beginning vogue for verismo operas

Mase·field \'mās-,fēld\ John 1878–1967 Eng. author; poet laureate (1930–67); author of *Salt Water Ballads*, etc., dramas, verse narratives, prose sketches, adventure novels, children's books, autobiographies

Mas·i·nis·sa or **Mas·si·nis·sa** \,ma-sə-'ni-sə\ *ca* 240–148 B.C. king of Numidia; under Roman protection, gained control of all of Numidia

Ma·son \'mā-s°n\ Charles 1728–1786 Eng. astron. & surveyor; surveyed with Jeremiah Dixon boundary line between Maryland and Pennsylvania (Mason-Dixon line)

Mason George 1725–1792 Am. statesman in Revolution; his criticism of Constitution largely responsible for adoption of Bill of Rights

Mas·sa·soit \ˌma-sə-ˈsȯit\ d 1661 Wampanoag Indian chief; negotiated peace with the Pilgrims and remained friendly with the whites all his life

Mas·sé·na \ˌma-sā-ˈnä, mə-ˈsā-nə\ André 1758–1817 Duc *de Rivoli;* Prince *d'Ess·ling* \des-lēŋ\ Fr. gen.; victorious under Napoléon in Italy but defeated in Portugal and Spain; supported restoration of Louis XVIII

Mas·se·net \ˌmas-ᵊn-ˈā, ma-ˈsnä\ Jules-Émile-Frédéric 1842–1912 Fr. composer; known for operas *Manon, Le Cid, Don Quichotte,* and for wide range of instrumental music

Mas·sey \ˈma-sē\ William Ferguson 1856–1925 N.Z. statesman; prime min. (1912–25)

Mas·sine \ma-ˈsēn\ Léonide 1896–1979 orig. *Leonid Fedorovich Miassin* Am. (Russ.-born) dancer & choreographer; one of the most important figures in ballet history; brought the avant-garde into ballet; created the symphonic ballet, etc.

Mas·sin·ger \ˈma-sᵊn-jər\ Philip 1583–1640 Eng. dram.; made thinly veiled observations on current politics in his plays, including *A New Way to Pay Old Debts, The City Madam*

Mas·son \ˈma-sᵊn\ David 1822–1907 Scot. editor & author; edited works of Goldsmith, Milton, Dequincey; wrote magnum opus *Life of Milton,* etc.

Mas·sys \ˈmä-ˌsīs\ or **Mat·sys** \ˈmät-sīs\ or **Mes·sys** \ˈme-sīs\ or **Met·sys** \ˈmet-sīs\ Quentin *ca* 1466–1530 Flem. painter; a leading representative of the early Flemish school of Antwerp

Mas·ters \ˈmas-tərz\ Edgar Lee 1869–1950 Am. author; best known for verse *Spoon River Anthology* (1915); also wrote novels, autobiography, biographies

Math·er \ˈma-thər, -thər\ Cotton 1663–1728 Am. clergyman & author; accepted idea of witchcraft trials and executions but opposed abuses; wrote many works on religious, scientific, historical, moral subjects

Mather Increase 1639–1723 *father of Cotton* Am. clergyman & author; pres. Harvard College (1685–1701); credited with ending executions for witchcraft

Ma·tisse \ma-ˈtēs, mə-\ Henri-Émile-Benoît 1869–1954 Fr. painter; a leader among Fauvists; created costumes for Diaghilev, illustrations, sculpture, paintings

Ma·tsuo \mät-ˈsü-ō, ˈmät-sü-ō\ Ba·shō \ˈbä-ˌshō\ 1644–1694 pseud. of *Matsuo Munefusa* Jp. haiku poet; revitalized *haiku* form with spirit of Zen Buddhism and evocative contrasts of natural phenomena

Ma·tsu·o·ka \ˌmat-sü-ˈwō-kə, ˌmät-, -(ˌ)kä\ Yōsuke 1880–1946 Jp. statesman; allied Japan with Axis powers and concluded nonaggression pact with Soviet Union

Mat·te·ot·ti \ˌma-tē-ˈō-tē, ˌmä-, -ˈȯ-\ Giacomo 1885–1924 Ital. socialist; murdered by Fascists 12 days after denouncing them, causing worldwide scandal

Mat·thew \ˈma-(ˌ)thyü *also* -(ˌ)thü\ Saint 1st cent. A.D. Christian apostle; traditionally regarded as author of first Gospel in the New Testament

Mat·thews \ˈma-(ˌ)thyüz\ (James) Brander 1852–1929 Am. educ. & author; first American professor of dramatic literature

Maugham \\'mȯm\\ (William) Somerset 1874–1965 Eng. nov. & dram.; author of novels *Of Human Bondage* (1915), *The Razor's Edge* (1944), etc., and short stories, plays, and autobiographies

Maul·din \\'mȯl-dᵊn\\ William Henry 1921– *Bill Mauldin* Am. cartoonist; gained fame first for his sympathetic, ironic portrayal of the WWII combat soldier and then for his editorial cartoons on American political and social issues

Mau·nou·ry \\ˌmō-nə-'rē\\ Michel-Joseph 1847–1923 Fr. gen.; in WWI checked von Kluck's drive on Paris

Mau·pas·sant \\ˌmō-pə-'säⁿ\\ (Henri-René-Albert-) Guy de 1850–1893 Fr. writer; gained renown as supreme master of the short story

Mau·riac \\mȯr-'yäk, ˌmȯr-ē-'äk\\ François 1885–1970 Fr. author; awarded 1952 Nobel prize for literature for his novels, essays, and poems

Mau·rice \\'mȯr-əs, 'mär-\\; *G* **Mo·ritz** \\'mȯr-əts, 'mȯr-\\ 1521–1553 elector of Saxony (1547–53) & gen.; supported Reformation and aided Charles V in various wars; later forced Charles to leave Germany and conclude Treaty of Passau

Maurice of Nassau 1567–1625 Prince of *Orange* Du. gen. & statesman; struggled against Spaniards

Mau·rois \\mȯr-'wä\\ André 1885–1967 pseud. of *Émile-Salomon⸗ Wilhelm Her·zog* \\er-zōg\\ Fr. writer; best known for biographies of Shelley, Disraeli, Byron, George Sand, etc.

Mau·ry \\'mȯr-ē, 'mär-\\ Matthew Fontaine 1806–1873 Am. naval officer & oceanographer; made wind and current charts of Atlantic, Pacific, and Indian Oceans

Mau·ser \\'maů-zər\\ Peter Paul 1838–1914 & his bro. Wilhelm 1834–1882 Ger. inventors; invented breech-loading gun known as "Mauser model," a pistol, a revolver, a repeating rifle, and the Mauser magazine rifle (last invented by Peter)

Maw·son \\'mȯs-ᵊn\\ Sir Douglas 1882–1958 Austral. explorer & geologist; leader of several Antarctic expeditions

Max·im \\'mak-səm\\ Sir Hiram Stevens 1840–1916 Brit. (Am.⸗ born) inventor; invented Maxim recoil-operated machine gun, a mousetrap, a steam-powered water pump, vacuum pumps, gas motors, engine governors, etc.

Maxim Hudson 1853–1927 *bro. of Sir Hiram* Am. inventor; invented high explosive maximite, smokeless powder stabillite, torpedo propellant motorite, process for making calcium carbide, etc.

Max·i·mil·ian \\ˌmak-sə-'mil-yən\\ 1832–1867 *bro. of Francis Joseph I of Austria* emp. of Mexico (1864–67); attempted reforms but abandoned by Napoléon III; captured by Juárez, executed

Maximilian I 1459–1519 Holy Rom. emp. (1493–1519); inaugurated many administrative reforms; engaged in unsuccessful war with France

Maximilian II 1527–1576 Holy Rom. emp. (1564–76); made disadvantageous truce with Turks; tolerant toward German Protestants

Max·well \\'maks-ˌwel, -wəl\\ James Clerk \\'klärk\\ 1831–1879 Scot. physicist; demonstrated that light is an electromagnetic wave; developed equations describing electric and magnetic forces and fields — **Max·wel·li·an** \\maks-'we-lē-ən\\ *adj*

May \\'mā\\ Sir Thomas Erskine 1815–1886 1st Baron *Farn·bor-*

ough \\'färn-,bər-ə, -,bə-rə, -b(ə-)rə\\ Eng. jurist; clerk of House of Commons (1871–86) and author of *Treatise on the Law, Privilege, Proceedings, and Usage of Parliament*, etc.

Ma·ya·kov·ski \\,mä-yə-'kȯf-kēh, -'kȯv-\\ Vladimir Vladimirovich 1893–1930 Russ. poet; leader of Futurist movement in Russia, characterized by use of technical innovations, crude language, grotesque images, declamatory manner

May·er \\'mī(-ə)r\\ Maria Goeppert 1906–1972 Am. (Ger.-born) physicist; awarded (with J.H.D. Jensen, E.P. Wigner) 1963 Nobel prize for physics for studies on nuclear shell structure

Mayo \\'mā-(,)ō\\ Charles Horace 1865–1939 & his bro. William James 1861–1939 Am. surgeons; cofounders of the Mayo Foundation, originators of modern procedures in goiter and neurosurgery (Charles) and abdomen, pelvis, kidney surgery (William)

Mays \\'māz\\ Willie Howard 1931–   Am. baseball player; gained fame with New York (later San Francisco) Giants (1951–52, 1954–72); had career total of 660 home runs and lifetime batting average of .302

Ma·za·rin \\,ma-zə-'ra[n]\\ Jules 1602–1661 Fr. cardinal & statesman; greatly strengthened France as a power in Europe by alliances and treaties, preparing the way for Louis XIV

Ma·zo·wie·cki \\,mä-zō-'vyet-skē\\ Tadeusz 1927–   prime min. of Poland (1989–91)

Maz·zi·ni \\mät-'sē-nē, mäd-'zē-\\ Giuseppe 1805–1872 Ital. patriot; involved in republican revolutions and democratic movements; championed Risorgimento movement for Italian unity

Mc·Adoo \\'ma-kə-,dü\\ William Gibbs 1863–1941 Am. administrator; president of company completing first tunnel under Hudson; U.S. senator (1933–38)

M'·Car·thy \\mə-'kär-thē *also* -tē\\ Justin 1830–1912 Irish writer & polit.; advocate of home rule; author of novels, biographies

Mc·Car·thy \\mə-'kär-thē *also* -tē\\ Eugene Joseph 1916–   Am. polit.; candidate for Democratic presidential nomination (1968); outspoken critic of the Vietnam War

McCarthy Joseph Raymond 1908–1957 Am. polit.; U.S. sen. from Wis. (1947–57); notorious for his sensational charges of communist subversion in high government circles; censured by Senate (1954) — **Mc·Car·thy·ite** \\mə-'kär-thē-,īt\\ *adj or n*

McCarthy Mary Therese 1912–1989 Am. writer; best known for novel *The Group* (1963) and for autobiography *Memories of a Catholic Girlhood* (1957)

Mc·Clel·lan \\mə-'kle-lən\\ George Brinton 1826–1885 Am. gen. & polit.; general in chief of the Union army early in the Civil War (1861–62); removed by Lincoln for nonaggressiveness; unsuccessful Democratic nominee for U.S. president (1864)

Mc·Clin·tock \\mə-'klin-tək\\ Barbara 1902–1992 Am. botanist; awarded 1983 Nobel prize for physiology or medicine for discovery that genes sometimes behave unexpectedly inside cells

Mc·Clos·key \\mə-'kläs-kē\\ John 1810–1885 1st Am. cardinal

Mc·Cloy \\mə-'klȯi\\ John Jay 1895–1989 Am. banker & govt. official; furnished loans to and supervised recovery of Germany after WWII

Mc·Clure \mə-ˈklu̇r\ Samuel Sidney 1857–1949 Am. (Irish-born) editor & publisher; established McClure Syndicate, first newspaper syndicate in U.S., and *McClure's Magazine*

Mc·Cor·mack \mə-ˈkȯr-mək, -mik\ John 1884–1945 Am. (Irish-born) tenor; well known for roles in opera and as concert singer, esp. of Irish songs

McCormack John William 1891–1980 Am. polit.; served as member (1929–70), speaker (1962–70), U.S. House of Representatives

Mc·Cor·mick \mə-ˈkȯr-mik\ Cyrus Hall 1809–1884 Am. inventor; invented (1831) and manufactured a successful reaping machine

McCormick Robert Rutherford 1880–1955 Am. newspaper publisher; involved with *Chicago Tribune, New York Daily News, Washington (DC) Times Herald* and used them to present his conservative views

Mc·Cul·lers \mə-ˈkə-lərz\ Carson 1917–1967 née *Smith* Am. writer; author of *The Heart is a Lonely Hunter* (1940), *Reflections in a Golden Eye* (1941), *The Member of the Wedding* (1946), etc.

Mc·Dow·ell \mək-ˈdau̇-(ə)l\ Ephraim 1771–1830 Am. surgeon; performed first recorded ovarian surgery in U.S.

McDowell Irvin 1818–1885 Am. gen.; Union commander during first year of the Civil War; lost both first and second battles at Bull Run (1861, 1862)

Mc·En·roe \ˈma-kᵊn-ˌrō\ John Patrick Jr. 1959– Am. tennis player; won many titles, including U.S. Open (1979, 1980, 1981, 1984), Wimbledon (1981, 1983, 1984); notorious for throwing temper tantrums

Mc·Gill \mə-ˈgil\ James 1744–1813 Canad. (Scot.-born) businessman & philanthropist; bequeathed funds and land for founding of McGill U.

Mc·Gov·ern \mə-ˈgə-vərn\ George Stanley 1922– Am. polit.; unsuccessful Democratic presidential nominee (1972)

Mc·Guf·fey \mə-ˈgə-fē\ William Holmes 1800–1873 Am. educ.; best known for his series of *Eclectic Readers,* for elementary schoolchildren

Mc·Ken·na \mə-ˈke-nə\ Siobhan \shə-ˈvȯn\ 1923?–1986 Irish actress; known for highly dramatic interpretations on English and Irish stage, as in *Playboy of the Western World* and *Saint Joan*

Mc·Kim \mə-ˈkim\ Charles Follen 1847–1909 Am. architect; a leader in American Neoclassical revival; works include the Boston Public Library, New York City Library, Morgan Library

Mc·Kin·ley \mə-ˈkin-lē\ William 1843–1901 25th pres. of the U.S. (1897–1901); acquired Cuba, Puerto Rico, Guam, Philippines, annexed Hawaii, Wake Island, Samoa; assassinated by an anarchist

Mc·Lu·han \mə-ˈklü-ən\ (Herbert) Marshall 1911–1980 Canad. educ.; expert on mass communications and author of *The Medium is the Massage* (with Q. Fiore), *Understanding Media,* etc.

Mc·Ma·hon \mək-ˈmä-(ə)n\ Sir William 1908–1988 prime min. of Australia (1971–72)

Mc·Mil·lan \mək-ˈmi-lən\ Edwin Mattison 1907–1991 Am. chem.; awarded (with G.T. Seaborg) 1951 Nobel prize for chemistry for work in discovering plutonium and other elements

Mc·Na·mara \ˌmak-nə-ˈmar-ə, ˈmak-nə-ˌmar-ə\ Robert Strange

1916–   U.S. secy. of defense (1961–68); played major role in U.S. involvement in Vietnam War; later became a critic of the nuclear arms race and of Vietnam War

Mc·Naugh·ton \mək-ˈnȯ-tᵊn\ Andrew George Latta 1887–1966 Canad. gen. & diplomat; commander of Canadian army in Great Britain (1942–44); co-inventor of cathode ray direction finder

Mead \ˈmēd\ Margaret 1901–1978 Am. anthropol.; author of *Coming of Age in Samoa* (1928), *Male and Female* etc.; controversial lecturer on contemporary social issues

Meade \ˈmēd\ George Gordon 1815–1872 Am. gen.; commander of army of the Potomac (1863–65); repulsed Lee's Confederate army at Gettysburg but failed to obtain decisive victory

Meade James Edward 1907–1996 Brit. econ.; awarded (with B. Ohlin) 1977 Nobel prize for economics for studies of international trade and finance

Means \ˈmēnz\ Russell Charles 1939–   Lakota Sioux activist; a leader in American Indian Movement; best known for leading 71-day siege at Wounded Knee, S.D., to focus attention on rights for Native Americans

Mea·ny \ˈmē-nē\ George 1894–1980 Am. labor leader; pres., American Federation of Labor-Congress of Industrial Organizations (1955–79)

Med·a·war \ˈme-də-wər\ Peter Brian 1915–1987 Eng. anatomist; awarded (with M. Burnet) 1960 Nobel prize for physiology or medicine for research in transplanting human organs

Me·dei·ros \mə-ˈder-əs, -ˌ(ˌ)ōs\ Humberto 1915–1983 Am. (Port.-born) cardinal

Me·di·ci, de' \ˈme-də-ˌchē\ Catherine — see CATHERINE DE MÉDICIS

Medici, de' Cosimo 1389–1464 *the Elder* Florentine financier & ruler; ruled through controlling appointments to chief offices; patron of literature and fine arts

Medici, de' Cosimo I 1519–1574 *the Great;* Duke of *Florence;* Grand Duke of *Tuscany;* capable but despotic and cruel ruler; patron of the arts who erected many buildings

Medici, de' Giulio — see CLEMENT VII

Medici, de' Lorenzo 1449–1492 *the Magnificent* Florentine statesman, ruler, & patron; immoral and tyrannical ruler but did much to make Florence prosperous; esp. influential in making Tuscan dialect Italy's national speech

Me·di·na-Si·do·nia \mə-ˈdē-nə-sə-ˈdōn-yə\ Duque de *d* 1619 *Alonso Pérez de Guzmán* Span. admiral; in command of "Invincible Armada" defeated by England (1588)

Meer van Delft, van der — see Jan VERMEER

Meh·ta \ˈmā-tə\ Zubin 1936–   Am. (Indian-born) conductor; musical director, Los Angeles Philharmonic Orchestra (1962–78), New York Philharmonic Orchestra (1978–91), Israel Philharmonic (1968–)

Meigh·en \ˈmē-ən\ Arthur 1874–1960 Canad. statesman; prime min. (1920–21; 1926)

Me·ir \me-ˈir\ Golda 1898–1978 orig. *Goldie Mabovitch,* later *Goldie Myerson* prime min. of Israel (1969–74)

Meis·so·nier \ˌmā-sᵊn-ˈyā\ Jean-Louis-Ernest 1815–1891 Fr. painter; best known for small genre pictures, often of military subjects, painted with great delicacy

Meit·ner \ˈmīt-nər\ Li·se \ˈlē-zə\ 1878–1968 Ger. physicist; known for work on disintegration products of radium, thorium, and actinium; accomplished (with Otto Hahn, Fritz Strassmann) the fission of uranium (1938)

Me·lanch·thon \mə-ˈlaŋ(k)-thən, -tən\ Philipp 1497–1560 orig. surname *Schwartzerd* Ger. scholar & religious reformer; noted for vast learning, skill in dialectics and exegesis, and moderation that tempered Luther's vehemence

Mel·ba \ˈmel-bə\ Dame Nellie 1861–1931 orig. *Helen Porter Mitchell* Austral. soprano; outstanding coloratura of her day

Mel·chers \ˈmel-chərz\ (Julius) Gari 1860–1932 Am. painter; excelled in genre pictures of Dutch peasant life, religious paintings, portraits, mural decorations

Mel·chi·or \ˈmel-kē-ˌȯr\ Lau·ritz \ˈlau̇-rəts\ Lebrecht Hommel 1890–1973 Am. (Dan.-born) tenor; considered the outstanding heldentenor of his day

Mel·lon \ˈme-lən\ Andrew William 1855–1937 Am. financier; endowed National Gallery of Art, Washington, D.C.

Mel·ville \ˈmel-ˌvil\ Herman 1819–1891 Am. author; wrote stories based on his seafaring experiences, esp. *Typee, Moby Dick* (1851), *Billy Budd, Foretopman*

Mem·ling \ˈmem-liŋ\ *or* **Mem·linc** \-liŋk\ Hans *ca* 1430–1494 Flem. painter; works included portraits and religious paintings

Me·nan·der \mə-ˈnan-dər\ 342–291 B.C. Greek dram.; author of more than 100 comedies noted for literary style, ingenuity of plot, and wit, and considered the zenith of New Comedy

Men·chú \ˈmen-ˌchü\ Rigoberta 1959–   Guatemalan human rights activist; awarded 1992 Nobel prize for peace for work to gain respect for the rights of Guatemala's Indian peoples

Mencius — see MENG-TZU

Menck·en \ˈmeŋ-kən, ˈmen-\ Henry Louis 1880–1956 Am. editor; author of *In Defense of Women, The American Language, Notes on Democracy,* etc. — **Menck·e·nian** \meŋ-ˈkē-nē-ən, men-\ *adj*

Men·del \ˈmen-dᵊl\ Gregor Johann 1822–1884 Austrian botanist; known for breeding experiments with peas; first to lay mathematical foundation of science of genetics — **Men·del·ian** \men-ˈde-lē-ən, -ˈdē-\ *adj*

Men·de·le·yev \ˌmen-də-ˈlā-əf\ Dmitry Ivanovich 1834–1907 Russ. chem.; known for devising periodic table classification of chemical elements by atomic weight

Men·dels·sohn \ˈmen-dᵊl-sən\ Moses 1729–1786 Ger. philos.; author of *Phaidon* in support of immortality of the soul and of translations into German of Psalms and Pentateuch, etc.

Mendelssohn–Bar·thol·dy \-bär-ˈtȯl-dē, -ˈthȯl-\ (Jakob Ludwig) Felix 1809–1847 *grandson of prec.* Ger. composer, pianist, & conductor; composed five symphonies, overtures including *A Midsummer Night's Dream,* concertos, chamber music, etc. — **Men·dels·sohn·ian** \ˌmen-dᵊl-ˈsō-nē-ən, -nyən\ *adj*

Mendès–France \maⁿ-des-fräⁿs\ Pierre 1907–1982 Fr. statesman; ended French involvement in Indochina; brought about Tunisian autonomy

Men·do·za \men-'dō-zə\ Antonio de *ca* 1490–1552 Span. colonial gov.; did much to alleviate exploitation of Indians and to improve their lives

Men·e·lik II \'me-n³l-(,)ik\ 1844–1913 emp. of Ethiopia (1889–1913); one of Ethiopia's greatest rulers; greatly expanded empire; repelled Italian invasion (1896); carried out modernization program

Men·em \'me₁nem, -nəm\ Carlos Saúl 1930–   pres. of Argentina (1989–   ); sought to resume diplomatic relations with Great Britain concerning Falkland Islands

Me·nén·dez de Av·i·lés \mə-'nen-dəs-dā₁ä-və-'lās\ Pedro 1519–1574 Span. navigator & explorer; built fort at St. Augustine; massacred French colony at Ft. Caroline; firmly established Spanish power in Florida

Me·nes \'mē-(,)nēz\ *fl ca* 3100 B.C. king of Egypt; first king of unified upper and lower Egypt; founder of Memphis

Mengs \'men(k)s\ Anton Raphael 1728–1779 Ger. painter; chief exponent of Neoclassicism; in his day widely regarded as greatest living painter

Meng–tzu \'məŋ-'dzü\ *ca* 371–*ca* 289 B.C. orig. *Meng K'o* L. *Mencius* \'men-ch(ē-)əs\ Chin. philos.; taught ethical system based on *jen* (magnanimity) and on belief in innate human goodness

Men·ning·er \'me-niŋ-ər\ Karl Augustus 1893–1990 Am. psychiatrist; one of the first U.S. physicians to receive psychoanalytic training; in Topeka, Kans., founded a psychiatric clinic, a sanitarium, and a foundation; a major influence on American psychiatry

Men·no Si·mons \'me-nō-'sē-mōns, -'sī-\ 1469–1561 Dutch religious reformer; active as organizer and leader of peaceful Anabaptist groups; Mennonite church named for him

Me·not·ti \mə-'nä-tē, -'nȯ-\ Gian Carlo 1911–   Am. (Ital.⸗born) composer; best known for television opera *Amahl and the Night Visitors* and for Pulitzer-prize winning operas *Amelia Goes to the Ball* and *The Consul*

Me·nu·hin \'men-yə-wən\ Yehudi \yə-'hü-dē\ 1916–   Am. violinist; famed as virtuoso, esp. for renditions of Bartók and Elgar

Men·zies \'men-(,)zēz\ Sir Robert Gordon 1894–1978 Austral. statesman; prime min. (1939–41; 1949–66); led Australia into ANZUS pact and SEATO

Mer·ca·tor \(,)mər-'kā-tər\ Gerardus 1512–1594 *Gerhard Kremer* Flem. cartographer; known for his map of the world employing Mercator projection

Mer·cer \'mər-sər\ John H. 1909–1976 *Johnny* Am. songwriter; composed lyrics for hundreds of popular songs including "Laura," "Moon River," "Days of Wine and Roses," etc.

Mercer Mabel 1900–1984 Am. (Brit.-born) cabaret singer; famed for distinctive singing style illuminating meaning of the lyrics; inspired singers Leontyne Price, Billie Holiday, Frank Sinatra, etc.

Mer·cier \mer-'syā, 'mer-sē₁ā\ Désiré-Joseph 1851–1926 Belg. cardinal & philos.; spiritual leader and spokesman of Belgians during German occupation of Belgium in WWI

Mer·e·dith \'mer-ə-dəth\ George 1828–1909 Eng. nov. & poet; acclaimed for stimulating thought, penetrating character analysis, humor, optimism; works include *The Ordeal of Richard Feverel, The Egoist*

Meredith Owen — see E. R. Bulwer-LYTTON

Mer·gen·tha·ler \'mər-gən-ˌthä-lər, 'mer-gən-ˌtä-\ Ottmar 1854–1899 Am. (Ger.-born) inventor; invented and then improved first Linotype typesetting machine

Mé·ri·mée \'mer-ə-ˌmā, ˌmā-rə-\ Prosper 1803–1870 Fr. writer; author of plays and short stories in classical style expressing Romantic themes

Mer·man \'mər-mən\ Ethel 1908?–1984 orig. surname *Zimmerman* Am. singer & actress; starred in Broadway musicals *Anything Goes, Annie Get Your Gun, Gypsy*, etc.; known for her clarion voice and brassy, belting delivery

Mer·ri·field \'mer-i-ˌfēld\ Robert Bruce 1921– Am. biochem.; awarded 1984 Nobel prize for chemistry for developing a rapid, automated method for making peptides

Mer·rill \'mer-əl\ James Ingram 1926–1995 Am. poet; known for finely crafted lyric and epic poems, esp. trilogy of epic poems published as *The Changing Light at Sandover* (1982)

Merrill Robert 1919– Am. baritone; at the Metropolitan Opera (from 1945) sang all the major baritone roles in the Italian and French repertories; known for the beauty and resonance of his voice

Mer·ton \'mər-t³n\ Thomas 1915–1968 Am. Roman Catholic monk & author; wrote autobiography *The Seven Storey Mountain* (1948); verse *Figures for an Apocalypse* (1948), etc., *Seeds of Contemplation* (1949), etc.

Mes·mer \'mez-mər, 'mes-\ Franz *or* Friedrich Anton 1734–1815 Ger. physician; experimented in magnetic therapeutics using séances; denounced in Vienna and Paris as an imposter

Mes·siaen \mes-yäⁿ\ Olivier-Eugène-Prosper-Charles 1908–1992 Fr. composer; regarded as most important French composer of his time; inspired by his Roman Catholic faith, created organ piece *La Nativité du Seigneur*, chamber piece *Quartuor pour la fin du temps*, symphony *Turangalila*, etc.

Mes·sa·la (*or* **Mes·sal·la**) **Cor·vi·nus** \mə-'sä-lə-ˌkȯr-'vi-nəs\ Marcus Valerius *ca* 64 B.C.–A.D. 8 Rom. gen. & statesman; commanded center of Octavian's victorious fleet at Actium; subjugated province of Aquitania

Mes·sa·li·na \ˌme-sə-'lī-nə, -'lē-\ Valeria *ca* A.D. 22–48 *3d wife of Rom. Emp. Claudius;* notorious for her licentious behavior and for instigating murderous court intrigues

Mes·ser·schmitt \'me-sər-ˌshmit\ Willy 1898–1978 Ger. aircraft designer & manuf.; designed all-metal M 18, Me 109 fighter, Me 262 (first jet flown in combat), etc.

Mes·sier \mäs-yā, 'me-sē-ˌā\ Charles 1730–1817 Fr. astron.; credited with discovery of 15 comets; compiled and published catalogue of nebulae still in some use

Meš·tro·vić \'mesh-trə-ˌvich, 'mes-\ Ivan 1883–1962 Am. (Yugoslavian-born) sculptor; works included *The Archangel Gabriel*, portraits and busts of Lady Cunard, Sir Thomas Beecham, President Masaryk, etc.

Me·tax·as \me-ˌtäk-'säs\ Ioannis 1871–1941 Greek gen. & dictator; led Greece into Western alliance (1940)

Metch·ni·koff \'mech-nə-ˌkȯf\ Élie 1845–1916 orig. *Ilya Ilich Mech·ni·kov* \'myäch-nyi-ˌkȯf\ Fr. (Russ.-born) zool. & bacteriol.;

awarded (with P. Ehrlich) 1908 Nobel prize for physiology or medicine for theory of phagocytosis as immunological defense

Met·ter·nich \\'me-tər-(,)nik, -(,)nik\\ Klemens Wenzel Nepomuk Lothar 1773–1859 Fürst *von Metternich* Austrian statesman; largely responsible for balance of power policy in Europe; acquiesced in suppression of liberal ideas or revolutionary movements — **Met·ter·nich·ian** \\,me-tər-'ni-kē-ən, -,kē-ən\\ *adj*

Mey·er \\'mī(-ə)r\\ Annie 1867–1951 née *Nathan* Am. educ. & writer; founder of Barnard College, Columbia U.

Mey·er·beer \\'mī-ər-,bir, -,ber\\ Giacomo 1791–1864 orig. *Jakob Liebmann Beer* Ger. composer; composer of operas in Italian and French styles, including *Les Huguenots, L'Africaine*, etc., and of instrumental music

Mey·er·hof \\'mī-ər-,hôf\\ Otto 1884–1951 Ger. biochem.; awarded (with A.V. Hill) 1922 Nobel prize for physiology or medicine for theory on the production of lactic acid in the muscles

Mi·chael \\'mī-kəl\\ *Romanian* **Mi·hai** \\mē-'hī\\ 1921– *Michael Hohenzollern* king of Romania (1927–30; 1940–47); helped overthrow Antonescu dictatorship (1944) and declared war on Germany; forced to accept communist government (1945) and then to abdicate

Mich·el \\'mi-kəl\\ Hartmut 1948– Ger. biochem.; awarded (with J. Diesendorfer and R. Huber) 1988 Nobel prize for physiology or medicine for revealing the structure of proteins essential to photosynthesis

Mi·chel·an·ge·lo \\,mī-kə-'lan-jə-,lō, ,mi-, ,mē-kə-'län-\\ 1475–1564 *Michelangelo di Lodovico Buonarroti Simoni* Ital. sculptor, painter, architect, & poet; best known for sculpture *Pietá*, colossal *David*, completion of architecture of St. Peter's (Rome), paintings on ceiling of Sistine Chapel; frequently considered the creator of the Renaissance — **Mi·chel·an·ge·lesque** \\-,lan-jə-'lesk\\ *adj*

Mi·che·let \\,mēsh-'lā, mē-shə-\\ Jules 1798–1874 Fr. hist.; first and greatest of the nationalist and romantic historians of France

Mi·chel·son \\'mī-kəl-sən\\ Albert Abraham 1852–1931 Am. (Ger.-born) physicist; awarded 1907 Nobel prize for physics for design of precise optical instruments and accurate measurements with them

Mich·en·er \\'mish-nər\\ (Daniel) Roland 1900– Canad. polit.; gov.-gen. (1967–74)

Mich·e·ner \\'mich-nər, 'mich-ə-\\ James Albert 1907– Am. author; author of epic novels including *Hawaii, Chesapeake, Texas*, etc.

Mi·chu·rin \\myi-'chür-yin\\ Ivan Vladimirovich 1855–1935 Soviet horticulturist; postulated complete heritability of acquired characteristics that as "Michurinism" became state doctrine

Mic·kie·wicz \\mits-'kyä-vich\\ Adam 1798–1855 Pol. poet; regarded as greatest Polish poet

Mid·dle·ton \\'mi-d°l-tən\\ Thomas 1570?–1627 Eng. dram.; author of tragedies *Women Beware Women, The Changeling* (with William Rowley), comedy *A Trick To Catch the Old-one*, etc.

Mies van der Ro·he \\,mēs-,van-də-'rō(-ə), ,mēz-\\ Ludwig 1886–1969 Am. (Ger.-born) architect; known esp. for developing neoclassical designs with exposed supports, glass-curtain walls, simple forms; leading exponent of International Style — **Mies·ian** \\'mē-sē-ən, 'mē-shən\\ *adj*

Miff·lin \\'mi-flən\ Thomas 1744–1800 Am. gen. in Revolution; involved in unsuccessful Conway cabal to replace Washington with Horatio Gates as commander in chief

Mi·haj·lo·vić \mi-'hī-lə-ˌvich\ Dragoljub 1893–1946 *Draža* \\'drä-zhə\ Yugoslav gen.; rival of communist partisans led by Tito; abandoned in favor of Tito by Allies

Mi·ki \'mē-kē\ Tak·eo \'tä-kā-ō\ 1907–1988 prime min. of Japan (1974–76)

Mi·ko·yan \ˌmē-kō-'yän\ Ana·stas \ˌä-nə-'stäs\ Ivanovich 1895–1978 Soviet polit.; head of Presidium (1964–65)

Miles \'mi(ə)lz\ Nelson Appleton 1839–1925 Am. gen.; led successful campaigns against Apache, Sioux, Nez Percé tribes; captured Geronimo

Mil·haud \mē-'yō\ Darius 1892–1974 Fr. composer; a pioneer of polytonality; composer of operas, dramatic music, symphonies, etc.

Mill \'mil\ James 1773–1836 Scot. philos., hist., & econ.; known as founder of philosophic radicalism; author of magnum opus *Analysis of the Mind* providing psychological basis for utilitarianism

Mill John Stuart 1806–1873 *son of James* Eng. philos. & econ.; developed utilitarian philosophy of Bentham by taking pleasure into account and infusing idealism

Mil·lais \'mi-ˌlā, mi-'lā\ Sir John Everett 1829–1896 Eng. painter; an originator of Pre-Raphaelite brotherhood; developed individual style, sense of brilliant color

Mil·lay \mi-'lā\ Edna St. Vincent 1892–1950 Am. poet; author of *Renascence and Other Poems, Second April*, etc.

Mil·ler \'mi-lər\ Arthur 1915–   Am. dram. & nov.; best known for plays *Death of a Salesman* (1949) and *The Crucible* (1953)

Miller (Alton) Glenn 1904–1944 Am. bandleader; organized orchestra (1938) that became one of the most popular "Big Bands" playing swing music, including hits "In the Mood," "Moonlight Serenade," "Tuxedo Junction"

Miller Henry 1891–1980 Am. writer; author of autobiographical novels notable for sexual candor and concern for self-realization, as *Tropic of Cancer*, etc.

Miller Joa·quin \wä-'kēn, wó-\ 1837–1913 pseud. of *Cincinnatus Hiner Miller* Am. poet; wrote poems portraying the majesty and excitement of the Old West, as in *Songs of the Sierras*; best known for poem "Columbus"

Miller Merton Howard 1923–   Am. econ.; awarded (with H.M. Markowitz and W.F. Sharpe) 1990 Nobel prize for economics for theories on corporate finance

Miller Perry Gilbert Eddy 1905–1963 Am. lit. critic & scholar; author of *The New England Mind, Roger Williams*, etc.

Miller William 1782–1849 Am. religious leader; believed in and prepared, with his followers (Millerites or Adventists), for Christ's coming in 1843 and 1844; organized Seventh-Day Adventists, etc., following the "Great Disappointment"

Mil·le·rand \mēl-räⁿ, mē-lə-\ Alexandre 1859–1943 Fr. statesman; pres. of France (1920–24)

Mil·les \'mi-ləs\ Carl 1875–1955 Swed. sculptor; created expressive rhythmical works that greatly influenced German Expressionism and 20th century American sculpture

Mil·let \mē-'yā, mi-'lā\ Jean-François 1814–1875 Fr. painter; famed for his sympathetic depictions of peasant life, as in *The Sower*, *The Gleaners*, *The Angelus*, etc.

Mil·lett \'mi-lət\ Katherine Murray 1934–   Am. feminist & artist; best known for feminist treatise *Sexual Politics*

Mil·li·kan \'mi-li-kən\ Robert Andrews 1868–1953 Am. physicist; awarded 1923 Nobel prize for physics for measuring the charge on electrons and working on the photoelectric effect

Mills \'milz\ Sir John 1908–   Brit. actor; often cast as upstanding, fundamentally decent Englishman; appeared in films *Great Expectations*, *Scott of the Antarctic*, *Ryan's Daughter*, etc.

Mil·man \'mil-mən\ Henry Hart 1791–1868 Eng. poet & hist.; known chiefly for historical works including *History of the Jews*, *History of Christianity*, etc.

Milne \'mil(n)\ Alan Alexander 1882–1956 Eng. poet & dram.; known esp. for juvenile books *Winnie the Pooh*, *The House at Pooh Corner*, verse *When We Were Very Young*, etc.

Mi·losz \'mē-lôsh\ Czeslaw 1911–   Pol. writer; awarded 1980 Nobel prize for literature for his poems

Mil·stein \'mil-ˌstīn, -ˌstēn\ César 1927–   Brit. (Argentine-born) immunologist; awarded (with N.K. Jerne and G.J. Kohler) 1984 Nobel prize for physiology or medicine for discoveries in immunology

Mil·stein \'mil-ˌstīn, -ˌstēn\ Nathan 1904–1992 Am. (Ukrainian-born) violinist; one of the leading violinists of the 20th century; known for technical mastery esp. in Romantic repertoire

Mil·ti·a·des \mil-'tī-ə-ˌdēz\ *ca* 554–?489 B.C. *the Younger* Athenian gen.; led successful attack on Persian force at Marathon

Mil·ton \'mil-t⁸n\ John 1608–1674 Eng. poet; blind in later life; best known for poems *L'Allegro*, *Il Penseroso*, *Lycidas*, masque *Comus*, pamphlet *Areopagitica* (1644), blank verse epics *Paradise Lost* (1667), *Paradise Regained* (1671), lyrical drama *Samson Agonistes* (1671) — **Mil·to·ni·an** \mil-'tō-nē-ən, -nyən\ *or* **Mil·ton·ic** \-'tä-nik\ *adj*

Mil·yu·kov \ˌmil-yə-'kóf, -'kóv\ Pavel Nikolayevich 1859–1943 Russ. polit. & hist.; a leader of liberal sentiment; fled to Paris after Bolshevik revolution

Min·nel·li \mə-'ne-lē\ Vincente 1913–1986 Am. film director; most famous for film musicals *Meet Me in St. Louis*, *An American in Paris*, *Gigi*

Mi·not \'mī-nət\ George Richards 1885–1950 Am. physician; awarded (with W.P. Murphy and G.H. Whipple) 1934 Nobel prize for physiology or medicine for researches on liver treatment of anemias

Min·ton \'min-t⁸n\ Sherman 1890–1965 Am. jurist; associate justice, U.S. Supreme Court (1949–56)

Min·u·it \'min-yə-wət\ *or* **Min·ne·wit** \'mi-nə-ˌwit\ Peter 1580–1638 Du. colonial administrator in America; purchased Manhattan Island from the Indians for trinkets valued at sixty guilders ($24)

Mi·ra·beau \'mir-ə-ˌbō\ Comte de 1749–1791 *Honoré-Gabriel Riqueti* Fr. orator & revolutionary; most important figure in first two years of French Revolution in advocacy of constitutional monarchy

Mi·ró \mē-ˈrō\ Joan \zhů-ˈän\ 1893–1983 Span. painter; developed painting style using curved, fantastic forms in abstract, humorous compositions of few colors

Mi·shi·ma \ˈmē-shi-ˌmä, mə-ˈshē-mə\ Yukio 1925–1970 Jp. writer; author of novels and stories exploring cultural dislocations of postwar Japan and resulting psychological disturbances

Mis·tral \mi-ˈsträl, -ˈstral\ Frédéric 1830–1914 Provençal poet; helped found Félibrige organization of Provençal poets and led Provençal renaissance; awarded (with J. Echegaray y Eizaguirre) 1904 Nobel prize for literature

Mis·tral \mi-ˈsträl, -ˈstral\ Gabriela 1889–1957 orig. *Lucila Godoy Alcayaga* Chilean poet & educ.; awarded 1945 Nobel prize for literature for her poems

Mitch·ell \ˈmi-chəl\ John 1870–1919 Am. labor leader; organized and directed successful miners' strike (1902)

Mitchell Margaret Munnerlyn 1900–1949 Am. nov.; author of *Gone With the Wind* (1936, Pulitzer prize)

Mitchell Maria 1818–1889 Am. astron.; established orbit of newly discovered comet; first woman elected to American Academy of Arts and Sciences

Mitchell Peter Dennis 1920–   Brit. chem.; awarded 1978 Nobel prize for chemistry for studies of cellular energy transfer

Mitchell William 1879–1936 *Billy Mitchell* Am. gen.; court-martialed and convicted for criticism of War and Navy departments for mismanagement of aviation service

Mit·ford \ˈmit-fərd\ Jessica Lucy 1917–   Eng.-born writer; known for her muckraking works on American institutions; wrote *The American Way of Death, The Trial of Dr. Spock,* etc.

Mitford Mary Russell 1787–1855 Eng. nov. & dram.; produced sketches of country life that became *Our Village* (5 vols.), her best known work

Mitford William 1744–1827 Eng. hist.; wrote *History of Greece,* long popular and highly esteemed

Mith·ra·da·tes VI Eu·pa·tor \ˌmi-thrə-ˈdā-tēz-ˈyü-ˌpā-tər\ *d* 63 B.C. *the Great* king of Pontus (120–63); had great military ability and proved one of most formidable opponents of Rome in three Mithradatic Wars

Mi·tro·pou·los \mə-ˈträ-pə-ləs\ Di·mi·tri \də-ˈmē-trē\ 1896–1960 Am. (Greek-born) conductor; noted for unorthodox style and for introducing modern works by Schoenberg, Berg, Krenek, etc.

Mit·ter·rand \ˌmē-ter-ˈäⁿ\ François-Maurice 1916–1996 pres. of France (1981–95); worked to nationalize industry and create jobs

Mi·ya·za·wa \ˌmē-ə-ˈzä-wə\ Kiichi 1919–   prime min. of Japan (1991–93)

Mo·bu·tu Se·se Se·ko \mə-ˈbü-(ˌ)tü-ˈsä-sä-ˈsä-(ˌ)kō\ 1930– orig. *Joseph-Désiré Mobutu* pres. of Zaire (1965–   )

Mo·di·glia·ni \ˌmò-dēl-ˈyä-nē, -dˈl-\ Amedeo 1884–1920 Ital. painter; known esp. for portraits and nudes executed in characteristic planar, asymmetric, elongated manner

Modigliani Franco 1918–   Am. (Ital.-born) econ.; awarded 1983 Nobel prize for economics for work on theories of personal saving and corporate finance

Mo·djes·ka \mə-'jes-kə\ Helena 1840–1909 Am. (Pol.-born) actress; excelled in serious dramatic roles, including Lady Macbeth, Juliet, Ophelia, Imogen, Ibsen's Nora, Dumas's Camille

Mo·ham·mad Re·za Pah·la·vi \mō-'ha-məd-ri-'zä-'pa-lə-(,)vē, -'hä-\ 1919–1980 shah of Iran (1941–79); ousted by growing popular opposition led mainly by Islamic fundamentalists

Mo·ham·med *var of* MUHAMMAD

Mois·san \mwä-'säⁿ\ Henri 1852–1907 Fr. chem.; awarded 1906 Nobel prize for chemistry for the discovery of flourine and the development of the electric furnace; also discovered silicon carbide

Mo·ley \'mō-lē\ Raymond Charles 1886–1975 Am. journalist; assistant secy. of state and member of "brain trust" group of advisers to Pres. F.D. Roosevelt

Mo·lière \mōl-'yer, 'mōl-\ 1622–1673 orig. *Jean-Baptiste Poquelin* Fr. actor & dram.; regarded as the greatest of French comedic writers; plays include *School for Wives, Tartuffe, Le Misanthrope*

Molina Tirso de — see TIRSO DE MOLINA

Mol·nár \'mōl-,när, 'mól-\ Fe·renc \'fer-ən(t)s\ 1878–1952 Hung. author; best known for short stories and for plays about contemporary life in Budapest, the latter including *Liliom, The Swan, The Red Mill*

Mo·lo·tov \'mä-lə-,tóf, 'mó-, 'mō-, -,tòv\ Vyacheslav Mikhaylovich 1890–1986 orig. surname *Skryabin* Soviet statesman; promoted global communism and fostered Cold War; known for production of Molotov cocktail, named for him

Molt·ke \'mólt-kə\ Helmuth Karl Bernhard 1800–1891 Graf *von Moltke* Pruss. field marshal; devised strategic and tactical command methods for modern mass armies engaged on broad fronts

Momm·sen \'mōm-zən\ Theodor 1817–1903 Ger. scholar & hist.; awarded 1902 Nobel prize for literature for *History of Rome* and *History of the Roman Provinces*

Monck *or* **Monk** \'məŋk\ George 1608–1670 1st Duke of *Al·be·marle* \'al-bə-,märl\ Eng. gen.; subjugated Scotland under Cromwell; organized Coldstream Guards; helped restore Charles II to throne

Mon·dale \'män-,dāl\ Walter Frederick 1928–   Am. polit.; vice pres. of the U.S. (1977–81); unsuccessful Democratic nominee for pres. (1984)

Mon·dri·an \'món-drē-,än\ Piet 1872–1944 *Pieter Cornelis Mondriaan* Du. painter; developed "neoplastic" aesthetic involving reduction of paintings to elements of straight lines, primary colors, noncolors

Mo·net \mō-'nä\ Claude 1840–1926 Fr. painter; perfected style of Impressionism; notable for producing series of the same subjects in various lighting conditions, as "Haystacks" and "Rouen Cathedral"

Mo·ne·ta \mō-'nā-tə\ Ernesto Teodoro 1833–1918 Ital. journalist & pacifist; awarded (with L. Renault) 1902 Nobel prize for peace for his work as head of the Lombard League for Peace

Mo·niz Antonio Egas — see EGAS MONIZ

Monk \'məŋk\ Meredith Jane 1942–   Am. composer, choreographer & performance artist; known for her innovative multimedia works mixing theatrical performance, video, film, etc.; composed strikingly original primitivist music

Monk Thelonious Sphere 1920–1982 Am. jazz musician; one of principal creators of "bop" style and noted for harmonic and rhythmic sophistication and humor

Mon·mouth \'mən-məth, 'män-\ Duke of 1649–1685 *James Scott, son of Charles II of England* Eng. rebel & claimant to the throne; defeated in battle, captured, and beheaded

Mon·net \mó-ne\ Jean-Omer-Marie-Gabriel 1888–1979 Fr. econ. & diplomat; responsible for the plan that successfully rebuilt and modernized France's ruined economy after WWII

Mo·nod \mó-nō\ Jacques-Lucien 1910–1976 Fr. biochem.; awarded (with F. Jacob and A. Livoff) 1965 Nobel prize for physiology or medicine for discoveries concerning genetic control of enzyme and virus synthesis

Mon·roe \mən-'rō\ James 1758–1831 5th pres. of U.S. (1817–25); period known as "era of good feeling"; acquired Florida; enacted Missouri Compromise legislation; promulgated Monroe Doctrine

Monroe Marilyn 1926–1962 orig. *Norma Jean Mor·ten·son* \'mór-tⁿn-sən\ Am. actress; starred in films *Gentlemen Prefer Blondes, Some Like It Hot, The Misfit,* etc.; celebrated in her time as a blonde sex symbol, later as a tragic figure exploited by Hollywood

Mon·ta·gna \mən-'tän-yə\ Bartolommeo *ca* 1450–1523 Ital. painter; founded school of Vicenza; created altarpieces, frescoes, etc.

Mon·ta·gu \'män-tə-,gyü, 'mən-\ Lady Mary Wortley 1689–1762 Eng. letter writer & poet; literary reputation rests chiefly on 52 Turkish embassy letters, written while her husband was stationed in Constantinople

Mon·taigne \män-'tān, mōⁿ-tenʸ\ Michel Eyquem de 1533–1592 Fr. essayist; famous for *Essais,* reflecting spirit of skepticism and inspired by classics and contemporary figures; exercised great influence on French and English literature

Mon·ta·le \mōn-'tä-(,)lä\ Eugenio 1896–1981 Ital. poet; awarded 1975 Nobel prize for literature for his poems

Mon·tana \(,)män-'ta-nə\ Joseph C Jr. 1956– Am. football player; quarterback, San Francisco 49ers (1979–93), Kansas City Chiefs (1993–95); led 49ers to Super Bowl victories (1982, 1985, 1990)

Mont·calm de Saint–Véran \mänt-'kälm-də-,saⁿ-vä-'rän, -'käm-\ Marquis de 1712–1759 *Louis-Joseph de Montcalm-Grozon* Fr. field marshal; commander in chief of French forces in Canada during Seven Years' War; mortally wounded at fall of Quebec

Mon·tes·pan \ˈmōⁿ-tes-pä̃, 'män-tə-,span\ Marquise de 1641–1707 née (*Françoise-Athénaïs*) *Rochechouart de Mortemart* mistress of Louis XIV; bore him six children later legitimated

Mon·tes·quieu \,män-təs-'kyü, -'kyə(r), -'kyœ̅\ Baron de *La Brède et de* 1689–1755 *Charles-Louis de Secondat* Fr. lawyer & polit. philos.; published *L'Esprit des lois,* seminal contribution to political theory, profound influence in Europe and America

Mon·tes·so·ri \,män-tə-'sōr-ē, -'sòr-\ Maria 1870–1952 Ital. physician & educ.; developed method for educating children based on developing child's initiative, sense and muscle training, and freedom through prepared materials and games

Mon·teux \mōⁿ-'tə(r), -'tœ̅\ Pierre 1875–1964 Am. (Fr.-born) conductor; noted as interpreter of 20th-century music

Mon·te·ver·di *or* **Mon·te·ver·de** \‚män-tə-'ver-dē, -'vər-\ Claudio 1567–1643 Ital. composer; highly influential in establishing new genres of opera and oratorio; leader in musical revolution of 16th century

Mon·te·zu·ma II \‚män-tə-'zü-mə\ *or* **Moc·te·zu·ma** \‚mäk-tə-\ 1466–1520 last Aztec emp. of Mexico (1502–20); held hostage by Spaniards and mortally wounded while trying to negotiate

Mont·fort \'mänt-fort, mȯⁿ-'fȯr\ Simon de 1165?–1218 *Simon IV de Montfort l'Amaury* Fr. soldier; at call of pope, led crusade against Albigenses, or Cathari

Mont·fort \'mänt-fort\ Simon de *ca* 1208–1265 Earl of *Leicester* Eng. soldier & statesman; long popularly revered as martyr and saint for role in Barons' War, leading to the beginning of modern Parliament

Mont·gol·fier \mänt-'gäl-fē-ər, -fē-‚ā\ Joseph-Michel 1740–1810 & his bro. Jacques-Étienne 1745–1799 Fr. inventors & balloonists; built hot-air balloon in which first manned ascent was made

Mont·gom·ery \(‚)mən(t)-'gom-rē, män(t)-, -'gäm-; -'gə-mə-, -'gä-\ Bernard Law 1887–1976 1st Viscount *Montgomery of Alamein* Brit. field marshal; commander in No. Africa (defeating Rommel), later in Sicily, Italy; led Normandy invasion (1944); led British and Canadian forces across Europe to ultimate victory in Germany

Montgomery Lucy Maud 1874–1942 Canad. nov.; author of *Anne of Green Gables, Anne of Avonlea,* etc.

Mont·mo·ren·cy \‚mänt-mə-'ren(t)-sē\ Anne 1493–1567 1st duc *de Montmorency* Fr. soldier; constable (1537); Catholic leader against Protestants

Mon·trose \män-'trōz\ 1st Marquess of 1612–1650 *James Graham* Scot. Royalist; in English Civil War, won victories over Parliamentary Scottish forces before being defeated, captured, and hanged

Moo·dy \'mü-dē\ Dwight Lyman 1837–1899 Am. evangelist; founded Northfield Seminary and Mount Hermon School; published (with Ira Sankey) *Sacred Songs and Solos, Gospel Hymns*

Moody William Vaughn 1869–1910 Am. poet & dram.; author of plays *The Great Divide, The Faith Healer,* etc.

Moon \'mün\ Sun Myung 1920–   Korean evangelist; founded (1954) the Holy Spirit Association for the Unification of World Christianity (Unification Church); followers known as Moonies

Moore \'mȯr, 'mȯr, 'mur\ George 1852–1933 Irish author; active in Irish literary revival; known for novels *Brook Kerith, Héloïse and Abélard,* etc.

Moore George Edward 1873–1958 Eng. philos.; developed system of Ideal Utilitarianism, a chief modern theory of ethics

Moore Henry 1898–1986 Brit. sculptor; developed style based on organic shapes and curves; best known for his undulating reclining nudes

Moore John Bassett 1860–1947 Am. jurist; judge, Permanent Court of International Justice; author of works on international law

Moore Marianne Craig 1887–1972 Am. poet; author of *Collected Poems* (Pulitzer prize), *To Be a Dragon, The Arctic Ox,* etc.

Moore Stanford 1913–1982 Am. biochem.; awarded (with W.H. Stein and C.B. Anfinsen) 1972 Nobel prize for chemistry for studies of enzymes

Moore Thomas 1779–1852 Irish poet; gained reputation as national lyrist of Ireland; wrote satirical verses; earned European reputation for *Lalla Rookh*, etc.

Mo·ra·via \mō-'rä-vē-ə\ Alberto 1907–1990 pseud. of *Alberto Pincherle* Ital. writer; became successful with novels *The Time of Indifference, Disobedience, The Conformist,* etc.

More \'mōr, 'mȯr\ Hannah 1745–1833 Eng. religious writer; devoted herself to social, political, and religious amelioration after writing for the popular stage

More Henry 1614–1687 Eng. philos.; a leading member of Cambridge Platonists; argued against Descartes and Hobbes

More Paul Elmer 1864–1937 Am. essayist & critic; associated with Irving Babbitt as champion of humanism

More Sir Thomas 1478–1535 *Saint* Eng. statesman & author; chancellor of England (1529–32); beheaded for refusing to accept Henry VIII as head of the Church of England; author of *Utopia* (1516)

Mo·reau \mȯ-rō\ (Jean-) Victor-Marie 1763–1813 Fr. gen.; headed Republican and Royalist conspiracy against Napoléon and exiled for complicity

Mor·gan \'mȯr-gən\ Daniel 1736–1802 Am. gen. in Revolution; defeated British at Cowpens; suppressed Whisky Rebellion

Morgan Sir Henry 1635–1688 Eng. buccaneer; for governor of Jamaica, robbed and raided in Panama, Cuba, Maracaibo, Gibraltar, Santa Catalina, etc.

Morgan John Hunt 1825–1864 Am. Confed. cavalry officer; famed for cavalry raids in Tennessee and Kentucky

Morgan John Pier·pont \'pir-ˌpänt\ 1837–1913 Am. financier; best known for government financing, reorganization of important railroads, industrial consolidations, etc.

Morgan John Pierpont 1867–1943 *son of J. P.* Am. financier; floated large loans for Allies during WWI and $1.7 billion in loans for postwar reconstruction

Morgan Thomas Hunt 1866–1945 Am. geneticist; awarded 1933 Nobel prize for physiology or medicine for discoveries relating to the laws and mechanisms of heredity

Morgan William Wilson 1906–1994 Am. astron.; studied and classified stars and galaxies; provided (1951) first evidence that the Earth's galaxy has spiral arms

Mor·gen·thau \'mȯr-gən-ˌthȯ\ Henry 1891–1967 U.S. secy. of the treasury (1934–45)

Mor·i·son \'mȯr-ə-sən, 'mär-\ Samuel Eliot 1887–1976 Am. hist.; author of *Builders of the Bay Colony, Admiral of the Ocean Sea* (Pulitzer prize), *John Paul Jones* (Pulitzer prize), etc.

Morison Stanley 1889–1968 Eng. type designer; known esp. for design of Times New Roman typeface

Mo·ri·sot \mȯ-rē-zō\ Berthe 1841–1895 Fr. painter; painted in Impressionist manner, with emphasis on design; works noted for delicate coloring

Mor·ley \'mȯr-lē\ Christopher Darlington 1890–1957 Am. writer; author of *The Haunted Book Shop, Thunder on the Left, Kitty Foyle,* etc.

Morley John 1838–1923 Viscount *Morley* Eng. statesman & writer; supporter of Gladstone and author of *Edmund Burke, Voltaire, Rousseau,* etc.

Mor·nay \mȯr-nā\ Philippe de 1549–1623 Seigneur *du Plessis= Marly;* usu. called **Du·ples·sis-Mor·nay** \dᴜᴇ-plä-sä-mȯr-ne\ Fr. Huguenot; became adviser to Henry of Navarre; outspoken champion of the Protestant cause during the French Wars of Religion (1562–98)

Mor·ris \'mȯr-əs, 'mär-\ Gou·ver·neur \ˌgə-və(r)-'nir\ 1752–1816 Am. statesman & diplomat; prepared report proposing system of decimal coinage, using terms dollar and cent

Morris Robert 1734–1806 Am. financier & statesman; helped American cause by arranging financing of supplies for Washington's armies

Morris William 1834–1896 Eng. poet, artist, & socialist; helped to found decorating firm which brought about reform in Victorian taste; started Kelmscott Press and published magnificent *Kelmscott Chaucer*

Mor·ri·son \'mȯr-ə-sən, 'mär-\ Herbert Stanley 1888–1965 Baron *Morrison of Lambeth* Eng. polit.; home secy., min. of home security, and member of war cabinet during WWII

Morrison Robert 1782–1834 Scot. missionary; translated New Testament and Old Testament into Chinese and completed *Chinese Grammar* and *Chinese Dictionary*

Morrison Toni 1931– orig. *Chloe Anthony Wofford* Am. novelist; examined in realistic detail the lives of African-Americans in *The Bluest Eye, Beloved* (Pulitzer prize), *Jazz,* etc.; awarded 1993 Nobel prize for literature

Morse \'mȯrs\ Samuel Finley Breese 1791–1872 Am. artist & inventor; invented Morse code; invented telegraph and sent first telegraph message, "What hath God wrought!"

Mor·ti·mer \'mȯr-tə-mər\ Roger de 1287–1330 1st Earl of *March* & 8th Baron of *Wigmore* Welsh rebel; compelled Edward II to abdicate and, with his paramour Queen Isabella, ruled through Edward III and procured murder of Edward II

Mor·ton \'mȯr-tᵊn\ Levi Parsons 1824–1920 Am. banker & polit.; vice pres. of the U.S. (1889–93)

Morton William Thomas Green 1819–1868 Am. dentist; devised process for using sulfuric ether as anesthetizing agent

Mos·by \'mȯz-bē\ John Singleton 1833–1916 Am. Confed. cavalry officer; credited by some with phrase "the Solid South"; commanded independent cavalry unit, Mosby's Rangers, raiding federal supplies

Moś·cic·ki \mȯsh-'chēt-skē, -'chit-\ Ignacy 1867–1946 Pol. chem.; pres. of Poland (1926–39); strong supporter of the dictatorship of Józef Piłsudski

Mo·ses \'mō-zəz *also* -zəs\ 14th cent.–13th cent. B.C. Hebrew prophet & lawgiver; according to biblical accounts, led Israelites out of Egypt; delivered Ten Commandments at Mt. Sinai

Moses Anna Mary née *Robertson* 1860–1961 *Grandma Moses* Am. painter; took up painting in her 70s and gained fame for primitive paintings of rural scenes and life

Moses Robert 1888–1981 Am. public official; responsible for the construction of highways, bridges, stadiums, public housing projects, etc. that transformed the character of N.Y. City; his projects greatly influenced construction in other cities

Mosley 244

Mos·ley \'mōz-lē\ Sir Oswald Er·nald \'ər-n°ld\ 1896–1980 Eng. polit.; founded British Union of Fascists (Blackshirts) (1932); founded Union Movement (1948)

Möss·bau·er \'mœs-,baù(-ə)r, 'mes-\ Rudolf Ludwig 1929– Ger. physicist; awarded with R. Hofstadter) 1967 Nobel prize for physics for research on gamma rays

Moth·er·well \'mə-thər-,wel, -wəl\ Robert 1915–1991 Am. artist; helped found Abstract Expressionism in New York; evolved a style of spontaneous painting of enormous images

Mo Ti — see MO-TZU

Mot·ley \'mät-lē\ John Lothrop 1814–1877 Am. hist.; author of *The Rise of the Dutch Republic, The Life and Death of John Barneveld.* etc.

Mo·ton \'mō-t°n\ Robert Russa 1867–1940 Am. educ.; principal of Tuskegee Normal and Industrial Institute (1915–35) and author of *Racial Good Will,* etc.

Mott \'mät\ John Raleigh 1865–1955 Am. religious leader; awarded (with E.G. Balch) 1946 Nobel prize for peace

Mott Lucretia 1793–1880 née *Coffin* Am. social reformer; a founder of Female Anti-Slavery Society, American Equal Rights Association, Free Religious Association; active in Underground Railroad

Mott Sir Nevill Francis 1905– Brit. physicist; awarded (with P.W. Anderson and J.H. Van Vleck) 1977 Nobel prize for physics for helping develop semiconductor devices

Mot·tel·son \'mō-t°l-sən, -(,)sön\ Ben Roy 1926– Dan. (Am.-born) physicist; awarded (with L.J. Rainwater and A.N. Bohr) 1975 Nobel prize for physics for work on the structure of the atomic nucleus

Mot·teux \mä-'tə(r), 'mä-\ Peter Anthony 1660–1718 Brit. (Fr.-born) dram. & translator; translated books IV and V of Rabelais and published free translation of Don Quixote

Mo–tzu \'mōd-'zə\ 470?–?391 B.C. orig. *Mo Ti* \'mō-'dē\ L. *Mi·cius* \'mē-sh(ē-)əs\ Chin. philos.; evolved philosophy that for a time rivaled Confucianism as leading Chinese school of thought; emphasized simplicity, universal love, religious sensibility

Moul·ton \'mōl-t°n\ Forest Ray 1872–1952 Am. astron.; a propounder of the planetesimal hypothesis of the origin of the solar system

Moul·trie \'mül-trē, 'mōl-\ William 1730–1805 Am. gen. in Revolution; repulsed British attack on Sullivan's Island in Charleston Harbor (1776); defended Charleston again (1779)

Mount·bat·ten \maunt-'ba-t°n\ Louis 1900–1979 1st Earl *Mountbatten of Burma* Brit. admiral; 1st gov.-gen. of India (1947–48); oversaw rapid transfer of power to native government and partition of Pakistan; chief of defense staff (1959–65)

Mountbatten Philip, Duke of Edinburgh — see Prince PHILIP

Mow·at \'mō-ət\ Farley McGill 1921– Canad. writer; author of novels set in the Canadian wilderness, including *People of the Deer, Never Cry Wolf, Tundra,* etc.

Mo·zart \'mōt-,särt\ Wolfgang Amadeus 1756–1791 Austrian composer; composed over 600 works in virtually every form, a body of work unexcelled in beauty, diversity, and profundity; works include operas *The Marriage of Figaro, Don Giovanni, The*

Magic Flute, etc. — **Mo·zart·ean** *or* **Mo·zart·ian** \mōt-'sär-tē-ən\ *adj*

Mu·bar·ak \mu̇-'bär-ək\ Muhammad Hosni 1929–   pres. of Egypt (1981–   ); continued Sadat's policies and work toward peace with Israel

Muench \'minch\ Aloisius Joseph 1889–1962 Am. cardinal

Mu·ga·be \mu̇-'gä-bē\ Robert Gabriel 1924–   prime min. of Zimbabwe (1980–87); executive pres. (1987–   )

Mug·ge·ridge \'mə-gə-ˌrij\ Malcolm Thomas 1903–1990 Brit. writer & social critic; author of *Chronicle of Wasted Time;* editor of *Punch;* associated with television series *Panorama*

Mu·ham·mad \mō-'ha-məd, -'hä- *also* mü-\ *ca* 570–632 *Abū al-Qāsim Muhammad ibn 'Abd Allāh ibn 'Abd al-Muṭṭalib ibn Hāshim* Arab prophet & founder of Islam; received prophetic call in vision and then periodic revelations that he held were from God and were later written down as the Qur'ān; preached message of Allāh's power and goodness, the duty of worship and generosity, and doctrine of last judgment — **Mu·ham·mad·an** \mō-'ha-mə-dən, -'hä- *also* mü-\ *adj or n*

Mu·ham·mad \mō-'ha-məd, mü-, -'hä-\ Elijah 1897–1975 orig. *E. Poole* Am. religious leader; directed growth of Black Muslim movement and of many related business activities

Muhammad XI \mō-'ha-məd, -'hä- *also* mü-\ *d* 1527 *Abū 'Abd Allāh Muhammad* Sp. *Bo·ab·dil* \bō-äv-'dēl\ last sultan of Granada; lost Granada to siege by forces of Ferdinand and Isabella, thus ending Muslim rule in Spain

Müh·len·berg \'myü-lən-ˌbərg\ Henry Melchior 1711–1787 Am. (Ger.-born) Lutheran clergyman; known as virtual founder of Lutheranism in America

Muir \'myu̇r\ John 1838–1914 Am. (Scot.-born) naturalist; helped gain establishment of Yosemite National Park and other forest reserves

Mul·ler \'mə-lər\ Hermann Joseph 1890–1967 Am. geneticist; awarded 1946 Nobel prize for physiology or medicine for work on artificial transmutation of the gene by X rays

Mül·ler \'myü-lər, 'mi-, 'mə-\ (Friedrich) Max 1823–1900 Brit. (Ger.-born) philologist; wrote *History of Ancient Sanskrit Literature, Contributions to the Science of Mythology,* etc.

Müller Johann 1436–1476 *Regiomontanus* Ger. astron.; a publisher of *Ephemerides ab anno 1475–1506* used by Columbus and other navigators; helped reform the calendar

Müller Karl Alexander 1927–   Swiss physicist; awarded (with J.G. Bednorz) 1987 Nobel prize for physics for discovery of superconductivity in a ceramic material

Müller Paul Hermann 1899–1965 Swiss chem.; awarded 1948 Nobel prize for physiology or medicine for discovery of insecticidal properties of DDT

Mul·li·ken \'mə-lə-kən\ Robert Sanderson 1896–1986 Am. chem. & physicist; awarded 1966 Nobel prize for chemistry for developing the molecular-orbital theory of chemical structure

Mul·lis \'mə-lis\ Kary Banks 1944–   Am. biochem.; awarded (with M. Smith) 1993 Nobel prize for chemistry for his method of copying genetic material

Mul·ro·ney \mǝl-'rü-nē\ (Martin) Brian 1939–   Canad. polit.; prime min. (1984–93); negotiated free trade agreement with U.S.

Mum·ford \'mǝm(p)-fǝrd\ Lewis 1895–1990 Am. writer; author of *The Story of Utopias* and *The City in History* discussing the negative effects of technology on society

Munch \'münch, 'mŭench\ Charles 1891–1968 Fr.-born conductor; known esp. for interpretations of Brahms, Debussy, Ravel

Munch \'mŭnk\ Edvard 1863–1944 Norw. painter; a forerunner of Expressionism in boldly subjective paintings of emotional distress in macabre scenes as *The Cry, Ashes*, etc.

Münch·hau·sen \'münk-,haŭ-zⁿn\ Karl Friedrich Hieronymus von 1720–1797 Baron *Mun·chau·sen* \'mǝn-,chaŭ-zⁿn, 'mün-\ Ger. hunter, soldier, & raconteur; his name now proverbially associated with absurdly exaggerated stories

Mu·ñoz Ma·rín \(,)mün-'yōs-mǝ-'rēn, -'yōz-\ Luis 1898–1980 Puerto Rican polit.; first elected gov. of Puerto Rico (1948–64); secured commonwealth status

Mun·ro \(,)mǝn-'rō\ Alice 1931–   née *Laidlaw* Canad. writer; author of stories about people of Scotch-Irish stock in rural Ontario; published story collections *Dance of the Happy Shades, Who Do You Think You Are?, The Progress of Love*, etc.

Munro Hector Hugh 1870–1916 pseud. *Saki* Scot. writer; produced collections of witty, satirical, sometimes fantastic short stories as *Reginald, The Square Egg*, etc., and novels

Mün·ster·berg \'mün(t)-stǝr-,bǝrg, 'myün(t)-, 'mǝn(t)-\ Hugo 1863–1916 Am. (Ger.-born) psychol.; known as pioneer in field of applied psychology

Mu·ra·sa·ki \,mür-ǝ-'sä-kē, ,myür-\ Shikibu 978?–?1026 Jp. court lady & nov.; author of *Genji monogatari* (*Tale of Genji*), generally considered the first full novel in the world and greatest classic of Japanese literature

Mu·rat \myü-'rä, mū-\ Joachim 1767–1815 Fr. gen.; marshal of France; king of Naples (1808–15); introduced Code Napoléon and other reforms; encouraged Italian nationalism

Mu·ra·ya·ma \,mü-rä-'yä-mä\ Tomiichi 1924–   prime min. of Japan (1994–96)

Mur·doch \'mǝr-dǝk, -,däk\ Dame (Jean) Iris 1919–   Brit. (Irish-born) writer; author of many novels imbued with subtle and humorous sensitivity to relationships, as *The Black Prince, The Sea, The Sea, The Good Apprentice*, etc.

Mu·ril·lo \myü-'ri-(,)lō, mù-'rē-(,)ō, myú-\ Bartolomé Esteban 1617–1682 Span. painter; known esp. as colorist in chiefly religious works, often softening Baroque manner with sentimental details

Mur·phy \'mǝr-fē\ Frank 1890–1949 Am. jurist; associate justice, U.S. Supreme Court (1940–49)

Murphy Robert Daniel 1894–1978 Am. diplomat; helped organize Berlin airlift; helped negotiate Korean armistice

Murphy William Parry 1892–1987 Am. physician; awarded (with G.R. Minot and G.H. Whipple) 1934 Nobel prize for physiology or medicine for discoveries on liver treatment for anemia

Mur·ray \'mǝr-ē, 'mǝ-rē\ (George) Gilbert Aimé 1866–1957 Brit. classical scholar; known chiefly for his critical editions of Euripides and Aeschylus and verse translations of Euripides

Murray Sir James Augustus Henry 1837–1915 Brit. lexicographer; helped plan and edit *New English Dictionary*, now *Oxford English Dictionary*

Murray Joseph Edward 1919–   Am. surgeon; awarded (with E.D. Thomas) 1990 Nobel prize for physiology or medicine for work in transplanting human organs and bone marrow

Murray Lindley 1745–1826 Am. grammarian; author of school-books including *Grammar of the English Language, English Reader, English Spelling Book*, etc.

Murray Philip 1886–1952 Am. labor leader; pres., Congress of Industrial Organizations (1940–52), and United Steel Workers of America (1942–52)

Mur·row \'mər-(,)ō, 'mə-(,)rō\ Edward Roscoe 1908–1965 Am. journalist; made notable broadcasts from London during Blitz (1941) and later involved with radio and television news series

Mu·si·al \'myü-zē-əl\ Stanley Frank 1920–   *Stan Musial* Am. baseball player; with St. Louis Cardinals (1941–63); one of baseball's greatest hitters; career batting average of .331

Mus·kie \'məs-kē\ Edmund Sixtus 1914–   Am. polit.; Democratic nominee for vice pres. (1968)

Mus·set \myü-'sā\ (Louis-Charles-) Alfred de 1810–1857 Fr. poet; achieved recognition with precocious poetry, Romantic but with a touch of ironic wit and glibness

Mus·so·li·ni \,mü-sə-'lē-nē, ,mù-\ Be·ni·to \bə-'nē-(,)tō\ 1883–1945 *Il Du·ce* \ēl-'dü-(,)chā\ Ital. Fascist premier (1922–43); conquered and annexed Ethiopia and Albania; entered WWII as ally of Germany; eventually defeated, deposed, shot

Mus·sorg·sky \mù-'sòrg-skē, -'zòrg-\ Mo·dest \mō-'dest\ Petrovich 1839–1881 Russ. composer; one of the most original and influential composers of the day; known esp. for opera *Boris Godunov*, piano piece *Pictures from an Exhibition*

Mustafa Kemal — see KEMAL ATATÜRK

Mu·tsu·hi·to \,müt-sə-'hē-(,)tō\ 1852–1912 *Mei·ji* \'mā-(,)jē\ emp. of Japan (1867–1912); his reign saw return of power to emperor, feudal system abolished, fiefs of great clans surrendered, and Western ideas and customs introduced

Mu·zo·re·wa \,mù-zə-'rā-wə\ Abel Tendekayi 1925–   prime min. of Zimbabwe Rhodesia (1979–80)

Muz·zey \'mə-zē\ David Saville 1870–1965 Am. hist.; author of *An American History, History of the American People*, etc.

Myr·dal \'mœr-,däl, 'mər-, 'mir-\ Alva 1902–1986 Swed. sociologist & diplomat; awarded (with A. Garcia Robles) 1982 Nobel prize for peace for contributions to the U.N. disarmament negotiations

Myrdal (Karl) Gunnar 1898–1987 Swed. econ.; awarded (with F. von Hayek) 1974 Nobel prize for economics for work in the theory of money and economic change and in the relationship between economic and social factors

My·ron \'mī-rən\ *fl ca* 480–440 B.C. Greek sculptor; considered one of the greatest Attic sculptors esp. for such works as *Discus Thrower*

N

Na·bo·kov \nə-'bȯ-kəf\ Vladimir Vladimirovich 1899–1977 Am. (Russ.-born) nov. & poet; known for novels *Lolita* (1955), *Pnin* (1957), *Pale Fire* (1962), *Ada* (1969), etc., and for earlier poems — **Na·bo·ko·vi·an** \na-bə-'kȯ-vē-ən\ *adj*

Na·der \'nā-dər\ Ralph 1934–   Am. consumer advocate; campaigner for consumer rights and protection through the establishment of effective lobbies

Nai·du \'nī-(,)dü\ Sarojini 1879–1949 Indian poet & reformer; first woman president of Indian National Congress; known as the "nightingale of India" for her poetry

Nai·paul \'nī-,pȯl\ Sir Vidiadhar Surajprasad 1932–   Trinidadian novelist; as one of Indian descent, wrote works concerned with exile and alienation among postcolonial peoples, including *A House for Mr. Biswas, A Bend in the River*, etc.

Na·ka·so·ne \nä-kə-'sō-nē\ Yasuhiro 1918–   prime min. of Japan (1982–87)

Na·math \'nā-məth\ Joseph William 1943–   *Joe Namath* Am. football player; quarterback, New York Jets (1965–77); led team to victory in first Super Bowl

Na·mier \'na-,mir\ Sir Lewis Bernstein 1888–1960 Brit. hist.; author of *England in the Age of the American Revolution, Europe in Decay*, etc.

Nā·nak \'nä-nək\ 1469–1539 founder of the Sikh faith in India

Nan·sen \'nän(t)-sən, 'nan(t)-\ Frid·tjof \'fri-,chȯf\ 1861–1930 Norw. arctic explorer, zool., & statesman; awarded 1922 Nobel prize for peace for directing repatriation of WWI prisoners and famine relief in Russia

Na·pier \'nā-pē-ər, -,pir; nə-'pir\ Sir Charles James 1782–1853 Brit. gen.; completed conquest of Sind and subdued hill tribes in India

Napier *or* **Ne·per** \'nā-pər\ John 1550–1617 Laird of *Mer·chis·ton* \'mər-kə-stən\ Scot. math.; invented and explained logarithms; pioneered in use of system of decimal notation, invented "Napier's bones," mechanical devices for computing

Napier Robert Cornelis 1810–1890 1st Baron *Napier of Mag·da·la* \'mag-də-lə\ Brit. field marshal; used special engineering skill in India, China, and Ethiopia to insure British victories

Na·po·léon I \nə-'pōl-yən, -'pō-lē-ən\ *or* **Napoléon Bo·na·parte** \'bō-nə-,pärt\ 1769–1821 emp. of the French (1804–15); as emperor became virtual master of most of Europe although lost control of seas to England; introduced educational and legal reforms, including codification of French laws as *Code Napoléon*; invaded Russia (1812), suffered terrible losses in retreat; gradually overwhelmed by Allies in Europe; abdicated at Fontainebleau and was exiled to Elba (1813); during the Hundred Days, reentered Paris, but defeated at Waterloo (1815); abdicated and surrendered and exiled on St. Helena — **Na·po·le·on·ic** \nə-,pō-lē-'ä-nik\ *adj*

Napoléon II 1811–1832 Duc *de Reichstadt*; son of *Napoléon I & Marie Louise*; named father's successor but not recognized by Allies; under control of Metternich

Napoléon III 1808–1873 *Louis-Napoléon*; son of *Louis Bonaparte*

& *nephew of* Napoléon I emp. of the French (1852–71); worked toward "Latin Empire" in Europe and America, but foiled by forces on both continents; captured and imprisoned during Franco-Prussian War; deposed by National Assembly

Nar·vá·ez \när-'vä-ˌäs\ Pánfilo *de ca* 1480–1528 Span. soldier; aided in conquest of Cuba; set out to conquer Florida

Nash \'nash\ John Forbes Jr. 1928–   Am. econ.; awarded (with J.C. Harsanyi and R. Selten) 1994 Nobel prize for economics for contributions to game theory

Nash Ogden 1902–1971 Am. poet; author esp. of humorous and prosodically unorthodox verse

Nash *or* **Nashe** \'nash\ Thomas 1567–1601 Eng. satirist & dram.; pioneered English picaresque novel; wrote and imprisoned for satire *The Isle of Dogs*

Nash Walter 1882–1968 prime min. of New Zealand (1957–60)

Na·smyth \'nā-ˌsmith, 'nāz-məth\ Alexander 1758–1840 Scot. painter; became "father of Scottish landscape art"

Nas·ser \'nä-sər, 'na-\ Ga·mal \gə-'mäl\ Ab·del \'äb-dᵊl\ 1918–1970 Egypt. polit.; pres. of Egypt (1956–70); nationalized Suez Canal; formed United Arab Republic; built Aswan High Dam on Nile; defeated in war with Israel (1967)

Nast \'nast\ Thomas 1840–1902 Am. (Ger.-born) cartoonist; credited with creating elephant and donkey symbols of political parties, American image of Santa Claus, etc.

Na·than \'nā-thən\ George Jean 1882–1958 Am. editor & drama critic; a founder and editor of *The American Mercury* and *The American Spectator*

Na·thans \'nā-thənz\ Daniel 1928–   Am. microbiologist; awarded (with W. Arber and H.O. Smith) 1978 Nobel prize for physiology or medicine for discoveries in molecular genetics

Na·tion \'nā-shən\ Car·ry \'kar-ē\ Amelia 1846–1911 née *Moore* Am. temperance agitator; armed with a hatchet, went on wrecking expeditions of places selling intoxicants throughout Kansas

Nat·ta \'nät-(ˌ)tä\ Giulio 1903–1979 Ital. chem.; awarded (with K. Ziegler) 1963 Nobel prize for chemistry for contributions to the understanding of polymers

Nav·ra·ti·lo·va \ˌna-vrə-tə-'lō-və, nə-ˌvrä-\ Martina 1956–   Am. (Czech-born) tennis player; won 54 Grand Slam events, including 9 singles titles at Wimbledon

Neb·u·cha·drez·zar II \ˌne-byə-kə-'dre-zər, -bə-\ *or* **Neb·u·chad·nez·zar** \-kəd-'ne-\ *ca* 630–562 B.C. Chaldean king of Babylon (605–562); captured and destroyed Jerusalem and carried Jews in exile to Babylon; restored Babylon and other cities

Nec·ker \nā-'ker, 'ne-kər\ Jacques 1732–1804 *father of Mme. de Staël* Fr. (Swiss-born) financier & statesman; his dismissal as director general of finance was immediate cause of storming of Bastille

Né·el \nā-el\ Louis-Eugène-Félix 1904–   Fr. physicist; awarded (with H.O.G. Alfvén) 1970 Nobel prize for physics for discovery of magnetic properties that apply to computer memories

Ne·he·mi·ah \ˌnē-(h)ə-'mī-ə\ 5th cent. B.C. Jewish leader; supervised rebuilding of Jerusalem; instituted religious reforms in the city

Neher **250**

Neh·er \\'nā(-ə)r\\ Erwin 1944–   Ger. biochem.; awarded (with B. Sakmann) 1991 Nobel prize for physiology or medicine for discovering how cells communicate with each other

Neh·ru \\'ner-(,)ü, 'nā-(,)rü\\ Ja·wa·har·lal \\jə-'wä-hər-,läl\\ 1889–1964 *son of Motilal* Indian nationalist; prime min. (1947–64); first prime min. of independent India; chief architect of politics of nonalignment

Nehru Pan·dit \\'pən-dət\\ Mo·ti·lal \\'mōt-ə-,äl\\ 1861–1931 Indian nationalist; formulated plan for dominion status for India; advocated campaign of civil disobedience

Neil·son \\'nē(ə)l-sən\\ William Allan 1869–1946 Am. (Scot.-born) educ.; pres., Smith College (1917–39); editor in chief, *Webster's New International Dictionary*, Second Edition (1934)

Nel·son \\'nel-sən\\ Horatio 1758–1805 Viscount *Nelson* Brit. admiral; naval commander during the Napoleonic wars; won crucial victories in the Battle of the Nile (1798) and Battle of Trafalgar (1805); infamous for his illicit love affair with Lady Hamilton

Nem·e·rov \\'ne-mə-,rȯf, -,rȯv\\ Howard 1920–1991 Am. writer; poet laureate (1988–90); known for literary prose works and blank verse

Ne·pos \\'nē-,päs, 'ne-\\ Cornelius *ca* 100–*ca* 25 B.C. Rom. hist.; friend of Catullus and Cicero; only extant work is a fragment of Roman biographical compendium, *De viris illustribus*

Ne·ri \\'ner-ē, 'nā-rē\\ Saint Philip 1515–1595 It. *Filippo Neri* Ital. founder (1564) of "Fathers of the Oratory", from which came name *oratorio* for a form of musical composition

Nernst \\'nern(t)st\\ Walther Hermann 1864–1941 Ger. physicist & chem.; awarded 1920 Nobel prize for chemistry for his discoveries concerning heat changes in chemical reactions

Ne·ro \\'nē-(,)rō, 'nir-(,)ō\\ A.D. 37–68 *Nero Claudius Caesar Drusus Germanicus* orig. *Lucius Domitius Ahenobarbus* Rom. emp. 54–68; reign became increasingly violent and despotic with murder of family members and advisers and, possibly, persecution of Christians; declared public enemy by Senate — **Ne·ro·ni·an** \\ni-'rō-nē-ən\\ *or* **Ne·ron·ic** \\-'rä-nik\\ *adj*

Ne·ru·da \\nā-'rü-də, -(,)thä\\ Pablo 1904–1973 *Neftalí Ricardo Reyes Basoalto* Chilean poet & diplomat; awarded 1971 Nobel prize for literature for his poems

Ner·va \\'nər-və\\ Marcus Cocceius *ca* A.D. 30–98 Rom. emp. (96–98); unable to repress excesses of praetorian guard

Ner·vi \\'ner-vē\\ Pier Luigi 1891–1979 Ital. engineer & architect; known for designs utilizing reinforced concrete cast in place, or prefabricated, achieving new versatility and beauty in material

Nes·to·ri·us \\ne-'stȯr-ē-əs, -'stȯr-\\ *d ca* 451 patriarch of Constantinople (428–431); preached doctrine that the divine and human natures of Christ were one in action but not one in person; deposed for heresy, but doctrine spread widely in Asia

Neu·rath \\'nȯi-,rät\\ Konstantin 1873–1956 Freiherr *von Neurath* Ger. diplomat; "protector" for Bohemia and Moravia (1939–41); imprisoned for war crimes

Nev·el·son \\'ne-vəl-sən\\ Louise 1900–1988 Am. (Russ.-born) sculptor; best known for white or gold environmental sculptures and later work with plexiglas and aluminum

Neville Richard — see Earl of WARWICK

Nev·in \'ne-vən\ Ethelbert Woodbridge 1862–1901 Am. composer; composed songs and short piano pieces published in *Water Scenes, In Arcady*, etc.; songs included "Mighty lak' a Rose"

Nev·ins \'ne-vənz\ Allan 1890–1971 Am. hist.; awarded Pulitzer prizes for *Grover Cleveland—A Study in Courage* and *Hamilton Fish—The Inner History of the Grant Administration*

New·bolt \'nü-ˌbōlt, 'nyü-\ Sir Henry John 1862–1938 Eng. author; wrote novels, renowned poetry as "Drake's Drum," and two-volume official history of the British Navy

New·comb \'nü-kəm, 'nyü-\ Simon 1835–1909 Am. (Canad.-born) astron.; secured international adoption of system of astronomical constants

New·man \'nü-mən, 'nyü-\ John Henry 1801–1890 Eng. cardinal & writer; acknowledged leader of the Tractarian, or Oxford, Movement; became Roman Catholic and produced *Apologia pro Vita Sua*

Newman Paul 1925–   Am. actor; known for his quirky portrayals of nonconformist loners; starred in films *The Hustler, Hud, Cool Hand Luke*, etc.

New·ton \'nü-t⁵n, 'nyü-\ Sir Isaac 1642–1727 Eng. math. & physicist; author of *Principia* (1687), one of the seminal works of modern science; laid the foundation of calculus; expanded human understanding of color and light; formulated three fundamental laws of mechanics, leading to the law of gravitation — **New·to·ni·an** \nü-'tō-nē-ən, nyü-, -nyən\ *adj*

Ney \'nā\ Michel 1769–1815 Duc *d'Elchingen*; Prince *de la Moskova* Fr. soldier; marshal of France; one of Napoleon's top marshals; rejoined him for the Hundred Days despite pledge to restored Bourbon monarchy; commanded Old Guard at Waterloo

Nich·o·las \'ni-k(ə-)ləs\ Saint 4th cent. Christian prelate; patron saint of Greece and Russia and of mariners, thieves, virgins, and children

Nicholas name of 2 czars of Russia: **I** 1796–1855 (reigned 1825–55); represented autocracy, post-Napoléonic reactionarism, militarism, bureaucracy; provoked Crimean War; **II** 1868–1918 (reigned 1894–1917); dissatisfaction with foreign and domestic policies resulted in Revolution; executed at Yekaterinburg with his family

Nicholas *Russ* **Ni·ko·lay Ni·ko·lay·e·vich** \'nyē-kə-ˌlī-ˌnyē-kə-'li(-ə)-ˌvyich\ 1856–1929 Russ. grand duke & army officer; commander in chief against Germany, Austria-Hungary in WWI; leader of monarchists in exile in France

Nicholas of Cu·sa \-'kyü-sə, -zə\ 1401–1464 Ger. cardinal, math. & philos.; anticipated Copernicus by belief in earth's rotation and revolution around sun

Nich·ols \'ni-kəlz\ Mike 1931–   orig. *Michael Igor Pesch·kow·sky* \pesh-'kóf-skē\ Am. stage & film director; best known for productions depicting the absurdities and tribulations of modern life; directed plays *The Odd Couple, The Prisoner of 2nd Avenue*, films *Who's Afraid of Virginia Woolf?, The Graduate*, etc.

Nich·ol·son \'ni-kəl-sən\ Ben 1894–1982 Brit. painter; influenced by Vorticism and Cubism and known for abstract or semiabstract still lifes and landscapes in which plane of picture is emphasized

Nicholson Jack 1937–   Am. actor; noted for his portrayals of rebellious outsiders, as in films *Five Easy Pieces, One Flew Over the Cuckoo's Nest, Prizzi's Honor,* etc.

Ni·ci·as \'ni-shē-əs, -sē-\ d 413 B.C. Athenian gen. & statesman; during the Peloponnesian War between Sparta and Athens commanded the failed siege of Syracuse

Nick·laus \'ni-klas\ Jack William 1940–   Am. golfer; won 71 tournaments, including 20 major championships; won U.S. Masters a record 6 times (1963, 1965, 1966, 1972, 1975, 1986)

Nic·o·lay \'ni-kə-,lā\ John George 1832–1901 Am. biographer; collaborator with John Jay in biography of Abraham Lincoln

Ni·co·let \,ni-kə-'lā, -'let\ Jean 1598–1642 Fr. explorer in No. America; first European to reach Lake Michigan-Wisconsin region

Ni·colle \nē-kól\ Charles-Jean-Henri 1866–1936 Fr. physician & bacteriol.; awarded 1928 Nobel prize for physiology or medicine for his work on typhus

Nic·ol·son \'ni-kəl-sən\ Sir Harold George 1886–1968 Eng. biographer & diplomat; author of biographies of Paul Verlaine, Tennyson, Byron, etc.

Nie·buhr \'nē-,búr, -bər\ Barthold Georg 1776–1831 Ger. hist., statesman, & philologist; known for his work *Römische Geschichte (Roman History),* which virtually created scientific historical scholarship

Niebuhr Rein·hold \'rīn-,hōld\ 1892–1971 Am. theol.; known for doctrine of Christian Realism, criticisms of Social Gospel liberalism — **Nie·buhr·ian** \nē-'búr-ē-ən\ *adj*

Niel·sen \'nē(ə)l-sən\ Carl August 1865–1931 Dan. composer; composed 6 symphonies, 2 operas, concertos, sonatas, quartets, piano pieces, etc.

Niem·ce·wicz \nyemt-'sā-vich\ Julian Ursyn 1758–1841 Pol. patriot & writer; involved in revolution and died in exile; wrote political comedy, song poems, first Polish historical novel

Nie·mey·er \'nē-,mī(-ə)r\ Oscar 1907–   in full Oscar Niemeyer *Soares Filho* Braz. architect; chief architect and co-ordinator of development of Brasilia

Nie·möl·ler \'nē-,mə(r)l-ər, -,mœl-\ (Friedrich Gustav Emil) Martin 1892–1984 Ger. Protestant theol.; publicly opposed Hitler and Nazi regime; released Declaration of Guilt by German churches after war

Nietz·sche \'nē-chə, -chē\ Friedrich Wilhelm 1844–1900 Ger. philos.; known for denouncing religion, for espousing doctrine of perfectibility of man, and for glorification of the superman (Übermensche) — **Nietz·sche·an** \-chē-ən\ *adj*

Night·in·gale \'ni-t°n-,gāl, -,tiŋ-\ Florence 1820–1910 Eng. nurse & philanthropist; organized nursing care during Crimean War and later founded first institution in the world to train nurses

Ni·jin·ska \nə-'zhin-skə, -'jin-\ Bro·ni·sła·wa \,brä-nə-'slä-və\ 1891–1972 *sister of following* Russ. (Pol.-born) dancer & choreographer; choreographed esp. works of Stravinsky, Poulenc, Ravel, Milhaud

Ni·jin·sky \nə-'zhin-skē, -'jin-\ Vas·lav \'vät-släf\ Fomich 1890–1950 Russ. dancer; rejected conventional ballet for free form of expression and known for powerful, graceful technique in ballets as *Les Sylphides, Pétrouchka, L'Après-midi d'un faune,* etc.

Nils·son \'nil-sən\ Birgit 1918–   Swed. soprano; leading Wagnerian soprano of her day, with a powerful voice and great physical presence and endurance

Nim·itz \'ni-məts\ Chester William 1885–1966 Am. admiral; commander in chief of U.S. Pacific fleet (1941–45) and chief of naval operations (1945–47)

Nin \'nēn\ Anaïs 1903–1977 Am. (Fr.-born) author; under influence of surrealism and psychoanalysis, wrote short stories, criticism, novels *House of Incest, Seduction of the Minotaur,* etc., and, published posthumously, *Diary*

Ni·ren·berg \'nir-ən-,bərg\ Marshall Warren 1927–   Am. geneticist; awarded (with R.W. Holley and H.G. Khorana) 1968 Nobel prize for physiology or medicine for explaining how genes determine the function of cells

Nit·ti \'ni-tē, 'nē-\ Francesco Saverio 1868–1953 Ital. econ. & polit.; prime min. (1919–20); author of *The Decadence of Europe, Bolshevism, Fascism, and Democracy,* etc.

Nix·on \'nik-sən\ Richard Milhous 1913–1994 Am. polit.; 37th pres. of the U.S. (1969–74); gradually withdrew U.S. ground forces from Vietnam and transferred combat role to South Vietnamese; imposed wage and price controls to stem inflation; reopened direct communications with People's Republic of China and visited that country; became first U.S. president to resign from office, having been threatened with impeachment for role in Watergate scandal — **Nix·on·esque** \,nik-sə-'nesk\ *or* **Nix·o·ni·an** \nik-'sō-nē-ən, -nyən\ *adj*

Nkru·mah \en-'krü-mə, eŋ-\ Kwa·me \'kwä-mē\ 1909–1972 prime min. (1952–60) & 1st pres. (1960–66) of Ghana; overthrown by coup

No·bel \nō-'bel\ Alfred Bernhard 1833–1896 Swed. manuf., inventor, & philanthropist; invented dynamite and over 100 other patented items; bequeathed fund of $9,200,000 for establishment of Nobel prizes, first awarded 1901

No·bi·le \'nò-bə-,lā\ Umberto 1885–1978 Ital. arctic explorer & aeronautical engineer; flew across north pole in airship *Norge,* designed by him, with Amundsen, Ellsworth

No·el–Ba·ker \,nō-əl-'bā-kər\ Philip John 1889–1982 Brit. polit.; awarded 1959 Nobel prize for peace for his work in promoting peace and disarmament

No·gu·chi \nō-'gü-chē\ Hideyo 1876–1928 Am. (Jp.-born) bacteriol.; discovered causative agent of syphilis and devised Noguchi test to diagnose disease

Noguchi Isamu 1904–1988 Am. sculptor; known for large-scale public sculpture, often of stone

Nor·dau \'nòr-,daù\ Max Simon 1849–1923 orig. *Süd·feld* \'züet-,felt\ Ger. (Hung.-born) physician, author, & Zionist; supported acceptance of East Africa as Jewish settlement; wrote critical and satirical works on moral and social questions, etc.

Nor·den·skiöld \'nùr-d'n-,shəld, -,shùld, -,shēld\ Baron (Nils) Adolf Erik 1832–1901 Swed. arctic explorer; accomplished Northeast Passage in the *Vega;* penetrated great sea ice barrier of Greenland

Nor·man \'nȯr-mən\ Jessye 1945– Am. soprano; known for her rich tone, broad register, and command of dynamics; made operatic debut as Elisabeth in Wagner's *Tannhäuser*

Nor·ris \'nȯr-əs, 'när-\ Benjamin Franklin 1870–1902 *Frank; bro. of C. G.* Am. nov.; a pioneer of American Naturalism in novels *Blix, McTeague,* etc.

Norris Charles Gilman 1881–1945 Am. nov.; author of *Brass, Bread, Hands,* etc.

Norris George William 1861–1944 Am. statesman; secured passage of act creating Tennessee Valley Authority; wrote the 20th Amendment to the Constitution

Nor·rish \'nȯr-ish\ Ronald George Wreyford 1897–1978 Brit. chem.; awarded (with M. Eigen and G. Porter) 1967 Nobel prize for chemistry for developing techniques to measure rapid chemical reactions

North \'nȯrth\ Christopher — see John WILSON

North Douglass Cecil 1920– Am. econ.; awarded (with R.W. Fogel) 1993 Nobel prize for economics for work in economic history

North Frederick 1732–1792 *Lord North* Eng. statesman; prime min. (1770–82); pursued ruinous policy leading to loss of American colonies

North Sir Thomas 1535–?1603 Eng. translator; translated Plutarch's *Lives* from the French, chief source of Shakespeare's knowledge of ancient history

Northcliffe Viscount — see Alfred C. W. HARMSWORTH

Nor·throp \'nȯr-thrəp\ John Howard 1891–1987 Am. biochem.; awarded (with J.B. Sumner and W.M. Stanley) 1946 Nobel prize for chemistry for preparing pure enzymes and virus proteins

Nor·ton \'nȯr-tᵊn\ Charles Eliot 1827–1908 Am. author & educ.; began first college course in fine arts as associated with social, cultural, and literary developments

Norton Thomas 1532–1584 Eng. lawyer & poet; collaborated with Thomas Sackville in blank-verse *Tragedy of Gorboduc,* earliest English tragedy

Nos·tra·da·mus \ˌnäs-trə-'dä-məs, ˌnōs-, -'dā-\ 1503–1566 *Michel de Notredame* or *Nostredame* Fr. physician & astrologer; produced *Centuries,* rhymed predictions in ambiguous phrasing

No·vel·lo \nō-'ve-(ˌ)lō\ Antonia Coello 1944– U.S. surgeon general (1990–93)

Noyes \'nȯiz\ Alfred 1880–1958 Eng. poet; author of poems *The Loom of Years,* etc., and of criticism, plays, short stories, novels

Nu·re·yev \nu̇-'rā-yəf\ Rudolf Hametovich 1938–1993 Russ.-born ballet dancer; became regular partner of Dame Margot Fonteyn; famed for strength, technique, emotional content of his dancing

Nut·ting \'nə-tiŋ\ Wallace 1861–1941 Am. antiquarian; author of *Old New England Pictures, The Clock Book, Furniture Treasury,* etc.

Nye \'nī\ Edgar Wilson 1850–1896 *Bill Nye* Am. humorist; author of humorous *Bill Nye's History of the United States,* etc.

O

Oates \'ōts\ Joyce Carol 1938–   Am. writer; author of novels depicting violence and evil in modern society, including *Them*, *Wonderland*, etc.

Oates Titus 1649–1705 Brit. fabricator of the Popish Plot; his false allegations of a Catholic grab for power created a wave of terror in London

O'·Boyle \ō-'boi(ə)l\ Patrick Aloysius 1896–1987 Am. cardinal

Obrenović Alexander I — see ALEXANDER

O'·Ca·sey \ō-'kā-sē\ Sean \'shón\ 1880–1964 orig. *John Casey* Irish dram.; wrote working-class plays as *The Plough and the Stars*, *Purple Dust*, etc.

Occleve — see Thomas HOCCLEVE

Ochoa \ō-'chō-ə\ Severo 1905–1993 Am. (Span.-born) biochem.; awarded (with A. Kornberg) 1959 Nobel prize for physiology or medicine for producing nucleic acid by artificial means

Ochs \'äks\ Adolph Simon 1858–1935 Am. newspaper publisher; acquired (1896) ownership of *The New York Times* and made it one of the world's outstanding newspapers

Ock·ham *or* **Oc·cam** \'ä-kəm\ William *of ca* 1285–?1349 Eng. philos.; best known for Occam's Razor, a philosophical rule that the simplest of competing theories be preferred to the more complex — **Ock·ham·is·tic** *or* **Oc·cam·is·tic** \,ä-kə-'mis-tik\ *adj*

O'·Con·nell \ō-'kä-nºl\ Daniel 1775–1847 Irish nationalist; united Irish Catholics under leadership of priests into league urging Irish claims

O'Connell William Henry 1859–1944 Am. cardinal

O'·Con·nor \ō-'kä-nər\ John Joseph 1920–   Am. cardinal; outspokenly conservative on issues such as abortion

O'Connor (Mary) Flannery 1925–1964 Am. writer; best known for short story collections *A Good Man Is Hard To Find*, *Everything That Rises Must Converge*, etc.

O'Connor Frank 1903–1966 pseud. of *Michael John O'Donovan* Irish author; known mainly for short story collections *The Wild Bird's Nest*, *Bones of Contention*, etc.

O'Connor Sandra Day 1930–   Am. jurist; associate justice, U.S. Supreme Court (1981–   ); first woman to hold this position

O'Connor Thomas Power 1848–1929 *Tay Pay* \'tā-'pā\ Irish journalist; founded radical newspapers, a literary paper, etc.; a supporter of Parnell

Octavius — see AUGUSTUS

Odets \ō-'dets\ Clifford 1906–1963 Am. dram.; author of plays of social protest, including *Waiting for Lefty*, *Golden Boy*, etc.

Odo·a·cer \'ō-də-,wā-sər, ,ä-\ *also* **Odo·va·car** *or* **Odo·va·kar** \-,vä-kər\ 433–493 1st barbarian ruler of Italy (476–493); terminated Western Roman Empire by abolishing title and office of emperor

Oe \'ō-e\ Ken·za·bu·rō \,ken-'zä-bü-rō\ 1935–   Jp. writer; wrote novels reflecting the concerns of Japan's rebellious post-WWII generation; best known to English readers for *The Silent Cry*; awarded 1994 Nobel prize for literature

Oeh·len·schlä·ger \\'ə(r)-lən-ˌshlä-gər, 'öel-\ Adam Gottlob 1779–1850 Dan. poet & dram.; a pioneer of the Romantic movement in Denmark; crowned as "king of the Scandinavian singers"

O'Fao·láin \ˌō-fə-'lón\ Seán \'shón\ 1900–1991 Irish author; known for novel *A Nest of Simple Folk* and for translations from Gaelic, *The Silver Branch*

Of·fen·bach \'ò-fən-ˌbäk, -ˌbäk\ Jacques 1819–1880 Fr. musician & composer; best known for opera (completed by Guiraud) *Tales of Hoffman*, operetta *La Vie parisienne*

O'Fla·her·ty \ō-'fla-(h)ər-tē\ Li·am \'lē-əm\ 1897–1984 Irish nov.; a leader of the Irish Renaissance with novels and short stories

Og·den \'òg-dən, 'äg-\ Charles Kay 1889–1957 Brit. psychol.; invented Basic English, simplified system of 850 words

Ogle·thorpe \'ō-gəl-ˌthòrp\ James Edward 1696–1785 Eng. philanthropist, gen., & founder of Georgia; colonized unemployed men freed from debtor's prison

Ögö·dei \'ō-gə-ˌdā\ *also* **Oga·dai** \-ˌdī\ *or* **Og·dai** \'ò-ˌdī\ *or* **Uge·dei** \'ü-gə-ˌdā\ 1185–1241 Mongol Khan (1229–41); attempted to organize empire set up by father Genghis and increased territory by marauding westward to Adriatic Sea

O'Hara \ō-'har-ə\ John Henry 1905–1970 Am. author; author of novels *Butterfield 8*, etc., short story collection *Pal Joey*, etc., plays, screenplays, and newspaper column

O'Hig·gins \ō-'hi-gənz, ō-'ē-gən(t)s\ Bernardo 1778–1842 *Liberator of Chile* Chilean soldier & statesman; defeated Spanish and became liberal dictator until himself deposed by revolution (1823)

Ohira \ō-'hir-ə\ Masayoshi 1910–1980 prime min. of Japan (1978–80)

Oh·lin \'ō-lin\ Bertil Gotthard 1899–1979 Swed. econ.; awarded (with J. Meade) 1977 Nobel prize for economics for studies of international trade and finance

Ohm \'ōm\ Georg Simon 1787–1854 Ger. physicist; discovered relationship between strength of electrical current, electromotive force, and the resistance of circuit (Ohm's law)

Ois·trakh \'òis-ˌtrak\ David Fyodorovich 1908–1974 Russ. violinist; acclaimed for exceptional technique and tone

O'Keeffe \ō-'kēf\ Georgia 1887–1986 Am. painter; esp. known for flowers, architectural scenes, still lifes in clear colors and surrealist feeling

O'Kel·ly \ō-'ke-lē\ Seán \'shón\ Thomas 1883–1966 Irish journalist; pres. of Republic of Ireland (1945–59)

O'Kelly Seu·mas \'shä-məs\ 1881–1918 Irish writer; author of plays, short stories, esp. *The Weaver's Grave*, and novel *The Lady of Deerpark*

Olaf \'ō-ləf, -ˌläf, -ˌlaf; 'ü-ˌläf\ name of 5 kings of Norway; esp. **Olaf I Trygg·va·son** \'trig-və-sən\ *ca* 964–1000 (reigned 995–1000); led Viking expedition to ravage coasts of England, France, Ireland; a great warrior and popular ruler; **Olaf II Har·alds·son** \'har-əl(d)-sən\ *Saint Olaf* 995?–1030 (reigned 1016–28); attempted to complete conversion of Norway to Christianity and devised religious code of 1024; patron saint of Norway; **Olaf V** 1903–1991 (reigned 1957–91); head of Norwegian armed forces until the end of German occupation

Olah \ˈō-(ˌ)lä\ George Andrew 1927–   Am. (Hung.-born) chem.; awarded 1994 Nobel prize for chemistry for his work in hydrocarbon research

Old·cas·tle \ˈōl(d)-ˌka-səl\ Sir John 1377?–1417 Baron *Cob·ham* \-ˈkä-bəm\ Eng. Lollard leader; hanged as heretic and traitor, and burned while hanging; model for Falstaff in *Henry IV*

Ol·den·bar·ne·velt \ˌōl-dən-ˈbär-nə-ˌvəlt\ Johan van 1547–1619 Du. statesman; a founding father of Dutch independence from Spain

O'Lea·ry \ō-ˈlir-ē\ Hazel Reid 1937–   U.S. secy. of energy (1993–)

Oli·vi·er \ō-ˈli-vē-ˌā\ Laurence Kerr 1907–1989 Baron *Olivier of Brighton* Eng. actor; famed for interpretation of great Shakespearean roles, films *Henry V, Hamlet, Richard III*, television *Brideshead Revisited*, etc.

Olm·sted \ˈōm-ˌsted, ˈäm-, -stəd\ Frederick Law 1822–1903 Am. landscape architect; planned Central Park in New York, grounds of Capitol, Washington, D.C., Boston park system, etc.

Omar Khay·yám \ˌō-ˌmär-ˌkī-ˈyäm, ˌō-mər-, -ˈyam\ 1048?–1122 Pers. poet & astron.; best known for his poems *Robā'iyāt*, known esp. through translation of Edward FitzGerald

Onas·sis \ō-ˈna-səs\ Jacqueline Kennedy 1929–1994 née *Bou·vier* \būˈvyä\ *wife of J. F. Kennedy* Am. socialite; as First Lady restored the White House and made it a salon for artists and performers; celebrated for her beauty, style, and indomitability in the aftermath of tragedy

O'·Neill \ō-ˈnē(ə)l\ Eugene Gladstone 1888–1953 Am. dram.; wrote plays *Strange Interlude, Mourning Becomes Electra, Long Day's Journey into Night*; awarded 1936 Nobel prize for literature

O'Neill Thomas Philip, Jr. 1912–1994 *Tip* Am. polit.; member (1953–87), speaker (1977–87), U.S. House of Representatives

On·ions \ˈən-yənz\ Charles Talbut 1873–1965 Eng. lexicographer; member of editorial staff of *Oxford English Dictionary*

On·sa·ger \ˈön-ˌsä-gər\ Lars 1903–1976 Am. (Norw.-born) chem.; awarded 1968 Nobel prize for chemistry for developing theory of irreversible chemical processes

Op·pen·heim \ˈä-pən-ˌhīm\ Edward Phillips 1866–1946 Eng. nov.; author of over 150 novels, short stories, plays of international espionage and intrigue

Op·pen·hei·mer \ˈä-pən-ˌhī-mər\ (Julius) Robert 1904–1967 Am. physicist; director (1942–45) of Manhattan Project which developed atomic bomb

Or·ca·gna \ȯr-ˈkän-yä\ Andrea *ca* 1308–*ca* 1368 *Andrea di Cione* Florentine painter, sculptor, & architect; known for work on Duomo, Florence, and on Orvieto cathedral

Or·czy \ˈȯrt-sē\ Baroness Em·mus·ka \ˈe-məsh-kə\ 1865–1947 Eng. (Hung.-born) nov. & dram.; best known for novel *The Scarlet Pimpernel*

Orff \ˈȯrf\ Carl 1895–1982 Ger. composer; known for lavish theatrical works, as *Carmina burana, Catulli carmina*, etc.

Or·i·gen \ˈȯr-ə-jən, ˈär-\ 185?–?254 Greek (Egypt.-born) Christian writer, teacher, & church father; produced textual studies on the Old Testament, defense of Christianity against Celsus, etc.

Or·lan·do \or-'lan-(,)dō, -'län-\ Vittorio Emanuele 1860–1952 Ital. statesman; resigned as president of Chamber of Deputies to protest Fascist election fraud (1925)

Or·man·dy \'or-mən-dē\ Eugene 1899–1985 Am. (Hung.-born) conductor; coconductor (1936–38), sole conductor (1938–80) of Philadelphia Orchestra; 44-yr. music directorship was longest in U.S. history; developed lush velvety "Philadelphia sound"

Oroz·co \ō-'rō-(,)skō\ José Clemente 1883–1949 Mex. painter; most important 20th-century muralist to work in fresco

Orr \'ȯr, 'ȯr\ Bobby 1948–   *Robert Gordon Orr* Am. (Canad.-born) hockey player; defenseman, Boston Bruins (1966–76); first defenseman to lead NHL in scoring; set seasonal defenseman records for goals (46), assists (102), and points (139)

Ør·sted \'ə(r)-stəd, 'ær-\ Hans Christian 1777–1851 Dan. physicist & chem.; founded science of electromagnetism

Or·te·ga y Gas·set \or-'tā-gə-,ē-gä-'set\ José 1883–1955 Span. philos., writer, & statesman; author of *Meditations of Quixote, The Theme of Our Time, The Revolt of the Masses,* etc.

Or·well \'or-,wel, -wəl\ George 1903–1950 pseud. of *Eric Blair* Eng. author; best known for political fable *Animal Farm* and Utopian novel *1984* (1949) that portrayed the archetypal totalitarian society — **Or·well·ian** \or-'we-lē-ən\ *adj*

Os·born \'äz-bərn, -,born\ Henry Fairfield 1857–1935 Am. paleontologist; as president of American Museum of Natural History (1908–35), introduced instructional content to museum displays

Os·borne \'äz-bərn, -,born, -,born\ John James 1929–1994 Brit. dram.; one of Britain's Angry Young Men; wrote plays *Look Back in Anger, The Entertainer,* etc.

Osborne Thomas Mott 1859–1926 Am. penologist; through Mutual Welfare League, gave prisoners a measure of self-government and responsibility

Os·car II \'äs-kər\ 1829–1907 king of Sweden (1872–1907) & of Norway (1872–1905); found problem of preserving union between Sweden and Norway impossible

Osce·o·la \,ä-sē-'ō-lə, ,ō-\ *ca* 1800–1838 Seminole Indian chief; leader of Seminoles during Second Seminole War; seized illegally and died in prison

Os·ler \'ōs-lər, 'ōz-\ Sir William 1849–1919 Canad. physician; instrumental in transforming the organization and curriculum of medical education, emphasizing the importance of clinical experience

Os·man I \ōs-'män\ 1258–*ca* 1326 founder of the Ottoman Empire; gradually controlled much Anatolian territory through long war with Byzantines

Os·me·ña \oz-'mān-yə, ōs-\ Sergio 1878–1961 pres. of Philippine Commonwealth (1944–46)

Os·si·etz·ky \,ä-sē-'et-skē\ Carl von 1889–1938 Ger. writer & pacifist; awarded 1935 Nobel prize for peace while in prison; award considered "a challenge and an insult" by Hitler government

Ossoli Marchioness — see Margaret FULLER

Ost·wald \'ōst-,wȯld, -,vȯld\ Friedrich Wilhelm 1853–1932 Ger. physical chem. & philos.; awarded 1909 Nobel prize for chemistry for work on catalysis, chemical equilibrium, rate of chemical reactions

Otis \'ō-təs\ Elwell Stephen 1838–1909 Am. gen.; suppressed Philippine insurrection (1899–1900)

Otis Harrison Gray 1837–1917 Am. gen. & journalist; served through Civil War and in Philippines; editor (from 1882) and owner (from 1886), Los Angeles *Times*

Otis James 1725–1783 Am. statesman in Revolution; among leaders in Massachusetts legislature upholding colonial cause and opposing sundry revenue acts

O'Toole \ō-'tül\ Peter 1932– Brit. actor; noted esp. for his intense portrayals of tormented heroes, as in films *Lawrence of Arabia, Becket, Lord Jim*, etc.

Ot·ter·bein \'ä-tər-ˌbīn\ Philip William 1726–1813 Am. (Ger.-born) clergyman; a founder of the United Brethren in Christ

Ot·to I \'ä-(ˌ)tō\ 912–973 *the Great* Holy Rom. emp. (936–973); defeated Magyars; marched into Rome and Byzantium; revived empire of Charlemagne; deposed Pope John XII

Ot·way \'ät-ˌwā\ Thomas 1652–1685 Eng. dram.; known esp. for his masterpiece, *Venice Preserved*, caricaturing Shaftesbury

Ouida — see Marie Louise de la RAMÉE

Ov·id \'ä-vəd\ 43 B.C.–?A.D. 17 *Publius Ovidius Naso* Rom. poet; best known for *Metamorphoses*, narrative poem recounting legends of miraculous transformation of forms from time of creation — **Ovid·ian** \ä-'vi-dē-ən\ *adj*

Ow·en \'ō-ən\ Robert 1771–1858 Welsh social reformer; based reforms on belief that human character is determined by environment; founded communities of "Owenites" based on cooperative principle

Owen Wilfred 1893–1918 Brit. poet; killed on Western Front and poems against war published posthumously

Ox·en·stier·na \'ük-sen-ˌsher-nä\ Count Axel Gustafsson 1583–1654 Swed. statesman; integral to wars and treaties involving Sweden with Denmark, Russia, Poland, Prussia, Germany, France (1612–54)

Oxford Earl of — see Robert HARLEY

Oza·wa \ō-'zau-ə\ Seiji 1935– Am. (Jp.-born) conductor; musical director, Boston Symphony (1973–); noted esp. for his vigorous conducting style and impassioned renditions of 19th-century Western symphonic works

P

Paa·si·ki·vi \'pä-sə-ˌkē-vē\ Ju·ho \'yü-(ˌ)hō\ Kusti 1870–1956 Finn. businessman; pres. of Finland (1946–56); negotiated end to Russo-Finnish War

Pa·ci·no \pə-'chē-(ˌ)nō\ Al 1940– *Alfred James Pacino* Am. actor; known for his highly visceral peformances in films *Serpico, Scent of a Woman, The Godfather* series, etc.

Pa·de·rew·ski \pa-də-'ref-skē, -'rev-\ Ignacy \ēn-'yäs\ Jan \'yän\ 1860–1941 Pol. pianist, composer, & statesman; a noted interpreter of Schumann, Chopin, Liszt, Beethoven; composer of an opera and instrumental pieces, esp. *Minuet in G;* worked for Polish cause in WWI

Pa·ga·ni·ni \ˌpä-gə-ˈnē-nē, ˌpä-\ Niccolò 1782–1840 Ital. violinist; revolutionized violin technique

Page \ˈpāj\ Geraldine 1924–1987 Am. actress; famed esp. for her interpretations of Tennessee Williams's heroines; appeared in stage and screen versions of *Summer and Smoke, Sweet Bird of Youth,* film *The Trip to Bountiful,* etc.

Page Thomas Nelson 1853–1922 Am. nov. & diplomat; wrote novels *Two Little Confederates, The Old South,* etc.

Page Walter Hines 1855–1918 Am. journalist & diplomat; urged U.S. intervention in WWI

Pag·et \ˈpa-jət\ Sir James 1814–1899 Eng. surgeon & pathologist; a founder of modern science of pathology

Pahlavi — see REZA SHAH PAHLAVI & MOHAMMAD REZA PAHLAVI

Paige \ˈpāj\ Satchel 1906?–1982 *Leroy Robert Paige* Am. baseball player; a pitcher of legendary prowess in the Negro Southern Association and Negro National League during 1930s and 1940s; became (1948) one of the first African-Americans to play in the major leagues

Paine \ˈpān\ Albert Bigelow 1861–1937 Am. author; author of *Mark Twain, A Biography,* etc.

Paine Thomas 1737–1809 Am. (Eng.-born) polit. philos. & author; best known for pamphlet *Common Sense* urging immediate declaration of independence from England

Pain·le·vé \paⁿ-lə-vä\ Paul 1863–1933 Fr. math. & statesman; min. of war (1917, 1925–29); premier of France (1917, 1925)

Pa·la·de \pə-ˈlä-dē\ George Emil 1912–   Am. (Romanian-born) biol.; awarded (with C. de Duve and A. Claude) 1974 Nobel prize for physics for their pioneer work in cell biology

Pa·le·stri·na \ˌpa-lə-ˈstrē-nə\ Giovanni Pierluigi da *ca* 1525–1594 Ital. composer; composed works that represent apex of composition in medieval church modes

Pa·ley \ˈpā-lē\ Grace 1922–   *orig. surname Goodside* Am. writer; known for her seriocomic portrayals of working-class New Yorkers in volumes of short stories, including *Enormous Changes at the Last Minute, Later the Same Day,* etc.

Paley William 1743–1805 Eng. theol. & philos.; wrote essay *Horae Paulinae* showing improbability of hypothesis that New Testament is a "cunningly devised fable"

Pal·grave \ˈpal-ˌgräv, ˈpȯl-\ Francis Turner 1824–1897 Eng. writer; published volumes of poetry, critical essays, and well known anthologies *Golden Treasury of the Best Songs and Lyrical Poems in the English Language,* etc.

Pal·la·dio \pə-ˈlä-dē-ˌō\ Andrea 1508–1580 Ital. architect; adapted principles of Roman architecture; devised Palladian motif of bay with rounded opening flanked by two squared openings — **Pal·la·di·an** \pə-ˈlä-dē-ən\ *adj*

Palma Tomás Estrada — see ESTRADA PALMA

Palm·er \ˈpä-mər, ˈpäl-mər\ Alice Elvira 1855–1902 née *Freeman; wife of G. H.* Am. educ.; pres., Wellesley Coll. (1882–88)

Palmer Arnold Daniel 1929–   Am. golfer; first to win the Masters Tournament four times; first to accumulate $1 million in prize money

Palmer Daniel David 1845–1913 Am. chiropractor; founder of chiropractic in America

Palmer George Herbert 1842–1933 Am. scholar & educ.; author of *The Odyssey of Homer* (translation), *The Field of Ethics*, etc.

Palmer James Alvin 1945–   *Jim Palmer* Am. baseball player; pitcher, Baltimore Orioles (1966–84); winner of Cy Young award (1973, 1975, 1976)

Palm·er·ston \'pä-mər-stən, 'päl-\ 3d Viscount 1784–1865 *Henry John Temple* Eng. statesman; prime min. (1855–58; 1859–65); one of most popular ministers in English history — **Palm·er·sto·nian** \,pä-mər-'stō-nē-ən, ,päl-, -nyən\ *adj*

Palm·gren \'päm-grən, 'pälm-\ Selim 1878–1951 Finn. pianist & composer; composer of operas, symphonic poem, concertos, piano pieces

Pā·ni·ni \'pä-nə-(,)nē, 'pän-yə-; pä-'nē-nē\ *fl ca* 400 B.C. Indian grammarian of Sanskrit; author of *Aṣṭādhyāyī*, oldest Sanskrit grammar and perhaps oldest extant grammar in the world

Pank·hurst \'paŋk-,hərst\ Emmeline 1858–1928 née *Goulden* Eng. suffragist; author of first woman-suffrage bill in Great Britain and of the Married Women's Property acts

Pan·ni·ni or **Pa·ni·ni** \pä-'nē-(,)nē\ Giovanni Paolo 1691–1765 Ital. painter; noted esp. for paintings of views of ancient Rome

Pa·nof·sky \pä-'nôf-skē\ Erwin 1892–1968 Am. (Ger.-born) art historian; author of books on medieval and Renaissance art, as *Albrecht Dürer, Gothic Architecture and Scholasticism*, etc.

Pa·o·li \'paù-lē, pä-ō-(,)lē\ Pasquale 1725–1807 Corsican patriot; as ruler after expulsion of Genoese, established more just and orderly government, built up navy, instituted schools

Pa·pan·dre·ou \,pä-pän-'drä-ü\ Andreas Georgios 1919–1996 prime min. of Greece (1981–89; 1993–96)

Pa·pen \'pä-pən\ Franz von 1879–1969 Ger. diplomat; instrumental in dissolving the Weimar Republic and allowing Adolf Hitler to assume chancellorship (1933)

Pap·pen·heim \'pä-pən-,hīm, 'pa-\ Gottfried Heinrich 1594–1632 Graf *zu Pappenheim* Ger. gen.; famed as cavalry commander in Thirty Years' War

Par·a·cel·sus \,par-ə-'sel-səs\ 1493–1541 pseud. of *Philippus Aureolus Theophrastus Bombast von Hohenheim* Swiss-born alchemist & physician; believed that diseases are specific entities rather than humors and can be cured by specific remedies

Pa·re·to \pə-'rā-(,)tō\ Vilfredo 1848–1923 Ital. econ. & sociol.; provided, with his theories of the superiority of the elite, basis for fascist ideology

Pa·ris \'pä-rēs, pə-\ (Bruno-Paulin-) Gaston 1839–1903 Fr. philologist; greatest French philologist of his time; helped found *Revue critique* (1866), *Romania* (1872)

Par·is \'par-əs\ Matthew *d* 1259 Eng. monk & hist.; a major source for record of European events between 1235 and 1259

Park Chung Hee \'pärk-'chəŋ-'hē\ 1917–1979 So. Korean leader (1961–79) & pres. (1963–79); guided economic growth of South Korea; assassinated

Park \\'pärk\\ Mungo 1771–1806 Scot. explorer; wrote about explorations of Gambia, Senegal, and Niger rivers in *Travels in the Interior Districts of Africa*

Par·ker \\'pär-kər\\ Dorothy 1893–1967 née *Rothschild* Am. writer; member of 1920's "Algonquin Round Table", known for acerbic wit

Parker Sir Gilbert 1862–1932 Canad. author; champion of imperialism; noted for portrayal of Canadian life and characters

Parker Matthew 1504–1575 Eng. theol.; sought to establish ecclesiastical forms midway between Romanism and Puritanism; oversaw formulation of Church of England doctrinal statements

Parker Robert Brown 1932– Am. nov.; best known for series of mystery novels featuring private detective Spenser

Parker Theodore 1810–1860 Am. Unitarian clergyman; associate of Transcendentalists; involved in social causes of the day

Parkes \\'pärks\\ Sir Henry 1815–1896 Austral. statesman; instituted free trade policy; reformed civil service; established compulsory free education; excluded Chinese immigrants, etc.

Park·man \\'pärk-mən\\ Francis 1823–1893 Am. hist.; published *England and France in North America* (7 vols.), *The Oregon Trail*, etc.

Parks \\'pärks\\ Rosa Lee 1913– Am. civil rights activist; her refusal to relinquish her seat on a Montgomery, Ala., bus to a white sparked a landmark civil rights boycott

Parley Peter — see Samuel Griswold GOODRICH

Par·men·i·des \\pär-'me-nə-ˌdēz\\ *b ca* 515 B.C. Greek philos.; founder of Eleatic school

Par·mi·gia·ni·no \\ˌpär-mi-jä-'nē-(ˌ)nō\\ *or* **Par·mi·gia·no** \\-mə-'jä-(ˌ)nō\\ 1503–1540 *Girolamo Francesco Maria Mazzuoli or Mazzola* Ital. painter; reacted against High Renaissance classicism and initiated Mannerism, esp. in portraits

Par·nell \\pär-'nel\\ Charles Stewart 1846–1891 Irish nationalist; the leader in the struggle for Irish Home Rule in the late 19th century

Parr Catherine — see CATHERINE

Par·ring·ton \\'par-iŋ-tən\\ Vernon Louis 1871–1929 Am. lit. hist.; known esp. for political liberalism and economic determinism of *Main Currents in American Thought*

Par·rish \\'par-ish\\ Maxfield Frederick 1870–1966 Am. painter; best known as illustrator for advertisements, magazines, books such as *Mother Goose in Prose*, Grahame's *Dream Days*, etc.

Par·ry \\'par-ē\\ Sir William Edward 1790–1855 Eng. explorer; attempted to reach North Pole from Spitzbergen (1827) and reached latitude 82° 45', not reached again until 1876

Par·sons \\'pär-s'nz\\ Talcott 1902–1979 Am. sociol.; developed general theoretical system for analysis of society in *Structure of Social Action, Social System*, etc.

Parsons William 1800–1867 3d Earl of *Rosse* Irish astron.; built "Leviathan" telescope incorporating his improvements and used it to study and name Crab Nebula, discover binary and triple stars, etc.

Pas·cal \\pa-'skal, pás-kál\\ Blaise 1623–1662 Fr. math. & philos.; founder of modern theory of probability; his studies in hydrodynamics and hydrostatic and atmospheric pressure led him to discover Pascal's law of pressure and principle of the hydraulic press, in *Pensées* presented his influential ideas on "inner religion"— **Pas·cal·ian** \pa-'ska-lē-ən\ *adj*

Pa·šić \'pä-(,)shich\ Nicola \'nē-kō-lä\ 1845–1926 Serbian & Yugoslav statesman; premier of Serbia and successor Yugoslavia (1906–26) with few interruptions; guided policy through WWI and creation of Yugoslavia

Pa·so·li·ni \,pä-sō-'lē-(,)nē\ Pier Paolo 1922–1975 Ital. film director, poet, & nov.; imparted his Marxist sensibility to such films as *Accattone, The Gospel According to Saint Matthew, Il Decamerone,* etc.

Passfield \'pas-,feld\ 1st Baron — see WEBB

Pas·sy \pa-'sē, pä-\ Frédéric 1822–1912 Fr. econ. & statesman; awarded first Nobel prize for peace (1901) for founding a French peace society (shared with J.-H. Dunant)

Passy Paul-Édouard 1859–1940 *son of prec.* Fr. phonetician; chief originator of the phonetic alphabet

Pas·ter·nak \'pas-tər-,nak\ Boris Leonidovich 1890–1960 Soviet (Russ.-born) poet, nov., & translator; awarded 1959 Nobel prize for literature for his novels, esp. *Dr. Zhivago*

Pas·teur \pas-'tər\ Louis 1822–1895 Fr. chem. & microbiologist; did pioneer work in the study of microorganisms and their effects; developed method of inoculating against anthrax and chicken cholera; developed cure and prevention for rabies — **Pas·teur·ian** \-ē-ən\ *adj*

Pa·ter \'pā-tər\ Walter Horatio 1839–1894 Eng. essayist & critic; interpreted the Humanism of Renaissance art and literature in *Studies in the History of the Renaissance*

Pat·more \'pat-,mōr, -,mȯr\ Coventry Kersey Dighton 1823–1896 Eng. poet; known esp. for poetic celebration of married love, *The Angel in the House*

Pa·ton \'pā-tᵊn\ Alan Stewart 1903–1988 So. African writer; wrote *Cry the Beloved Country* (1948), bringing world attention to South African apartheid

Pat·rick \'pa-trik\ Saint 5th cent. A.D. apostle & patron saint of Ireland; a leader in conversion of Irish race to Catholicism

Pat·ti \'pa-tē, pä-\ Adelina 1843–1919 Am. (Span.-born) soprano; considered one of the greatest coloratura singers of the 19th century in operas of Bellini, Rossini, Gounod, etc.

Pat·ti·son \'pa-tə-sən\ Mark 1813–1884 Eng. scholar & author; investigated Continental systems of education; wrote *Life of John Milton,* etc.

Pat·ton \'pa-tᵊn\ George Smith 1885–1945 *Old Blood and Guts* Am. gen.; one of finest practitioners of mobile tank warfare as demonstrated in North Africa, Sicily, Europe during WWII

Paul \'pȯl\ Saint *d bet* 62 and 68 A.D. Jewish name *Saul* early Christian apostle & missionary; zealous opponent of Christianity until conversion on road to Damascus; went on missionary journeys to Asia Minor, Greece; founded many churches to which he sent epistles (Pauline epistles of New Testament)

Paul name of 6 popes: esp. **III** 1468–1549 (pope 1534–49); began Counter-Reformation; commissioned Michelangelo to construct the new St. Peter's, paint *Last Judgment* and Sistine Chapel ceiling, etc.; **V** 1552–1621 (pope 1605–21); forbade English Catholics to

swear allegiance to king; encouraged missions to Latin America;
VI (*Giovanni Battista Montini*) 1897–1978 (pope 1963–78); issued
encyclicals for clerical celibacy, against birth control

Paul I 1754–1801 emp. of Russia (1796–1801); made reforms in
treatment of serfs, but antagonized nobility and army; assassinated

Paul I 1901–1964 king of Greece (1947–64)

Paul Alice 1885–1977 Am. suffragist; a leader in the campaign for
a woman suffrage amendment to the U.S. Constitution; wrote
(1923) the first constitutional amendment mandating equal rights

Paul Jean — see RICHTER

Paul \'paúl\ Wolfgang 1913–1993 Ger. physicist; awarded (with
H.G. Dehmelt and N. Ramsey) 1989 Nobel prize for physics for
isolating and measuring single atoms

Paul–Bon·cour \'pôl-(,)bôⁿ-'kúr\ Joseph 1873–1972 Fr. lawyer &
statesman; known for support of League of Nations and for work
in French resistance to German occupation

Paul·ding \'pôl-diŋ\ James Kirke 1778–1860 Am. author; prominent in literary war with English writers and in advocating use of
American scenes and material in literature

Pau·li \'paú-lē\ Wolfgang 1900–1958 Am. (Austrian-born) physicist; awarded 1945 Nobel prize for physics for his discovery of the
Pauli exclusion principle

Pau·ling \'pô-liŋ\ Li·nus \'lī-nəs\ Carl 1901–1994 Am. chem.;
awarded 1954 Nobel prize for chemistry for work on the forces
that hold matter together

Pau·lus \'paú-ləs\ Friedrich 1890–1957 Ger. field marshal;
commander of German 6th army; captured at Stalingrad, ending
German offense in Russia

Pau·lus \'pô-ləs\ Julius 2d–3d cent. A.D. Rom. jurist; one of greatest of Roman jurists

Pau·sa·ni·as \pô-'sā-nē-əs\ *fl* A.D. 143–176 Greek traveler & geographer; author of *Periegesis of Greece,* valuable source of information on topography, local history, religion, architecture, sculpture

Pa·va·rot·ti \,pä-və-'rä-(,)tē, ,pa-, -'rô-\ Luciano 1935– Ital.
tenor; performed in operatic houses and concert halls worldwide;
celebrated for the purity of his voice and ability to reach the highest notes in a tenor's range

Pav·lov \'päv-,lòf, 'pav-, -,lòv\ Ivan Petrovich 1849–1936 Russ.
physiol.; awarded 1904 Nobel prize for physiology or medicine for
work on the physiology of digestion; best known for experiment
demonstrating conditioned reflex in a dog — **Pav·lov·ian** \pav-
'lò-vē-ən, -'lò-; -'lò-fē-\ *adj*

Pav·lo·va \'pav-lə-və, pav-'lō-\ Anna 1882–1931 Russ. ballerina;
famed for dance creations such as *Le Cygne (The Swan), Papillons
(Butterflies),* etc.

Pay·ton \'pā-t³n\ Walter Jerry 1954– Am. football player;
with Chicago Bears (1975–88); regarded as greatest running back
in football history; set records for total career rushing yardage
(16,726 yards), most combined career yards gained (rushing and
pass receiving; 21,803 yards), etc.

Paz \'päs, 'päz\ Octavio 1914– Mex. author; author of poems,
essays, literary criticism, etc.; awarded 1990 Nobel prize for literature

Pea·body \'pē-,bä-dē, -bə-dē\ Endicott 1857–1944 Am. educ.; a founder and first head of Groton School, Groton, Mass.

Peabody George 1795–1869 Am. merchant & philanthropist; founded and endowed Peabody Institute, Baltimore; Peabody Institute, Peabody, Mass.; Peabody Museums, Harvard and Yale, etc.

Pea·cock \'pē-,käk\ Thomas Love 1785–1866 Eng. nov. & poet; author of satirical and Romantic novels, esp. *Nightmare Abbey*

Peale \'pē(ə)l\ family of Am. painters: Charles Willson 1741–1827; painted over 1000 portraits, including Washington, Franklin, Jefferson, etc.; & his bro. James 1749–1831; miniaturist; painted miniatures of George and Martha Washington; & Charles's son Rembrandt 1778–1860; best known for portraits of illustrious contemporaries

Peale Norman Vincent 1898–1993 Am. Protestant clergyman; famed for his "applied Christianity," whereby people were encouraged to think positively; wrote inspirational books, including best= selling *The Power of Positive Thinking*, etc.

Pear·son \'pir-sᵊn\ Karl 1857–1936 Eng. math.; applied statistics to biological problems, esp. evolution, heredity

Pearson Lester Bowles 1897–1972 prime min. of Canada (1963–68); awarded 1957 Nobel prize for peace for efforts to solve Suez crisis of 1956

Pea·ry \'pir-ē\ Robert Edwin 1856–1920 Am. polar explorer; usually credited with being first to reach North Pole (April 6, 1909)

Pe·der·sen \'pē-dər-sən\ Charles John 1904–1989 Am. (Korean= born) chem.; awarded (with J.-M. Lehn and D.J. Cram) 1987 Nobel prize for chemistry for development of and work with artificial molecules

Pe·dro \'pā-drō, -drü\ Dom; name of 2 emps. of Brazil: **I** 1798–1834 (reigned as emp. 1822–31; as king of Portugal 1826); **II** 1825–1891 (reigned 1831–1889); worked for abolition of slavery and for economic progress; forced to abdicate on proclamation of republic

Peel \'pē(ə)l\ Sir Robert 1788–1850 Eng. statesman; instituted first disciplined police force in London (called *bobbies* after him); imposed income tax; eased punitive measures against Catholics and Jews, etc.

Peele \'pē(ə)l\ George 1556–1596 Eng. dram. & poet; wrote tragedies, folk plays, pastorals, etc.

Pei \'pā\ Ieoh Ming 1917–   Am. (Chin.-born) architect; designer of such innovative structures as John Hancock Tower, Boston, and glass pyramids at the Louvre, Paris

Peirce \'pərs, 'pirs\ Charles Sanders 1839–1914 Am. physicist, math., & logician; founder of pragmatism, pragmaticism, and semiotics; now viewed as most original thinker and greatest logician of his time — **Peirc·ean** \'pər-sē-ən, 'pir-\ *adj*

Pei·sis·tra·tus *or* **Pi·sis·tra·tus** \pi-'sis-trə-təs, pə-\ *d* 527 B.C. Athenian tyrant; reign noted for religious and civic reforms, expansion of trade and industry, internal tranquility, external neutrality

Pe·la·gius \pə-'lā-j(ē-)əs\ *ca* 354–after 418 Brit. monk & theol.; refuted Augustinian doctrines of predestination and total depravity

Pe·lop·i·das \pə-'lä-pə-dəs\ *d* 364 B.C. Theban gen.; responsible for a brief period of Theban preeminence in ancient Greece

Pel·ti·er \'pel-tē-ər, ˌpel-tē-'ā\ Leonard 1944–   Ojibwa-Lakota activist; a leader in the American Indian movement; his conviction and imprisonment for the murder of two FBI agents at South Dakota's Pine Ridge Reservation became a cause célèbre

Pe·ña \'pe-nyə, 'pā-\ Federico Fabian 1947–   U.S. secy. of transportation (1993–   )

Pen·de·rec·ki \ˌpen-də-'ret-skē\ Krzysztof 1933–   Pol. composer; composer of avant garde music including *Threnody for the Victims of Hiroshima*, operas, St. Luke passion, etc.

Penn \'pen\ Sir William 1621–1670 Eng. admiral; commanded fleet sent against Spanish possessions in America

Penn William 1644–1718 *son of prec.* Eng. Quaker & founder of Pennsylvania; made peace treaties with Indians; supervised laying out of Philadelphia; granted liberal charter to colony

Pen·nell \'pe-nᵊl, pə-'nel\ Joseph 1857–1926 Am. etcher; known for illustrations of books about travels with his wife in Europe and for vivid drawings of industrial activities

Pen·rose \'pen-ˌrōz, pen-'rōz\ Roger 1931–   Brit. math. & physicist; with Stephen Hawking proved that all matter within a black hole collapses to a singularity (a geometric point in space where mass is compressed to infinite density and zero volume)

Pen·zi·as \'pent-sē-əs\ Arno Allan 1933–   Am. (Ger.-born) physicist; awarded (with R. Wilson) 1978 Nobel prize for physics for the discovery of cosmic microwave background radiation

Pé·pin III \'pe-pən\ 714?–768 *the Short* king of the Franks (751–768); founded Carolingian dynasty and bestowed sovereignty of Ravenna on pope (Donation of Pépin)

Pepys \'pēps\ Samuel 1633–1703 Eng. diarist; author of unique 9-year diary written in shorthand, with foreign words and invented ciphers, offering candid picture of his life and the life of his times — **Pepys·ian** \'pēp-sē-ən\ *adj*

Per·cy \'pər-sē\ Sir Henry 1364–1403 *Hotspur* Eng. soldier; revolted (1403) with his father and Owen Glendower; slain in battle of Shrewsbury

Percy Thomas 1729–1811 Eng. antiquarian & poet; awakened interest in English and Scottish traditional songs and influenced Romantic poets with his *Reliques of Ancient English Poetry* (*Percy's Reliques*)

Percy Walker 1916–1990 Am. writer; author of darkly comical novels as *The Moviegoer, The Thanatos Syndrome*, etc.

Per·el·man \'per-əl-mən (*his own pron.*), 'pər(-ə)l-\ Sidney Joseph 1904–1979 Am. writer; known for humorous essays, books, screenplays including *Horsefeathers, Around the World in Eighty Days* (Academy award), etc.

Per·es \'per-(ˌ)ez\ Shimon 1923–   orig. surname *Perski* Israeli polit.; prime min. (1984–86, 1995–   ); foreign min. (1986–88, 1992–95); awarded (with Y. Arafat, Y. Rabin) 1994 Nobel peace prize for their efforts to create peace in the Middle East

Pé·rez Gal·dós \'per-əs-(ˌ)gäl-'dōs\ Benito 1843–1920 Span. writer; published a series of historical romances and novels reflecting contemporary life and its problems

Pérez Ro·dri·guez \-ˌröth-'rē-gäs\ Carlos Andrés 1922–   pres. of Venezuela (1974–79, 1989–93)

Per·go·le·si \ˌpər-gə-'lā-zē, ˌper-gə-'lā-sē\ Giovanni Battista

1710–1736 Ital. composer; composed operas; his comic intermezzo *La serva pardona* precipitated *guerre des bouffons* between lovers of French and Italian opera in Paris

Per·i·cles \'per-ə-,klēz\ *ca* 495–429 B.C. Athenian statesman; responsible for the full flowering of Athenian democracy and the Athenian empire; his administration marked Athens' political and cultural apex; achievements included construction of the Acropolis — **Per·i·cle·an** \,per-ə-'klē-ən\ *adj*

Per·kins \'pər-kənz\ Frances 1882–1965 Am. public official; as U.S. secy. of labor supervised New Deal labor legislation, esp. Fair Labor Standards Act

Perl·man \'pər(-ə)l-mən, 'perl-\ Itzhak 1945–   Am. (Israeli-born) violinist; known for his brilliant virtuosity

Pe·rón \pā-'rōn, pə-\ Juan Domingo 1895–1974 Argentine polit.; pres. of Argentina (1946–55, 1973–74); brought about economic reforms and public works, but administration marked by graft, suppression of civil liberties

Pe·rot \pə-'rō\ (Henry) Ross 1930–   Am. businessman; independent candidate for U.S. president (1992)

Per·rault \pə-'rō, pe-\ Charles 1628–1703 Fr. writer; best known for *Contes de ma mère l'oye (Tales of My Mother Goose)*

Per·rin \pe-'raⁿ(n), pe-\ Jean-Baptiste 1870–1942 Fr. physicist; awarded 1926 Nobel prize for physics for work on the discontinuous structure of matter and for discovery of equilibrium of sedimentation

Per·ry \'per-ē\ (Mary) Antoinette 1888–1946 Am. actress & director; founder (1941) of the American Theatre Wing, which posthumously named its annual Antoinette Perry (Tony) Awards after her

Perry Bliss 1860–1954 Am. educ. & critic; author of *The American Mind*, etc.; editor, Cambridge editions of the major American poets

Perry Matthew Calbraith 1794–1858 Am. commodore; obtained treaty with Japanese granting U.S. trading rights, beginning of Japanese contact with western powers

Perry Oliver Hazard 1785–1819 *bro. of prec.* Am. naval officer; sent famous message, "We have met the enemy and they are ours," after defeating British on Lake Erie during War of 1812

Perry Ralph Barton 1876–1957 Am. philos. & educ.; noted as founder of new Realism school in American Pragmatic philosophy

Perry William James 1927–   U.S. secy. of defense (1994–   )

Perse St. John — see Aléxis Saint-Léger LÉGER

Per·shing \'pər-shiŋ, -zhiŋ\ John Joseph 1860–1948 *Black Jack* Am. gen.; American commander in Europe during WWI; destroyed German resistance with Meuse-Argonne offensive (1918)

Per·sius \'pər-shəs, 'pər-sē-əs\ A.D. 34–62 *Aulus Persius Flaccus* Rom. satirist; author of six satires of a high moral tone, composed in hexameters

Pe·ru·gi·no \,per-ə-'jē-(,)nō\ *ca* 1450–1523 *Pietro di Cristoforo Vannucci* Ital. painter; a master of the early Renaissance; teacher of Raphael

Per·utz \pə-'rüts\ Max Ferdinand 1914–   Brit. (Austrian-born) chem.; awarded (with J.C. Kendrew) 1962 Nobel prize for chemistry for studies on globular proteins

Pe·ruz·zi \pə-'rüt-sē, pä-\ Baldassare 1481–1536 Ital. architect & painter; a leading artist of the High Renaissance and one of earliest to try illusionist architectural painting (*quadratura*)

Pes·ta·loz·zi \,pes-tə-'lät-sē\ Johann Heinrich 1746–1827 Swiss educ.; influenced schools throughout Europe and America with his emphasis on using objects to develop powers of observation and reasoning

Pé·tain \pā-ta⁽ⁿ⁾\ Philippe 1856–1951 Fr. gen.; became national hero for his victory at Battle of Verdun in WWI; marshal of France; premier of Vichy France (1940–44); convicted (1945) of collaboration with enemy

Pe·ter \'pē-tər\ Saint *d* ca 64 A.D. *Simon Peter* one of twelve Apostles; made Jerusalem headquarters for preaching in Palestine (ca. 33–44 A.D.); established see of Antioch; probable author of two New Testament epistles

Peter I 1672–1725 *the Great* czar of Russia (1682–1725); acquired ports on Baltic and Caspian Seas; renowned for introducing western European civilization into Russia and raising Russian status — **Pe·trine** \'pē-,trīn\ *adj*

Peter I 1844–1921 king of Serbia (1903–21); a liberal and an advocate of constitutional government

Peter II 1923–1970 king of Yugoslavia (1934–45); after German invasion, set up government in London; reign ended when Yugoslavia became republic

Peter Cla·ver \'kläv-ər\ Saint 1581–1654 Span. Jesuit missionary; known as "Apostle of the Negroes" for ministrations to newly arrived African slaves in Colombia despite official opposition

Peter Lom·bard \'läm-,bärd\ ca 1095–1160 L. *Petrus Lombardus* Ital. theol.; produced *Sententiarum libri IV*, the official textbook in medieval theological schools and important in forming church doctrine

Peter the Hermit ca 1050–1115 Fr. preacher of the 1st Crusade; led his followers into Asia Minor where they were destroyed by the Turks; he survived to help conquer Jerusalem

Pe·ters \'pā-tərz, -tərs\ Carl 1856–1918 Ger. explorer; instrumental in establishing a German protectorate in East Africa; discovered traces of ancient cities along the Zambezi

Pe·tő·fi \'pe-tə-fē\ Sán·dor \'shän-,dór\ 1823–1849 Hung. poet; among the finest of Hungary's lyric poets

Pe·trarch \'pē-,trärk, 'pe-\ 1304–1374 It. *Francesco Petrarca* Ital. poet; known chiefly for *Canzoniere* or *Rime*, sonnets and odes written to Laura, an idealized lover; greatest scholar of his time for his study of classical manuscripts — **Pe·trarch·an** \pē-'trär-kən, pe-\ *adj*

Pe·trie \'pē-trē\ Sir (William Matthew) Flin·ders \'flin-dərz\ 1853–1942 Eng. Egyptologist; investigated pyramids at Giza and other Egyptian antiquities; developed principle of sequence dating by potsherds

Pe·tro·ni·us \pə-'trō-nē-əs\ *d* A.D. 66 in full prob. *Titus Petronius Niger* Rom. satirist; generally regarded as author of *Satyricon*, satirical picaresque romance extant in fragments — **Pe·tro·ni·an** \-nē-ən\ *adj*

Pet·ty \'pe-tē\ Richard 1937– Am. automobile racer; won Daytona 500 and NASCAR national championship 7 times each

Petty Sir William 1623–1687 Eng. polit. econ.; an author of first book on vital statistics; stated that price depends on labor necessary for production; made first estimate of national income and first discussion of velocity of money, etc.

Pevs·ner \'pevz-nər\ Antoine 1886–1962 *bro. of Naum Gabo* Fr. (Russ.-born) sculptor & painter; with brother, a pioneer of constructivist style

Pevsner Sir Nikolaus 1902–1983 Brit. (Ger.-born) art hist.; authority on English architecture and author of *An Outline of European Architecture*

Phae·drus \'fē-drəs\ 5th cent. B.C. Greek philos.; contemporary of Plato and Socrates; one of Plato's dialogues named for him

Phaedrus ca 15 B.C.–ca A.D. 50 Rom. fabulist; author of *Fabulae Aesopiae*, chiefly versification of fables of Aesop cycle

Phid·i·as \'fi-dē-əs\ *fl ca* 490–430 B.C. Greek sculptor; regarded as greatest of ancient Greek sculptors; created sculptures on the Parthenon, statue *Athene Parthenos*, etc.

Phil·ip \'fi-ləp\ 1639?–1676 *Met·a·com·et* \,me-tə-'kä-mət\ Wampanoag Indian chief; waged King Philip's War on New England colonists; his death marked end of Indian resistance to white settlement

Philip name of 6 kings of France: esp. **II** *or* **Philip Augustus** 1165–1223 (reigned 1179–1223); one of the greatest Capetian kings; made France a power in Europe; **IV** (*the Fair*) 1268–1314 (reigned 1285–1314); his reign, one of most momentous of medieval era, marked by new developments of French monarchy and restriction of feudal usages; **VI** 1293–1350 (reigned 1328–50); first Valois king; reign saw beginning of Hundred Years' War with England

Philip name of 5 kings of Spain: esp. **II** 1527–1598 (reigned 1556–98); developed Inquisition; failed to quell revolt in Netherlands; lost naval supremacy in defeat of Armada; **V** 1683–1746 (reigned 1700–24, 1724–46); founder of Bourbon dynasty in Spain; began War of Spanish Succession and joined in War of Austrian Succession

Philip II 382–336 B.C. king of Macedon (359–336); proved himself a military genius in his gradual conquest of all Greece; prepared the way for his son Alexander the Great

Philip III 1396–1467 *the Good* Duke of Burgundy (1419–67); added to territory and made Burgundy most wealthy and prosperous of all European states

Philip Prince 1921–   *consort of Queen Elizabeth II of Great Britain* 3d Duke of Edinburgh

Phil·ips \'fi-ləps\ Ambrose 1674–1749 *Nam·by-Pam·by* \,nam-bē-'pam-bē\ Eng. poet & dram.; infamous for his sentimental, insipid poetry that was much ridiculed by Alexander Pope and the inspiration for his derisive nickname

Phil·lips \'fi-ləps\ Wendell 1811–1884 Am. orator & reformer; abolitionist and later advocate of prohibition, penal reform, woman suffrage, etc.

Phill·potts \'fil-,päts\ Eden 1862–1960 Eng. nov. & dram.; author of realistic, often tragic novels of Devonshire, historical novels, mystery and fairy stories, poems, plays

Phi·lo Ju·dae·us \'fī-(,)lō-jü-'dē-əs, -'dā-\ *ca* 13 B.C.–A.D. 45 to 50

Jewish philos. of Alexandria; often regarded as forerunner of Christian theology in his attempt to reconcile revealed religion of Jews with Greek philosophy

Pho·ci·on \\'fō-sē-ˌän\\ *ca* 402–318 B.C. Athenian gen. & statesman; ruled as virtual dictator in Athens after Alexander the Great's death, but under control of neighboring Macedonia

Phyfe \\'fīf\\ Duncan 1768–1854 Am. (Scot.-born) cabinetmaker; renowned for excellence and artistic beauty of his Neoclassical furniture

Pi·af \\pē-'af\\ Edith \\ā-'dēt\\ 1915–1963 orig. *Edith Giovanna Gassion* Fr. singer; famous for her dramatic interpretations of cabaret songs in a throaty voice redolent of tragedy

Pia·get \\pyä-'zhä\\ Jean 1896–1980 Swiss psychol.; known for investigation of thought processes, esp. in children; regarded as the major figure in 20th-century developmental psychology — **Piaget·ian** \\ˌpē-ə-'je-tē-ən, pyä-'zhä-ən\\ *adj*

Pi·card \\pē-'kär, pi-'kärd\\ Jean 1620–1682 Fr. astron.; first to apply telescope to measurement of angles from which he was able to compute size of earth

Pi·cas·so \\pi-'kä-(ˌ)sō, -'ka-\\ Pablo 1881–1973 Span. painter & sculptor in France; generally recognized as greatest and most influential artist of the 20th century for technique, style, output; with Georges Braque, the creator of Cubism

Pic·card \\pi-'kär, -'kärd\\ Auguste 1884–1962 Swiss physicist; investigated radioactivity and atmospheric electricity in ascents to record height in a balloon and to record depth in a bathyscape

Piccard Jacques-Ernest-Jean 1922– *son of Auguste* Swiss (Belg.-born) oceanographer; made (1960) record descent of 35,800 ft. into the Mariana Trench in the Pacific Ocean

Pick·er·ing \\'pi-k(ə-)riŋ\\ Edward Charles 1846–1919 & his bro. William Henry 1858–1938 Am. astron.; Edward renowned for work in stellar photometry and spectroscopy; William predicted existence of 9th planet. Together, established observation station at Arequipa, Peru

Pick·ett \\'pi-kət\\ George Edward 1825–1875 Am. Confed. gen.; made unsuccessful famous charge across Cemetery Ridge, Battle of Gettysburg, often considered turning point of Civil War

Pi·co del·la Mi·ran·do·la \\'pē-(ˌ)kō-ˌde-lə-mə-'ran-də-lə, -'rän-\\ Conte Giovanni 1463–1494 Ital. humanist; a leading scholar of Italian Renaissance; emphasized human dignity based on free will

Pierce \\'pirs\\ Franklin 1804–1869 14th pres. of the U.S. (1853–57); made Gadsden Purchase; opened Northwest for settlement; failed to deal with rising sectionalism and increasingly violent slavery issue

Pie·ro del·la Fran·ces·ca \\'pyer-ō-ˌde-lə-fran-'ches-kə, -frän-\\ *or* **de' Fran·ces·chi** \\-dā-fran-'ches-kē, -frän-\\ *ca* 1420–1492 Ital. painter; considered a master of perspective and a major contributor to the Italian Renaissance

Pike \\'pīk\\ Zebulon Montgomery 1779–1813 Am. gen. & explorer; explored headwaters of Mississippi, Arkansas, Red rivers; discovered peak named for him; stimulated expansion into Texas

Pi·late \\'pī-lət\\ Pon·tius \\'pän-chəs, 'pən-chəs\\ *d* after A.D. 36 Rom. procurator of Judea (26–*ca* 36); presided at the trial of Jesus and responsible for the order for death by crucifixion

Pił·sud·ski \pil-'süt-skē, -'züt-\ Józef Klemens 1867–1935 Pol. gen. & statesman; a fighter for Polish independence (from 1892); first pres. (1918–22) of the newly independent Poland

Pin·chot \'pin-ˌshō\ Gifford 1865–1946 Am. conservationist & polit.; first professional American forester; governor of Pennsylvania (1923–27, 1931–35)

Pinck·ney \'pink-nē\ Charles Cotesworth 1746–1825 Am. statesman & diplomat; aroused intense feeling in France and U.S. with report on "XYZ Affair" in which French treaty negotiators requested bribe

Pin·dar \'pin-dər, -ˌdär\ ca 522–ca 438 B.C. Greek poet; author of 44 complete extant *Epinicia* (Odes of Victory) for victories in national games — **Pin·dar·ic** \pin-'dar-ik\ adj

Pi·ne·ro \pə-'nir-(ˌ)ō, -'ner-\ Sir Arthur Wing 1855–1934 Eng. dram.; defined new era of modern drama with a series of problem plays; also wrote plays reflecting current manners and morals, satirical comedies, etc.

Pin·ker·ton \'pin-kər-tᵊn\ Allan 1819–1884 Am. (Scot.-born) detective; established first private detective agency in U.S

Pi·no·chet Ugar·te \ˌpē-nō-'chet-ü-'gär-tā\ Augusto 1915– Chilean gen.; pres. of Chile (1974–90); leader of coup that overthrew Marxist government of Allende

Pin·ter \'pin-tər\ Harold 1930– Eng. dram.; author of *The Birthday Party*, *The Caretaker*, etc., in which sense of menace emerges from a second or third layer of unspoken meaning — **Pinter·esque** \ˌpin-tə-'resk\ adj

Pin·tu·ric·chio \ˌpin-tə-'rē-kē-ˌō\ ca 1454–1513 *Bernardino di Betto di Biago* Ital. painter; leading historical painter of Umbrian school; known for his highly decorative frescoes

Pin·zón \pin-'zōn\ Martín Alonso ca 1441–1493 & his bro. Vicente Yáñez ca 1460–ca 1523 Span. navigators & explorers; commanded the *Pinta* and *Niña* on expedition with Columbus; Vicente Yáñez later explored coast of Brazil, north to Costa Rica, south perhaps to La Plata

Pioz·zi \pē-'ôt-sē\ Hester Lynch 1741–1821 *Mrs. Thrale* \'thrā(ə)l\ Eng. writer; engaged in twenty-year friendship with Dr. Johnson; edited his letters and wrote volume of anecdotes about him

Pi·ran·del·lo \ˌpir-ən-'de-(ˌ)lō\ Luigi 1867–1936 Ital. author; awarded 1934 Nobel prize for literature for his plays, including *Six Characters in Search of an Author*; an important innovator in modern drama — **Pi·ran·del·li·an** \-'de-lē-ən\ adj

Pi·ra·ne·si \ˌpir-ə-'nā-zē\ Giambattista 1720–1778 Ital. architect, painter, & engraver; made series of engravings of classical architecture which contributed to 18th-century Neoclassical movement and to interest in archaeology

Pire \'pir\ Dominique Georges 1910–1969 Belg. clergyman & humanitarian; awarded 1958 Nobel prize for peace for aid to postwar displaced persons

Pi·sa·no \pi-'sä-(ˌ)nō, -'zä-\ Giovanni ca 1250–after 1314 & his father Nicola ca 1220–1278 (or 1284) Ital. sculptors; Giovanni was chief Italian sculptor of Middle Ages and founder of Italian Gothic style; Nicola represented apex of Romanesque style; first important precursor of Renaissance

Pisistratus — see PEISISTRATUS

Pis·sar·ro \pə-'sär-(,)ō\ Camille 1830–1903 Fr. painter; identified with Impressionist school and later with pointilism

Pis·ton \'pis-tən\ Walter Hamor 1894–1976 Am. composer; composed symphonies, ballet, instrumental pieces in Neoclassical style with Romantic overtones

Pit·man \'pit-mən\ Sir Isaac 1813–1897 Eng. phonographer; invented shorthand system based on phonetic principles

Pitt \'pit\ William 1708–1778 Earl of *Chatham; the Elder Pitt* Eng. statesman; chief cabinet min. during Seven Years' War (1756–63); secured vast empire for Britain by bringing about defeats of French in India, Africa, Canada, on seas

Pitt William 1759–1806 *the Younger Pitt; son of prec.* Eng. statesman; prime min. (1783–1801, 1804–06) during French Revolution and early Napoleonic era; instituted new taxes and fiscal reforms; empowered the office of prime min.

Pitt–Riv·ers \'pit·'riv-vərz\ Augustus Henry 1827–1900 Eng. archaeol.; adopted sociological approach to excavations of prehistoric, Roman, Saxon sites in Wiltshire

Pi·us \'pī-əs\ name of 12 popes: esp. **II** (*Enea Silvio Piccolomini* or *Ae·ne·as Sil·vi·us* \i-'nē-əs-'sil-vē-əs\ or *Syl·vi·us* \'sil-vē-əs\) 1405–1464 (pope 1458–64); a leader of the Humanists, patron of learning, and prolific writer; **VII** 1742–1823 (pope 1800–23); restored Jesuit order; **IX** 1792–1878 (pope 1846–78); proclaimed dogmas of Immaculate Conception and papal infallibility; lost greater part of papal holdings and lost temporal power; pontificate longest in history; **X** 1835–1914 (pope 1903–14); inaugurated reform and revision in music and church law; **XI** (*Ambrogio Damiano Achille Ratti*) 1857–1939 (pope 1922–39); signed Lateran Treaty with Mussolini; issued encyclicals against Communism and Nazism; **XII** (*Eugenio Pacelli*) 1876–1958 (pope 1939–58); maintained neutrality in WWII; accepted modern biblical scholarship

Pi·zar·ro \pə-'zär-(,)ō\ Francisco *ca* 1475–1541 Span. conquistador; conquered Peru and founded Lima as new capital

Planck \'pläŋk\ Max Karl Ernst Ludwig 1858–1947 Ger. physicist; awarded 1918 Nobel prize for physics for stating the quantum theory of light

Plan·tin \pläⁿ-taⁿ\ Christophe *ca* 1520–1589 Fr. printer; published *Biblia polyglotta,* fixing original text of Old and New Testaments

Plath \'plath\ Sylvia 1932–1963 Am. poet; author of confessional poems in *The Colossus, Ariel,* etc.; published semi-autobiographical novel *The Bell Jar* under pseudonym Victoria Lucas

Pla·to \'plā-(,)tō\ *ca* 428–348 (or 347) B.C. Greek philos.; disciple of Socrates and teacher of Aristotle; with them laid philosophical foundations of Western culture

Plau·tus \'plȯ-təs\ Titus Maccius *ca* 254–184 B.C. Rom. dram.; writer of comedies adapted from Greek originals, creating Roman literary idiom — **Plau·tine** \'plȯ-,tīn\ *adj*

Ple·kha·nov \plə-'kä-,nȯf, pli-'kä-\ Georgy Valentinovich 1857–1918 Russ. Marxist philos.; credited with greatly influencing development of Socialist thought and policy in Russia, esp. his theory of two-phase revolution

Ple·ven \plā-'ven\ René 1901–1993 Fr. polit.; premier (1950–51, 1951–52); his plan for a unified European army led to the creation of NATO

Pliny \'pli-nē\ A.D. 23–79 *Gaius Plinius Secundus; Pliny the Elder* Rom. scholar; studied and wrote in fields of history, rhetoric, natural science, military tactics

Pliny A.D. 61 (or 62)–*ca* 113 *Gaius Plinius Caecilius Secundus; Pliny the Younger; nephew of prec.* Rom. author; best known for 9 books of letters on literary, social, political, domestic themes

Plo·ti·nus \plō-'tī-nəs\ A.D. 205–270 Rom. (Egypt.-born) philos.; chief exponent of Neoplatonism — **Plo·tin·i·an** \-'ti-nē-ən\ *adj*

Plu·tarch \'plü-,tärk\ *ca* A.D. 46–after 119 Greek biographer & moralist; best known for *Parallel Lives,* character studies of famous Greeks and Romans from age of Theseus and Romulus to his own — **Plu·tarch·an** \plü-'tär-kən\ *or* **Plu·tarch·ian** \-kē-ən\ *adj*

Po·ca·hon·tas \,pō-kə-'hän-təs\ *ca* 1595–1617 *dau. of Powhatan* Am. Indian; said by Captain John Smith in his *Generall Historie of Virginia* to have saved his life from Powhatan's warriors

Pod·gor·ny \päd-'gòr-nē\ Nikolay Viktorovich 1903–1983 Soviet polit.; head of Presidium (1965–77)

Poe \'pō\ Edgar Allan 1809–1849 Am. poet & short-story writer; creator of the American Gothic tale and of detective fiction genre; works include stories "The Tell-Tale Heart," "The Cask of Amontillado," "The Murders in the Rue Morgue," poem "The Raven," etc.

Poin·ca·ré \,pwaⁿ-,kä-'rā\ Jules-Henri 1854–1912 Fr. math.; reconstituted analytical mathematics; worked on electromagnetic theory of light; contributed to theory of numbers and topology, etc.

Poincaré Raymond 1860–1934 *cousin of J. H.* Fr. statesman; pres. of France (1913–20); sustained patriotism through war

Po·lan·yi \pō-'län-yē\ John Charles 1929– Canad. (Ger.-born) chem.; awarded (with D.R. Herschbach, Y.T. Lee) 1986 Nobel prize for chemistry for pioneering research on basic chemical reactions

Pole \'pōl, 'pül\ Reginald 1500–1558 Eng. cardinal; archbishop of Canterbury (1556–58); a powerful figure under Roman Catholic queen Mary Tudor; attempted to restore ecclesiastical system disrupted by Henry VIII

Po·len·ta \pō-'len-tə\ Francesca da *d* 1283 (or 1284) *Fran·ces·ca da Ri·mi·ni* \,fran-'ches-kə-dä-'ri-mə-(,)nē, ,frän-, -'rē-\ Ital. noblewoman famous for tragic adulterous love affair; story immortalized in Dante's *Inferno,* plays by Pellico, Heyse, etc., operas by Götz, Rachmaninoff, etc.

Po·li·tian \pə-'li-shən\ 1454–1494 *Angelo Poliziano* or *Angelo Ambrogini* Ital. classical scholar & poet; one of foremost classical scholars of the Renaissance

Polk \'pōk\ James Knox 1795–1849 11th pres. of the U.S. (1845–49); settled Oregon boundary; won Mexican War and annexed California and most of Southwest

Pol·lio \'pä-lē-,ō\ Gaius Asinius 76 B.C.–A.D. 4 Rom. soldier, orator, & polit.; with Caesar in Civil War and later with Mark Antony; built first library in Rome and patronized literature; wrote history of civil wars

Pol·lock \'pä-lək\ Sir Frederick 1845–1937 Eng. jurist; author of authoritative textbooks on law

Pol·lock (Paul) Jackson 1912–1956 Am. painter; a leading exponent of Abstract Expressionism and Action Painting with technique of dripping or pouring paint on canvas

Po·lo \'pō-(,)lō\ Mar·co \'mär-(,)kō\ 1254–1324 Venetian traveler; famous for his journey from Europe to China, his 17-year stay in the court of Kublai Khan; his account, known in English as *The Travels of Marco Polo*, was highly popular and influential for centuries

Po·lyb·i·us \pə-'li-bē-əs\ *ca* 200–*ca* 118 B.C. Greek hist.; wrote 40-volume *Histories* of Rome from 220 to 146 B.C.

Pol·y·carp \'pä-li-,kärp\ Saint 2d cent. Christian martyr & Apostolic Father; bishop of Smyrna; very influential because of righteousness and attacks on heresies; burned at stake during persecution of Christians

Pol·y·cli·tus *or* **Pol·y·clei·tus** \,pä-li-'klī-təs\ 5th cent. B.C. Greek sculptor & architect; credited with perfecting the abstract proportion which characterizes Greek sculpture; executed mainly bronze statues of young athletes

Po·lyc·ra·tes \pə-'li-krə-,tēz\ *d ca* 522 B.C. tyrant of Samos; master of the Aegean basin and notorious for piracy

Pol·y·do·rus \,pä-li-'dōr-əs, -'dor-\ 1st cent. B.C. Rhodian sculptor; a collaborator in carving the famous sculptural group Laocoön

Pol·yg·no·tus \,pä-lig-'nō-təs\ *ca* 500–*ca* 440 B.C. Greek painter; regarded as leading representative of Greek painting of his century; executed monumental murals

Pom·pa·dour \'päm-pə-,dōr, -,dor, -,dúr\ Madame de 1721–1764 *Jeanne-Antoinette Poisson; mistress of Louis XV;* patronized authors and artists and guided French taste to its apex

Pom·pey \'päm-pē\ 106–48 B.C. *Gnaeus Pompeius Magnus; the Great* Rom. gen. & statesman; a member of First Triumvirate; defeated at Pharsalus in civil war with Caesar

Pom·pi·dou \'päm-pi-,dü\ Georges-Jean-Raymond 1911–1974 Fr. polit.; premier (1962–68) & pres. (1969–74) of France; continued policies of de Gaulle

Ponce de Le·ón \,pän(t)-sə-,dā-lē-'ōn, ,pänts-də-, -'lē-ən\ Juan 1460–1521 Span. explorer; discovered Florida while searching for island of Bimini, reputedly the location of a Fountain of Youth

Pon·chi·el·li \,pōn-kē-'e-lē\ Amilcare 1834–1886 Ital. composer; composed operas *I promessi sposi, La gioconda,* etc., and ballets and sacred music

Pons \'pänz, 'pōⁿs\ Lily 1904–1976 Am. (Fr.-born) soprano; reigning diva at the Metropolitan Opera for 30 years; famed for French and Italian coloratura parts

Pon·selle \pän-'sel\ Rosa Melba 1897–1981 Am. soprano; sang coloratura roles in Italian and French opera at Metropolitan Opera (1918–37)

Pon·ti·ac \'pän-tē-,ak\ *ca* 1720–1769 Ottawa Indian chief; led Pontiac's War (1763–64), an intertribal resistance to British power in the Great Lakes area

Pon·top·pi·dan \,pän-'tä-pə-,dan\ Henrik 1857–1943 Dan. nov.; awarded (with K. Gjellerup) 1917 Nobel prize for literature for his novels; realistically depicted contemporary Danish life

Pon·tor·mo \pōn-'tȯr-(,)mō\ Jacopo da 1494–1557 orig. *J. Carrucci* Ital. painter; painter of Florentine Mannerist school; pupil of da Vinci, di Cosimo, del Sarto

Pope \'pōp\ Alexander 1688–1744 Eng. poet; best known for poems *An Essay on Criticism,* the mock-epics *The Rape of the Lock* and *Dunciad* and *Essay on Man,* last widely quoted, etc.; famed for his caustic wit and his ongoing literary feuds — **Pop·ian** *also* **Popean** \'pō-pē-ən\ *adj*

Pope John 1822–1892 Am. gen.; Union general in the Civil War; defeated at Second Battle of Bull Run

Por·son \'pȯr-s²n\ Richard 1759–1808 Eng. scholar; best known for important contributions to knowledge of meter and texts

Por·tal \'pȯr-t²l, 'pȯr-\ Charles Frederick Algernon 1893–1971 1st Viscount *Portal of Hungerford* Brit. air marshal; chief of the British Air Staff during WWII

Por·ter \'pȯr-tȯr, 'pȯr-\ Cole Albert 1891–1964 Am. composer & lyricist; known for urbane, witty lyrics and sinuous music; composed for musicals and songs "You Do Something to Me," "Night and Day," "I've Got You Under My Skin," etc.

Porter David 1780–1843 & his son David Dixon 1813–1891 Am. naval officers; David harassed British shipping in the Pacific during War of 1812; his was first U.S. warship in Pacific waters; David Dixon fought in Civil War; as superintendent, U.S. Naval Academy (1865–69), improved curriculum and instruction

Porter Eliot Furness 1901–1990 Am. photographer; known for his color photographs of richly detailed landscapes; credited with establishing color photography as an art form

Porter Gene 1868–1924 née *Stratton* Am. nov.; author of sentimental novels and stories including *A Girl of the Limberlost, Laddie,* etc.

Porter Sir George 1920–   Brit. chem.; awarded (with M. Eigen and R.G.W. Norrish) 1967 Nobel prize for chemistry for developing techniques to measure rapid chemical reactions

Porter Katherine Anne 1890–1980 Am. writer; author of novel *Ship of Fools,* essays, short stories including *The Leaning Tower, Collected Short Stories,* etc.

Porter Noah 1811–1892 Am. philos. & lexicographer; author of *The Human Intellect,* etc.; editor of *Webster's American Dictionary of the English Language* (1864), etc.

Porter Rodney Robert 1917–1985 Brit. biochem.; awarded (with G.M. Edelman) 1972 Nobel prize for physiology or medicine for discovery of the chemical structure of antibodies

Porter William Sydney 1862–1910 pseud. *O. Hen·ry* \(')ō-'hen-rē\ Am. short-story writer; stories known for dramatic trick endings, including "The Gift of the Magi," "The Ransom of Red Chief," etc.

Portland Duke of — see BENTINCK

Post \'pōst\ Emily 1872–1960 née *Price* Am. columnist & writer; wrote on subject of manners and social etiquette

Po·tem·kin \pə-'tyȯm(p)-kən, pō-'tem(p)-\ Grigory Aleksandrovich 1739–1791 Russ. field marshal & statesman; favorite of Catherine II; built fleet and harbor in Black Sea; annexed Crimea

Pot·ter \'pä-tər\ Beatrix 1866–1943 Brit. writer & illustrator; famous for children's books, including *The Tale of Peter Rabbit*, featuring animal characters and their watercolor illustrations

Potter Paul *or* Paulus 1625–1654 Du. painter; best known for paintings of animals in rural settings

Pou·lenc \'pü-ˌlaŋk\ Fran·cis \frän-sēs\ 1899–1963 Fr. composer; a member of "Les Six;" composed orchestral, vocal, choral works, and songs regarded as among finest of 20th century

Pound \'paùnd\ Ezra Loomis 1885–1972 Am. poet; a major influence on 20th-century U.S. and English literature, esp. through *Cantos* and other poems, translations, criticism — **Pound·ian** \'paùn-dē-ən\ *adj*

Pound Roscoe 1870–1964 Am. jurist; advocate of "sociological jurisprudence," whereby legal codes and traditions are adjusted to contemporary social conditions

Pound·mak·er \'paùnd-ˌmā-kər\ 1826–1886 Canad. Cree chief; a leader in unsuccessful Riel Rebellion in Saskatchewan (1885)

Pous·sin \pü-saⁿ\ Nicolas 1594–1665 Fr. painter; noted for scriptural and mythological subjects; his paintings in the classical style influenced generations of painters

Pow·ell \'paù(-ə)l\ Adam Clayton 1908–1972 Am. clergyman & polit.; African-American pastor of Harlem's Abyssinian Baptist Church; member, U.S. House of Representatives (1965–67, 1969–71); known for liberal legislation, flamboyant lifestyle, opposition to racism, and successful defeat of an attempt to unseat him

Pow·ell \'pō-əl, 'paù(-ə)l\ Anthony 1905–   Eng. writer; best known for novels in series *A Dance to the Music of Time*

Powell Cecil Frank 1903–1969 Brit. physicist; awarded 1950 Nobel prize for physics for work on photography of nuclear processes

Powell \'paù(-ə)l\ Colin Luther 1937–   Am. gen.; came to prominence during Persian Gulf War; chairman of joint chiefs of staff (1989–93), being first African-American to occupy that office

Powell John Wesley 1834–1902 Am. geologist & explorer; explored Green and Colorado rivers; published folio atlases for U.S. Geological Survey and first classification of American Indian languages

Powell Lewis Franklin 1907–   Am. jurist; associate justice, U.S. Supreme Court (1972–87)

Pow·ell \'pō-əl, 'paù(-ə)l\ Michael Latham 1872–1963 Brit. film director, writer, & producer; with Eric Pressburger made original films notable for the use of color, such as *The Red Shoes, Black Narcissus, The Tales of Hoffman*, etc.

Pow·ers \'paù(-ə)rz\ Hiram 1805–1873 Am. sculptor; executed important works in Neoclassical style including *Greek Slave, The Last of the Tribe*

Pow·ha·tan \ˌpaù-ə-'tan, paù-'ha-tᵊn\ 1550?–1618 *Wa-hun-sen-a=cawh* or *Wahunsonacock; father of Pocahontas* Am. Indian chief; head of Algonquian Confederacy of Powhatan in eastern Virginia

Pow·ys \'pō-əs\ John Cow·per \'kü-pər\ 1872–1963 & his bros. Theodore Francis 1875–1953 & Llewelyn 1884–1939 Eng. authors; John wrote the novels *Wolf Solent, Owen Glendower*, etc.; Theodore wrote allegorical novels of good and evil, life and death, in a rural village; Llewelyn wrote stories and impressions of African life

Pra·do Ugar·te·che \\'prä-(,)dō-,ü-gär-'tä-chē\\ Manuel 1889–1967 Peruvian banker; pres. of Peru (1939–45, 1956–62)

Pra·ja·dhi·pok \\prə-'chä-ti-,päk\\ 1893–1941 king of Siam (1925–35); twice forced to submit to constitutional government and finally abdicated

Pratt \\'prat\\ Edwin John 1883–1964 Canad. poet; leading Canadian poet of his time; known esp. for narrative poem *Brébeuf and His Brethren*

Prax·it·e·les \\prak-'si-t³l-,ēz\\ *fl* 370–330 B.C. Athenian sculptor; regarded as greatest Attic sculptor of his century; created graceful, sensuous forms — **Prax·it·e·le·an** \\(,)prak-,si-t³l-'ē-ən\\ *adj*

Pre·ble \\'pre-bəl\\ Edward 1761–1807 Am. naval officer; commander of U.S. naval forces during the Tripolitan War (1801–05)

Pregl \\'prä-gəl\\ Fritz 1869–1930 Austrian chem.; awarded 1923 Nobel prize for chemistry for inventing a method of microanalyzing organic substances

Pre·log \\'pre-,lōg\\ Vladimir 1906– Swiss (Bosnian-born) chem.; awarded (with J.W. Cornforth) 1975 Nobel prize for chemistry for work on the chemical synthesis of important organic compounds

Pres·cott \\'pres-kət *also* -,kät\\ William Hickling 1796–1859 Am. hist.; known for his works on Spanish history

Pres·ley \\'prez-lē\\ Elvis Aron 1935–1977 Am. singer; first white rock and roll singer to achieve superstardom; created the archetype of the rock star as sexy, sneering rebel; sold over 500 million records in his lifetime

Pre·to·ri·us \\pri-'tōr-ē-əs, -'tȯr-\\ Andries Wilhelmus Jacobus 1798–1853 & his son Marthinus Wessels 1819–1901 So. African Du. colonizers & soldiers; Andries won from British acknowledgment of independence of Transvaal Boers; district and town of Pretoria named for him; Marthinus won from British recognition of independence of Orange Free State; saw later reannexation of country

Pré·vost d'Ex·iles \\prā-'vō-,deg-'zē(ə)l\\ Antoine-François 1697–1763 Fr. abbé & writer; author of *Histoire du Chevalier des Grieux et de Manon Lescaut*, basis of operas by Massenet and Puccini

Price \\'prīs\\ (Mary) Le·on·tyne \\lē-'än-,tēn; 'lē-ən-,, 'lä-\\ 1927– Am. soprano; noted for her interpretations of esp. Verdi and Barber; pioneering African-American in operatic world

Pride \\'prīd\\ Thomas *d* 1658 Eng. parliamentary commander; conducted a expulsion of Presbyterians from House of Commons known as Pride's Purge; a signer of death warrant of Charles I

Priest·ley \\'prēst-lē\\ John Boynton 1894–1984 Eng. author; best remembered for novels *The Good Companions, Ansel Pavement, Lost Empires*, play *An Inspector Calls*, etc.

Priestley Joseph 1733–1804 Eng. clergyman & chem.; best known for discovery of "dephlogisticated air," now called oxygen

Pri·go·gine \\prə-'gȯ-zhən, -,(,)gō-'zhēn\\ Ilya 1917– Belg. (Russ.-born) chem.; awarded 1977 Nobel prize for chemistry for contributions to nonequilibrium thermodynamics

Pri·mo de Ri·ve·ra y Or·ba·ne·ja \'prē-(,)mō-thä-ri-'ver-ə-,ē,ór-bə-'nä-(,)hä\ Miguel 1870–1930 Marqués *de Estella* Span. gen. & polit.; dictator (1923–30) following coup d'état

Primrose Archibald Philip — see ROSEBERY

Prior \'prī(-ə)r\ Matthew 1664–1721 Eng. poet; known for occasional poems, neat epigrams, and for elegance and grace of his familiar verse

Pris·cian \'pri-shən, 'pri-shē-ən\ *fl* A.D. 500 *Priscianus Caesariensis* Latin grammarian at Constantinople; known for his *Institutionis grammaticae,* standard grammar textbook in medieval European schools

Pro·clus \'prō-kləs, 'prä-\ 410?–485 Greek philos.; regarded as last of great teachers of Neoplatonism; vigorous defender of paganism

Pro·co·pi·us \prə-'kō-pē-əs\ 6th cent. Byzantine hist.; wrote narratives of Persian, Vandal, and Gothic wars in time of Justinian, etc.

Pro·kho·rov \,pró-kə-'róf\ Aleksandr Mikhaylovich 1916– Russ. physicist; awarded (with C.H. Townes and N.G. Basov) 1964 Nobel prize for physics for developing masers and lasers

Pro·kof·iev \prə-'kóf-yəf, -,yef, -,yev\ Sergey Sergeyevich 1891–1953 Russ. composer; produced music for ballets, films, operas, symphonies, etc., including *Peter and the Wolf, Romeo and Juliet, Cinderella,* etc. — **Pro·kof·iev·ian** \-,kóf-'ye-vē-ən\ *adj*

Pro·per·tius \prō-'pər-sh(ē-)əs\ Sextus *ca* 50–*ca* 15 B.C. Rom. poet; author of chiefly amatory verse to his mistress "Cynthia" and others

Pro·tag·o·ras \prō-'ta-gə-rəs\ *ca* 485–410 B.C. Greek philos.; the first and best known of the Sophists; his philosophy epitomized in saying "Man is the measure of all things" — **Pro·tag·o·re·an** \-,ta-gə-'rē-ən\ *adj*

Prou·dhon \prü-dōⁿ\ Pierre-Joseph 1809–1865 Fr. journalist; regarded as father of anarchism

Proust \'prüst\ Marcel 1871–1922 Fr. nov.; introduced exhaustive psychological analysis as a recognized element in fiction in series *A la recherche du temps perdu* — **Proust·ian** \'prü-stē-ən\ *adj*

Prynne \'prin\ William 1600–1669 Eng. Puritan pamphleteer; his persecution by Charles I intensified the hostility between king and Parliament in years preceding English Civil Wars

Prze·val·sky \,pər-zhə-'väl-skē, ,pshə-'väl-\ Nikolay Mikhaylovich 1839–1888 Russ. explorer; in exploration of west central China, eastern Tibet, Gobi Desert, discovered wild camel, early type of horse (now known as Przhewalski's horse), etc.

Ptol·e·my \'tä-lə-mē\ name of 15 kings of Egypt 323–30 B.C., comprising the Ptolemaic or Macedonian dynasty — **Ptol·e·ma·ic** \,tä-lə-'mā-ik\ *adj*

Ptolemy 2d cent. A.D. *Claudius Ptolemaeus* Alexandrian astron.; in *Almagest* described Ptolemaic, heliocentric system of astronomy and geography

Puc·ci·ni \pü-'chē-nē\ Giacomo 1858–1924 Ital. composer; composed operas, most with tragic love themes, *La Bohème, Tosca, Madame Butterfly,* incomplete *Turandot,* etc. — **Puc·ci·ni·an** \-nē-ən\ *adj*

P'u–i \'pü-ē, -'yē\ Henry 1906–1967 *Hsüan-T'ung* Chin. emp. (1908–12); last of Manchu dynasty; puppet emp. of Manchukuo (1934–45)

Pu·las·ki \pə-'las-kē, pyü-\ Kazimierz 1747–1779 Pol. soldier in Am. Revolution; general, chief of cavalry, and commander of guerrilla group known as the Pułaski Legion

Pu·lit·zer \'pù-lət-sər (*family's pron.*), 'pyü-\ Joseph 1847–1911 Am. (Hung.-born) journalist; helped create the modern newspaper; established Pulitzer prizes for achievement in American journalism, letters, and music

Pull·man \'pùl-mən\ George Mortimer 1831–1897 Am. inventor; helped design Pullman railroad car with convertible berths, dining car, chair car, vestibule car

Pu·pin \pyü-'pēn, pü-\ Michael Idvorsky 1858–1935 Am. (Hung.-born) physicist & inventor; improved long-distance telephony; developed method for short-exposure x-ray photography

Pur·cell \(,)pər-'sel\ Edward Mills 1912–   Am. physicist; awarded (with F. Bloch) 1952 Nobel prize for physics for developing magnetic measurement methods for atomic nuclei

Pur·cell \'pər-səl, (,)pər-'sel\ Henry ca 1659–1695 Eng. composer; composed for every public event of Charles II, incidental music for 43 plays, chamber music, operas *Dido and Aeneas*, etc.

Pur·chas \'pər-chəs\ Samuel ca 1577–1626 Eng. compiler of travel books; known esp. for *Purchas, his Pilgrimages*, on religions of all ages

Pur·ky·ně *or* **Pur·kin·je** \'pùr-kən-,yā\ Jan Evangelista 1787–1869 Bohemian physiol.; known for observations and discoveries in physiology and microscopic anatomy, and for recognizing fingerprints as means of identification

Pu·sey \'pyü-zē\ Edward Bouverie 1800–1882 Eng. theol.; leader of Oxford Movement; influential in revival of confession in English Church and endeavored to unite English and Roman churches

Push·kin \'pùsh-kən\ Aleksandr Sergeyevich 1799–1837 Russ. poet; introduced Romanticism and the Byronic hero into Russian literature — **Push·kin·ian** \pùsh-'ki-nē-ən\ *adj*

Put·nam \'pət-nəm\ Israel 1718–1790 Am. gen. in Revolution; famed as an Indian fighter during French and Indian War but generally unsuccessful as a Revolutionary commander

Putnam Rufus 1738–1824 *cousin of prec.* Am. gen. in Revolution; in charge of defensive works around Boston and New York and rebuilt West Point defenses; led colony to Marietta, Ohio, first organized settlement in Northwest Territory

Pu·vis de Cha·vannes \pᵫ-vē-də-shä-vän, -vēs-; pyü-vē(s)-də-shä-'vän\ Pierre-Cécile 1824–1898 Fr. painter & muralist; best known for murals for the Boston public library

Pye \'pī\ Henry James 1745–1813 Eng. poet laureate (1790–1813); author of ludicrously tame patriotic verses and epic *Alfred*

Pyle \'pī(ə)l\ Ernest Taylor 1900–1945 *Ernie Pyle* Am. journalist; famous for columns about ordinary soldiers during WWII; killed during Okinawa campaign

Pym \'pim\ John 1584–1643 Eng. statesman; a leader in events leading up to Civil War; led Parliament in seizing power of taxation and rejecting peace negotiations

Pyn·chon \'pin-chən\ Thomas 1937–   Am. writer; author of novels *V*, *The Crying of Lot 49*, *Gravity's Rainbow*, etc.; noted for his use of black humor and fantasy to dramatize alienation in modern society — **Pyn·chon·esque** \,pin-chə-'nesk\ *adj*

Pyr·rhus \'pir-əs\ 319–272 B.C. king of Epirus (306–302, 297–272 B.C.); defeated Romans at Heraclea, but heavy losses in victory gave rise to phrase "Pyrrhic victory"

Py·thag·o·ras \pə-'tha-gə-rəs, pī-\ *ca* 580–*ca* 500 B.C. Greek philos. & math.; generally credited with theory of functional significance of numbers in the objective world and in music — **Py·thag·o·re·an** \pə-,tha-gə-'rē-ən\ *adj*

Q

Qad·da·fi — see GADHAFI

Qua·dros \'kwä-,drōs\ Jânio da Silva 1917–1992 pres. of Brazil (1960–61)

Quarles \'kwȯr(-ə)lz, 'kwär(-ə)lz\ Francis 1592–1644 Eng. poet; wrote *Emblemes* and *Hièroglyphikes of the life of Man*, most popular books of verse in 17th century

Qua·si·mo·do \kwä-'zē-mə-,dō\ Salvatore \,säl-vä-'tō-(,)rä\ 1901–1968 Ital. poet & critic; a leading Hermetic poet; author of introverted and symbolist books of verse

Quayle \'kwā(ə)l\ Sir (John) Anthony 1913–1989 Brit. actor & director; famed for directing and acting in plays produced by the Shakespeare Memorial Theatre (later Royal Shakespeare) Company and for appearance in film *Lawrence of Arabia*

Quayle James Danforth 1947– *Dan Quayle* Am. polit.; vice pres. of the U.S. (1989–93)

Queensberry Marquis of — see DOUGLAS

Quercia, della Jacopo — see JACOPO DELLA QUERCIA

Ques·nay \kā-'nā\ François 1694–1774 Fr. physician & econ.; wrote articles for the *Encyclopédie* that formulated the theoretical basis of the physiocratic school of economics

Que·zon y Mo·li·na \'kā-,sȯn-,ē-mə-'lē-nə\ Manuel Luis 1878–1944 pres. of the Philippine Commonwealth (1935–44)

Quid·de \'kvi-də, 'kwi-\ Ludwig 1858–1941 Ger. hist. & pacifist; awarded (with F. Buisson) 1927 Nobel prize for peace

Quil·ler–Couch \'kwi-lər-'küch\ Sir Arthur Thomas 1863–1944 pseud. *Q* Eng. author; author of many romances, short stories, and novels, esp. on Cornwall and the sea, and of criticism and verse

Quin·cy \'kwin-zē, 'kwin(t)-sē\ Josiah 1744–1775 Am. lawyer; pamphleteer in pre-Revolutionary agitation

Quine \'kwīn\ Willard Van Orman 1908– Am. philos.; investigated philosophical issues within a systematic linguistic framework

Quintero Serafín & Joaquín — see ALVAREZ QUINTERO

Quin·til·ian \kwin-'til-yən\ *ca* A.D. 35–*ca* 100 *Marcus Fabius Quintilianus* Rom. rhetorician; author of *Institutio oratoria* containing principles of rhetoric and a practical exposition of Roman education and educational methods

Qui·ri·no \ki-'rē-(,)nō\ Elpidio 1890–1956 pres. of the Philippine Republic (1948–53); suppressed communist Huk movement;

brought economic gains, but permitted graft and corruption; failed to solve social problems

Quoirez Françoise — see Françoise SAGAN

R

Ra·be·lais \'ra-bə-ˌlā, ˌra-bə-'lā\ François *ca* 1483–1553 Fr. humorist & satirist; author of novels known as *Gargantua and Pantagruel;* noted for racy humor and satirical content — **Ra·be·lai·sian** \ˌra-bə-'lā-zhen, -zē-ən\ *adj*

Ra·bi \'rä-bē\ Isidor Isaac 1898–1988 Am. (Austrian-born) physicist; awarded 1944 Nobel prize for physics for recording the magnetic properties of atomic nuclei

Ra·bin \rä-'bēn\ Yitzhak 1922–1995 prime min. of Israel (1974–77, 92–95); awarded (with S. Peres, Y. Arafat) 1994 Nobel peace prize for efforts to create peace in the Middle East

Rabinowitz Solomon — see Shalom ALEICHEM

Rach·ma·ni·noff \'räk-'mä-nə-ˌnof\ Sergey Vasilyevich 1873–1943 Russ. composer, pianist, & conductor; composed symphonies, piano concertos (esp. Nos. 2 and 3), orchestral works, operas, songs, etc.

Ra·cine \ra-'sēn, rə-\ Jean 1639–1699 Fr. dram.; author of tragedies often based on classical themes, including *Britannicus, Bérénice, Phèdre* — **Ra·cin·ian** \ra-'si-nē-ən, rə-\ *adj*

Rack·ham \'ra-kəm\ Arthur 1867–1939 Brit. illustrator; known for imaginative, stylized illustrations, esp. for children's books

Rad·cliffe \'rad-ˌklif\ Ann 1764–1823 née *Ward* Eng. nov.; most original and distinguished writer of Gothic romances, as *The Mysteries of Udolpho;* fond of vivid description, startling events and horrors

Ra·detz·ky \rə-'det-skē\ Joseph 1766–1858 Graf *Radetzky von Radetz* Austrian field marshal; served against Napoléon, defeated Sardinians, captured Venice

Rae \'rā\ John 1813–1893 Scot. explorer; surveyed and mapped 1400 miles of Canadian Arctic coast

Rae·burn \'rā-(ˌ)bərn\ Sir Henry 1756–1823 Scot. painter; fashionable Edinburgh portrait painter of Scott, Hume, Boswell, etc.

Rae·der \'rā-dər\ Erich 1876–1960 Ger. admiral; commander in chief of German Navy (1928–43); pursued an aggressive naval strategy

Rae·mae·kers \'rā-ˌmä-kərz, -kərs\ Louis 1869–1956 Du. cartoonist; known esp. for anti-German cartoons in Amsterdam *Telegraaf* during WWI

Raf·san·ja·ni \ˌräf-sän-'jä-nē\ Ali Akbar Hashemi 1934–   pres. of Iran (1989–   )

Rag·lan \'ra-glən\ 1st Baron 1788–1855 *FitzRoy James Henry Somerset* Brit. field marshal; British commander in chief during Crimean War; his ambiguous order at Battle of Balaklava led to disastrous cavalry charge of the Light Brigade

Rai·mon·di \rī-'män-dē, -'mōn-\ Marcantonio *ca* 1480–*ca* 1534 Ital. engraver; leading Italian line engraver of the Renaissance, first to reproduce designs of other artists

Rai·nier III \rə-'nir, ra-, rā-\ 1923– prince of Monaco (1949–)

Rains \'rānz\ Claude 1889–1967 Am. (Brit.-born) actor; known for roles in films *Casablanca, Notorious, Lawrence of Arabia,* etc.

Rain·wa·ter \'rān-,wȯ-tər, -,wä-\ L(eo) James 1917–1986 Am. physicist; awarded (with A.N. Bohr and B.R. Mottelson) 1975 Nobel prize for physics for work on the structure of the atomic nucleus

Ra·ja·go·pa·la·cha·ri \'rä-jə-(,)gō-,pä-lə-'chär-ē\ Chakravarti 1879–1972 Indian polit.; gov.-gen. of India (1948–50)

Ra·leigh *or* **Ra·legh** \'rȯ-lē, 'rä- *also* 'ra-\ Sir Walter 1554–1618 Eng. courtier, navigator, & hist.; a favorite of Queen Elizabeth I; made several unsuccessful attempts to colonize along American coast, including the Lost Colony at Roanoke Island, N.C.; introduced potato and tobacco to England and Ireland

Ra·ma·krish·na \,rä-mə-'krish-nə\ 1836–1886 Hindu religious; preached the essential unity of all religions and looked upon as sainted wise man by Hindus

Ra·man \'rä-mən\ Sir Chan·dra·se·kha·ra \,chən-drə-'shä-kə-rə\ Venkata 1888–1970 Indian physicist; awarded 1930 Nobel prize for physics for discovering the Raman effect (when light traverses a transparent material, some of the light changes in wavelength)

Ra·meau \ra-'mō\ Jean-Philippe 1683–1764 Fr. composer; considered greatest French musical dramatist and leading theorist of the day; also known for his harpsichord music

Ra·mée \rə-'mā\ Marie Louise de la 1839–1908 pseud. *Oui·da* \'wē-də\ Eng. nov.; wrote melodramatic romances of fashionable life and later of Italian peasant life

Ra·món y Ca·jal \rə-'mōn-(,)ē-kə-'häl\ Santiago 1852–1934 Span. histologist; awarded (with C. Golgi) 1906 Nobel prize for physiology or medicine for studies of nerve tissue

Ra·mos \'rä-(,)mōs\ Fidel V. 1928– pres. of the Philippines (1992–)

Ram·say \'ram-zē\ Allan 1686–1758 Scot. poet; maintained the poetic traditions of Scotland by writing Scots poetry and preserving the works of earlier Scottish poets

Ramsay James Andrew Broun 1812–1860 10th Earl & 1st Marquis of *Dal·hou·sie* \dal-'haü-zē\ Brit. colonial administrator; as governor general of India, annexed much territory, developed resources, reformed administration, established public works and transportation system, instituted Westernizing social reforms

Ramsay Sir William 1852–1916 Brit. chem.; awarded 1904 Nobel prize for chemistry for discovering helium, neon, xenon, and krypton and determining their place in the periodic table

Ram·ses \'ram-,sēz\ *or* **Ram·e·ses** \'ra-mə-,sēz\ name of 11 kings of Egypt: esp. **II** (reigned 1304–1237 B.C.); reign marked last peak of Egyptian imperial power; famed for his massive building programs and many colossal statues bearing his likeness; **III** (reigned 1198–1166 B.C.); checked invasions of Libyans and Sea Peoples; last years filled with internal disturbances

Ram·sey \\'ram-zē\\ (Arthur) Michael 1904–1988 archbishop of Canterbury (1961–74)

Ramsey Norman Foster 1915–   Am. physicist; awarded (with H.G. Dehmelt and W. Paul) 1989 Nobel prize for physics for work that led to the atomic clock

Rand \\'rand\\ Ayn \\'īn\\ 1905–1982 Am. (Russ.-born) writer; espoused her philosophy of objectivism and "rational selfishness" in novels *Atlas Shrugged, The Fountainhead,* etc.

Ran·dolph \\'ran-ˌdälf\\ Asa Philip 1889–1979 Am. labor leader; director of March on Washington for Jobs and Freedom (1963), largest civil rights demonstration in U.S. history

Randolph Edmund Jennings 1753–1813 Am. statesman; instrumental in the drafting and ratification of the U.S. Constitution; attorney general and later secy. of state in Washington's cabinet

Randolph John 1773–1833 *John Randolph of Roanoke* Am. statesman; staunch advocate of doctrine of states' rights and consistent opponent of efforts toward a strong centralized government

Ran·jit Singh \\'rən-jət-'siṇ\\ 1780–1839 *Lion of the Punjab* founder of Sikh kingdom; consolidated most of Punjab into Sikh kingdom

Ran·ke \\'räṇ-kə\\ Leopold von 1795–1886 Ger. hist.; a founder of the modern school of history; champion of objective writing based on source material

Ran·som \\'ran(t)-səm\\ John Crowe 1888–1974 Am. educ. & poet; member of Southern poetical circle The Fugitives; founder of the *Kenyon Review,* author of *The New Criticism,* the manifesto of an influential critical school

Rao \\'raü, 'rä-ō\\ Pamulaparti Venkata Narasimha 1921–   prime min. of India (1991–   )

Ra·pha·el \\'ra-fē-əl, 'rä-, 'rä-\\ 1483–1520 It. *Raffaello Sanzio* Ital. painter; a master of the Italian High Renaissance; famed for religious pictures, esp. Madonna series; numerous works include Vatican frescoes *Disputa* and *School of Athens* — **Ra·pha·el·esque** \\ˌra-fē-ə-'lesk, ˌrä-, ˌrä-\\ *adj*

Rask \\'rask, 'räsk\\ Rasmus Kristian 1787–1832 Dan. philologist & orientalist; a founder of modern science of linguistics

Ras·mus·sen \\'ras-mə-sən, 'räs-ˌmü-s°n\\ Knud Johan Victor 1879–1933 Dan. explorer & ethnologist; authority on the Greenland Eskimo; made first recorded sledge crossing of Melville Bay

Ras·pu·tin \\ra-'spyü-t°n, -'spü-, -'spü-\\ Grigory Yefimovich 1872–1916 Russ. mystic; powerful personage in court of Czar Nicholas II and Czarina Alexandra for his healing abilities over their hemophiliac son

Rausch·en·berg \\'raü-shən-ˌberg\\ Robert 1925–   Am. artist; incorporated wide range of trash and debris with splashes of paint in collages and "combines"

Ra·vel \\rə-'vel, ra-\\ Mau·rice \\mȯ-'rēs\\ 1875–1937 Fr. composer; known esp. for ballet *Boléro,* orchestration of Mussorgsky's *Pictures from an Exhibition,* piano music, etc. — **Ra·vel·ian** \\rə-'ve-lyən, ra-, -'lē-ən\\ *adj*

Raw·lings \\'rȯ-liṇz\\ Marjorie Kinnan 1896–1953 Am. writer; wrote novels and stories set in backwoods Florida, esp. *The Yearling*

Raw·lin·son \'rȯ-lən-sən\ Sir Henry Cres·wicke \'kre-zik\ 1810–1895 Eng. orientalist; deciphered Old Persian cuneiform inscriptions, key to expanding knowledge of ancient Near East

Ray \'rā\ John 1627–1705 Eng. naturalist; often called "father of English natural history" through work on plants and insects; established the species as the ultimate unit of taxonomy

Ray Satyajit 1921–1992 Indian film director, writer, & producer; India's foremost filmmaker; known for poetic narratives of Bengali life as *Pather Panchali, Aparajito,* and *Apu Sansar*

Ray·burn \'rā-(,)bərn\ Samuel Taliaferro 1882–1961 Am. polit.; member (1913–61), speaker (1940–46, 1949–53, 1955–61), U.S. House of Representatives; instrumental in passing New Deal program

Ray·leigh \'rā-lē\ Lord 1842–1919 *John William Strutt* Eng. math. & physicist; awarded 1904 Nobel prize for physics for studying the density of gases and discovering argon

Read \'rēd\ George 1733–1798 Am. statesman in Revolution; instrumental in causing Delaware to be first state to ratify Constitution

Read Sir Herbert 1893–1968 Eng. writer; chief advocate and interpreter of British art movements (from 1930s)

Reade \'rēd\ Charles 1814–1884 Eng. nov. & dram.; drew attention to social ills in several polemic novels; best known for historical romance *The Cloister and the Hearth*

Read·ing \'re-diŋ\ 1st Marquis of 1860–1935 *Rufus Daniel Isaacs* Brit. statesman; viceroy of India (1921–26)

Rea·gan \'rā-gən\ Ronald Wilson 1911–   Am. actor & polit.; 40th pres. of the U.S. (1981–89); achieved a significantly lower rate of inflation; lowered personal income taxes; greatly increased defense spending while reducing expenditures on social programs — **Rea·gan·esque** \,rā-gə-'nesk\ *adj*

Ré·au·mur \,rā-ō-'myu̇r, -'mü̇r\ René-Antoine Ferchault de 1683–1757 Fr. naturalist & physicist; worked on the production of steel and iron; isolated and investigated role of gastric juice, etc.

Ré·ca·mi·er \rā-'ka-mē-,ā, rā-kȧ-myā\ Jeanne-Françoise-Julie-Adélaïde 1777–1849 Fr. society hostess; with wit and charm, attracted notables in politics and the arts to her salon in Paris

Red Cloud \'red-,klau̇d\ 1822–1909 Sioux Indian chief; conducted Red Cloud's War (1865–67), a successful harassment of government efforts to develop the Bozeman Trail in Wyoming and Montana

Red·mond \'red-mənd\ John Edward 1856–1918 Irish polit.; prominent organizer of Home Rule propaganda and forces

Re·don \rə-'dōⁿ\ Odilon 1840–1916 Fr. artist; a Postimpressionist and a forerunner of Surrealists

Reed \'rēd\ John 1887–1920 Am. journalist, poet, & communist; an eyewitness to the 1917 Bolshevik Revolution in Russia, which he recounted in *Ten Days that Shook the World*

Reed Stanley Forman 1884–1980 Am. jurist; associate justice, U.S. Supreme Court (1938–57)

Reed Thomas Brackett 1839–1902 Am. polit.; responsible for adoption by the House of Representatives of Reed's Rules, whereby speaker can expedite legislation favored by majority party

Reed Walter 1851–1902 Am. army surgeon; proved that yellow fever is transmitted by mosquito *Aëdes aegypti*, leading to eradication of carriers and disease; Walter Reed Hospital, Washington, D.C., named for him

Reg·u·lus \\'re-gyə-ləs\\ Marcus Atilius *d ca* 250 B.C. Rom. gen.; subject of legendary account of his heroic endurance as a captive in Carthage

Rehn·quist \\'ren-ˌkwist, 'ren-kwəst\\ William Hubbs 1924– Am. jurist; chief justice U.S. Supreme Court (1986–)

Reich \\'rīsh, 'rīk\\ Robert Bernard 1946– U.S. secy. of labor (1993–)

Reich \\'rīk\\ Wilhelm 1897–1957 Austrian psychol.; known for theory of repressive action of society on personality and restoration of integrity through "orgone" energy — **Reich·ian** \\'rī-kē-ən\\ *adj*

Reich·stein \\'rīk-ˌshtīn, -ˌstīn\\ Tadeus 1897– Swiss (Pol.-born) chem.; awarded (with P.S. Hinch and E.C. Kendall) 1950 Nobel prize for physiology or medicine for discoveries on cortisone and ACTH

Reid \\'rēd\\ Thomas 1710–1796 Scot. philos.; founder of the Scottish or "common sense" school

Reid Whitelaw 1837–1912 Am. journalist & diplomat; editor, New York Tribune (1872–1905); on commission that negotiated peace following Spanish-American War

Rei·ner \\'rī-nər\\ Fritz 1888–1963 Am. (Hung.-born) conductor of Cincinnati Symphony; music director of Metropolitan Opera, Chicago Symphony, etc.

Rein·hardt \\'rīn-ˌhärt\\ Max 1873–1943 orig. surname *Goldmann* Austrian theater director; one of the first directors to be seen as a primary creative force in the staging of a dramatic work

Re·marque \\rə-'märk\\ Erich Maria 1898–1970 Am. (Ger.-born) nov.; known esp. for *All Quiet on the Western Front*

Rem·brandt \\'rem-ˌbrant *also* -ˌbränt\\ 1606–1669 in full *Rembrandt Harmensz* (or *Harmenszoon*) *van Rijn* (or *Ryn*) Du. painter; leading representative of the Dutch school of painting; master of chiaroscuro, luxuriant brushwork, brilliant color; known for psychological insight in his portraits and self-portraits — **Rembrandt·esque** \\ˌrem-ˌbran-ˈtesk, -ˌbrän-\\ *adj*

Rem·ing·ton \\'re-miŋ-tən\\ Frederic 1861–1909 Am. artist; known as animal painter and illustrator of scenes from the American West

Rem·sen \\'rem(p)-sən, 'rem-zən\\ Ira 1846–1927 Am. chem.; discovered saccharin

Re·nan \\rə-'nä(n)\\ Joseph Ernest 1823–1892 Fr. philologist & hist.; a leader of the school of critical philosophy in France

Re·nault \\rə-'nō\\ Louis 1843–1918 Fr. jurist & pacifist; awarded 1907 Nobel prize for peace for organizing and representing France at peace conferences

Re·ni \\'rā-nē\\ Guido 1575–1642 Ital. painter; known for classical idealism of his religious and mythological subjects

Ren·ner \\'re-nər\\ Karl 1870–1950 pres. of Austria (1945–50)

Re·no \\'rē-(ˌ)nō\\ Janet 1938– U.S. atty. gen. (1993–)

Re·noir \\'ren-ˌwär, rən-'\\ Jean 1894–1979 *son of P.-A.* Fr. film director & writer; made such classics as *La Grande Illusion, The Rules of the Game, The River*

Re·noir \'ren-ˌwär\ Pierre-Auguste 1841–1919 Fr. painter; a leader among the Impressionists but later adopted more formal technique; best known for figure paintings, landscapes, flowers

Ren·wick \'ren-(ˌ)wik\ James 1818–1895 Am. architect; known for Gothic revival designs

Rep·plier \'re-ˌplir, -plē-ər\ Agnes 1855–1950 Am. essayist; author of *Books and Men, Points of View,* etc.

Re·spi·ghi \rə-'spē-gē, re-\ Ottorino 1879–1936 Ital. composer; known for his orchestral colorism

Res·ton \'res-tən\ James Barrett 1909–1995 Am. journalist; reporter & editor, *New York Times* (1939–89); famed Washington, D.C., insider

Retz \'rets, *Fr* re(s)\ Cardinal de 1613–1679 *Jean-François-Paul de Gondi* Fr. ecclesiastic & polit.; wrote *Memoires,* valuable source of information on contemporary life

Reuch·lin \'rȯi-klən; -ˌklēn, rȯi-\ Johannes 1455–1522 *Cap·nio* \'kap-nē-ˌō\ Ger. humanist; promoter of Greek and Hebrew studies in Germany; champion of modern (Reuchlian) pronunciation of Greek

Reu·ter \'rȯi-tər\ Baron Paul Julius von 1816–1899 orig. *Israel Beer Josaphat* Brit. (Ger.-born) journalist; founded Reuter's News Agency

Reu·ther \'rü-thər\ Walter Philip 1907–1970 Am. labor leader; pres. of United Automobile Workers (1946–70)

Re·vere \ri-'vir\ Paul 1735–1818 Am. patriot & silversmith; his ride from Boston to Lexington to warn that British were coming was celebrated by Longfellow in *The Midnight Ride of Paul Revere*

Rex·roth \'reks-ˌrȯth\ Kenneth 1905–1982 Am. writer; associated with the literary Beat generation; wrote *In What Hour, The Dragon and the Unicorn, Alternative Society,* etc.

Rey·mont \'rā-ˌmänt\ *or* **Rej·ment** \'rā-ˌment\ Wła·dy·sław \vlä-'di-ˌsläf\ Sta·ni·sław \stä-'nē-ˌsläf\ 1867–1925 Pol. nov.; awarded 1924 Nobel prize for literature for *Chłopi (The Peasants)*

Rey·naud \rā-'nō\ Paul 1878–1966 premier of France (1940); at time of France's surrender to Germany resigned rather than conclude armistice

Reyn·olds \'re-nᵊl(d)z\ Sir Joshua 1723–1792 Eng. painter; leading figure in 18th-century British art; known esp. for his portraits in the continental Grand Style; his *Discourses Delivered at the Royal Academy* important in art critical theory

Re·za Shah Pah·la·vi \ri-'zä-'shä-'pä-lə-(ˌ)vē, -'shō-\ 1878–1944 *father of Mohammad Reza Pahlavi* shah of Iran (1925–41); modernized country; emancipated women

Rhee \'rē\ Syng·man \'siŋ-mən, 'sig-\ 1875–1965 So. Korean polit.; pres. of So. Korea (1948–60); assumed dictatorial powers until forced to resign

Rhodes \'rōdz\ Cecil John 1853–1902 Brit. administrator & financier in So. Africa; obtained territory north of Bechuanaland, named it Rhodesia (now Zimbabwe); by will endowed scholarships for education at Oxford for students from British Empire, U.S., and Germany

Rhond·da \'rän-də, -thə\ 1st Viscount 1856–1918 *David Alfred Thomas* Brit. industrialist & administrator; as controller of ministry of food (1917–18), stabilized prices and set up system of rationing

Rhys \'rēs\ Jean 1890–1979 orig. *Ella Gwendolen Rees William* West Indian nov.; best known for *Wide Sargasso Sea,* a prequel to Charlotte Brontë's classic *Jane Eyre*

Rib·ben·trop \'ri-bən-ˌträp, -ˌtrōp\ Joachim von 1893–1946 Ger. diplomat; aided in organizing Nazi government and negotiated pacts and alliances with Britain, Russia, Japan, Italy

Ri·be·ra \rē-'ber-ə\ José (or Jusepe) de 1591–1652 *Lo Spa·gno·let·to* \ˌlō-ˌspän-yə-'le-(ˌ)tō\ Span. painter & etcher in Naples; a leading painter of the Neapolitan school; known esp. for dramatic realism and use of light and shadow

Ri·car·do \ri-'kär-(ˌ)dō\ David 1772–1823 Eng. econ.; regarded as first to systematize economics, advocated laissez-faire doctrines; his Iron Law of Wages maintained that workers' wages were doomed to subsistence level

Rice \'rīs\ Anne 1941–   née O'Brien Am. nov.; best known for the Vampire Chronicles, series of novels beginning with *Interview with the Vampire*

Rice Elmer Leopold 1892–1967 orig. *Elmer Reizenstein* Am. dram.; author of *On Trial, Street Scene* (Pulitzer prize), etc.

Rich \'rich\ Adrienne Cecile 1929–   Am. poet; known esp. for deeply personal free-form verse that increasingly became informed by a lesbian/feminist aesthetic

Rich Bernard 1917–1987 *Buddy Rich* Am. musician; a jazz drummer of legendary, lightning-fast virtuosity; led the Buddy Rich Big Band

Rich·ard \'ri-chərd\ name of 3 kings of England: **I** (*Coeur de Li·on* \ˌkər-də-'lī-ən, -ˈlē-; -lē-ˈōⁿ\) 1157–1199 (reigned 1189–99); during Third Crusade conquered Cyprus, Acre, Jaffa; captured in Austria, ransomed by England; hero of romantic legends; **II** 1367–1400 (reigned 1377–99); defeated by Henry of Bolingbroke (later Henry IV), deposed by Parliament, imprisoned; **III** 1452–1485 (reigned 1483–85); suspected of murdering Edward V and his brother Richard; suppressed rebellion of Duke of Buckingham, but defeated and killed by Earl of Richmond (later Henry VII)

Rich·ards \'ri-chərdz\ Ann 1933–   orig. *Dorothy Ann Willis* Am. polit.; governor of Texas (1991–95)

Richards Dickinson Woodruff 1895–1973 Am. physician; awarded (with A.F. Cournand and W. Forssman) 1956 Nobel prize for physiology or medicine for using a catheter to chart the interior of the heart

Richards Theodore William 1868–1928 Am. chem.; awarded 1914 Nobel prize for chemistry for determining the atomic weights of many elements

Rich·ard·son \'ri-chərd-sən\ Henry Handel 1870–1946 pseud. of *Ethel Florence Lindesay Richardson* Austral. nov.; author of *The Getting of Wisdom, The End of Childhood* (short stories), etc.

Richardson Henry Hobson 1838–1886 Am. architect; pioneer of Romanesque revival in U.S.; pioneer in development of indigenous American architectural style

Richardson Sir Owen Willans 1879–1959 Eng. physicist; awarded 1928 Nobel prize for physics for studying electron emission by hot metals

Richardson Sir Ralph David 1902–1983 Brit. actor; celebrated for his performances on stage as Uncle Vanya, Falstaff, etc. and in films *The Heiress, Long Day's Journey Into Night,* etc.

Richardson Samuel 1689–1761 Eng. nov.; author of *Pamela: or Virtue Rewarded, Clarissa; or the History of a Young Lady,* etc.; a pioneer in the development of the epistolary novel

Ri·che·lieu \'ri-shə-ˌlü, -shəl-ˌyü; rē-shə-lyœ\ Duc de 1585–1642 Armand-Jean du Plessis Fr. cardinal & statesman; controlled Louis XIII and directed French domestic and foreign policies toward royal absolutism and weakening of Hapsburgs

Ri·chet \rē-'shā\ Charles Robert 1850–1935 Fr. physiol.; awarded 1913 Nobel prize for physiology or medicine for studying allergies caused by foreign substances

Rich·ter \'rik-tər\ Burton 1931– (with S.C.C. Ting) 1976 Nobel prize for physics for discovery of the elementary nuclear *psi,* or *J,* particle

Richter Charles Francis 1900–1985 Am. seismologist; helped devise scale to measure strength of earthquakes, named for him

Rich·ter \'rik-tər, 'rik-\ Jean Paul Friedrich 1763–1825 pseud. *Jean Paul* \'zhän-ˌpaul\ Ger. writer; author of novels and of works on pedagogy, art, philosophy, politics

Ric·i·mer \'ri-sə-mər\ Flavius *d* 472 Rom. gen.; effective sovereign of the Western Roman Empire, deposing and installing emperors at his will

Rick·en·back·er \'ri-kən-ˌba-kər\ Edward Vernon 1890–1973 Am. aviator; credited with 26 air victories during WWI

Rick·o·ver \'ri-ˌkō-vər\ Hyman George 1900–1986 Am. admiral; supervised adaptation of nuclear power to propel ships, the first of which was the submarine *Nautilus*

Ride \'rīd\ Sally Kristen 1951– Am. astronaut; first U.S. woman to fly in space

Ridg·way \'rij-ˌwā\ Matthew Bunker 1895–1993 Am. gen.; commander of 82nd Airborne Division during WWII; directed invasion of Sicily, first large-scale airborne operation in army history

Rid·ley \'rid-lē\ Nicholas *ca* 1503–1555 Eng. reformer & martyr; denounced Queens Mary and Elizabeth as illegitimate; on Mary's accession declared a heretic, excommunicated, condemned, burned alive

Rie·fen·stahl \'rē-fən-ˌshtäl\ Leni 1902– orig. *Berta Helene Amalie Riefenstahl* Ger. filmmaker; extolled the power and pageantry of the Nazi movement in cinematically brilliant documentaries, including *Triumph of the Will, Olympia*

Ri·el \rē-'el\ Louis 1844–1885 Canad. insurgent; led Métis in opposition to incorporation of Northwest Territories into Canadian dominion; eventually surrendered, tried for treason, hanged

Rie·mann \'rē-ˌmän\ Georg Friedrich Bernhard 1826–1866 Ger. math.; provided foundation for theory of relativity with his ideas on geometry; many mathematical theorems, concepts named for him — **Rie·mann·ian** \rē-'mä-nē-ən\ *adj*

Rien·zo \'ryent-sō\ Cola *di* 1313–1354 prename *Niccolò* Ital. leader; made himself dictatorial head of Roman state twice; hero of opera by Wagner, novel by Bulwer-Lytton

Ries·man \'rēs-mən\ David 1909–   Am. social scientist; co-author of study of urban middle class *The Lonely Crowd*

Riis \'rēs\ Jacob August 1849–1914 Am. (Dan.-born) social reformer; active in improving slum conditions in schools and tenements of lower New York City

Ri·ley \'rī-lē\ James Whit·comb \'hwit-kəm, 'wit-\ 1849–1916 Am. poet; wrote dialect poems dealing with scenes of simple life, marked by gentle humor, pathos, sincerity, naturalness

Riley Richard Wilson 1933–   U.S. secy. of education (1993–)

Ril·ke \'ril-kə, -kē\ Rai·ner \'rī-nər\ Maria 1875–1926 Ger. poet; developed style of lyrical poetry called "Ding-Gedicht," used in his finest poetry *Duineser Elegien* and *Die Sonnette an Orpheus*

Rim·baud \raⁿ(m)-'bō, 'ram-\ (Jean-Nicholas-) Arthur 1854–1891 Fr. poet; leading influence on Symbolist movement; best known for prose poems *Illuminations*

Rimini Francesca da — see POLENTA

Rim·sky–Kor·sa·kov \,rim(p)-skē-'kȯr-sə-,kȯf, -,kȯv, -,kȯr-sə-\ Nikolay Andreyevich 1844–1908 Russ. composer; best known for suite *Sheherazade*, "Flight of the Bumble Bee," etc.

Rine·hart \'rīn-,härt\ Mary 1876–1958 née *Roberts* Am. writer; author of mysteries and romances including *The Circular Staircase*, *The Breaking Point*, *The Frightened Wife*, etc.

Rí·os \'rē-,ōs\ Juan Antonio 1888–1946 pres. of Chile (1942–46)

Rip·ley \'ri-plē\ George 1802–1880 Am. lit. critic & socialist; involved in Transcendental movement; organized communal Brook Farm; founded and edited *Harper's New Monthly Magazine* (1850–54); literary critic, *New York Tribune* (1849–80)

Ritch·ie \'ri-chē\ Jean 1922–   Am. singer & folklorist; compiled numerous volumes of traditional American folksongs esp. of the Appalachians; noted for her recordings of folksongs and dulcimer music

Ri·ve·ra \ri-'ver-ə\ Diego 1886–1957 Mex. painter; a leader of Mexican politico-social school of painting; best known for leftist-oriented murals on native historical themes

Riv·ers \'ri-vərz\ Larry 1923–   Am. artist; an Abstract Expressionist and a forerunner of Pop art; known for ironic approach to historical subjects and realistic paintings

Ri·zal \ri-'zäl, -'säl\ José Protasio 1861–1896 Filipino patriot; advocated reform of Spanish rule and provided main stimulus to revolution of 1896–98

Riza Shah Pahlavi *var of* REZA SHAH PAHLAVI

Riz·zio \'rit-sē-,ō\ *or* Ric·cio \'ri-chē-,ō\ David *ca* 1533–1566 Ital. musician, secy. & favorite of Mary, Queen of Scots

Robbe–Gril·let \,rȯb-bə-grē-'yā\ Alain 1922–   Fr. writer; leader of the *nouveau roman* genre with novels *Le Voyeur*, *La Jalousie* (*Jealousy*), etc.

Robbia, della Luca — see DELLA ROBBIA

Rob·bins \'rä-bənz\ Frederick Chapman 1916–   Am. physician; awarded (with J.F. Enders and T.H. Weller) 1954 Nobel prize for physiology or medicine for discovering a simple method of growing polio virus in laboratory suspensions

Robbins Jerome 1918–   Am. dancer & choreographer; best known for choreographing *On the Town*, *West Side Story*, *Fiddler on the Roof*, etc.

Robert I \'rä-bərt\ *d* 1035 *the Devil* Duke of Normandy (1027–35) *father of William the Conqueror*

Robert I 1274–1329 *the Bruce* \'brüs\ king of Scotland (1306–1329); gradually drove English out of Scotland and forced Edward III to recognize Scotland's independence and Robert's right to throne

Robert Guis·card \-gē-'skär\ *ca* 1015–1085 *Robert de Hauteville* Norman mil. leader; became duke of Apulia, eventually extending Norman rule over Naples, Calabria, and Sicily

Rob·erts \'rä-bərts\ Sir Charles George Douglas 1860–1943 Canad. poet; considered father of Canadian literature; best remembered for simple lyrics about the scenery and rural life of New Brunswick and Nova Scotia and for short stories with woodland settings

Roberts Frederick Sleigh 1832–1914 1st Earl *Roberts* Brit. field marshal; commander in Second Afghan War (1878–80) and South African War (1899–1902)

Roberts Kenneth 1885–1957 Am. nov.; author of historical novels *Arundel, Northwest Passage,* etc.

Roberts Owen Josephus 1875–1955 Am. jurist; associate justice, U.S. Supreme Court (1930–45)

Roberts Richard John 1943– Am. (Brit.-born) biol.; awarded (with P.A. Sharp) 1993 Nobel prize for physiology or medicine for discoveries regarding the structure and function of genes

Rob·ert·son \'rä-bərt-sən\ William 1721–1793 Scot. hist.; author of *History of Scotland, History of America, History of the Reign of Emperor Charles V*

Robe·son \'rōb-sən\ Paul Bustill 1898–1976 Am. actor & singer; appeared in *Emperor Jones* (play and film), *Show Boat* (play and film), *Othello,* etc., and performed concerts

Robes·pierre \'rōbz-,pir, -,pyer; ,rō-bes-'pyer\ Maximilien=François-Marie-Isidore de 1758–1794 Fr. revolutionary; recognized as leader of radical Montagnards and responsible for much of Reign of Terror; overthrown and guillotined by Thermidorians

Rob·in·son \'rä-bən-sən\ Edwin Arlington 1869–1935 Am. poet; best known for short dramatic poems set in fictional New England town, including "Richard Cory," "Miniver Cheevy," etc.

Robinson George Frederick Samuel 1827–1909 1st Marquis & 2d Earl of *Ripon* Brit. statesman; as governor general of India (1880–84) instituted new Afghan policy, encouraged development of self-government, etc.

Robinson Jack Roosevelt 1919–1972 *Jackie Robinson* Am. baseball player; with Brooklyn Dodgers (1947–56); first African=American to play in U.S. major leagues

Robinson James Harvey 1863–1936 Am. hist.; a pioneer in new methods and content of history teaching, focusing on social, scientific, intellectual, artistic progress

Robinson Sir Robert 1886–1975 Eng. chem.; awarded 1947 Nobel prize for chemistry for studies in plant biology, esp. in alkaloid molecular structures

Robinson Sugar Ray 1921–1989 orig. *Walker Smith* Am. boxer; won world championships in both welterweight and middleweight divisions; in 201 professional bouts scored 109 knockouts; known for his dazzling footwork, lightning speed, and combination punches

Ro·cham·beau \ˌrō-sham-ˈbō\ Comte de 1725–1807 *Jean-Baptiste-Donatien de Vimeur* Fr. field marshal; commanded French force that helped Washington's Continental army defeat Cornwallis at Yorktown

Rock \ˈräk\ John 1890–1984 Am. obstetrician-gynecologist; with G. Pincus and M.C. Chang developed first effective oral contraceptive ("the Pill"), which revolutionized sexual mores, population control, and status of women

Rocke·fel·ler \ˈrä-ki-ˌfe-lər\ John Davison father 1839–1937 Am. oil magnate & philanthropist; dominant in oil business; established and endowed Rockefeller Inst. for Medical Research, Rockefeller Foundation, etc.; benefactor of U. of Chicago; & son 1874–1960; planned and built Rockefeller Center, N.Y. City, and restored Colonial Williamsburg, Va.

Rockefeller Nelson Aldrich 1908–1979 *grandson & son of prec.* Am. polit.; vice pres. of the U.S. (1974–77)

Rock·ing·ham \ˈrä-kiŋ-əm, *US also* -kiŋ-ˌham\ 2d Marquis of 1730–1782 *Charles Watson-Wentworth* Eng. statesman; prime min. (1765–66, 1782); repealed Stamp Act; favored independence for American colonies

Rock·ne \ˈräk-nē\ Knute \ˈnüt\ Kenneth 1888–1931 Am. (Norw.-born) football coach; built Notre Dame into national collegiate football power; instituted substitution of entire team during game

Rock·well \ˈräk-ˌwel, -wəl\ Norman 1894–1978 Am. illustrator; known for his American genre paintings, many on covers of *Saturday Evening Post*

Rod·bell \ˈräd-ˌbel\ Martin 1925–   Am. biochem.; awarded (with A.G. Gilman) 1994 Nobel prize in physiology or medicine for work in discovering G proteins that help control fundamental life processes

Ro·de \ˈrō-thə\ Hel·ge \ˈhel-gə\ 1870–1937 Dan. poet; leader of an anti-rationalist movement opposing materialism and Darwinism and championing mysticism

Rod·gers \ˈrä-jərz\ Richard 1902–1979 Am. composer; collaborated with Lorenz Hart on musical comedies *On Your Toes, Babes in Arms,* etc.; with Oscar Hammerstein on *Oklahoma!, South Pacific, The King and I,* etc.

Ro·din \rō-ˌdan(n)\ (François-)Auguste(-René) 1840–1917 Fr. sculptor; often regarded as sculpture's greatest portraitist esp. for monumental statues of Victor Hugo and Honoré de Balzac; equally famous for "The Thinker" and "The Kiss" — **Ro·din·esque** \ˌrō-ˌda-ˈnesk\ *adj*

Rod·ney \ˈräd-nē\ George Bryd·ges \ˈbri-jəz\ 1718–1792 1st Baron *Rodney* Eng. admiral; effective in defeating Spanish and Dutch in Caribbean Sea

Ro·drí·guez Pe·dot·ti \ˌroth-ˈrē-gäs-pā-ˈdȯt-tē\ Andrés 1923–   pres. of Paraguay (1989–93)

Roeb·ling \ˈrō-bliŋ\ John Augustus 1806–1869 Am. (Ger.-born) civil engineer; designed suspension bridges at Niagara Falls, at Cincinnati; made preliminary plans for Brooklyn Bridge

Roentgen — see RÖNTGEN

Roe·rich \\'rər-ik, 'rer-\\ Nikolay Konstantinovich 1874–1947 Russ. painter; landscape painter known esp. for designing monumental historical sets for Diaghilev's Ballets Russes

Roeth·ke \\'ret-kė, 'reth-\\ Theodore 1908–1963 Am. poet; author of collections of lyrical poems *Open House, The Waking* (Pulitzer prize), *The Far Field*, etc.

Rog·ers \\'rä-jərz\\ Bruce 1870–1957 Am. printer & book designer; designed Montaigne and Centaur typefaces; designed over 400 books, including Oxford Lectern Bible

Rogers Carl Ranson 1902–1987 Am. psychol.; developed open therapy sessions and encounter groups

Rogers Ginger 1911–1995 orig. *Virginia Katherine McMath* Am. dancer & actress; best known as partner of Fred Astaire in 10 classic film musicals, beginning with *Flying Down to Rio*

Rogers Henry Hut·tle·ston \\'hə-t³l-stən\\ 1840–1909 Am. financier; devised machinery for separating naphtha from crude oil; originated idea of pipeline oil transportation; in charge of Standard Oil financial interests

Rogers Robert 1731–1795 Am. frontiersman; headed Rogers' Rangers, using Indian fighting techniques in French and Indian War and later Queen's Rangers, royalist force defeated by Continental army

Rogers William Penn Adair 1879–1935 *Will Rogers* Am. actor & humorist; rope artist with accompanying monologue laced with homespun humor

Ro·get \\rō-'zhā, 'rō-,\\ Peter Mark 1779–1869 Eng. physician & scholar; author of *Thesaurus of English Words and Phrases*

Rohr·er \\'rōr-ər\\ Heinrich 1933– Swiss physicist; awarded (with G. Binnig and E. Ruska) 1986 Nobel prize for physics for invention of the scanning tunneling microscope

Roh Tae Woo \\'rō-'tā-'ü, 'nō-, -'wü\\ 1932– pres. of So. Korea (1988–93)

Ro·kos·sov·sky \\,rä-kə-'sóf-skė, -'sóv-\\ Konstantin Konstantinovich 1896–1968 marshal of Soviet Union; crushed German resistance before Stalingrad in WWII; marched through Poland

Rolfe \\'rälf\\ John 1585–1622 Eng. colonist; discovered method of curing tobacco, making it the basis of Virginia's trade and prosperity in colonial period

Rol·land \\rō-'läⁿ, rȯ-\\ Romain 1866–1944 Fr. author; awarded 1915 Nobel prize for literature for novel cycle *Jean-Christophe* and collected pacifist manifestos

Röl·vaag \\'rōl-,väg\\ Ole \\'ō-lə\\ Ed·vart \\'ed-,värt\\ 1876–1931 Am. (Norw.-born) educ. & nov.; achieved fame with *Giants in the Earth;* a founder of Norwegian-American Historical Association

Ro·mains \\rō-'maⁿ\\ Jules 1885–1972 pseud. of *Louis-Henri-Jean Farigoule* Fr. author; a founder and chief exponent of literary movement *Unanimisme*, emphasizing human groups over individual personalities; wrote 27-volume epic *Men of Good Will*

Romano Giulio — see GIULIO ROMANO

Ro·ma·nov *or* **Ro·ma·noff** \\rō-'mä-nəf, 'rō-mə-,näf\\ Michael 1596–1645 1st czar (1613–45) of Russ. Romanov dynasty (1613–1917)

Rom·berg \'räm-,bərg\ Sigmund 1887–1951 Am. (Hung.-born) composer; composed music for *The Student Prince, The Desert Song,* etc.

Rom·mel \'rä-məl\ Erwin Johannes Eugen 1891–1944 *the Desert Fox* Ger. field marshal; commander of German forces in Africa (1941–43); won spectacular victories early in WWII; defeated by British at el-Alamein

Rom·ney \'räm-nē, 'rəm-\ George 1734–1802 Eng. painter; fashionable portraitist of the English aristocracy

Ron·sard \rōⁿ-'sär\ Pierre de 1524–1585 Fr. poet; chief member of poets' group La Pléiade; devoted to uplifting French language by using classical and Italian models

Rönt·gen *or* **Roent·gen** \'rent-gən, 'rənt-, -jən; 'ren-chən, 'rən-\ Wilhelm Conrad 1845–1923 Ger. physicist; awarded first Nobel prize for physics (1901) for his discovery of X rays

Roo·se·velt \'rō-zə-vəlt (*Roosevelts' usual pron.*), -,velt *also* 'rü-\ (Anna) Eleanor 1884–1962 *née* Roosevelt, *wife of F.D.* Am. humanitarian & writer; widely admired for support of liberal causes and humanitarian concerns

Roosevelt Franklin Del·a·no \'de-lə-,nō\ 1882–1945 32d pres. of the U.S. (1933–45); only president elected for 3rd and 4th terms; developed reforms and projects known as the New Deal; guided U.S. through WWII — **Roo·se·velt·ian** \,rō-zə-'vel-tē-ən, -sh(ē-)ən\ *adj*

Roosevelt Theodore 1858–1919 26th pres. of the U.S. (1901–09); acquired Canal Zone and began Panama Canal; awarded 1906 Nobel prize for peace for ending Russo-Japanese War

Root \'rüt, 'rút\ Elihu 1845–1937 Am. lawyer & statesman; awarded 1912 Nobel prize for peace for settling the problem of Japanese immigration to California and organizing the Central American Peace Conference

Ro·rem \'rōr-əm, 'rȯr-\ Ned 1923–   Am. composer; created songs, symphonies, operas, much instrumental music, ballets, and published critical essays and diaries

Ro·sa \'rō-zə\ Salvator 1615–1673 Ital. painter & poet; leading painter of Neapolitan school; known for wildly romantic landscapes, marine paintings, battle scenes

Rose \'rōz\ Peter Edward 1942–   *Pete Rose* Am. baseball player; with Cincinnati Reds (1963–78, 1984–87), Philadelphia Phillies (1979–83); had career total of 4,256 hits, highest in all of baseball; later banned from baseball for illicit betting

Rose·bery \'rōz-,ber-ē, -b(ə-)rē\ 5th Earl of 1847–1929 *Archibald Philip Prim·rose* \'prim-,rōz\ Eng. statesman; prime min. (1894–95); opposed Irish home rule; pushed imperialist policy toward Boers

Rose·crans \'rō-zə-,kranz, 'rōz-,kran(t)s\ William Starke 1819–1898 Am. gen.; Union commander in the Civil War, remembered for his career-breaking defeat in the Battle of Chickamauga (Sept. 1863)

Ro·sen·berg \'rō-z'n-,bərg, -,berg\ Alfred 1893–1946 Ger. Nazi & writer; considered the ideologist of Nazism; developed the notion that Germans were the embodiment of Nordic racial purity

Ro·sen·wald \'rō-z'n-,wȯld\ Julius 1862–1932 Am. merchant & philanthropist; did much to aid Negro education in the South

Ross \'ròs\ Betsy 1752–1836 née *Griscom* reputed maker of 1st Am. flag

Ross Sir James Clark 1800–1862 Scot. explorer; determined position of north magnetic pole; discovered Ross Sea and Victoria Land in Antarctic

Ross Sir John 1777–1856 *uncle of prec.* Scot. explorer; made expeditions in search of Northwest Passage

Ross Sir Ronald 1857–1932 Brit. physician; awarded 1902 Nobel prize for physiology or medicine for working on malaria and discovering how malaria is transmitted

Rosse Earl of — see William PARSONS

Ros·sel·li·ni \,rò-se-'lē-nē\ Roberto 1906–1977 Ital. film director; renowned as a pioneer of Italian Neorealist movement with films *Open City*, *Paisan*, etc.

Ros·set·ti \rō-'ze-tē, -'se-\ Christina Georgina 1830–1894 *sister of D.G.* Eng. poet; published her best verse in *Goblin Market and Other Poems*

Rossetti Dante Gabriel 1828–1882 Eng. painter & poet; with Holman Hunt, Millais, and others, founded Pre-Raphaelite school of painting and published poetry *Ballads and Sonnets*

Ros·si \'rò-sē\ Bruno 1905–1993 Am. (Ital.-born) physicist; studied cosmic rays and developed X-ray astronomy

Ros·si·ni \rò-'sē-nē, rə-\ Gio·ac·chi·no \jō-ə-'kē-(,)nō\ Antonio 1792–1868 Ital. composer; leading representative of bel canto school of opera and one of the last masters of opera buffa; composed *The Barber of Seville, Otello, William Tell*, etc. — **Ros·si·ni·an** \-'sē-nē-ən\ *adj*

Ros·tand \rò-stäⁿ, 'räs-,tand\ Edmond 1868–1918 Fr. poet & dram.; author of many plays, esp. *Cyrano de Bergerac*

Ro·ta \'rō-(,)tä\ Nino 1911–1979 Ital. composer; known esp. for musical scores for all of Fellini's films, *The Godfather*, etc.

Roth \'ròth\ Philip 1933– Am. writer; author of comic works examining modern Jewish-American society, esp. stories *Goodbye Columbus* and novel *Portnoy's Complaint*

Roth·ko \'räth-(,)kō\ Mark 1903–1970 Am. (Russ.-born) painter; a leading figure in Abstract Expressionism; his use of color as the sole means of expression resulted in finely nuanced works

Roth·schild \'ròth(s)-,child, 'ròs-, G 'rōt-,shilt\ Mayer Amschel 1744–1812 Ger. financier; founder of a banking dynasty with branches in Frankfurt, London, Paris, Vienna, and Naples; greatly influenced the economic and political course of Europe

Rothschild Nathan Mayer 1777–1836 *son of prec.* financier in London

Rou·ault \rü-'ō\ Georges 1871–1958 Fr. painter; in an Expressionist style painted religious scenes and secular subjects, as tragic clowns and prostitutes, with a deeply religious sensibility

Rou·get de Lisle \(,)rü-'zhä-də-'lē(ə)l\ Claude-Joseph 1760–1836 Fr. army officer & composer; known as composer of words and music of *La Marseillaise*, French national anthem

Rous \'raüs\ Francis Peyton 1879–1970 Am. pathologist; awarded (with C.B. Huggins) 1966 Nobel prize for physiology or medicine for discovery of tumor-inducing viruses

Rous·seau \rù-'sō, 'rü-,\ Henri-Julien-Félix 1844–1910 *le Douanier* Fr. painter; known for richly colored primitive paintings, esp. of jungles and wild beasts

Rousseau Jean-Jacques 1712–1778 Fr. (Swiss-born) philos. & writer; known for writings advocating superiority of savage state, opposing private property, insisting that the rightful political authority is the general will; influenced modern pedagogical movements — **Rous·seau·esque** \,rü-sō-'esk, ,rü-\ *or* **Rous·seau·ian** \-'sō-ē-ən\ *adj*

Rousseau (Pierre-Étienne-) Théodore 1812–1867 Fr. painter; leader of the Barbizon school of painting; painted landscapes from direct observation of nature

Rowe \'rō\ Nicholas 1674–1718 Eng. poet & dram.; poet laureate (1715–18); first modern editor of Shakespeare

Row·land·son \'rō-lən(d)-sən\ Thomas 1756–1827 Eng. caricaturist; created a series of plates, illustrated works of Smollett, Goldsmith, etc., and *Baron Munchausen*

Row·ley \'rō-lē, 'raù-\ William 1585?–?1642 Eng. actor & dram.; collaborator with Thomas Middleton on *The Changeling*, etc.

Ro·xas y Acu·ña \'rō-,häs-,ē-ə-'kün-yə\ Manuel 1892–1948 Philippine statesman; first pres. of the Philippine Republic (1946–48)

Roy·all \'ròi(-ə)l\ Kenneth Claiborne 1894–1971 Am. statesman; first secy. of the Army (1947–49) under newly organized Defense Department

Royce \'ròis\ Josiah 1855–1916 Am. philos.; developed philosophy of Idealism, emphasizing individuality and will rather than intellect

Rub·bia \'rü-bē-ə\ Carlo 1934– Ital. physicist; awarded (with S. van der Meer) 1984 Nobel prize for physics for contributions to the discovery of W and R subatomic particles

Ru·bens \'rü-bənz\ Peter Paul 1577–1640 Flem. painter; painted in Baroque style landscapes, portraits, and esp. historical and sacred subjects; known for his masterly use of color and the sensuous exuberance esp. of his female nudes — **Ru·ben·esque** \,rü-bə-'nesk\ *adj* — **Ru·ben·si·an** \rü-'ben-zē-ən\ *adj*

Ru·bin \'rü-bən\ Robert Edward 1938– U.S. secy. of treasury (1995–)

Ru·bin·stein \'rü-bən-,stīn\ An·ton \än-'tòn\ 1829–1894 Russ. pianist & composer; made many concert tours; composed operas, symphonies, concertos, etc.

Rubinstein Arthur 1887–1982 Am. (Pol.-born) pianist; acclaimed as one of the 20th century's greatest pianists

Rubinstein Helena 1870–1965 Am. (Pol.-born) beautician & businesswoman; founded beauty salons and manufacturing facilities for her line of cosmetics; established cosmetics as a major industry

Rud·olf \'rü-,dälf\ 1858–1889 archduke & crown prince of Austria; excluded from government because of liberal views; committed suicide with Baroness Marie Vetsera

Rudolf I 1218–1291 Holy Rom. emp. (1273–91); 1st of the Hapsburgs; concentrated power in Austria

Ru·dolph \'rü-,dòlf, -,dälf\ Wilma Glodean 1940–1994 Am. athlete; overcame polio and other childhood diseases to become world-class runner; won three Olympic gold medals (1960)

Ruis·dael *or* **Ruys·dael** \'rīz-ˌdäl, 'rīs-\ Jacob van 1628 (or 1629)–1682 & his uncle Salomon van *ca* 1602–1670 Du. painters; Jacob often considered greatest Dutch landscape painter

Rumford Count — see Benjamin THOMPSON

Run·cie \'rən(t)-sē\ Robert Alexander Kennedy 1921– archbishop of Canterbury (1980–91)

Rund·stedt \'růn(t)-ˌshtet\ Karl Rudolf Gerd von 1875–1953 Ger. field marshal; instrumental in fall of France (1940); commander in chief on western front (1942–45); regarded as the ablest of the Nazi generals

Ru·ne·berg \'rü-nə-ˌbərg, -ˌber-ē\ Johan Ludvig 1804–1877 Finn. poet; considered the greatest Finnish poet

Run·yon \'rən-yən\ (Alfred) Da·mon \'dā-mən\ 1884–1946 Am. author; known esp. for slang-filled stories about Broadway characters, esp. *Guys and Dolls* — **Run·yon·esque** \ˌrən-yə-'nesk\ *adj*

Ru·pert \'rü-pərt\ Prince 1619–1682 Count *Palatine of Rhine* & Duke of *Bavaria* Eng. (Ger.-born) Royalist gen. & admiral; dominant figure of Royalist forces in English Civil War; a founder of Hudson's Bay Co.

Rush \'rəsh\ Benjamin 1745–1813 Am. physician & patriot; signed Declaration of Independence; established first free dispensary in U.S.

Rush Richard 1780–1859 *son of prec.* Am. diplomat & statesman; negotiated Rush-Bagot Agreement with Great Britain, providing for disarmament on the Great Lakes after War of 1812

Rush·die \'rəsh-(ˌ)dē, 'rush-\ (Ahmed) Salman 1947– Brit. (Indian-born) writer; best known for death sentence passed on him by Ayatollah Khomeini of Iran for his novel *Satanic Verses*

Rusk \'rəsk\ (David) Dean 1909–1994 U.S. secy. of state (1961–69); known for his unwavering defense of U.S. policy in Vietnam

Rus·ka \'rüs-kə\ Ernst August Friedrich 1906–1988 Ger. physicist; awarded (with G. Binnig) 1986 Nobel prize for physics for invention of electron microscope

Rus·kin \'rəs-kən\ John 1819–1900 Eng. essayist, critic, & reformer; one of the chief arbiters of public taste in Victorian England; championed the Gothic Revival in architecture and J.M.W. Turner in painting — **Rus·kin·ian** \ˌrəs-'ki-nē-ən\ *adj*

Rus·sell \'rə-səl\ Bertrand Arthur William 1872–1970 3d Earl *Russell* Eng. math. & philos.; awarded 1950 Nobel prize for literature for his philosophic writings; also known for his work in mathematical logic and his pacifism

Russell Bill 1934– *William Felton Russell* Am. basketball player; with Boston Celtics (1956–69); regarded as one of the greatest defensive centers in basketball history; first African-American to coach a major professional sports team in U.S.

Russell Charles Taze 1852–1916 Am. religious leader; organized International Bible Students' Assn. (1872); began to preach that second coming had occurred invisibly, the end of the world to follow this "Millenial Age" in 1914

Russell George William 1867–1935 pseud. Æ \'ā-'ē\ Irish poet; a leader of the Irish literary Renaissance; interested in theosophy, the origins of religion, and mystical experience

Russell John 1792–1878 1st Earl *Russell of Kingston Russell* Brit. statesman; prime min. (1846–52, 1865–66); leader in the fight for passage of Reform Bill of 1832

Russell Lillian 1861–1922 *Helen Louise Leonard* Am. singer & actress; excelled in comic-opera roles; famed for her beauty and flamboyant lifestyle

Rus·tin \'rəs-tən\ Bayard 1910–1987 Am. civil rights leader

Ruth \'rüth\ George Herman 1895–1948 *Babe Ruth* or *the Babe* Am. baseball player; outfielder, New York Yankees (1920–34); hit 60 home runs in 1927 (record for 154-game season) and 714 in career — **Ruth·ian** \'rü-thē-ən\ *adj*

Ruth·er·ford \'rə-thə(r)-fərd, -thə(r)-\ Ernest 1871–1937 1st Baron *Rutherford of Nelson* Brit. physicist; awarded 1908 Nobel prize for chemistry for discovering that radioactive elements change into other elements

Rutherford Joseph Franklin 1869–1942 Am. leader of Jehovah's Witnesses; imprisoned (1918–19) for stand against military service and encouragement of conscientious objectors

Rut·ledge \'rət-lij\ John 1739–1800 Am. statesman & jurist; member of Constitutional Convention; chief justice, U.S. Supreme Court (1795); served one term but Senate voted against confirmation

Rutledge Wiley Blount \'blənt\ 1894–1949 Am. jurist; associate justice, U.S. Supreme Court (1943–49)

Ru·žič·ka \'rü-,zhich-kə, -,zich-, -,zhits-\ Leopold 1887–1976 Swiss (Croatian-born) chem.; awarded (with A. Butenandt) 1939 Nobel prize for chemistry for work on polymethylenes

Ryan \'rī-ən\ (Lynn) Nolan Jr. 1947– Am. baseball player; in major leagues (1966–93); held over 50 major league records, including most seasons pitched (27), most strikeouts (5,714), and most no-hitters (7)

Ry·der \'rī-dər\ Albert Pinkham 1847–1917 Am. painter; excelled in landscapes, marines, and figure paintings, esp. Romantic or allegorical compositions

Rydz–Śmig·ły \'rits-'shmē-glē\ Edward 1886–1941 Pol. gen.; one of most powerful men of Poland (1936–39); fled to Romania on German occupation

Ryle \'rī(ə)l\ Sir Martin 1918–1984 Brit. astron.; awarded (with A. Hewish) 1974 Nobel prize for physics for his use of small radio telescopes to "see" into space

S

Saa·ri·nen \'sär-ə-nən\ Ee·ro \'er-(,)ō\ 1910–1961 Am. architect; best known for Memorial Arch, St. Louis

Saarinen (Gottlieb) Eliel 1873–1950 *father of prec.* Finn. architect; foremost architect of his day in Finland

Saa·ve·dra La·mas \sä-'vä-drə-'lä-məs, -'vä-thrə-\ Carlos 1878–1959 Argentine lawyer & diplomat; awarded 1936 Nobel prize for peace for helping end Chaco War

Sa·ba·tier \,sa-bə-'tyā\ Paul 1854–1941 Fr. chem.; awarded (with F.A.V. Grignard) 1912 Nobel prize for chemistry for his method of using nickel as a hydrogenation catalyst (shared with F.A.V. Grignard)

Sa·ba·ti·ni \,sa-bə-'tē-nē, sä-\ Rafael 1875–1950 Eng. (Ital.-born) author; writer chiefly of historical romances, including *Scaramouche, Captain Blood*, etc.

Sa·bin \'sā-bin\ Albert Bruce 1906–1993 Am. physician; developed live-virus vaccine against poliomyelitis

Sac·a·ga·wea *also* **Sac·a·ja·wea** \,sa-kə-jə-'wē-ə\ 1786?–1812 Am. Indian guide; acted as interpreter for Lewis and Clark expedition

Sac·co \'sa-(,)kō\ Nicola 1891–1927 & **Van·zet·ti** \van-'ze-tē\ Bartolomeo 1888–1927 Am. (Ital.-born) anarchists; their conviction and execution on charges of robbery and murder were widely attributed to their political beliefs and prompted worldwide protests and lingering controversy

Sachs \'zäks, 'saks\ Hans 1494–1576 Ger. poet & Meistersinger; depicted as central figure in Wagner's opera *Die Meistersinger von Nürnberg*

Sachs \'saks, 'zäks\ Nelly 1891–1970 Swed. (Ger.-born) dram. & poet; awarded (with S.Y. Agnon) 1966 Nobel prize for literature for poetry and plays about the Jewish people

Sack·ville \'sak-,vil\ Thomas 1536–1608 1st Earl of *Dorset* Eng. poet & diplomat; wrote (with Thomas Norton) *Tragedy of Gorboduc,* earliest English tragedy; announced her death sentence to Mary, Queen of Scots

Sackville–West \-'west\ Victoria Mary 1892–1962 *Vita* Eng. writer; author of novels *The Edwardians, All Passion Spent,* etc., and poetry, essays

Sä·dät \sə-'dat, -'dät\ Anwar el- 1918–1981 pres. of Egypt (1970–81); awarded (with Israeli Premier M. Begin) 1978 Nobel prize for peace for efforts to settle Arab-Israeli conflict

Sade, de \də-'säd\ Comte Donatien-Alphonse-François 1740–1814 Marquis *de Sade* Fr. writer of erotica; notorious for his sexual compulsiveness and history of sexual abuse; wrote novels, plays, and stories graphically describing various sexual perversions, including the one named after him, sadism

Sa·gan \'sā-gən\ Carl Edward 1934– Am. astronomer; studied planetary atmospheres and surfaces and the origin of life on Earth; popularized astronomy through books and television shows

Sa·gan \sä-'gäⁿ\ Françoise 1935– pseud. of *Françoise Quoi·rez* \kwä-rā\ Fr. writer; best known for novels *Bonjour tristesse (Good Morning Sadness)* and *Un Certain Sourire (A Certain Smile)*

Sage \\'sāj\\ Russell 1816–1906 Am. financier; associated with Jay Gould in extensive stock market operations and security promotion

St. Den·is \\sānt-'de-nəs, sənt-\\ Ruth 1878–1968 Am. dancer & choreographer; influenced almost every phase of American dance, esp. with use of philosophical themes, Oriental dance forms and costumes

Sainte–Beuve \\sant-'bœv; sānt-'bə(r)v, sənt-\\ Charles-Augustin 1804–1869 Fr. critic & author; considered leading literary critic of his time; best known for *Port-Royal*, a history of the Cistercian abbey of Port-Royal

Saint–Gau·dens \\sānt-'gȯ-dᵊnz, sənt-\\ Augustus 1848–1907 Am. (Irish-born) sculptor; often considered foremost American sculptor of late 19th century; renowned esp. for Shaw Memorial, Boston, and Mrs. Henry Adams Memorial, Washington, D.C.

St. John Henry — see BOLINGBROKE

St. Johns \\sānt-'jänz\\ Adela Rogers 1894–1988 Am. journalist; wrote news and feature articles for Hearst newspapers; known esp. as one of journalism's preeminent sob sisters for her knack for finding any story's emotional angle

Saint–Just \\saⁿ-zhūēst; sānt-'jəst, sənt-\\ Louis-Antoine-Léon de 1767–1794 Fr. revolutionary; active in bringing on Reign of Terror; arrested and guillotined in Thermidorian Reaction

St. Lau·rent \\saⁿ-lò-räⁿ\\ Louis Stephen 1882–1973 Canad. polit.; prime min. (1948–57)

Saint–Pierre — see BERNARDIN DE SAINT-PIERRE

Saint–Saëns \\saⁿ-säs\\ (Charles-) Camille 1835–1921 Fr. composer; composed opera *Samson et Dalila*, symphonic poem *Danse Macabre*, *Carnaval des Animaux*, etc.; wrote criticism, poetry, essays, plays

Saints·bury \\'sānts-,ber-ē, -b(ə-)rē\\ George Edward Bateman 1845–1933 Eng. critic; wrote *A History of Elizabethan Literature*, *A History of Criticism*, etc.

Saint–Si·mon \\saⁿ-sē-mōⁿ\\ Claude-Henri de Rouvroy 1760–1825 Comte de Saint-Simon Fr. philos. & social scientist; founded Christian Socialism, combining teachings of Jesus with ideas of science and industrialism

Saint–Simon Louis de Rouvroy 1675–1755 Duc de Saint-Simon Fr. soldier, statesman, & writer; best known for his *Mémoires*, covering 1694–1723 and an invaluable source of information on court affairs

Sai·on·ji \\sī-'än-jē, -'òn-\\ Prince Kimmochi 1849–1940 Jp. statesman; member of the oligarchy that effected the Meiji Restoration, which restored power to the emperor

Sa·kha·rov \\'sä-kə-,rȯf, -,räf; 'sak-ə-, -,rȯv\\ Andrey Dmitriyevich 1921–1989 Russ. physicist; awarded 1975 Nobel prize for peace for work in promoting peace and opposing violence and brutality

Sa·ki \\'sä-kē\\ — see H. H. MUNRO

Sak·mann \\'zäk-,män, 'säk-\\ Bert 1942– Ger. biochem.; awarded (with E. Neher) 1991 Nobel prize for physiology or medicine for discovering how cells communicate with one another

Sal·a·din \\'sa-lə-dēn, -dən; ,sa-lə-'dēn\\ 1137 (or 1138)–1193 *Salāh Ad-dīn Yūsuf Ibn Ayyūb* Syrian commander & vizier in Egypt; captured Jerusalem (1187), ending 88-year occupation by the

Christian Crusaders; considered founder of the Ayyūbid dynasty and the greatest of all Muslim heroes

Sa·lam \sä-'läm\ Abdus 1926–   Pakistani physicist; awarded (with S.L. Glashow and S. Weinberg) 1979 Nobel prize for physics for developing a principle that unifies the weak nuclear force and electromagnetic force

Sa·la·zar \ˌsa-lə-'zär, ˌsä-\ Antonio de Oliveira 1889–1970 Port. dictator (1932–68); carried out economic reforms and development

Sa·li·nas de Gor·ta·ri \sä-'lē-näs-thä-gȯr-'tä-rē\ Carlos 1948–   pres. of Mexico (1988–94)

Sal·in·ger \'sa-lən-jər\ Jerome David 1919–   Am. nov.; best known for novel *Catcher in the Rye*

Salisbury 1st Earl of & 3d Marquis of — see CECIL

Salk \'sȯ(l)k\ Jonas Edward 1914–1995 Am. physician; developed first vaccine against poliomyelitis

Sal·lust \'sa-ləst\ *ca* 86–35 (or 34) B.C. *Gaius Sallustius Crispus* Rom. hist. & polit.; regarded as one of Latin's great stylists; noted esp. for his narratives of contemporary political rivalries; credited with development of the monograph — **Sal·lus·ti·an** \sə-'ləs-tē-ən, sa-\ *adj*

Sa·lo·me \sə-'lō-mē, 'sa-lə-(ˌ)mä\ 1st cent. A.D. Judaean princess; brought about death of John the Baptist by asking for his head as a reward from Herod Antipas for her dancing

Sal·o·mon \'sa-lə-mən\ Haym 1740–1785 Am. (Pol.-born) merchant and financier; helped maintain American credit during Revolution with cash advances; also gave financial aid to many patriot leaders

Sam·o·set \'sa-mə-ˌset, sə-'mä-sət\ *d* 1653? Abenaki tribal leader; a firm friend of the Pilgrims at Plymouth, extending to them the surprise greeting "Welcome, Englishmen!" and later introducing them to Massasoit

Sam·per Pi·za·no \'säm-per-pē-'sä-nō\ Ernesto 1950–   pres. of Colombia (1994–   )

Sam·u·el \'sam-yə-wəl, -yəl\ *ca* 11th cent. B.C. early Hebrew judge; annointed Saul and David king

Sam·u·el·son \'sam-yə(-wə)l-sən\ Paul Anthony 1915–   Am. econ.; awarded 1970 Nobel prize for economics for raising the level of scientific analysis in economic theory

Sam·u·els·son \'sam-yə(-wə)l-sən\ Bengt I. 1934–   Swed. biochem.; awarded (with S.K. Bergstrom and J.R. Vane) 1982 Nobel prize for physiology or medicine for discoveries regarding prostaglandins and related substances

Sánchez de Bustamante y Sirvén Antonio — see BUSTAMANTE Y SIRVÉN

Sand \'sand, 'sän(d, sä\ George 1804–1876 pseud. of *Amandine-Aurore-Lucie* (or *-Lucile*) *Du·de·vant* \düed-väⁿ, düē-də-\ née *Dupin* Fr. writer; noted for her novels, her liaisons, esp. with Chopin, her unconventionality, and her championship of women

Sand·burg \'san(d)-ˌbȯrg\ Carl 1878–1967 Am. author; considered the poet of America's common people; also known for *Abraham Lincoln: The Prairie Years, Abraham Lincoln: The War Years*

San·gal·lo \sän-'gäl-(ˌ)lō, sän-\ Giuliano da 1445?–1516 Florentine architect & sculptor; helped Raphael design and build Saint Peter's Basilica; also known as military engineer

Sang·er \\'saŋ-ər\\ Frederick 1918–   Brit. chem.; awarded 1958 Nobel prize for chemistry for discovering the structure of the insulin molecule

Sanger Margaret 1883–1966 née *Higgins* Am. birth-control leader; important in U.S. and world birth control and population control movements

San Mar·tin \\,san-(,)mär-'tēn, ,sän-\\ José de 1778–1850 So. Am. soldier & statesman; national hero in Argentina; liberated Argentina, Chile, Peru from Spanish rule

San·ta An·na \\,san-tə-'a-nə, ,sän-tə-'ä-nə\\ Antonio López de 1794–1876 Mex. gen., revolutionary, & pres.; as pres. of Mexico during Texas Revolution (1836) conducted famed siege at the Alamo but defeated by Sam Houston at San Jacinto; commanded troops against U.S. in Mexican War until defeated by Winfield Scott

San·tan·der \\,sän,tän-'der, ,san-tan-\\ Francisco de Paula 1792–1840 Colombian gen. & polit.; a commander in Simón Bolívar's army of liberation; regarded as founder of Colombia

San·ta·ya·na \\,san-tə-'yä-nə, ,san-tē-'ä-, ,sän-\\ George 1863–1952 Am. (Span.-born) poet & philos.; major contributor to aesthetics, literary criticism, speculative philosophy; known esp. for *The Sense of Beauty*, *The Life of Reason*, novel *The Last Puritan*

San·tos–Du·mont \\,san-təs-dü-'mänt, -dyü-; sän-tōs-dᵫ-'mōⁿ\\ Alberto 1873–1932 Fr. (Braz.-born) aviation pioneer; made first official powered flight in Europe; produced "Demoiselle" or "Grasshopper" monoplanes, forerunners of modern light plane

Sa·pir \\sə-'pir\\ Edward 1884–1939 Am. (Pomeranian-born) anthropol. & linguist; a founder of ethnolinguistics and principal developer of American school of structural linguistics

Sap·pho also **Psap·pho** \\'sa-(,)fō\\ *fl ca* 610–*ca* 580 B.C. Greek poet; author of lyric poems on themes of love and personal relationships, often with other women

Sar·da·na·pa·lus or **Sar·da·na·pal·lus** \\,sär-d°n-'a-p(ə-)ləs, -d°n-ə-'pā-ləs\\ king of Assyria; sometimes identified with Ashurbanipal (reigned 668–627 B.C.); according to Diodorus Siculus, known for his sybaritic way of life

Sar·dou \\sär-'dü\\ Victorien 1831–1908 Fr. dram.; known as a craftsman of bourgeois drama, very popular in its day

Sar·gent \\'sär-jənt\\ John Sing·er \\'siŋ-ər\\ 1856–1925 Am. painter; known chiefly for elegant portraits of the Edwardian gentry; caused a scandal with his portrait of famed Parisian beauty known as "Madame X"

Sar·gon II \\'sär-,gän, -gən\\ king of Assyria (722–705 B.C.); consolidated Assyrian empire, putting down continual rebellions

Sa·roy·an \\sə-'rȯi-ən\\ William 1908–1981 Am. writer; author of short stories, plays, novels, memoirs with a wryly humorous bent

Sar·tre \\'särtrᵊ\\ Jean-Paul 1905–1980 Fr. philos., dram., & nov.; major exponent of philosophy of existentialism; best known works include novel *Nausea*, philosophical treatise *Being and Nothingness*, play *No Exit*; awarded 1964 Nobel prize for literature — **Sar·tre·an** or **Sar·tri·an** \\'sär-trē-ən\\ *adj*

Sas·soon \\sa-'sün, sə-\\ Siegfried Lorraine 1886–1967 Eng. writer; author of anti-war and devotional verse and of autobiographical prose works

Sa·tie \sȧ-'tē, sä-\ Erik-Alfred-Leslie 1866–1925 Fr. composer; composed spare, unconventional, often witty avant-garde music that influenced esp. Debussy, Ravel, Poulenc, Milhaud

Sa·ud \sä-'üd\ 1902–1969 king of Saudi Arabia (1953–64); continued program of modernization; deposed by brother Faisal

Saul \'sȯl\ 11th cent. B.C. first king of Israel (ca. 1020–1000); protector, later rival, of David; defeated, killed by Philistines in battle; succeeded by David

Saul — see PAUL

Saus·sure \sō-sūer\ Ferdinand de 1857–1913 Swiss linguist; gave stimulus and direction to modern linguistics with his posthumous *Cours de linguistique générale (General Linguistics Course)* — **Saus·sur·ean** *also* **Saus·sur·ian** \sō-'sūr-ē-ən, sȯ-\ *adj*

Sav·age \'sa-vij\ Michael Joseph 1872–1940 prime min. of New Zealand (1935–40); instituted economic recovery measures, educational and social security reforms

Savage Richard 1697?–1743 Eng. poet; his difficult life recounted in Samuel Johnson's celebrated *Account of the Life of Mr. Richard Savage*

Sa·vo·na·ro·la \ˌsä-və-nə-'rō-lə, sə-ˌvä-nə-'rō-\ Gi·ro·la·mo \ji-'rō-lə-ˌmō\ 1452–1498 Ital. reformer; renowned for his attacks against a corrupt clergy; upon fall of the Medici, sole leader of Florence; overthrown, convicted of heresy, and executed

Saxe \'saks\ Hermann-Maurice 1696–1750 Comte *de Saxe* Fr. gen.; made innovations in military training, esp. in musketry; served in War of Polish Succession, of Austrian Succession; conquered Austrian Netherlands, etc.

Saxo Gram·mat·i·cus \ˌsak-(ˌ)sō-grə-'ma-ti-kəs\ *ca* 1150–after 1216 Dan. hist.; author of *Gesta Danorum*, the first important history of Denmark and first important work of Danish literature; his legend of *Amleth* is thought to be source of Shakespeare's *Hamlet*

Say·ers \'sā-ərz, 'serz\ Dorothy Leigh 1893–1957 Eng. writer; author of mystery stories featuring detectives Lord Peter Wimsey or Montague Egg, religious plays, translation of Dante, etc.

Sca·lia \skə-'lē-ə\ Antonin 1936– Am. jurist; associate justice, U.S. Supreme Court (1986–)

Scal·i·ger \'ska-lə-jər\ Joseph Justus 1540–1609 Fr. scholar; his works on establishing chronology in antiquity helped put study of history on scientific basis

Scaliger Julius Caesar 1484–1558 *father of prec.* Ital. physician; best known for his philosophical and scientific writings and commentaries on Greek authors

Scanderbeg — see SKANDERBEG

Scar·lat·ti \skär-'lä-tē\ (Pietro) Alessandro Gaspare 1660–1725 & his son (Giuseppe) Domenico 1685–1757 Ital. composers; Alessandro noted for thematic development, chromatic harmony, development of opera; Domenico composed over 500 sonatas for harpsichord with innovative harmony and form

Scar·ron \ska-'rōⁿ\ Paul 1610–1660 Fr. author; foremost French exponent of the burlesque; remembered solely for novel *Le Roman comique*

Schacht \'shäkt, 'shäkt\ (Horace Greeley) Hjal·mar \'yäl-ˌmär\ 1877–1970 Ger. financier; president of the Reichsbank (1923–30,

1933–39); credited with halting the ruinous inflation that threatened the Weimar Republic

Schal·ly \'sha-lē\ Andrew Victor 1926– Am. (Pol.-born) physiol.; awarded (with R. Guillemin and R. Yallow) 1977 Nobel prize for physiology or medicine for research concerning the role of hormones in the chemistry of the body

Scharn·horst \'shärn-ˌhȯrst\ Gerhard Johann David von 1755–1813 Pruss. gen.; developed modern general staff system; helped develop the "shrinkage system" of army training, which created reserves of trained men

Schar·wen·ka \shär-'veŋ-kə\ (Ludwig) Philipp 1847–1917 & his bro. (Franz) Xaver 1850–1924 Ger. pianists & composers; Philipp wrote orchestral, choral and chamber music, instrumental music, and songs; Xaver composed concertos, an opera, a symphony, etc.

Schaw·low \'shȯ-(ˌ)lō\ Arthur Leonard 1921– Am. physicist; awarded (with N. Bloembergen and K. Siegbahn) 1981 Nobel prize for physics for role in the development of laser spectroscopy

Schei·de·mann \'shī-də-ˌmän\ Philipp 1865–1939 Ger. polit.; proclaimed establishment of Weimar Republic; became its first chancellor

Schel·ling \'she-liŋ\ Friedrich Wilhelm Joseph von 1775–1854 Ger. philos.; a leading figure of German Idealism; critical of Hegel's philosophy — **Schel·ling·ian** \she-'liŋ-ē-ən\ adj

Schia·pa·rel·li \skē-ˌä-pə-'re-lē, ˌska-\ Giovanni Virginio 1835–1910 Ital. astron.; observed numerous double stars; reported markings on Mars, calling them "channels" (misunderstood in English as "canals")

Schick \'shik\ Béla \'bā-lə\ 1877–1967 Am. (Hung.-born) pediatrician; discovered Schick test for determining susceptibility to diphtheria

Schiff \'shif\ Dorothy 1903–1989 Am. newspaper publisher; owner and later editor in chief of *New York Post*, keeping it a crusading liberal daily while adding human-interest stories, comics, gossip columnists, and other tabloid features

Schil·ler \'shi-lər\ (Johann Christoph) Friedrich von 1759–1805 Ger. poet & dram.; regarded as second only to Goethe in German literature and as first among German dramatists; renowned esp. for *The Robbers, Wallenstein, William Tell,* etc.

Schin·dler \'shind-lər\ Oskar 1908–1974 Ger. humanitarian; during WWII operated an enamelware factory and later a bogus munitions factory that became safe havens for Jews who otherwise would have perished in death camps

Schi·rach \'shē-ˌräk, -ˌräk\ Baldur von 1907–1974 Ger. Nazi polit.; national director of Hitler Youth movement (1933–45)

Schle·gel \'shlā-gəl\ August Wilhelm von 1767–1845 Ger. author; helped found *Athenäum*, journal of German Romanticism; known esp. for his translations of Shakespeare's plays

Schlegel Friedrich von 1772–1829 *bro. of prec.* Ger. philos. & writer; inspired much of German Romantic movement with his philosophy; wrote lyric poems, novel, drama, philosophy; influential for notion of a universal, historical, and comparative literary scholarship

Schlei·cher \\'shlī-kər, -kər\\ Kurt von 1882–1934 Ger. soldier & polit.; chancellor of Germany (Dec. 1932–Jan. 1933) until succeeded by Hitler; murdered by SS during "night of the long knives"

Schlei·er·ma·cher \\'shlī-ər-ˌmä-kər, -ˌkər\\ Friedrich Ernst Daniel 1768–1834 Ger. theol. & philos.; considered founder of modern Protestant theology

Schle·sing·er \\'shlä-ziŋ-ər, 'shle-sin-jər\\ Arthur Meier father 1888–1965 & son 1917– Am. historians; Arthur Sr. wrote on American social and urban developments; Arthur Jr. wrote *A Thousand Days: John F. Kennedy in the White House*, etc.

Schley \\'shlī, 'slī\\ Winfield Scott 1839–1909 Am. admiral; at center of controversy over assignment of credit for American victory over Spanish fleet at Santiago de Cuba during Spanish-American War

Schlie·mann \\'shlē-ˌmän\\ Heinrich 1822–1890 Ger. archaeol.; often considered modern discoverer of prehistoric Greece; excavated Troy, Mycenae, Boeotia

Schmidt \\'shmit\\ Helmut 1918– chancellor of West Germany (1974–82)

Schna·bel \\'shnä-bəl\\ Ar·tur \\'är-ˌtür\\ 1882–1951 Austrian pianist & composer; specialized in performing Beethoven, Brahms, Schubert; composed piano works and works for voice, orchestra

Schnitz·ler \\'shnits-lər\\ Arthur 1862–1931 Austrian physician, dram. & nov.; known for psychological dramas that dissected turn-of-the-century Viennese bourgeois life

Schoen·berg \\'shə(r)n-ˌbərg, 'shœn-ˌberk\\ Arnold Franz Walter 1874–1951 Am. (Austrian-born) composer; one of the foremost composers of the 20th century; the first to use atonality, a composition method based on a series of 12 tones — **Schoen·berg·ian** \\-ˌbər-gē-ən\\ *adj*

Scho·field \\'skō-ˌfēld\\ John McAllister 1831–1906 Am. gen.; Union commander in the Civil War; defeated Hood at Franklin and Nashville; general in chief, U.S. army (1888–95)

Scho·pen·hau·er \\'shō-pən-ˌhaú(-ə)r\\ Arthur 1788–1860 Ger. philos.; chief exponder of pessimism and of the irrational impulses of life arising from the will; influenced Existentialism and Freudian psychology — **Scho·pen·hau·er·ian** \\ˌshō-pən-ˈhaú-(ə-)rē-ən\\ *adj*

Schrief·fer \\'shrē-fər\\ John Robert 1931– Am. physicist; awarded (with J. Bardeen and L.N. Cooper) 1972 Nobel prize for physics for work on superconductivity

Schrö·ding·er \\'shrœ-diŋ-ər, shrä-\\ Erwin 1887–1961 Austrian physicist; awarded (with P. Dirac) 1933 Nobel prize for physics for discovering new forms of atomic theory

Schu·bert \\'shü-bərt, -ˌbert\\ Franz Peter 1797–1828 Austrian composer; created the German lied (art song) by setting a poem by Goethe to music; noted for the melody and harmony of his songs and chamber music — **Schu·bert·ian** \\shü-'bər-tē-ən, -'ber-\\ *adj*

Schultz \\'shülts\\ Theodore 1902– Am. econ.; awarded (with A. Lewis) 1979 Nobel prize for economics for research into the economic problems of developing countries

Schulz \\'shülts\\ Charles Monroe 1922– Am. cartoonist; creator of comic strip "Peanuts"

Schu·man \'shü-ˌmän, -mən\ Robert 1886–1963 Fr. statesman; developed the Schuman Plan (1950) to promote European economic and military unity

Schu·man \'shü-mən\ William Howard 1910–1992 Am. composer; composed 10 symphonies, concertos, ballets, and choral and orchestral works

Schu·mann \'shü-ˌmän, -mən\ Robert 1810–1856 Ger. composer; one of the greatest Romantic composers; renowned esp. for piano music and songs

Schu·mann–Heink \'shü-mən-'hīŋk\ Ernestine 1861–1936 née *Roessler* Am. (Austrian-born) contralto; known for interpretation of operas of Wagner and Richard Strauss and of German art songs

Schur·man \'shür-mən, 'shər-\ Jacob Gould 1854–1942 Am. philos. & diplomat; author of *Kantian Ethics and the Ethics of Evolution, The Ethical Import of Darwinism,* etc.

Schurz \'shürts, 'shərts\ Carl 1829–1906 Am. (Ger.-born) lawyer, gen., & polit.; a supporter of high moral standards in government, civil rights, civil service reform, etc.

Schusch·nigg \'shùsh-(ˌ)nik, -(ˌ)nig\ Kurt von 1897–1977 Austrian statesman; attempted to prevent Hitler from occupying Austria

Schuy·ler \'skī-lər\ Philip John 1733–1804 Am. gen. & statesman; member, Continental Congress (1775–77, 1778–80); commanded northern department of Continental army until early setbacks prompted his replacement

Schwartz \'shwörts\ Melvin 1932– Am. physicist; awarded (with L.M. Lederman and J. Steinberger) 1988 Nobel prize for physics for their work on subatomic neutrinos

Schwarz·kopf \'shwörts-ˌköf, 'shwörts-\ H. Norman 1934– Am. gen.; commander of Operation Desert Storm in Persian Gulf War

Schwarz·kopf \'shvärts-ˌköpf\ (Olga Maria) Elisabeth Friederike 1915– Ger. (Pol.-born) soprano; sang major operatic roles in opera houses around the world; famed for her interpretations of German art songs

Schweit·zer \'shwīt-sər, 'shvīt-, 'swīt-\ Albert 1875–1965 Fr. theol., philos., missionary physician, & music scholar; founder of Lambaréné Hospital, French Equatorial Africa; awarded 1952 Nobel prize for peace for his work in behalf of "The Brotherhood of Nations"

Schwing·er \'shwiŋ-ər\ Julian Seymour 1918– Am. physicist; awarded (with S. Tomonaga and R.P. Feynman) 1965 Nobel prize for physics for basic work in quantum electrodynamics

Scip·io \'si-pē-ˌō, 'ski-\ **Aemilianus Af·ri·ca·nus** \-ˌa-frə-'ka-nəs, -'kä-, -'kä-\ **Numantinus** Publius Cornelius 185 (or 184)–129 B.C. *Scipio the Younger* Rom. gen.; famed for his destruction of Carthage, thereby ending the Third Punic War, and for his subjugation of Spain

Scipio Africanus Publius Cornelius 236–184 (or 183) B.C. *Scipio the Elder* Rom. gen.; crushed Hannibal at Zama; regarded as Rome's greatest general up to time of Julius Caesar

Sco·field \'skō-ˌfēld\ (David) Paul 1922– Brit. actor; renowned for his powerful, insightful performances on stage and screen, esp. in *A Man For All Seasons, King Lear,* etc.

Scopes \'skōps\ John Thomas 1900–1970 Am. teacher; precipitated Scopes (or "Monkey") trial for teaching evolution in defiance of Tennessee state law; convicted, but decision reversed on technicality

Scor·se·se \skȯr-'sä-sē, -'se-, -sə\ Martin 1942–   Am. film director; known for such grittily realistic films as *Raging Bull*, *Taxi Driver*, *Good Fellas*, etc.

Scott \'skät\ Dred \'dred\ 1795?–1858 Am. slave; central figure in notorious Dred Scott Case, in which U.S. Supreme Court declared that slaves were mere property and had no rights

Scott Sir George Gilbert 1811–1878 Eng. architect; led Gothic revival, esp. in England, building and restoring cathedrals

Scott Robert Falcon 1868–1912 Eng. polar explorer; reached South Pole shortly after Roald Amundsen's expedition; perished on return journey

Scott Sir Walter 1771–1832 Scot. poet & nov.; invented the historical novel with *Waverly*, *Rob Roy*, *Ivanhoe*, etc.

Scott Winfield 1786–1866 Am. gen.; commanding general of U.S. army (1841–61); in Mexican War, captured Vera Cruz, occupied Mexico City; Whig candidate for president (1852)

Scotus Duns — see DUNS SCOTUS

Scotus John — see ERIGENA

Scria·bin *or* **Skrya·bin** \skrē-'ä-bən\ Aleksandr Nikolayevich 1872–1915 Russ. composer; created 3 symphonies, tone poems, piano works

Scribe \skrēb\ Augustin-Eugène 1791–1861 Fr. dram.; master of the neatly plotted, tightly constructed "well-made" play; wrote or co-wrote over 350 successful plays

Scu·dé·ry \,skü-də-'rē, skü̇-dā-rē\ Madeleine de 1607–1701 *Sa·pho* \sȧ-fō\ Fr. poet, nov., & hostess of literary salon; known esp. for her *romans à clef* that were very popular in her day

Sea·borg \'sē-,bȯrg\ Glenn Theodore 1912–   Am. chem.; awarded (with E.M. McMillan) 1951 Nobel prize for chemistry for work on discovering plutonium and other elements

Sears \'sirz\ Richard Warren 1863–1914 Am. merchant; established mail-order business that eventually became Sears, Roebuck & Co.

See \'sē\ Thomas Jefferson Jackson 1866–1962 Am. astron. & math.; known esp. for investigations of double stars, the ether, the cause of universal gravitation and magnetism, etc.

Seeckt \'zākt\ Hans von 1866–1936 Ger. army officer; successfully remodeled army under Weimar Republic

See·ger \'sē-gər\ Peter 1919–   *Pete Seeger* Am. folksinger; began modern revival of folk music with protest songs "Where Have All the Flowers Gone," "Little Boxes," etc.

Se·fe·ri·a·des \,se-fer-'yä-thēs\ Giorgos Stylianou 1900–1971 pseud. *George Se·fer·is* \se-'fer-ēs\ Greek diplomat & poet; awarded 1963 Nobel prize for literature for his poems

Se·go·via \sā-'gō-vyə, -vē-ə\ Andrés 1893?–1987 Span. guitarist & composer; generally acclaimed as the foremost guitarist of his time; credited with restoring the guitar as an instrument for serious music esp. by demonstrating its expressive and technical potential

Se·grè \sə-'grā, sā-\ Emilio Gino 1905–1989 Am. (Ital.-born) physicist; awarded (with O. Chamberlain) 1959 Nobel prize for physics for work in demonstrating the existence of the antiproton

Sei·fert \'zī-fərt\ Jaroslav 1901–1986 Czech poet; awarded 1984 Nobel prize for literature, first Czech so honored

Se·ja·nus \si-'jā-nəs\ Lucius Aelius d A.D. 31 Rom. conspirator; favorite of emperor Tiberius; allegedly poisoned emperor's son and had Agrippina banished; executed by Tiberius

Sel·den \'sel-dən\ George Baldwin 1846–1922 Am. lawyer & inventor; first American to receive patent for gasoline-driven car

Selden John 1584–1654 Eng. jurist & antiquarian; wrote history of civil government before Norman conquest, study of polytheism, exposition of rabbinical law, etc.

Se·leu·cus I Ni·ca·tor \sə-,lü-kəs-'nī-,kā-tər\ 358 (to 354)–281 B.C. Macedonian gen. & founder of Seleucid dynasty; conquered eastern regions to the Indus; included Syria and Asia Minor in empire

Sel·kirk \'sel-,kərk\ Alexander 1676–1721 Scot. marooned sailor; the original of Defoe's hero Robinson Crusoe

Sel·ten \'zel-t⁹n, 'sel-\ Reinhard 1930– Ger. econ.; awarded (with J.C. Harsanyi and J.F. Nash, Jr.) 1994 Nobel prize for economics for contributions to game theory

Se·me·nov \sə-'my○-nəf\ Nikolay Nikolayevich 1896–1986 Soviet chem.; awarded (with C. Hinshelwood) 1956 Nobel prize for chemistry for work on chemical chain reactions

Semmes \'semz\ Raphael 1809–1877 Am. Confed. admiral; commanded Confederate commerce destroyers *Sumter* and *Alabama*

Sen·e·ca \'se-ni-kə\ Lucius Annaeus 4 B.C.?–A.D. 65 Rom. statesman, dram., & philos.; tutor and adviser to emperor Nero; author of philosophical works and tragedies; his tragedies esp. *Thyestes* had great influence on Renaissance writers and esp. English dramatists including Shakespeare — **Sen·e·can** \-kən\ *adj*

Sen·ghor \sen-'gòr, sän-'gòr\ Léopold Sédar 1906–   first pres. of Senegal (1960–80)

Sen·nach·er·ib \sə-'na-kə-rəb\ d 681 B.C. king of Assyria (704–681); invaded Palestine and captured many cities of Judah; destroyed Babylon; may have waged second campaign against Jerusalem

Se·quoya *or* **Se·quoy·ah** *or* **Se·quoia** \si-'kwòi-ə\ ca 1760–1843 George Guess Cherokee Indian scholar; formed syllabary of Cherokee language; taught thousands to read and write; name perpetuated in giant *Sequoia* and in Sequoia National park

Ser·kin \'sər-kən\ Rudolf 1903–1991 Am. (Bohemian-born) pianist; with violinist Adolph Busch founded Vermont's Marlboro Music Festival

Ser·ra \'ser-ə\ Ju·ní·pe·ro \hü-'nē-pə-,rō\ 1713–1784 orig. *Miguel José* Span. missionary in Mexico & California; founded mission at San Diego, first European settlement in Upper California

Ser·to·ri·us \(,)sər-'tòr-ē-əs, -'tòr-\ Quintus ca 123–72 B.C. Rom. gen. & statesman; became independent ruler of most of Spain; allied with Mediterranean pirates and Mithradates II against Rome

Ser·ve·tus \(,)sər-'vē-təs\ Michael 1511?–1553 Span. *Miguel Serveto* Span. theol. & physician; regarded as a heretic by both Roman

Catholics and Protestants; opposed Trinitarianism and infant baptism; discovered pulmonary circulation of blood

Ser·vice \'sər-vəs\ Robert William 1874–1958 Canad. writer; known as the "Canadian Kipling" for rollicking ballads of the "Frozen North," as "The Shooting of Dan McGrew," novels

Ses·sions \'se-shənz\ Roger Huntington 1896–1985 Am. composer; created 8 symphonies, violin concerto, piano pieces, chamber music, etc.

Se·ton \'sē-tᵊn\ Saint Elizabeth Ann née *Bayley* 1774–1821 *Mother Seton* Am. religious leader; first native-born American canonized by Roman Catholic Church

Seton Ernest Thompson 1860–1946 orig. surname *Thompson* Am. (Eng.-born) writer & illustrator; founder of modern school of animal fiction writing

Seu·rat \sə-'rä\ Georges 1859–1891 Fr. painter; founder of Neo≠Impressionism and an originator of pointillism; painted compositions consisting of tiny discrete dots of pure color that create an overall shimmering effect

Seuss — see Theodor Seuss GEISEL

Se·ve·rus \sə-'vir-əs\ Lucius Septimius A.D. 146–211 Rom. emp. (193–211); named emperor by his soldiers; restructured government on military basis and reformed judicial system

Sé·vi·gné \,sā-(,)vēn-'yā, sā-'vēn-(,)yā\ Marquise de 1626–1696 née *(Marie) de Rabutin-Chantal* Fr. letter writer; recorded in letters to her daughter events of daily interest in Paris and Brittany; a notable literary stylist

Sew·ard \'sü-ərd, 'sù(-ə)rd\ William Henry 1801–1872 Am. statesman; secy. of state (1861–69); famous for stating the "irrepressible conflict" between freedom and slavery as opposing and enduring forces; negotiated purchase of Alaska from Russia (Seward's Folly, 1867)

Sew·ell \'sü-əl\ Anna 1820–1878 Brit. writer; author of *Black Beauty: The Autobiography of a Horse*

Sey·mour \'sē-,mōr, -,mór\ Jane 1509?–1537 *3d wife of Henry VIII of England & mother of Edward VI*

Seyss–In·quart \'zīs-,iŋk-,värt\ Ar·tur \'är-,túr\ 1892–1946 Austrian Nazi polit.; chancellor of Austria at the time of its annexation by Germany

Shack·le·ton \'sha-kəl-tən\ Sir Ernest Henry 1874–1922 Brit. polar explorer; involved in numerous Antarctic expeditions; unsuccessful in ultimate goal of reaching the South Pole

Shad·well \'shad-,wel, -wəl\ Thomas 1642?–1692 Eng. dram.; poet laureate (1688–92); satirized by Dryden in *Absalom and Achitophel* and *MacFlecknoe*

Shaf·ter \'shaf-tər\ William Rufus 1835–1906 Am. gen.; received surrender of Santiago de Cuba (1898)

Shaftes·bury \'shaf(t)s-,ber-ē, -b(ə-)rē\ 1st Earl of 1621–1683 *Anthony Ashley* Coo·per \'kü-pər, 'kù-\ Eng. polit.; played important role in sucession dispute; satirized by Dryden in *Absalom and Achitophel;* encouraged anti-Catholic Terror

Shāh Ja·hān \'shä-jə-'hän\ 1592–1666 Mogul emp. of India (1628–57 or 58); reign marked height of Mughal power and golden age of Muslim architecture in India; built esp. Tāj Mahal

Shahn \\'shän\\ Ben 1898–1969 Am. (Lithuanian-born) painter; devoted his art to political and social causes, as Sacco and Vanzetti trial, Tom Mooney trial, etc.

Shake·speare \\'shāk-ˌspir\\ William 1564–1616 Eng. dram. & poet; often considered greatest writer of plays and poetry of all time; celebrated for creating characters of great psychological depth and for presenting in his plays virtually the entire range of human emotion and experience; greatest works include tragedies *Hamlet, King Lear, Othello,* and *Macbeth* — **Shake·spear·ean** *or* **Shake·spear·ian** *also* **Shake·sper·ean** *or* **Shake·sper·ian** \\shāk-'spir-ē-ən\\ *adj*

Sha·la·la \\shə-'lā-lə, -'lä-\\ Donna Edna 1941–   U.S. secy. of health & human services (1993–   )

Sha·mir \\shə-'mēr\\ Yitzhak 1914–   orig. surname *Yizernitzky* prime min. of Israel (1983–92)

Sha·piro \\shə-'pir-(ˌ)ō\\ Karl Jay 1913–   Am. poet & critic; known for mastery of wide variety of poetic forms; author also of criticism and a novel

Sha·rif \\shä-'rēf\\ Nawaz 1949–   prime min. of Pakistan (1990–93)

Sharp \\'shärp\\ Phillip Allen 1944–   Am. biol.; awarded (with R.J. Roberts) 1993 Nobel prize for physiology or medicine for discoveries regarding the structure and function of genes

Sharpe \\'shärp\\ William Forsyth 1934–   Am. econ.; awarded (with H.M. Markowitz and M.H. Miller) 1990 Nobel prize for economics for theories on corporate finance

Shas·tri \\'shäs-trē\\ Lal \\'läl\\ Bahadur 1904–1966 prime min. of India (1964–66)

Shaw \\'shò\\ George Bernard 1856–1950 Brit. (Irish-born) author; a founding member of the Fabian society; leading British playwright since the 17th century; works include *Caesar and Cleopatra, Pygmalion,* and *Saint Joan;* awarded 1925 Nobel prize for literature

Shaw Thomas Edward — see T. E. LAWRENCE

Shawn \\'shòn\\ Ted 1891–1972 Am. dancer & choreographer; created a vigorous, masculine dance technique, as in *Olympiad,* etc.

Shays \\'shāz\\ Daniel 1747?–1825 Am. soldier & insurrectionist; led Shays' Rebellion in western Massachusetts in opposition to high taxes and treatment of debtors

Shee·ler \\'shē-lər\\ Charles 1883–1965 Am. painter & photographer; known esp. for industrial-commercial assignments and for Precisionist paintings of industrial subjects

Shel·don \\'shel-dən\\ William Herbert 1898–1977 Am. psychologist & physical anthropologist

Shel·ley \\'she-lē\\ Mary Woll·stone·craft \\'wùl-stən-ˌkraft\\ 1797–1851 née *Godwin;* wife of P. B. Eng. nov.; author of *Frankenstein* (1818), *The Fortunes of Perkin Warbeck,* etc.

Shelley Percy Bysshe \\'bish\\ 1792–1822 Eng. poet; one of greatest English Romantic poets; poems include "Ode to the West Wind," "To a Skylark," "Hymn to Intellectual Beauty," etc. — **Shel·ley·an** \\'she-lē-ən\\ *or* **Shel·ley·esque** \\ˌshe-lē-'esk\\ *adj*

Shen·stone \\'shen-ˌstōn, 'shen(t)-stən\\ William 1714–1763 Eng. poet; influential in reviving the ballad; author of "The Schoolmistress" and other poems of rustic virtue and simplicity

Shep·ard \\'she-pərd\\ Alan Bartlett 1923–   Am. astronaut; the first American in space (May 5, 1961)

Sher·a·ton \\'sher-ə-t²n\\ Thomas 1751–1806 Eng. furniture designer; known for his refined Neoclassical designs

Sher·i·dan \\'sher-ə-d²n\\ Philip Henry 1831–1888 Am. gen.; Union cavalry commander during the Civil War, his brilliant victories esp. in Virginia were critical to the defeat of the Confederacy

Sheridan Richard Brins·ley \\'brinz-lē\\ 1751–1816 Irish dram. & orator; foremost among writers of comedies of manners with *The Rivals, The School for Scandal, The Critic,* etc.

Sher·man \\'shər-mən\\ James Schoolcraft 1855–1912 vice pres. of the U.S. (1909–12)

Sherman John 1823–1900 *bro. of W. T.* Am. statesman; congressman (1855–61), senator (1861–77, 1881–97); instrumental in the establishment of a national banking system and a return to the gold standard

Sherman Roger 1721–1793 Am. jurist & statesman; only person to sign all four of Declaration of Independence, Articles of Association, Articles of Confederation, Federal Constitution

Sherman William Tecumseh 1820–1891 Am. gen.; made famous march through Georgia from Chattanooga to Atlanta to Savannah, then northward through South and North Carolina; received Johnston's surrender at end; known for saying "War is hell"— **Sher·man·esque** \\,shər-mə-'nesk\\ *adj*

Sher·iff \\'sher-əf\\ Robert Cedric 1896–1975 Eng. writer; successful with play *Journey's End;* wrote novels, plays, film, scripts

Sher·ring·ton \\'sher-iŋ-tən\\ Sir Charles Scott 1857–1952 Eng. physiol.; awarded (with E.D. Adrian) 1932 Nobel prize for physiology or medicine for discoveries on the function of neurons

Sher·wood \\'shər-,wu̇d *also* 'sher-\\ Robert Emmet 1896–1955 Am. dram.; member of Algonquin Round Table; author of award-winning plays *Idiot's Delight, Abe Lincoln in Illinois,* etc.

Shev·ard·nad·ze \\,she-vər(d)-'näd-zə\\ Eduard Amvrosiyevich 1928– Soviet foreign min. (1985–90, 1991); pres. of Georgia (1992–)

Shev·chen·ko *or* **Šev·čen·ko** \\shef-'cheŋ-(,)ko̅\\ Taras Hryhorovych 1814–1861 Ukrainian poet; the father of Ukrainian national literature

Shi·de·ha·ra \\,shē-də-'här-ə\\ Kijūrō Baron 1872–1951 Jp. statesman; advocated peaceful foreign policy (Shidehara diplomacy, 1924–27, 1929–31); premier (1945–46)

Shi·ge·mit·su \\,shē-gə-'mit-(,)sü, ,shi-\\ Mamoru 1887–1957 Jp. diplomat; signed Japanese surrender to the Allies (Sept. 2, 1945)

Shih Huang–ti — see CH'IN SHIH HUANG TI

Shin·well \\'shin-,wel, -wəl\\ Emanuel 1884–1986 Brit. polit.; nationalized mines (1946); notable for his aggressive political stance

Shi·rer \\'shir-ər\\ William Lawrence 1904–1993 Am. author; wrote *The Rise and Fall of the Third Reich,* etc.

Shir·ley \\'shər-lē\\ James 1596–1666 Eng. dram.; author of popular plays and of masques second only to Jonson's

Shock·ley \\'shä-klē\\ William Bradford 1910–1989 Am. physicist; awarded (with J. Bardeen and W.H. Brattain) 1956 Nobel prize for physics for inventing the transistor

Sho·lo·khov \\'shȯ-lə-,kȯf, -,kȯv\\ Mikhail Aleksandrovich 1905–1984 Soviet (Russ.-born) nov.; best known for tetralogy

Tikhy Don, translated into English as *And Quiet Flows the Don* and *The Don Flows Home to the Sea*

Sho·sta·ko·vich \\,shäs-tə-'kō-vich, ,shòs-, -'kó-\ Dmi·try \də-'mē-trē\ Dmitriyevich 1906–1975 Soviet (Russ.-born) composer; attacked by government for avant-garde works during Stalin's life; composed 15 symphonies, operas, ballets, etc.

Shull \'shəl\ Clifford G. 1915–   Am. physicist; awarded (with B.N. Brockhouse) 1994 Nobel prize for physics for research on using neutron beams to probe the structure of atoms

Shultz \'shûlts\ George Pratt 1920–   U.S. secy. of labor (1969–70); secy. of the treasury (1972–73); secy. of state (1982–89)

Shute \'shüt\ Nev·il \'ne-vəl\ 1899–1960 pseud. of *Nevil Shute Norway* Eng. aeronautical engineer & writer; noted for combining technical detail with fictional narrative, as in esp. *On the Beach, A Town Like Alice*

Shver·nik \'shver-nik\ Nikolay Mikhaylovich 1888–1970 Soviet polit.; chairman of the Presidium (1946–54)

Si·be·lius \sə-'bāl-yəs, -'bā-lē-əs\ Jean \'zhän, 'yän\ 1865–1957 Finn. composer; leading Finnish composer of his generation; known esp. for *Finlandia*

Sick·les \'si-kəlz\ Daniel Edgar 1825–1914 Am. gen. & polit.; instrumental in obtaining Central Park for New York City

Sid·dhār·tha Gau·ta·ma \si-'där-tə-'gaù-tə-mə, -'gō-\ *ca* 563–*ca* 483 B.C. *The Bud·dha* \'bü-də, 'bù-\ Indian philos. & founder of Buddhism; formulated and taught doctrine of "four noble truths" and "chain of causation"

Sid·dons \'si-dⁿnz\ Sarah 1755–1831 née *Kemble* Eng. actress; acknowledged as queen of the stage for role as Isabella in *Fatal Marriage*; esp. renowned for Lady Macbeth, her greatest role

Sid·ney \'sid-nē\ Sir Philip 1554–1586 Eng. poet, statesman, & soldier; wrote *The Arcadia*, most important prose fiction of 16th century England; celebrated for sonnet cycle *Astrophel and Stella;* considered ideal gentleman of his age

Sieg·bahn \'sēg-,bän\ Kai Manne 1918–   Swed. physicist; awarded (with N. Bloembergen, A.L. Schawlow) 1981 Nobel prize for physics for his contribution to the development of high=resolution electron spectroscopy

Siegbahn Karl Manne Georg 1886–1978 Swed. physicist *father of prec.*; awarded 1924 Nobel prize for physics for working with the X-ray spectroscope

Sie·mens \'sē-mənz\ Sir William 1823–1883 Brit. (Ger.-born) inventor; invented regenerative steam engine and improved Siemens steel process; laid first cable between Britain and U.S.

Sien·kie·wicz \shen-'kyä-vich\ Henryk 1846–1916 pseud. *Litwas* Pol. nov.; best known for *Quo Vadis?,* historical novel of ancient Rome; awarded 1905 Nobel prize for literature for his novels

Sie·yès \sē-,ā-'yes\ Emmanuel-Joseph 1748–1836 Fr. revolutionary; leading theorist of the concept of popular sovereignty at start of French Revolution; chief organizer of coup d'état that raised Napoléon to power

Sig·is·mund \'si-gəs-mənd\ 1368–1437 Holy Rom. emp. (1433–37); defeated twice in crusades against Turks; inaugurated Council of Constantine (1414)

Sigs·bee \'sigz-bē\ Charles Dwight 1845–1923 Am. admiral; in command of battleship *Maine* when it was blown up in Havana harbor (1898)

Si·gurds·son \'si-gərd-sən, -gərth-\ Jón \'yōn\ 1811–1879 Icelandic statesman & author; regarded as chiefly responsible for Denmark's grant of constitution to Iceland; published works on Iceland

Si·kor·ski \sə-'kȯr-skē\ Władysław 1881–1943 Pol. gen. & statesman; after German conquest of Poland (1939), commanded Polish army in France and headed Polish government in exile

Si·kor·sky \sə-'kȯr-skē\ Igor Ivan 1889–1972 Am. (Russ.-born) aeronautical engineer; developed first practical American helicopter (1939)

Sil·ko \'sil-(ˌ)kō\ Leslie Marmon 1948– Laguna Pueblo nov. & poet; best known for novel *Ceremony*, which drew on her Native American heritage

Sil·lan·pää \'si-lən-ˌpä\ Frans Eemil 1888–1964 Finn. nov.; awarded 1939 Nobel prize for literature for his novels, first Finnish writer so honored

Sills \'silz\ Beverly 1929– orig. *Belle Silverman* Am. soprano; best known for her association with New York City Opera Company as singer (1955–61, 1963–80), director (1979–89); acclaimed for her bel canto roles

Si·lo·ne \si-'lō-nē\ Ignazio 1900–1978 pseud. of *Secondo Tranquilli* Ital. author; gained fame with anti-Fascist novels stressing need for social reforms in Italy

Si·me·non \ˌsē-mə-'nōⁿ\ Georges-Joseph-Christian 1903–1989 Fr. (Belg.-born) writer; best known for his more than 80 detective novels featuring Inspector Maigret; one of the most widely published authors of the 20th century

Sim·e·on Sty·li·tes \'si-mē-ən-stə-'lī-tēz, -ˌstī-\ Saint ca 390–459 Syrian ascetic & pillar dweller; passed last 30 years of his life atop a 50-foot pillar, preaching and making converts

Simms \'simz\ Phillip 1956– Am. football player; quarterback, New York Giants (1979–94); MVP award, Super Bowl XXI

Simon — see Saint PETER

Si·mon \'sī-mən\ Saint 1st cent. A.D. one of the twelve Apostles

Si·mon \sē-'mōⁿ\ Claude 1913– Fr. writer; leading exponent of the French *nouveau roman* ("new novel"), mixing narration and stream of consciousness; awarded 1985 Nobel prize for literature

Si·mon \'sī-mən\ 1st Viscount 1873–1954 *John Allsebrook Simon* Brit. jurist & statesman; major supporter of Neville Chamberlain's policy of appeasement toward Nazi Germany

Simon Herbert Alexander 1916– Am. econ.; awarded 1978 Nobel prize for economics for research on the decision-making process in business

Simon Neil 1927– Am. dram.; wrote *Barefoot in the Park, The Odd Couple, Lost in Yonkers*, etc.

Si·mon·i·des \si-'mä-nə-ˌdēz\ **of Ceos** ca 556–ca 468? B.C. Greek poet; first known Greek poet to have written on commission for fees; wrote earliest recorded ode for Olympic victor

Simp·son \'sim(p)-sən\ Orenthal James 1947– Am. football player; running back, Buffalo Bills (1969–78); had career total of

11,236 yards gained rushing; acquitted of murder charges in sensational cause célèbre (1995)

Sims \'simz\ William Sow·den \'saù-dᵊn\ 1858–1936 Am. admiral; promoted convoy system in WWI; commanded American naval operations in European waters (1917–19)

Si·na·tra \sə-'nä-trə\ Frank 1915– *Francis Albert Sinatra* Am. singer & actor; acclaimed as one of the greatest singers of popular songs of his time; starred in films *From Here to Eternity, Guys and Dolls, The Manchurian Candidate,* etc.

Sin·clair \sin-'kler, siŋ-\ Upton Beall \'bel\ 1878–1968 Am. writer & polit.; author of topical and polemical novels *The Jungle, The Money Changers,* etc.

Sing·er \'siŋ-ər\ Isaac Ba·shev·is \bə-'she-vəs\ 1904–1991 Am. (Pol.-born) author; awarded the 1978 Nobel prize for literature for his Yiddish-language novels and short stories portraying Jewish life; best known works include novels *The Family Moskat, The Magician of Lublin,* etc.

Singer Isaac Merrit 1811–1875 Am. inventor; best known for development of improved sewing machine

Singh \'siŋ, 'siⁿ-hə\ Vishwanath Pratap 1931– prime min. of India (1989–90)

Si·quei·ros \si-'kā-(,)rōs\ David Alfaro 1896–1974 Mex. painter; known esp. for murals distinguished by sharp delineation, striking colors, political content

Si·rāj–ud–Daw·lah \sə-,räj-ə-'daù-lə\ *ca* 1732–1757 nawab of Bengal (1756–57); his reign witnessed the beginning of British domination of India; responsible for tragedy of Black Hole of Calcutta

Sis·ley \'siz-lē, sēs-lē\ Alfred 1839–1899 Fr. (Eng.-born) painter; a creator of French Impressionism and known esp. for landscapes

Sis·mon·di \sis-'män-dē, sēs-mōⁿ-dē\ Jean-Charles-Léonard Simonde de 1773–1842 Swiss hist. & econ.; a pioneer theorist on nature of economic crises and risks of limitless competition, overproduction, underconsumption

Sit·ter \'si-tər\ Willem de 1872–1934 Du. astron.; enunciated theory of an expanding universe

Sit·ting Bull \si-tiŋ-'bùl\ *ca* 1831–1890 Sioux leader; a leader in Sioux War; and with Gall and Crazy Horse defeated Custer at battle of the Little Big Horn (1876)

Sit·well \'sit-,wel, -wəl\ Sir George Reres·by \'rirz-bē\ 1860–1943 & his 3 children: Dame Edith 1887–1964; Sir Osbert 1892–1969; & Sa·chev·er·ell \sə-'she-və-rəl\ 1897–1988 Eng. authors; George was author of *Tales of My Native Village,* etc.; Edith was known for her formidable personality, Elizabethan dress, eccentric opinions, and revolt against Georgian poetry; Osbert wrote satirical and serious poetry and novels; Sacheverell wrote books on art and architecture as well as volumes of poetry

Skan·der·beg or **Scan·der·beg** \'skan-dər-,beg\ 1405–1468 orig. *George Kas·tri·o·ti* \,käs-trē-'ō-(,)tē\ Turk. *Is·kan·der Bey* \i-skän-'der-'bā\ Albanian hero; repulsed 23 Turkish invasions, including armies of Murad II

Skeat \'skēt\ Walter William 1835–1912 Eng. philologist; compiled *Etymological English Dictionary;* popularized philology

Skel·ton \'skel-t°n\ John *ca* 1460–1529 Eng. poet; developed an original style of caustic satire replete with slang, grotesque words, Latin quotations, etc. — **Skel·ton·ic** \skel-'tä-nik\ *adj*

Skin·ner \'ski-nər\ Burrhus Frederic 1904–1990 Am. psychol.; a leading proponent of behaviorism and operant conditioning; inventor of the Skinner box; known esp. for *Walden Two*, a description of a utopia based on behavioral engineering — **Skin·ner·ian** \ski-'nir-ē-ən, -'ner-\ *adj*

Skinner Cornelia Otis 1901–1979 *dau. of Otis* Am. actress; wrote, produced, directed series of "monodramas"; acted in *Candida*, *Major Barbara*, etc.

Skinner Otis 1858–1942 Am. actor; played leading roles esp. in Shakespeare plays, *Kismet*, etc.

Sko·da \'skō-də, 'shkȯ-(,)dä\ Emil von 1839–1900 Czech engineer & industrialist; manufactured military equipment, esp. large cannon and artillery

Sla·ter \'slā-tər\ Samuel 1768–1835 Am. (Eng.-born) industrialist; regarded as founder of American cotton industry; founded first U.S. cotton mill in Pawtucket, R.I. (1793)

Sli·dell \slī-'del, *by collateral descendants* 'slī-d°l\ John 1793–1871 Am. Confed. diplomat; participant in the Trent Affair during the Civil War, in which he and James M. Mason were seized by Union forces from the British steamer *Trent* en route to France

Sloan \'slōn\ John French 1871–1951 Am. painter; gained fame as member of "The Eight" or "Ashcan School;" known for dark, anecdotal portraits of working people

Slo·cum \'slō-kəm\ Henry Warner 1827–1894 Am. gen.; fought at Gettysburg; with Sherman on march to the sea and through Carolinas

Slo·nim·sky \slō-'nim(p)-skē\ Nicolas 1894–1996 Am. (Russ.-born) composer & musicologist; author of *Music Since 1900*; editor of *Baker's Biographical Dictionary of Musicians*, etc.

Sme·ta·na \'sme-t°n-ə\ Be·dřich \'be-dər-,zhik\ 1824–1884 Czech composer; founder of Czech national school of music; best known for opera *Bartered Bride* and symphonic poem *Má vlast (My Country)*

Smigły–Rydz Edward — see RYDZ-ŚMIGŁY

Smith \'smith\ Adam 1723–1790 Scot. econ.; produced *Inquiry into the Nature and Causes of the Wealth of Nations*, laying foundation of science of political economy and exerting influence throughout world

Smith Alfred Emanuel 1873–1944 Am. polit.; first Catholic to run for president; lost to Herbert Hoover (1928)

Smith Bessie 1894 (or 1898)–1937 Am. blues singer; known for emotional intensity, personal involvement, earthy realism of her style

Smith David 1906–1965 Am. sculptor; executed abstract welded metal sculptures, as *Medals of Dishonor*, *Royal Bird*, etc.

Smith Edmund Kirby — see KIRBY-SMITH

Smith Hamilton Othanel 1931–   Am. microbiologist; awarded (with W. Arber and D. Nathans) 1978 Nobel prize for medicine or physiology for discoveries in molecular genetics

Smith John *ca* 1580–1631 Eng. explorer & colonist; captured at Jamestown by Indians, condemned to death, and by legend saved by Pocahontas

Smith Joseph 1805–1844 Am. founder of Mormon Church; discoverer and self-described translator of *The Book of Mormon*, which together with the Bible, became the theological foundation of his church

Smith Kate 1909–1986 *Kathryn Elizabeth Smith* Am. singer; introduced some 700 popular songs, including "When the Moon Comes Over the Mountain," "God Bless America," etc.

Smith Margaret Chase 1897–1995 Am. polit.; member, U.S. House of Representatives (1940–49), U.S. Senate (1949–73); one of the first to speak out against Sen. Joseph McCarthy and his inquisition against alleged communists in U.S. government

Smith Michael 1932–   Canad. (Brit-born) biochem.; awarded (with K.B. Mullis) 1993 Nobel prize for chemistry for his method of altering DNA molecules

Smith Sydney 1771–1845 Eng. essayist; produced *Letters of Peter Plymley* in defense of Catholic emancipation; championed parliamentary reform, etc.

Smith Walter Be·dell \bə-'del\ 1895–1961 Am. gen. & diplomat; negotiated and accepted surrenders of Italy and Germany in WWII

Smith William 1769–1839 Eng. geologist; founder of stratigraphical geology; his geologic map of England and Wales became prototype for modern geologic maps

Smith-Dor·ri·en \'smith-'dȯr-ē-ən, -'där-\ Sir Horace Lockwood 1858–1930 Brit. gen.; served in Zulu War, Egyptian War, Sudan, Bengal, Punjab, Boer War, WWI, etc.

Smith·son \'smith-sən\ James 1765–1829 Brit. chem. & mineralogist & benefactor of Smithsonian Inst.

Smol·lett \'smä-lət\ Tobias George 1721–1771 Brit. author; renowned for his satirical, picaresque novels, including *Roderick Random, Peregrine Pickle, Humphry Clinker*, etc.; acclaimed for his rendering of comic characters

Smuts \'sməts, 'smœts\ Jan \'yän\ Christiaan 1870–1950 So. African field marshal; prime min. (1919–24, 1939–48)

Smyth \'smith\ Henry DeWolf 1898–1986 Am. physicist; played key role in development of atomic bomb

Snell \'snel\ George 1903–   Am. research geneticist; awarded (with B. Benacerraf and J. Dausset) 1980 Nobel prize for physiology or medicine for discoveries concerning the genetic regulation of the body's immune system

Snor·ri Stur·lu·son \'snȯr-ē-'stər-lə-sən, ˌsnär-\ 1179–1241 Icelandic statesman & hist.; author of works on Norse mythology and early history

Snow \'snō\ Charles Percy 1905–1980 Baron *Snow* Eng. nov. & physicist; author of 11-volume sequence of novels, *Strangers and Brothers* and of *The Two Cultures and the Scientific Revolution*, etc.

Snow·den \'snō-dᵊn\ Philip 1864–1937 1st Viscount *Snowden of Ick·orn·shaw* \'i-ˌkȯrn-ˌshȯ\ Eng. polit.; as chancellor of the exchequer, cut government expenditures and secured abandonment of gold standard

Snow·don \'snō-dᵊn\ Earl of — see ARMSTRONG-JONES

Sny·der \'snī-dər\ John Wesley 1895–1985 Am. banker & administrator; U.S. secy. of treasury (1946–53); designed U.S. reconstruction programs for nations devastated by WWII

Sny·ders \'snī-dərs\ Frans 1579–1657 Flem. painter; known for hunting scenes and animals in combat

Soar·es \'swär-ish\ Mário 1924–   prime min. of Portugal (1976–78, 1983–85) & pres. (1986–   )

Sobieski John — see JOHN III SOBIESKI

So·ci·nus \sō-'sī-nəs\ Faustus 1539–1604 *Fausto Soz·zi·ni* or *So·ci·ni* or *Soz·i·ni* \sōt-'sē-nē\ Ital. theol.; developed anti-Trinitarian doctrine into Socinianism; denounced by Inquisition; strongly influenced Unitarianism

Soc·ra·tes \'sä-krə-ˌtēz\ *ca* 470–399 B.C. Greek philos.; developer of philosophical thought concerned with the analysis of the character and conduct of human life; famous for his injunction "know thyself;" remembered for his conviction on charges of impiety and death by drinking poisonous hemlock — **So·crat·ic** \sə-'kra-tik, sō-\ *adj*

Sod·dy \'sä-dē\ Frederick 1877–1956 Eng. chem.; awarded 1921 Nobel prize for chemistry for studying radioactive substances and isotopes

Sö·der·blom \'sə(r)-dər-ˌblüm, 'sœ-\ Nathan 1866–1931 Swed. theol.; awarded 1930 Nobel prize for peace for his ecumenical activities

So·do·ma \sō-'dō-mə\ Il 1477–1549 *Giovanni Antonio Bazzi* Ital. painter; influenced by da Vinci and esp. Raphael; works show transition from High Renaissance to Mannerist style

Sol·o·mon \'sä-lə-mən\ 10th cent. B.C. *son of David* king of Israel; under his rule Israel rose to height of greatness; noted for wealth, wisdom; builder of Solomon's Temple in Jerusalem; reputed author of Old Testament books Proverbs, Song of Solomon, Ecclesiastes, Wisdom of Solomon

So·lon \'sō-lən, -ˌlän\ *ca* 630–*ca* 560 B.C. Athenian lawgiver; instituted profound legal reforms; considered first great poet of Athens; one of the Seven Wise Men of Greece

So·low \'sō-lō\ Robert Merton 1924–   Am. econ.; awarded 1987 Nobel prize for developing a mathematical model that identified technology as the dominant factor in long-term economic growth

Sol·ti \'shōl-tē\ Sir Georg 1912–   orig. *György Solti* Brit. (Hung.-born) conductor; as musical director of Chicago Symphony Orchestra (1969–91) reestablished its international standing

Sol·zhe·ni·tsyn \ˌsōl-zhə-'nēt-sən, ˌsȯl-\ Aleksandr Isayevich 1918–   Russ. nov.; awarded 1970 Nobel prize for literature for his novels, including *One Day in the Life of Ivan Denisovich, Cancer Ward, The Gulag Archipelago,* etc.

Som·er·ville \'sə-mər-ˌvil\ Sir James Fownes 1882–1949 Brit. admiral; commander in both World Wars

Sond·heim \'sänd-ˌ(h)īm\ Stephen Joshua 1930–   Am. composer & lyricist; renowned for unorthodox, groundbreaking musical dramas as *Company, Sweeney Todd: The Demon Barber of Fleet Street, Sunday in the Park With George,* etc.

Son·tag \'sän-₁tag\ Susan 1933–   Am. writer; best known for her philosophical essays on modern culture, as her influential "Notes on 'Camp'," an examination of camp humor

Soong Ai–ling \'sù̇ŋ-'ī-₁liŋ\ 1888–1973 *wife of H. H. K'ung*

Soong Ch'ing–ling \-'chiŋ-'liŋ\ 1892–1981 *wife of Sun Yat-sen*

Soong Mei–ling \-'mā-'liŋ\ 1897–   *wife of Chiang Kai-shek*

Soong Tzu–wen *or* **Tse–ven** *or* **Tsŭ–wên** \-'tsù̇-'wən\ 1894–1971 *T. V. Soong; bro. of prec.* Chin. financier & statesman; financed Kuomintang party; min. of finance, Nationalist government; founded Bank of China

Soph·o·cles \'sä-fə-₁klēz\ *ca* 496–406 B.C. Greek dram.; ranked with Aeschylus and Euripides as greatest Greek dramatists; wrote *Oedipus Rex, Antigone, Philoctetes,* etc. — **Soph·o·cle·an** \₁sä-fə-'klē-ən\ *adj*

Sor·del·lo \sȯr-'de-(₁)lō\ *ca* 1200–before 1269 Ital. troubadour; wrote, in Provençal, love songs, satires, a lament, a didactic poem, etc.

So·rol·la y Bas·ti·da \sə-'rȯl-yə-ē-bä-'stē-də, -'rȯl-ə-, -'stē-thə\ Joaquín 1863–1923 Span. painter; known for genre paintings, landscapes, beach scenes in conservative Impressionist style marked by contrasts of light and shade, brilliant colors, vigorous brushstrokes

So·to, de \thä-'sōt-(₁)ō, di-\ Hernando 1496 (or 1499 or 1500)–1542 Span. explorer; explored territory of present Florida, Alabama, Tennessee, Mississippi, Arkansas, Oklahoma, and Louisiana; sighted and crossed Mississippi River

Soult \sült\ Nicolas-Jean de Dieu 1769–1851 Duc *de Dal·ma·tie* \dȧl-mȧ-sē\ Fr. soldier; marshal of France; fought for Napoléon and for Louis XVIII; responsible for conquest of Algeria

Sou·sa \'sü-zə, 'sü-sə\ John Philip 1854–1932 *the March King* Am. bandmaster & composer; composed about 140 military marches, including "Semper Fidelis," "Washington Post March," "Stars and Stripes Forever," etc.

Sou·ter \'sü-tər\ David 1939–   Am. jurist; associate justice, U.S. Supreme Court (1990–   )

South \'saů̇th\ Robert 1634–1716 Eng. clergyman; best known for his vigorous, pithy, clear sermons

Sou·they \'saů̇-thē, 'sə-thē\ Robert 1774–1843 Eng. author; poet laureate (1813–43); remembered best for his shorter poems, letters, and biographical and historical works

Sou·tine \sü-'tēn\ Chaim 1893–1943 Fr. (Lith.-born) painter; works characterized by thick impasto, agitated brushwork, convulsive rhythms, disturbing psychological content

So·yin·ka \shó-'yiŋ-kä\ Wo·le \'wó-lā\ 1934–   Nigerian dram. & poet; awarded 1986 Nobel prize for literature for poems and novels, the first black African so honored

Spaak \'späk\ Paul-Henri Charles 1899–1972 Belg. lawyer & polit.; premier (1938–39, 1947–50); secy.-gen. of NATO (1957–61); helped draft charters of Benelux, U.N., NATO, Common Market

Spaatz \'späts\ Carl 1891–1974 Am. gen.; chief of U.S. bombing force in Germany (1944) and Japan (1945); first chief of staff of an independent U.S. air force

Spal·ding \'spȯl-diŋ\ Albert 1888–1953 Am. violinist & composer; wrote suite for orchestra, violin concerti, other violin pieces

Spark \\'spärk\\ Muriel Sarah 1918–   née *Camberg* Brit. writer; best known for novels *Memento Mori, The Prime of Miss Jean Brodie*, etc.

Sparks \\'spärks\\ Jar·ed \\'jar-əd, 'jer-\\ 1789–1866 Am. hist.; published *The Writings of George Washington, The Works of Benjamin Franklin*, etc.

Spar·ta·cus \\'spär-tə-kəs\\ d 71 B.C. Rom. slave & insurrectionist; defeated several Roman armies sent against him before being beaten by Crassus and killed in battle

Spell·man \\'spel-mən\\ Francis Joseph 1889–1967 Am. cardinal

Spe·mann \\'shpā-,män\\ Hans 1869–1941 Ger. embryologist; awarded 1935 Nobel prize for physiology or medicine for discovering the organizer effect in the growth of an embryo

Spen·cer \\'spen(t)-sər\\ Herbert 1820–1903 Eng. philos.; one of few modern thinkers to attempt systematic account of all cosmic phenomena, including mental and social principles; leading exponent of social Darwinism; coined phrase "survival of the fittest"

Spen·der \\'spen-dər\\ Stephen Harold 1909–1995 Eng. poet & critic; associated with Auden and Day-Lewis; wrote *Poems from Spain, The Generous Days*, etc.

Speng·ler \\'shpeŋ-lər, 'speŋ-\\ Oswald 1880–1936 Ger. philos.; author of *Der Untergang des Abendlandes (The Decline of the West)* predicting the eclipse of Western civilization

Spen·ser \\'spen(t)-sər\\ Edmund 1552–1599 Eng. poet; author of *The Faerie Queene*, etc.; "the Poet's Poet," he excelled in richness and beauty of imagination; invented Spenserian stanza — **Spen·se·ri·an** \\spen-'sir-ē-ən\\ *adj*

Sper·ry \\'sper-ē\\ Elmer Ambrose 1860–1930 Am. inventor; best known for invention of gyroscope compasses and stabilizers for ships and airplanes

Sperry Roger Wolcott 1913–1994 Am. psychobiologist; awarded (with D.H. Hubel and T.N. Wiesel) 1981 Nobel prize for physiology or medicine for research on the organization and functioning of the brain

Spiel·berg \\'spē(ə)l-,bərg\\ Steven 1947–   Am. motion-picture director, writer, & producer; notably successful with wide range of films, many requiring fantastic special effects, including *Jaws, Empire of the Sun*, Indiana Jones series, *Jurassic Park, Schindler's List*, etc. — **Spiel·berg·ian** \\,spēl-'bər-gē-ən\\ *adj*

Spil·lane \\spə-'lān\\ Mickey 1918–   orig. *Frank Morrison Spillane* Am. writer; known esp. for series of hard-boiled detective novels featuring Mike Hammer and marked by violence, sexual frankness, and even sadism

Spi·no·za \\spi-'nō-zə\\ Benedict de 1632–1677 Hebrew prename *Baruch* Du. philos.; viewed as most eminent expounder of rational pantheism

Spit·te·ler \\'shpi-t⁵l-ər, 'spi-\\ *see* footnote... Carl 1845–1924 pseud. *Felix Tan·dem* \\'tän-,dem\\ Swiss writer; awarded 1919 Nobel prize for literature for his epics, stories, and essays

Spitz \\'spits\\ Mark Andrew 1950–   Am. swimmer; first athlete to win seven gold medals in a single Olympic Games (1972)

Spock \\'späk\\ Benjamin McLane 1903–   Am. physician; wrote *The Common Sense Book of Baby and Child Care*, ubiquitous guide to the rearing of children; later became avid pacifist

Spode \\'spōd\ Josiah 1754–1827 Eng. potter; credited with developing hybrid porcelain that became the standard English bone china

Spru·ance \\'sprü-ən(t)s\ Raymond Ames 1886–1969 Am. admiral; in charge of conquest of Gilbert and Marshall Islands (1943–44)

Spy·ri \\'shpir-ē, 'spir-\ Johanna 1827–1901 née *Heusser* Swiss author; author of beloved children's book *Heidi*

Squan·to \\'skwän-(,)tō\ d 1622 *Tisquantum* \tə-'skwän-təm\ Pawtuxet interpreter & guide; served as translator between Massasoit and the Pilgrims at Plymouth; taught colonists basic farming skills

Staël, de \də-'stäl, -stȧl\ Mme. Anne-Louise-Germaine 1766–1817 née *Necker* Baronne *de Staël-Holstein* Fr. writer & hostess of literary salon; during French Revolution maintained literary salons in Paris and Switzerland; wrote several literary and political essays that are important documents in the development of European Romanticism; also known for novels, plays, memoirs

Staf·ford \\'sta-fərd\ Jean 1915–1979 Am. writer; noted esp. for her deftly drawn characters in numerous short stories and in novels as *Boston Adventure*

Ståhl·berg \\'stȯl-,bərg, -,ber-ē\ Kaarlo Ju·ho \\'yü-(,)hȯ\ 1865–1952 Finn. statesman; first president of the Finnish republic (1919–25)

Stair Viscount & Earl of — see DALRYMPLE

Sta·lin \\'stä-lən, 'stȧ-, -,lēn\ Joseph 1879–1953 *Iosif Vissarionovich Dzhu·gash·vi·li* \,jü-gəsh-'vē-lē\ Soviet leader; virtual dictator of U.S.S.R. after death of Lenin; reformed, improved, expanded Soviet society, industry, territory with singleminded ruthlessness, building up Soviet Union as rival to U.S. for world leadership

Stan·dish \\'stan-dish\ Myles *or* Miles 1584?–1656 Am. colonist; leader among Pilgrims at Plymouth colony; by unsubstantiated legend had John Alden propose unsuccessfully to Priscilla Mullens on his behalf

Stan·is·lav·sky \,sta-ni-'släf-skē\ Konstantin 1863–1938 pseud. of *Konstantin Sergeyevich Alekseyev* Russ. actor, director, & producer; founder of the Moscow Art Theatre; best known for his influential "method" system of acting

Stan·is·ław I \\'sta-nə-,slȯv, -,släv\ Lesz·czyń·ski \lesh-'chin-skē\ 1677–1766 king of Poland (1704–09, 1733–35); largely a pawn in the continual struggle by foreign powers to dominate Poland

Stan·ley \\'stan-lē\ Edward George Geoffrey Smith 1799–1869 Earl of *Derby* Brit. statesman; prime min. three times; one of greatest parliamentary orators; also accomplished classical scholar

Stanley Sir Henry Morton 1841–1904 orig. *John Rowlands* Brit. explorer; led expedition into central Africa to find David Livingstone, greeting him with famous "Dr. Livingstone, I presume?"; explored Congo region and opened it up to European trade and political organization

Stanley Wendell Meredith 1904–1971 Am. biochem.; awarded (with J.H. Northrop and J.B. Sumner) 1946 Nobel prize for chemistry for preparing pure enzymes and virus proteins

Stan·ton \\'stan-tᵊn\ Edwin McMasters 1814–1869 Am. lawyer & secy. of war (1862–68); guided war department through Civil War;

his dismissal by President Johnson resulted in unsuccessful impeachment proceedings

Stanton Elizabeth 1815–1902 née *Cady* Am. suffragist; helped launch woman suffrage movement by organizing first U.S. women's rights convention (1848, Seneca Falls, N.Y.)

Stan·wyck \'stan-(,)wik\ Barbara 1907–1990 orig. *Ruby Stevens* Am. actress; known esp. for playing strong-willed, independent women in films as *Stella Dallas, Double Indemnity,* and *Sorry, Wrong Number*

Star·hem·berg \'stär-əm-,bərg, 'shtär-əm-,berk\ Ernst Rüdiger 1899–1956 Fürst *von Starhemberg* Austrian polit.; head of right-wing Vaterländische Front (1934–36)

Stark \'stärk\ Harold Raynsford 1880–1972 Am. admiral; commander in European waters (1942–45)

Stark \'shtärk, 'stärk\ Johannes 1874–1957 Ger. physicist; awarded 1919 Nobel prize for physics for discovering Stark effect of spectra in electric fields

Stark \'stärk\ John 1728–1822 Am. gen. in Revolution; best known for victory in battle of Bennington and as member of court-martial convicting Major André

Starr \'stär\ Bart 1934–   *Bryan Bartlett Starr* Am. football player; quarterback, Green Bay Packers (1956–71); led Packers to five NFL championships and two Super Bowl victories (1967, 1968)

Sta·tius \'stā-sh(ē-)əs\ Publius Papinius *ca* A.D. 45–96 Rom. poet; under Domitian, author of lyric verse in *Silvae* and of epics *The-baid* and *Achilleid* (left unfinished)

Stau·bach \'stȯ-,bäk\ Roger Thomas 1942–   Am. football player; quarterback, Dallas Cowboys (1969–79); led Cowboys to two Super Bowl victories (1972, 1978)

Stau·ding·er \'shtau̇-diŋ-ər, 'stau̇-\ Hermann 1881–1965 Ger. chem.; awarded 1953 Nobel prize for chemistry for discovering a way to synthesize fiber

Steele \'stē(ə)l\ Sir Richard 1672–1729 Brit. essayist & dram.; founder of journals *The Tatler, The Spectator,* etc.

Steen \'stän\ Jan 1626–1679 Du. painter; his paintings marked by humor, expert use of color, subtle capturing of facial expression in biblical and classical subjects, portraits, scenes of everyday life

Ste·fans·son \'ste-fən-sən\ Vil·hjal·mur \'vil-,yȧl-mər\ 1879–1962 Am. (Canad.-born) explorer; explored Canadian and Alaskan Arctic regions; conducted ethnographical and zoological studies among Eskimos

Stef·fens \'ste-fənz\ (Joseph) Lincoln 1866–1936 Am. journalist; initiated and helped write muck-raking articles in *McClure's Magazine;* later supported revolutionaries in Europe

Steg·ner \'steg-nər\ Wallace Earle 1909–1993 Am. writer; known for his novels, biographies, essays, and historical studies celebrating the American West

Stei·chen \'stī-kən\ Edward Jean 1879–1973 Am. photographer; pioneer in photography as art form; known for portraits of Greta Garbo, Charlie Chaplin, etc.

Stein \'stīn\ Gertrude 1874–1946 Am. writer; best remembered for the artistic and literary salon she kept in Paris between the wars

Stein William Howard 1911–1980 Am. biochem.; awarded (with C.B. Anfinsen and S. Moore) 1972 Nobel prize for chemistry for fundamental contributions to the chemistry of enzymes

Stein \'shtīn, 'stīn\ (Heinrich Friedrich) Karl 1757–1831 Freiherr *vom und zum Stein* Pruss. statesman; accomplished reforms in administration, taxation, civil service; abolished serfdom

Stein·beck \'stīn-ˌbek\ John Ernst 1902–1968 Am. nov.; awarded 1962 Nobel prize for literature for his novels, which included *The Grapes of Wrath* (1939), *The Pearl, Of Mice and Men*, etc.

Stein·berg·er \'stīn-ˌbər-gər\ Jack 1921– Am. (Ger.-born) physicist; awarded (with L.M. Lederman and M. Schwartz) 1988 Nobel prize for physics for work on subatomic neutrinos

Stei·nem \'stī-nəm\ Gloria 1934– Am. feminist writer & editor; a leader in the women's movement; a founder and editor of *Ms.* magazine

Stei·ner \'stā-ner, 'stī-nər\ (Francis) George 1929– Fr. writer; known for his literary criticism examining the relationship between literature and society esp. in light of modern history

Steiner Maximilian Raoul Walter 1888–1971 Am. (Austrian-born) composer & conductor; best known for film scores, including those for *King Kong, Gone With the Wind, Casablanca*, etc.

Stein·metz \'shtīn-ˌmets, 'stīn-\ Charles Proteus 1865–1923 Am. (Ger.-born) electrical engineer; patented over 200 inventions, including improvements on generators and motors

Stel·la \'ste-lə\ Frank Philip 1936– Am. painter; a leading figure in the Minimal Art movement; known esp. for paintings that were austere yet monumental in the simplicity of their design

Sten·dhal \sten-'däl, stan-, *F* staⁿ-däl\ 1783–1842 pseud. of *Marie= Henri Beyle* \'bel\ Fr. writer; chiefly known for Romantic novels, among most important in French, esp. *Le Rouge et le noir* (1830; *The Red and the Black*), *La Chartreuse de Parme* (1839; *The Chart= erhouse of Parma*) — **Sten·dhal·ian** \-'dä-lē-ən\ *adj*

Sten·gel \'steŋ-gəl\ Casey 1891–1975 *Charles Dillon Stengel* Am. baseball player & manager; manager, New York Yankees (1949–60); led Yankees to 7 World Series victories; also remembered for his mangled English known as "Stengelese"

Ste·phen \'stē-vən\ *ca* 1097–1154 king of England (1135–54); involved in battle for throne with Matilda, daughter of Henry I and empress of Germany; eventually submitted and acknowledged Henry of Anjou (Henry II) his heir

Stephen Sir Leslie 1832–1904 Eng. philos., critic, & biographer; wrote biographies of Pope, Swift, George Eliot, Hobbes; first editor of *Dictionary of National Biography*

Ste·phens \'stē-vənz\ Alexander Hamilton 1812–1883 Am. polit.; vice pres. of the Confed. states (1861–65)

Stephens James 1882–1950 Irish poet & nov.; author of pantheistic fairy tales set in Dublin slums and poems about animals

Ste·phen·son \'stē-vən-sən\ George 1781–1848 Eng. inventor & founder of railroads; devised miner's safety lamp; patented successful locomotive engines

Stephenson Robert 1803–1859 *son of George* Eng. engineer; chief engineer of first railway into London; known also for his bridges

Stern \\'stərn\ Isaac 1920–   Am. (Russ.-born) violinist; through tours and concerts has become known as one of the world's greatest violinists

Stern Otto 1888–1969 Am. (Ger.-born) physicist; awarded 1943 Nobel prize for physics for discovering the molecular beam method of studying the atom

Stern·berg \\'stərn-,bərg\ George Miller 1838–1915 Am. physician & bacteriol.; first to demonstrate the plasmodium of malaria and the bacilli of tuberculosis and of typhoid fever

Sterne \\'stərn\ Laurence 1713–1768 Brit. nov.; best known for novel *The Life and Opinions of Tristram Shandy*, with eccentric humor and unconventional indecorum

Stet·tin·i·us \stə-'ti-nē-əs, ste-\ Edward Reilly 1900–1949 Am. financier & statesman; U.S. secy. of state (1944–45); helped to established the United Nations

Steu·ben \\'stü-bən, 'styü-, 'shtöi-\ Baron Friedrich Wilhelm Ludolf Gerhard Augustin von 1730–1794 Pruss.-born gen. in Am. Revolution; trained Continental army and became trusted adviser to Washington

Ste·vens \\'stē-vənz\ John 1749–1838 Am. inventor; made first seagoing steamship, the *Phoenix*, which went from New York to Philadelphia

Stevens John Paul 1920–   Am. jurist; associate justice, U.S. Supreme Court (1975–   )

Stevens Risë 1913–   Am. mezzo-soprano; known esp. for roles in operas *Mignon, Der Rosenkavalier, Carmen,* etc.

Stevens Thaddeus 1792–1868 Am. polit.; instrumental in preparation of 14th Amendment; proposed impeachment of President Johnson and managed the trial

Stevens Wallace 1879–1955 Am. poet; author of poems exploring the relationship of reality and imagination

Ste·ven·son \\'stē-vən-sən\ Ad·lai \\'ad-lē, -(,)lā\ Ewing 1835–1914 Am. polit.; vice pres. of U.S. (1893–97)

Stevenson Adlai Ewing 1900–1965 *grandson of prec.* Am. polit.; Democratic candidate for pres. of U.S. (1952, 1956)

Stevenson Robert Louis Balfour 1850–1894 Scot. author; best known for novels *Treasure Island, Kidnapped, The Strange Case of Dr. Jekyll and Mr. Hyde,* etc.

Stew·art \\'stü-ərt, 'styü-; 'st(y)ù(-ə)rt\ Du·gald \\'dü-gəld\ 1753–1828 Scot. philos.; major exponent of the Scottish "common sense" school of philosophy, holding doctrines of natural realism, empiricism, and intuitionism

Stewart Jackie 1939–   *John Young Stewart* Brit. automobile racer; started in 99 races; won record 27 world championships (1965–73)

Stewart James Maitland 1908–   Am. actor; renowned esp. for his portrayals of naive, self-effacing, but stalwart heroes in films *Mr. Smith Goes to Washington, It's a Wonderful Life, The Spirit of St. Louis,* etc.

Stewart Potter 1915–1985 Am. jurist; associate justice, U.S. Supreme Court (1959–81)

Stewart Robert 1769–1822 Viscount *Cas·tle·reagh* \\'ka-səl-,rā\ Eng. statesman; led coalition against Napoléon and secured Napoléon's removal to St. Helena; controlled outcome of Congress of

Vienna and did his best to oppose Metternich's retaliatory attitude towards France

Steyn \'stīn\ Marthinus Theunis 1857–1916 So. African statesman; guerilla leader during South African War; later resisted Botha's program of conciliation

Stieg·litz \'stē-glǝts, -ˌglits\ Alfred 1864–1946 Am. photographer; often called the father of modern photography for his efforts to establish it as a form of art

Stig·ler \'sti-glǝr\ George J. 1911–1991 Am. econ.; awarded 1982 Nobel prize for economics for research on industrial organizations, markets, and regulation

Stil·i·cho \'sti-li-ˌkō\ Flavius ca 365–408 Rom. gen. & statesman; one of the last great Roman military commanders in the West; led several campaigns against the invading barbarians

Still \'stil\ Andrew Taylor 1828–1917 Am. founder of osteopathy

Stil·well \'stil-ˌwel, -wǝl\ Joseph Warren 1883–1946 Am. gen.; commanded U.S. forces in China, Burma, India (1942); commanded 10th Army in the Pacific until war's end

Stim·son \'stim(p)-sǝn\ Henry Lewis 1867–1950 Am. statesman; U.S. secy. of war (1911–13, 1940–45); chief adviser to Roosevelt and Truman on atomic policy; advised use of atomic bombs against Japan

Stin·nes \'shti-nǝs, 'sti-\ Hugo 1870–1924 Ger. industrialist; served as head of industrial production during WWI in Germany and occupied Belgium; controlled vast interests

Stir·ling \'stǝr-liŋ\ James Frazer 1926–1992 Brit. architect; leading exponent of postmodernism in architecture; helped to develop New Brutalist style, emphasizing functional aesthetics and materials; works included Neue Staatsgalerie in Stuttgart, Germany

Stock·hau·sen \'shtók-ˌhaú-zǝn, 'stäk-\ Karlheinz 1928– Ger. composer & theorist; known for compositions combining electronic sounds and traditional instruments

Stock·mar \'stäk-ˌmär\ Christian Friedrich 1787–1863 Baron *von Stockmar* Anglo-Belg. statesman; adviser to Queen Victoria and arranged her marriage to Prince Albert

Stock·ton \'stäk-tǝn\ Francis Richard 1834–1902 *Frank R. Stockton* Am. writer; best known as author of story "The Lady or the Tiger" and of humorous novels

Stod·dard \'stä-dǝrd\ Richard Henry 1825–1903 Am. poet & critic; served as center of cultural life in New York for 30 years; wrote unoriginal and now dated verse

Sto·ker \'stō-kǝr\ Bram 1847–1912 Brit. writer; published horror tale *Dracula*, etc.

Stokes \'stōks\ Sir Frederick Wilfrid Scott 1860–1927 Eng. engineer & inventor; invented Stokes trench mortar

Sto·kow·ski \stǝ-'kóf-skē, -'kóv- *also* -'kaú-\ Leopold Antoni Stanislaw Boleslawowicz 1882–1977 Am. (Eng.-born) conductor; known for lush interpretations of the classics, showmanship, and popularizing of classical music, as in Walt Disney's *Fantasia*

Stone \'stōn\ Edward Durell 1902–1978 Am. architect; a leading exponent of International Style; works included John F. Kennedy Center for the Performing Arts in Washington, D.C.

Stone Harlan Fiske 1872–1946 Am. jurist; chief justice U.S. Supreme Court (1941–46); advocate of judicial self-restraint

Stone Irving 1903–1989 orig. surname *Tennenbaum* Am. writer; known for fictionalized biographies of Van Gogh (*Lust for Life*), Michelangelo (*The Agony and the Ecstasy*), etc.

Stone Lucy 1818–1893 Am. suffragist; a founder of woman suffrage movement; retained her own name after marriage to protest laws applying to married women

Stone Oliver William 1946–   Am. filmmaker; known for his visceral, cinematically virtuosic films on controversial subjects, including *Platoon, JFK, Nixon*, etc.

Stone Sir (John) Richard Nicholas 1913–1991 Eng. ecòn.; awarded 1984 Nobel prize for economics for developing methods of measuring the performance of national economies

Stoph \'shtôf, 'stôf\ Willi 1914–   prime min. of East Germany (1976–89)

Stop·pard \'stä-ˌpärd\ Tom 1937–   orig. *Tomas Strauss·ler* \'straùs-lər\ Brit. (Czech-born) playwright; known esp. for ingeniously plotted, verbally brilliant plays including *Rosencrantz and Guildenstern Are Dead, Jumpers, The Real Thing*, etc.

Sto·ry \'stōr-ē, 'stòr-ē\ Joseph 1779–1845 Am. jurist; associate justice, U.S. Supreme Court (1811–45); with James Kent, considered a founder of equity jurisprudence in U.S.

Story William Wetmore 1819–1895 *son of prec.* Am. sculptor; works included *Cleopatra*, described in Hawthorne's novel *The Marble Fawn*

Stout \'staùt\ Rex Todhunter 1886–1975 Am. writer; author of detective stories featuring the reclusive aesthete Nero Wolfe and his extroverted legman Archie Goodwin

Stow \'stō\ John 1525–1605 Eng. hist. & antiquarian; collected and transcribed manuscripts, produced histories as *A Survey of London*, a standard authority on Old London

Stowe \'stō\ Harriet Elizabeth 1811–1896 née *Beecher* Am. author; best known as author of *Uncle Tom's Cabin, or Life Among the Lowly*, important in making slavery a moral issue in the North

Stra·bo \'strā-(ˌ)bō\ 64 (or 63) B.C.–after A.D. 23 Greek geographer; wrote *Geographical Sketches* describing Europe, Asia, India, Syria, etc.

Stra·chey \'strā-chē\ (Evelyn) John St. Loe 1901–1963 Eng. socialist; author of *The Coming Struggle for Power, The Nature of Capitalist Crisis*, etc.

Strachey (Giles) Lytton 1880–1932 Eng. biographer; with *Eminent Victorians* established a new style of ironic, elegant, witty, irreverent biography as a work of art

Stra·di·va·ri \ˌstra-də-'vär-ē, -'var-, -'ver-\ Antonio 1644–1737 L. *Antonius Strad·i·var·i·us* \ˌstra-də-'var-ē-əs, -'ver-\ Ital. violin maker; considered greatest of all violin makers; set modern proportions of violin

Straf·ford \'stra-fərd\ 1st Earl of 1593–1641 *Thomas Wentworth* Eng. statesman; for his attempt to consolidate the sovereign power of Charles I, he was impeached and executed by a hostile Parliament

Stras·berg \'stras-ˌbərg\ Lee 1901–1982 orig. *Israel Strassberg* Am. (Pol.-born) theater director & teacher; leading American exponent of "Method acting," which calls for the actor to draw upon his or her own emotional experience and memory; shaped a whole generation of stage and film actors

Stratford de Redcliffe Viscount — see Stratford CANNING

Strath-co-na \strath-'kō-nə\ **and Mount Royal** 1st Baron 1820–1914 *Donald Alexander Smith* Canad. (Scot.-born) railroad builder & polit.; instrumental in building the Canadian Pacific Railway

Straus \'shtraùs, 'straùs\ Oscar 1870–1954 Fr. (Austrian-born) composer; best known as composer of operetta *Der tapfere Soldat (The Chocolate Soldier)*

Strauss \'shtraùs, 'straùs\ David Friedrich 1808–1874 Ger. theol. & philos.; interpreted the Bible on basis of Hegelian dialectic; caused enormous controversy by describing Gospels as "historical myth"

Strauss Johann father 1804–1849 & his sons Johann Baptist 1825–1899 & Josef 1827–1870 Austrian composers; Johann composed waltzes, polkas, galops, etc.; Johann Baptist was known as the Waltz King for compositions such as *The Blue Danube, Tales from the Vienna Woods*, etc.; Josef conducted family orchestra in turn and composed many dances

Strauss Ri·chard \'ri-ˌkärt, -ˌkärt\ 1864–1949 Ger. composer; regarded as leader of the New Romantic school; composed operas *Der Rosenkavalier, Ariadne auf Naxos*, etc., tone poems *Also sprach Zarathustra, Ein Heldenleben*, etc. — **Strauss·ian** \'strau-sē-ən, 'shtrau-\ *adj*

Stra·vin·sky \strə-'vin(t)-skē\ Igor \'ē-ˌgòr\ Fyodorovich 1882–1971 Am. (Russ.-born) composer; known esp. for ballets *Firebird, Pétrouchka, Rite of Spring*; one of greatest composers of 20th century and a pioneering modernist of seminal influence — **Stra·vin·sky·an** *or* **Stra·vin·ski·an** \-skē-ən\ *adj*

Streep \'strēp\ Meryl 1949– orig. *Mary Louise Streep* Am. actress; known esp. for the exceptional versatility of her performances in films *Sophie's Choice, Out of Africa, The Bridges of Madison County*, etc.

Strei·cher \'shtrī-kər, 'strī-, -ˌkər\ Julius 1885–1946 Ger. Nazi administrator; notorious for his anti-Semitic campaign (from 1919) and involvement in Munich Putsch

Strei·sand \'strī-ˌsand\ Barbara 1942– orig. *Barbara Joan Streisand* Am. singer, actress, & director; renowned for her compelling interpretations of popular songs on stage and screen and for her tour de force performances in films as *Funny Girl, The Way We Were, The Prince of Tides* (which she also directed)

Stre·se·mann \'shtrā-zə-ˌmän, 'strā-\ Gustav 1878–1929 Ger. polit.; chiefly responsible for restoration of Germany's international status after WWI; awarded (with A. Briand) 1926 Nobel peace prize for his policy of reconciliation and negotiation

Strij·dom \'strī-dəm, 'strā-\ Johannes Gerhardus 1893–1958 prime min. of So. Africa (1954–58); pursued policy of strict apartheid

Strind·berg \'strin(d)-ˌberg, Sw 'strind-ˌber-ē\ August 1849–1912 Swed. dram. & nov.; considered greatest writer of modern Sweden; profoundly influenced European and American dramatists in Naturalistic novels, stories, and esp. plays as *The Father, Miss Julie, The Ghost Sonata*, etc. — **Strind·berg·ian** \strin(d)-'bər-gē-ən\ *adj*

Stroess·ner \'stres-nər\ Alfredo 1912–   pres. of Paraguay (1954–89)

Stru·en·see \'shtrü-ən-ˌzā, 'strü-\ Johann Friedrich 1737–1772 Graf *Struensee* Dan. (Ger.-born) physician & polit.; as court physician gained complete dominance over Christian VII; as lover of Queen Caroline Matilda, condemned, tortured, and beheaded by conspiracy of nobles

Stu·art \'stü-ərt, 'styü-\ 'st(y)ú(-ə)rt\ — see CHARLES I & MARY STUART

Stuart Charles *the Young Pretender* — see CHARLES EDWARD

Stuart Gilbert Charles 1755–1828 Am. painter; one of the leading portrait painters of her era; best known for portrait of George Washington

Stuart James Ewell Brown 1833–1864 *Jeb Stuart* Am. Confed. gen.; cavalry commander; known for his spectacular raids, sometimes encircling the Union army, and for his intelligence-gathering operations

Stuart James Francis Edward *the Old Pretender* — see JAMES EDWARD

Stubbs \'stəbz\ George 1724–1806 Eng. painter; known chiefly for masterly paintings of animals, esp. horses

Stubbs William 1825–1901 Eng. hist. & prelate; considered founder of the systematic study of English medieval constitutional history

Stülp·na·gel \'shtúlp-ˌnä-gəl, 'stúlp-, 'shtu̇lp-\ Karl Heinrich von 1886–1944 Ger. gen.; commander of occupied France (1942–44); a chief conspirator in plot to assassinate Hitler (July 1944); executed

Stur·ges \'stər-jəs\ Preston 1898–1959 orig. *Edmond Preston Biden* \'bī-dᵊn\ Am. film director & writer; known for sophisticated film satires as *The Lady Eve, Sullivan's Travels, The Miracle of Morgan's Creek,* etc.

Sturluson — see SNORRI STURLUSON

Stur·sa \'shtúr-sə\ Jan \'yän\ 1880–1925 Czech sculptor; regarded as a leader of the modern Czech school of sculpture

Stuy·ve·sant \'stī-və-sənt\ Peter *ca* 1610–1672 Du. colonial administrator in America; director general of all Dutch possessions in New World; headquartered in New Amsterdam (later New York); remembered for despotic administration and failure to prevent British seizure of the colony

Styne \'stīn\ Jule 1905–1994 orig. *Julius Kerwin Stein* Am. (Brit.-born) composer; known for popular ballads and for scores for Broadway musicals *Gentlemen Prefer Blondes, Gypsy, Funny Girl,* etc.

Sty·ron \'stī-rən\ William 1925–   Am. writer; author of *The Confessions of Nat Turner, Sophie's Choice,* etc.

Sua·rez Gon·zá·lez \'swär-əz-gən-'zä-ləs\ Adolfo 1932–   prime min. of Spain (1976–81)

Su·choc·ka \sü-'kȯt-ˌskä\ Hanna 1946–   prime min. of Poland (1992–93)

Suck·ling \'sə-kliŋ\ Sir John 1609–1642 Eng. Cavalier poet; famous for wit and prodigality and for inventing game cribbage; wrote words "Why so pale and wan, fond lover?" etc.

Su·cre \'sü-(ˌ)krä\ Antonio José de 1795–1830 So. Am. liberator; a chief commander under Simón Bolívar; liberator of Gran Colombia (now Ecuador); first president of newly liberated Upper Peru (now Bolivia)

Sue \\`sü, sū̄e\\ Eugène 1804–1857 orig. *Marie-Joseph Sue* Fr. nov.; noted for sea stories, novels of high society, and esp. later novels championing Socialism and set in Paris underworld

Sue·to·ni·us \\swē-`tō-nē-əs, ̩sü-ə-`tō-\\ *ca* A.D. 69–after 122 *Gaius Suetonius Tranquillus* Rom. biographer & hist.; author of biographies of Roman literary figures (*De viris illustribus*) and lives of first eleven emperors (*De vita Caesarum*)

Su·gi·ya·ma \\ ̩sü-gē-`yä-mə\\ Hajime 1880–1945 Jp. field marshal; chief of general staff during WWII

Su·har·to \\ sə-`här-(̩)tō, sù-\\ 1921–   pres. of Indonesia (1967–   ); notable for his conservatism, nationalistic policies, and fervent anticommunism

Su·kar·no \\sü-`kär-(̩)nō\\ 1901–1970 pres. of Indonesian Republic (1945–1967); obtained independence from the Netherlands; instituted authoritarian regime of "Guided Democracy"; corrupt and extravagant; deposed by coup d'état

Sü·ley·man *or* **So·li·man** *or* **Su·lei·man I** \\`sü-lā-̩män, -li-\\ 1494 (or 1495)–1566 *the Magnificent* Ottoman sultan (1520–66); his reign considered high point of Ottoman civilization in military, administrative, social, cultural arenas

Sul·la \\`sə-lə\\ 138–78 B.C. *Lucius Cornelius Sulla Felix* Rom. gen. & polit.; involved in civil war with Marius; dictator of Rome (82–79), reorganizing Senate and judiciary and founding military colonies throughout Italy

Sul·li·van \\`sə-lə-vən\\ Sir Arthur Seymour 1842–1900 Eng. composer; collaborator with librettist W.S. Gilbert on such distinctively English comic operettas as *H.M.S. Pinafore, The Pirates of Penzance, The Mikado*, etc.

Sullivan John 1740–1795 Am. gen. in Revolution; best remembered for his retaliatory attacks against the Iroquois and Loyalists in the Mohawk Valley of New York

Sullivan John Lawrence 1858–1918 Am. boxer; noted for blustering personality and fabled strength

Sullivan Louis Henri 1856–1924 Am. architect; regarded as the father of modern functionalism in architecture, esp. by his designs of the skyscraper

Sul·ly \\`sə-lē, (̩)sə-`lē, sū̄e-lē\\ Duc de 1560–1641 *Maximilien de Béthune Baron de Ros·ny* \\də-rō-`nē\\ Fr. statesman; min. to Henry IV and superintendent of finances; instrumental in rehabilitating France after the Wars of Religion (1562–98)

Sul·ly \\`sə-lē\\ Thomas 1783–1872 Am. (Eng.-born) painter; one of leading portrait painters of his day, completing some 2000 portraits including Lafayette, Jefferson, Madison, etc.

Sul·ly Prud·homme \\sū̄e-lē-prü-`dəm\\ 1839–1907 pseud. of *René-François-Armand Prudhomme* Fr. poet & critic; a leader of the French Parnassian movement, a reaction against the excesses of French Romanticism; awarded first (1901) Nobel prize for literature

Sum·ner \\`səm-nər\\ Charles 1811–1874 Am. statesman & orator; a leader in Congress among the opponents of slavery; victim of notorious assault by Rep. Preston S. Brooks of South Carolina that left him permanently impaired

Sumner James Batcheller 1887–1955 Am. biochem.; awarded (with W.M. Stanley and J.H. Northrop) 1946 Nobel prize for chemistry for discovering that enzymes can be crystallized

Sumner William Graham 1840–1910 Am. sociol. & educ.; prolific publicist of Social Darwinism

Sun·day \'sən-dē\ William Ashley 1862–1935 *Billy Sunday* Am. evangelist; preached a fundamentalist theology in a flamboyant style

Sun Yat–sen \'sùn-'yät-'sen\ 1866–1925 orig. *Sun Wen* or *Sun Chung-shan* Chin. statesman; leader of the Kuomintang (Nationalist Party); instrumental in overthrowing the Manchu dynasty; first provisional president of Republic of China (1911–12); regarded as the father of modern China

Surrey Earl of — see Henry HOWARD

Sur·tees \'sər-(ˌ)tēz\ Robert Smith 1803–1864 Eng. nov. & editor; co-founder of *New Sporting Magazine* and contributor of sketches of Mr. John Jorrocks, a fox-hunting cockney grocer

Suth·er·land \'sə-thər-lənd\ Earl Wilbur, Jr. 1915–1974 Am. physiol.; awarded 1971 Nobel prize for physiology or medicine for his discovery of cyclic AMP and demonstration of its role in metabolic processes in animals

Sutherland Dame Joan 1926–   Austral. soprano; world renowned for coloratura roles in Donizetti's *Lucia di Lammermoor,* Bellini's *Norma,* etc.

Sut·ter \'sə-tər, 'sü-\ John Augustus 1803–1880 orig. *Johann August Suter* Am. (Ger.-born) pioneer; the discovery (1848) of gold on his land along the Sacramento River precipitated the California Gold Rush

Sutt·ner \'zùt-nər, 'sùt-\ Bertha 1843–1914 née *Kinsky* Baroness *von Suttner* Austrian writer & pacifist; credited with influencing Alfred Nobel in establishment of Nobel prize for peace; awarded 1905 Nobel prize for peace for her pacifism and for founding Austrian Society of Friends of Peace

Su·vo·rov \sü-'vór-əf, -'vär-\ Aleksandr Vasilyevich 1729–1800 Russ. field marshal; gained reputation as successful and unorthodox tactician in the Russo-Turkish War of 1787–91 and in the French Revolutionary Wars

Sved·berg \'sved-ˌbərg, *Sw* -ˌber-ē\ The *or* Theodor 1884–1971 Swed. chem.; awarded 1926 Nobel prize for chemistry for his work on dispersions and on colloid chemistry

Sver·drup \'sver-drəp\ Harald Ulrik 1888–1957 Norw. meteorologist & oceanographer; explained equatorial countercurrents; helped develop method of predicting surf and breakers

Sver·rir \'sver-ər\ *ca* 1149–1202 *Sverrir Si·gurds·son* \'si-gərd-sən\ king of Norway (1184–1202); one of Norway's greatest kings; built strong monarchy with support of peasantry

Swe·den·borg \'swē-d³n-ˌbórg\ Emanuel 1688–1772 orig. *Svedberg* Swed. philos. & religious writer; wrote works on psychical and spiritual interpretation of the Bible; Church of New Jerusalem founded by his followers — **Swe·den·bor·gian** \ˌswē-d³n-'bór-j(ē)ən, -'bór-gē-ən\ *adj*

Swee·linck \'swā-liŋk\ Jan Pieterszoon 1562–1621 Du. organist & composer; famous as organ teacher; composed much sacred and secular vocal music in the French and Dutch polyphonic tradition

Sweet \'swēt\ Henry 1845–1912 Eng. phonetician; chief founder of modern phonetics

Swift \'swift\ Gustavus Franklin 1839–1903 Am. meat packer; commissioned development of refrigerator car and made first shipment of dressed meat to eastern U.S. cities; used by-products to make oleo margarine, soap, glue, fertilizer, etc.

Swift Jonathan 1667–1745 Eng. writer and cleric; most famous for satires *Gulliver's Travels, A Tale of a Tub*, "A Modest Proposal"; considered the greatest prose satirist in English — **Swift·ian** \'swif-tē-ən\ *adj*

Swin·burne \'swin-(,)bərn\ Algernon Charles 1837–1909 Eng. poet; known esp. for verse drama *Atalanta in Calydon* and poetry collections *Poems and Ballads* and *Songs Before Sunrise* — **Swin·burn·ian** \swin-'bər-nē-ən\ *adj*

Sylva Carmen — see ELIZABETH Queen of Romania

Sy·ming·ton \'sī-miŋ-tən\ (William) Stuart 1901–1988 Am. industrialist & polit.; U.S. senator from Missouri (1953–77); critic of the Vietnam War

Sy·monds \'si-mən(d)z, 'sī-\ John Addington 1840–1893 Eng. scholar; published *Renaissance in Italy*, a classic authority, *A Problem in Modern Ethics*, a pioneering work on homosexuality, and translations and biographies

Sy·mons \'si-mənz, 'sī-\ Arthur William 1865–1945 Brit. poet & critic; first English champion of French Symbolist poets; author of Impressionistic *fin de siècle* lyrics

Synge \'siŋ\ John Millington 1871–1909 Irish poet & dram.; promoter of Celtic revival of 1890s; wrote masterpiece drama *Playboy of the Western World*, etc.

Synge Richard Laurence Millington 1914–   Brit. biochem.; awarded (with A.P. Martin) 1952 Nobel prize for chemistry for developing the partition chromatography process for separating compounds

Szell \'sel, 'zel\ George 1897–1970 Am. (Hung.-born) conductor; conductor of the Cleveland Orchestra (1946–70); acclaimed for the clarity, balance, and intensity of his performances

Szent–Györ·gyi \sänt-'jōrj, -'jōr-jē\ Albert von Nagyrapolt 1893–1986 Am. (Hung.-born) chem.; awarded 1937 Nobel prize for chemistry for discoveries in connection with oxidation in tissues, vitamin C, and fumaric acid

Szi·lard \'zi-,lärd, zə-'lärd\ Leo 1898–1964 Am. (Hung.-born) physicist; instrumental in developing Manhattan Project; with Enrico Fermi created the first sustained nuclear chain reaction; later turned to biology and peaceful uses of atomic energy

Szold \'zōld\ Henrietta 1860–1945 Am. Zionist & founder of Hadassah

T

Tac·i·tus \\'ta-sə-təs\\ Cornelius *ca* A.D. 56–*ca* 120 Rom. hist.; known for *Historiae*, covering reigns from Galba to Domitian, *Annals*, history of the Julian emperors following Augustus, etc. — **Tac·i·te·an** \\,ta-sə-'tē-ən\\ *adj*

Taft \\'taft\\ Lo·ra·do \\lə-'rä-(,)dō\\ 1860–1936 Am. sculptor; important influence on the development of sculpture in the Middle West

Taft Robert Alphonso 1889–1953 *son of W. H.* Am. polit.; called "Mr. Republican" for his traditional conservatism; sponsored Taft-Hartley Labor Relations Act

Taft William Howard 1857–1930 27th pres. of the U.S. (1909–13); chief justice U.S. Supreme Court (1921–30)

Ta·gore \\tə-'gōr, -'gór\\ Sir Ra·bin·dra·nath \\rə-'bin-drə-,nät\\ 1861–1941 Indian poet; awarded 1913 Nobel prize for literature

Taine \\'tän, 'ten\\ Hippolyte-Adolphe 1828–1893 Fr. philos. & critic; a leading exponent of French Positivism; applied scientific method to study of humanities

Tait \\'tāt\\ Archibald Campbell 1811–1882 archbishop of Canterbury (1869–82)

T'ai-tsu — see CHAO K'UANG-YIN

Ta·ke·shi·ta \\tä-'kä-shə-,tä\\ Noboru 1924–   prime min. of Japan (1987–89)

Tall·chief \\'tól-,chēf\\ Maria 1925–   Am. dancer; one of four Native American stars with Ballets Russes de Monte Carlo in 1940s; memorable for roles created for her by Balanchine

Tal·ley·rand–Pé·ri·gord \\,ta-lē-,ran(d)-,per-ə-'gór, *F* tàl-rän-\\ Charles-Maurice de 1754–1838 Prince *de Bénévent* Fr. statesman; a political survivor who held high office during French Revolution, Napoléonic era, restoration of Bourbon monarchy, and under King Louis-Philippe

Ta·ma·yo \\tə-'mī-(,)ō\\ Rufino 1899–1991 Mex. painter; developed style combining pre-Columbian motifs with modern European art

Tamerlane *or* **Tamburlaine** — see TIMUR

Tamm \\'täm, 'tam\\ Igor Yevgenyevich 1895–1971 Soviet physicist; awarded (with P.A. Cherenkov and I.M. Frank) 1958 Nobel prize for physics for discovering and interpreting the Cherenkov effect in studying high-energy particles

Tan \\'tan\\ Amy 1952–   Am. writer; examined the lives of Chinese immigrant women and the very different ones of their American daughters in novels esp. *The Joy Luck Club*

Tan·cred \\'tan-krəd\\ 1078?–1112 Norman leader in 1st Crusade

Tan·dy \\'tan-dē\\ Jessica 1909–1994 Am. (Brit.-born) actress; came to fame as Blanche DuBois in *Streetcar Named Desire* on stage; often acted with her husband, Hume Cronyn; won 1989 Academy award for film *Driving Miss Daisy*

Ta·ney \\'tó-nē\\ Roger Brooke 1777–1864 Am. jurist; chief justice U.S. Supreme Court (1836–64); remembered principally for decision he delivered in Dred Scott case

Tan·ge \\'tän-gā\\ Kenzo 1913–   Jp. architect; best known for Hiroshima Peace Center, National Gymnasium for 1964 Olympic Games, etc.

T'ang T'ai Tsung \\'tän-'tī-'dzùṇ\\ 600–649 orig. *Li Shih-min* \\'le-

'shir-'min\ Chin. emp.; often considered greatest Chinese emperor for reunification of China and institution of thorough reforms; his reign a high point of Chinese culture and administration

Tan·guy \tän-'gē\ Yves 1900–1955 Am. (Fr.-born) artist; Surrealist known esp. for landscapes with familiar forms in bizarre environments

Tar·bell \'tär-bəl\ Ida Minerva 1857–1944 Am. author; best known for her muckraking *The History of the Standard Oil Company*

Tar·dieu \tär-'dyə(r), -'dyœ\ André-Pierre-Gabriel-Amédée 1876–1945 Fr. statesman; premier of France (1929–30, 1932)

Tar·king·ton \'tär-kiŋ-tən\ (Newton) Booth 1869–1946 Am. nov.; best known for satirical, sometimes romanticized depictions of Midwesterners, esp. *Penrod, Alice Adams, The Magnificent Ambersons*, etc.

Tas·man \'taz-mən\ Abel Janszoon 1603?–?1659 Du. navigator & explorer; explored Tasmania, New Zealand, Tonga, and Fiji Islands

Tas·so \'ta-(,)sō, 'tä-\ Tor·qua·to \tôr-'kwä-(,)tō\ 1544–1595 Ital. poet; known esp. for *Gerusalemme liberata* (later revised as *Gerusalemme conquistata*), heroic epic dealing with capture of Jerusalem during First Crusade

Tate \'tāt\ (John Orley) Allen 1899–1979 Am. poet & critic; a member of the "Fugitives" group of poets; a leading exponent of the "New Criticism"

Tate Nahum 1652–1715 Brit. dram.; poet laureate (1692–1715); credited with hymns, author of libretto of Purcell's *Dido and Aeneas*; best known poem "Panacea: a Poem upon Tea"

Ta·tum \'tā-təm\ Edward Lawrie 1901–1975 Am. biochem.; awarded (with G.W. Beadle and J. Lederberg) 1958 Nobel prize for physiology or medicine for work in biochemical genetics

Taube \'taúb\ Henry 1915–   Am. (Canad.-born) chem.; awarded 1983 Nobel prize for chemistry for research on the transfer of electrons between molecules in chemical reactions

Taw·ney \'tó-nē\ Richard Henry 1880–1962 Eng. economic hist.; successful campaigner for social reforms as adviser to governmental bodies

Tay·lor \'tā-lər\ (James) Bay·ard \'bī-ərd, 'bā-\ 1825–1878 Am. writer; noted for writings on his travels to California gold rush, Egypt, Asia Minor, Syria, Europe, India, China, and Japan

Taylor (Joseph) Deems 1885–1966 Am. composer & music critic; composer of symphonic poems, cantata, suites for orchestra, operas, etc.

Taylor Edward 1645?–1729 Am. clergyman & poet; considered foremost poet of colonial America

Taylor Elizabeth Rosemond 1932–   Am. actress; famed for her roles in films *National Velvet, Cleopatra, Who's Afraid of Virginia Woolf?*, etc. and for her colorful personal life; in later years known for her fund-raising efforts for AIDS research

Taylor Jeremy 1613–1667 Eng. prelate & author; wrote *Liberty of Prophesying, Holy Living, Holy Dying*, etc.

Taylor Joseph Hooton 1941–   Am. physicist; awarded (with R.A. Hulse) 1993 Nobel prize for physics for discovery of pulsars

Taylor Lawrence 1959–   Am. football player; linebacker, New York Giants (1981–95); Most Valuable Player award, NFL (1986)

Taylor Maxwell Davenport 1901–1987 Am. gen.; a pioneer in airborne warfare during WWII esp. in Normandy and the Netherlands

Taylor Richard Edward 1929–   Canad. physicist; awarded (with J. Friedman and H. Kendall) 1990 Nobel prize for physics for experiments that proved the existence of subatomic quarks

Taylor Tom 1817–1880 Eng. dram.; wrote or adapted over one hundred dramatic pieces esp. *Our American Cousin*

Taylor Zachary 1784–1850 12th pres. of the U.S. (1849–50); hero of the Mexican War esp. Battle of Buena Vista

Tchai·kov·sky \chī-'kȯf-skē, chə-, -'kȯv-\ Pyotr Ilich 1840–1893 Russ. composer; best known for opera *Eugen Onegin;* ballets *Swan Lake, Sleeping Beauty, Nutcracker Suite,* symphonies, etc. — **Tchai·kov·sky·an** *or* **Tchai·kov·ski·an** \-skē-ən\ *adj*

Teas·dale \'tēz-,dāl\ Sara 1884–1933 Am. poet; author of numerous volumes of verse, including *Rivers to the Sea, Love Songs,* etc.

Te·cum·seh \tə-'kəm(p)-sə, -sē\ *or* **Te·cum·tha** \-'kəm(p)-thə\ *or* **Ti·kam·the** \-'kəm(p)-thə, -'käm(p)-\ 1768–1813 Shawnee Indian chief; attempted to form an Indian confederation to resist white encroachment; fought with British in War of 1812 after Battle of Tippecanoe and helped capture Detroit

Ted·der \'te-dər\ 1st Baron 1890–1967 *Arthur William Tedder* Brit. air marshal; instrumental in the defeat of Germany on the Western Front during WWII as a result of his bombing of German communications and providing air support for ground operations

Teil·hard de Char·din \tā-,yär-də-shár-'daⁿ\ Pierre 1881–1955 Fr. philos. & paleontologist; known for theory that humanity is evolving, mentally and socially, toward a final spiritual unity

Tek·a·kwitha \,te-kə-'kwi-thə\ *or* **Teg·a·kwitha** \,te-gə-\ *or* **Teg·a·kouita** \,te-gə-'kwi-tə\ Ka·teri \'kä-tə-rē\ 1656–1680 *Lily of the Mohawks* Am. Indian religious; first North American Indian proposed for canonization in Roman Catholic Church

Te·le·mann \'tā-lə-,män, 'tē-\ Georg Philipp 1681–1767 Ger. composer; compositions included over 50 operas, cantatas, concertos, oratorios, Passions, much chamber music, etc.

Tel·ler \'te-lər\ Edward 1908–   Am. (Hung.-born) physicist; with Fermi produced first nuclear chain reaction; worked on Manhattan Project; advocated use of nuclear energy for peaceful purposes

Téllez Gabriel — see TIRSO DE MOLINA

Tem·in \'te-mən\ Howard Martin 1934–1994 Am. oncologist; awarded (with D. Baltimore and R. Dulbecco) 1975 Nobel prize for physiology or medicine for research on how certain viruses affect the genes of cancer cells

Tem·ple \'tem-pəl\ Frederick 1821–1902 archbishop of Canterbury (1896–1902)

Temple Shirley 1928–   Am. actress & polit.; child star in 1930s in films including *Bright Eyes, The Little Colonel,* etc.; later became ardent Republican and ambassador

Temple Sir William 1628–1699 Brit. statesman; involved in conducting foreign policy toward Netherlands; helped arrange marriage of Dutch ruler William of Orange and Princess Mary of England (later British monarchs)

Temple William 1881–1944 *son of Frederick* archbishop of Canterbury (1942–44)

Templewood Viscount — see HOARE

Teng Hsiao-p'ing *or* **Deng Xiao-ping** \'dəŋ-'shaủ-'piŋ\ 1904– Chin. Communist leader (1977–); instituted sequence of reforms to modernize China

Te-niers \tə-'nirs, tā-'nyä\ David *the Elder* 1582–1649 & *the Younger* 1610–1690 Flem. painters; the Elder painted chiefly religious subjects; the Younger was renowned as genre, landscape, and portrait painter

Ten-niel \'ten-yəl\ Sir John 1820–1914 Eng. cartoonist & illustrator; known for his work in *Punch* and his illustrations for *Alice's Adventures in Wonderland* and *Through the Looking-Glass*

Ten-ny-son \'te-nə-sən\ Alfred 1809–1892 1st Baron *Tennyson* known as **Alfred, Lord Tennyson** Eng. poet; poet laureate (1850–92); best known for poems "Charge of the Light Brigade," *The Idylls of the King*, etc. — **Ten-ny-so-nian** \ˌte-nə-'sō-nē-ən, -nyən\ *adj*

Ter-borch *or* **Ter Borch** \tər-'bȯrk, -'bȯrk\ Gerard 1617–1681 Du. painter; known for portraits and interior genre paintings

Ter-brug-ghen \tər-'brü-gən\ Hendrik 1588–1629 Du. painter; paintings, influenced by Caravaggio's chiaroscuro style, include masterpiece *St. Sebastian Tended by Irene and Her Maid*

Ter-ence \'ter-ən(t)s\ 186 (or 185)–?159 B.C. *Publius Terentius Afer* Rom. dram.; regarded as a master of Roman comedy; plays, modeled on Menander, distinguished for purity of language and realism

Te-re-sa \tə-'rā-zə, -'rē-sə\ Mother 1910– *Agnes Gonxha Bojaxhiu* Albanian religious in India; awarded 1979 Nobel prize for peace for aiding India's poor

Teresa of Avila Saint 1515–1582 Span. Carmelite & mystic; founded many convents and monasteries; famous for her mystical visions

Te-resh-ko-va \ˌter-əsh-'kȯ-və, -'kō-\ Valentina Vladimirovna 1937– Soviet (Russ.-born) cosmonaut; first woman to go into space (1963)

Ter-hune \(ˌ)tər-'hyün\ Albert Payson 1872–1942 Am. author; best known as author of books about dogs, esp. collies, including *Lad, a Dog; Lad of Sunnybank*, etc.

Ter-ry \'ter-ē\ (Alice) Ellen 1847–1928 Eng. actress; known for her roles in Shakespeare, Wills, Tennyson, etc.; carried on famous "paper courtship" (letter correspondence) with G.B. Shaw who wrote several parts for her

Ter-tul-lian \(ˌ)tər-'təl-yən\ *ca* A.D. 155 (or 160)–after 220 *Quintus Septimius Florens Tertullianus* church father; as initiator of ecclesiastical Latin, instrumental in shaping the vocabulary and thought of Western Christianity

Tes-la \'tes-lə\ Nikola 1856–1943 Am. (Croatian-born) electrical engineer & inventor; discovered principle of rotating magnetic field, basis of most alternating-current machinery

Tet-zel *or* **Te-zel** \'tet-səl\ Johann *ca* 1465–1519 Ger. Dominican monk; his preaching on indulgences provoked Luther to publish his 95 theses

Thack·er·ay \\'tha-k(ə-)rē\\ William Makepeace 1811–1863 Eng. author; acquired reputation as novelist of first rank with *Vanity Fair, Pendennis*, etc. — **Thack·er·ay·an** \-k(ə-)rē-ən-ən\ *adj*

Tha·les \\'thā-(ˌ)lēz\\ **of Miletus** 625?–?547 B.C. Greek philos.; gained fame in his own day by predicting eclipse of the sun; considered by Aristotle to be the father of Greek philosophy — **Tha·le·sian** \thə-'lē-zhən\ *adj*

Thant \\'thant, 'thänt\ U \\'ü\ 1909–1974 Burmese U.N. official; secy.-gen. (1961–71)

Tharp \\'thärp\ Twyla 1942– Am. dancer & choreographer; known for dances marked by glib movements, humorous poses, and social commentary; founded Twyla Tharp Dance Company

Thatch·er \\'tha-chər\ Margaret Hilda 1925– née *Roberts* Brit. prime min. (1979–90); first woman party leader in Britain; noted for very conservative approach to economic and social issues; Britain's longest-serving prime min. since 1827

Thayer \\'thar, 'ther, 'thā-ər\ Sylvanus 1785–1872 *father of West Point* Am. army officer & educ.; established military organization, academic standards, methods of instruction used at West Point

Thei·ler \\'tī-lər\ Max 1899–1972 Am. (So. African-born) microbiologist; awarded 1951 Nobel prize for physiology or medicine for research on yellow fever

The·mis·to·cles \thə-'mis-tə-ˌklēz\ *ca* 524–*ca* 460 B.C. Athenian gen. & statesman; began development of port of Piraeus, convinced Athens to boost naval strength, led Athens to victory over Persians at Salamis (480 B.C.)

The·oc·ri·tus \thē-'ä-krə-təs\ *ca* 310–250 B.C. Greek poet; regarded as creator of pastoral poetry

The·o·dor·ic \thē-'ä-də-rik\ 454?–526 *the Great* king of the Ostrogoths (493–526); gradually conquered all of Italy, Sicily, Dalmatia, part of German lands, with capital at Ravenna

The·o·do·sius I \thē-ə-'dō-sh(ē-)əs\ 347–395 *the Great* Rom. gen. & emp. (379–395); accepted Nicene Creed as universal norm for Christian orthodoxy; briefly controlled East and West after defeat of Maximus

The·o·phras·tus \ˌthē-ə-'fras-təs\ *ca* 372–*ca* 287 B.C. Greek philos. & naturalist; disciple and successor of Aristotle; best known for his character sketches (Charaktēres) delineating moral types

The·o·rell \ˌtā-ə-'rel\ Axel Hugo Theodor 1903–1982 Swed. biochem.; awarded 1955 Nobel prize for physiology or medicine for discoveries on the nature and action of oxidation enzymes

Theresa Saint — see TERESA OF AVILA

Thes·pis \\'thes-pəs\ 6th cent. B.C. Greek poet; reputed founder of tragic drama

Thiers \tē-'er\ Louis-Adolphe 1797–1877 Fr. statesman & hist.; led rehabilitation of France after Franco-Prussian War; first pres. of Third Republic after Paris Commune crushed; author of *Histoire de la révolution française*, etc.

Thom·as \\'tä-məs\ Saint 1st cent. A.D. one of twelve Apostles; according to biblical account, doubted resurrection of Jesus until he had physical proof

Tho·mas \tô-'mä\ (Charles-Louis-)Ambroise 1811–1896 Fr. composer; best known for operas *Mignon, Françoise de Rimini, Hamlet*, etc.

Thom·as \\'tä-məs\\ Augustus 1857–1934 Am. dram.; wrote or adapted some 70 plays noted for use of native material

Thomas Clarence 1948–   Am. jurist; associate justice, U.S. Supreme Court (1991–   )

Thomas Dyl·an \\'di-lən\\ Marlais 1914–1953 Welsh poet; works included verse collections *The Map of Love, Deaths and Entrances,* etc.; prose *Adventures in the Skin Trade,* etc.; radio play *Under Milk Wood*

Thomas Edward Donnall 1920–   Am. physician; awarded (with J.E. Murray) 1990 Nobel prize for physiology or medicine for work in transplanting human organs and bone marrow

Thomas Helen 1920–   Am. journalist; reporter (1943–74), White House bureau chief (1974–   ), U.P.I.; first woman journalist to head White House bureau

Thomas Lowell Jackson 1892–1981 Am. traveler, journalist, & author; made T.E. Lawrence famous for his exploits in the Arabian Desert; radio and newsreel newscaster; wrote over 50 books, including *With Lawrence in Arabia*

Thomas Norman Mat·toon \\ma-'tün, mə-\\ 1884–1968 Am. socialist polit.; helped found American Civil Liberties Union; Socialist candidate for president (1928–48); advocated many measures now in law

Thomas Seth 1785–1859 Am. clock manuf.; made clocks by mass production method

Thomas (Christian Friedrich) Theodore 1835–1905 Am. (Ger.-born) conductor; exercised great influence on development of a knowledge and appreciation of symphonic music

Thomas à Becket — see BECKET

Thomas à Kem·pis \\ə-'kem-pəs, (,)ä-'kem-\\ 1379 (or 1380)–1471 orig. *Thomas Hemerken* Du. ecclesiastic & writer; famed as reputed writer of religious classic *De Imitatione Christi* (*Imitation of Christ*)

Thomas Aqui·nas \\ə-'kwī-nəs\\ Saint 1224 (or 1225)–1274 It. *Tommaso d'Aquino* Ital. religious & philos.; outstanding figure of Scholastic philosophy, integrating Aristotle's philosophy with Christianity

Thomas of Er·cel·doune \\'ər-səl-,dün\\ fl 1220–1297 *Thomas the Rhymer* and *Thomas Learmont* Scot. seer & poet; probable author of *Sir Tristrem;* linked in popular lore with Merlin and other seers

Thomp·son \\'täm(p)-sən\\ Benjamin 1753–1814 Count *Rum·ford* \\'rəm(p)-fərd\\ Brit. (Am.-born) physicist & statesman; introduced improvements in heating and cooking equipment; known for studies of heat and friction; argued that heat is a form of motion

Thompson Dorothy 1894–1961 Am. journalist; one of the most famous journalists of her time; remembered for her exposure of the Nazi menace

Thompson Francis 1859–1907 Eng. poet; member of the Aesthetic movement; best known for poem "The Hound of Heaven"

Thompson Sir John Sparrow David 1844–1894 Canad. statesman; prime min. (1892–94)

Thom·son \\'täm(p)-sən\\ Sir George Pag·et \\'pa-jət\\ 1892–1975 *son of Sir Joseph John* Eng. physicist; awarded (with C. Davisson) 1937 Nobel prize for physics for discovering the diffraction of electrons by crystals

Thomson James 1700–1748 Scot. poet; published *The Seasons* giving leading place to description of nature and paving the way for emotional treatment by Romantic poets

Thomson James 1834–1882 *B. V.* or *Bysshe Vanolis* Scot. poet; wrote, chiefly in despairing and atheistic mood, *Sunday up the River*, etc.

Thomson John Arthur 1861–1933 Scot. biol.; attempted to popularize biology and correlate science and religion in lectures and writings

Thomson Sir Joseph John 1856–1940 Eng. physicist; awarded 1906 Nobel prize for physics for studying electrical discharge through gases

Thomson Virgil Garnett 1896–1989 Am. composer & critic; influenced by Les Six; wrote operas, symphonies, ballets, choral and chamber music, etc.

Thomson William — see Baron KELVIN

Tho·reau \thə-'rō, thô-; 'thôr-(,)ō, 'thər-(,)ō\ Henry David 1817–1862 orig. *David Henry Thoreau* Am. writer; associated with Transcendentalists; devoted himself to study of nature and to writing at Walden Pond; best known for book *Walden, or Life in the Woods* — **Tho·reau·vi·an** \thə-'rō-vē-ən, thô-\ adj

Tho·rez \tô-'rez\ Maurice 1900–1964 Fr. polit.; member of French Communist party and leader of leftist causes

Thorn·dike \'thôrn-,dīk\ Edward Lee 1874–1949 Am. psychol.; founder of experimental animal psychology and a pioneer in the study of animal intelligence

Thorndike Lynn 1882–1965 Am. historian; author of *The History of Medieval Europe, A History of Magic and Experimental Science*, etc.

Thorndike Dame (Agnes) Sybil 1882–1976 Brit. actress; known esp. for versatility in modern and classic dramas

Thorn·ton \'thôrn-tⁿn\ William 1759–1828 Am. architect; won competition for design of Capitol building, Washington, D.C.

Thorpe \'thôrp\ James Francis 1866–1953 *Jim Thorpe* Am. athlete; won decathlon and pentathlon in 1912 Olympic Games; also played professional baseball and football; one of the greatest all-around athletes in sports history

Thor·vald·sen or **Thor·wald·sen** \'tôr-,wôl-sən, 'thôr-; 'tûr-,väl-sən\ Ber·tel \'ber-tⁿl\ 1768 (or 1770)–1844 Dan. sculptor; first internationally acclaimed Danish artist; a leader in the classical revival

Thras·y·bu·lus \,thra-sə-'byü-ləs\ d 388 B.C. Athenian gen.; instrumental in effecting return of democratic government to Athens after reign of Thirty Tyrants; influential in galvanizing opposition to Sparta

Thu·cyd·i·des \thü-'si-də-,dēz, thyü-\ d ca 401 B.C. Greek hist.; for his *History of the Peloponnesian War*, regarded as first critical historian and greatest historian of antiquity — **Thu·cyd·i·de·an** \(,)thü-,si-də-'dē-ən, (,)thyü-\ adj

Thur·ber \'thər-bər\ James Grover 1894–1961 Am. writer; notable for his humorous drawings, essays, and short stories, esp. "The Secret Life of Walter Mitty"; author of *My Life and Hard Times, The Thurber Carnival*, etc. — **Thur·ber·esque** \,thər-bə-'resk\ adj

Thut·mo·se \thüt-'mō-sə\ name of 4 kings of Egypt: esp. **III** *d* 1450 B.C. (reigned 1504–1450 B.C.); one of the greatest Egyptian kings; brought Egypt to zenith of its power

Thys·sen \'ti-s°n\ Fritz 1873–1951 Ger. industrialist; a principal financial backer of Nazi party; aided in Hitler's rise to power

Tib·bett \'ti-bət\ Lawrence Mervil 1896–1960 Am. baritone; principal baritone at Metropolitan opera esp. in Italian roles (1925–50)

Ti·be·ri·us \tī-'bir-ē-əs\ 42 B.C.–A.D. 37 *Tiberius Claudius Nero Caesar Augustus* Rom. emp. (14–37); at first wise and beneficent; later, esp. under influence of Sejanus, vicious, cruel, and tyrannical

Ti·bul·lus \tə-'bə-ləs\ Albius *ca* 55–*ca* 19 B.C. Rom. poet; known for clear and unaffected style and exquisiteness of feeling and expression in elegiac verse

Tieck \tēk\ (Johann) Ludwig 1773–1853 Ger. author; center of literary society in Berlin; author of novels, plays, narrative collection, criticism, translations, lyric poems

Tie·po·lo \tē-'ā-pə-,lō, -'e-\ Giovanni Battista 1696–1770 Ital. painter; style marked by use of chiaroscuro, control, underlying melancholy in frescoes, easel pictures, portraits, etchings

Tif·fa·ny \'ti-fə-nē\ Charles Lewis 1812–1902 Am. jeweler; opened store in New York City (1837, with J.B. Young)

Tiffany Louis Comfort 1848–1933 *son of C.L.* Am. painter & stained-glass artist; developed process of making uniquely beautiful opalescent glass called "Favrile"; a leader of Art Nouveau movement

Tig·lath–pi·le·ser III \'ti-,glath-(,)pī-'lē-zər-, -pə-\ *d* 727 B.C. king of Assyria (745–727); subjugated Israel and Samaria; defeated Philistines; captured Gaza, Damascus, etc.

Til·den \'til-dən\ Samuel Jones 1814–1886 Am. polit.; lost 1876 presidential election to Rutherford B. Hayes by one electoral vote by decision of Electoral Commission

Til·dy \'til-dē\ Zoltán \'zōl-,tän\ 1889–1961 Hung. polit.; first pres. of Hungarian Republic (1946–48); forced to resign by Soviet pressure; min. in Nagy's revolutionary government (1956)

Til·lich \'ti-lik, -lik\ Paul Johannes 1886–1965 Am. (Ger.-born) theol.; attempted to synthesize traditional Christianity and modern culture in *Systematic Theology*

Til·lot·son \'ti-lət-sən\ John 1630–1694 Eng. prelate; archbishop of Canterbury (from 1691)

Til·ly \'ti-lē\ Graf von 1559–1632 *Johann Tser·claes* \tsər-'kläs\ Bavarian gen.; outstanding commander of forces of Catholic League in Germany during Thirty Years' War; took Magdeburg by storm (1611)

Ti·mo·shen·ko \,ti-mə-'shen̠-(,)kō\ Semyon \səm-'yón\ Konstantinovich 1895–1970 Soviet marshal; credited with halting German drive on Moscow; directed defense of Stalingrad; directed winter offensive (1942–43)

Tim·o·thy \'ti-mə-thē\ Saint 1st cent. A.D. disciple of the Apostle Paul

Tim·ur \ti-(,)mùr\ *or* **Timur Lenk** \-'leṇk\ 1336–1405 E. *Tam·er·lane* \'ta-mər-,lān\ *or* **Tam·bur·laine** \'tam-bər-,lān\ Turkic conqueror; remembered esp. for the barbarity of his conquests from India and Russia to the Mediterranean Sea; transformed Samarkand into a center of culture

Tin·ber·gen \'tin-ˌber-kə(n)\ Jan 1903–1994 Du. econ.; awarded (with Ragnar Frisch) 1969 Nobel prize for economics for work in econometrics

Tinbergen Nikolaas 1907–1988 *bro. of Jan* Du. ethologist; awarded (with K.Z. Lorenz and K. von Frisch) 1973 Nobel prize for physiology or medicine for studies on animal behavior

Ting \'tiŋ\ Samuel Chao Chung 1936– Am. physicist; awarded (with B. Richter) 1976 Nobel prize for physics for discovery of the elementary psi, or J, particle

Ting·ley \'tiŋ-lē\ Katherine Augusta 1847–1929 née *Westcott* Am. theosophist; merged the Theosophical Society into new Universal Brotherhood

Tin·to·ret·to \ˌtin-tə-'re-(ˌ)tō\ *ca* 1518–1594 *Jacopo Robusti* Ital. painter; one of the greatest Mannerist painters of the Venetian school; influenced by Michelangelo's design and Titian's coloring

Ti·pu *or* **Tip·pu Sul·tan** \ˌti-(ˌ)pü-'sùl-ˌtän\ 1749 (or 1753)–1799 sultan of Mysore (1782–99); defeated in Third Mysore War and forced to cede half his kingdom

Tir·pitz \'tir-pəts, 'tər-\ Alfred von 1849–1930 Ger. admiral; credited with creating formidable German high-seas fleet (1897–1916)

Tir·so de Mo·li·na \'tir-(ˌ)sō-ˌdā-mə-'lē-nə\ *ca* 1584–1648 pseud. of *Gabriel Te·llez* \'tā(l)-yäth\ Span. dram.; one of greatest dramatists of Spanish Golden Age; introduced Don Juan into literature in tragedy *El burlador de Sevilla*

Ti·se·li·us \tə-'sä-lē-əs, -'zā-\ Arne Wilhelm Kaurin 1902–1971 Swed. biochem.; awarded 1948 Nobel prize for chemistry for studies concerning the nature of serum proteins

Ti·so \'tē-(ˌ)sō\ Josef *or* Joseph 1887–1947 Slovak priest & polit.; pres. of Slovakia (1939–45), a puppet state controlled by Germany

Titch·e·ner \'ti-chə-nər\ Edward Bradford 1867–1927 Am. psychol.; known as foremost exponent of structural psychology

Ti·tian \'ti-shən\ *ca* 1488–1576 *Tiziano Vecellio* Ital. painter; one of greatest painters of history; known esp. for his handling of color and depiction of human character — **Ti·tian·esque** \ˌti-shə-'nesk\ *adj*

Ti·to \'tē-(ˌ)tō\ 1892–1980 orig. *Josip Broz* \'bròz, 'bròz\ usu. called *Marshal Tito* leader of Yugoslavia (1943–80); conducted policy of nonalignment with Soviet Union or the West; established ties with other nonaligned nations in Africa, Asia, Latin America

Ti·tus \'tī-təs\ A.D. 39–81 *Titus Flavius Vespasianus* Rom. emp. (79–81); reign marked by great beneficence and by solicitude for welfare of people; completed Colosseum

To·bin \'tō-bən\ James 1918– Am. econ.; awarded 1981 Nobel prize for economics for his analyses of financial markets and their effect on how businesses and families spend and save money

Tocque·ville \'tōk-ˌvil, 'tōk-, 'täk-, -ˌvēl, -vəl\ Alexis-Charles-Henri Clérel de 1805–1859 Fr. statesman & author; gained fame with *De la démocratie en Amérique*, giving perceptive analysis of American political and social systems of the early 19th century

Todd \'täd\ Sir Alexander Robertus 1907– Brit. chem.; awarded 1957 Nobel prize for chemistry for his work on the protein composition of cells

Todt \\'tōt\\ Fritz 1891–1942 Ger. military engineer; built West Wall and Atlantic Wall of defenses along French and Belgian coasts

To·gliat·ti \\tōl-'yä-tē\\ Pal·mi·ro \\päl-'mē-(,)rō\\ 1893–1964 Ital. polit.; made Italian communist party most powerful communist party in western Europe

Tō·gō \\'tō-(,)gō\\ Marquis Heihachirō 1848–1934 Jp. admiral; in Russo-Japanese war, won great battle at Tsushima, annihilating Russian fleet with brilliant, innovative maneuvers

Tō·jō \\'tō-(,)jō\\ Hideki 1884–1948 Jp. gen. & polit.; prime min. (1941–44); hanged as war criminal

To·ku·ga·wa \\tō-kù-'gä-wə\\ Ieyasu 1543–1616 orig. *Matsudaira Takechiyo* Jp. shogun (1603–05); founder of last Jp. shogunate (1603–1867)

To·land \\'tō-lənd\\ Gregg 1904–1948 Am. cinematographer; renowned for his innovative, masterly use of chiaroscuro and wide depth of field in films *Wuthering Heights, Citizen Kane,* etc.

Tol·kien \\'tòl-,kēn\\ John Ronald Reuel 1892–1973 Eng. author; best known as writer of fantasies *The Hobbit,* trilogy *The Lord of the Rings,* etc. — **Tol·kien·esque** \\,tòl-(,)kē-'nesk\\ adj

Tol·ler \\'tò-lər, 'tä-\\ Ernst 1893–1939 Ger. dram. & polit.; leader of social revolutionary movements in Germany after WWI; wrote verse, Expressionist plays, autobiography

Tol·stoy \\tòl-'stòi, tòl-', täl-', tòl-', 'tòl-', 'täl-\\ Count Lev Nikolayevich 1828–1910 Russ. nov., philos., & mystic; author of great novels *War and Peace* and *Anna Karenina;* after spiritual transformation, developed a form of Christian anarchism and devoted himself to social reform — **Tol·stoy·an** *also* **Tol·stoi·an** \\-ən\\ adj

Tom·baugh \\'täm-,bò\\ Clyde William 1906–   Am. astron.; discovered Pluto (1930) and galactic star clusters

Tom·ma·si·ni \\,tä-mə-'zē-nē\\ Vincenzo 1878–1950 Ital. composer; works included operas, ballets, symphonic poems, string quartets, instrumental and vocal compositions

To·mo·na·ga \\,tō-mə-'nä-gə, -mō-\\ Shin'ichirō 1906–1979 Jp. physicist; awarded (with J.S. Schwinger and R.P. Feynman) 1965 Nobel prize for physics for basic work in quantum electrodynamics

Tomp·kins \\'täm(p)-kənz\\ Daniel D. 1774–1825 Am. polit.; vice pres. of the U.S. (1817–25)

Tone \\'tōn\\ (Theobald) Wolfe 1763–1798 Irish revolutionary; leader of an unsuccessful attempt to overthrow English rule in Ireland with the aid of a French military force

To·ne·ga·wa \\,tō-nə-'gä-wa\\ Susumu 1939–   Am. (Jp.-born) biol.; awarded 1987 Nobel prize for physiology or medicine for discoveries on how genes change to produce antibodies against specific disease agents

Tooke \\'tùk\\ (John) Horne 1736–1812 Eng. polit. radical & philologist; leading agitator for parliamentary reform; worked on behalf of American colonies; wrote treatise on etymology of English

Toombs \\'tümz\\ Robert Augustus 1810–1885 Am. polit.; known for aggressive defense of Southern position on slavery question

Tor·que·ma·da \\,tòr-kə-'mä-də, -thə\\ Tomás de 1420–1498 Span. grand inquisitor; persuaded Ferdinand and Isabella to expel Jews

(1492); made grand inquisitor by Innocent VIII (1487) and organized Inquisition in Spain; notorious for his severity and cruelty

Tor·ri·cel·li \ˌtȯr-ə-ˈche-lē, ˌtär-\ Evangelista 1608–1647 Ital. math. & physicist; made improvements on the telescope; invented barometer

Tos·ca·ni·ni \ˌtäs-kə-ˈnē-nē, ˌtȯs-\ Ar·tu·ro \är-ˈtu̇r-(ˌ)ō\ 1867–1957 Ital. conductor; known for his dynamic interpretations of Beethoven, Verdi, Wagner

Tou·louse–Lau·trec (–Mon·fa) \tü-ˌlüz-lō-ˈtrek(-mōⁿ-ˈfä)\ Henri-Marie-Raymond de 1864–1901 Fr. painter; painted popular entertainers and scenes of Parisian night life; achieved fame with poster *La Goulue at the Moulin Rouge*

Tour·neur \ˈtər-nər\ Cyril *ca* 1575–1626 Eng. dram.; author of *The Atheist's Tragedie* and *The Revenger's Tragedie*

Tous·saint–Lou·ver·ture \ˈtü-ˌsaⁿ-ˈlü-vər-ˌtu̇r, -ˌtyu̇r\ *ca* 1743–1803 orig. *François-Dominique Toussaint* Haitian gen. & liberator; briefly established Haiti as a black-governed French protectorate

Townes \ˈtau̇nz\ Charles Hard 1915– Am. physicist; awarded (with N.G. Basov and A.M. Prokhorov) 1964 Nobel prize for physics for developing masers and lasers

Toyn·bee \ˈtȯin-bē\ Arnold Joseph 1889–1975 Eng. hist.; known for 12-volume *A Study of History;* divided history into 21 developed and 5 "arrested" civilizations

Tra·cy \ˈtrā-sē\ Spencer 1900–1967 Am. actor; remembered esp. for costarring with Katharine Hepburn in battle-of-the-sexes films *Woman of the Year, Adam's Rib, Guess Who's Coming to Dinner,* etc.

Tra·jan \ˈtrā-jən\ A.D. 53–117 orig. *Marcus Ulpius Traiánus* usu. called *Germanicus* Rom. emp. (98–117); reorganized administration of provinces; improved and constructed many buildings (esp. Trajan's forum), roads, and bridges

Trapp \ˈtrap, ˈträp\ Maria Augusta von 1905–1987 Am. (Austrian-born) singer & musician; leader of the Trapp Family Singers, whose story became basis for the musical *The Sound of Music*

Trau·bel \ˈtrau̇-bəl\ Helen 1903–1972 Am. soprano; known esp. for Wagnerian roles

Tree \ˈtrē\ Sir Herbert Draper Beerbohm 1853–1917 Eng. actor-manager; lauded esp. for stage versions of Dickens

Treitsch·ke \ˈtrīch-kə\ Heinrich von 1834–1896 Ger. hist.; advocated authoritarian power politics, unity of Germany through Prussian might, colonial expansion

Tre·vel·yan \tri-ˈvel-yən, -ˈvil-\ George Macaulay 1876–1962 Eng. hist.; author of *History of England, England under Queen Anne, The English Revolution,* etc.

Trevelyan Sir George Otto 1838–1928 *father of prec.* Eng. polit., biographer, & hist.; chief secy. for Ireland (1882–84); secy. for Scotland (1886, 1892–95); author of *The American Revolution,* etc.

Trol·lope \ˈträ-ləp\ Anthony 1815–1882 Eng. nov.; author of some 50 novels, including series "Barsetshire Chronicles," "Parliamentary series," etc. — **Trol·lo·pi·an** \trä-ˈlō-pē-ən\ *adj*

Tromp \ˈtrȯmp, ˈträmp\ Maarten Harpertszoon 1598–1653 Du. admiral; defeated Spanish fleet and Spanish-Portuguese fleet (1639), thus signalling the decline of Spain as a sea power

Trots·ky \'trät-skē *also* 'tròt-\ Leon 1879–1940 *orig.* Lev Davidovich Bronstein Russ. communist leader; major theorist in October Revolution (1917); expelled from Communist party and exiled after Lenin's death; murdered in Mexico — **Trots·ky·ist** \'trätskē-ist\ *adj* — **Trots·ky·ite** \-skē-ˌīte\ *adj*

Tru·deau \trü-(ˌ)dō, trü-'\ Pierre Elliott 1919–   Canad. polit.; prime min. (1968–79, 1980–84)

Tru·ji·llo Mo·li·na \trü-'hē-(ˌ)yō-mə-'lē-nə\ Rafael Leónidas 1891–1961 Dominican gen. & polit.; pres. of Dominican Republic (1930–38, 1942–52)

Tru·man \'trü-mən\ Harry S. 1884–1972 33d pres. of the U.S. (1945–53); established "containment" policy against Soviet Union, Truman Doctrine, Marshall Plan, NATO, Central Intelligence Agency, U.S. into Korean War

Trum·bull \'trəm-bəl\ John 1756–1843 Am. painter; painted portraits of contemporary notables; creator of pictures for Capitol rotunda, Washington, D.C.

Trumbull Jonathan 1710–1785 *father of prec.* Am. statesman; guided and encouraged Connecticut industry in supplying Continental army with food and munitions

Trump \'trəmp\ Donald John 1946–   Am. real estate developer; known for his high-profile real estate developments including New York City's Trump Tower and Atlantic City's Taj Mahal casino, etc.

Truth \'trüth\ Sojourner *ca* 1797–1883 Am. evangelist & reformer; as freed slave, gained national fame as preacher for abolition and woman suffrage

Ts'ao Chan \'tsaù-'jän\ 1715?–1763 Ts'ao Hsüeh-ch'in Chin. nov.; author of major part of *Hung lou meng* (*Dream of the Red Chamber*), considered greatest Chinese novel

Tschaikovsky *var of* TCHAIKOVSKY

Tu Fu \'tü-'fü\ 712–770 Chin. poet; one of greatest poets of China; wrote anti-war poems, satires, lyrics

Tub·man \'təb-mən\ Harriet *ca* 1820–1913 Am. abolitionist; an escaped slave, called "Moses of her people" for helping over 300 slaves escape to North on the Underground Railroad

Tubman William Vacanarat Shadrach 1895–1971 Liberian lawyer; pres. of Liberia (1944–71); instituted government, education, and social reforms

Tuch·man \'tək-mən\ Barbara 1912–1989 Am. hist.; author of *The Guns of August, A Distant Mirror: The Calamitous 14th Century, The March of Folly: From Troy to Vietnam,* etc.

Tu·dor \'tü-dər, 'tyü-\ Antony 1908 (or 1909)–1987 Am. (Brit.= born) ballet dancer & choreographer; known for *Lilac Garden, Pillar of Fire, Romeo and Juliet,* etc.

Tul·sī·dās \ˌtùl-sē-'däs\ 1543?–1623 Hindu poet; called the greatest poet of medieval Hindustan

Tup·per \'tə-pər\ Sir Charles 1821–1915 Canad. polit.; prime min. (1896); strong advocate of Canadian federation; responsible for making Nova Scotia a province and for completion of Canadian Pacific Railway

Tu·renne \tü-'ren\ Vicomte de 1611–1675 Henri de La Tour d'Auvergne marshal of France; important in Thirty Years' War, in the civil war of the Fronde (1648–53), in the French invasion of the

Spanish Netherlands, and in the third Dutch War; one of history's greatest military leaders

Tur·ge·nev \túr-'gän-yəf, -'gen-\ Ivan Sergeyevich 1818–1883 Russ. nov.; best known for novel *Fathers and Sons*

Tur·got \túr-'gō\ Anne-Robert-Jacques 1727–1781 Baron *de l'Aulne* \'lōn\ Fr. statesman & econ.; instituted reforms in economy and trade; abolished some feudal privileges, etc.

Tur·ner \'tər-nər\ Frederick Jackson 1861–1932 Am. hist.; influenced treatment of American history by emphasizing significance of the frontier in national development

Turner Joseph Mallord William 1775–1851 Eng. painter; perhaps greatest landscapist of 19th century; in mature period, sought to convey impressions of nature, using more dreamlike and poetic effects, brilliant color and light

Turner Nat 1800–1831 Am. slave insurrectionist; convinced of his divine inspiration, led (1831) failed slave uprising

Turner Ted 1938– *Robert Edward Turner* television executive; founder of Turner Broadcasting System; pioneer in the use of satellite and cable technology

Tut·ankh·a·men \,tü-,taŋ-'kä-mən, -,tän-\ *or* **Tut·ankh·a·ten** \-'kä-t⁴n\ *ca* 1370–1352 B.C. king of Egypt (1361–1352 B.C.); controlled by advisers during much of his reign; restored religion of Amon; tomb discovered intact (1922) by Howard Carter

Tutu \'tü-,tü\ Desmond Mpilo 1931– So. African clergyman & polit. activist; awarded 1984 Nobel prize for peace for leading nonviolent campaign against racial segregation in his country

Twacht·man \'twäkt-mən\ John Henry 1853–1902 Am. painter; one of the first American Impressionists; known for scenes of nature veiled in cool, shimmering light

Twain Mark — see CLEMENS

Tweed \'twēd\ William Marcy 1823–1878 *Boss Tweed* Am. polit.; head of the Tweed Ring; controlled New York City finances and swindled treasury of $30 to 200 million

Tweedsmuir — see BUCHAN

Ty·ler \'tī-lər\ Anne 1941– Am. writer; author of novels *Dinner at the Homesick Restaurant, The Accidental Tourist, Breathing Lessons,* etc.

Tyler John 1790–1862 10th pres. of the U.S. (1841–45); administration marked by party conflict, annexation of Texas to Union, etc.

Tyler Wat \'wät\ *or* Walter *d* 1381 Eng. leader of Peasants' Revolt (1381); presented to Richard II demands for abolition of serfdom, freedom of labor and trade, amnesty for rebels; killed on presenting second set of demands

Tyn·dale *or* **Tin·dal** *or* **Tin·dale** \'tin-d⁴l\ William *ca* 1494–1536 Eng. reformer & translator; published version of the Bible that was basis of Authorized Version of 1611

Tyn·dall \'tin-d⁴l\ John 1820–1893 Brit. physicist; studied diffusion of light by large molecules and dust (Tyndall effect); showed sky is blue because of atmospheric particles, etc.

Tyr·whitt–Wil·son \'tir-ət-'wil-sən\ Gerald Hugh 1883–1950 14th Baron *Ber·ners* \'bər-nərz\ Eng. composer; composed ballets, comic opera, piano pieces, etc.

Ty·son \'tī-sᵊn\ Michael Gerald 1966–   *Mike Tyson* Am. boxer; winner of heavyweight championships (1986–90); youngest heavyweight champion in history

Tz'u–hsi \'tsü-'shē\ 1835–1908 Chin. empress dowager; *concubine of Emperor I-chu, mother of Tsai-ch'un;* virtual dictator of China as co-regent (1875–1889) and again when emperor attempted reforms

U

Uc·cel·lo \ü-'che-(,)lō\ Paolo 1397–1475 orig. *Paolo di Dono* Florentine painter; attempted to reconcile late Gothic and early Renaissance styles; known esp. for studies in foreshortening, perspective

Udall \'yü-,dȯl, 'yü-dᵊl\ Nicholas 1505–1556 Eng. schoolmaster & dram.; author of *Ralph Roister Doister*, earliest English comedy, modeled on Plautus' *Miles Gloriosus*

Ugar·te \ü-'gär-tē\ Manuel 1874–1951 Argentine writer; constant critic of U.S. activities in South America; creator of phrase "Colossus of the North"; author of short stories, political works, literary history

Uh·land \'ü-,länt\ Johann Ludwig 1787–1862 Ger. poet & hist.; influenced by Romanticism; a founder of modern medieval studies

Ul·bricht \'ul-(,)brikt, -(,)brikt\ Walter 1893–1973 East German polit.; persecuted Trotskyites and communist deviationists for Stalin (1933–45); exercised complete control in East Germany (1960–73); erected Berlin Wall (1961)

Ul·fi·las \'ul-fə-,läs, 'əl-, -,ləs, -,las\ *or* Goth. **Wul·fi·la** \'wul-fə-lə\ *ca* 311–*ca* 382 Gothic missionary; translated Bible into Gothic

Ul·pi·an \'əl-pē-ən\ *d* A.D. 228 *Domitius Ulpianus* Rom. jurist; author of many legal commentaries, later constituting one-third of Justinian's *Digest*

Um·ber·to \(,)əm-'ber-(,)tō\ name of 2 kings of Italy: **I** 1844–1900 Duke of *Savoy* (reigned 1878–1900); worked to unify Italy; formed Triple Alliance with Germany and Austria-Hungary; ended colonial policy in Africa; **II** 1904–1983 Prince of *Piedmont;* Count of *Sarre* (reigned 1946)

Una·mu·no y Ju·go \,ü-nə-'mü-(,)nō-ē-'hü-(,)gō\ Miguel de 1864–1936 Span. philos. & writer; early exponent of Existentialism

Un·cas \'əŋ-kəs\ 1588?–?1683 Pequot Indian chief; leader of independent Mohegan tribe, a division of the Pequots

Und·set \'ùn-,set\ Sigrid \'si-grē, -grəd\ 1882–1949 Norw. nov.; author of novels portraying plight of women, esp. trilogy *Kristin Lavransdatter;* awarded 1928 Nobel prize for literature

Uni·tas \yü-'nī-təs\ John Constantine 1933–   *Johnny Unitas* Am. football player; quarterback, Baltimore Colts (1957–62); many career records included at least one touchdown pass in 47 consecutive games

Uno \'ü-(,)nō\ Sousuke 1922–   prime min. of Japan (1989)

Un·ter·mey·er \\'ən-tər-ˌmī(-ə)r\\ Louis 1885–1977 Am. poet; author of verse and editor of many anthologies

Up·dike \\'əp-ˌdīk\\ John Hoyer 1932–   Am. writer; best known for series of novels *Rabbit Run, Rabbit Redux, Rabbit at Rest*, etc.

Up·john \\'əp-ˌjän\\ Richard 1802–1878 Am. (Eng.-born) architect; a founder of American Institute of Architects; created, in Gothic Revival style, many churches and chapels

Up·ton \\'əp-tən\\ Emory 1839–1881 Am. gen. & author; wrote important works on tactics

Ur·ban \\'ər-bən\\ name of 8 popes: esp. **II** (*Odo* \\'ō-(ˌ)dō\\ *of Lagery*) *ca* 1035–1099 (pope 1088–99); opposed antipope Clement III; preached First Crusade; strengthened the Papacy as a political entity

Urey \\'yūr-ē\\ Harold Clayton 1893–1981 Am. chem.; awarded 1934 Nobel prize for chemistry for discovery of heavy hydrogen

Ur·quhart \\'ər-kərt, -ˌkärt\ *or* **Ur·chard** \\ər-chərd\\ Sir Thomas 1611–1660 Scot. author & translator; author of *Epigrams*, etc.; translator of *Works of Mr. Francis Rabelais*, Books I, II, III

Ussh·er \\'ə-shər\\ James 1581–1656 Irish prelate; propounder of a scheme of biblical chronology, long accepted, according to which the creation took place 4004 B.C.

Utril·lo \\yü-'tri-(ˌ)lō, ˌyü-trē-'ō, ˌūē-\\ Maurice 1883–1955 Fr. painter; known for his paintings of Parisian street scenes, esp. of the Montmartre district

V

Val·de·mar \\'väl-də-ˌmär, 'val-\ *or* **Wal·de·mar** \\'wȯl-\\ name of 4 kings of Denmark: esp. **I** 1131–1182 (reigned 1157–82); ended Wend (Slav) threat to shipping; won independence from Holy Rom. emp.; greatly increased Danish defenses and army

Valdes Peter — see WALDO

Val·di·via \\val-'dē-vē-ə\\ Pedro de *ca* 1498–1553 Span. conquistador; led expedition into Chile and founded Santiago (1541), Concepción (1550), Valdivia (1552)

Va·lens \\'vā-lənz, -ˌlenz\\ 328?–378 Rom. emp. of the East (364–378); subdued Visigoths (367-369); unfair treatment of them led to war (377–78)

Val·en·tin·ian \\ˌva-lən-'ti-nē-ən, -'tin-yən\ *L* **Val·en·tin·i·a·nus** \\'va-lən-ˌti-nē-'ā-nəs\\ name of 3 Rom. emperors in the West: **I** 321–375 (reigned 364–375); forced to contend with barbarian invasions in Gaul, Illyricum, Africa; **II** 371–392 (reigned 375–392); driven out of Italy by Magnus Maximus (387) and murdered at Vienna; **III** 419–455 (reigned 425–455); controlled first by mother as regent, then by Aetius; much of Europe overrun by Vandals, Visigoths, etc.

Valera Eamon de — see DE VALERA

Va·le·ra y Al·ca·lá Ga·lia·no \\və-'ler-ə-ē-ˌal-kə-'lä-ˌga-lē-'ä-(ˌ)nō, -ˌäl-kə-, -ˌgä-\\ Juan 1824–1905 Span. writer & statesman; author of

Veb·len \'ve-blən\ Thor·stein \'thȯr-,stīn\ Bunde 1857–1929 Am. sociol. & econ.; noted for trenchant social criticism esp. *The Theory of the Leisure Class* in which he coined the phrase "conspicuous consumption"— **Veb·le·ni·an** \ve-'blē-nē-ən\ *adj*

Ve·ga \'vā-gə\ Lo·pe \'lō-(,)pā\ de 1562–1635 *Lope Félix de Vega Carpio* Span. dram.; founder of Spanish national drama; reputed author of about 1800 plays and several hundred shorter dramatic pieces; known for comic character the *gracioso*

Ve·láz·quez \və-'las-kəs, -'läs-, -kwiz, -(,)kās\ Diego Rodríguez de Silva 1599–1660 Span. painter; court painter to Philip IV; known for portraits of the royal family, including Philip IV, Infanta Margarita, Infanta Maria, etc., court jesters, dwarfs, Pope Innocent X; renowned for his rich, expressive brushwork, mastery of color, and psychological profundity; one of the giants of Western art

Ven·dôme \vän(n)-'dōm\ Duc de 1654–1712 *Louis-Joseph* Fr. soldier; fought in Dutch campaign (1672), War of Grand Alliance (1689–97), War of Spanish Succession (1701–14)

Ve·ni·zé·los \,ve-nə-'zā-ləs, -'ze-ləs\ Eleuthérios 1864–1936 Greek statesman; organized Balkan League (1912); expanded Greek territory during Second Balkan War; championed Allied cause in WWI; premier (1910–1920, 1924, 1928–32, 1933)

Ver·di \'ver-dē\ Giuseppe Fortunio Francesco 1813–1901 Ital. composer; credited, along with Richard Wagner, with developing opera into fully integrated art form (*dramma per musica*); noted for masterpieces *Otello, Falstaff, Aïda, La traviata,* etc. — **Ver·di·an** \-ən\ *adj*

Ve·re·ker \'ver-ə-kər\ John Standish Surtees Prendergast 1886–1946 6th Viscount *Gort* \'gȯrt\ Brit. soldier; chief of British forces in France and Belgium (1939–40); relieved during evacuation of Dunkirk (1940); high commissioner of Palestine and Trans-Jordan (1944–45)

Ve·re·shcha·gin \,ver-əsh-'chä-gən, ,ver-ə-'shä-\ Vasily Vasilyevich 1842–1904 Russ. painter; known esp. for historical paintings depicting Russia's invasion by Napoleon in 1812

Vergil — see VIRGIL

Ver·laine \ver-'län, -'len\ Paul 1844–1896 Fr. poet; associated with Parnassians, then a leading Symbolist; author of some of most musical verse in French including *Romances sans paroles* (*Songs Without Words*)

Ver·meer \vər-'mer, -'mir\ Jan 1632–1675 also called *Jan van der Meer van Delft* \van-dər-'mer-van-'delft, -'mir-\ Du. painter; one of the masters of Dutch art; renowned esp. for genre scenes in which he recorded the soft play of natural light with unparalleled subtlety and lucidity

Verne \'vərn, 'vern\ Jules \'jülz, 'zhᵫl\ 1828–1905 Fr. writer; helped create genre of science fiction with novels *Voyage to the Center of the Earth, Twenty Thousand Leagues Under the Sea, Around the World in Eighty Days,* etc.

Ver·ner \'ver-nər\ Karl Adolph 1846–1896 Dan. philologist; propounded Verner's law explaining exceptions to Grimm's law of phonetic shifts in Indo-European languages

Ver·nier \ver-'yā, 'vər-nē-ər\ Pierre *ca* 1580–1637 Fr. math.; invented Vernier caliper for making accurate measurements of linear magnitudes

Ver·non \\'vər-nən\\ Edward 1684–1757 Eng. admiral; called "Old Grog"; first to issue rum diluted with water (grog)

Ve·ro·ne·se \\,ver-ə-'nā-sē, -zē\\ Paolo 1528–1588 orig. *Paolo Caliari* Ital. painter; a chief painter of Venetian school; works notable for large scale, large number of figures, rich color, illusionist composition, frequently in architectural frameworks

Ver·ra·za·no *or* **Ver·raz·za·no** \\,ver-ə-'zä-(,)nō, -ət-'sä-\\ Giovanni da 1485?–?1528 Florentine navigator & explorer; explored coast of North America from Cape Fear probably to Cape Breton; sighted New York and Narragansett Bays

Ver·roc·chio \\və-'rò-kē-,ō\\ Andrea del 1435–1488 orig. *Andrea di Michele Cione* Florentine sculptor & painter; after Donatello, leading sculptor of Tuscan school; teacher of Leonardo da Vinci

Verulam — see Francis BACON

Ve·rus \\'vir-əs\\ Lucius Aurelius A.D. 130–169 orig. *Lucius Ceionius Commodus* Rom. emp. (161–169); ruled jointly with Marcus Aurelius

Ver·woerd \\fər-'vùrt, fer-\\ Hendrik Frensch 1901–1966 So. African polit.; prime min. (1958–66); applied rigorous policy of apartheid

Ve·sa·li·us \\və-'sā-lē-əs, -'zā-\\ Andreas 1514–1564 Belg. anatomist; repudiated ancient traditional theories and revolutionized practice of medicine by careful description of human anatomy based on dissecting cadavers; wrote and illustrated first comprehensive textbook of anatomy

Ve·sey \\'vē-zē\\ Denmark *ca* 1767–1822 Am. slave insurrectionist; mastermind of aborted slave revolt in and around Charleston, S.C.

Ves·pa·sian \\ve-'spā-zh(ē-)ən\\ A.D. 9–79 *Titus Flavius Sabinus Vespasianus* Rom. emp. (69–79); initiator of a vast building program that included the Forum, Temple of Peace, and the beginning of the Colosseum; his fiscal and administrative reforms brought political stability to the empire

Ves·puc·ci \\ve-'spü-chē, -'spyü-\\ Amer·i·go \\ə-'mer-i-,gō, *It* ,ä-mə-'rē-(,)gō\\ 1454–1512 L. *Amer·i·cus Ves·pu·cius* \\ə-'mer-ə-kəs,-ves-'pyü-sh(ē-)əs\\ Ital. navigator & explorer; navigator of expedition under Alonso de Ojeda (1499–1500) that first sighted American mainland; first to realize that Columbus had encountered not Asia but a "New World"; his name given to new lands by Martin Waldseemüller, publisher of his accounts

Vi·co \\'vē-kō\\ Giambattista 1668–1744 Ital. philos.; a forerunner of cultural anthropology, known esp. for attempt to discover and organize laws common to evolution of all society in *Scienza Nuova*

Victor Em·man·u·el I \\'vik-tər-i-'man-yə-wəl\\ 1759–1824 king of Sardinia (1802–21); all dominions occupied by French (1802–14), restored (1815)

Victor Emmanuel II 1820–1878 king of Sardinia-Piedmont (1849–61) & 1st king of a united Italy (1861–78)

Victor Emmanuel III 1869–1947 king of Italy (1900–46); acquiesced in Fascist seizure of power and Mussolini's rise; reign marked end of Italian monarchy

Vic·to·ria \\vik-'tōr-ē-ə, -'tòr-\\ 1819–1901 *Alexandrina Victoria* queen of Great Britain (1837–1901); recognized as symbolizing new conception of British monarchy and a unified empire — **Vic·to·ri·an** \\vik-'tōr-ē-ən\\ *adj*

Victoria Tomás Luis de *ca* 1548–1611 Span. composer; with Palestrina and Orlando di Lasso, outstanding composer of 16th century

Vi·da \'vē-də\ Marco Girolamo *ca* 1490–1566 Ital. poet; best known for his Latin epic *Christias*

Vi·dal \vē-'däl, 've-ˌdäl\ Gore 1925– orig. *Eugene Luther Vidal* Am. writer; notorious for his iconoclasm and irreverence; known esp. for play *The Best Man*, satirical novel *Myra Breckenridge*, historical novel *Burr*, etc.

Vi·gée–Le·brun \vē-ˌzhā-lə-'brəⁿ(n), -'brœⁿ\ Marie-Louise-Élisabeth 1755–1842 Fr. painter; best known for portraits, including those of English princesses Victoria and Adelaide, Lord Byron, Mme. de Staël, many of Marie Antoinette

Vi·gno·la \vēn-'yō-lə\ Giacomo da 1507–1573 *Giacomo Ba·roz·zi* \bä-'rót-sē\ Ital. architect; with Palladio and Giulio Romano, leader of Mannerist architecture in Italy; built first church with an oval dome; wrote standard text on architecture

Vi·gny \vēn-'yē\ Alfred-Victor de 1797–1863 Fr. author; a leader among French Romantics; known esp. for drama *Chatterton* and historical novel *Cinq-Mars*

Vil·la \'vē-yə\ Francisco usu. called Pan·cho \'pän-(ˌ)chō, 'pan-\ 1878–1923 orig. *Doroteo Arango* Mex. bandit & revolutionary; guerrilla leader who fought against the regimes of Porfirio Díaz and Victoriano Huerta

Vil·la–Lo·bos \ˌvē-lə-'lō-(ˌ)bōsh, -(ˌ)bōs, -bəs\ Heitor \'ā-ˌtór\ 1887–1959 Braz. composer; known for applying classical forms and techniques to Afro-Brazilian themes, including 9 *Bachianas brasileiras*, etc.

Vil·lard \və-'lär(d)\ Oswald Garrison 1872–1949 Am. journalist; editor (1918–32) and owner (1918–35) *The Nation*

Vil·lars \vi-'lär\ Claude-Louis-Hector 1653–1734 Duc *de Villars* Fr. soldier; marshal of France; Louis XIV's most successful commander in the War of the Spanish Succession (1701–14)

Ville·neuve \ˌvēl-'nə(r)v, -'nœv\ Pierre-Charles-Jean-Baptiste-Silvestre de 1763–1806 Fr. admiral; commander of fleet designed to invade England; defeated by Nelson at Trafalgar (1805)

Vil·liers \'vil-yərz, 'vi-lərz\ George 1592–1628 1st Duke of *Buckingham* \'bə-kiŋ-əm, US also -ˌkiŋ-ham\ Eng. courtier & polit.; notable for series of political and military failures

Villiers George 1628–1687 2d Duke of *Buckingham, son of prec.* Eng. courtier & dram.; engaged in intrigues and caused much scandal for personal immorality

Vil·lon \vē-'yōⁿ also -'lō\ François 1431–after 1463 orig. *François de Montcorbier* or *Des Loges* Fr. poet; produced highly lyrical, technically accomplished, emotional and learned works

Vil·lon \vē-'lōⁿ, -'yōⁿ\ Jacques 1875–1963 orig. *Gaston Duchamp*; *bro. of Marcel Duchamp* Fr. painter; worked in Impressionist, Fauvist, and Cubist manners

Vin·cent de Paul \'vin(t)-sənt-də-'pól\ Saint 1581–1660 Fr. religious; founder of the Congregation of the Mission (Lazarists or Vincentians)

Vinci, da Leonardo — SEE LEONARDO DA VINCI

Vi·no·gra·doff \ˌvi-nə-'gra-ˌdóf\ Sir Paul Gavrilovitch 1854–1925 Brit. (Russ.-born) jurist & hist.; authority on early laws and customs in England

Vin·son \'vin(t)-sən\ Frederick Moore 1890–1953 Am. jurist; chief justice U.S. Supreme Court (1946–53)

Viol·let–le–Duc \vyė-ə-'lä-lə-'dük, -'dyük; vyȯ-le-lə-dük\ Eugène Emmanuel 1814–1879 Fr. architect; a leader in the Gothic revival in France; designed the restoration of many medieval buildings in France

Vir·chow \'fir-(,)kō, 'vir-\ Rudolf 1821–1902 Ger. pathologist; one of the preeminent physicians of the 19th century; a pioneer in the modern concept of pathological processes by his application of the cell theory to pathology

Vir·gil also **Ver·gil** \'vər-jəl\ 70–19 B.C. *Publius Vergilius Maro* Rom. poet; greatest of Roman poets; works include *Georgics, Eclogues (Bucolica),* and great epic *Aeneid* — **Vir·gil·ian** also **Ver·gil·ian** \(,)vər-'ji-lē-ən\ *adj*

Vir·ta·nen \'vir-tə-,nen\ Art·tu·ri \'är-tə-rē\ Ilmari 1895–1973 Finn. biochem.; awarded 1945 Nobel prize for chemistry for development of method of protecting silage from destructive fermentation

Vi·tru·vi·us \və-'trü-vē-əs\ *fl* 1st cent. B.C. *Marcus Vitruvius Pollio* Rom. architect & engineer; author of *De architectura,* for many centuries accepted as final authority on classical architecture

Vi·val·di \vi-'väl-dē, -'vȯl-\ Antonio Lucio 1678–1741 Ital. composer; considered most original and influential Italian composer of his day; an innovator in form, orchestration, and technique; known esp. for four violin concertos collectively known as *The Four Seasons*

Vla·di·mir I \'vla-də-,mir, vlə-'dē-,mir\ Saint *ca* 956–1015 grand prince of Kiev (980–1015); consolidated rule from Baltic to Ukraine; first Russian ruler to accept Christianity

Vla·minck \vlə-'maŋk\ Maurice de 1876–1958 Fr. painter; a member of Fauvist group; later influenced by Cézanne; developed personal style of Expressionism

Vo·gler \'fō-glər\ Georg Joseph 1749–1814 Abt \'äpt, 'apt\ *or* Abbé *Vogler* Ger. composer & writer; best known for theoretical and pedagogical works

Vol·stead \'väl-,sted, 'vȯl-, 'vōl-, -stəd\ Andrew John 1860–1947 Am. legislator; author of Volstead Act (1919) to enforce Eighteenth Amendment, prohibition of manufacture and sale of alcoholic beverages

Vol·ta \'vōl-tə, 'väl-, 'vȯl-\ Conte Alessandro Giuseppe Antonio Anastasio 1745–1827 Ital. physicist; invented the electrophorus and the voltaic pile; the volt, electrical unit, is named for him

Vol·taire \vōl-'tar, väl-, vȯl-, -'ter\ 1694–1778 orig. *François-Marie Arouet* Fr. writer; gained fame as defender of victims of religious intolerance, but known chiefly as master of satire; works included tragedies, philosophical satire *Candide, Dictionnaire philosophique,* poems, etc. — **Vol·tair·ean** *or* **Vol·tair·ian** \-'tar-ē-ən, -'ter-\ *adj*

Von Braun Wernher — see BRAUN

Von Eu·ler \fȯn-'ȯi-lər\ Ulf Svante 1905–1983 Swed. physiol.; awarded (with J. Axelrod and B. Katz) 1970 Nobel prize for physiology or medicine for discoveries of the role played by certain chemicals in transmitting nerve impulses

Von·ne·gut \'vä-ni-gət\ Kurt 1922– Am. writer; author of novels *Slaughterhouse Five, Cat's Cradle, Deadeye Dick,* etc.

Vo·ro·shi·lov \\,vȯr-ə-'shē-,lȯf, ,vär-, -,lȯv\\ Kliment Yefremovich 1881–1969 Soviet marshal; chairman of the Presidium (1953–60)

Vor·ster \\'fȯr-stər\\ Balthazar Johannes 1915–1983 prime min. of Republic of So. Africa (1966–78); rigidly enforced apartheid policies

Voz·ne·sen·sky \\,väz-nə-'sen(t)-skē\\ Andrey 1933– Soviet (Russ.-born) poet; one of the most prominent of the generation of writers that emerged after the Stalinist era; condemned during 1963 government crackdown against "excessively experimental" artistic styles

Vries, de \\də-'vrēs\\ Hugo Marie 1848–1935 Du. botanist & geneticist; deduced laws of heredity similar to those of Mendel; discovered Mendel's work (1900)

Vuil·lard \\vwē-'yär\\ (Jean-)Édouard 1868–1940 Fr. painter; developed with Pierre Bonnard, Intimist style, marked by small scenes, subtle colors and composition

Vy·shin·sky \\və-'shin(t)-skē\\ Andrey Yanuaryevich 1883–1954 Soviet lawyer, polit., & diplomat; prosecutor in Great Purge trials (1934–38); U.N. representative (1949–54)

W

Waals, van der \\'van-dər-,wȯlz\\ Johannes Diderik 1837–1923 Du. physicist; awarded 1910 Nobel prize for physics for studying the relationship of liquids and gases

Wace \\'wās, 'wäs\\ ca 1100–after 1174 Anglo-Norman poet; author of two poetical chronicles in Norman French, *Roman de Brut* and *Roman de Rou*

Wag·ner \\'väg-nər\\ (Wilhelm) Ri·chard \\'ri-,kärt, -,kärt\\ 1813–1883 Ger. composer; originator of the music drama and pioneer in the development of the leitmotiv; composed operas *Tannhäuser, Lohengrin,* cycle *Der Ring des Nibelungen, Tristan und Isolde,* etc. — **Wag·ne·ri·an** \\väg-'nir-ē-ən, -'ner-\\ *adj*

Wagner von Jau·regg *or* **Wagner–Jau·regg** \\-'yaù-,rek\\ Julius 1857–1940 Austrian neurologist & psychiatrist; awarded 1927 Nobel prize for physiology or medicine for discovering the fever treatment for paralysis

Wain·wright \\'wān-,rīt\\ Jonathan Mayhew 1883–1953 Am. gen.; defended Bataan and Corregidor until forced to surrender (1942)

Wainwright Richard father 1817–1862 & his son 1849–1926 Am. naval officers; father was naval commander in Civil War under Farragut; son in Spanish-American war and after

Waite \\'wāt\\ Morrison Remick 1816–1888 Am. jurist; chief justice U.S. Supreme Court (1874–88); wrote over 1000 opinions, many interpreting post-Civil War constitutional amendments

Waks·man \\'waks-mən, 'waks-\\ Sel·man \\'sel-mən\\ Abraham 1888–1973 Am. (Ukrainian-born) microbiologist; awarded 1952 Nobel prize for physiology or medicine for work in the discovery of streptomycin

Wal·cott \'wȯl-(,)kät\ Derek Alton 1930–   West Indian poet & playwright; awarded 1992 Nobel prize for literature for novels and poems

Wald \'wȯld\ George 1906–   Am. biol.; awarded (with R. Granit and H.K. Hartline) 1967 Nobel prize for physiology or medicine for their findings about the chemical and physiological processes of the eye

Wald Lillian D. 1867–1940 Am. social worker; founder and organizer of public-health nursing service, Henry Street Settlement in New York City

Waldemar — see VALDEMAR

Wal·der·see \'väl-dər-,zā, 'wȯl-\ Alfred von 1832–1904 Ger. soldier; commander of European forces in China during Boxer rebellion (1900–01)

Wald·heim \'vält-,hīm\ Kurt 1918–   Austrian U.N. official; secy.-gen. (1972–82); pres. of Austria (1986–92)

Wal·do \'wȯl-(,)dō, 'wäl-\ *or* **Val·des** \'val-(,)däs, 'väl-\ Peter *d* before 1218 Fr. religious leader; founded movement known as Pauperes or Pauperes Spiritu (later Waldenses)

Wa·łe·sa \vä-'len(t)-sə, wä-; vä-'weⁿ-sə\ Lech \'lek, 'lek\ 1943–   Pol. polit.; instrumental in launching Solidarity movement that brought end to communist government; awarded 1983 Nobel prize for peace; pres. of Poland (1990–95)

Walk·er \'wȯ-kər\ Alice Malsenior 1944–   Am. writer; best known as author of *The Color Purple, Possessing the Secret of Joy,* etc.

Walker Francis Am·a·sa \'a-mə-sə\ 1840–1897 Am. econ.; widely known as advocate of international bimetallism

Walker William 1824–1860 Am. military adventurer; invaded Lower California with "colonists" (1853), Nicaragua (1855); made himself president of Nicaragua but ousted with help of Cornelius Vanderbilt (1857)

Wal·lace \'wä-ləs\ Alfred Russel 1823–1913 Eng. naturalist; originated independently a theory of natural selection (1858) published jointly with Darwin's

Wallace George Corley 1919–   Am. polit.; governor of Alabama (1963–67, 1971–79, 1983–87); began as ardent segregationist but later moved to a more liberal position

Wallace Henry Agard \'ä-gärd\ 1888–1965 Am. agriculturist, editor, & polit.; vice pres. of the U.S. (1941–45)

Wallace Lewis 1827–1905 *Lew Wallace* Am. lawyer, gen., & nov.; on military court that tried conspirators in Lincoln's assassination; author of novels *The Fair God, Ben Hur,* etc.

Wallace Sir William *ca* 1270–1305 Scot. patriot; leader of resistance forces in early years of struggle to liberate Scotland from English rule

Wal·lach \'wä-lək, 'väl-\ Otto 1847–1931 Ger. chem.; awarded 1910 Nobel prize for chemistry for work on alicyclic substances

Wal·len·berg \'wä-lən-,bərg, *Sw* -,ber-ē\ Raoul 1912–1947? Swed. diplomat & hero of the Holocaust; saved up to 100,000 Hungarian Jews

Wal·len·stein \'vä-lən-,shtīn, 'wä-lən-,stīn\ Albrecht Eusebius Wenzel von 1583–1634 Duke of *Friedland and Mecklenburg;*

Prince of *Sagan* Austrian gen.; commanding gen. in the armies of Holy Roman emp. Ferdinand II during Thirty Years' War

Wal·ler \'wä-lər\ Edmund 1606–1687 Eng. poet; author of graceful, elegant *Poems*, etc.; made heroic couplet fashionable

Waller Thomas Wright 1904–1943 *Fats Waller* Am. pianist & composer; achieved commercial success by blend of jazz and comic manner; influenced by "stride" style and first jazz musician to master organ; composed songs, including "Ain't Misbehavin'," "Honeysuckle Rose," etc.

Wal·pole \'wȯl-ˌpōl, 'wäl-\ Horace 1717–1797 orig. *Horatio* 4th Earl of *Or·ford* \'ȯr-fərd\ Eng. author; author of *The Castle of Otranto*, forerunner of Gothic romances; known for charming, vivacious, often brilliant letters

Walpole Sir Hugh Seymour 1884–1941 Eng. nov.; known for novels *Fortitude, Jeremy* and series on life of English boy, tetralogy *Rogue Herries*, etc.

Walpole Sir Robert 1676–1745 1st Earl of *Orford; father of Horace* Eng. statesman; managed transfer of power to House of Commons; first to unify cabinet government under prime min. — **Wal·pol·ian** \wȯl-'pō-lē-ən, wäl-\ *adj*

Wal·ter \'väl-tər, 'wȯl-\ Bruno 1876–1962 orig. *Bruno Schle·sing·er* \'shlā-ziŋ-ər\ Am. (Ger.-born) conductor; noted for interpretations of Mozart, Mahler, Bruckner

Wal·ters \'wȯl-tərz\ Barbara 1931–   Am. broadcast journalist; known esp. as an interviewer, first on television's "Today Show," then on "The Barbara Walters Special"; became (1976) first woman to anchor a network news program ("ABC Evening News")

Wal·ther von der Vo·gel·wei·de \'väl-tər-ˌfȯn-dər-'fō-gəl-ˌvī-də\ *ca* 1170–*ca* 1230 Ger. minnesinger & poet; wrote love songs, including "Unter den Linden," moral and didactic poems, and political and religious songs championing German independence and unity

Wal·ton \'wȯl-tⁿn\ Ernest Thomas Sinton 1903–1995 Irish physicist; awarded (with J. Cockcroft) 1951 Nobel prize for physics for work on the transmutation of nuclei by artificially accelerated atomic particles

Walton Izaak \'ī-zik, -zək\ 1593–1683 Eng. writer; best known for masterpiece *The Compleat Angler, or the Contemplative Man's Recreation*, dialogues with anecdotes, country scenery, verse, etc.

Walton Sir William Turner 1902–1983 Eng. composer; set poems of Edith Sitwell to music; composed symphonies, operas, etc., and music for Laurence Olivier's films of *Henry V, Hamlet, Richard III*

Wan·a·ma·ker \'wä-nə-ˌmā-kər\ John 1838–1922 Am. merchant; developed largest retail men's clothing store in U.S. (by 1871)

Wang \'waŋ\ An 1920–1990 Am. (Chin.-born) computer engineer; invented (1948) a magnetic core memory for computers; founded (1951) Wang Laboratories, which became known for desktop calculators and office computers

Wang Ching–wei \'wäŋ-'jiŋ-'wä\ 1883–1944 Chin. polit.; pres. of Kuomintang government (1932–38); became strongly pro-Japanese; puppet ruler of occupied China (1940–44)

War·beck \'wȯr-ˌbek\ Perkin 1474–1499 Flem. imposter & pretender to the English throne; pretended to be Richard, the youngest duke of York, who was presumed murdered with his brother King Edward V in the Tower of London

War·burg \'wȯr-ˌbərg, 'vär-ˌbůrk\ Otto Heinrich 1883–1970 Ger. biochem.; awarded 1931 Nobel prize for physiology or medicine for discovering that enzymes aid in respiration by tissues

Ward \'wȯrd\ Aaron Montgomery 1843–1913 Am. merchant; established Chicago drygoods business that became great mail-order house of Montgomery Ward & Co.

Ward Ar·te·mas \'är-tə-məs\ 1727–1800 Am. gen. in Revolution; forced British evacuation of Boston

Ward Artemus — see Charles Farrar BROWNE

Ward Barbara 1914–1981 Baroness *Jackson of Lodsworth* Eng. econ.; influential adviser to the Vatican, the U.N., the World Bank

Ward Sir Joseph George 1856–1930 N.Z. statesman; prime min. (1906–12, 1928–30)

Ward Mary Augusta 1851–1920 *Mrs. Humphry Ward* née *Arnold* Eng. nov.; best known for spiritual romance *Robert Elsmere*

War·hol \'wȯr-ˌhȯl, -ˌhōl\ Andy 1927?–1987 Am. artist & film-maker; a pioneer of Pop Art movement; known for his paintings of banal objects as Campbell's soup cans and for statement that in the future everyone will be famous for 15 minutes — **War·hol·ian** \(ˌ)wȯr-'hō-lē-ən, -'hō-\ *adj*

War·ner \'wȯr-nər\ Charles Dudley 1829–1900 Am. editor & essayist; best known for collections of essays; collaborated with Mark Twain on *The Gilded Age*

War·ren \'wȯr-ən, 'wär-\ Earl 1891–1974 Am. jurist; chief justice U.S. Supreme Court (1953–69); noted for opinions in landmark cases *Brown v. Board of Education*, *Miranda v. Arizona*

Warren Gou·ver·neur \ˌgə-və(r)-'nir\ Kemble 1830–1882 Am. gen.; made crucial battlefield decision at Battle of Gettysburg (July 2, 1863) that led to Union victory

Warren Joseph 1741–1775 Am. physician & gen. in Revolution; on Committee of Safety that sent Paul Revere and William Dawes to Lexington to warn of danger (Apr. 18, 1775)

Warren Robert Penn 1905–1989 Am. author & educ.; poet laureate (1986–87); winner of three Pulitzer prizes for poems and novels, including *All the King's Men*

War·ton \'wȯr-tⁿn\ Thomas 1728–1790 Eng. lit. hist. & critic; poet laureate (1785–90); earned reputation with *Observations on the Faerie Queene of Spenser*; wrote *The History of English Poetry* (to end of Elizabethan age)

War·wick \'wär-ik, *US also* 'wȯr-ik, 'wȯr-ˌwik\ Earl of 1428–1471 Richard Nev·ille \'ne-vəl\; *the Kingmaker* Eng. soldier & statesman; powerful figure in first half of Wars of the Roses; obtained crown for Yorkist Edward IV (1461); restored to power deposed Lancastrian Henry VI (1470–71)

Wash·ing·ton \'wȯ-shiŋ-tən, 'wä-, *chiefly Midland also* 'wȯr- *or* 'wär-\ Book·er \'bů-kər\ Tal·ia·ferro \'tä-lə-vər\ 1856–1915 Am. educ.; first president and principal developer of Tuskegee Institute; influential spokesman for black Americans esp. after 1895

Washington George 1732–1799 Am. gen.; commander in chief of the Continental Army during the American Revolution (1775–83); 1st pres. of the U.S. (1789–97); established many precedents that permanently shaped the character of the office of pres.; universally regarded as father of his country — **Wash·ing·to·nian** \ˌwȯ-shiŋ-'tō-nē-ən, ˌwä-, -'wȯr-, ˌwär-, -nyən\ *adj*

Was·mo·sy \'wäs-'mō-sē\ Juan Carlos 1939– pres. of Paraguay (1993–)

Was·ser·mann \'wä-sər-mən, 'vä-\ August von 1866–1925 Ger. bacteriol.; discovered (1906) Wassermann reaction, basis for universal blood-serum test for syphilis

Was·ser·stein \'wä-sər-ˌstīn\ Wendy 1950– Am. dram.; best known for *The Heidi Chronicles*

Wa·ters \'wȯ-tərz, 'wä-\ Ethel 1896–1977 Am. actress & singer; known for Broadway roles in *Blackbirds, Member of the Wedding,* etc.; film roles in *The Sound and the Fury, Pinky,* etc.

Wat·son \'wät-sən\ James Dewey 1928– Am. geneticist; awarded (with F.H.C. Crick and M.H.F. Wilkins) 1962 Nobel prize for physiology or medicine for work on DNA

Watson John 1850–1907 pseud. *Ian Mac·lar·en* \mə-'klar-ən\ Scot. clergyman & author; wrote *Beside the Bonnie Brier Bush* (1894) and other "kailyard school" portrayals of humble Scottish life

Watson John Broadus 1878–1958 Am. psychol.; a leading exponent, codifier, and popularizer of behaviorism

Watson Thomas Sturges 1949– Am. golfer; winner of 32 tournaments on U.S. tour, 5 British Open tournaments, 1 U.S. Open, 2 Masters

Watson Sir (John) William 1858–1935 Eng. poet; author of lyrical, political, and esp. occasional verse

Watson–Watt \-'wät\ Sir Robert Alexander 1892–1973 Scot. physicist; instrumental in the development of radar to detect German air raids (1940)

Watt \'wät\ James 1736–1819 Scot. inventor; invented modern condensing steam engine and double-acting engine; which did much to propel the Industrial Revolution

Wat·teau \wä-'tō, vä-\ (Jean-) Antoine 1684–1721 Fr. painter; known esp. for his charming, lyrical, Rococo style, reflecting influences of contemporary theater and opera

Wat·ter·son \'wä-tər-sən, 'wȯ-\ Henry 1840–1921 Am. journalist & polit.; editor, Louisville (Ky.) *Courier-Journal* (1868–1918); a strong voice on many issues of the day

Watts \'wäts\ George Frederic 1817–1904 Eng. painter & sculptor; painted series of about 300 portraits of distinguished contemporaries; works noted for obscurely symbolic elements

Watts Isaac 1674–1748 Eng. theol. & hymn writer; composed 600 hymns including "O God, Our Help in Ages Past," "There is a Land of Pure Delight," etc.

Watts–Dun·ton \-'dən-tᵊn\ Walter Theodore 1832–1914 Eng. critic & poet; friend of Rossetti, mentor of C. Swinburne; author of verse, novels, sonnets, essays, etc.

Waugh \'wȯ\ Evelyn Arthur St. John 1903–1966 Eng. writer; considered finest satirical novelist in English in his day; works included *Vile Bodies, Brideshead Revisited, The Loved One,* etc.

Wa·vell \'wä-vəl\ 1st Earl 1883–1950 Archibald Percival Wavell Brit. field marshal; viceroy of India (1943–47); destroyed Italian armies in North Africa and Middle East; defeated by Rommel; in command of Allied forces in Southwest Pacific (1942) and in India and Burma (1942)

Wayne \'wān\ Anthony 1745–1796 *Mad Anthony* Am. gen. in Revolution; involved in battles of Brandywine, Germantown, Monmouth, Stony Point, Yorktown, etc.; decisively defeated Indians at battle of Fallen Timbers (near Toledo) and negotiated treaty (1795)

Wayne John 1907–1979 orig. *Marion Michael Morrison; the Duke* Am. actor; known esp. for his roles as a gruff, tough, but fundamentally decent man of action in usu. war and western films, including *Stagecoach, Sands of Iwo Jima, True Grit,* etc.

Webb \'web\ Beatrice 1858–1943 née *Potter; wife of S.J.* Eng. socialist

Webb Sidney James 1859–1947 1st Baron *Passfield* Eng. socialist; a founder of Fabian Society; author of *Socialism in England;* anticipated welfare state with report in favor of Poor Law (1909)

We·ber \'vā-bər\ Carl Maria von 1786–1826 Ger. composer & conductor; a leading creator of German Romanticism and nationalism in music; works included 9 operas, orchestral works, concertos, much piano music, etc.

Weber Ernst Heinrich 1795–1878 Ger. physiol.; considered a founder of experimental psychology

Weber Max 1864–1920 Ger. sociol. & econ.; a chief theorist of liberal imperialism; best known for thesis linking Protestantism and capitalism — **We·be·ri·an** \vā-'bir-ē-ən\ *adj*

Web·er \'we-bər\ Max 1881–1961 Am. (Russ.-born) painter; produced paintings influenced by Fauvism, Cubism, Hasidic Jewish themes

We·bern \'vā-bərn\ Anton von 1883–1945 Austrian composer; student of Schoenberg, associate of Berg in developing theory of atonality and practice of 12-tone composition

Web·ster \'web-stər\ Daniel 1782–1852 Am. statesman & orator; gained fame as orator for constitutional speeches in reply to Hayne (1830) and Calhoun (1833); as senator from Mass. (1827–41, 1845–50) opposed Mexican War and annexation of Texas; supported Clay's compromise measures on slavery (1850)

Webster John *ca* 1580–*ca* 1625 Eng. dram.; demonstrated tragic power and poetic genius in *The White Devil* and *The Duchess of Malfi*

Webster Noah 1758–1843 Am. lexicographer & author; known esp. for his *American Spelling Book* and *American Dictionary of the English Language* (1828)

Wed·e·mey·er \'we-də-ˌmī-ər\ Albert Coady 1897–1989 Am. gen.; principal author of 1941 Victory Program, a comprehensive plan for U.S. involvement in WWII that included a "Germany first" strategy; instrumental in planning D-Day invasion

Wedg·wood \'wej-ˌwu̇d\ Josiah 1730–1795 Eng. potter; developed his firm into one of world's leading producers of domestic and decorative ceramics

Weems \'wēmz\ Mason Locke 1759–1825 *Parson Weems* Am. clergyman & biographer; author of *The Life and Memorable Actions of George Washington* (1800), with popular stories about Washington, including tale of hatchet and cherry tree

We·ge·ner \'vā-gə-nər\ Alfred Lothar 1880–1930 Ger. geophysicist & meteorologist; originated Wegener hypothesis of continental drift

Weill \'wī(ə)l, 'vī(ə)l\ Kurt \'kurt\ 1900–1950 Am. (Ger.-born) composer; with librettist Bertolt Brecht created revolutionary operas of sharp social satire, including *Rise and Fall of the City of Mahagonny* and *The Threepenny Opera*; with librettist Maxwell Anderson composed Broadway musicals *Knickerbocker Holiday*, etc.

Wein·berg \'wīn-,bərg\ Steven 1933–   Am. physicist; awarded (with S.L. Glashow and A. Salam) 1979 Nobel prize for physics for developing a principle unifying weak nuclear force and electromagnetism

Wein·ber·ger \'wīn-,bər-gər\ Caspar Willard 1917–   U.S. secy. of defense (1981–87)

Weir \'wir\ Robert Walter 1803–1889 Am. painter; best known for *Embarkation of the Pilgrims* for U.S. Capitol Rotunda

Weis·mann \'vīs-,män, 'wīs-mən\ August Friedrich Leopold 1834–1914 Ger. biol.; developed theory of germ plasm, contending that only variations of germ plasm are inherited

Weiss·mul·ler \'wīs-,mə-lər\ Johnny 1904–1984 *Peter John Weissmuller* Am. swimmer & actor; winner of 5 Olympic gold medals; holder of 67 world records in swimming in the 1920s; best known for his role as Tarzan in 12 films beginning with *Tarzan the Ape Man*

Weiz·mann \'vīts-mən, 'wīts-\ Chaim \'kīm, 'hīm\ Azriel 1874–1952 Israeli (Russ.-born) chem.; 1st pres. of Israel (1949–52)

Welch \'welch, 'welsh\ William Henry 1850–1934 Am. pathologist; opened first pathology laboratory in U.S.; discovered *Clostridium welchii* (1892), agent of gas gangrene

Wel·ler \'we-lər\ Thomas Huckle 1915–   Am. virologist; awarded (with J.F. Enders and F.C. Robbins) 1954 Nobel prize for physiology or medicine for discovering a simple method of growing polio virus in laboratory suspensions

Welles \'welz\ (George) Or·son \'ȯr-sᵊn\ 1915–1985 Am. film & theater director, writer, producer, & actor; renowned as one of the greatest directors in film history; creator of landmark *Citizen Kane* (1941), acclaimed for its brilliant use of cinematic narrative, dramatic lighting, dynamic editing; notorious for erratic career

Welles Gideon 1802–1878 Am. polit. & writer; U.S. secy. of navy under Abraham Lincoln and Andrew Johnson; his *Diary of Gideon Welles* a prime source of information and insight about the era

Welles Sumner 1892–1961 Am. diplomat; laid foundation for "good neighbor" policy in Latin America

Welles·ley \'welz-lē\ 1st Marquis of 1760–1842 *Richard Colley Wellesley* Brit. statesman; gov.-gen. of India (1797–1805); greatly enlarged the British Empire in India

Wel·ling·ton \'we-liŋ-tən\ 1st Duke of 1769–1852 *Arthur Wellesley; the Iron Duke* Brit. gen. & statesman; commander during the Napoleonic Wars, first distinguishing himself during Peninsular War in Spain (1808–14); best known for important role in defeat of Napoléon at Waterloo (1815); prime minister (1828–30)

Wells \'welz\ Herbert George 1866–1946 Eng. nov. & hist.; wrote series of fantastic scientific romances including *The Time Machine* (1895), *The Invisible Man* (1897), *The War of the Worlds* (1898), etc.; also wrote *Tono-Bungay* (1908), *Outline of History* (1920, rev. ed 1931) — **Wells·ian** \'wel-zē-ən\ *adj*

Wel·ty \'wel-tē\ Eudora 1909–   Am. writer; author of novels and short stories set in a small Mississippi town, including *The Robber Bridegroom, The Ponder Heart, The Optimist's Daughter,* etc.

Wen·ces·las \'wen(t)-sə-,slòs, -slàs\ *G* **Wen·zel** \'ven(t)-səl\ 1361–1419 king of Germany & Holy Rom. emp. (1378–1400) & (as Wenceslas IV) king of Bohemia (1378–1419); a weak ruler whose reign was constantly beset by wars and princely rivalries and eventually virtual anarchy

Wen·dell \'wen-d'l\ Barrett 1855–1921 Am. scholar; author of *Cotton Mather, Puritan Priest; A Literary History of America,* etc.

Went·worth \'went-(,)wərth\ William Charles 1790–1872 Austral. statesman; helped bring about Constitution Act (1842) giving colonial self-government to New South Wales; secured new colonial constitution (1855), etc.

Wer·fel \'ver-fəl\ Franz 1890–1945 Ger. author; author of volumes of Expressionist verse, plays, and esp. novel *The Song of Bernadette*

Wer·ner \'ver-nər\ Alfred 1866–1919 Swiss chem.; awarded 1913 Nobel prize for chemistry for coordination theory on the arrangement of atoms

Wes·ley \'wes-lē, 'wez-\ Charles 1707–1788 *bro. of John* Eng. Methodist preacher & hymn writer; author of several thousand hymns, including "Love divine, all loves excelling," "Hark, the herald angels sing," "Christ the Lord is ris'n today," etc.

Wesley John 1703–1791 Eng. theol., evangelist, & founder of Methodism

West \'west\ Benjamin 1738–1820 Am. painter; gained fame for historical paintings, including *The Death of Wolfe, Death on the Pale Horse,* etc.

West Jessamyn 1902–1984 Am. writer; best known for her short stories about American Quakers esp. collection *Friendly Persuasion*

West Nathanael 1903–1940 orig. *Nathan Wallenstein Weinstein* Am. nov.; author of satiric novels *Miss Lonelyhearts, Day of the Locust,* etc.

West Dame Rebecca 1892–1983 pseud. of *Cicily Isabel Andrews* née *Fairfield* Eng. critic & nov.; author of *The Meaning of Treason* and *A Train of Powder* from Nürnberg trials and of novels *The Judge,* etc.

West Thomas — see DE LA WARR

Wes·ter·marck \'wes-tər-,märk\ Edward Alexander 1862–1939 Finn. philos. & anthropol.; author of *The History of Human Marriage, Ethical Relativity,* etc.

Wes·ting·house \'wes-tiŋ-,haús\ George 1846–1914 Am. inventor; pioneer in introducing in America high-voltage alternating-current single-phase electrical system; took out more than 400 patents

West·more·land \west-'mōr-,lənd, -'mòr-\ William Childs 1914–   Am. general; controversial commander of American combat troops in Vietnam during the years (1964–68) of peak American involvement in the war there

Wes·ton \'wes-t'n\ Brett 1911–1993 Am. photographer; member of Group f/64, which championed "straight" photography over pictorialism; known esp. for his close-ups of plant leaves, coastal rocks, etc. that revealed their inherent abstract designs

Weston Edward 1886–1958 *father of prec.* Am. photographer; one of the most influential photographers of the 20th century; developed a photographic aesthetic that emphasized abstract form and sharp resolution of detail; known esp. for his photographs of sand dunes and female nudes in natural settings

Wet, de \də-'vet\ Christiaan Rudolf 1854–1922 Boer soldier & polit.; became legendary as guerilla leader against British; organized unsuccessful Afrikaner rebellion (1914)

Wey·den \'vī-d⁽ə⁾n, 'vā-\ Rogier van der 1399?–1464 Flem. painter; most influential painter of the day; noted esp. for realistic clarity, color in chiefly religious pictures

Wey·gand \vā-gäⁿ\ Maxime 1867–1965 Fr. gen.; commander in chief of Allied armies in France; unable to prevent German victory (1940)

Whar·ton \'hwȯr-t⁽ə⁾n, 'wȯr-\ Edith Newbold 1862–1937 née *Jones* Am. nov.; author of *The House of Mirth, Ethan Frome, The Age of Innocence,* etc.

Whate·ly \'hwāt-lē, 'wāt-\ Richard 1787–1863 Eng. theol., logician, & social reformer; as Anglican archbishop of Dublin, supported proposals to lessen intense Catholic-Protestant rivalry; author of *Logic, Rhetoric, Christian Evidence,* etc.

Wheat·ley \'hwēt-lē, 'wēt-\ Phillis 1753?–1784 Am. (African-born) poet; regarded as a prodigy in Boston; published *Poems on Various Subjects, Religious and Moral*

Wheat·stone \'hwēt-ˌstōn, 'wēt-, *chiefly Brit* -stən\ Sir Charles 1802–1875 Eng. physicist & inventor; invented the concertina (1829); demonstrated velocity of electricity in a conductor; invented the Wheatstone bridge for measuring electrical resistances

Whee·ler \'hwē-lər, 'wē-\ Joseph 1836–1906 Am. gen.; almost continuously in the field during Civil War; known for his efforts to promote North-South reconciliation

Wheeler William Almon 1819–1887 Am. polit.; vice pres. of the U.S. (1877–81)

Whee·lock \'hwē-ˌläk, 'wē-\ Eleazar 1711–1779 Am. clergyman & educ.; founder (1769) and first president of Dartmouth College

Whip·ple \'hwi-pəl, 'wi-\ George Hoyt 1878–1976 Am. pathologist; awarded (with G.R. Minot and W.P. Murphy) 1934 Nobel prize for physiology or medicine for discoveries on liver treatment for anemia

Whis·tler \'hwis-lər, 'wis-\ James Abbott McNeill 1834–1903 Am. painter & etcher; noted for his striking full-length portraits and paintings of nocturnal London, etc.; instrumental in introducing modern French painting in England; best known for *Arrangement in Grey and Black, No. 1: The Artist's Mother,* popularly called *Whistler's Mother* — **Whis·tler·ian** \hwis-'lir-ē-ən, wis-\ *adj*

White \'hwīt, 'wīt\ Andrew Dickson 1832–1918 Am. educ. & diplomat; helped organize Cornell U.; president of Cornell (1868–85); chairman, U.S. delegation to Hague Peace Conference (1899)

White Byron Raymond 1917–   Am. jurist & polit.; associate justice, U.S. Supreme Court (1962–93)

White Edward Douglass 1845–1921 Am. jurist; chief justice U.S. Supreme Court (1910–21); known for enunciation of "rule of reason" for interpretation and application of antitrust laws

White Elwyn Brooks 1899–1985 Am. journalist & writer; best known for *The Elements of Style* and children's novels *Stuart Little, Charlotte's Web, The Trumpet of the Swan*

White Gilbert 1720–1793 Eng. clergyman & naturalist; author of classic *Natural History and Antiquities of Selbourne*

White Patrick Victor Martindale 1912–1990 Austral. writer; awarded 1973 Nobel prize for literature for his novels

White Stanford 1853–1906 Am. architect; designed Casino at Newport, R.I., Madison Square Garden, Washington Arch, several buildings for U. of Va., etc.

White Stewart Edward 1873–1946 Am. writer; author chiefly of western adventure stories

White Theodore Harold 1915–1986 Am. writer; best known for *The Making of the President, 1960* and *The Making of the President, 1964*

White William Allen 1868–1944 Am. journalist & writer; known for developing Emporia (Kans.) *Gazette* into one of most notable small papers of U.S.

White·field \'hwīt-ˌfēld, 'hwit-, 'wīt-, 'wit-\ George 1714–1770 Eng. Methodist revivalist; toured Great Britain and America; credited with inspiring foundation of more than 50 colleges and universities in U.S.

White·head \'hwīt-ˌhed, 'wīt-\ Alfred North 1861–1947 Eng. math & philos.; author of *The Principles of Natural Knowledge, Science and the Modern World, Aims of Education*, etc.

Whitehead William 1715–1785 Eng. dram.; poet laureate (1757–85); known for his most successful play, the comedy *School for Lovers*

Whit·man \'hwīt-mən, 'wīt-\ Marcus 1802–1847 & his wife Narcissa 1808–1847 née *Prentiss* Am. missionaries & pioneers; missionaries to Cayuse, Walla Walla, Umatilla tribes; instrumental in securing Oregon country for U.S.

Whitman Walt \'wȯlt\ 1819–1892 orig. *Walter* Am. poet; best known as author of *Leaves of Grass*; saw himself as great poet of democracy; well-known poems include "Song of Myself," "I Sing the Body Electric," etc. — **Whit·man·esque** \ˌhwīt-mə-'nesk, ˌwit-\ *or* **Whit·man·ni·an** \hwīt-'mä-nē-ən, wit-\ *adj*

Whit·ney \'hwīt-nē, 'wīt-\ Eli 1765–1825 Am. inventor; invented cotton gin (1793); devised system of manufacturing interchangeable parts for guns

Whitney Gertrude Vanderbilt 1875–1942 Am. sculptor & art patron; founded (1930) Whitney Museum of American Art in New York City

Whitney Josiah Dwight 1819–1896 Am. geologist; measured highest peak in Calif., named Mt. Whitney for him

Whitney William Dwight 1827–1894 *bro. of J.D.* Am. philologist; noted as scholar in Sanskrit and in linguistic science, etc.; editor of 1864 *Webster's Dictionary*, etc.

Whit·ta·ker \'hwi-ti-kər, 'wit-\ Charles Evans 1901–1973 Am. jurist; assoc. justice, U.S. Supreme Court (1957–62)

Whit·tier \'hwit-tē-ər, 'wit-\ John Greenleaf 1807–1892 Am. poet; author of well known poems "Massachusetts to Virginia," "Snow=Bound," "Barefoot Boy," etc.; wrote books including *Legends of New England of Prose and Verse*, etc.

Wic·lif or **Wick·liffe** var of WYCLIFFE

Wi·dor \vē-'dòr\ Charles-Marie 1844–1937 Fr. organist & composer; composed ballets, operas, organ symphonies, etc.

Wie·land \'vē-,länt\ Christoph Martin 1733–1813 Ger. author; works, chief representatives of the Rococo in German literature, included novels and romances establishing genre of *Bildungsroman*, and fantastic tale *Dschinnistan* on which Mozart based *Magic Flute*

Wieland Heinrich 1877–1957 Ger. chem.; awarded 1927 Nobel prize for chemistry for studying gall acids and related substances

Wien \'vēn\ Wilhelm 1864–1928 Ger. physicist; awarded 1911 Nobel prize for physics for discoveries on the heat radiated by black objects

Wie·ner \'wē-nər\ Norbert 1894–1964 Am. math.; best known as founder of cybernetics (a term he coined)

Wie·schaus \'wē-,shaús\ Eric F. 1947–   Am. biol.; awarded (with E.B. Lewis, C. Nuesslein-Volhard) 1995 Nobel prize for physiology or medicine for discoveries about how genes control early embryonic development

Wie·sel \vē-'zel, wē-\ El·ie \'e-lē\ 1928–   Am. (Rom.-born) writer; awarded 1986 Nobel prize for peace for his vigorous efforts on behalf of victims of oppression and racial discrimination

Wie·sel \'vē-səl\ Torsten N. 1924–   Swed. neurobiologist; awarded (with R.W. Sperry and D.H. Hubel) 1981 Nobel prize for physiology or medicine for research on the organization and functioning of the brain

Wig·gin \'wi-gən\ Kate Douglas 1856–1923 Am. writer & educ.; author of *Rebecca of Sunnybrook Farm,* etc.; a founder of California Kindergarten Training School

Wig·ner \'wig-nər\ Eugene Paul 1902–1995 Am. (Hung.-born) physicist; awarded (with M.G. Mayer and J.H. Jensen) 1963 Nobel prize in physics for contributions to the understanding of atomic nuclei and elementary particles

Wil·ber·force \'wil-bər-,fòrs, -,fòrs\ William 1759–1833 Eng. philanthropist & abolitionist; won abolition of slave trade (1807); act abolishing slavery passed one month after his death

Wil·bur \'wil-bər\ Richard Purdy 1921–   Am. poet & translator; poet laureate (1987–88); published widely acclaimed translation of Molière; wrote lyrics for musical *Candide;* published *New and Collected Poems,* etc.

Wilde \'wī(ə)ld\ Oscar Fingal O'Flahertie Wills 1854–1900 Irish writer; spokesman for art for art's sake; published poems, novel *The Picture of Dorian Gray,* fairy tales, tragedy, comedies including *The Importance of Being Earnest;* tried on charge of sodomy, convicted, imprisoned — **Wil·de·an** \'wil-dē-ən\ *adj*

Wil·der \'wil-dər\ Billy 1906–   orig. *Samuel Wilder* Am. (Austrian-born) film director & writer; known esp. for hard-edged, even cynical melodramas and comedies, including *Double Indemnity, Sunset Boulevard,* and *Some Like It Hot*

Wil·der Thornton Niven 1897–1975 Am. author; best known for plays *Our Town, The Skin of Our Teeth, The Matchmaker,* etc. and for novel *The Bridge of San Luis Rey,* etc.

Wi·ley \'wī-lē\ Harvey Washington 1844–1930 Am. chem. & reformer; led campaign against food adulteration; instrumental in securing passage of Food and Drugs Act (1906)

Wil·hel·mi·na \,wil-(,)hel-'mē-nə, ,wi-lə-'mē-\ 1880–1962 queen of the Netherlands (1890–1948); encouraged Dutch resistance during German occupation in WWII

Wilkes \'wilks\ Charles 1798–1877 Am. naval officer & explorer; established that Antarctica is a continent

Wilkes John 1725–1797 Eng. polit.; championed Parliamentary reform, colonial rights in American Revolution, civil rights, freedom of press, etc.

Wil·kins \'wil-kənz\ Sir George Hubert 1888–1958 Australian explorer; pioneered the use of the submarine for polar research

Wilkins Mary Eleanor — see Mary E. FREEMAN

Wilkins Maurice Hugh Frederick 1916– Brit. biophysicist; awarded (with J.D. Watson and F.H.C. Crick) 1962 Nobel prize for physics for work on DNA

Wilkins Roy 1901–1981 Am. civil rights leader; executive director (1955–77) of the National Association for the Advancement of Colored People

Wil·kin·son \'wil-kən-sən\ Ellen Cicely 1891–1947 Eng. feminist & polit.; active in woman suffrage and labor movements

Wilkinson Sir Geoffrey 1921– Brit. chem.; awarded (with E. Fischer) 1973 Nobel prize for chemistry for work on organometallic compounds

Wilkinson James 1757–1825 Am. gen. & adventurer; served in American Revolution; after the war conspired to turn Kentucky region over to Spain; represented U.S. in taking over Louisiana Purchase; implicated in Aaron Burr's conspiracy but acquitted

Will \'wil\ George Frederick 1941– Am. journalist; known for his conservative commentary on national and international events in print and broadcast media

Wil·lard \'wi-lərd\ Emma 1787–1870 née *Hart* Am. educ.; pioneer in field of higher education for women; established and directed several schools, including Troy Female Seminary (now Emma Willard School, 1821–38)

Willard Frances Elizabeth Caroline 1839–1898 Am. educ. & reformer; devoted herself to temperance movement

Will·cocks \'wil-käks\ Sir William 1852–1932 Brit. engineer; designed dam at Aswan, Egypt; undertook irrigation work in South Africa (1901), Mesopotamia (1911)

Wil·liam \'wil-yəm\ name of 4 kings of England: **I** (*the Conqueror*) *ca* 1028–1087 (reigned 1066–87); invaded England (1066) and defeated Harold at Hastings; completed conquest (1070); established feudal system; ordered compilation of Domesday Book, etc.; **II** (*Ru·fus* \'rü-fəs\) *ca* 1056–1100 (reigned 1087–1100); provoked insurrection of barons by ruthless, shortsighted, rapacious rule; **III** 1650–1702 (reigned 1689–1702—see MARY); **IV** 1765–1837 (reigned 1830–37); caused long political crisis by obstructing Second Reform Bill; last English sovereign to attempt to force a ministry (Sir Robert Peel's) on unwilling majority

William I 1533–1584 *the Silent* prince of Orange & founder of the Du. Republic; leader in independence from Spain

William I 1797–1888 *Wilhelm Friedrich Ludwig* king of Prussia (1861–88) Ger. emp. (1871–88); generally acceded to policies of Bismarck

William II 1859–1941 *Friedrich Wilhelm Viktor Albert* Ger. emp. & king of Prussia (1888–1918); dominant force of Central Powers at beginning of WWI; by 1918 saw defeat but refused to surrender; abdicated

William 1882–1951 *Friedrich Wilhelm Victor August Ernst* crown prince of Germany (1888–1918); renounced rights to crowns of Prussia and German Empire (1918)

William of Malmes·bury \\'mämz-₁ber-ē, 'mälmz-, -b(ə-)rē\\ *ca* 1090–*ca* 1143 Eng. hist.; wrote *Gesta regum Anglorum, Gesta pontificum Anglorum, Historia novella* bringing his English history to 1142

Wil·liams \\'wil-yəmz\\ Elizabeth 1943–   *Betty Williams* Irish peace worker; awarded (with M. Corrigan) 1976 Nobel prize for peace for organizing a movement to end Protestant-Catholic fighting in Northern Ireland

Williams John Towner 1932–   Am. conductor & composer; conductor, Boston Pops Orchestra (1980–95); known esp. for composing scores for films *Jaws, Star Wars, E.T., Schindler's List,* etc.

Williams Ralph Vaughan — see VAUGHAN WILLIAMS

Williams Roger 1603?–1683 Am. (Eng.-born) clergyman & founder of Rhode Island colony; founded Providence (1636), first settlement in Rhode Island; famous as apostle of religious toleration and advocate of democracy and liberal government

Williams Ted 1918–   *Theodore Samuel Williams* Am. baseball player; outfielder, Boston Red Sox (1939–60); two-time winner of baseball's Triple Crown (best batting average, most home runs, and most runs batted in during a single season); lifetime batting average of .344 (.406 in 1941)

Williams Tennessee 1911–1983 orig. *Thomas Lanier Williams* Am. dram.; wrote *Cat on a Hot Tin Roof, The Glass Menagerie, A Streetcar Named Desire;* created a world in which an aura of romantic gentility masks feelings of frustration and anger

Williams William Carlos 1883–1963 Am. writer; author of verse, stories, essays, and novels including trilogy *White Mule, In the Money, The Build-Up*

Wil·lis \\'wil-əs\\ Nathaniel Parker 1806–1867 Am. editor & writer; wrote *Poetical Scripture Sketches, Fugitive Poetry,* etc.

Will·kie \\'wil-kē\\ Wendell Lewis 1892–1944 Am. polit.; Republican nominee for president (1940)

Wil·loch \\'vi-lək\\ Kå·re \\'kôr-ə\\ Isaachsen 1928–   prime min. of Norway (1981–86)

Will·stät·ter \\'vil-₁shte-tər, 'wil-₁ste-\\ Richard 1872–1942 Ger. chem.; awarded 1915 Nobel prize for chemistry for research on chlorophyll and other coloring matter in plants

Wil·son \\'wil-sən\\ Charles Thomson Rees 1869–1959 Scot. physicist; awarded (with A.H. Compton) 1927 Nobel prize for physics for discovering a method of tracing the paths of ions

Wilson Edmund 1895–1972 Am. writer; author of influential criticism of literature and politics, including *Axel's Castle, To the Finland Station, Patriotic Gore,* etc.

Wilson Sir (James) Harold 1916–1995 Brit. prime min. (1964–70, 1974–76)

Wilson Henry 1812–1875 orig. *Jeremiah Jones Colbath* Am. polit.; founder of Free-Soil party (1848); helped found Republican party; vice pres. of the U.S. (1873–75)

Wilson John 1785–1854 pseud. *Christopher North* Scot. author; friend of Wordsworth, Southey, Coleridge, DeQuincey; published poetry, prose fiction, critical essays, etc.

Wilson Kenneth G. 1936–   Am. physicist; awarded 1982 Nobel prize for physics for his method of analyzing the behavior of matter when it changes form

Wilson Robert Woodrow 1936–   Am. physicist; awarded (with A. Penzias) 1978 Nobel prize for physics for developing the 'big bang' theory of creation

Wilson (Thomas) Wood·row \'wu̇-ˌdrō\ 1856–1924 28th pres. of the U.S. (1913–21); oversaw 17th, 18th, 19th amendments, Child Labor Law; maintained neutrality in WWI until 1917, then made it a crusade to "make the world safe for democracy"; a leading advocate of the League of Nations; awarded 1919 Nobel prize for peace — **Wil·so·ni·an** \wil-'sō-nē-ən\ *adj*

Winck·el·mann \'viŋ-kəl-ˌmän, 'wiŋ-kəl-mən\ Johann Joachim 1717–1768 Ger. archaeol. & art hist.; defined Greek aesthetic and essentially created Neoclassical movement in the arts

Win·daus \'vin-ˌdau̇s\ Adolf Otto Reinhold 1876–1959 Ger. chem.; awarded 1928 Nobel prize for chemistry for studying sterols and their connection with vitamins

Win·disch·grätz \ˌvin-dish-'grets\ Alfred Candidus Ferdinand 1787–1862 Fürst *zu Windischgrätz* Austrian field marshal; suppressed uprisings in Prague and Vienna (1848) helped place Francis Joseph I to throne

Windsor Duke of — see EDWARD VIII

Win·frey \'win-frē\ Oprah 1954–   Am. talk show host; host of "The Oprah Winfrey Show" (1985–)

Win·gate \'win-ˌgāt, -gət\ Orde \'ȯrd\ Charles 1903–1944 Brit. gen.; recognized as expert in irregular mobile tactics in Ethiopia, China, Burma

Wingate Sir (Francis) Reginald 1861–1953 Brit. gen.; involved in reconquest of Sudan (1896–98); governor general of Sudan (1899–1916); high commissioner of Egypt (1917–19)

Wins·low \'winz-ˌlō\ Edward 1595–1655 gov. of Plymouth colony (1633, 1636, 1644)

Win·sor \'win-zər\ Justin 1831–1897 Am. librarian & hist.; a founder of American Library Association (1876)

Win·throp \'win(t)-thrəp\ John 1588–1649 1st gov. of Mass. Bay colony; foremost Puritan founder of New England; opposed religious dissident Anne Hutchinson; presided at court that banished her

Winthrop John 1606–1676 *son of prec.* gov. of Connecticut colony (1657, 1659–76)

Winthrop John 1638–1707 *son of prec.* gov. of Connecticut colony (1698–1707)

Wise \'wīz\ Stephen Samuel 1874–1949 Am. (Hung.-born) rabbi; a leader in democratization of Reform Judaism, in civic reform, and in Zionist movement

Wise·man \\'wīz-mən\\ Nicholas Patrick Stephen 1802–1865 Eng. cardinal & author; first Roman Catholic cardinal to reside in England since the Reformation; first archbishop of Westminster

Wiss·ler \\'wis-lər\\ Clark 1870–1947 Am. anthropol.; author of *North American Indians of the Plains, The American Indian*, etc.

Wis·ter \\'wis-tər\\ Owen 1860–1938 Am. nov.; author of *The Virginian*, which established the cowboy as an American folk hero

With·er \\'wi-thər\\ George 1588–1667 Eng. poet & pamphleteer; imprisoned twice for libelous pamphlets and satire; his best verse collected in *Juvenalia*

Witt, de \\də-'vit\\ Johan 1625–1672 Du. statesman; rebuilt Dutch navy after First Dutch War with England; restored finances, extended commerce in Far East; concluded successful Second Anglo-Dutch War

Wit·te \\'vi-tə\\ Sergey Yulyevich 1849–1915 Russ. statesman; negotiated Treaty of Portsmouth; first constitutional premier of the Russian Empire

Wit·te, de \\də-'vi-tə\\ Emanuel 1617–1692 Du. painter; chief master of Dutch architectural painting; known also for genre scenes

Wit·te·kind \\'vi-tə-‚kint\ *or* **Wi·du·kind** \\'vē-də-\ *d ca* 807 Saxon warrior; leader of Saxons against Charlemagne

Witt·gen·stein \\'vit-gən-‚shtīn, -‚stīn\\ Ludwig Josef Johan 1889–1951 Brit. (Austrian-born) philos.; exerted great influence on logical positivism, linguistic analysis, semantics — **Witt·gen·stein·ian** \\‚vit-gən-'shtī-nē-ən, -'stī-\ *adj*

Wit·tig \\'vi-tik\\ Georg 1897–1987 Ger. chem.; awarded (with H.C. Brown) 1979 Nobel prize for chemistry for developing compounds capable of producing chemical bonds useful in the manufacture of drugs and in other industrial processes

Wode·house \\'wúd-‚haús\\ Sir Pel·ham \\'pe-ləm\\ Grenville 1881–1975 Am. (Eng.-born) writer; best known as author of humorous novels centered about Bertie Wooster and Jeeves, the ultimate "gentleman's gentleman"

Wof·fing·ton \\'wä-fiŋ-tən\\ Margaret *ca* 1714–1760 Peg Woffington Irish actress; known for playing "breeches parts" (male roles played a female actor); played chief roles in comedy and tragedy, esp. as elegant women of fashion

Wol·cott \\'wúl-kət\\ Oliver 1726–1797 *son of Roger* Am. polit.; signer of Declaration of Independence; governor of Connecticut (1796–97)

Wolcott Oliver 1760–1833 *son of prec.* Am. polit.; governor of Connecticut (1817–27)

Wolcott Roger 1679–1767 Am. colonial administrator; governor of Connecticut (1751–54)

Wolf \\'vȯlf\\ Friedrich August 1759–1824 Ger. philologist; argued that the *Iliad* and *Odyssey* are the work of several authors; championed the study of classical antiquity

Wolf Hugo Philipp Jakob 1860–1903 Austrian composer; strongly influenced by Liszt and Wagner; composed over 300 songs, opera, instrumental works, etc.

Wolfe \\'wúlf\\ Charles 1791–1823 Irish poet; author of short stirring elegy "The Burial of Sir John Moore at Corunna"

Wolfe James 1727–1759 Brit. gen.; completed British conquest of North America with capture of Quebec from French

Wolfe Thomas Clayton 1900–1938 Am. nov.; author of *Look Homeward, Angel; Of Time and the River,* etc.

Wolff *or* **Wolf** \ˈvȯlf\ Christian 1679–1754 Freiherr *von Wolff* Ger. philos. & math.; chief German spokesman of the Enlightenment, 18th-century philosophical movement

Wolff \ˈvȯlf\ Kaspar Friedrich 1734–1794 Ger. anatomist; advanced the germ-layer theory of embryonic development

Wol·fram von Esch·en·bach \ˈwu̇l-frəm-vän-ˈe-shən-ˌbäk, ˈvȯl-ˌfräm-, -ˌbäk\ *ca* 1170–*ca* 1220 Ger. poet & minnesinger; author of epic *Parzival,* basis of Wagner's libretto of his opera *Parsifal*

Wol·las·ton \ˈwu̇-lə-stən\ William Hyde 1766–1828 Eng. scientist; devised metallurgical techniques that were basis of modern industrial processes; discovered palladium and rhodium

Woll·stone·craft \ˈwu̇l-stən-ˌkraft\ Mary 1759–1797 *wife of William Godwin & mother of M.W. Shelley* Eng. feminist & writer; known esp. for *Vindication of the Rights of Women*

Wolse·ley \ˈwu̇lz-lē\ 1st Viscount 1833–1913 *Garnet Joseph Wolseley* Brit. field marshal; served in Second Burmese War, Crimean War, Sepoy Mutiny, etc.; instrumental in modernizing British army

Wol·sey \ˈwu̇l-zē\ Thomas *ca* 1475–1530 Eng. cardinal & statesman; dominated the government of Henry VIII (1515–1529); the anticlerical character of English Reformation was a reaction to his unpopularity

Wood \ˈwu̇d\ Grant 1892–1942 Am. painter; evolved sharply realistic style; best known for painting *American Gothic*

Wood Leonard 1860–1927 Am. physician & gen.; army chief of staff (1910–14); gov.-gen. of Philippines (1921–27)

Wood·ward \ˈwu̇d-wərd\ Robert Burns 1917–1979 Am. chem.; awarded 1965 Nobel prize for chemistry for syntheses of complex organic substances

Woolf \ˈwu̇lf\ (Adeline) Virginia 1882–1941 née *Stephen* Eng. author; a central figure in Bloomsbury group; made original contribution to form of the novel, stressing psychological minutiae of experience in *Mrs. Dalloway, To the Lighthouse, Orlando,* etc.

Wooll·cott \ˈwu̇l-kət\ Alexander 1887–1943 Am. writer; remembered chiefly as a leader of famed Algonquin Round Table

Wool·ley \ˈwu̇-lē\ Sir Charles Leonard 1880–1960 Eng. archaeol.; notable for research and writings on the Sumerians

Wool·worth \ˈwu̇l-(ˌ)wərth\ Frank Winfield 1852–1919 Am. merchant; developed extensive chain of five-and-ten-cent stores throughout the U.S.

Worces·ter \ˈwu̇s-tər\ Joseph Emerson 1784–1865 Am. lexicographer; chief rival of Noah Webster in the mid 19th century

Worde \ˈwȯrd\ Wynkyn de *d* 1534? Eng. (Alsatian-born) printer; first printer in England to use italic type (1524)

Words·worth \ˈwərdz-(ˌ)wərth\ William 1770–1850 Eng. poet; poet laureate (1843–50); wrote (with S.T. Coleridge) *Lyrical Ballads* (1798), considered one of the first and greatest works of English Romantic movement; known esp. for poems "Lines composed a few miles above Tintern Abbey," "Intimations of Immortality," etc. — **Words·worth·ian** \ˌwərdz-ˈwər-thē-ən, -thē-\ *adj*

Wot·ton \'wü-t°n, 'wä-\ Sir Henry 1568–1639 Eng. diplomat & poet; best known for poem "You Meaner Beauties of the Night"

Wran·gel \'raŋ-gəl\ Baron Pyotr Nikolayevich 1878–1928 Russ. gen.; commanded volunteer White Russian army (from 1920)

Wren \'ren\ Sir Christopher 1632–1723 Eng. architect; greatest English architect of his time; designed and built 53 churches in London, including St. Paul's Cathedral; a founder of the Royal Society

Wright \'rīt\ Frank Lloyd 1867–1959 Am. architect; chief theorist and practitioner of "Prairie school" of architecture; showed mastery of space, form, human-centered design; generally regarded as American architecture's greatest creative genius

Wright Joseph 1734–1797 *Wright of Derby* Eng. painter; known for candlelight or fireside scenes and as pioneer in depiction of industrial scenes

Wright Or·ville \'ȯr-vəl\ 1871–1948 & his bro. Wilbur 1867–1912 Am. pioneers in aviation; made first successful flight in a motor-powered airplane at Kill Devil Hills, near Kitty Hawk, N.C. (1903)

Wright Richard 1908–1960 Am. author; wrote fiction dealing with the prejudice, alienation, and suffering of fellow urban American blacks, including novels *Native Son*, etc., stories, autobiography, nonfiction

Wright Willard Huntington 1888–1939 pseud. *S. S. Van Dine* \van-'dīn, vən-\ Am. writer; creator of detective Philo Vance in series of novels

Wundt \'vůnt\ Wilhelm 1832–1920 Ger. physiol. & psychol.; founder of experimental psychology; believed psychology must be based on experience, known through introspection

Wu-ti — see HAN WU TI

Wy·att *or* **Wy·at** \'wī-ət\ Sir Thomas 1503–1543 Eng. poet & diplomat; introduced the sonnet (with his creation of concluding rhymed couplet), *ottava rima* and *terza rima* verse forms, and French rondeau into English literature

Wych·er·ley \'wi-chər-lē\ William 1640–1716 Eng. dram.; best known for *The Country Wife* and *The Plain Dealer*, comedies satirizing social customs and human foibles

Wyc·liffe \'wi-,klif, -kləf\ John *ca* 1330–1384 Eng. religious reformer & theol.; developed politico-ecclesiastical theories requiring church to give up possessions; attacked church beliefs and practices; initiated first translation of Bible into English; considered forerunner of Protestant Reformation — **Wyc·liff·ian** \wi-'kli-fē-ən\ *adj*

Wy·eth \'wī-əth\ Andrew Newell 1917–   Am. painter; known esp. for his tempera paintings in muted earth tones naturalistically depicting the inhabitants and landscapes around Pennsylvania's Brandywine Valley and Maine's central coast

Wyeth Newell Convers 1882–1945 *father of A. N.* Am. painter; best known for illustrations of Stevenson's novels (*Treasure Island, Kidnapped*, etc.) and edition of *Robin Hood*

Wyld \'wī(ə)ld\ Henry Cecil Kennedy 1870–1945 Eng. lexicographer; edited *Universal Dictionary of the English Language*

Wy·ler \\'wī-lər\\ William 1902–1981 Am. (Ger.-born) film director; noted for finely crafted pictorial compositions in films *Wuthering Heights, The Best Years of Our Lives, The Heiress,* etc.

Wy·lie \\'wī-lē\\ Elinor Morton 1885–1928 *Mrs. William Rose Benét,* née *Hoyt* Am. poet & nov.; author of verse *Nets to Catch the Wind, Black Armour,* etc., novel *The Orphan Angel,* etc.

Wylie Philip Gordon 1902–1971 Am. writer; best known for non-fiction *Generation of Vipers* (1942)

Wynd·ham \\'win-dəm\\ George 1863–1913 Eng. polit. & writer; as chief secy. for Ireland (1900–05), adopted conciliatory program to maintain union, promote economic development; edited North's version of Plutarch's *Lives,* Shakespeare's poems

X

Xan·thip·pe \\zan-'thi-pē, -'ti-\\ 5th cent. B.C. *wife of Socrates;* proverbial for her peevish scolding and quarrelsome temper

Xa·vi·er \\'zāv-yər, 'zā-vē-ər, ig-'zā-\\ Saint Francis 1506–1552 Span. *Francisco Ja·vier* \\hä-'vyer\\ Span. Jesuit missionary; helped found Jesuit order (1534); missionary in Goa, India, and Japan

Xe·noc·ra·tes \\zi-'nä-krə-ˌtēz\\ 396–314 B.C. Greek philos.; credited with classical distinction among mind, soul, and body

Xe·noph·a·nes \\zi-'nä-fə-ˌnēz\\ *ca* 560–*ca* 478 B.C. Greek philos.; wrote poems ridiculing anthropomorphism in religion, immorality of Olympian gods

Xen·o·phon \\'ze-nə-fən\\ *ca* 431–*ca* 352 B.C. Greek hist.; wrote *Anabasis,* highly regarded by ancient literary critics and an important influence on Latin literature

Xer·xes I \\'zərk-ˌsēz\\ *ca* 519–465 B.C. *the Great* king of Persia (486–465); invaded Greece by bridging Hellespont; invasion ultimately failed, signalling beginning of decline of Achaemenid Empire

Y

Yale \\'yā(ə)l\\ Elihu 1649–1721 Eng. (Am.-born) colonial administrator in India; gave books and goods to Collegiate School, which took name Yale College (1718)

Yal·ow \\'ya-ˌlō\\ Rosalyn Sussman 1921– Am. med. physicist; awarded (with R. Guillemin and A. Schally) 1977 Nobel prize for physiology or medicine for research concerning the role of hormones in the body's chemistry

Ya·ma·ga·ta \\ˌyä-mə-'gä-tə\\ Prince Aritomo 1838–1922 Jp. gen. & statesman; advocated adoption of Western military weapons and techniques; chiefly responsible for modernization of army

Ya·ma·mo·to \ˌyä-mə-ˈmō-(ˌ)tō\ Isoroku 1884–1943 Jp. admiral; devised Japanese naval strategy in the Pacific including attack on Pearl Harbor

Ya·ma·shi·ta \ˌyä-ˈmä-shi-ˌtä\ Tomoyuki 1885–1946 Jp. gen.; commanded Japanese forces in Malayan and Philippine campaigns

Yang Chen Ning \ˈyäŋ-ˈjən-ˈniŋ\ 1922–   Chin. physicist; awarded (with T.D. Lee) 1957 Nobel prize for physics for work disproving the law of conservation of parity

Yeats \ˈyāts\ William Butler 1865–1939 Irish poet & dram.; awarded 1923 Nobel prize for literature for his poems; leader of Irish literary revival with poems, essays, plays; best known poems include "The Wild Swans at Coole," "Sailing to Byzantium," "The Second Coming," etc. — **Yeats·ian** \ˈyāt-sē-ən\ adj

Yelt·sin \ˈyelt-sən, ˈyel-sin\ Boris Nikolayevich 1931–   pres. of Russian Federation (1990–   )

Yen Hsi–shan \ˈyen-ˈshē-ˈshän\ 1883–1960 Chin. gen.; successfully opposed Japanese in northern China (1935–37)

Yer·kes \ˈyər-kēz\ Charles Ty·son \ˈtī-sᵊn\ 1837–1905 Am. financier; invested in railroads, Philadelphia transit system, etc.

Yev·tu·shen·ko \ˌyef-tə-ˈsheŋ-(ˌ)kō\ Yevgeny Aleksandrovich 1933–   Soviet (Russ.-born) writer; a leader among the post-Stalin Russian poets calling for a Soviet literature based on aesthetic rather than political standards; known esp. for love lyrics and poems that were meditations on contemporary concerns

Yo·nai \ˈyō-ˌnī\ Mitsumasa 1880–1948 Jp. admiral & statesman; min. of navy (1937–39, 1944–45); prime min. (1940)

York \ˈyȯrk\ Alvin Cullum 1887–1964 Am. soldier; in battle of Argonne (1918), singlehandedly captured 132 German soldiers

Yo·shi·hi·to \ˌyō-shi-ˈhē-(ˌ)tō\ 1879–1926 emp. of Japan (1912–26); during reign, Japan joined Allies in WWI and became leading world power

You·mans \ˈyü-mənz\ Vincent 1898–1946 Am. composer; wrote scores for Broadway musicals including No, No, Nanette with songs "Tea for Two" and "I Want to Be Happy"

Young \ˈyəŋ\ Andrew Jackson, Jr. 1932–   Am. polit.; with Martin Luther King Jr., a leader in the Southern Christian Leadership Conference; U.S. ambassador to U.N. (1977–79)

Young Brig·ham \ˈbri-gəm\ 1801–1877 Am. Mormon leader; succeeded Joseph Smith as head of Mormon church (1844); directed and superintended mass migration of Mormons to Salt Lake City, Utah

Young Cy 1867–1955 Denton True Young Am. baseball player; winner of more major league games than any other pitcher in baseball history, his victory total being variously recorded as 509 or 511; the annual awards for best pitcher in the American and National Leagues named in his honor

Young Edward 1683–1765 Eng. poet; best known for Night Thoughts which gave rise to school of "graveyard poets"

Young Francis Brett 1884–1954 Eng. nov.; author of Dark Tower, They Seek a Country, A Man About the House, etc.

Young Owen D. 1874–1962 Am. lawyer; involved in plan for German reparations after WWI

Young Whitney Moore 1921–1971 Am. civil rights leader; executive director, National Urban League (1961–71); advocated "domestic Marshall Plan," much of which was included in Pres. Lyndon Johnson's antipoverty program

Young·hus·band \\'yəŋ-ˌhəz-bənd\\ Sir Francis Edward 1863–1942 Brit. explorer & author; explored mountains between China and Kashmir, Pamir mountains, forbidden city of Lhasa; wrote *Heart of a Continent, Everest: The Challenge,* etc.

Your·ce·nar \\ˌyür-sə-'när\\ Marguerite 1903–1987 orig. surname *de Crayencour* Fr. author; best known for erudite, meditative works of psychological insight, esp. novel *Mémoires d'Hadrien* about 2nd-century Roman emperor; first woman elected to Académie Française

Yp·si·lan·tis \\ˌip-sə-'lan-tē\\ Alexandros 1792–1828 & his bro. Demetrios 1793–1832 Greek revolutionaries; Alexandros was in command of secret organization Philiki Extairia; defeated by Turks (1821); Demetrios fought in war for Greek independence (1821); commander in chief, Greek forces (1828–30)

Yüan Shih–k'ai \\yü-'än-'shir-'kī, -'shē\\ 1859–1916 Chin. soldier & statesman; pres. of China (1913–16); restored Confucianism

Yu·ka·wa \\yü-'kä-wə\\ Hideki 1907–1981 Jp. physicist; awarded 1949 Nobel prize for physics for predicting the existence of the meson

Yung–lo \\'yüŋ-'lō\\ 1360–1424 orig. *Chu Ti;* often called *Ch'eng Tsu* Chin. emp. (1402–24); his reign considered pinnacle of Ming dynasty's power

Z

Zagh·lūl \\zag-'lül\\ Sa'd \\'säd\\ 1857–1927 *Sa'd Zaghlūl Pasha ibn Ibrāhīm* Egypt. statesman; premier of Egypt (1924); active advocate of Egyptian independence

Za·har·i·as \\zə-'har-ē-əs\\ Babe 1914–1956 *Mildred Ella Zaharias* née *Di·drik·son* \\'dē-drik-sən\\ Am. athlete; regarded as one of the greatest female athletes in sports history; excelled in basketball, track and field events, baseball, swimming, figure skating, and above all golf; won Olympic gold medals for 80-meter hurdles and javelin throw (1932)

Za·ha·roff \\zə-'här-əf, -ˌôf\\ Sir Basil 1849–1936 orig. *Basileios Zacharias* Fr. (Russ.-born) banker & armament contractor; Allied intelligence agent in WWI

Za·ï·mis \\zä-'ē-məs, -mēs\\ Alexandros 1855–1936 Greek statesman; helped bring about annexation of Crete; president of Republic of Greece (1929–35)

Zang·will \\'zaŋ-ˌgwil, -ˌwil\\ Israel 1864–1926 Eng. dram. & nov.; author of plays and novels on Jewish themes and themes of international amity

Zech·a·ri·ah \\ˌze-kə-'rī-ə\\ *fl* 520–518 B.C. Hebrew prophet; with Haggai, persuaded Jews to rebuild the Temple

Ze·dil·lo Pon·ce de Le·ón \\sā-'thē-(ˌ)yō-'pón-sā-(ˌ)thä-lā-'ón\\ Ernesto 1951– pres. of Mexico (1994–)

Zee·man \\'zā-ˌmän, -mən\\ Pieter 1865–1943 Du. physicist; awarded (with H.A. Lorentz) 1902 Nobel prize for physics for discovering the Zeeman effect of magnetism on light

Zef·fi·rel·li \\ˌze-fə-'re-lē\\ Franco 1923–   orig. *Gian-Franco Corsi* Ital. opera, film, and theater director; noted for the authentic detail and opulence of his productions including opera *La Traviata* and films *Taming of the Shrew*, *Romeo and Juliet*, etc.

Zeng·er \\'zeŋ-gər, -ər\\ John Peter 1697–1746 Am. (Ger.-born) journalist & printer; acquitted in libel trial in decision regarded as fundamental in establishing freedom of the press in America

Ze·no of Citium \\'zē-(ˌ)nō-əv-'si-sh(ē-)əm\\ *ca* 335–*ca* 263 B.C. Greek philos. & founder of Stoic school

Zeno of Elea \\'ē-lē-ə\\ *ca* 495–*ca* 430 B.C. Greek philos.; famed for paradoxes that contributed to development of logical rigor

Ze·no·bia \\zə-'nō-bē-ə\\ *d* after A.D. 274 queen of Palmyra (267 to 268–272); ambitious to extend power over Roman empire in the East; defeated (271–72) by Emperor Aurelian

Zeph·a·ni·ah \\ˌzef-ə-'nī-ə\\ *or* **So·pho·ni·as** \\ˌsä-fə-'nī-əs, ˌsō-\\ 7th cent. B.C. Hebrew prophet

Zep·pe·lin \\ˌtse-pə-'lēn, 'ze-p(ə-)lən\\ Ferdinand Adolf August Heinrich 1838–1917 Graf *von Zeppelin* Ger. gen. & aeronaut; constructed first airship of rigid type known as Zeppelin (1900)

Zer·ni·ke \\'zer-ni-kə, 'zər-\\ Frits 1888–1966 Du. physicist; awarded 1953 Nobel prize for physics for invention of phase contrast microscope

Zeux·is \\'zük-səs\\ 5th cent. B.C. Greek painter; works not extant, but painted chiefly genre and mythological scenes and still lifes; by legend, birds pecked at his realistic grapes

Zhao Zi·yang *or* **Chao Tzu-yang** \\'jaù-(d)zə-'yäŋ\\ 1919– Chin. polit.; premier (1980–87); gen. secy. of Chinese Communist party (1987–89)

Zhda·nov \\zhə-'dä-nəf, 'shtä-\\ Andrey Aleksandrovich 1896–1948 Soviet polit.; after WWII, directed policy severely restricting Soviet cultural activities

Zhu·kov \\'zhü-ˌkóf, -ˌkóv\\ Georgy Konstantinovich 1896–1974 Soviet marshal; defended Moscow against Germans (1941); broke sieges of Stalingrad, Leningrad (1942–43); commanded final assault on Berlin; in charge of Soviet occupation force (1945–46)

Zieg·feld \\'zig-ˌfeld, 'zēg- *also* -ˌfēld, -fəld\\ Florenz 1869–1932 Am. theatrical producer; introduced the "revue" with *The Follies of 1907*, followed by annual editions known as *Ziegfeld's Follies*

Zieg·ler \\'tsē-glər\\ Karl 1898–1973 Ger. chem.; awarded (with G. Natta) 1963 Nobel prize for chemistry for production of organometallic compounds

Zim·mer·mann \\'zi-mər-mən, 'tsi-mər-ˌmän\\ Arthur 1864–1940 Ger. statesman; sent "Zimmermann telegram" to Mexico (1917), intercepted by British, that helped lead U.S. into WWI

Zi·nov·yev *or* **Zi·nov·iev** \\zý-'nóf-yəf\\ Grigory Yevseyevich 1883–1936 orig. *Ovsel Gershon Aronov Radomylsky* Soviet revolutionary; a close associate of Lenin in the Bolshevik Party up to the October Revolution; a leading figure in the Soviet Union's Communist Party until falling victim to Stalin's Great Purge

Zins·ser \\'zin(t)-sər\\ Hans 1878–1940 Am. bacteriol.; demonstrated method of immunizing against some varieties of typhus

Zin·zen·dorf \\'zin-zən-ˌdȯrf, 'tsin-sən-\ Nikolaus Ludwig 1700–1760 Graf *von Zinzendorf* religious reformer; instrumental in reviving and establishing Moravian Brethren (Renewed Church of the United Brethren)

Žiž·ka \\'zhish-kə\ Count Jan *ca* 1376–1424 Bohemian gen. & Hussite leader; revolutionized warfare with mobile artillery; his innovation largely ignored for two centuries

Zog I \\'zōg\ 1895–1961 prename *Ahmed Bey Zogu* king of the Albanians (1928–39); pursued policy of close collaboration with Italy; driven from Albania by Italian invasion (1939)

Zo·la \\'zō-lə, 'zō-ˌlä, zō-'lä\ Émile 1840–1902 Fr. nov.; founder of the Naturalist movement in literature; author of *Thérèse Raquin*, series of 20 novels *Les Rougon-Macquart*, trilogy *Les Trois Villes*, etc.; also known for his defense of Alfred Dreyfus in the famous essay "J'accuse" — **Zo·la·esque** \\ˌzō-lə-'esk, -lä-\ *adj*

Zorn \\'sȯrn, 'zȯrn\ Anders Leonhard 1860–1920 Swed. painter, etcher, & sculptor; painted esp. Swedish subjects, nudes, portraits; etchings included nudes and portraits of contemporary literary luminaries

Zo·ro·as·ter \\'zōr-ə-ˌwas-tər, 'zȯr-\ *Old Iranian* **Zar·a·thu·shtra** \\ˌzar-ə-'thüsh-trə, -'thash-, -'thüs-, -'thəs-\ *ca* 628–*ca* 551 B.C. founder of Zoroastrianism; reputed author of the *Gāthās*, oldest and holiest part of the Avesta (Zoroastrian scriptures)

Zor·ri·lla y Mo·ral \\zə-'rē-yə-ˌē-mə-'räl\ José 1817–1893 Span. poet & dram.; major figure of nationalist wing of Spanish Romantic movement; author esp. of lyrical historical *leyendas* ("legends")

Zsig·mon·dy \\'zhig-ˌmȯn-dē\ Richard 1865–1929 Ger. chem.; awarded 1925 Nobel prize for chemistry for his method of studying colloids

Zu·lo·a·ga y Zabaleta \\ˌzü-lə-'wä-gə-ˌē-ˌzä-vä-'lä-tə\ Ignacio 1870–1945 Span. painter; known esp. for landscapes, portrayals of popular Spanish types (gypsies, bullfighters, beggars, etc.), portraits of women

Zur·ba·rán \\ˌzùr-bə-'rän\ Francisco de 1598–1664 Span. painter; court painter to Philip IV; known for religious paintings and monastic portraits marked by naturalism, tenebrism, idealized figures, shadowed forms

Zweig \\'zwīg, 'swīg, 'tsvīk\ Arnold 1887–1968 Ger. author; author of plays *Bonaparte in Jaffa*, etc., novels *The Time is Ripe*, etc.

Zweig Stefan 1881–1942 Austrian writer; best known for his psychoanalytical biographies, novels

Zwing·li \\'zwiŋ-glē, 'swiŋ-, -lē; 'tsfiŋ-lē\ Huldrych 1484–1531 Swiss Reformation leader; by his preaching, established Reformation in Switzerland (1522) — **Zwing·li·an** \\'zwiŋ-glē-ən, 'swiŋ-, -lē-; 'tsfiŋ-lē-\ *adj*